CONTENTS

KU-024-478

Introduction   **1**

TERESA CREMIN AND CATHY BURNETT

SECTION 1

BECOMING A TEACHER   3

1.1 Primary teaching: A personal perspective   5

COLIN RICHARDS

'Acrostic' teaching • A sense of style • Teaching: Science, craft or art?
• Enactive, pre-active and post-active primary teaching • The personal
qualities and knowledge required of primary teachers • The purposes of
primary teaching

1.2 Becoming a professional in the current context   17

SAMANTHA TWISELTON AND JANET GOEPEL

Professionalism – theory and research • Becoming professional – the process
• Raising your awareness through mapping your journey • Additional
complexity according to school context • Ofsted • Teachers' Standards

1.3 Making the most of your placements   32

JANE WARWICK AND MARY ANNE WOLPERT

Establishing effective dispositions • Reflective teaching • Evaluating your
lessons • Working with school mentors • Making the most of learning
conversations • Challenging professional conversations • Progression
through placements

SECTION 2

EXPLORING THE NATURE OF LEARNING AND TEACHING

SECTION 7

RECENT DEVELOPMENTS

391

FIGURES

TABLES

TASKS

LEARNING TO TEACH IN THE PRIMARY SCHOOL

How do you become an effective primary school teacher? What do you need to be able to do? What do you need to know?

Flexible, effective and creative primary school teachers require subject knowledge, an understanding of their pupils and how they learn, a range of strategies for managing behaviour and organising environments for learning and the ability to respond to dynamic classroom situations.

The fourth edition of this bestselling textbook has been fully updated with the latest research and initiatives in the field, as well as the most recent changes to the National Curriculum across the UK. Twenty-four new authors have contributed, sharing their expertise and experience as practitioners. New units have been included on:

- Becoming a professional in the current context
- Building inclusive communities of engaged learners
- Understanding schools' aims and enacting your own
- Teaching for social justice
- Reading
- Grammar and punctuation
- Mastery in mathematics
- The value of outdoor learning
- Primary education in a digital age.

A selection of extra tasks have been woven throughout, with an emphasis on innovative, reflective practice, and new 'vivid examples' bring each unit's argument to life in a classroom context. In addition, each unit contains M-level tasks and further reading to assist with research assignments, and differences in the National Curriculum and policy in Scotland, Wales and Northern Ireland are highlighted.

Providing a comprehensive but accessible introduction to teaching and learning in the primary school, covering everything a trainee needs to know in order to gain QTS, this accessible and engaging text-book is essential reading for *all* students training to be primary school teachers.

This textbook is supported by a free companion website with additional resources for instructors and students (www.routledge.com/cw/cremin) and an accompanying series of books on Teaching Creatively across the curriculum.

Teresa Cremin is Professor of Education (Literacy) at The Open University, UK. A former primary teacher and teacher educator, she has served as President of the UK Reading Association and the UKLA, and Board Member of the Cambridge Primary Review Trust, BookTrust and the Poetry Archive. She has led and contributed to research on creativity and on teachers' literate identities and practices and has published widely in these areas (https://researchrichpedagogies.org/research/).

Cathy Burnett is Professor of Literacy and Education at Sheffield Hallam University, UK, where she leads the Language and Literacy Education Research Group. She worked for many years as a primary teacher and teacher educator and is currently President Elect for the UKLA. She has published widely for professional and academic readerships and has led and contributed to research projects associated with literacy, digital media, teacher identities and uses of new technologies in classrooms.

THE LEARNING TO TEACH IN THE PRIMARY SCHOOL SERIES
Series Editor: Teresa Cremin, The Open University, UK

Teaching is an art form. It demands not only knowledge and understanding of the core areas of learning, but also the ability to teach these creatively and foster learner creativity in the process. *The Learning to Teach in the Primary School Series* draws upon recent research which indicates the rich potential of creative teaching and learning, and explores what it means to teach creatively in the primary phase. It also responds to the evolving nature of subject teaching in a wider, more imaginatively framed twenty-first-century primary curriculum.

Designed to complement the textbook, *Learning to Teach in the Primary School*, the well-informed, lively texts offer support for student and practising teachers who want to develop more creative approaches to teaching and learning. Uniquely, the books highlight the importance of the teachers' own creative engagement and share a wealth of research informed ideas to enrich pedagogy and practice.

Titles in the series:

Teaching Music Creatively, 2nd Edition
Pam Burnard and Regina Murphy

Teaching Design and Technology Creatively
Clare Benson and Suzanne Lawson

Teaching Outdoors Creatively
Edited by Stephen Pickering

Teaching History Creatively, 2nd Edition
Edited by Hilary Cooper

Teaching Geography Creatively, 2nd Edition
Edited by Stephen Scoffham

Teaching Science Creatively, 2nd Edition
Dan Davies and Deb McGregor

Teaching English Creatively, 2nd Edition
Teresa Cremin

Teaching Mathematics Creatively, 2nd Edition
Linda Pound and Trisha Lee

Teaching Religous Education Creatively
Edited by Sally Elton-Chalcraft

Teaching Physical Education Creatively
Angela Pickard and Patricia Maude

Applying Cross-Curricular Approaches Creatively
The Connecting Curriculum
Jonathan Barnes

LEARNING TO TEACH IN THE PRIMARY SCHOOL

Fourth edition

**Edited by
Teresa Cremin and
Cathy Burnett**

Routledge
Taylor & Francis Group

LONDON AND NEW YORK

Fourth edition published 2018
by Routledge
2 Park Square, Milton Park, Abingdon, Oxon, OX14 4RN

and by Routledge
711 Third Avenue, New York, NY 10017

Routledge is an imprint of the Taylor & Francis Group, an informa business

First edition published by Routledge 2006
Third edition published by Routledge 2014

British Library Cataloguing-in-Publication Data
A catalogue record for this book is available from the British Library

Library of Congress Cataloging-in-Publication Data
Names: Cremin, Teresa, 1959– editor of compilation. | Burnett, Cathy, editor of compilation.
Title: Learning to teach in the primary school / edited by Teresa Cremin and Cathy Burnett.
Description: Fourth edition. | New York : Routledge, 2018. | Series: Learning to Teach in the Primary School Series
Identifiers: LCCN 2017043813 | ISBN 9781138211049 (Hardback) | ISBN 9781138211063 (Paperback) | ISBN 9781315453736 (eBook)
Subjects: LCSH: Elementary school teaching – Great Britain. | Elementary school teachers – Training of – Great Britain.
Classification: LCC LB1556.7.G7 L43 2018 | DDC 372.1102–dc23
LC record available at https://lccn.loc.gov/2017043813

ISBN: 978-1-138-21104-9 (hbk)
ISBN: 978-1-138-21106-3 (pbk)
ISBN: 978-1-315-45373-6 (ebk)

Typeset in Interstate and Helvetica
by Florence Production Ltd, Stoodleigh, Devon, UK

Visit the companion website: www.routledge.com/cw/cremin

CONTRIBUTORS

Dr Jonathan Barnes has wide experience in all sectors of education. His current role in teacher education involves teaching music and geography and researching the relationship between the arts and well-being. He is author of Cross Curricular Learning 3-14 and writes regularly on creative approaches to staff and student development.

Eve Bearne's research interests while at the University of Cambridge Faculty of Education have been concerned with diversity and inclusion, specifically gender, language and literacy. She was a member of the research team for the Cambridge gender project Raising Boys' Achievement. She edited *Differentiation and Diversity* (Routledge) and has written and edited a range of books about language, literacy and inclusion: *Literacy and Community: Developing a Primary Curriculum through Partnerships* and *Inclusive Approaches to Teaching Literacy in the Secondary School*, both for the United Kingdom Literacy Association.

Dr Adam Boddison is the Chief Executive for nasen with responsibility for strategic direction and operational delivery across the full breadth of nasen's activity. Prior to this, Adam held a number of senior education roles including Director of the Centre for Professional Education at the University of Warwick, Academic Principal for IGGY (an educational social network for gifted teenagers) and as West Midlands Area Coordinator for the Further Mathematics Support Programme. In addition to a range of teaching and leadership posts in both primary and secondary schools, Adam has a portfolio of education research and international education projects.

Des Bowden was formerly Head of Geography at Newman University, Birmingham. He spent 2 years lecturing in Geomorphology at the University of Sierra Leone (Njala University College) and has worked in further education. Des has carried out research in Iceland, Sierra Leone, Malawi, the Gambia and India and, like most geographers, he is widely travelled. He is now co-director of B&C Educational Ltd, which is a small company specialising in three interrelated activities: developing and publishing curriculum resource materials for primary schools; working to promote the value of the global dimension and global citizenship in primary schools through CPD courses and curriculum development; and planning and running study visits to the Gambia for primary school staff (heads, teachers, LAs and governors). Since 2010, many primary schools in the West Midlands have developed sustainable partnerships with schools in The Gambia.

Dr Virginia Bower is a Senior Lecturer and Programme Director in the School of Teacher Education and Development at Canterbury Christ Church University. She has completed her doctorate based on supporting children with English as an additional language and is particularly interested in how bilingual approaches might be adopted in primary schools, to support all learners. Dr Bower is the author of four publications: *Creative Ways to Teach Literacy, Games, Ideas and Activities for Primary Poetry, Developing Early Literacy 0-8* and *Supporting Children with English as an Additional Language* (forthcoming).

Jo Bowers is Senior Lecturer in Primary Education and Literacy Coordinator for the School of Education at Cardiff Metropolitan University. She teaches English and history courses to PGCE primary students and a number of other literacy-related courses on undergraduate education programmes. Her subject specialism is Primary English. Prior to this appointment, she was a primary school teacher for 20 years and a literacy coordinator for 15 of them. She is the Welsh regional representative for the United Kingdom Literacy Association (UKLA) and is on the editorial board for the English Association's literacy journal for primary teachers, English 4-11. She has a lifelong interest in children's literature and developing children's reading for pleasure and currently co-leads a children's literature Special Interest Group with two UKLA literacy colleagues. She has completed a research project supporting student teachers' subject knowledge of children's literature. Her other main areas of interest are using philosophical enquiry to develop thinking skills and talk in the primary classroom. She wrote the boxes on Wales.

Mark Boylan is a Professor of Education at Sheffield Hallam University. Mark's background is in mathematics teaching and mathematics teacher education. He led the design of the Yorkshire Mathematics Specialist Teacher (MaST) programme for primary teachers. Much of Mark's current work involves research of policy initiatives in mathematics education. He leads the longitudinal evaluation of the Mathematics Teacher Exchange: China-England, a government-funded programme of exchange visits with Shanghai teachers aimed at promoting mastery methods in English schools. He is also research lead for the Embodying Mathematics Project – a curriculum and professional development project in partnership with Complicité Theatre Company.

Cathy Burnett is Professor of Literacy and Education at Sheffield Institute of Education, Sheffield Hallam University, where she worked in primary teacher education for many years, teaching on undergraduate, postgraduate and Masters-level courses of initial and continuing teacher education. Prior to arriving at Sheffield Hallam University, she worked as a primary teacher, for various theatre-in-education companies and for Derby City Education Service. She has published widely for professional and academic audiences, including several books and many journal articles and book chapters focused on literacy education, enquiry and professional education and the connections between literacy and technology. Her books include *New Literacies around the Globe* (published by Routledge and co-edited with Julia Davies, Guy Merchant and Jennifer Rowsell), *The Case of the iPad: Mobile Literacies in Education* (with Guy Merchant, Alyson Simpson and Maureen Walsh, for Springer) and *Literacy, Media, Technology: Past, Present and Future* (with Becky Parry and Guy Merchant, for Bloomsbury). Her research review – *The digital age and its implications for learning and teaching in the primary school* – was commissioned by the Cambridge Primary Review Trust. Cathy has a longstanding commitment to creative approaches to literacy education and to using enquiry as a mode of professional development. Her most recent research focuses on the relationship between new technologies and literacies within and beyond educational contexts. She was previously an editor of the journal *Literacy* and has led and contributed to a series of research and evaluation projects funded by organisations such as Booktrust, United Kingdom Literacy Association (UKLA), JISC and the Education Endowment Fund. Cathy is President Elect and joint Research Convener for the UKLA and also co-convenes the UKLA Digital Literacies special interest group.

Jenny Carey is Course Leader for the Early Years Teacher Specialism at the University of Strathclyde, which provides Masters-level study for early years practitioners. She also works on both undergraduate and postgraduate initial teacher education courses, contributing to teaching and learning and to language and literacy programmes. Her work with undergraduate and Masters-level students has guided her interest in teacher reflection and curriculum implementation. Jenny's current research explores factors that affect 9-year-old children's engagement with learning in school settings, focusing on the perspectives held by children and teachers about the learning opportunities, pedagogical approaches and interactions. She wrote the boxes on Scotland.

Elizabeth Carruthers is a National Leader of Education and is Head Teacher of Redcliffe Nursery School, Children's Centre, National Teaching School and Research Base, Bristol. She has taught in all phases of education but her focus for the past 20 years has been on birth to 8 years. She has published articles and books on mathematics education and her work with Maulfry Worthington was recommended by the Williams Mathematics Review, 2008. She is presently studying for a PhD in Mathematics Education, at Bristol University, partly funded by the Martin Hughes Scholarship Fund.

Liz Chamberlain is a Senior Lecturer in Education at The Open University, where she is Programme Leader for the Education Studies (Primary) degree. Liz has worked in higher education for a decade, supporting both initial teaching students and practising teachers. Prior to working in HE, Liz held a variety of positions including English Subject Leader, Leading Literacy Teacher and Assistant Head Teacher, and taught in a number of primary schools in London, Devon, Southampton, and in Malaysia. Liz's specialism is Primary English, and she was the Strategic Consultant on the DfE-funded Everybody Writes project, working closely with both the Book Trust and the National Literacy Trust. Liz is a case-study researcher who has a focus on capturing what it means for children to be writers. In particular, her main expertise is as a literacy case-study researcher with a focus on developing writers' experiences of writing, both in and out-of-school.

Dr Roland Chaplain is a Chartered Psychologist and Associate Fellow of the British Psychological Society. He is an Educational Consultant and the Behaviour Management Specialist in The Faculty of Education, University of Cambridge, UK, where he designed and teaches the Behaviour Management Training and Support Programme to all PGCE trainees. The quality of this programme has been highlighted in all recent Ofsted inpections at Cambridge. He has experience as a teacher, head teacher and senior lecturer in psychology. As an educational consultant Roland also provides behaviour management training to schools and ITT providers. He has produced many books, chapters and journal articles on classroom management, behaviour disorders and teacher stress. His latest book, *Teaching Without Disruption in the Primary School* (2nd edition) – published by Routledge in 2016 – is an extremely practical book underpinned by contemporary educational, psychological and neuroscientific research.

Dr Helen Childerhouse is Senior Lecturer in the School of Education at The University of Lincoln. She has 14 years' experience of teaching a diverse range of early years and primary learners in mainstream schools. Helen has a particular interest in pupil well-being and special educational needs and has recently completed research focusing on primary teachers' perceptions of what it is like to support learners who are considered to experience social, emotional and behavioural difficulties. She has taught in universities for the last 10 years on undergraduate and postgraduate teacher education programmes.

Pam Copeland is former Citizenship Lead at Newman University, Birmingham, and a Director of B and C Educational (www.primary-school-resources.com). She and her business partner produce and publish their own global teaching resources, offer curriculum consultancy to primary schools, and lead groups of primary teachers and heads to the Gambia as part of their CPD course on the global dimension in the curriculum.

Dr Ayshea Craig is the Programme Leader for the Primary PGCE Courses at UCL Institute of Education. She worked as a primary school teacher in the Midlands before taking a Masters degree in Mathematics Education at Warwick University and studying for a PhD in Education at IOE. Ayshea has undergraduate and Masters degrees in mathematics from Cambridge University. She is interested in all aspects of primary teacher education and the teaching and learning of mathematics including the broader social, cultural, political and historical context of its place in education systems and value to society. Ayshea has worked on research projects on teachers' pedagogical responses to testing and on mainstream provision for primary school pupils with statements for special educational needs.

Professor Teresa Cremin is Professor of Education (Literacy) at The Open University. Her sociocultural research focuses mainly on teachers' identities as readers and writers and the potential influence of these on both their classroom practice and their students' literate identities and practices. She also researches creativity and creative pedagogical practice. An ex-teacher and teacher-educator, Teresa worked in initial teacher education for nearly 20 years and now undertakes research and consultancy for numerous organisations. Her research is frequently co-participative, involving teachers as researchers both in schools and in children's homes. A Fellow of the Academy of Social Sciences, the Royal Society of the Arts and the English Association, Teresa is also a member of the ESRC Peer Review College, a Trustee of the UK Literacy Association, convenor of the British Educational Research Association's Special Interest Group on Creativity and co-editor of the journal *Thinking Skills and Creativity*. Previously she has been a board member of BookTrust and the Poetry Archive, a Director of the Cambridge Primary Review Trust, President of UKLA and UKRA and editor of the journal *Literacy*. Teresa has written and edited nearly thirty books. Forthcoming and current volumes include: *Experiencing Reading for Pleasure in the Digital Age* (Sage, 2018); *Writer Identity and the Teaching and Learning of Writing; Storytelling in Early Childhood: Enriching Language, Literacy and Culture* (Routledge, 2017, edited collections); *Teaching English Creatively* (Routledge, 2015); *Researching Literacy Lives: Building Home School Communities* (Routledge, 2015); and *Building Communities of Engaged Readers: Reading for Pleasure* (Routledge, 2014).

Louise Cunningham is a secondary-trained Physical Education teacher and has more than 17 years' teaching experience in middle years education. She has been a subject lead for PE, PSHE and Citizenship for a number of years before more recently specialising in special educational needs. She is currently researching effective teaching methods for inclusion of challenging pupils in alternative provision for her final year of an MA at the University of Bedfordshire. Louise has worked in partnership with the local authority to set up an alternative provision for primary-aged children with social, emotional and mental health needs and continues to manage this provision alongside her role as SENDCO in a mainstream primary school.

Lyn Dawes worked as a teacher in primary and middle schools before lecturing in Science and English at Bedford, Northampton and Cambridge Universities. She now provides workshops for education professionals with a focus on Talk for Learning. Lyn has authored and co-authored several books for teachers, including *Talk Box* (KS1) and *Talking Points* (KS2), both David Fulton publications, and *Teaching Primary Science* (Sage). She has a chapter in the classic *The Articulate Classroom*, edited by Prue Goodwin. Lyn is a committee member of Oracy Cambridge and is a governor at Water Hall School.

Bernadette Duffy originally trained as an early years teacher at the West London Institute of Higher Education and later studied at the Froebel College. During the last 38 years she has worked in a variety of early years settings. Bernadette has been a member of a number of Department for Education advisory committees and was the early years expert on the prime minister's National Council for Education Excellence and part of the Expert Group for the Early Years Foundation Stage Review. Bernadette is the author of *Supporting Creativity and Imagination in the Early Years* and co-editor with Dame Gillian Pugh of *Contemporary Issues in the Early Years*. She has also contributed to a wide range of other publications. Bernadette is a Vice President of the British Association for Early Childhood Education and a trustee of the Froebel Trust. Bernadette was made an OBE in 2005.

Dr Sally Elton-Chalcraft is Reader in Education at the University of Cumbria. She has published in the areas of intercultural education, religious education and spirituality, creative teaching and learning in the primary stage, and research methods. Her recent research projects include collaborative work investigating the imposition of fundamental British values into teacher education and school settings; an evaluation of leadership courses with an emphasis on BME and women aspirant leaders; and a collaborative research project with other Cathedrals Group universities to culminate in some fit-for-purpose guidelines for ethical research in school settings. She has been lead investigator collecting data over two summers in six Indian states studying the impact of Christian faith in schools and also attitudes towards SEN. Currently, she is leading an investigation into the successes and challenges of creating a studio (free) school within a multi-academy trust.

Jo Evans is CEO of St Christopher's Multi Academy Trust in Devon. She has a very strong research-informed background, being part of the Cambridge Primary Review Trust. She has been a leader in a range of rural and city schools, in the last 7 years taking one school from special measures to outstanding and the most recent from good to outstanding. This has been achieved through her resolve to provide a principled approach to education. Jo has recently been involved in the creation of the Church of England Professional Qualification for Headship.

Dr Robert Fisher taught in schools in the UK, Africa and Hong Kong before becoming a teacher trainer and professor of education at Brunel University. His PhD was awarded for research into philosophy for children and his many books include *Teaching Thinking*, *Teaching Children to Think*, *Teaching Children to Learn*, *Creative Dialogue*, the *Stories for Thinking* series and *Brain Games for Your Child*. He gives lectures and conference presentations on teaching thinking and philosophy for children and continues to write, but spends more time since retiring on painting, sculpting and dancing Argentine tango.

Alison Fox is a Senior Lecturer at the Faculty of Wellbeing, Education and Language Studies at The Open University, UK. After training as a secondary school science teacher, Alison moved into initial teacher training and research about and for the support of beginning teachers. She has been involved in the Teaching and Learning Research Programme 'Learning how to learn: In classrooms, in schools and in networks' project (2002–06), which investigated the development of assessment for learning practices across five local authorities the Department for Education-funded 'Schools and continuing professional development in England – State of the Nation' project (2008) and an evaluation of the National College for Teaching and Leadership's leadership curriculum provision (2012–16). She works through school-university partnerships and Masters provision to support practitioner enquiry, and her current research interests are in supporting initial teacher education and teachers' professional learning, particularly as it relates to their networking activities.

Angela Gill is an Assistant Professor in the School of Education at Durham University, working with undergraduate and postgraduate students in primary education. She has worked for more than 20 years in primary schools in County Durham and North Somerset. While teaching, Angela was subject leader for English and phonics, which sparked a particular interest in the subject. She has written several books and articles, about phonics and other primary English topics, including a best-selling book about teaching systematic synthetic phonics in the primary school.

Professor Caroline Gipps was, until July 2011, Vice Chancellor at the University of Wolverhampton. Previously she was Deputy Vice Chancellor at Kingston University and Dean of Research at the Institute of Education, London. Trained as a psychologist, test developer and a qualified teacher, she carried out research on assessment in the school system for more than 20 years. Research projects have included a 6-year study of the introduction of the National Curriculum assessment programme into primary schools; a seminal study of teacher feedback to learners; and the teaching, assessment and feedback strategies used by 'expert' classroom teachers.

Dr Janet Goepel is a Senior Lecturer in Primary Education at Sheffield Hallam University. She teaches Special Educational Needs and Inclusion to primary undergraduate and postgraduate students as well as in-service teachers on the Special Educational Needs Coordinators (SENCOs) Masters-level award. Janet's doctoral thesis concerned the professionalism of doctors and teachers in working together to support children with special educational needs. She has presented papers on this theme in the UK and in Australia to both teachers and health professionals. She has also presented at conferences on teacher professionalism and published papers on this theme. Janet has contributed chapters to several books and has co-authored a book entitled *Inclusive Primary Teaching: A Critical Approach to Equality and Special Educational Needs* (Critical Publishing, 2015).

Dr Stephen Griffin is Co-Leader of the Education and Multi Professional Practice Department at Newman University. A former primary school deputy head teacher, Stephen has taught extensively in a range of educational settings from KS1 to KS3. His research interests focus on the implementation of neuroscientifically informed learning theory in schools, teacher agency and the impact of educational consultancy upon educational change in school.

Previously a Primary and Early Years Teacher, **Dr Emese Hall** is Senior Lecturer in Art Education at the Graduate School of Education, University of Exeter, where she has worked since 2005. She is the current Programme Director of the Primary PGCE, tutors on the MA (Ed) Creative Arts in Education Programme, and supervises doctoral and Masters research. Her research interests encompass professional learning, drawing, reflective practice, communication and creativity. She is a member of both the University of Exeter's Centre for Research in Professional Learning and Lesson Study Network. Emese is also a council and forum member of the National Society for Education in Art and Design (NSEAD), a former member of the Expert Subject Advisory Group for Art and Design Education and a former regional coordinator of the Cambridge Primary Review Trust. In addition, she is founder of the South West NSEAD Regional Network Group, Exeter Area Art Educators.

Kathy Hall is Professor of Education at University College Cork. She teaches and researches in the areas of professional learning, inclusion, literacy and assessment. She is currently leading a Teaching Council-commissioned national, longitudinal evaluation of professional learning and school placement in response to major policy changes in teacher education in Ireland. She supervises a large number of PhD studies on a variety of themes related to her research and publications. She is co-chair of the Standing Conference on Teacher Education North and South (SCoTENS) an organisation established in 2003 following the broader peace dynamic to promote understanding, research and policy on teacher education in both parts of the island of Ireland. Recent authored books include *Learning, Culture and Neuroscience* (Routledge) with Curtin and Rutherford and *Research Methods for Pedagogy* (Bloomsbury) with Nind and Curtin.

Eleanore Hargreaves is Reader in Learning and Pedagogy at the UCL Institute of Education, London University. She taught in the primary phase in England and abroad before entering the NFER's Department of Assessment and Measurement in 1992. Later, she registered with the UCL Institute of Education for a PhD exploring the roles of assessment in primary education. Since then she has led MA modules on learning, teaching and assessment and carried out research into these areas. She currently leads the MA in Effective Learning and Teaching. Her first book was as co-author of *What Makes a Good Primary School Teacher?* (Routledge, 2000) and her most recent, sole-authored book is *Children's Experiences of Classrooms* (Sage, 2017). Her work in formative assessment, especially feedback, has led her to carry out educational consultancies in a range of countries, including Egypt, Hong Kong, Macedonia and Pakistan.

Donna Hazzard is a Principal Lecturer at St Mary's University College, Queen's University, Belfast where she is Course Team Leader for Literacy and Chair of the Master's degree programme. Currently she is in her final year of doctoral study. Her research draws on Bourdieu's conceptual tools as an analytical framework to explore the extent to which adopting a socially just literacy pedagogy that cultivates a critical perspective, might help student teachers understand the socially constructed nature of literacy. Donna has been the United Kingdom Literary Association's Northern Ireland representative since 2005 and is editor of the spring edition of UKLA News. She wrote the boxes on Northern Ireland.

Dr Jenny Houssart has a background in primary teaching and taught across the primary age range before becoming an Advisory Teacher for a local authority, specialising in primary mathematics. She then moved into higher education, where she worked in initial teacher education, on courses for teaching assistants and on a range of other postgraduate and undergraduate programmes. She is author of *Low Attainers in Primary Mathematics* and joint editor of *Supporting Mathematical Thinking* and *Listening Counts: Listening to Young Learners of Mathematics* and has written a range of research and professional publications, mainly related to primary mathematics. Her recent research has focused on the role of teaching assistants in primary schools.

Dr Hanneke Jones was born in the Netherlands, where she trained as a teacher in Amsterdam. After living in Greece with her English husband and son, she worked as a primary teacher in north-east England for 13 years, before taking up her position as a teacher educator on the Primary PGCE course at Newcastle University. In her PhD, she focused on Creative Thinking in the Community of Enquiry, and her areas of expertise lie in social justice (related to poverty), creativity and innovative pedagogy. Her teaching on the Primary PGCE/SD course includes these areas as well as a SAPERE training course in Philosophy for Children. She lives in Northumberland and enjoys reading, swimming and cycling in her spare time.

Peter Kelly is Reader in Comparative Education and Convenor of the Comparative Social Policy Research Group in the Institute of Education at Plymouth University, UK, where he has worked since 2003. His work focuses on comparing social policy and pedagogy and their effects on educational inequality in Europe. Formerly, he led the International Masters Programme at Plymouth. Currently, he leads the module Researching Education Practice in the Education Doctorate and is Director of Studies for both professional doctorate and PhD students. He is also a tutor on the MA (Education) Programme, which provides practice-focused Masters-level study in all areas of education.

Rebecca Kennedy is an independent consultant specialising in English. She has a range of experience teaching, supporting primary schools in the West Midlands and as an external moderator. Rebecca works as an Associate Consultant with the Centre for Literacy in Primary Education (CLPE), training and writing for the Power of Reading project. Her professional interests are children's reading and writing, multimodality and children's literature. She has contributed to several United Kingdom Literacy Association publications and is on the editorial board of the magazine *English 4-11*.

Andreas O. Kyriakides works as a primary school teacher in Cyprus. He is also a Scientific Collaborator in the Department of Educational Studies of the European University Cyprus. In the field of teacher education, he is interested, not only in training prospective teachers to acquire a mathematics knowledge base, but also in sharpening their sensitivity to the complexities of learning and directing their attention to practices and constructs that can inform preferences when teaching mathematics.

Roger McDonald is a Senior Lecturer in the Department of Primary Education at the University of Greenwich. Roger initially worked as a primary school teacher for 16 years and then became a deputy head teacher in Kent and Medway schools. Roger holds a National Professional Qualification for Headship (NPQH). As a primary school teacher Roger became interested in the power of picture books across the age ranges, as well as the significant impact music could have on children's writing. He developed the use of drama within his classroom and eventually across the school to support children's imaginative and emotional engagement with texts. This interest led to a successful completion of his Masters degree and also the invitation to take part in associate tutoring at Canterbury Christ Church University. It was the experience of researching and working with students that supported Roger in securing a post to teach in the Primary Department at the University of Greenwich in 2012. Since joining the university, he has lectured on both the PGCE and BA routes into teaching. In addition, he oversees the School Direct (Salaried) route as well as supporting students in their final school experience. Currently, Roger is engaged in research surrounding the notion of literacy teaching and development of the imagination.

Jane Medwell began her career as a primary teacher and taught and carried out research at the Universities of Wales, Exeter, Plymouth and Warwick. She is currently Associate Professor at the University of Nottingham, where she is Director of Postgraduate Research in the School of Education. She has completed a number of research projects on aspects of literacy teaching and learning and, more recently, the teaching and learning of languages in primary schools. She is currently researching the teaching of handwriting and its relationship with composing, the teaching of languages in primary schools and the use and effects of homework. She is also leading a project for the International Baccalaureate organisation exploring enquiry-led teaching in primary schools. Jane is the author/editor of more than twenty books and more than sixty articles/chapters on aspects of literacy/language teaching.

Dr Elaine Millard began her career as an English teacher working in a variety of 11–18 comprehensive schools in Sheffield and Nottingham. From 1998 to 1990, she worked as an advisory teacher for Nottingham LEA, preparing both primary and secondary schools for the introduction of the English National Curriculum. In 1991, she joined Sheffield University's School of Education and was one of the main originators of its influential Masters degree in Literacy. Elaine is past chair of the National Association for the Teaching of English. Her most influential publication is *Differently Literate* (Falmer Press), which presents research into the differences between boys' and girls' responses to the reading curriculum.

Debra Myhill is Professor of Education at the University of Exeter, UK. Her research has focused particularly on young people's composing processes and their metacognitive awareness of them; the interrelationship between metalinguistic understanding and writing; the talk-writing interface; and the teaching of writing. She is Director of the Centre for Research in Writing, which promotes interdisciplinary research, drawing on psychological, sociocultural and linguistic perspectives on writing. Over the past 15 years, she has led a series of research projects in these areas, in both primary and secondary schools, and has conducted several commissioned research studies. Debra runs numerous professional education courses for teachers, examining the practical classroom implications of her research on the teaching of writing, and, in 2014, her research team was awarded the Economic and Social Research Council award for Outstanding Impact in Society.

Jane Payler is Professor of Education (Early Years) at the Open University. Jane has taught, examined, researched, published and practised in early years education and care for more than 25 years. She has taught and developed curricula for early years students on vocational courses through to university doctoral level. She has previously worked as an NHS health education officer and a crèche supervisor and has run a preschool. Jane was closely involved in the development of Early Years Professional Status and Early Years Teacher in England. Her publications and research have focused on interprofessional practice, professional development and young children's learning experiences. She is currently Co-Director of the Children's Research Centre at the Open University.

Alison Peacock, DBE, DL, DLitt, is Chief Executive of the Chartered College of Teaching. The Chartered College opened membership in January 2017 and aims to provide a professional body 'by teachers, for teachers'. She is a regular columnist for *TES* and has spent the majority of her career working as both teacher and researcher. Alison has worked in partnership with educational researchers to document her innovative work as a teacher and creative school leader. Throughout her career, Alison has sought to teach and lead in a manner that encourages the voice of the child, building a trusting environment for dialogue that enriches understanding and builds communities of lifelong learning. Until December 2016, Alison was Head Teacher of The Wroxham School and Educational Research Centre, in Hertfordshire. She led the school out of special measures less than a year after her appointment as Head Teacher (January 2003), and it was subsequently judged by Ofsted to be outstanding (2006, 2009, 2013). Alison's teaching career spans primary, secondary and advisory roles. Alison is advising the Welsh government on Curriculum and Assessment and was appointed by the DfE as a member of the Commission for Assessment Without Levels and as a member of the ITT Expert Group and CPD Expert Group. She is a trustee of Teach First and a member of the Royal Society Education Committee. In July 2014, Alison was awarded an honorary doctorate from the University of Brighton and, in May 2015, appointed as a Deputy Lieutenant of Hertfordshire. In December 2015, Alison was appointed as Visiting Professor for the University of Hertfordshire.

Alison Pickering taught in primary schools in inner London and Sydney, Australia, prior to her appointment as Deputy Head Teacher of a primary school in Richmond-upon-Thames. She was Course Director for undergraduate routes into teaching at the School of Education, Kingston University. Her main areas of interest are primary science, cross-curricular approaches to learning and creative approaches to assessment.

Stephen Pickering is the Course Leader for Primary and Outdoor Education and a Senior Lecturer in Education at the University of Worcester. He sits on the editorial board of Primary Geography and is a consultant for the Geographical Association. Stephen has written widely for the Geographical Association and TIDE, as well as being the editor of *Teaching Outdoors Creatively* (2017) and contributing a chapter to S. Scoffham's *Teaching Geography Creatively* (2013, 2nd edn 2017), both for Routledge. Stephen is a qualified Forest School Leader and Earth Education Leader. His research interests include learning and teaching outdoors, geographical education, the global dimension, global citizenship and literature as a vehicle for learning.

Dr John Potter is Reader in Media in Education at University College London Institute of Education, in the UCL Knowledge Lab. His research, teaching, doctoral supervision and publications are focused on media education, new literacies and the changing nature of teaching and learning in response to the pervasive use in wider culture of digital media. He has a background in primary and secondary education, as a teacher, advisor and teacher-educator in East London for many years. He is the author of *Digital Media and Learner Identity: The New Curatorship* (Palgrave, 2012), which explored children's video production, building a theory of curation as a new literacy practice in digital media, and co-author, with Keith Turvey and Jeremy Burton, of *Primary Computing and Digital Technologies* (Learning Matters/Sage, 2016). He is co-editor, with Rebecca Eynon, of the journal *Learning, Media and Technology*.

Dr Noel Purdy is Director of Research and Scholarship and Head of Education Studies (with responsibility for Special Educational Needs) at Stranmillis University College, Queen's University, Belfast. He is the Northern Chair of SCoTENS, the all-Ireland Standing Conference on Teacher Education North and South, a network of thirty-seven colleges of education, university education departments, teaching councils, curriculum councils, education trade unions and education centres, with a responsibility for and interest in teacher education. A qualified teacher, Dr Purdy taught Modern Languages in two post-primary schools in Northern Ireland but has also taught in Germany and Switzerland. He is a Fellow of the Leadership Foundation for Higher Education and a Senior Fellow of the Higher Education Academy. He served as chair of the Northern Ireland Anti-Bullying Forum 2013-16 and President of nasen in Northern Ireland 2014-16.

Colin Richards is Emeritus Professor of Education at the University of Cumbria and has been a visiting professor at the Universities of Leicester, Warwick and Newcastle. A former primary school teacher and deputy head, he was an HMI from 1983 to 1996 specialising in primary education and in teacher education and holding the post of Staff Inspector (Curriculum 5-16), followed by that of Ofsted's Specialist Adviser for Primary Education. Since leaving Ofsted, he has maintained a keen but critical interest in the issues of standards, primary and secondary education, the school curriculum, governance and inspection. He is Chair of Governors of a Cumbrian secondary school that has voted twice not to seek academy status. He has served on a number of primary school governing bodies and has recently stood down as a National Leader of Governance. As a critic of much (though not all) of past and present government education policy, he is a frequent contributor to the national press (in particular to *The Guardian*, *The Observer*, *The Independent*, the *TES* and *Schools Week*). He also tweets at @colinsparkbridg.

Dr Carol Robinson is an Associate Professor in the Education Research Centre at the University of Brighton. She is a trained teacher and has experience of teaching in secondary schools as well as teaching both primary- and secondary-aged pupils in pupil referral units. Carol's research interests combine theoretical and empirical work focusing on the voices, experiences, rights and empowerment of children and young people, and she has published widely in this area. Carol has led several pupil voice projects in primary, secondary and special schools, helping staff to develop ways of listening to the voices of children and young people. She also led the 'Pupils' Voices' strand of the University of the Cambridge Primary Review of Education in England.

Sue Rogers, PhD, is Professor of Early Years Education at the UCL Institute of Education, University College London, UK. She has a long-standing interest in curriculum and pedagogy in early years education, the benefits of play-based learning, and effective child-adult interactions in educational settings. Recent work has focused on the use of research evidence in professional learning and educational practice as a way of improving expertise and skills in the early years workforce. Alongside leading several funded projects concerned with both early years pedagogy and professional learning, she has published widely in the field of early childhood education, including several books: *SAGE Guide to Early Years and Primary Education* (Sage, 2016, with Wyse), *Exploring Education and Early Childhood* (Routledge, 2015, with Wyse, Jones and Davies), *Adult Roles in the Early Years* (Open University Press, 2012, with Janet Rose), *Rethinking Play and Pedagogy: Concepts, Contexts and Cultures* (Routledge, 2011), and *Inside Role Play in Early Childhood Education: Researching Children's Perspectives* (Routledge, 2008, with Julie Evans).

Dr Janet Rose is currently Principal of Norland College, a specialist, vocational early years higher education institution. Until recently, she was a Reader in Education (Associate Professor) and the Early Education Award Leader at Bath Spa University. She has run various undergraduate and postgraduate early childhood degrees and teacher training programmes at several universities.

She formerly worked as a primary teacher in schools and a range of early years settings. She has her own consultancy and ran workshops for 0-3s for many years, both in England and abroad. She has worked closely with the National College of Teaching and Learning, as well as numerous local authorities and professional organisations around the country. She is frequently invited to present at national and international conferences and is the author of a wide range of publications. These include co-authoring a book on *The Role of the Adult in Early Years Settings* and one on *Health and Well-being in the Early Childhood*.

John Ryan is Associate Professor in Primary Education at Nottingham University. He has wide experience in teacher education and has previously worked at the University of Birmingham as the Director of Primary Education and Newman University as a Senior Lecturer. Prior to working at universities, John worked and held senior positions in a range of primary schools, teaching and leading from Reception to Year 6. His main research interests are in the field of professional identities and character education, and he recently co-authored the book *Teaching Character in the Primary Classroom*.

Mary Scanlan is a Senior Lecturer in Education at the University of Winchester, where she is Early Years Subject Lead and teaches on the English team. Mary is also Module Leader for the BEd/MEd research modules, and is currently exploring ITE and research-informed practice. Mary is an experienced infant, nursery and primary school teacher and has taught in a variety of settings. She worked at the University of Bristol on the Home School Knowledge Exchange project, and her PhD explored how home and school can work together to support children's literacy learning. Mary is a Senior Fellow of the HEA.

Kieron Sheehy's research interests are within the broad field of inclusive education, often focusing on how teaching approaches or services can be developed to successfully support diverse groups of learners. He supervises research within this area and has a particular interest in addressing issues for those who might be stigmatised and excluded within educational systems. This has encompassed examining the relationship between new technologies and assessment, and developing practical pedagogies for inclusive classrooms. Currently, he is working with colleagues in East Java to develop Signalong Indonesia, a signed communication approach to support inclusive classrooms and school communities.

Dr Heather Smith is a Senior Lecturer at the University of Newcastle and Docent Professor of Multicultural Teacher Education at Helsinki University, Finland. Her underlying interest lies in equity in education. She draws primarily on critical race theory, critical whiteness and sociocultural theory in her research. She is the Principal Investigator for the ROMtels (Roma Translanguaging enquiry learning space) Erasmus+ Project, which looks to improve education for Roma pupils (https://research.ncl.ac.uk/romtels/).

Vivien Townsend is a doctoral student at Manchester Metropolitan University. Her PhD research is on how primary school teachers are implementing the 2014 National Curriculum for mathematics, and this has led to an interest in 'mastery'. In 2016, she presented a paper - 'The mastery curriculum in England: A battle with dominant discourses of ability and accountability' - at the International Congress for Mathematics Education. She is particularly interested in inconsistencies in how the term 'mastery' is used within schools and more widely across the educational landscape. Vivien has worked as a primary school teacher, a local authority adviser and, most recently, a freelance primary mathematics consultant. Through her consultancy, she has led networks for mathematics subject leaders and provided the mathematics input at Leicester and Leicestershire Primary SCITT. She is an accredited NCETM PD Lead and is also a member of ATM, MA, NAMA, BERA and BSRLM.

Jo Trowsdale's research is concerned with the practice of 'art making' as a site for transdisciplinary, more personally meaningful learning that stimulates pupils' affective as well as cognitive dimensions. She is a Principal Teaching Fellow in the Centre for Education Studies at the University of Warwick. Jo has extensive experience in teacher development, particularly in primary- and secondary-phase drama, and has a long-standing research interest in developing young people through the arts and creativity. She continues to work directly with schools, teachers, pupils and artists, and is currently researching the role of the arts in STEAM (science, technology, engineering, arts and mathematics) education. This builds on her early work enabling professional artists and educators to develop, collaboratively, innovative and significant learning experiences, and her directorship of the Creative Partnerships programme (2002–10).

Professor Samantha Twiselton is the Director of Sheffield Institute of Education at Sheffield Hallam University. She uses her research and practice in the development of teacher expertise, and curriculum design to help develop school-embedded approaches to teacher development. Sam has been heavily involved in influencing government policy on teacher education and was recently a member of the advisory panel for the Department for Education Carter Review of ITT and a member of the DfE Expert Behaviour Management Panel chaired by Tom Bennett. She is now working on ITE and NQT/RQT follow-up to this regionally and with the DfE through a number of projects. She is an affiliate member and strong supporter of the Chartered College of Teaching, as her role has exposed her to so many sources of evidence that the teaching profession needs a powerful and authoritative voice.

Jane Warwick taught for 15 years in primary schools, taking on various leadership roles including induction tutor for NQTs. She worked as a local authority science advisor and support teacher for PE. Since 2000, she has worked in teacher education at the University of Cambridge, where she been the Primary PGCE Course Manager since 2006. She has responsibility for all aspects of the course, including partnerships with schools, preparing trainees for placements and mentor training, which is a particular research interest. Other current research interests include supporting male trainees in primary and supporting trainees' well-being.

David Waugh is Subject Leader for Primary English at Durham University. He has published extensively on Primary English. David is a former deputy head teacher, was Head of the Education Department at the University of Hull and was Regional Adviser for ITT for the National Strategies from 2008 to 2010. He has written and co-written or edited more than forty books on primary education. As well as his educational writing, David also writes children's stories and regularly teaches in schools. His latest novel, *The Wishroom*, was written with forty-five children from fifteen East Durham schools. Now semi-retired, David does regular voluntary work in schools using his novels as a stimulus for a range of literacy activities.

Janice Wearmouth has many years' experience of teaching and research work in schools and universities, in the UK and overseas. In her research work, she brings together a concern for the learner whose educational experience is problematic with a concern for professionals who have to deal with, and mitigate, the problems that are experienced and facilitate opportunities for learning. Since 2000, she has been researching and publishing on issues related to literacy difficulties, behavioural concerns in schools, teacher professional development and inclusion, and special educational needs and disability, with colleagues in New Zealand, at the University of Waikato, and in the UK.

Louise Wheatcroft is a Senior Lecturer in Primary English working on initial teacher training courses at Birmingham City University. Before that, she was a primary school teacher and literacy coordinator in Birmingham primary schools. She has also taught English and worked in teacher training abroad during her time working with Voluntary Services Overseas in the Maldives. She is interested in literacies and changing literacy practices, and her research interest centres on student teachers' digital lives and their classroom practices.

Mary Anne Wolpert taught for 12 years in primary schools, latterly as an English specialist, and has been an English consultant for two local authorities. She has worked in teacher education at the University of Cambridge since 2005 and is an Affiliated Lecturer at the Faculty of Education. As Deputy Course Manager for the Primary PGCE, she focuses on developing partnerships with schools, preparing trainees for placements and coordinating the Professional Studies course. Her current research interests encompass reading comprehension and reading for pleasure, as well as literacy interventions in phonics and writing.

David Wray taught in primary schools in the United Kingdom for 10 years and is currently Professor Emeritus at the University of Warwick. He has served as President of the United Kingdom Reading Association and edited its journal for 8 years. He has published more than fifty books and more than 150 chapters and articles on aspects of literacy teaching and is best known for his work on developing teaching strategies to help students access the curriculum through literacy. His major publications include *Extending Literacy* (Routledge), *Developing Children's Non-Fiction Writing* (Scholastic), *Literacy in the Secondary School* (Fulton) and *Teaching Literacy Effectively* (Routledge Falmer). More recently, he has begun new research programmes exploring the importance and teaching of handwriting, renewing the concept of readability and evaluating the educational use of mobile learning devices.

Dominic Wyse is Professor of Early Childhood and Primary Education at University College London (UCL), Institute of Education (IOE), and Academic Head of the Department of Learning and Leadership. Dominic is a Fellow of the Academy of Social Sciences, an elected member of the British Educational Research Association (BERA) Council, and a Fellow of the Royal Society for the Encouragement of Arts, Manufactures and Commerce (RSA). The main focus of Dominic's research is curriculum and pedagogy. Key areas of work are the teaching of writing (e.g. *How Writing Works*, Cambridge University Press), reading and creativity. Dominic has extensive experience of funded research projects that he has disseminated in numerous peer-reviewed research journal articles and books. These books include major international research volumes for which he is the lead editor (e.g. *The BERA/SAGE Handbook of Educational Research* and *The SAGE Handbook of Curriculum, Pedagogy and Assessment*) and bestselling books for students, teachers and educators (e.g. *Teaching English, Language and Literacy*, 4th edn). His most recent book is *A Guide to Early Years and Primary Teaching* (published by Sage). He has been an editor, and on the editorial board, of internationally recognised research journals. He is currently an editor of the *Curriculum Journal*, one of the journals of BERA.

INTRODUCTION

Teresa Cremin and Cathy Burnett

So you want to become a primary teacher? Or you are already one and want to revisit your understanding of the two-way traffic between research and practice? Then you have found the right book! We wonder what brought you to this career choice and what kind of teacher you are or want to become. Do you see teaching as a vocation – a craft – a profession? The world of education is changing, and, with the advance of technology and global uncertainty, we also need to ask ourselves what kinds of teacher do the children of tomorrow need? For instance, do they need:

- curriculum deliverers
- concept builders
- creative practitioners
- reflective practitioners
- possibility thinkers
- passionate, principled pedagogues
- artistically engaged professionals?

Where do you see yourself? Perhaps there are more areas of overlap than distinctions here, but exploring your conception of teachers, and of teaching and learning, will be key to your professional journey and can be enabled through this handbook. *Learning to Teach in the Primary School* aims to support you during your initial education as a teacher, and through your NQT year and beyond, regardless of the route through which you enter the profession.

In developing this, the fourth edition of the text, we reviewed the value, contemporary relevance and research underpinning the book and identified additional themes and issues that deserved inclusion in order to ensure comprehensive coverage of both policy and practice in primary education. We also reviewed the style and format in order to increase the accessibility and connection to the classroom, such that research-informed practice examples are offered in an engaging manner. We invited twenty-four new authors and have worked with forty-one ongoing authors, all of whom are experts in their various fields, to bring their area to life. We are delighted that in this edition, for the first time, we have academics co-authoring with teachers and head teachers and, throughout, a strong sense of the sharing of perspectives and understandings that draw upon rich accounts of practice from diverse classrooms across the UK. The authors' voices and views shine through. All seek to provoke discussion and debate in order to enable your development as a reflective practitioner, now and on into the future. They recognise, as we do, that teaching is a professional and artistic enterprise and that, at the heart of the practice of education, is the relationship between teacher and pupil. It is this relationship that sets the tone for everything that happens in the classroom, and it is this relationship that influences the development of positive attitudes and dispositions, as well as growth in knowledge, skills and understanding.

So this book is not a collection of 'tips for teachers'. You will find within its pages a great deal of very practical advice about primary teaching, strategies to support you and activities you can use in the classroom, but the book goes far beyond this. In compiling it, we aimed to offer you practical advice and support, but also a rationale for why such advice might be useful, where it comes from, on what basis it has been formulated, and how you might evaluate its usefulness. Of course, teaching is never a neutral activity. It is always informed by particular experiences, beliefs and commitments, and the recommendations and perspectives found in this handbook are no exception. We hope that, as you read and reflect critically on the units, you will review your own beliefs and commitments and find inspiration for translating these into practice. In short, this book is intended to be both practical and theoretical, a professional resource that is a prompt for reflection, a source of new knowledge and support for tomorrow. This reflects our view of teaching as a highly skilled, knowledgeable, professional activity.

The book, therefore, will help move you on in your development as a professional by providing you with background insights into a range of issues that affect the decisions you make in the classroom, and illustrating how such insights affect your classroom practice. Our intention is that this book will work alongside the other experiences on your journey, providing a practical introduction to the complex knowledge, skills, understanding and attitudes that teachers need to acquire, and to the theories underpinning them.

The book is divided into key sections, each exploring and explaining critical issues, such as teaching and learning, curriculum and assessment, diversity and inclusion, and it also attends to recent significant developments and partnerships in practice. It closes by looking forwards to your professional development. Each unit within these sections contains an introduction to the key concepts and learning activities for student teachers, presented in the form of tasks. There are also annotated lists of suggested reading for students, tutors and mentors who want to explore topics in more detail. A number of tasks and suggestions for further reading are labelled as particularly appropriate for Masters-level (M-level).

The text can be used in a very flexible way, as pre-reading or follow-up for taught sessions or work in schools, as support for assignments, as part of a conversation with your mentor or tutor or within your group. However you use it, we hope it will help inspire in you the same deep interest in and commitment to primary education that our contributors express.

Education is an endlessly fascinating subject, and, of course, teaching children is a highly challenging and creative activity. Enjoy the experience – we hope it will be engaging and satisfying for all involved and that this book will support you on your professional learning journey as you commence your career as a primary teacher.

SECTION 1
BECOMING A TEACHER

PRIMARY TEACHING

A personal perspective

Colin Richards

INTRODUCTION

Primary teaching is an immensely complicated business – much more complicated than government ministers and most other politicians realise. It involves so many different elements and dimensions. It changes in form and substance from minute to minute, hour to hour, lesson to lesson, class to class and year to year. Some people see it as a scientific activity, involving the selection of the best ways to 'deliver' material to young minds; others stress its artistic side and place emphasis on the 'feel' or style of teaching. So what is this enterprise called primary teaching? It is the purpose of this introductory unit to open this up for discussion.

OBJECTIVES

By the end of this unit, you should be beginning to:

- form a view of the nature of primary teaching;
- develop an awareness of the personal qualities and skills you require as a primary teacher;
- form views as to the purposes of primary teaching;
- be overawed, yet excited, at the responsibility of being a primary school teacher.

'ACROSTIC' TEACHING

When you begin teaching you will be surprised at the range of different types of writing that the children are expected to engage in. Children have to learn to write narrative accounts, imaginative stories, descriptions of their 'experiments', diaries, letters, poems, and so on. Some are introduced to acrostics and enjoy the challenge these present. What are acrostics? They are poems or other compositions in which certain letters in each line form a word or words.

I have used an acrostic when giving an introductory talk to students at the beginning of their course of teacher education. You will notice that I don't call them 'trainees' and I don't talk of 'teacher training'. They, like you, are not being introduced to a simple, straightforward, uncontroversial activity in which they can be trained to perform like machine operators on a production line or like speakers using autocues.

You are being inducted into a very complex professional activity – illustrated, for example, by the fact that the text you are reading contains over forty units and is just an introduction that will need complementing with further professional development when you are in post! It is not the easy, straightforward activity beloved of politicians such as Michael Gove, Nick Gibb or Boris Johnson in search of sound bites and easy votes. It's a very demanding set of activities that require intellect, emotional intelligence, imagination and sensitivity – all of which are not easy to acquire or to assess.

Here's the acrostic:

```
T    . . . . . . . .
E    . . . . . . . .
A    . . . . . . . .
C    . . . . . . . .
H    . . . . . . . .
I    . . . . . . . .
N    . . . . . . . .
G    . . . . . . . .
```

I have asked my students, and I am asking you, to characterise primary teaching using eight adjectives corresponding to the eight letters.

 Task 1.1.1 The nature of primary teaching

What do you think primary teaching is like? What does it feel like? What kind of activity is it? Complete your acrostic and share it with fellow students.

Of course, there are no right or wrong answers here, and an activity as complex as primary teaching cannot be captured in just eight words. As 'a starter for eight', I offer you my 'take' on primary teaching:

T iring: Primary teaching is very demanding work – very demanding physically, as you have to cope with a class of very active, growing human beings all requiring your attention; very demanding emotionally, as you have to deal with a myriad of social interactions and situations occurring in a crowded classroom; very demanding intellectually, as you have to translate complex ideas in your head into terms that children can understand.

E xhilarating: Primary teaching is equally (but paradoxically) invigorating work – especially when both you and the children get 'fired up' with enthusiasm for a particular activity, topic or piece of work. That 'buzz' needs to be experienced to be appreciated. It cannot be measured, but it can be experienced and should be treasured.

A musing: Primary teaching is enlivened by countless amusing incidents during the course of a day or a week. Some children are natural, self-conscious comedians; others are unintentionally so; primary classrooms provide endless scope for amusement. 'Never a dull moment' captures this characteristic.

C haotic: Primary teaching can appear (and sometimes is) chaotic, as unforeseen circumstances arise and have to be coped with; as the government, testing agencies, Ofsted inspectors, parents, the head teacher and children make conflicting demands that have somehow to be met; and as the daily business of fostering the learning of twenty, thirty, or even more, lively and, to a degree, unpredictable youngsters has to be managed.

H ectic: Primary teaching occurs in an extremely busy place called a classroom, where a multitude of activities (some intended by the teachers, others unintended!) take place simultaneously, and where nothing or nobody stands or sits still for long. Stamina, patience, resilience, grit and an ability to cope with the unexpected are at a premium. These qualities are impossible to 'train' or 'measure', but they can be fostered and ought to be appreciated.

I nspiring: Primary teaching can be inspiring. You can be inspired by the amazing abilities children can reveal, for example in the creative arts; you can be inspired by the personal qualities of kindness and consideration children can show to one another and to you; you can be inspired by the fact that children with unbelievably difficult home circumstances come to school and manage to learn at all; you can be inspired by the work of your colleagues in your own school and in others, from whom you can learn so much. You can be inspired and, on occasion, you can inspire!

N ever-ending: Primary teaching is not a 'nine till four' occupation. In fact, it's not so much an occupation as a way of life. It is never complete, never mastered, never perfected and never 'sorted'. There is always more to learn and more to do for the children in your class. Teaching can take over your whole life with its never-ending demands, but you have to learn to temper these demands with your own personal needs. Doing this can be conscience-wracking, but is absolutely essential – to your own and, indirectly, your children's well-being. Work load is a very real issue that you, your school and the government need to address and manage.

G ratifying: Primary teaching can be intensely gratifying (despite some inevitable frustrations). Teaching a child to read, seeing another child's delight on mastering a skill, telling a story that captivates the whole class, having a lesson that goes really well – such activities can and will give you tremendous satisfaction. But don't expect it from every single lesson. You cannot be 'outstanding' or even 'good' all the time, or expect outstanding or good results from every child all the time – despite the fact that some head teachers and inspectors seem to expect this.

A SENSE OF STYLE

You can see from my completed acrostic that I believe that primary teaching is an extremely complex activity. It's an amalgam of so many elements – emotional, intellectual, physical, spiritual and social. It changes subtly in form, substance and 'feel', minute to minute, hour to hour, lesson to lesson, class to class, and year to year. It involves qualities such as 'respect', 'concern', 'care', 'commitment' and 'intellectual integrity', which are impossible to define but which are deeply influential in determining the nature of life in classrooms. The ends and means of education and the aims and methods of teaching are inextricably interwoven. As well as being a practical activity, teaching needs to be conducted with a strong sense of moral purpose – you are doing it primarily to benefit others, not yourself! The word 'style' captures something of what I am trying to convey – a sense of considered professional judgement, of personal response, of quality, of distinctive style, which each practitioner (including you!) needs to foster. You need to develop your own style; don't be misled into believing that there is an 'approved' or 'set' style from China, Singapore or wherever, that will 'deliver' (horrible word!) the results. Primary teaching involves far more than the routine repetition of established procedures; it goes well beyond establishing and maintaining a well-organised, orderly classroom, though that's important. It cannot be pinned down in a few straightforward sentences or in a political sound bite or in a brief inspection report (or, for that matter, in my simple acrostic!).

TEACHING: SCIENCE, CRAFT OR ART?

Some educational researchers, such as Coe and Waring (2017), Hattie (2012) and Muijs and Reynolds (2001), seem to believe that it is possible to create a science of teaching based on the social sciences. They believe that it is possible to study teaching by comparing the results of different methods in terms of the outcomes they produce in children, and thereby arrive at objective findings as to which teaching methods are effective in which contexts. You will come across books with titles such as *Effective Teaching*, which claim to provide scientifically defensible evidence on which to base decisions about how to teach. But don't be afraid to question their conclusions.

Some educationists, such as Marland (1975), regard teaching as a craft – a set of difficult and complex techniques that can be picked up from, or taught by, skilled practitioners and that can be honed and perfected over the years. Currently, many politicians also have this view of teaching, though they tend to see it as much more straightforward than the educationists do. You will come across government documents such as 'The importance of teaching' and books with titles such as *The Craft of the Classroom* that embody this approach. Be questioning of these too.

Others, such as Eisner (1979) and Bennett (2012), regard teaching as an art – a complex creative activity concerned with the promotion of human learning and involving imagination, sensitivity and personal response and an indefinable element of professional judgement, none of which can be taught directly by another person (though they can be learned indirectly). Treat Eisner's and Bennett's views with respect: they are close to the truth as I see it, but question them too.

 Task 1.1.2 Teaching: Science, craft or art?

Based on your experience of teaching at school, at university or on this course, how would you characterise teaching – as science, art or craft? Try to justify your answer to fellow students.

Again, as in the response to Task 1.1.1, there are no absolutely right or wrong answers.

From what I have written already, you can see that I characterise teaching as very largely an art, although an art also involving some craft skills that can be taught and even trained for. I do not see that there can ever be an 'objective' science of teaching, involving the rigorous definition of methods and the clear measurement of outcomes in national tests or through other means. I believe that such a science is logically impossible, as 'the power to teach' is a highly complex amalgam of judgement, technique and personal qualities whose assessment is inevitably subjective and can never be susceptible to quantification or measurement by social scientists and educational researchers. However, that perspective is my own personal one. Treat it critically. Other educationists have different ideas of the nature of teaching, including some who even subscribe to the notion of 'the science of the art of teaching'!

ENACTIVE, PRE-ACTIVE AND POST-ACTIVE PRIMARY TEACHING

What kinds of activity are involved in being a primary teacher? What should the balance be between the different kinds?

To outsiders (government ministers such as Nick Gibb in particular!) and perhaps too many primary-age children (though we don't know because we haven't asked them!), 'teaching' conjures up an image of an adult in front of a class describing, explaining, instructing or demonstrating something to his or her pupils. This is *enactive teaching* – teaching in action, the 'full frontal' interaction of teacher and children. Of course, enactive teaching doesn't only take place in classrooms – it occurs in the hall, in the school grounds and on school trips. Nor does it always involve direct interaction with a whole class of children – the teacher may be teaching individuals or groups, or may be setting up activities where children learn for themselves, for example. There has been a considerable amount of research into enactive teaching in English primary schools – referred to in other parts of this book, such as Section 2. However, there is far more to teaching than enactive teaching, even though the latter is the core activity.

There is *pre-active teaching*, involving the preparation and planning for children's learning, the organisation of the classroom, the collection and organisation of teaching resources, the management of visits or activities outside the classroom and the briefing of other adults who work with children. Interestingly, there has been little research into how primary teachers actually plan, prepare and organise their work. But there is no doubt it takes up a lot of time – before and after school and in the school holidays. Pre-active teaching is essential to the success of enactive teaching – hence the emphasis on planning and managing learning in Section 3 of this book.

There is also *post-active teaching*, which involves considered reflection on practice, writing up evaluations, marking children's work, making assessments of children's progress and keeping records. At its best, this feeds into pre-active teaching, as reflection and assessment inform planning and preparation. There is plenty of advice available on assessment and record-keeping (see Section 5) but, again, a dearth of research into how teachers actually engage in post-active teaching – you might consider undertaking some research of your own later in your career!

But there is still more to primary teaching as a professional activity. Teachers have to engage in a variety of extra-class activities – administrative tasks, staff meetings, clubs, consultations with parents and attendance at professional development courses, which relate indirectly to teaching but can't be fitted into my neat (too neat?) threefold classification. There was some interesting work carried out more than 20 years ago by Campbell and Neill (1994) into the nature of primary teachers' work, especially the amount of time devoted to a variety of activities. The research makes interesting reading, although the categories the researchers used are rather different from my classification, and the findings may now be somewhat dated. Campbell and Neill found that, on average, the 374 infant and junior teachers in their study spent 52.6 hours a week on professional activity – subdivided into 18.3 hours for teaching (i.e. enactive teaching), 15.7 hours for preparation/marking (i.e. an amalgam of pre-active and post-active teaching), 14.1 hours on administration, 7.2 hours on professional development (including staff meetings and reading) and 4.5 hours on a ragbag of other activities that didn't fit into any of their other categories. Clearly, this research gave the lie to the idea of primary teaching as a '9 to 3.30 occupation'!

More recently, this has been backed up by a government workload survey carried out in 2013 that showed an increase in working hours for all categories of teachers compared with 2010. Primary classroom teachers' hours had increased by more than 9 hours a week to 59.3. Classroom teachers spent 19 hours a week teaching, 10.6 hours on lesson planning and preparation for tests, 9.7 hours on assessment, making and report-writing, and 4 hours a week on aspects of school management (Department for Education, 2014). Primary teaching is not getting any easier in terms of workload!

One of the most surprising findings of the 1994 and 2013 surveys was the relatively small proportion of the teachers' total work time devoted to what I have called enactive teaching, that is, about a third. Given the pressures of national testing and Ofsted inspections, it is not so surprising that, between 1994 and the present, there has been a large (I would say 'disproportionate') increase in the amount of time devoted to assessment record-keeping and data-recording – activities that have contributed massively to current concerns about teacher workloads. Enactive teaching requires a large input of pre-active teaching if it is to be successful, and it needs to be followed up by considerable, though far less, post-active activity to ensure a professional cycle of planning-teaching-assessment-reflection-planning-teaching-assessment . . . ad infinitum. Remember, primary teaching is 'never-ending'!

THE PERSONAL QUALITIES AND KNOWLEDGE REQUIRED OF PRIMARY TEACHERS

Task 1.1.3 The characteristics of a good teacher

In a small group, consider what makes a good teacher, and what knowledge and personal qualities s/he needs.

Would children come up with the same answers? Discuss the issue with a small group of primary-aged children.

There has been little research into how children view good teachers. More than 40 years ago, Philip Taylor and Frank Musgrove asked both primary- and secondary-aged children and received very similar answers from both. In their words:

> Pupils expect teachers to teach. They value lucid exposition, the clear statement of problems and guidance in their solution. Personal qualities of kindness, sympathy and patience are secondary, appreciated by pupils if they make the teacher more effective in carrying out his primary, intellectual task . . . there appears to be little demand by pupils that teachers shall be friends or temporary mothers and fathers.
>
> (Musgrove and Taylor, 1969: 17)

Much more recently, the Cambridge Review asked children what they looked for in a good teacher:

> Children described the best teachers as being those who listened, were kind and 'understood how you feel'. A good teacher, they suggested, should:
>
> * 'really know their stuff'
> * be able to make learning fun
> * know everyone's names
> * tell you things in advance so that you know what a lesson is about
> * give you a permanent record of what you learn
> * be able to explain things clearly so that you understand
> * have lots of energy and enthusiasm.
>
> (Alexander, 2010: 148)

How do these two sets of findings compare with the results of your small group discussions?

The knowledge required to be a primary teacher has changed considerably since the introduction of what was then teacher training in the nineteenth century, but the personal qualities needed have remained the same. The following paragraph captures something of what is required:

> Teaching involves a lot more than care, mutual respect and well-placed optimism. It demands knowledge and practical skills; the ability to make informed judgements, and to balance pressures

and challenges; practice and creativity; interest and effort; as well as an understanding of how children learn and develop.

(Department for Education and Skills and Teacher Training Agency, 2002: 4)

Tongue in cheek, I can characterise the expectations of teachers held currently by the government and the wider society as representing:

a set of demands which properly exemplified would need the expertise of Leonardo da Vinci, the knowledge of a Mastermind winner, the diplomatic understanding and charm of Barack Obama, the histrionic skills of Helen Mirren, the determination of Mo Farah or Laura Trott, and the saintliness of Pope Francis, coupled with the omniscience of God.

Admittedly, this is over the top, but it does represent the inflated expectations of us as teachers. None of us is a perfect human being (nor, for that matter, are the children in our classes, their parents or our politicians), but those inflated expectations are a powerful influence on how many teachers view themselves and on causing so many to feel guilty about falling short. We can aspire to educational sainthood but hardly hope to achieve it – not even the writers in this book. However, in its pursuit, we can at least aspire to show such qualities as 'care', 'respect', 'optimism', 'interest' and 'effort', required of us, quite properly in my view, by officialdom.

The knowledge required of you as primary teachers is of seven kinds – each important, though one (the second) is, in my view, more important than the others. As the government emphasises (rather too much?), you certainly need subject-content knowledge – an understanding of the main concepts, principles, skills and content of the areas that you will have to teach. That's a tall order, given that the curriculum you are required to teach in Key Stages 1 and 2 involves a large range of subjects, as well as cross-curricular areas such as personal and social education, and given the wide curriculum required in early years settings. You can't assume that you have the required subject knowledge as a result of your own education, whether at school, college or university. You will need to audit and, where necessary, top up your subject knowledge by reading or attending courses. Begin now in a small way, if you haven't done this already.

The second kind of knowledge involves the application of subject knowledge in teaching your children – sometimes termed, rather grandly, 'pedagogical subject knowledge'. This crucially important area involves knowing how to make the knowledge, skills and understanding of subjects accessible and meaningful to children – how best to represent particular ideas; what illustrations to use; what demonstrations or experiments to employ; what stories to tell; what examples to draw on; what kinds of explanation to offer; how to relate what needs to be taught to children's experiences or interests, and so on. You will begin to develop this applied expertise in your course of initial teacher education; you will need to add to it through continuing professional development and through your own reading; and, over time, you will add to it from 'the wisdom of practice' – your colleagues' and hopefully your own. Membership of associations such as the Chartered College of Teaching, the Cambridge Primary Review Trust and the National Association for Primary Education can also enhance your expertise and wider understanding of primary education. Application of subject knowledge also draws on knowledge of children's development, including aspects of how children learn and what motivates them; of developmental sequences (in so far as we can identify them); and of learning difficulties and other special needs (see Sections 2 and 6 of this book).

You also need to develop curriculum knowledge, that is, knowledge of National Curriculum requirements, now particularly (and obsessively?) detailed for English and mathematics. But you also need to know about school policies, guidelines and schemes of work, and about the range of published materials and sources available as 'tools of the trade' to help you teach your class. You cannot be expected to keep abreast of developments in every area, but you can be expected to know to whom to turn for advice in your school.

There are yet more areas of professional knowledge you need to acquire. According to Shulman (1987), these include general pedagogical knowledge (including teaching strategies, techniques, behaviour management and classroom organisation), knowledge of educational contexts (ranging from the workings of small groups and the ways in which schools are organised, run, financed and governed, to the characteristics of communities and cultures) and knowledge of educational ends, purposes and values. To these I should add knowing how to collect, analyse and use performance data. It's particularly important to know the limitations as well as the uses of data. Data can raise issues for you to consider; data should inform, but never override, your professional judgement. You know the children in your class far better than any test.

You can see that primary teaching involves much more than knowledge of how to teach 'reading, writing and number' - a view too many politicians, local and national, seem to hold. Being a primary teacher involves lifelong learning and being something of a mini-polymath!

THE PURPOSES OF PRIMARY TEACHING

The state first provided elementary education for children of primary-school age in the latter half of the nineteenth century. The state system complemented a rather chaotic and ad hoc collection of schools run by religious organisations. Now, more than 95 per cent of children aged from 4 to 11 attend state primary schools and are taught by teachers in local authority (LA) schools, in academies or in free schools. LA schools have to work to, and academies and free schools have to 'have regard to', national requirements and guidelines, such as the National Curriculum and testing arrangements.

Since the nineteenth century, primary teaching has served a variety of purposes; although the relative importance of these has changed over time, as a primary teacher, you will play a part in fulfilling these purposes. You will need to form your own view of their relative importance and decide how best to fulfil them, or possibly subtly subvert aspects of them, in the best interests of your pupils.

One major purpose of primary teaching has been, and is, *instruction* - here broadly conceived to include helping children acquire:

- procedural knowledge:
    - helping children to acquire and use information, for example learning and applying the four rules of number, learning how to spell, learning how to conduct fair tests in science;
- conceptual knowledge:
    - helping children to understand ideas;
    - helping children to understand principles, for example learning the importance of chronology in history or basic scientific principles;
- skills:
    - helping children to acquire manipulative and other physical skills, such as cutting, handwriting or gymnastics;
    - helping children to acquire complex skills, such as learning how to read and interpret texts using a variety of strategies, or word-processing skills;
- metacognitive knowledge:
    - helping children to be more knowledgeable about how they learn and how they can improve their learning.

Over time, the relative importance of these components has changed. In the nineteenth century, most emphasis was placed on *procedural knowledge* and *skills acquisition*, often of an elementary kind.

The latter half of the twentieth century saw an increasing emphasis on *conceptual knowledge* and more advanced *skills acquisition*. Currently, there is a growing interest in fostering *metacognitive knowledge* (see Section 2), but also a re-emphasis by the government on procedural and factual knowledge. As a primary teacher in the first part of the twenty-first century, you will need to foster all four components – not an easy task!

A second major purpose of primary teaching has been, and is, *socialisation*. Children need to be introduced into a wider society than the home; they need to be able to relate to their peers and to work with them. They need to be inducted into the norms and values of British society (though these are difficult to define!), but also be aware of wider international values such as sustainability and human rights. They need to be socialised into the 'strange' world of school, which operates very differently from most homes and involves a great deal of fundamental but often unacknowledged learning – graphically captured (for all time?) in Philip Jackson's brilliant first chapter in his *Life in Classrooms* (1968). As a teacher, especially if you are an early years teacher, you will be a very significant and influential agent in children's socialisation. This process has always been a major purpose of primary teaching, especially in the nineteenth century, when large numbers of children entered formal education for the first time and had to be compelled to 'accept their place in society', as the Victorians might have put it. But it is still very significant today – partly as a result of our increasingly complex, rich, multicultural society, in which the values of tolerance and respect for others are so much needed and where they can be fostered and reinforced from the minute children enter school. Contemporary children need to find a place – a comfortable, affirming, respected place – in our society. Primary teachers need to help them find it and make it their own.

Linked to socialisation is another function of primary teaching. Teachers are concerned with children's *welfare* – physical, mental, emotional and social. Primary schools are the most accessible 'outposts' of the welfare state as far as most parents and children are concerned. They are crucially important points of contact, especially for economically disadvantaged families. In the late nineteenth and early twentieth centuries, primary teachers were particularly concerned for children's physical welfare – as illustrated by the introduction of school meals and medical inspections and the emphasis placed on physical training. In very recent years, there has been a resurgence of concern about children's welfare. Especially in the area of welfare, it is not easy to decide on the limits of teachers' care for their children (Nias, 1997). But there is another aspect to welfare – your own. You need to be fit and well for your own sake, as well as for your class. You need to look after your own well-being, and this involves difficult choices about what to do and what not to do among the million and one things you could do. Welfare, your children's as well as your own, is yet another dimension to primary teaching – no wonder your course of teacher education is so crowded, and this book so long!

There is a fourth function of primary teaching – and one about which I feel rather uncomfortable. Traditionally, primary teaching has also involved the *classification* of children in order to 'sort' them out for their secondary education. Classification wasn't a major purpose in Victorian times – the working-class children who were taught in the state elementary schools were not expected to go on to any form of secondary education. However, in the first three-quarters of the twentieth century, primary teachers played a major part in identifying children of different abilities and preparing them for different forms of secondary education – grammar, secondary modern and, to a far lesser extent, technical education. That classification function still applies in those parts of the country that retain selective schools and may well increase more widely if the government of the day succeeds in establishing more selective schools. Currently, a more insidious form of classification influences the practice of many primary teachers as a result of the introduction of national testing and the emphasis on assessing children's progress in relation to official criteria. Too often, children are classified in terms of how far they are meeting age-related, official expectations in such a way that they begin to define themselves in ways that narrow their views of themselves and their ability to learn. As a primary teacher, you will need to work within the system as it is, but you also have a professional duty to lobby to change it, if, like me, you feel it works against the interests of children in your care.

Task 1.1.4 The purposes of primary teaching

In pairs, consider the relative importance of the four purposes of primary teaching. Make a list of the kinds of activity teachers engage in related to each of the four purposes. Primary teachers in other countries do not necessarily see their role in these terms (see Alexander, 2000). Should any of these purposes *not* apply, or be given far less emphasis in primary teaching in the United Kingdom? Why?

SUMMARY

The importance of primary teaching

I hope that, by now, you have realised how demanding primary teaching is and how important it is, especially to the children themselves. Philip Jackson reminds us that children spend around 7,000 hours in primary school, spread over 6 or 7 years of their young lives. There is no other activity that occupies as much of the child's time as that involved in attending school.

> Apart from the bedroom there is no single enclosure in which he spends a longer time than he does in the classroom. During his primary school years he is a more familiar sight to his teacher than to his father, and possibly even his mother.
>
> (Jackson, 1968: 5)

As a child's teacher, you are an incredibly (and frighteningly!) significant person: your teaching will help shape attitudes to learning at a most sensitive period in children's development. After all:

> These seven years are among the most vivid of our existence. Every day is full of new experiences; the relatively static seems permanent; time seems to last much longer; *events and individuals leave deeper impressions and more lasting memories than later in life*. Without discussing what are the happiest years, we may at least agree that every stage of life should be lived for its own sake as happily and fully as possible. *We must above all respect this right on behalf of children, whose happiness is a good deal at the mercy of circumstances and people beyond their control.*
>
> (Scottish Education Department, 1946: 5; my italics)

To return to my acrostic, becoming a primary school teacher is demanding, difficult and exhausting and at times can be a fazing experience. But it is also immensely rewarding, incredibly fascinating, never for a moment boring (unless you make it so!), often very humorous and, because never-ending, always unfinis . . .

Hopefully, you are up for it?

ANNOTATED FURTHER READING

Alexander, R. (2000) *Culture and Pedagogy: International Comparisons in Primary Education*, Oxford, UK: Blackwell.
A fascinating analysis of primary teaching as practised in France, Russia, India, the United States and England.

Alexander, R. (ed.) (2010) *Children, Their World, Their Education*, London: Routledge.
The most recent and authoritative review of English (not UK) primary education – full of valuable and fascinating information and ideas, though less good at getting 'inside' what it is to be a primary teacher.

Cremin, T. (2009) 'Creative teachers, creative teaching', in A. Wilson (ed.) *Creativity in Primary Education*, 2nd edn, Exeter, UK: Learning Matters, pp. 36–46.
This explores the characteristics and personal qualities of creative teachers and creative primary teaching.

Jackson, P. (1968) *Life in Classrooms*, New York: Holt, Rinehart & Winston.
This offers a complementary but rather different view of teaching primary-aged children from that offered in this unit. Almost 50 years on, it is still the most evocative description of life as lived in classrooms.

FURTHER READING TO SUPPORT M-LEVEL STUDY

Nias, J. (1997) 'Would schools improve if teachers cared less?', *Education 3–13*, 25(3): 11–22.
This is a challenging, critical perspective on the role of education and care in the education of primary-aged children.

Guerriero, S. and Revai, N. (2017) 'Knowledge based teaching and the evolution of a profession', in S. Guerriero (ed.) *Pedagogical Knowledge and the Changing Nature of the Teaching Profession*. Paris: OECD.
This chapter offers a conceptual framework for teacher competence that is based on teacher learning (through ITE, CPD and informal opportunities). It provides a contemporary take on teachers' professional competence and how this relates to student learning and recognises the importance of teachers' affective motivational competences and beliefs.

Richards, C. (2011) 'What could be – for contemporary policy and practice: Challenges posed by the work of Edmond Holmes', *Forum*, 53(3): 451–61.
This discusses critically the role of the primary school teacher – from both a contemporary perspective and from a historical one. It illustrates some of the perennial issues facing primary education.

REFERENCES

Alexander, R. (2000) *Culture and Pedagogy: International Comparisons in Primary Education*, Oxford, UK: Blackwell.

Alexander, R. (ed.) (2010) *Children, Their World, Their Education*, London: Routledge.

Bennett T. (2012) *Teacher: Mastering the Art and Craft of Teaching*, London: Continuum.

Campbell, R.J. and Neill, S. (1994) *Primary Teachers at Work*, London: Routledge.

Coe, R. and Waring, M. (2017) *Research Methods and Methodologies in Education*, London: Sage.

Department for Education. (2014) *Teachers' Workload Diary Survey: Research Report*, London: Department for Education.

Department for Education and Skills (DfES) and Teacher Training Agency (TTA). (2002) *Qualifying to Teach: Professional Standards for Qualified Teacher Status and Requirements for Initial Teacher Training*, London: DfES/TTA.

Eisner, E. (1979) *The Educational Imagination*, New York: Collier-Macmillan.

Hattie, J. (2012) *Visible Learning for Teachers: Maximizing Impact on Learning*, London: Routledge.

Jackson, P. (1968) *Life in Classrooms*, New York: Holt, Rinehart & Winston.

Marland, M. (1975) *The Craft of the Classroom*, London: Heinemann Educational.

Muijs, D. and Reynolds, D. (2001) *Effective Teaching: Evidence and Practice*, London: Paul Chapman.

Musgrove, F. and Taylor, P. (1969) *Society and the Teacher's Role*, London: Routledge & Kegan Paul.

Nias, J. (1997) 'Would schools improve if teachers cared less?', *Education 3-13*, 25(3): 11-22.

Scottish Education Department. (1946) *Primary Education*, Edinburgh: His Majesty's Stationery Office.

Shulman, L. (1987) 'Knowledge and teaching: Foundations of the new reforms', *Harvard Educational Review*, 57: 1-22.

BECOMING A PROFESSIONAL IN THE CURRENT CONTEXT

Samantha Twiselton and Janet Goepel

INTRODUCTION

There is so much more to becoming a teacher who truly *feels like* a real professional than meets the eye! This is because it not only involves meeting the standards as stipulated but also includes grappling with the behaviours, knowledge, skills and (most importantly) beliefs and values you think are needed to make you *feel* like you are a professional. This unit will help you examine the journey you are on to becoming a true professional in relation to both the technical things you need to be able to demonstrate and to the processes, challenges and tensions you are likley to face along the way.

OBJECTIVES

By the end of this unit, you should be able to:

1 understand that the term 'professionalism' has multiple definitions;
2 make sense of what this means to you in a range of different contexts;
3 begin to plan for how to take control of your own professionalism as demands on you change over time.

PROFESSIONALISM – THEORY AND RESEARCH

We all have notions as to what we mean by 'being professional'. For most of us this includes ways in which we behave and present ourselves, including, for example, how we dress. It also includes what we do and how we do it: for example, what time we arrive and how much preparation we have done before we get there. We consider someone to be professional if they carry out a required task well and if they are polite and punctual. They often require some distinct or expert knowledge or skill that guides professional practice (Hilferty, 2008: 162). The most basic definition of being professional for teachers is of being paid to teach (Tichenor and Tichenor, 2005: 90). This idea is similar to how someone who practises their sport as their means of income is viewed, and is in contrast to an amateur who might be involved in their sport in their spare time but for whom this is not their source of income. However, it is also suggested that being professional involves high standards of delivery (Demirkasimoğlu, 2010: 2048), and that this means still being professional even 'when no-one is looking' (Hargreaves and Fullen, 2012: 5).

Although theoretical perspectives might help to form a definition of professionalism, it is interesting to consider what teachers themselves consider professionalism to be and look like. One study found that teachers identified characteristics such as being resilient, keeping composure, being caring, nurturing, friendly, patient, well organised and open to new ideas as important expressions of being professional (Tichenor and Tichenor, 2005). Additionally, this study found that teachers thought that being professional involved being a good communicator with parents and children, being a good role model and showing respect. A more recent project found that teachers felt they had a professional responsibility to improve their practice, and that they had an intrinsic desire to do the best job they could in becoming a better teacher and in meeting the needs of their pupils (Poet, Rudd and Kelly, 2010). The use of self-reflection as well as peer feedback was seen as an important tool for developing professional practice.

What is clear is that the definition of professionalism is subject to change over time, through different influences, such as political and social change, and from different perspectives (Demirkasimoğlu, 2010: 2050). An important element of being able to be fully professional is concerned with having the authority to decide how to carry out practice, to be autonomous. Unlike the medical profession or law, teachers do not have a strong, independent professional body that regulates their performance and maintains the standing of the profession. Instead, teachers' day-to-day work and professional expectations are set out in the Teachers' Standards developed by the Department for Education (2011), and matters relating to teacher's personal and professional conduct are regulated by the National College of Teaching and Leadership (NCTL). The NCTL – which has responsibility for the supply and training of high-quality teachers, as well as teacher regulation and the development of policy for education – is a government agency rather than a professional body. This means that teachers often feel like they have little say in their own working practices and behaviours. They may feel themselves to have little autonomy. For many practising teachers, the requirement by the government to carry out their professional practice in particular ways, according to priorities that may not fit their own particular school environment and may not tally with their own view of professionalism, is a challenge that has to be reconciled.

The Chartered College of Teaching

Although it is true to say that the functions carried out by the General Teaching Council for England (GTCE) have been taken on by the NCTL, it is also fair to say that these were rather narrowly defined when it was being considered what a professional body can mean to a profession's sense of supporting its members to be professionals in the fullest sense. The Chartered College of Teaching came into being in 2016, with its founding CEO taking up her appointment in January 2017. This body has aspirations to support and represent the teaching profession in a way that goes much further than the GTCE. Although it is still in the early stages of development, its plans are rapidly developing, and free membership is available for student teachers.

In Northern Ireland . . .

The General Teaching Council for Northern Ireland (GTCNI) is the regulating body for the teaching profession in Northern Ireland. In *Teaching: The Reflective Profession* (2007), the GTCNI present their model of the Reflective and Activist Practitioner along with a Code of Values and Professional Practice that comprises twenty-seven teacher professional competences.

Source: General Teaching Council for Northern Ireland. (2007) *Teaching: The Reflective Profession*, Belfast, GTCNI. Available at www.gtcni.org.uk/userfiles/file/The_Reflective_Profession_3rd-edition.pdf (accessed 11 October 2017).

In Northern Ireland . . .

The Department of Education for Northern Ireland (DENI) launched the Teacher Professional Learning Strategy in March 2016. The overall aim of the strategy is 'to empower the teaching profession to strengthen its professionalism and expertise to meet the challenging educational needs of young people in the 21st century' (DENI, 2016: 4). This is based on the vision that every teacher is a learning leader, accomplished in working collaboratively with all partners in the interests of children and young people.

Source: Department of Education for Northern Ireland (DENI). (2016) *Learning Leaders: A Strategy for Teacher Professional Learning*, Bangor, NI: DENI. Available at http://dera.ioe.ac.uk/25762/1/strategy-document-english.pdf (accessed 8 November 2017).

Task 1.2.1 Professionalism: Theory and research

Based on the definitions of professionalism given above and teachers' own views of professionalism as shown in the research, write your own definition of professionalism.

How will this definition of professionalism influence your practice as a trainee teacher?

BECOMING PROFESSIONAL – THE PROCESS

When you are learning how to become a teacher, you will no doubt be focused on achieving the expectations set out in the Teachers' Standards (2011). These are the measure used to assess whether you can gain the right to begin practising as a newly qualified teacher (NQT; at the time of writing we are awaiting further detail about proposed reforms to Qualified Teacher Status (QTS) that the White Paper (Department for Education (DfE), 2016a) announced). In achieving these standards by the end of the ITE phase, you are expected to take on the values and behaviours they set out and, by doing so, to be accepted into the profession. However, it is important to recognise that fulfilling the Standards is only part of what becoming a professional teacher is about. Becoming professional is a process that begins as you start your course (or even at the point you decide to become a teacher) to learn to be a teacher and continues throughout your professional life.

RAISING YOUR AWARENESS THROUGH MAPPING YOUR JOURNEY

Task 1.2.2 Plotting your journey to being a teacher to date

Draw a horizontal line across a paper. Mark the right hand end as being TODAY – where you are right now on your journey to being a teacher.

1   The left hand end of the line should be the first point in your life you can identify as being formative in your decision to become a teacher – even though it was probably not the point at which you decided. For example, it could be an inspirational teacher or experience

you had as a pupil, a series of baby-sitting experiences when you realised you were fascinated by young children, something in your studies that made you inspired to help others learn, and so on

2 Add other key points in your life to the line that you think have played a role in helping you decide what kind of teacher you would like to become.

3 Add other key points in your life to the line that you think have played a role in helping you decide the kind of teacher you *don't* want to become (in both cases, try not to restrict your experiences to things that have just involved teachers and consider broader influences).

4 Compare with someone else on your course – what are the similarities and differences?

5 Looking ahead to the next bit of the line – the next steps on your journey to becoming a teacher – what kinds of experience and support do you think you need to become the kind of teacher you want to be?

6 Has the process of looking back and thinking forwards raised any interesting thoughts or questions? Have your ideals about the 'perfect teacher' changed over time?

There are many factors that influence the kind of professional you may become, and the starting point is your own identity. Each of us has multiple identities that involve our ethnicity, gender, religion, culture, position in the family and other relationships. These identities form who you are, your values and your behaviours. As you begin to take on the professional identity of a teacher, your own personal identity will transform into this new, but ever-evolving personal and professional identity. It is a process that is never completed, no matter how long you are a teacher.

As you begin to take on a professional identity as a teacher, it is likely that you will become aware of challenges and tensions that require you to respond to them. Professional identity tensions are considered to be 'internal struggles between the teacher as a person and the teacher as a professional' and as such create 'identity dissonance' (Pillen, Den Brok and Beijard, 2013: 86-7). These dissonances may not be readily reconcilable as they are linked with a teacher's values, beliefs and perceptions and may challenge who you are. Although these tensions by their very nature may be uncomfortable or stressful, they are instrumental in developing professionalism in a way that adhering to Teachers' Standards alone may not. An example of tensions that may occur for you as a trainee teacher is shown in the following story.

Lisa's story

Lisa was working in her placement school. She had previously worked as a teaching assistant for a year in a special school before starting on her course. She had seen how the class teacher in the special school had made personalised provision for each of the pupils in her class and how each of them had been encouraged to record their work in many different ways, to show understanding. In the placement school, the teacher did not seem to differentiate the work for children's different learning approaches and insisted that children should write the learning objective at the beginning of every piece of work, before anything else was attempted. Some children had no other work in their books, as they found the writing process difficult and laborious. Lisa wanted to make more personalised provision for different learners and was also keen to introduce different ways of recording children's work, but the class teacher told her she had to abide by the school policy of writing out the learning objective at the beginning of each lesson. Lisa found this situation created a tension between the values she held concerning individual provision, what her previous experience in a special school had taught her and the requirements of the placement school. Lisa is obviously experiencing 'identity dissonance'. She will need to find a way of managing the relationships with others in the school, identify what she is willing to compromise in terms of her values and practice, negotiate differences of practice and expectation and allow this experience to shape her professional identity.

How you respond to identity dissonances you encounter will influence the kind of professional you will become, and, in negotiating your way through these tensions, you will develop a stronger sense of belonging to the profession (Steinert *et al.*, 2014). This process is known as socialisation and is represented in the following model, which has been adapted from Steinert *et al.* (2014).

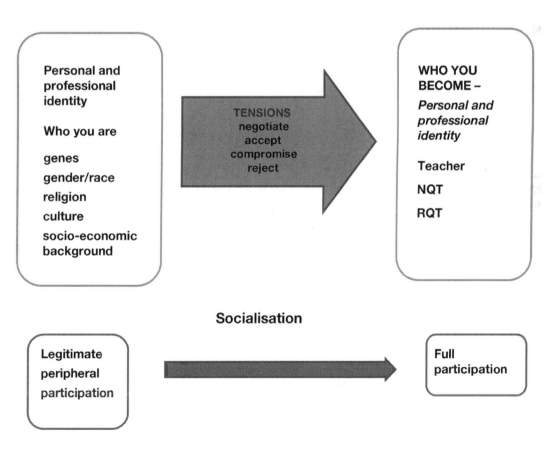

FIGURE 1.2.1 Taking on teacher professional identity through socialisation

Task 1.2.3 Developing professionalism

Consider the diagram in Figure 1.2.1.

1 What personal characteristics make up your personal identity?
2 What challenges and tensions have you faced already in developing professionalism?
3 Consider whether you accepted, rejected, negotiated or found a compromise for these challenges?
4 Why did you make the decision you did about these challenges or tensions?
5 How is this contributing to your professional development?

As can be seen from the diagram in Figure 1.2.1, it is the process of becoming a teacher that is important, and it is through this process that professionalism is developed. It is also through this process that you will move from peripheral participation within the profession to becoming a full participant.

It is easy as a trainee teacher to be unquestioning about what you are required to do in order to become a professional. However, as shown in the socialisation model, the process of becoming a professional is not without its tensions and challenges, each of which needs to be negotiated, accepted or rejected, or a compromise must be reached. Clark states boldly that, 'student teachers must, first and foremost, be disabused of any illusions they may have that their education system is either designed or equipped to turn them into the very best teacher they can be. They must do this for themselves' (2016: 41). However, she goes on to acknowledge that teachers must accept the expectations placed upon them, but that they should have the freedom to interpret them within the complexity of the workplace and through the uniqueness of the individual who is becoming professional. Therefore, as a trainee teacher, it is not just a matter of achieving the Teachers' Standards, but of coming to terms with challenges and tensions in applying the standards to practice.

A similar model of developing a professional identity as a teacher is outlined by Hargreaves and Fullen (2012). They call the personal characteristics of the socialisation model (Steinert *et al.*, 2014) human capital. This is concerned with personal resources such as being caring, friendly, patient and resiliant. The socialisation process is concerned with the importance of developing relationships with colleagues and others in the learning community, such as parents, teaching assistants and professionals from other agencies. Such relationships are seen as a resource, a way of increasing knowledge and generating trust between different groups of people. This is referred to as building social capital (Hargreaves and Fullen, 2012: 90). A third element of developing a professional identity is called decisional capital. This is developed over time and relates to the ability to make 'discretionary judgements' (ibid.: 92), to make wise decisions where there are no guidelines or given ways of managing a situation. Together, human capital, social capital and decisional capital make up professional capital, which is considered to be a vital concept in bringing together what is required to produce high standards for teachers.

Task 1.2.4 Building social capital

1 How can you build up relationships of trust with teachers, teaching assistants, parents and children?
2 What knowledge, insights and understanding have you gained through working with teachers, teaching assistants, parents and children on placement?
3 How has building social capital with others in your placement school helped you to develop your professional identity as a teacher?

ADDITIONAL COMPLEXITY ACCORDING TO SCHOOL CONTEXT

Every school is different, and every location brings its own unique set of challenges and opportunities for the pupils and teachers learning and teaching within it. This means that what is considered to be optimal professional behaviour is also likely to vary from one placement or school setting to another. Depending on the context, there will be a number of variables that will impact on how you experience this as a student teacher:

*   The legal status of your school: for example, it is a local authority school, a member of a multi-academy trust, a stand-alone academy, a free school, a faith school; there may well be specific practices and expectations that go with this. It is a good idea to find out as much as you can about this in advance.
*   Your status in the school: if your training route is, for example, Salaried School Direct or Teach First, you may be employed by the school and have contractual obligations. It may also be that you are not currently employed by the school, but there is an intention to employ you in the future. In all cases, it can be helpful to consider that you have similar obligations to a school you are training in as you would if you were an employed teacher there.
*   The Ofsted category of your school and where it is on a school improvement journey: this is likely to have an impact on the kinds of behaviour it prioritises both for pupils and teachers. It is helpful to find out about this before you visit and to tune yourself in as soon as you arrive.

This is an example from one particular type of student teacher:

When I took up my salaried School Direct place there were a number of things (both good and bad) that made me feel different from the other trainnees on different routes at various times in the school. Firstly I started at the beginning of the July before the academic year when the others were there. This made me feel like I 'belonged' right from the beginning and I was treated like a member of staff by pupils and adults. This was mostly lovely but it did sometimes mean I was expected to know more than I did and in the early days I had to keep deciding whether to go along with this expectation or to remind them I was so inexperienced – both options felt like they carried a risk. Being there right at the start of the school year definitely gave me an enormous advantage when it came to seeing new classes being set up and routines and ground rules established. By the time the other trainees started many of the things the teachers worked so hard on at the beginning had become routine and therefore invisible, yet I knew they were really important to the success of the lessons.

Ofsted and other forms of school accountability

The word 'accountability' in education is often interpreted negatively as ever-increasing pressure on schools and teachers. Given the high stakes involved, this is not surprising. However, accountability in its broadest sense should provide important support for school improvement and be a source of professional aspiration.

OFSTED

Ofsted, the Office for Standards in Education, Children's Services and Skills, is a govenment body set up to inspect schools and other childcare/educational institutions and judge their effectiveness. During the inspection, inspectors will observe lessons, check records and gather a range of evidence to inform their judgements, including speaking to staff, governors, pupils and parents and scrutinising pupils' work.

If you are in a school when it is being inspected, try not to panic! Although this may be a natural response, most of the pressure during an inspection should be borne by the senior leadership team. However, this does not mean there may not be some disconcerting changes in the way people behave, as they react to pressure in a range of ways. It is important to note that the vast majority of inspectors are reasonable and understanding, and the experience can be very positive and developmental, whether you are directly involved or observing from a distance.

TEACHERS' STANDARDS

The Teachers' Standards apply to trainee teachers working towards QTS, to those completing their NQT year and to those who are more experienced teachers and wish to apply to access the upper pay range. The more experienced you become, the greater the depth and breadth of knowledge, skill and understanding you will be required to demonstrate in meeting the Standards within the role you are carrying out and the context in which you are working (DfE, 2011: 7). Additionally, the Standards are used as a means of ensuring teachers are accountable through Ofsted inspections and annual appraisal. The Standards are divided into two parts, with a preamble that summarises the values and behaviours that you, as a teacher, must demonstrate throughout your career. Part One of the Standards relates to the practice of teaching and is divided into eight subdivided standards, and Part Two is concerned with personal and professional conduct. These are discussed in more detail below.

Teachers' Standards Part One

1 Set high expectations which inspire, motivate and challenge pupils

This standard requires you as a teacher to believe that all children can make progress, and your teaching should provide the environment that enables children to flourish. As a teacher, you are a role model for children, and your attitudes are fundamental to children's attitudes towards themselves and towards others. Your classroom should be a safe environment where mistakes are learning opportunities, positive relationships are fostered, and activities are engaging and stimulating and are designed with the expectation of every child doing their best.

2 Promote good progress and outcomes by pupils

When you are on your placement in school and working as a trainee teacher, you will be working towards this standard, which makes it clear that you will be held accountable for the attainment, progress and outcomes for your pupils. This standard is concerned with ensuring that you know how children learn, that you teach in a way that builds on prior learning and encourages pupils to take responsibility for their own learning.

3 Demonstrating good subject and curriculum knowledge

It is obvious that, before you can teach something, you must know what it is you are going to teach. Having a good knowledge of the curriculum means knowing what has been taught before, what will be taught next, and how what you are teaching now links these together. Primary teachers are required to teach a wide range of subjects, and therefore their subject knowledge needs to be extensive. It is easy as a trainee teacher to consider that, as you have taken a subject at a higher level yourself, this means that your own subject knowledge is sufficient. However, having good subject knowledge is about knowing, not just what should be taught, but how it can be taught. This pedagogical knowledge is fundamental. You may yourself have experienced being taught by someone with a great depth of knowledge but who has not communicated this to you in a way you could understand. Although their subject knowledge is good, their pedagogical knowledge is lacking, and, without good pedagogical knowledge, subject knowledge has little meaning.

4 Plan and teach well structured lessons

Ewens (2014: 62) identifies that planning is a means to an end. As a trainee teacher, you are likely to engage in detailed planning, ensuring every aspect is covered and no eventuality is unaccounted for. The structure of the plan may take up much of your thought, and trainee teachers I have worked with have often thought hard about what activities they will use and how they will produce exciting lessons. What is important in lesson planning is to know what you want the children to learn and how you will know if this has been achieved. When a trainee teacher on placement was asked how well she thought the lesson that had just been observed had gone, she replied that it had gone well, as the children had enjoyed the lesson. Although there is no denying that enjoyment of a lesson is important, there was no mention of what she wanted the children to learn or whether any of them had learned this. Her planning was centred on an exciting activity that had engendered enthusiasm in the children, and yet the focus of the lesson was concerned with knowledge the children already had. Additionally, the trainee's reflection on her lesson showed that she did not understand that an effective lesson required children to learn rather than be entertained.

5 Adapt teaching to respond to the strengths and needs of all pupils

All of our classes in school demonstrate a wide range of diversity. This provides a challenge for even the most experienced teacher. All children should be included in the classroom, and this does not just mean that they are present, but that they are involved in the learning activities and are fully a part of the social aspects of the classroom too.

Inclusive practice flows from inclusive beliefs. Yet, as Ewens (2014: 80) points out, the current policies that teachers are working within require children with special educational needs (SENs) to be supported in order to 'catch up' rather than to be engaged in suitable challenges, whatever their starting point might be. This highlights a dilemma for inclusive teachers who may understand that some of their children, owing to their particular learning difficulties, may not 'catch up', but are nonetheless capable of learning, albeit in different ways. Other children who may benefit from differentiated approaches include those living in poverty, travellers, children who are high achievers, children with English as an additional language (EAL), children with social or mental health difficulties and children who are asylum seekers or refugees. All of these children will require you to understand their needs and to 'use and evaluate distinctive teaching approaches to engage and support them' (DfE, 2011: 12).

6 Make accurate and productive use of assessment

Whereas Teachers' Standard 2 (TS 2) requires teachers to be accountable for children's progress, TS 6 requires teachers to assess children's progress. Teachers engage in formative assessment in order to inform them of the level of children's understanding and to plan their teaching in order to support children's further development, whereas summative assessment is undertaken at the end of a piece of work and is usually part of a reporting system, such as weekly spelling tests or end-of-year assessments. Although you may have the freedom as a professional to employ what formative assessment methods you feel are appropriate, you will also be required to collect summative data in order to track pupils' progress and to enable school improvement targets to be set.

7 Manage behaviour effectively to ensure a good and safe learning environment

When talking with trainee teachers at the beginning of their course, I hear concerns about 'controlling' behaviour in the classroom. Although it is important to have clear expectations about classroom routines and behaviours, it is also important to enable children to take responsibility for their own choices and behaviours. Children are more likely to choose to behave well if they know they are accepted, respected and included, and if they consider their teacher to be fair. Therefore, establishing a good, safe learning environment depends on the kind of relationship you create with the children in your class, as well as behaviour management strategies.

8 Fulfil wider responsibilities

The school environment involves much more than what goes on inside the classroom. Schools are communities, and, as a trainee teacher, you are expected to contribute to it. This involves the relationships you establish and the way you work, not only with your teaching colleagues, but with other adults, including support staff. Additionally, you are expected to develop effective communication with parents and carers, which involves listening to them as well as talking with them and developing shared responsibility for the child's learning.

Task 1.2.5 Meeting the Teachers' Standards

Jake had a troubled home life. His mother did her best to look after him and his brother, but she was an alcoholic, and it was a struggle. His father worked long hours. Jake and his brother tried to look after each other. During Jake's Y6 year and just before he sat his SATs in May, he took a friend home after school and found that his mother had taken an overdose and died. This was clearly a very distressing event, and Jake became unable to concentrate in regular lessons. The school was sympathetic to Jake's situation, but was also aware that he was due to sit his SATs very soon. Jake had been in a booster group for SATs, but he was no longer able to concentrate even in the small group and became disruptive and difficult to manage.

How would you answer the following questions?

1 What do you think Jake's needs are at this time?
2 What are the tensions the class teacher is facing in trying to meet Jake's needs while being aware that it is SATs week soon?
3 What approaches could the class teacher use to support Jake's needs?
4 How can the class teacher balance making provision for Jake with effective teaching for the rest of the children in the class?
5 What Teachers' Standards might be addressed by responding professionally to this situation, and do you think there is any tension in trying to meet all of these standards?

It is important to remain aware that the kind of professional practice required to achieve the Standards has been set by the government and has a relationship to how the government perceives the purpose of education. Every 3 years, a global survey is carried out in the countries that are members of the Organisation for Economic Co-operation and Development (OECD), and as a result countries are ranked giving them a position within the global market. Most governments are keen to increase their standing within this global market and therefore set educational standards accordingly. Sachs (2016: 417) pulls no punches with her assertion that, 'teachers . . . are often held captive to the short-term political rhetoric and interests of a particular government at the time', and that this leads to a compliant teaching profession who are constantly required to respond to the latest government initiative and strategy. Elements of this can be seen in Part Two of the Teachers Standards discussed below.

Teachers' Standards Part Two: Personal and professional conduct

Part Two of the Teachers' Standards is related to personal and professional conduct and sets expectations for you as a trainee teacher and throughout your professional practice, not only for setting high academic standards, but also for being concerned for the wider well-being of the children you will teach. This relates to behaviours both 'within and outside school' (DfE, 2011: 14). Part Two of the Standards makes it clear that you are required to 'treat pupils with dignity' and to build relationships around mutual respect and, in doing so, will 'uphold public trust' (ibid.). Part Two also sets out an expectation that teachers must have an understanding and regard for statutory frameworks, as well as the policies and practices of the school. Clearly there is a link between statutory requirements and school policy and procedures, as school practice must always reflect what is required by law. It is therefore important for you to be aware of statutory frameworks and to act within them.

Understanding statutory frameworks and high standards of ethics and behaviour

As a teacher, whether a trainee or of many years' experience, you are required to 'have regard for the need to safeguard pupils' well being' and to 'not undermine fundamental British values' (DfE, 2011: 14). It is important for you to understand the legislative requirements that accompany these statements. The DfE published statutory guidance in 2016 (2016b) that details the responsibilities of schools and colleges with regard to the safeguarding of all children and young people. This includes types of abuse and neglect, what school staff should know and do, as well as how any matters of safeguarding should be managed. Statistics available on the NSPCC website state that there are 93,000 children in care in the UK and more than 57,000 children identified as needing protection from abuse, and more than 23,000 children and young people contacted Child Line about abuse in 2015 (NSPCC, 2016). It is clear that all teachers should be attentive to safeguarding matters. Every school is required to have a designated person who is responsible for safeguarding. It is important that you should know who this is when you are on placement or working in school, and that you know what you should do if you become aware of a matter that could be concerned with child protection. You should also become acquainted with the school's safeguarding policy, as this will support you in complying with legislative requirements, as well as your ability to fulfil the requirements of Part Two of the Standards.

It is, of course, vitally important that you adhere to strict ethical codes yourself in regard to your professional and personal behaviour with children, both on the school premises and beyond. You also need to be aware of your reputation as a teacher or trainee teacher and be wise about what you are prepared to make public about yourself, through social media for example. Comments or posts that you consider to be allowable in a social domain on social media may not be acceptable in the professional domain. If parents, colleagues or employers become aware of these, you may be subject to criticism or even disciplinary action. If this occurs, then the public trust that teachers are required to uphold in Part Two of the Standards is seriously damaged.

In regard to 'not undermining fundamental British values', it is important to understand the statutory frameworks that underpin this part of the Standards (DfE, 2011: 14). The term 'fundamental British values' is taken from the Prevent Strategy (HM Government, 2011). This is related to the prevention of radicalisation and extremism, as well as terrorism, through attacks by extremist groups such as Al-Qaida. At the time of writing, government sources consider that a terrorist attack is highly likely, and the threat level is high; therefore, addressing this is seen as a priority, and schools are at the forefront of this, along with other agencies such as police, security and border control. Although the Prevent Strategy guidance is not statutory, the Counter-Terrorism and Security Act 2015 to which it relates is. Therefore, you are bound by law to comply with its requirements, and this is monitored through Ofsted.

However, carrying out this statutory requirement in practice is a complex matter. Davies (2015) discusses how, in some schools, Muslim children have become fearful of speaking in class, in case their comments are misinterpreted, and teachers would rather avoid controversial issues such as religion and extremism. Additionally, the term 'fundamental British values' is seen as problematic, both in terms of defining what they are and in the implicit assumption that 'immigrants' do not adhere to such values. Additionally, research by Elton-Chalcraft *et al.* (2017) identified that 47 per cent of student teachers participating in her study were unclear about what British values are, suggesting tokenistic responses such as queueing, being polite and caring for animals. Elton-Chalcraft *et al.* (2017) go on to suggest that, to avoid such simplistic notions, it is important for trainees to have the opportunity to examine who is British, how and why they are, as well as there being multiple ways of being British, in order to more fully understand the term British values.

The DfE (2014) defines British values as 'democracy, the rule of law, individual liberty, and mutual respect and tolerance of those with different faiths and beliefs'. Schools are required to teach a broad and balanced curriculum and to ensure that children are safe from a range of views that are extremist or designed to radicalise them. Within the broad and balanced curriculum, schools are expected to promote the spiritual, moral, social and cultural (SMSC) development of pupils. This involves enabling pupils to have strong self-esteem and confidence, be able to distiguish between right and wrong, accept responsibility for their own behaviour and make a positive contribution to the lives of others. Furthermore, it concerns engendering a respect for others, for democracy and for law, as well as a desire for 'tolerance and harmony between different cultural traditions' (DfE, 2014: 5).

Task 1.2.6 Teaching fundamental British values

When you are on placement, your class teacher asks you to include fundamental British values in your approach.

1 What do you understand this to mean?
2 How might you promote diversity and tolerance in your classroom?
3 How might you teach children to respect those from different faiths, cultures and religions?
4 Supposing your class is all white British. How would you teach fundamental British values to the children in this class in a meaningful way?
5 A pupil mentions during a lesson that they have seen a video of suicide bombings. What would you do?

SUMMARY

Although the Teachers' Standards are an important and necessary framework for you to adhere to, it is clear that being professional is more than just the meeting of standards. Baggini (2005: 7) considers that the way teachers respond to imposed standards demonstrates the extent to which they may be professional. Having to attain imposed goals and outcomes, even though they may be at odds with personal and professional beliefs and ideals, is demanding and requires teacherly wisdom. The kind of professionalism this demands is not easily attained and takes time to develop. As a trainee, it is likely that the professionalism you demonstrate will be centred on meeting the Teachers' Standards, but, as you continue as a teacher, the professionalism that you demonstrate is likely to extend beyond adherence to the Standards, to the development of collaborative networks, the fostering of relationships of trust and the ability to make wise decisions in 'situations of unavoidable uncertainty' (Hargreaves and Fullen, 2012: 93). In this way, you will be continuing to develop your own professional identity as a teacher.

 ## ANNOTATED FURTHER READING

Eaude, T. (2011) *Thinking Through Pedagogy for Primary and Early Years*, Exeter, UK: Learning Matters.
> A book designed to help students explore the complexities of teaching in the primary and early years.

Ewens, T. (2014) *Reflective Primary Teaching (Critical Teaching)*, Northwich, UK: Critical Publishing.
> This book provides a detailed outline of each of the Teachers' Standards and provides a critical analysis of what they mean and how they can be achieved. Each chapter is supported by research and outlines some of the complexities of working to meet the Standards and provides practical activities and reflections to support deeper thinking and understanding.

Glazzard, J. (2016) *Learning to be a Primary Teacher: Core Knowledge and Understanding (Critical Teaching)*, Northwich, UK: Critical Publishing.
> This book is a comprehensive guide to becoming a primary teacher. It takes a critical approach and outlines complex issues, supported by research and current educational thinking. The final chapter provides a detailed explanation of professionalism and its practical implications.

 ## FURTHER READING TO SUPPORT M-LEVEL STUDY

Davies, L. (2015) 'Security, extremism and education: Safeguarding or surveillance?', *British Journal of Educational Studies*, 64(1): 1-19.
> Davies considers the relationship between security and extremism and the implications for education. She examines the UK's Prevent Strategy and proposes a human rights approach as a way of promoting greater personal and national security.

Hargreaves, A. and Fullan, M. (2013) 'The power of professional capital', *Journal of Staff Development*, 34(3): 36-9.
> The authors consider two approaches of professionalism, the business model and the professional capital approach. It outlines the importance of developing decisional capital as part of professional

capital and shows how different career stages provide the means for decisional capital to be developed.

Sachs, J. (2016) 'Teacher professionalism: Why are we still talking about it?', *Teachers & Teaching*, 22(4): 413-25. In this paper, Sachs outlines what she considers shapes teacher professionalism, arguing that the teaching profession has become controlled or compliant through the requirement to adhere to externally imposed expectations. She proposes that teachers should take control of their own professional development through engagement in teacher and classroom research, thereby defining and developing their own professional identity.

 ## RELEVANT WEBSITES

Department for Education: www.gov.uk/government/publications/teachers-standards
This website details the Teachers' Standards, with further information and how they should be used.

Department for Education: https://www.gov.uk/government/uploads/system/uploads/attachment_data/file/380595/SMSC_Guidance_Maintained_Schools.pdf
This further document details how fundamental British values can be promoted in schools as part of SMSC education.

The Jubilee Centre for Character and Virtues: www.jubileecentre.ac.uk/1610/character-education
The Jubilee Centre is associated with Birmingham University. The website provides a set of resources that teachers can use and adapt to develop the personal qualities or 'character' of the pupils in their class.

National College of Teaching and Leadership (NCTL): www.gov.uk/government/organisations/national-college-for-teaching-and-leadership
This website provides information about routes to teaching, professional development, teachers' workload and teacher misconduct.

The Chartered College of Teaching: www.collegeofteaching.org/teachers

Reflective teaching: www.reflectiveteaching.co.uk
A website that is constantly updated with articles to encourage reflective practice.

 ## REFERENCES

Baggini, J. (2005) 'What professionalism means for teachers today', *Education Review*, 18: 5-11.

Clark, L. (2016) *Teacher Status and Professional Learning: The Place Model*, Northwich, UK: Critical Publishing.

Davies, L. (2015) 'Security, extremism and education: Safeguarding or surveillance?', *British Journal of Educational Studies*, 64(1): 1-19.

Demirkasımoğlu, N. (2010) 'Defining "teacher professionalism" from different perspectives', *Procedia - Social & Behavioral Sciences*, 9: 2047-51.

Department for Education. (2011) *Teachers Standards*. Retrieved from https://www.gov.uk/government/uploads/system/uploads/attachment_data/file/283566/Teachers_standard_information.pdf (accessed 12 October 2017).

Department for Education. (2014) *Promoting Fundamental British Values as part of SMSC in Schools - Departmental Advice for Maintained Schools*. Retrieved from www.gov.uk/government/uploads/system/uploads/attachment_data/file/380595/SMSC_Guidance_Maintained_Schools.pdf.

Department for Education. (2016a) *Educational Excellence Everywhere*. Retrieved from https://www.gov.uk/govern-ment/uploads/system/uploads/attachment_data/file/508447/Educational_Excellence_Everywhere.pdf (accessed 12 October 2017).

Department for Education. (2016b) *Keeping Children Safe in Education: Statutory Guidance for Schools and Colleges*. Retrieved from https://www.gov.uk/government/uploads/system/uploads/attachment_data/file/550511/Keeping_children_safe_in_education.pdf (accessed 12 October 2017).

Elton-Chalcraft, S., Lander, V., Revell, L., Warner, D. and Whitworth, L. (2017) 'To promote, or not to promote fundamental British values? Teachers' standards, diversity and teacher education', *British Education Research Journal*, 43(1): 29-48.

Ewens, T. (2014) *Reflective Primary Teaching (Critical Teaching)*, Northwich, UK: Critical Publishing.

Hargreaves, A. and Fullen, M. (2012) *Professional Capital: Transforming Teaching in Every School*. London and New York: Routledge.

Hilferty, F. (2008) 'Theorising teacher professionalism as an enacted discourse of power', *British Journal of Sociology of Education*, 29(2): 161-73.

HM Government. (2011) *Prevent Strategy*. Retrieved from https://www.gov.uk/government/uploads/system/uploads/attachment_data/file/97976/prevent-strategy-review.pdf (accessed 12 October 2017).

NSPCC. (2016) *Preventing Abuse*. Retrieved from www.nspcc.org.uk/preventing-abuse/ (accessed 12 October 2017).

Pillen, M.T., Den Brok, P.J. and Beijaard, D. (2013) 'Profiles and change in beginning teachers' professional identity tensions', *Teaching & Teacher Education*, 34: 86-97.

Poet, H., Rudd, P. and Kelly, J. (2010) *How Teachers Approach Practice Improvement*, London: General Teaching Council for England.

Sachs, J. (2016). 'Teacher professionalism: Why are we still talking about it?', *Teachers & Teaching*, 22(4): 413-25.

Steinert, Y., Cruess, R., Cruess, S., Boudreau, D., Snell, L. and Hafferty, F. (2014, August) *From Professionalism to Professional Identity Formation: A Journey not a Destiny*. Symposium presented at AMEE Conference, Milan, Italy.

Tichenor, M.S. and Tichenor, J.M. (2005) 'Understanding teachers' perspectives on professionalism', *The Professional Educator*, 27: 89-95.

MAKING THE MOST OF YOUR PLACEMENTS

Jane Warwick and Mary Anne Wolpert

INTRODUCTION

> The steepest learning curve for a student teacher naturally takes place in the classroom itself.
>
> (Chris, a primary PGCE trainee)

In this unit, we examine how you can make the most of the opportunities afforded by your placements and how day-to-day experience of working with children in school will give you understanding of why theory and research are integral to effective teaching. We discuss the importance of being a reflective practitioner and examine how the dispositions you present and the relationships you develop on placement are key factors to becoming an effective teacher. As the quotation from Chris above suggests, classroom experiences provide crucial, yet sometimes challenging, learning opportunities, and we offer vignettes from recent trainees who provide insghts into significant elements of their school placements.

OBJECTIVES

This unit will help you to understand:

- dispositions that will maximise your learning during school placements;
- the importance of reflection and how lesson evaluations inform practice;
- the role of mentors and how learning conversations with colleagues inform professional development.

ESTABLISHING EFFECTIVE DISPOSITIONS

> Becoming an expert teacher . . . is a transformative process rather than simply the acquisition of skills.
>
> (Wilson, 2013: 44)

In order for you to make sense of your experience across placements during your course, it will be helpful to understand dispositions towards your learning. Hagger *et al.* (2008), in their study of 1-year PGCE trainees, defined five different dimensions to professional learning that trainee teachers

TABLE 1.3.1 Five dimensions according to which the variation among the student teachers' accounts of their learning from experience were analysed

Dimension	Orientation		
Intentionality: the extent to which learning is planned	Deliberative	← →	Reactive
Frame of reference: the value ascribed to looking beyond their experience in order to make sense of it	Drawing on a range of sources to shape and make sense of experience	← →	Exclusive reliance on the experience of classroom teaching
Response to feedback: disposition towards receiving feedback and the value attributed to it	Effective use of feedback to further learning	← →	Tendency to be disabled by critical feedback
Attitude to context: attitude to the positions in which student teachers find themselves and the approaches they take to the school context	Acceptance of the context and ability to capitalise on it	← →	Tendency to regard the context as constraining
Aspiration: the extent of their aspirations for their own and their pupils' learning	Aspirational as both learners and teachers	← →	Satisfaction with current level of achievement

Source: Hagger *et al.* (2008: 167)

take (see Table 1.3.1). Having an understanding of these dimensions and their associated orientations will equip you to become a competent professional learner and teacher.

Hagger *et al.* (2008) argue that the degree of intentionality – the extent to which the learning is planned – is key. One end of the continuum is represented by a 'deliberative' approach to learning, and the other by a reactive approach to experiences. Novice teachers who take the first, proactive approach actively seek feedback on their teaching and advice from more experienced colleagues, showing an 'enthusiasm to experiment with their teaching' (p. 169). In contrast, trainees with a 'reactive approach' show 'an abdication of responsibility' (p. 168) and have difficulty identifying their future learning needs.

Within the second dimension (frame of reference), Hagger *et al.* found differences in the extent to which trainees recognised the value of looking beyond their own experience. Trainees with a proactive disposition drew on a range of sources, such as appropriate research findings and discussions with mentors and tutors, whereas those exhibiting a 'reactive' disposition relied more exclusively on individual classroom experience. Third, dispositions towards receiving feedback ranged from those trainees who made effective use of feedback and those who were defensive and perceived the feedback as criticism. We explore this dimension more fully below. Attitude to school context was similarly characterised as a continuum ranging from trainees who accepted and capitalised on the position in which they found themselves to those who regarded the context as a constraint on their progress. Finally, Hagger *et al.* identified an aspirational orientation. At one end were trainees who constantly sought to develop professional practice and the ways in which they, and pupils, learn. At the other end were those who were complacent about their own level of performance and that of the learners.

Task 1.3.1 Dimensions and their associated orientations

Consider the five dimensions (Table 1.3.1) and their associated orientations. Where would you place yourself on each continuum? What evidence do you have to support this judgement? Thinking about your personal context, what actions do you think might be necessary for you to move towards more positive orientations in each of the dimensions?

REFLECTIVE TEACHING

> Teaching is a complex and highly skilled activity which, above all, requires classroom teachers to exercise judgement in deciding how to act.
>
> (Pollard *et al.*, 2014: 68)

While on placement, you need to develop skills that will enable you to analyse and reflect upon your practice in order to make increasingly appropriate judgements about teaching and learning. Teachers' Standard 4 (DfE, 2012) requires teachers to 'reflect systematically on the effectiveness of lessons and approaches to teaching'.

Reflection about an episode in the classroom starts as a series of 'questioning thoughts' (McGregor and Cartwright, 2011: 1), which will help understanding of what, when and how the event happened. These initial thoughts will become more purposeful when you start to analyse why the event happened in the way it did, especially as you become more familiar with the context and the children with whom you are working. Such questions need to be followed by consideration of how you might have behaved or done things differently, and how to improve the situation in future. This is not to suggest that reflection should only happen when things go wrong; the habit of reflection is something that needs to be developed in relation to *all* aspects of your professional work, including successful lessons.

Reflection should be a conscious activity: 'reflection at its most effective comes with growing professional knowledge based on the acquisition of theory and its critical application to practice' (Cartwright, 2011: 56). Your reading of educational research is essential to help you reflect on, and make sense of, your classroom experiences. According to Pollard *et al.* (2014), there are seven characteristics of reflective teaching (see Figure 1.3.1). Through engaging in reflective action that stems from professional thinking, rather than merely having intuitive reactions to classroom situations, teachers can raise their standards of professional competence. This process, Pollard *et al.* argue, is cyclical in nature, mediated through collaboration and dialogue with colleagues and arises through evidence-based enquiry. While you are on placements, discussions with your mentor and other colleagues will help you to gain confidence in analysing and reflecting on your teaching.

This concept of reflection in and on activity has been extended to include the notion of reflexivity, which requires, 'not just the ability to reflect about what has happened and what one has done, but the ability to reflect on the way in which one has reflected' (Moore, 2004: 148). In addition, when teachers are reflexive, they take into account the impact and implications that they bring to, and have on, a particular learning situation (Sewell, 2012). This means that you should consider how your values, dispositions and possible biases might influence your teaching. You will be expected to provide evidence of your reflective and reflexive practice through discussion and recordings in more formal documentation. In the next section, we show examples of trainees' evaluations of their teaching as a tool for helping you to do this.

Reflective teaching:

1 implies an active concern with aims and consequences, as well as means and technical efficiency;

2 is applied in a cyclical or spiralling process;

3 requires competence in methods of evidence-based classroom enquiry;

4 requires attitudes of open-mindedness, responsibility and whole-heartedness;

5 is based on teacher judgement, informed by evidence-based enquiry and insights from other research;

6 along with professional learning and personal fulfilment, is enhanced through collaboration and dialogue with colleagues;

7 enables teachers creatively to mediate externally developed frameworks for teaching and learning.

FIGURE 1.3.1 The seven characteristics of reflective teaching
Source: Pollard *et al.* (2014: 76)

EVALUATING YOUR LESSONS

> The lesson does not end when the bell goes!
>
> (Hattie, 2012: 145)

Evaluating the impact of your teaching on children's learning is a fundamental part of the planning, teaching and assessment cycle; lesson evaluations are key to demonstrating reflection and will help you understand and develop your practice. These could take the form of reflective journals or diaries, annotations of individual lesson plans and sequences of lessons, or detailed, 'formal' evaluations of individual lessons.

Beginner teachers often have a tendency to focus their reflections on aspects of their own performance in the classroom and, most notably, how they manage behaviour. Burn *et al.* (2000) found trainees focused on four categories related to their own practice: 'their actions, their planning, the resources used (materials they had made themselves or existing resources) and their own affective state (usually judgements about their nervousness, but sometimes reflections on their sense of exhaustion)' (2000: 272). We argue that, in addition to your teaching, the focus on pupil learning is a crucial element of lesson evaluations.

To be effective and formative, lesson evaluations should focus on specific elements of learning and teaching and avoid repetition and description. They should also link to previous targets set by your mentor, other school colleagues, tutors or yourself. Consider the following elements in structuring your evaluations:

1   the successes of the lesson;
2   the children's learning;
3   your teaching;
4   implications for your future practice.

The successes of the lesson

Beginning teachers tend to make broad judgements about the successes of the lesson. For example, comments such as 'all the children enjoyed the lesson and understood the learning objective' or 'the lesson went well' are typical. Compare these comments with the example below to see a more analytical approach that identifies specific evidence to support the judgements made.

The children's learning

When reflecting upon and analysing children's learning, consider the following questions:

- What did the children actually learn and do?
- To what extent did the children meet the learning objective?
- To what extent did children maintain interest and effort?
- Were there any misconceptions/errors for all children? If so, how will they be addressed?
- Were there any barriers to learning?

In the examples in the tables, the trainees identified explicitly what the children learned, linked to the lesson learning objectives and success criteria. Judgements were made based on the learning outcomes. (Names of children have been removed.)

TABLE 1.3.2 An example of appropriate comments that highlight successes of a lesson

Question	Comment	Specific evidence
What were the successes of the lesson?	The children took pride in their work and made a lot of effort. Children were engaged and able to work in pairs, threes or independently effectively. Overall, the timings were well planned and appropriate. The lesson was accessible to all pupils, with self-differentiation taking place in the creative writing of poetry. Higher achievers were able to work on their own while less confident pupils could support each other. Children learned about important aspects of poetry such as the importance of reading it aloud and listening to it being read. The quality of work was high; they all wanted to read their poems, which demonstrated how much they had enjoyed the lesson.	Mentor was pleased with the letters and lesson had gone well. She said it was carefully planned, although she had a few points that we could adapt and improve upon. The final pieces of work were finished on time and were of a satisfactory or good standard.

It is important to get feedback from other professionals.

The quality of the children's work forms a key source of evidence.

TABLE 1.3.3 An example of appropriate comments that relate to children's learning

Question	Comment	Specific evidence
What did the children actually learn and do?	The children learned to identify characters and their emotions and descriptions.	Work produced showed a clear understanding of the characters' emotions, and the following lesson for literacy showed that the concept of character descriptions had been learned through the application in a different context (which was commented on by the teacher). Children also showed they had learned to predict what would happen next by the discussion I had; some managed to draw what they thought would happen next.
Were there any unexpected outcomes?	Some learned to predict what would happen next in the story.	

Evidence from a range of sources supports judgements.

Your teaching

Initially, analysing your teaching tends to be easier than reflecting on children's learning. However, in order to avoid writing a descriptive narrative that focuses on you, consider the following questions through the eyes of the children:

- How effective was the lesson/activity plan?
- How effectively did I manage behaviour?
- To what extent was my modelling and explanation clear throughout the lesson?
- Was the timing appropriate?
- Was the use of other adults efficient, and did it support the learning?

TABLE 1.3.4 An example of critical comments that relate to evaluation of the teaching

Question	Comment	Specific evidence
How effective was the lesson/ activity plan? Consider: (1) timings; (2) pace	The pace of the lesson went well. Activities were 10–15 minutes to encourage the children to maintain interest while allowing them time to apply their skills. Resources were prepared before the lesson and included use of whiteboards. However, children spent a large proportion of time on the carpet, partly due to the layout and size of the class. I would have preferred the children to return to their class seats, but I would not have been able to speak to all of them effectively, and it would be more difficult to engage them. Need to keep the activities on the carpet short and snappy to maintain interest and levels of concentration.	Teacher feedback, observations *Reflections explicitly state an issue that will have impacted on children's motivation and concentrations levels. Importantly a change of practice has been identified.*

Question	Comment	Specific evidence
To what extent was my modelling and explanation clear throughout the lesson?	I modelled the process of creating words and then the process of joining words together to create a line of poetry. Used the words 'sneaky', 'sly' and simile 'as slow as a turtle' to show that it didn't have to be a literal description; I wanted the children to tell me what words/images evoked for them. This worked well; most children identified interesting words and used comparisons and alliteration. However, the blue group simply copied the words I wrote down. Need to be clearer about what I expect the children to do, and ask children who struggled to repeat to me what they have to do with an example.	Teacher feedback, pupil response *Individual children who either exceeded or did not meet the learning objective are identified which will inform future planning.*

Implications for your future practice

This is at the heart of why time should be spent writing lesson evaluations on placements; it is the 'So what?', 'What do I do next?'. To have an impact on your future teaching, evaluations must include an action plan that focuses both on children's learning and your own practice.

Task 1.3.2 Lesson evaluations

Using the suggested four sections of a lesson evaluation outlined above, reflect upon and evaluate a recent lesson you have taught. What evidence have you found to support your analysis? Discuss this with your mentor and identify an aspect of your lesson evaluation that informs your targets for development.

TABLE 1.3.5 An example of the implications for future practice identified after teaching a lesson

Children's learning	Importance of modelling both pushes and pulls before asking children to do each task. I learned how time-consuming practical investigations are (in future I will allocate longer) and how important it is to keep the focus on science and make recording as simple as possible. In future I will keep the written aspect to a minimum. I also learned how valuable the interactive science clips are on the IWB. I will definitely use these again.
In my role as a teacher	If children aren't giving me the answers I am hoping for, I will use thinking time, talk partners and group discussions. I will add this into future plans.
	To have confidence to keep discussing concepts and extend the discussion if the children are still engaged.

It is important to be aware that lesson evaluations should:

- be analytical and critical, rather than descriptive;
- have a specific focus;
- reflect on the impact of the lesson through learners' eyes;
- identify implications for future practice.

WORKING WITH SCHOOL MENTORS

> It is really important to remember that mentors . . . provide feedback in order for you to become a better teacher.
>
> (Becky, a primary PGCE trainee)

The DfE (2016) defines a mentor working with a trainee teacher as 'a suitably-experienced teacher who has formal responsibility to work collaboratively with the ITT partnership to help ensure the trainees receives the highest-quality training'. As Hobson (2016) states, the mentoring process is:

> a one to one relationship between a relatively inexperienced teacher (the mentee) and a relatively experienced teacher (the mentor), which aims to support the mentee's learning, development and well-being, and their integration into the cultures of both the organisation in which they are employed and the wider profession.
>
> (Hobson, 2016: 88)

Mentors will provide you with access to a range of increasingly self-directed learning opportunities to scaffold your development and help you respond to the changing demands of your course. It is helpful to conceive of them as 'significant narrators' (Sfard and Prusak, 2005: 833) who have a major role to play in the building of your emerging professional identify as a teacher.

According to research involving BEd trainees, immediate professional support and advice from school mentors are valued (Laker, Laker and Lea, 2008) by beginning teachers. Then, as they progress through a series of school placements, a definite pattern of progression is identified that moves from formal to more informal sources of support, namely fellow trainees and teacher colleagues in the wider school community. Forming these social relationships is vital in helping you move from somewhat 'peripheral participation' (Lave and Wenger, 1991) in the school workforce to becoming a member of a community of practice.

In this vignette, Charlotte (a primary PGCE trainee) reflects on her experiences of working with mentors during her training:

> In my first two placements, my mentors were one of the most important influences in how I learned to teach. Mentors allow you to see the role of a teacher from the inside out. I learned from observing, discussing and questioning with them about what goes on in the classroom. They guided me but I realised it was essential that I took responsibility for finding out as much as possible from their wealth of knowledge and experience during the time I spent with them. This involved me asking questions and for advice, but also going to them with ideas.

> My mentors were there to redirect. I shared my plans with them which gave me opportunities to explain my vision and ideas. This allowed them to see how I was thinking and, moreover, how I had taken on board advice and used it to adapt my planning and teaching. At times I did not fully understand what my mentors were saying and quickly learned that I shouldn't feel embarrassed about asking what I sometimes thought were obvious questions: I realised later that some pieces of advice can remain dormant, until that 'eureka moment' when the suggestion gains its meaning.

MAKING THE MOST OF LEARNING CONVERSATIONS

> I soon came to realise that these were not tests she was setting me.
>
> (Luke, a primary PGCE trainee)

In order to make sense of the complexity of learning and teaching, it is vital that your development is scaffolded through dialogue with more experienced practitioners. Being involved in professional conversations about your teaching with school colleagues and tutors is essential to supporting your professional development.

Receiving and responding to feedback are intrinsically linked with beliefs about learning. The term feedback may seem to imply a one-way process, in which feedback discourse is characterised by the 'expert' providing a 'gift' (Askew and Lodge, 2000: 4) to support improvement. Askew and Lodge (2000) offer a second model of discourse in which feedback is a two-way process, enabling the development of understanding through the use of open questioning and shared insight. We prefer to consider their third model of feedback – a co-constructive discourse that involves a reciprocal process of learning. Here, feedback is a dialogue, formed by 'loops' connecting the trainee and the mentor that illuminate learning (Askew and Lodge, 2000). We therefore use the term learning conversation, as this indicates the necessary active involvement of the trainee in the dialogue.

Dweck (1986) outlines the motivational processes that affect learning and how learners vary in their beliefs about success, their 'goal orientation', about learning and their responses to difficult tasks. She defines a 'positive learning orientation', or 'growth mindset' as one that focuses on 'improving one's competence', with a belief that effort leads to success and a belief in one's ability to improve and learn. On the other hand, a more negative pattern focuses on 'performance orientation', in which one is more concerned with 'proving one's competence'. This is associated with negative effects for learners, such as greater helplessness, reduced help-seeking and reduced use of learning strategies. As Hagger *et al.* (2008) demonstrate, trainees who adopt a 'defensive stance' and 'those who are disabled by critical feedback' have a tendency to blame others, including the pupils, to explain their difficulties or lack of progress.

Teachers' Standard 8 (DfE, 2012) states that teachers need to 'take responsibility for improving teaching through appropriate professional development, responding to advice and feedback from colleagues'. The preceding discussion illuminates how this responsibility should be conceived positively, and how advice and feedback should be responded to in order to optimise your learning during placements.

In this vignette, Nicola reflects on learning conversations with her mentor and how these enabled her to become a more effective teacher. As you read this, consider how Nicola's positive dispositions were essential to this process.

> I was apprehensive about the initial feedback meeting and acutely aware that this very experienced teacher had not just closely observed everything I had done in my first lesson but also scrutinised my planning. 'So', he asked 'how do you think the lesson went?' Admittedly, the whole lesson had gone by in a blur. Finding myself more self-conscious than when I had actually been standing up in front of the class, I responded with a hopeful 'Ok?' Together we reviewed and analysed several aspects of the lesson: positives were highlighted whilst areas of improvement tactfully suggested.
>
> One observation my mentor made was that I hadn't made full use of the classroom teaching assistant. This really surprised me, I had considered that my planning for the teaching assistant was good and had spoken to her just before the lesson. To help clarify his point, my mentor showed me the comprehensive directions he'd written on his own lesson plans for his teaching assistant and explained how resources had been modified for her to use. Arrangements were then made for me to spend time shadowing a teaching assistant, observing how she worked and discussing what we could do to help each other in the classroom. As a result, I found myself more effectively deploying support staff for the benefit of my pupils. The mentoring feedback process prevented me from being insular, at times even a little defensive about my teaching. Instead I understood the need to be open to advice.

CHALLENGING PROFESSIONAL CONVERSATIONS

> Feedback thrives on error . . . knowing this error is fundamental to moving towards success.
>
> (Hattie, 2012: 115)

Learning to teach does not merely involve acquiring a body of knowledge and skills or the mimicking of experienced teachers, but requires changes in cognition and perception in order to interpret school experience, which, at times, can be stressful (Wilson, 2013). One of the challenges is that the classroom is a constantly changing, unique environment that requires the teacher to make decisions and judgements. These will be influenced, not only by rational thinking, but also by previous experiences and emotions (Demetriou, Wilson and Winterbottom, 2009).

In order to 'think' like a teacher, trainees need be able to make deliberative judgements through understanding interrelated elements impacting on the classroom and relationships, based on responses to learning conversations, which can sometimes be challenging. It is important to reflect on the key messages of professional conversations and analyse both emotional and deliberative responses in order to move towards a constructive outcome.

Receiving and responding to feedback on a lesson you have put hours of work into can sometimes feel very difficult, as though your efforts were wasted. In the following passage, Becky describes her approach to ensure that the conversations with her mentor remained constructive.

> Initially, I found receiving feedback to be a daunting process, particularly if a lesson hadn't quite gone according to plan. I would try to focus on the positives and remind myself of the journey that I was on in developing my teaching practice. This then helped me to prepare for discussing aspects of the lesson that hadn't been as successful. I viewed receiving feedback as a tool in developing my teaching practice, rather than as a type of criticism. I found this mindset to be crucial during feedback sessions which in turn have enabled me to develop my teaching practice and become a reflective practitioner.

It is not always easy to remain as rational and positive as Becky during challenging feedback sessions; the tendency might be to have an emotional response and lose sight of the constructive nature of the feedback process. If you find yourself in this situation, working through the following questions might enable you to move towards a 'cooler action' and help you 'think like a teacher' (Wilson, 2013):

*   *Summary*: description of conversation. What did you hear?
*   *Initial reaction*: What's your intuitive response?
*   *Emotional response*: How do you feel about what happened?
*   *Evidence*: What are the facts?
*   *Action*: What are you going to do to address the issue?
*   *Timescale*: When will things happen?
*   *Support*: What help do you need to achieve a satisfactory outcome

Task 1.3.3 Reflecting on learning conversations

Think about a professional conversation you have found challenging (for example, with a parent or colleague) and replay it in your head. Make notes using the prompts above in order to reflect and learn from the experience so that there is a positive outcome.

Developing these positive dispositions and skills will help you develop professional resilience that is required during your training year and throughout your future career (Day and Kington, 2008).

In summary, it is important to be:

*   receptive, open-minded and active in these learning conversations;
*   aware of how you learn and the strategies you find effective in order that you can talk explicitly to your mentors about the approach that suits you;
*   aware of your attitude towards engaging with learning conversations; this includes how you present yourself through your body language, tone of voice and level of engagement;
*   'deliberative' during challenging professional conversations to avoid an emotional response.

PROGRESSION THROUGH PLACEMENTS

> Professional identity . . . is negotiated through experience and the sense that is made of that experience.
>
> (Sachs, 2005: p15)

As you move through your placements, within a school or to a different school, you may find that you feel your practice has regressed – this is perfectly natural and should be expected as challenges are presented in the process of enculturation within a new setting. The learning journey of a trainee teacher is not a linear, predictable or straightforward process, so it is inevitable that some points during the year will be more challenging than others. Wilson (2103) identifies February as the low point of a specific trainee's pre-service training.

In this vignette, Luke describes his progression through a 1-year PGCE course. As you read this passage, consider how Luke's role in the professional dialogue sessions changes, as he becomes more experienced and develops his professional identity by becoming an active participant.

Perhaps the most valuable moments of my teacher training attributed to my successful completion were the open, effective and professional conversations that occurred between myself and my mentors. Despite originally assuming that these feedback meetings would be wholly led by the mentors, the way in which these sessions occurred evolved throughout my practice as I became more confident in discussing myself as a practitioner – a notion that was initially rather nerve-wracking.

The feedback I received during my first placement acknowledged the aspects of my teaching that I had consciously attempted to implement and also sensitively highlighted elements of my practice that I had failed to consider. I agreed with all the feedback that was provided and targets that were set, yet never really commented on or questioned the feedback. It was certainly not the case that the mentor made me feel uncomfortable in doing so, but I was just glad to have the opinion of a professional, as at the time in my training I felt merely like a teaching 'imposter' and so allowed the mentor to fully lead the evaluation.

By my second placement, I was teaching sequences of lessons, which allowed me to feel more in control of the progression of the children's learning. During feedback meetings, I was praised on elements of my practice that I had not consciously intended to incorporate. Some strategies and approaches were becoming natural to me and this allowed me to stress less about constantly demonstrating 'good practice'. Instead, I could focus on the areas of my teaching that were mutually decided to be the most in need of addressing. I was certainly beginning to trust myself to contribute more to the professional discussion.

My final placement mentor would frequently question my decision to implement certain strategies and ask for my opinion in regards to my teaching. Although initially my heart would skip a beat as I tried to think of the correct response, I soon came to realise that these were not tests she was setting me. Instead, she was encouraging me to truly interrogate my practice.

Before I knew it, I was driving the discussions, stating the strengths and areas to adapt that I had observed during my own lessons. Finally, I had learned to not only look to my mentors for support, but also to rely on, and believe in, myself. During my placements, I began to realise the importance of instantly self-reflecting upon lessons prior to having a discussion with my mentor. It was valuable to realise that over time, my judgements and my mentors' correlated. It was empowering to discover that my judgements as a practitioner were akin to those of experienced teachers and really allowed me to believe in myself as a teacher.

Every route into teaching will have different expectations for the specific characteristics and build-up of responsibilities in school placements during the course. Training providers will take into account your prior experience of working with children and teaching and your personal subject knowledge in order to individualise the training programme for you.

Task 1.3.4 Reflecting on teaching experiences

Reflect on a particular experience or episode from which you have gained significant insight into an aspect of your learning about teaching while on placement. Write an account that analyses the links between this experience in school and some aspect of your reading of educational research.

SUMMARY

As a beginning practitioner, it may be difficult to understand what an experienced teacher does to be effective, but gradually, as you progress through your school placements, you will develop an understanding of the craft, science and art of teaching. Becoming a reflexive practitioner is crucial to this process. Your placements will be some of the most challenging experiences of your training, but being proactive is vital, and having an aspirational disposition for both you and the children will make the process more positive, increasing the likelihood that you will successfully gain QTS. Progressing through school placements may sometimes feel like a rollercoaster, as you will undoubtedly experience highs and lows. During intensive, stressful periods, it is important that you take care of yourself and, as far as possible, retain a work–life balance. Make time for *all* the SPICES of life – the Spiritual, Physical, Intellectual, Creative, Emotional and Social aspects, some of which are easy to forget during school placements. First-hand experiences in schools are obviously vital in your preparation to become a teacher, and in this unit we have attempted to articulate considerations that will help you to become a successful, 'fully developed professional' who has control of their own professional development and continues learning.

ANNOTATED FURTHER READING

McGregor, D. and Cartwright, L. (2011) *Developing Reflective Practice: A Handbook for Beginning Teachers*, Maidenhead, UK: Open University Press.
> This practical guide explains some of the best-known theories on reflective practice. The very real problems faced by beginning teachers are brought to life through the use of rich case studies, as well as extracts drawn from the reflective journals of those starting their teaching career.

Hattie, J. (2012) *Visible Learning for Teachers: Maximizing Impact on Learning*, London: Routledge.
> Written with trainee teachers in mind and championing student teacher perspectives, this book links the biggest ever research project on teaching strategies to practical classroom implementation and includes step-by-step guidance on topics such as lesson preparation, interpreting learning and feedback during the lesson and post-lesson discussions.

Robinson, C., Bingle, B. and Howard, C. (2015) *Your Primary School-Based Experience: A Guide to Outstanding Placements*, Northwich, UK: Critical Publishing.

> This is an essential companion for primary trainee teachers. It focuses on the school-based experience and provides both practical strategies and opportunities for reflection, so trainees are challenged to critically evaluate their learning in order to improve attainment and succeed.

 ## FURTHER READING TO SUPPORT M-LEVEL STUDY

Hagger, H., Burn, K., Mutton, T. and Brindley, S. (2008) 'Practice makes perfect? Learning to learn as a teacher', *Oxford Review of Education*, 34(1): 159-78.

> This article presents research conducted with twenty-five student teachers, following a 1-year postgraduate course within two well-established, school-based partnerships. The authors' findings show that the success the trainees had in making the most of their placements was determined by their attitudes and dispositions.

Day, C. and Kington, A. (2008) 'Identity, wellbeing and effectiveness: The emotional contexts of teaching', *Pedagogy, Culture & Society*, 16(1): 7-23.

> This article links research on dispositions and developing teachers' indentity. It does not directly focus on trainee teachers and their placements, but it does illustrate how these issues are relevant beyond the training year and how they impact on longer-term professional development.

Caires, S., Almeida, L. and Vieira, D. (2012) 'Becoming a teacher: Student teachers' experiences and perceptions about teaching practice', *European Journal of Teacher Education*, 35(2): 163-78.

> This study focuses on the experiences of 295 student teachers. Their feelings, cognitions and perceptions regarding teaching practice were analysed. Results emphasise some of the positive perceptions and difficulties experienced during this period.

 ## RELEVANT WEBSITES

Reflective Teaching: http://reflectiveteaching.co.uk

> The resources on this website are designed to support the development of high-quality professional judgement and evidence-informed practice. It has further links to the Teaching and Learning Research Programme (TLRP).

Visible Learning: https://visible-learning.org/2014/08/john-hattie-mind-frames-teachers/

> This website contains useful information and videos about how to make learning visible as an aid for teachers to evaluate their own teaching. According to John Hattie, visible learning and teaching occur when teachers see learning through the eyes of students and help them become their own teachers.

Education Support Partnership: www.educationsupportpartnership.org.uk/about-us

> This UK charity is dedicated to improving the health and well-being of people working in education. It champions good mental health and well-being of teachers, with a wide range of tools to support and help improve professional and organisational development.

Acas (Advisory, Conciliation and Arbitration Service): www.acas.org.uk/index.aspx?articleid=3799

> This website contains free and impartial information and advice about workplace relations, including challenging conversations and how to manage them. The website contains useful information, videos and strategies to support this aspect of your professional development.

REFERENCES

Askew, S. and Lodge, C. (2000) 'Gifts, ping-pong and loops – linking feedback and learning', in S. Askew (ed.) *Feedback for Learning*, London: RoutledgeFalmer.

Burn, K., Hagger, H., Mutton, T. and Everton, T. (2000) 'Beyond concerns with self: The sophisticated thinking of beginning student teachers', *Journal of Education for Teaching*, (26)3: 259–78.

Cartwright, L. (2011) 'How consciously reflective are you?', in D. McGregor and L. Cartwright, *Developing Reflective Practice: A Handbook for Beginning Teachers*, Maidenhead, UK: Open University Press.

Day, C. and Kington, A. (2008) 'Identity, wellbeing and effectiveness: The emotional contexts of teaching', *Pedagogy, Culture & Society*, 16(1): 7–23.

Demetriou, H., Wilson, E. and Winterbottom, M. (2009) 'The role of emotion in teaching: Are there differences between male and female newly qualified teachers' approaches to teaching?', *Educational Studies*, 35(4): 449–73.

Department for Education (DfE). (2012) *Teachers' Standards*. Retrieved from www.gov.uk/government/publications/teachers-standards (accessed 8 November 2017).

Department for Education (DfE). (2016) *National Standards for School-Based Initial Teacher Training (ITT) Mentors*, London: Department for Education. Retrieved from https://www.gov.uk/government/uploads/system/uploads/attachment_data/file/536891/Mentor_standards_report_Final.pdf (accessed 16 November 2016).

Dweck, C. (1986) 'Motivational processes affecting learning', *American Psychologist*, 41: 1040–8.

Hagger, H., Burn, K., Mutton, T. and Brindley, S. (2008) 'Practice makes perfect? Learning to learn as a teacher', *Oxford Review of Education*, 34(1): 159–78.

Hattie, J. (2012) *Visible Learning for Teachers: Maximizing Impact on Learning*, London: Routledge.

Hobson, A.J. (2016) 'Judgementoring and how to avert it: Introducing ONSIDE Mentoring for beginning teachers', *International Journal of Mentoring & Coaching in Education*, 5(2): 87–110.

Laker, A., Laker, J.C. and Lea, S.J. (2008) 'Sources of support for pre-service teachers during school experience', *Mentoring & Tutoring*, 16(2): 125–40.

Lave, J. and Wenger, E. (1991) *Situated Learning: Legitimate Peripheral Participation*, Cambridge, UK: Cambridge University Press.

McGregor, D. and Cartwright, L. (2011) *Developing Reflective Practice: A Handbook for Beginning Teachers*, Maidenhead, UK: Open University Press.

Moore, A. (2004) *The Good Teacher: Dominant Discourses in Teaching and Teacher Education*, London: Routledge.

Pollard, A. with Black-Hawkins, K., Cliff-Hodges, G., Dudley, P., James, M., Linklater, H., Swaffield, S., Swann, M., Turner, F., Warwick, P., Winterbottom, M. and Wolpert M.A. (2014) *Reflective Teaching in Schools*, 4th edn, London: Bloomsbury.

Sachs, J. (2005) 'Teacher education and the development of professional identity: Learning to be a teacher', in P. Denicolo and M. Kompf (eds) *Connecting Policy and Practice: Challenges for Teaching and Learning in Schools and Universities*, Oxford, UK: Routledge, pp. 5–21.

Sewell, K. (2012) *Doing Your PGCE at M-Level*, 2nd edn, London: Sage.

Sfard, A. and Prusak, A. (2005) 'Telling identities: In search of an analytical tool for investigating learning as a culturally shaped activity', *Educational Researcher*, 34(4): 14–22.

Wilson, E. (2013) 'Building social capital in teacher education through university–school partnerships', in M. Evans (ed.) *Teacher Education and Pedagogy Theory, Policy and Practice*. Cambridge, UK: Cambridge University Press.

SECTION 2
EXPLORING THE NATURE OF LEARNING AND TEACHING

LOOKING AT CHILDREN

Jane Payler and Mary Scanlan

INTRODUCTION

Why do primary teachers need to have a good understanding of child development? Every child you teach will be unique, each growing up in a family with its own culture and range of experiences. Those home and community experiences form the very basis of children's developmental trajectories. Children draw upon knowledge and experience from their wider life to make sense of learning in the classroom. Teachers need to know about child development so that the classroom experiences we offer acknowledge the uniqueness of each pupil throughout the primary school, ensuring all can progress.

Although the priorities of statutory curricula are subject to continual change, and different priorities take precedence at various times, what remains unchanging is the teacher's responsibility for providing the best educational experience for all children within the given constraints. In this unit, the phrase *educational experience* means the total (school) experience of every child. The role of the teacher is conceptualised here as catering for each child's unique needs and providing an environment in which every child can make progress across all areas of development.

The unit first examines the *nature* of child development and explores three areas of development foundational to learning: physical, social and emotional, and communication and language. It then introduces some of the key child development theorists and explores how their research has impacted on classroom practice. It will emphasise that our knowledge of child development is open to challenge, that developmental norms are socially constructed, and that they have often been based on Western industrialised childhoods. The unit will equip you to think critically about learning and teaching perspectives, and raise questions for you to reflect on. The unit will help you to understand how you can support your pupils using knowledge of child development and why this is so important.

OBJECTIVES

By the end of this unit, you should:

- understand the holistic nature of child development;
- be familiar with key theorists in child development and their ideas;
- understand the importance of your role in supporting the development of the children you teach.

SITUATED, HOLISTIC DEVELOPMENT

Drawing on extensive research over many decades, we know that human development:

- continues throughout the life-course;
- is holistic, with interrelated, rather than separate, domains;
- is socioculturally-historically situated and occurs through participation.

Consider the following vignettes:

> Aileen is 3 weeks old and lying in her crib. She wakes from sleep. Her tummy feels empty and hurts. She feels cold and uncomfortable. She begins to cry loudly. Her mother picks her up and holds her close. Aileen senses comforting contact and a familiar smell. She hears her mother's soothing voice and can see her face up close. She turns her head instinctively to feed, her hands tucked in close to her chest. As she feeds, she watches her mother's face and listens to her voice. She feels warm; she finds the suckling soothing and the discomfort in her tummy lessens.

> Aileen is now 8 months old. She sits up on the floor and reaches for the wooden hoop in the basket near to her. She grasps it, turns it around in her hands, passing it from one to the other, and puts it in her mouth. She feels the smooth wood and the rounded shape. Her brother, aged 3 years, sits nearby, searching through the basket rapidly. She watches and listens as he finds the wooden spoon, bangs it noisily in a plastic cup, and pretends to eat from it while making appreciative yum-yum noises. She gurgles in response and smiles. 'Want some, Aileen?' he asks, meeting her gaze.

Child development is often researched, discussed and written about as if it occurs in separate domains and is the same for all children. You may have read about cognitive, social, physical, emotional, language and moral aspects of development. But, as illustrated in the two vignettes above, we know that human development occurs holistically, with all domains interrelated and influencing each other. In the first vignette, Aileen appears initially to be driven by her physical sensations. However, her experiences in having her needs met are the foundations of her social development (someone else tends to me with care), communication (voice and facial expressions are directed at me; I can return the gaze) and emotional development (I feel responded to with warmth when I am in need), and in turn these are associated with the pleasurable physical sensations of food, warmth and comfort. In the second vignette, Aileen's physical changes - she is now able to sit, see further and handle items - enable her to reach out, grasp more accurately and explore with hands and mouth. Previous interesting experiences drive her curiosity and exploration, as do observing and interacting with her older sibling.

Although interrelatedness may seem obvious when discussing a baby's development, we can lose sight of the importance of attending to *all* domains of development once children are older and in school, and forget how each domain affects another. Yet physical changes, emotional insecurity, adapting to new social situations or learning a new language all influence cognition. Thus, all developmental domains are important to learning and are of concern to teachers.

Human development is not only holistic, but also situated. It takes place in the specific situations that make up children's life experiences. Those life experiences are woven through with culture and history, passed on from one generation to the next, infused throughout our social lives (Rogoff, 2003). How a child develops in a particular time in history, in a particular place and family, in a specific society with its language and cultural tools will be different to another child from a different time and place. It is the child's *changing participation over time within social situations* that constitutes development (Rogoff, 2003; Fleer and Hedegaard, 2010). Therefore, understanding something of children's home and community cultures will help you to understand what each child brings with him or her to school, in terms of their individual development and how that might differ to *your* individual experiences of development.

Given the explanation that human development is holistic rather than domain-specific, there are arguably foundational aspects to development that can help our understanding of cognitive development and learning. You will read more about the nature of learning in the next unit, 2.2. In this unit, we indicate some of the key aspects of development that could be seen as foundational to learning.

Physical development

The importance of physical movement and sensory exploration in young children's development has long been known - for example, Piaget's conceptualisation of the child as a learner interacting with their environment from birth (see below) - and recent advances in neuroscience have further evidenced this interconnectedness between brain and body development (Nurse, 2009). As seen in the vignette above, Aileen's physical progress is closely connected to other areas of development. We note her rapid development in the first year, a move from dependency to growing independence as she gains control over her body. Physical development (along with communication and language development and personal social and emotional development) is one of the *prime* areas in the Early Years Foundation Stage (EYFS) curriculum (DfE, 2017). This official recognition highlights the fact that achievement in later areas is problematic without this solid foundation. For example, handwriting is a complex activity involving well-developed gross (shoulder and arm) and fine (pincer grasp) motor skills, in addition to manipulative prowess and good hand-eye coordination. It is important, though, that physical development is seen as vital for the well-being and development of every child, and not as something important only for school 'readiness'. O'Connor and Daly (2016: 2) identify six interconnected areas of physical development:

- growth and control (of limbs, muscles);
- motor development leading to bipedal mobility (upright on two legs);
- inhibition of primitive reflexes;
- sensory development of the vestibular (balance) and proprioceptive (awareness of one's own body) systems;
- fine and gross motor skills;
- mastery of a range of physical skills such as locomotion and manipulation.

In physical growth, defined as increases in height, weight, size and power, we should again acknowledge individual *and* cultural differences. Hereditary factors, nutrition and lifestyle all impact on individual growth, and cultural factors are also linked to physical features such as stature (Doherty and Hughes, 2014).

Motor development means the child's growing ability to use their body in a variety of ways. *Gross motor skills* concern managing large muscles - pulling, pushing, bending and twisting. *Locomotor skills* are linked but involve movement - running, jumping and skipping. *Fine motor skills* involve the smaller muscles and hand-eye coordination, used in activities such as threading, tying shoelaces and turning book pages (Cooper and Doherty, 2010). Physical development usually begins in a head-to-toe (cephalocaudal) and centre-to-outwards (proximodistal) sequence. Gaining mastery over a range of physical skills similarly underpins the physical education programmes of study in the National Curriculum in KS1 and KS2, together with a focus on competition and cooperation (DfE, 2013).

It has been argued that we have been moving to a *disembodied* educational system focusing on narrow cognitive competences that ignore the importance of bodily movement (Tobin, 2004; Goddard Blyth, 2005). Goddard Blyth stresses that it is primarily through movement that neurological development is promoted, suggesting that some diagnosed problems such as dyspraxia are based on the unwanted retention of primitive reflexes present at birth. More recently, there has been interest in spontaneous *movement play*: play that develops the vestibular and proprioceptive systems (Archer and Siraj, 2015a; O'Connor and Daly, 2016). 'Movement play is about children moving in specific ways as they go through a developmental sequence of significant movement patterns that link the body and the brain' (Archer and Siraj, 2015b: 1). Given current concerns regarding young children's obesity levels and lack of fitness (HM Government, 2016), teachers have a vital role to play in promoting the physical development and well-being of the pupils they teach.

Task 2.1.1 Time to move?

Consider the opportunities available for physical movement in a class you know. Over a day, record:

- how much time children are required to sit still;
- how much time children are free to move about;
- opportunities for movement play;
- whether those opportunities are available indoors or outside.

How well do you feel that children's physical development is supported in the classroom?

Social and emotional development

Humans are social animals with powerful psychologic drives fuelling interdependency. Research by Deci and Ryan (2000, 2002) suggests that throughout our lives we try to establish and maintain feelings of *relatedness*, *autonomy* and *competence*. Clearly, for very young children, relatedness begins as total dependency. But, even from birth, babies seek out and contribute to their relationships with others through reciprocal facial expressions (Meltzoff and Moore, 1983). The need to seek out and be part of close relationships with others continues throughout our lifetimes (Morris, 2015). Our individual blueprint for how we understand and form those close relationships, however, is developed through our earliest experiences of bonding with our primary carers, and predicated on the care, attention and responsiveness we receive. This bonding is known as *attachment* and is the earliest form of relatedness. It explains the deep-seated need for affectional bonds between a baby/child and their closest carers and, although its specific characteristics vary across cultures, it occurs internationally (Van Ijzendoorn and Sagi-Schwartz, 2008). Early attachment experiences have a strong impact on our subsequent relationships throughout childhood and into adulthood. That is not to say that early experiences are entirely deterministic; on the contrary, as humans we are highly adaptive and continue to learn from experiences throughout life. Nonetheless, early attachment is very influential on how children subsequently try to make relationships and try to make *sense* of relationships. You will refresh your knowledge of attachment theory in Unit 3.5.

Relationships with people other than their closest carers also continue to be important to children's social and emotional development. Longitudinal research by Dunn and colleagues showed the importance of sibling relationships in fostering young children's development (Dunn, 1988). Being aware of the value of sibling relationships can offer scope when teachers might need strategies to help younger children feel more secure, or help children going through a difficult time. Friendships also play a valuable role in children's development. Research by Broadhead shows that, when playing or working with established friends, children add to each other's ideas and sustain more complex creations, experience a sense of belonging, and have opportunities to achieve greater depth and exploration from drawing on their joint and separate experiences (Broadhead, 2006, 2009; Broadhead and Burt, 2012; Broadhead and Chesworth, 2015). Being with a best friend can help children to cope with difficult situations (Adams, Bruce Santo, and Bukowski, 2011), measurably reducing the level of the stress hormone cortisol, suggesting that friendships should be respected and facilitated as far as possible in classroom organisation and routines.

Communication and language

Returning to Aileen, we can see how her language development is being promoted within her usual family environment. She knows to communicate by vocalising her needs through crying, making eye contact, gurgling and smiling. She also listens carefully; her mother's voice soothes her distress, and she watches her older sibling, observing both his verbal and nonverbal behaviours. Aileen is demonstrating three key aspects of language: *expressive* (speaking), *receptive* (listening) and *understanding*.

Communication is vital, and the way in which language develops has been the subject of much investigation (Whitehead, 2010). Research explored the puzzle of how infants learned to speak so well without direct focused instruction, and, in the 1950s, Chomsky identified what he termed the Language Acquisition Device (LAD). He theorised that young children were born with an innate ability to learn language and were sensitive to the linguistic features within their environment and that children learned language through imitation. However, his theories were critiqued for not acknowledging the importance of emotional relationships and the surrounding social context in promoting language development. Bruner (1975), following a Vygotskian social learning perspective, stressed the importance of opportunities for babies both to experience language interactions and to observe language interactions between others. His Language Acquisition Support System (LASS) acknowledged the way in which adults scaffold children's language development. He also identified *infant-directed speech*, the way in which adult speech is modified when talking to young children, for example speaking in slower, shorter, less complex sentences. Kersner (2015) has since argued that language learning is influenced by a combination of imitation, innate ability and adult-child interaction.

A *preverbal* stage in language development is often referred to in which babies' needs are expressed through cries and physical action. They listen and, from about 4 months, use vocal play with sounds such as 'ah' and 'oo'. From about 6 months, babies 'babble', producing strings such as 'dadada'. At about 9 months, babies use jargon, where the intonation patterns of speech are practised (Kersner, 2015). The *verbal stage* then builds on this foundation. First words are introduced from about the age of 1, and two-word phrases are used from about the age of 2. By the third year, the development of a grammatical structure becomes apparent. Helped by adult-child interaction, children gradually develop the use of tenses, plurals and word order and begin to speak in more complex sentences.

Spoken language is highlighted in the English programmes of study in the National Curriculum for KS1 and KS2: 'Teachers should therefore ensure the continual development of pupils' confidence and competence in spoken language and listening skills' (DfE, 2013: 14-15). In any primary class, there can be a wide range of speech, language and communication needs (SLCN). Development in this area is dependent on a range of factors, including age and experience. Some children are adept at masking language difficulties, and others may appear to have alternative challenges. Again, the holistic nature of development needs to be recognised, as a child with language processing difficulties might present with apparent behavioural issues (appearing to ignore instructions), and a child who finds it difficult to make themselves understood might risk becoming socially isolated (Cross, 2015). Teachers need to be alert to possible underlying issues and their importance. Recent research highlights the impact that poor language skills can have on achievement:

> One child in five starts primary school in England without the language skills they need to succeed, a figure that rises to one in three of the poorest children . . . one in four children who struggled with language at age five did not reach the expected standard in English at the end of primary school compared with one in 25 children who had good language skills at age five.
>
> (Save the Children, 2016: 1)

It is vital that teachers are confident to assess and support children's language development. The Bercow Report (Bercow, 2008) reviewed SLCN services, with one outcome being the setting up of the Better Communication Research Programme (BCRP). Findings from this programme have underpinned a range of materials for teachers, including tools to audit communication-friendly classrooms in an effort to improve practice (BCRP, 2013). Further outputs are available online (please see the Relevant websites section).

Task 2.1.2 Reflecting on speech language and communication needs

Please spend some time looking at online support materials in the area of SCLN.

- Ensure you feel confident and knowledgeable regarding any issues in language development in the classes you are teaching.
- Reflect on your role as a teacher. How might you support development in this area?
- Download the *Communication Supporting Classroom Observation Tool* and use this to audit your communication provision.

KEY THEORISTS OF CHILD DEVELOPMENT

Jean Piaget was a Swiss biologist who became fascinated by psychology and the way in which young children learn to think. Writing from the 1920s to the 1970s, his work focused on the importance of active experiential learning (Piaget, 1929), moral (Piaget, 1932) and cognitive development (Piaget, 1953).

Piaget's conceptualisation of human development was that of a 'staged theory', the idea that children need to successfully complete each of a set of defined stages to reach their full intellectual potential. These stages moved from the physically situated *sensorimotor* stage (birth to 2 years) through the *pre-operational* stage, in which the child's social development allows them to be less egocentric (2-7 years), to the *concrete-operational* stage (7-11 years), in which, Piaget argued, logical thought was enabled. The final stage was *formal operations* (11+ years), in which children were able to think both logically and hypothetically. He believed that successful negotiation through these stages was achieved through the child's active interaction with their environment, both socially and physically. Piaget is also well known for his conceptualisation of how children acquire knowledge. His *schema theory* argued that young children are born with the mental ability to interact with others and their environment to gain knowledge. As these experiences increase, they create files or *schemas* of representations and information. One of the key ways in which children gain this knowledge is through their language interactions with those around them. When a child can understand everything in their immediate world, they are said to be in a state of balance or *equilibrium*, which is disturbed when they come across something new they cannot understand. *Disequilibrium* allows children to challenge and develop their current understanding. These ideas and some critiques of his theory are discussed more fully in Unit 2.2.

Although Piaget's theories of child development were not conceived to be applicable to classroom practice, they were highly influential in the 1960s. In the USA, his ideas of active learning underpinned the innovative High/Scope approach to education, which drew on his conceptualisation of the child as an intrinsically motivated learner placed within a supportive environment (Hohmann and Weikart, 1995). In the UK, his influence was seen in the Plowden Report (1967), which advocated a move from a teacher-led, formal transmission curriculum model to a more child-centred discovery approach.

Lev Vygotsky was a Russian psychologist studying development and writing primarily during the 1920s and 1930s. His ideas did not become widely available in the West until the 1960s and were popularized from the early 1980s onwards. Vygotsky's theory suggests that human development is socially formed. Although Piaget acknowledged the role of socialisation in providing experiences on which the child operates to actively construct his or her cognitive development, the 'social' was seen as an overlay to intrapersonal development (Piaget, 1995: 278). Vygotsky, on the other hand, understood the social not simply as setting the *parameters* for learning, but in *actively forming* the higher mental functions in partnership with the child's spontaneous development, mediated by psychological 'tools' and interpersonal communication. Vygotsky saw a complex interrelationship between instruction and development, where one sometimes leads the other (Vygotsky, 1986: 184).

Although often recognised as contributing most to our understanding of the impact of social and cultural determinants of development, Vygotsky clearly acknowledged biological aspects of development. Similarly, Vygotsky noted that children's concept formation occurred along dual lines, with different forms of childhood experience leading to different types of concept development. Although 'scientific concepts' (schooled, more abstract and logical concepts) originated in the highly structured nature of classroom activity, 'spontaneous concepts' (empirically rich and disorganised) emerged from 'a child's own reflections on everyday experiences' (Kozulin's introduction to Vygotsky, 1986: xxxiv). Scientific and spontaneous concepts are inextricably interwoven, each acting on the other.

For Vygotsky, two things are key in forming shifts in children's development. The first is the *zone of proximal development* (ZPD), of which you will learn more in Unit 2.2. The ZPD points to the fact that children can do more with the guidance of someone more competent than alone. The zone varies for each child and for their specific period of development. The second key idea is that of '*crises*'. Note, though, that crises in this context do not mean something catastrophic or bad is happening to the child. Crises refer instead to the times at which something *changes* for the child, biologically or in terms of gaining competence, which result in a change in the child's motivations. This in turn challenges the way that the child relates to others, as relationships will have been based on the child's previous biological state or level of competence (Hedegaard, 2009). Hedegaard gives the example of a 1-year-old baby whose relationships with her parents and her environment change as a result of her biological and competence shifts in being able to walk. How her parents relate to her and care for her changes, owing to her increased mobility.

For the teacher, there are a number of implications to be taken into account from Vygotsky's theory of child development:

- Children bring with them individual and distinctive ways of being and thinking, based on their earlier everyday 'spontaneous' social and cultural experiences.
- Children need to be able to draw on these, as well as on new experiences, interaction and teaching, to make sense of the world.
- Such experiences work in partnership with biological development. No matter what the experiences and the level of sensitive teaching, it is not possible to teach a 6-month-old baby to ride a bicycle. Most teachers will not be working with 6-month-old babies, but the principle remains true of older children, too. However, teaching is vital to help children to progress. See the later section on age-in-cohort.
- The relationship between the teacher, the pedagogy and each child is dynamic and constantly evolving, influenced by shifting experiences, biology and levels of competence.

Jerome Bruner, a psychologist writing and researching from the 1950s to late 1990s, shared Vygotsky's view that culture and context are vital to understanding learning and development. Bruner added to our understanding of the processes involved when a more competent person guides the activity of another person in the ZPD, explaining the nature of adults' *scaffolding* children's participation through graduated support (Wood, Bruner and Ross, 1976). Like Vygotsky, Bruner emphasised the importance of *language* in human development. In particular, he examined the role of story or *narrative* in helping humans to make sense of their lives and their place in it (Bruner, 1991). He emphasised the vital role that children's questions play in demonstrating their thinking, and how attending to and responding to children's questions could further extend thinking and understanding. Bruner introduced the notion that even the most complex of subjects could be explained gradually, to children of any age, in appropriate terms and revisited to further develop understanding through the *spiral curriculum* (Bruner, 1991).

Urie Bronfenbrenner's seminal work, *The Ecology of Human Development*, was published in 1979. In it, he argued that every aspect of experience that impacted on the developing child, such as family structure, social circumstances, economic positioning and political factors, needed to be seen holistically rather than separately. He argued that, not only was acknowledgement of the different environments in which the child grew up important, but also the relationships between them. Thus, his ecological systems theory was 'a nested arrangement of structures, each contained within the next' (Bronfenbrenner, 1977: 514). As each child was part of a different set of structures, all children's developmental experiences were unique. In his original work, Bronfenbrenner identified four structures or layers that surrounded the child and impacted on their development. The child's immediate layer he termed the *microsystem* – for young children, largely comprising home and school. Here, children learned rules and socially acceptable behaviour. The next layer was the *mesosystem*, which was the set of relationships formed by participants within the microsystem, for example relationships between the home and the school. Bronfenbrenner argued that good relationships in the mesosystem supported the child. He suggested that effective partnerships between home and school would be beneficial to the child's education, and indeed research has evidenced this positive impact (e.g. Goodall and Vorhaus, 2011). His third layer was the *exosystem*, which indirectly impacted on the child. This comprised elements such as the family's economic circumstances, local neighbourhood and influences such as the media. Bronfenbrenner's fourth layer was the *macrosystem*, which he identified as the cultural practices, laws and customs that govern society.

Bronfenbrenner later acknowledged that he had not sufficiently recognised the part played by the individual child in the process of development, for example their resilience (Christensen, 2010). Later, he also added the *chronosystem*, showing that human ecology changes over time, in response to both external and internal changes. In terms of the school curriculum, Bronfenbrenner's influence can perhaps be seen most clearly in the Early Years Foundation Stage (DfE, 2017), in which three of the four themes, the Unique Child, the Enabling Environment and Positive Relations, can be viewed as being influenced by his theoretical perspectives.

Barbra Rogoff, currently professor at the University of California, Santa Cruz, has extended our knowledge of the processes involved in children developing and learning in their home and community cultures. Her research has emphasised that human development is something that happens through children's *participation* in the routine ways of doing things in their cultures. This means that children learn through taking an active part in the *everyday practices* of daily life with their families and others in their homes, villages and towns. How young children take part changes over time and according to the situations in which they are taking part (Rogoff, 2003). She explained in more detail how participation in activities is an *apprenticeship in thinking* and how children come to *appropriate* what they learn, that is to understand and use knowledge or skills for their own purposes (Rogoff, 1990). Children do so through being alongside and participating at gradually higher levels in adults' everyday and cultural activities. Through her research in cultures around the world, Rogoff has helped to demonstrate the cultural and participatory nature of human development. It is a powerful way to remind us all to step outside our *own* experiences, to question our assumptions about human development and to view it as richly varied.

Marianne Hedegaard, a Danish psychologist, proposed a further extension of Vygotsky's sociocultural historical theory of children's development. Hedegaard's model of human development takes into account not only the societal conditions and the institutional practices that shape developmental experiences, but also the individual child's different participation through activity as they move *between* several different institutions (Hedegaard, 2009, 2012). Institutions such as home, school or preschool, after-school clubs, church, and so on each have their own values and practices. To fully understand children's development, we need to consider how each child experiences participating in these institutions in societies in their *individual trajectories*; it is the child's perspective and his or her trajectory that are unique. What is of interest to teachers here is that, in addition to taking account of children's sociocultural backgrounds and their growing competence, along with biological changes, teachers need to think about how children experience and make sense of the different contexts in which they live. What is each child's cumulative story? Taking such a view can help teachers to understand, for example, how seemingly small incidents can cause distress or low self-esteem when they are actually experienced by the child as part of a *set* of experiences, with cumulative effect across different contexts.

Luis Moll, too, was influenced by Vygotsky, particularly the view that human thinking needs to be understood in relation to an individual's social and historical surroundings. Working with James Greenberg and focusing on low-income Hispanic students and their families in Arizona, in the USA, Moll carried out ethnographic research allowing him to map the cultural and social resources that families enjoyed (Moll and Greenberg, 1990). These resources were termed *funds of knowledge*: an 'operations manual of essential information and strategies households need to maintain their wellbeing' (Greenberg, 1989:2). Moll then worked with teachers in schools to explore how these funds of knowledge might support pupils' literacy development in the classroom. When they found out, for example, that many family members were employed in the building trade, a module was devised that allowed pupils to draw on this fund of knowledge to support learning in the classroom. Additionally, parents and community members were invited into school to share their expertise at an academic rather than a social level. Moll argued that this style of teaching and learning exemplified Vygotsky's ZPD where 'the child learns of things that far exceed the limits of his actual and even potential immediate experience' (Vygotsky, 1987: 180). For a more recent exploration regarding how practices can support the child within the school curriculum, see Scanlan (2012).

CHALLENGING NORMS, STAGES AND DEFICIT VIEWS

Although more recent child development research, such as that by Barbara Rogoff, has included information about children developing in cultures across the world, there is no doubt that the field of child development has in the past been dominated by research based on children from Western, Educated, Industrialised, Rich and Democratic (WEIRD) societies (see, for example, Karasik *et al.*, 2010). The research and the ensuing conceptions of how children *are* at set developmental stages have passed into popular use as developmental milestones and are routinely used to assess how well babies and children are developing (see, for example, Sheridan, 1997). Such norms can mean that children who have experienced different sociocultural backgrounds are measured against the dominant view of child development, as if the milestones can be applied universally to all children. It can give a view of some children as perhaps 'deficient' and in need of reparation. Less helpful still, it can be taken to imply a level of innate ability that is fixed and therefore indicative of future educational achievement and life outcomes.

Thinking in terms of *norms*, or averaging of levels according to the sample used, immediately places some children below or above the norm and gives rise to conceptions of 'below average' or 'above average' children. When such implications of universal developmental norms become part of routine and unquestioned practice, it is time to pause and think critically about what they mean, the evidence on which they are based and the implications of adhering to them unthinkingly. There is a tendency in English schools towards a concept of natural, fixed ability (see, for example, Bourne, 2000). How readily have the terms low-, mid- and high-ability become stalwarts of classroom practice for grouping or categorising children? Notions of universal development also leave disabled children or those with specific learning difficulties 'outside the box'. As Rix and Parry (2014) explain in their critique of *Development Matters*, the child development charts that supported the English Early Years Foundation Stage Statutory Framework (Early Education, 2012):

> Disabled children may simply not develop in an area designated by the Framework; this then becomes identified as an individual need. Consequently, practitioners may feel encouraged to find a remedy for weakness rather than building on strengths and be more likely to design individualized solutions rather than engage with wider social learning opportunities.
>
> (Rix and Parry, 2014: 210)

When a teacher is faced with concerns to identify and put in place interventions to support children who are 'falling behind', however, there are understandable tensions for that teacher to grapple with. Nonetheless, an understanding of human development should alert us to the rich variety of diverse childhoods and thus to diverse development. Teachers need to be aware of the variety of children's development, to be aware of children engaging with and building from the range of cultural, social, community, institutional, biological and home heritages. Understanding these as contexts and resources for children's development and learning can help teachers to work effectively and inclusively (Payler and Georgeson, 2017).

Task 2.1.3 Exploring childhoods

Map the range of *childhoods* evident for children in a classroom you are familiar with. Using a different post-it note for each aspect, noting distinctive elements of their childhoods. Mount them all on a large sheet of paper. Now reflect and make notes on the paper about:

- how much you know about each child's developmental contexts and individual childhood;
- what you need to find out;
- how the diversity is reflected in your classroom practices.

We turn now to two examples of the ways in which being aware of influences on children's apparent development could support teachers in making sound decisions.

Age-in-cohort

Are children born in the autumn cleverer than those born in the summer? It sounds like a preposterous statement. Yet, there is a strong body of evidence showing that children's relative age within their school cohort is associated with different levels of academic *attainment*. In particular in England, autumn-born children consistently attain at higher levels than those born in the summer (Armstrong, 1966; Bell and Daniels, 1990; Campbell, 2014; TACTYC, 2015). Further, summer-born children are significantly over-represented among children diagnosed with special educational needs (Martin *et al.*, 2004; Sykes, Bell and Rodeiro, 2009). Exactly why this pattern of achievement should exist, we are not yet certain. What common sense tells us is that autumn-born children are not likely to be generally more academically able than summer-born children. However, it is probable that the relative immaturity of summer-born children in age-cohort classes is an important factor, including differences in absolute age at time of assessment (Crawford, Dearden and Greaves, 2013). One example of differential achievement is in the phonics check, which has been administered to all children in England at the end of Year 1 since 2012. Using data from freedom-of-information requests, Clark has shown that success in the test is closely related to age, with a clear gradient in pass rate, month on month, according to month of birth. In 2014, 82 per cent of the oldest children passed the check, but only 65 per cent of the youngest (Clark, 2014).

Teacher *perceptions* of children's ability and attainment are also associated with the child's birth month, with older children more likely to be judged 'above average' by their teachers (Campbell, 2014). Relatively younger children tend more often to be placed in the lowest in-class ability groups, and relatively older children in the highest groups (Campbell, 2014). Daniels, Shorrocks-Taylor and Redfern (2000) found that teacher expectations of the youngest children in their classes affected the tasks that were given to children and the children's performance. They showed that summer-born children's results in standard tests at the end of Key Stage 1 were not significantly affected by spending seven or nine terms at school, because they remained the youngest in their class. Campbell's research convincingly shows that in-class 'ability grouping' may be instrumental in contributing to the effect of age-in-cohort on children's academic achievement. Perhaps, then, teachers need to think carefully about decisions to group children according to perceptions of ability and to be more aware of age-related factors.

Task 2.1.4 Reviewing age-in-cohort consequences

Review the ways in which age-in-cohort is reflected in the processes and structures in your classroom or one you are visiting.

- Write down the names of the six children you think of as the highest achieving and the six lowest achieving.
- Now check whether your perceptions of ability relate to children's birth dates.
- If ability grouping is used, check whether there are links between the groups and children's ages-in-cohort.

Disrupted childhoods

A growing body of research has examined the effects of disrupted childhoods on children's development (Garmezy and Rutter, 1985; MacFarlane and Van Hooff, 2009; Masten and Narayan, 2012). Although natural disasters, war and terrorism might sometimes seem remote from the everyday life of the primary classroom, in recent years, our awareness of close-to-home disaster events and of migrant children's experiences has been sharpened. Exposure to such experiences inevitably affects children, but the nature and extent of the experiences, together with interventions in the aftermath, play an influential role in shaping how children's development is affected (Masten and Narayan, 2012). There are cumulative effects of repeat exposure to traumas, and the age at which exposure takes place has a differential effect on children: in some ways worse in early childhood; in other ways worse in later childhood. Stress can affect brain development; the effects of trauma can be passed on to the next generation through biological, behavioural or socioeconomic processes; effects on one part of life can have a negative effect on other parts, such as managing at school (Masten and Narayan, 2012: 233). However, there are also ways in which the effects of trauma can be made more manageable for children. *Protective factors* for the longer-term consequences of trauma include attachment relationships and continuing, consistent care from parents and close caregivers, as well as promotion of children's sense of agency and self-efficacy – in other words, their being encouraged to believe that they have some control over their own lives. Further, re-establishing steady routines, including schooling, and opportunities to play and socialise with their peers are all important aspects that can help protect children from longer-term damage (Masten and Narayan, 2012).

For teachers, the implications for practice are to:

- become aware of the individual circumstances of children's experiences;
- understand that each child may react differently to similar events, depending on previous and subsequent experiences and the protective factors available to them;
- encourage a sense of agency and self-esteem;
- work closely with children's parents, families and communities to support their role in being the child's 'first line of defence'.

SUMMARY

In this unit, we have argued that an understanding of child development is important for all primary teachers, not just those teaching the youngest children. We have illustrated how areas of learning are interconnected and highlighted that, as teachers, we need to take a holistic overview of learning and development. We have also explored the work of key theorists, particularly those who take a sociocultural perspective, one in which the importance of a child's world and their participation within it are acknowledged. Different conceptualisations of child development can impact on policy and practice in classrooms. For example, the work of Hedegaard means teachers need to be proactive in both finding out about, and acknowledging, the out-of-school social worlds of the children they teach, thereby creating an inclusive classroom. Similarly, our understanding regarding the links between poverty, disruption and development means teachers can use this knowledge to plan specific interventions in the classroom, such as individualised support or sharing knowledge and resources with parents and carers to enhance the home learning environment.

Furthermore, although an in-depth knowledge of child development is essential for every teacher, it is equally important that we are able to critique standardised models of progression. Young children are all unique at birth and continue to grow and develop in different ways, dependent on a wide range of factors, such as environment and experience. In the same way, we are all unique as teachers; a wide range of differing experience and knowledge supports our practice, and this understanding of, and reflection on, our own individuality should underpin the learning experiences we offer to the children we teach.

ANNOTATED FURTHER READING

Morris, K. (2015) *Promoting Positive Behaviour in the Early Years*, Maidenhead, UK: Open University Press.
>   This book gives a highly readable account of research and theory relating to children's social and emotional development and their impact on behaviours. Strategies are helpful and constructive, with currency beyond the early years.

FURTHER READING TO SUPPORT M-LEVEL STUDY

Archer, C. and Siraj, I. (2015a) 'Measuring the quality of movement-play in Early Childhood Education settings: Linking movement-play and neuroscience', *European Early Childhood Education Research Journal*, 23(1): 21–42.
>   This article explores the links between research in neuroscience, movement and neurological dysfunction in relation to young children's learning and development. It explores whether practitioner intervention can result in improved movement experiences for children. It introduces a scale to assess the quality of young children's movement-play.

Fleer, M. and Hedegaard, M. (2010) 'Children's development as participation in everyday practices across different institutions', *Mind, Culture, & Activity*, 17(2): 149-68.
> This article builds on the theoretical approach in Hedegaard (2009) and applies it to a study of a child across different institutions. It highlights the processes involved in development and emphasises the importance of knowing about children's participation in settings beyond school or nursery.

Hedegaard, M. (2009) 'Children's development from a cultural-historical approach: Children's activity in everyday local settings as foundation for their development', *Mind, Culture, & Activity*, 16(1): 64-82.
> This interesting article attempts to set out a theoretical approach that takes account both of individual psychology and of children operating in concrete, everyday institutions infused with societal values. It is well illustrated with extracts from research.

RELEVANT WEBSITES

activematters: www.activematters.org/library/
> A website dedicated to early years physical development.

AFASIC Voice for Life: www.afasic.org.uk/

DfE: http://advanced-training.org.uk/module5/M05U12.html
> The DfE has produced research-based training materials for practitioners, including this one, which focuses on SLCN.

The Communication Trust: www.thecommunicationtrust.org.uk

OpenLearn, *Attachment in the Early Years*: www.open.edu/openlearn/health-sports-psychology/childhood-youth/early-years/attachment-the-early-years/content-section-0
> A free online course produced by the Open University.

ICAN Children's Communication Charity: www.ican.org.uk/

REFERENCES

Adams, R.E., Bruce Santo, J. and Bukowski, W.M. (2011) 'The presence of a best friend buffers the effects of negative experiences', *Developmental Psychology*, 47(6): 1786-91.

Archer, C. and Siraj, I. (2015a) 'Measuring the quality of movement-play in Early Childhood Education settings: Linking movement-play and neuroscience', *European Early Childhood Education Research Journal*, 23(1): 21-42.

Archer, C. and Siraj, I. (2015b) *Encouraging Physical Development through Movement Play*, London: Sage

Armstrong, H.G. (1966) 'A comparison of the performance of summer and autumn-born children at eleven and sixteen', *British Journal of Educational Psychology*, 36(1): 72-6.

Bell, J.F. and Daniels, S. (1990) 'Are summer-born children disadvantaged? The birthdate effect in education', *Oxford Review of Education*, 16(1): 67-80.

Bercow, J. (2008) *The Bercow Report: A Review of Services for Children and Young People with Speech, Language and Communication Needs*, Nottingham, UK: DCSF Publications.

Better Communication Research Programme. (2013) *Communication Supporting Classroom Observation Tool*. The Communications Trust. Retrieved from www.thecommunicationtrust.org.uk/media/93866/tct_bcrp_csc_final.pdf (accessed 16 October 2017).

Bourne, J. (2000) 'New imaginings of reading for a new moral order. A review of the production, transmission and acquisition of a new pedagogic culture in the UK', *Linguistics & Education*, 11(1): 31-45.

Broadhead, P. (2006) 'Developing an understanding of young children's learning through play: The place of observation, interaction and reflection', *British Educational Research Journal*, 32(2): 191-207.

Broadhead, P. (2009) 'Conflict resolution and children's behaviour: Observing and understanding social and cooperative play in early years educational settings', *Early Years*, 29(2): 105-18.

Broadhead, P. and Burt, A. (2012) *Understanding Young Children's Learning Through Play: Building Playful Pedagogies*, London: Routledge.

Broadhead, P. and Chesworth, L. (2015) 'Friendship, culture and playful learning', in J. Moyles, *The Excellence of Play*, 4th edn, Maidenhead, UK: Open University Press, chap. 9, pp. 94-105.

Bronfenbrenner, U. (1977) 'Toward an experimental ecology of human development', *American Psychologist*, 32: 513-31.

Bronfenbrenner, U. (1979) *The Ecology of Human Development*, Cambridge, MA: Harvard University Press.

Bruner, J.S. (1975) 'The ontogenesis of speech acts', *Journal of Child Language*, 2(1): 1-20.

Bruner, J.S. (1991) 'The narrative construction of reality', *Critical Inquiry*, 18(1): 1-21.

Campbell, T. (2014) 'Stratified at seven: In class ability grouping and the relative age effect', *British Educational Research Journal*, 40(5): 749-71.

Christensen, J. (2010) 'Proposed enhancement of Bronfenbrenner's development ecology model', *Educational Inquiry*, 1(2): 101-10.

Clark, M. (2014) *An Evidence-based Critique of Synthetic Phonics in Literacy Learning*. Retrieved from: https://ukla.org/downloads/M_Clark_Primary_First_Article_on_synthetic_phonics_1.pdf (accessed 16 October 2017).

Cooper, L. and Doherty, J. (2010). *Physical Development*, London: Continuum.

Crawford, C., Dearden, L. and Greaves, E. (2013) *When You Are Born Matters: Evidence for England*. Retrieved from https://www.ifs.org.uk/comms/r80.pdf (accessed 27 May 2013).

Cross, M. (2015) 'Links between social, mental and emotional health difficulties, and communication needs', in M. Kersner and J.A. Wright, *Supporting Young Children with Communication Problems*, London: Routledge, pp. 86-103.

Daniels, S., Shorrocks-Taylor, D. and Redfern, E. (2000) 'Can starting summer-born children earlier at infant school improve their National Curriculum results?', *Oxford Review of Education*, 26(2): 207-20.

Deci, E.L. and Ryan, R.M. (2000) 'The "what" and "why" of goal pursuits: Human needs and the self-determination of behaviour', *Psychological Inquiry*, 11(4): 227-68.

Deci, E.L. and Ryan, R.M. (2002) *Handbook of Self-determination Research*, Rochester, NY: University of Rochester Press.

Department for Education. (2013) *The National Curriculum in England: Framework Document*, London: Crown Copyright. Retrieved from www.gov.uk/government/collections/national-curriculum (accessed 10 November 2017).

Department for Education (DfE). (2017) *Statutory Framework for the Early Years Foundation Stage*, London: DfE. Retrieved from www.gov.uk/government/publications/early-years-foundation-stage-framework−2 (accessed 16 October 2017).

Doherty, J. and Hughes, M. (2014) *Child Development: Theory and Practice 0-11*, Harlow, UK: Pearson.

Dunn, J. (1988) *The Beginnings of Social Understanding*, Oxford, UK: Blackwell.

Early Education. (2012) *Development Matters in the Early Years Foundation Stage*, London: Early Education.

Fleer, M. and Hedegaard, M. (2010) 'Children's development as participation in everyday practices across different institutions', *Mind, Culture, & Activity*, 17(2): 149-68.

Garmezy, N. and Rutter, M. (1985) 'Acute reactions to stress', in M. Rutter and L. Hersov (eds) *Child and Adolescent Psychiatry: Modern Approaches*, 2nd edn, Oxford, UK: Blackwell Science, pp. 152-76.

Goddard Blythe, S. (2005) *The Well Balanced Child: Movement and Early Learning*, 2nd edn, Stroud, UK: Hawthorne Press.

Goodall, J. and Vorhaus, J. (2011) *Review of Best Practice in Parental Engagement: Research Report*, DFE-RR156, London: DfE.

Greenberg, J.B. (1989) Funds of knowledge: Historical constitution, social distribution and transmission. Paper presented at the annual meetings of the Society of Applied Anthropology, Santa Fe, NM.

Hedegaard, M. (2009) 'Children's development from a cultural-historical approach: Children's activity in everyday local settings as foundation for their development', *Mind, Culture, & Activity*, 16(1): 64–82.

Hedegaard, M. (2012) 'Analyzing children's learning and development in everyday settings from a cultural-historical wholeness approach', *Mind, Culture, & Activity*, 19(2): 127–38.

HM Government. (2016) *Childhood Obesity: A Plan for Action*. Retrieved from https://www.gov.uk/government/uploads/system/uploads/attachment_data/file/546588/Childhood_obesity_2016__2__acc.pdf (accessed 7 March 2017).

Hohmann, M. and Weikart, D.P. (1995) *Educating Young Children: Active Learning Practices for Preschool and Child Care Programs*, Ypsilanti, MI: High/Scope Press.

Karasik, L.B., Adolph, K.E., Tamis-LeMonda, C.S. and Bornstein, M.H. (2010) 'WEIRD walking: Cross-cultural research on motor development', *Behavioral & Brain Sciences*, 33(2-3): 95–6.

Kersner, M. (2015) 'The development of communication: Speech and language acquisition', in M. Kersner and J.A. Wright (eds) *Supporting Young Children with Communication Problems*, London: Routledge, pp. 13–25.

Kozulin, A. (1986) 'Introduction', in L. Vygotsky, *Thought and Language*, revised and edited by A. Kozulin, Cambridge, MA: MIT Press, pp. xi–lvi.

MacFarlane, A.C. and Van Hooff, M. (2009) 'Impact of child exposure to disaster on adult mental health: 20-year longitudinal follow-up study', *British Journal of Psychiatry*, 195: 142–8.

Martin, R.P., Foels, P., Clanton, G. and Moon, K. (2004) 'Season of birth is related to child retention rates, achievement, and rate of diagnosis of specific LD', *Journal of Learning Disabilities*, 37(4): 307–17.

Masten, A.S. and Narayan, A.J. (2012) 'Child development in the context of disaster, war, and terrorism: Pathways of risk and resilience', *Psychology*, 63: 227–57.

Meltzoff, A.N. and Moore, M.K. (1983) 'Newborn infants imitate adult facial gestures', *Child Development*, 54(3): 702–9.

Moll, L. and Greenberg, J. (1990) 'Creating zones of possibilities: Combining social contexts for instruction', in L. Moll (ed.) *Vygotsky and Education*, Cambridge, UK: Cambridge University Press.

Morris, K. (2015) *Promoting Positive Behaviour in the Early Years*, Maidenhead, UK: Open University Press.

Nurse, A.D. (2009) *Physical Development in the Early Years Foundation Stage*, Abingdon, UK: Routledge.

O'Connor, A. and Daly, A. (2016) *Understanding Physical Development in the Early Years: Linking Bodies and Minds*. London: David Fulton.

Payler, J. and Georgeson, J. (2017) 'Social class and culture: Bridging divides through learner agency', in J. Moyles, J. Georgeson and J. Payler (eds) *Beginning Teaching, Beginning Learning*, 5th edn, Maidenhead, UK: Open University Press, chap. 16, pp. 203–14.

Piaget, J. (1929) *The Child's Conception of the World*, London: Routledge & Kegan Paul.

Piaget, J. (1932) *The Moral Judgement of the Child*, London: Routledge & Kegan Paul.

Piaget, J. (1953) *The Origin of Intelligence in the Child*, London: Routledge & Kegan Paul.

Piaget, J. (1995) *Sociological Studies*, London: Routledge.

Plowden Report. (1967) *Children and Their Primary Schools: A Report of the Central Advisory Council for England*, London: HMSO.

Rix, J. and Parry, J. (2014) 'Without foundation: The DfE Framework and its creation of need', in J. Moyles, J. Payler and J. Georgeson (eds) *Early Years Foundations: Critical Issues*, Maidenhead, UK: Open University Press, chap. 18, pp. 203–14.

Rogoff, B. (1990) *Apprenticeships in Thinking. Cognitive Development in Social Context*, Oxford, UK: Oxford University Press.

Rogoff, B. (2003) *The Cultural Nature of Human Development*, Oxford, UK: Oxford University Press.

Save the Children. (2016) *Early Language Development and Children's Primary School Attainment in English and Maths: Key Findings*, London: Save the Children.

Scanlan, M. (2012) '"Cos um it like put a picture in my mind of what I should write": An exploration of how home-school partnership might support the writing of lower achieving boys', *Support for Learning*, 27(1): 4-10.

Sheridan, M.D. (1997) *From Birth to Five Years: Children's Developmental Progress* (revised by M. Frost and A. Sharma), London, New York: Routledge.

Sykes, E.D.A., Bell, J.F. and Rodeiro, C.V. (2009) 'Birthdate effects: A review of the literature from 1990-on', Unpublished paper, University of Cambridge.

TACTYC. (2015) *Written Evidence Submitted by TACTYC to the Education Select Committee Evidence Check: Starting School Enquiry.* Retrieved from http://data.parliament.uk/writtenevidence/committeeevidence. svc/evidencedocument/education-committee/evidence-check-starting-school/written/18334.pdf (accessed 16 October 2017).

Tobin, J. (2004) 'The disappearance of the body in early childhood education', in L. Bresler (ed.) *Knowing Bodies Knowing Minds: Towards Embodied Teaching and Learning*, Dordrecht, Netherlands: Kluwer Academic.

Van Ijzendoorn, M.H. and Sagi-Schwartz, A. (2008) 'Cross-cultural patterns of attachment: Universal and contextual dimensions', in J. Cassidy and P.R. Shaver (eds) *Handbook of Attachment: Theory, Research, and Clinical Applications*, 2nd edn, New York: Guilford Press, pp. 880-905.

Vygotsky, L. (1986) *Thought and Language*, revised and edited by A. Kozulin, Cambridge, MA: MIT Press.

Vygotsky, L. (1987) 'Speech and thinking', in L.S. Vygotsky, *Collected Works* (Vol. 1; R. Rieber and A. Carton, eds; N. Minick, trans.), New York: Plenum, pp. 39-285.

Whitehead, M. (2010) *Language and Literacy in the Early Years 0-7*, London: Sage.

Wood, D., Bruner, J. and Ross, G. (1976) 'The role of tutoring in problem-solving', *Journal of Child Psychology & Psychiatry*, 17: 89-100.

LOOKING AT LEARNING

David Wray

INTRODUCTION

Learning is paradoxical in nature. It can sometimes appear to be very simple. All of us are learning all the time, after all, from the myriad experiences we encounter in our daily lives. Learning is so simple that we rarely question its presence: it is as natural to our existence as eating and drinking. Yet, when we encounter difficulties in learning something, we no longer take the learning process for granted. Learning can suddenly seem very difficult indeed. I remember trying numerous ways of learning Latin declensions at school until it suddenly struck me I could make a nursery rhyme of them: *lupus, lupe, lupum, lupi, lupi, lupo*. This revelation worked so well, I still have this (useless) knowledge down pat even now.

Learning is a natural process. Yet, understanding how we learn is not so straightforward. The existence of numerous definitions and theories of learning and the fierce debates about these theories show the complexity of the process. So, what is this simple, yet complex, thing called 'learning'? And does it matter how we define it? Will that actually make a difference to our teaching?

OBJECTIVES

After reading this unit you should be able to:

1 recognise and describe the main elements of the major theoretical approaches to learning;
2 understand the implications of each of these approaches for classroom teaching.

APPROACHES TO LEARNING

Although there are many different approaches to learning, there are three basic schools of thought: behaviourist, constructivist (often referred to as 'cognitivist') and social constructivist. In this unit, I will provide a brief introduction to each theory, including a short historical introduction and a discussion of the view of knowledge presupposed by the theory and of its implications for teaching.

BEHAVIOURISM

Brief history

Behaviourism began as a reaction against the dominance of Freud and Jung, who maintained that the study of consciousness was the primary object of psychology. Their methods relied on introspection – first-person reports of feelings and experiences, both conscious and subconscious. Behaviourists rejected introspective methods as subjective and unquantifiable. Instead, they focused on observable, quantifiable events and behaviour. They argued that, as it is not possible to observe objectively what occurs in the mind, scientific theories should take into account only observable indicators such as behaviour. What happens in the mind during processes such as learning would forever be inside 'the black box' and thus not knowable. All that psychologists could do was to observe the behaviours resulting from such internal states.

What is knowledge?

Behaviourists view knowledge as a repertoire of behaviours. Skinner argued that it is not the case that we use knowledge to guide our action; rather, 'knowledge is action, or at least rules for action' (1976: 152). It is a set of passive, largely mechanical responses to environmental stimuli. So, for instance, the behaviourist would argue that to say someone knows Shakespeare is to say that this person has a certain repertoire of behaviour with respect to Shakespeare (p. 152).

Knowledge that is not actively expressed in behaviour can be explained as behavioural capacities. For example, 'I know a Siamese cat when I see one' can be seen as effectively equivalent to 'I have the capacity to identify a Siamese cat although I am not now doing so' (p. 154). If knowledge is seen as a repertoire of behaviours, someone can be said to understand something if they possess the appropriate repertoire of behaviour. No reference to unobservable cognitive processes is necessary (pp. 156-7).

What is learning?

From a behaviourist perspective, the transmission of information from teacher to learner is essentially the transmission of the response appropriate to a certain stimulus. Thus, the point of education is to present the learner with the appropriate repertoire of behavioural responses to specific stimuli and to reinforce those responses through an effective reinforcement schedule (Skinner, 1976: 161). This requires consistent repetition of the material, broken down into small, progressive sequences of tasks, alongside continuous positive reinforcement. Without positive reinforcement, learned responses will quickly become extinct. This is because learners will continue to modify their behaviour until they do receive some positive reinforcement.

How should you teach?

Behaviourist teaching methods tend to rely on so-called 'skill and drill' exercises to provide the consistent repetition necessary for the effective reinforcement of response patterns. Other methods include question (stimulus) and answer (response) sequences in which questions are of gradually increasing difficulty, guided practice and regular reviews of material. Behaviourist methods also typically rely heavily on the use of positive reinforcements, such as verbal praise, good marks and prizes. Behaviourists test the degree of learning using methods that measure observable behaviour, such as tests and examinations.

Behaviourist teaching methods have proved most successful in areas where there is a 'correct' response or easily memorised material. For example, whereas behaviourist methods have proved to be successful in teaching structured material, such as facts and formulae, scientific concepts and foreign language vocabulary, their usefulness in teaching comprehension and composition is questionable.

Behaviourist theories of learning have had a renaissance in the field of behaviour management. Positive behaviour management is usually taken to involve rewarding acceptable behaviour in pupils (catch them being good - CBG) and ignoring unacceptable behaviour. Thus, so the theory goes, pupils will be encouraged to repeat the acceptable behaviour, and the unacceptable will gradually die away. Note that it has usually been argued that theoretically, unacceptable behaviour, if met with a negative response by the teacher, may in fact be perceived by the pupil as having been rewarded (any attention being better than none for some pupils!) and thus will not fade away but be continued. Ignoring it is better. This argument makes good sense theoretically, but you might find it difficult to implement practically!

It is also true, of course, that the reward (positive feedback) that a pupil gains following unacceptable behaviour may come, not from the teacher, but from others in the class. The class clown tends to get his or her rewards from peers rather than from teachers.

Task 2.2.1 A behaviourist approach to teaching

Behaviourist approaches to teaching tend to rely on three basic principles:

1 Break down the desirable end behaviour into small steps.
2 Teach – that is, stimulate and reinforce – each of these steps in the learner.
3 Reinforce increasingly long chains of behaviour until the full end behaviour is finally achieved.
   • Think of a teaching event in which you might employ such a set of principles for your teaching. Share your suggestions with colleagues and discuss how applicable this approach might be to teaching.
   • Before reading the following section of this unit, discuss with your colleagues what you consider to be the main limitations of behaviourism as a theory of learning.

Task 2.2.2 Skinner versus Chomsky

One of the most significant challenges to behaviourist views of learning came in the field of language acquisition. Skinner's attempt to explain this from a behaviourist perspective came in 1957, in his book *Verbal Behavior*. This produced a devastating review from noted linguist Noam Chomsky. This review can be read at www.chomsky.info/articles/1967—.htm, and a wider attack on behaviourism can be found at www.chomsky.info/articles/19711230.htm (both accessed 17 October 2017).

When you have read either, or both, of these articles, try to produce a bullet-point summary of the differences between Skinner and Chomsky in terms of their views about learning.

CONSTRUCTIVISM

Brief history

A dissatisfaction with behaviourism's strict focus on observable behaviour led psychologists such as Jean Piaget to demand an approach to learning theory that paid more attention to what went on 'inside the learner's head'. An approach developed that focused on mental processes rather than observable behaviour – cognition rather than action. Common to most constructivist approaches is the idea that knowledge comprises symbolic mental representations, such as propositions and images, together with a mechanism that operates on those representations. Knowledge is seen as something that is actively constructed by learners based on their existing cognitive structures. Therefore, it relates strongly to their stage of cognitive development. Understanding the learner's existing intellectual framework is central to understanding the learning process.

The most influential exponent of constructivism was the Swiss child psychologist Jean Piaget. Piaget rejected the idea that learning was the passive assimilation of given knowledge. Instead, he proposed that learning is a dynamic process comprising successive stages of adaptation to reality, during which learners actively construct knowledge by creating and testing their own theories of the world. Piaget's theory has two main strands: first, an account of the mechanisms by which cognitive development takes place; and, second, an account of the four main stages of cognitive development through which, he claimed, all children pass.

The basic principle underlying Piaget's theory is the principle of equilibration (balancing): all cognitive development progresses towards increasingly complex but *stable* mental representations of the world. Such stability is threatened by the input of new ideas, and so equilibration takes place through a process of adaptation. One of the reasons why humans have often been resistant to new ideas is this inbuilt need for stability in their concepts of the world. Think about the centuries during which people were convinced that the Sun orbited the Earth, rather than vice versa. It was not until evidence of the falsity of such a belief was overwhelming that most people made the destabilising mental shift to a new set of ideas.

Such adaptation might involve the assimilation of new information into existing cognitive structures or the accommodation of that information through the formation of new cognitive structures. As an example of this, consider what happens when you enter a novel situation – say, going into a new restaurant. Normally, although you have never been in this particular restaurant before, you will have experience of many similar environments, and thus know what to expect. You know the sequence of events (waiter brings menu, leaves you for a while, returns to ask for your order, etc., etc.) – you know what is expected of you. The 'new' aspects of this restaurant (location, orientation of the room, design of the menus, particular specialist dishes, etc.) are simply new elements of information that you need to assimilate into your mental maps of the world (schemas). If, less usually, this restaurant is way outside your previous experience (suppose it is your first visit to a Japanese restaurant), the process of learning might be more radical. There may be details about the cutlery, plates, order of the courses, appropriate drinks, and so on, to come to terms with, and these new features need to be accommodated into an expanded schema of 'restaurant'. Thus, learners adapt and develop by assimilating and accommodating new information into existing cognitive structures.

Piaget also suggested that there are four main stages in the cognitive development of children. In their first 2 years, children pass through a sensorimotor stage, during which they progress from cognitive structures dominated by instinctive drives and undifferentiated emotions (they do not care who picks them up, as long as they satisfy the basic physical drives of hunger, comfort, etc.) to more organised systems of concrete concepts and differentiated emotions (not anyone will do as a food provider – it has to be Mum or Dad). At this stage, children's outlook is essentially egocentric in the sense that they are unable to take into account others' points of view.

The second stage of development lasts until around 7 years of age. Children begin to use language to make sense of reality. They learn to classify objects using different criteria and to manipulate numbers. Children's increasing linguistic skills open the way for greater levels of social action and communication with others.

From the ages of 7 to 12 years, children begin to develop logic, although they can only perform logical operations on concrete objects and events.

In adolescence, children enter the formal operational stage, which continues throughout the rest of their lives. Children develop the ability to perform abstract intellectual operations and learn how to formulate and test abstract hypotheses, without referring to concrete objects. Most importantly, children develop the capacity to appreciate others' points of view, as well as their own.

Piaget's theory was widely accepted from the 1950s until the 1970s. Then, researchers such as Margaret Donaldson began to find evidence that young children were not as limited in their thinking as Piaget had suggested (Donaldson, 1978). Researchers found that, when situations made 'human sense' (Donaldson's term) to children, they could engage in mental operations at a much higher level than Piaget had predicted. His theory, particularly that aspect related to the above stages of development, is not now as widely accepted, although it has had a significant influence on later theories of cognitive development.

What is knowledge?

Behaviourists maintain that knowledge is a passively absorbed repertoire of behaviours. Constructivists reject that claim, arguing instead that knowledge is actively constructed by learners, and that any account of knowledge makes essential references to the cognitive structures within the learner's mind. Each learner interprets experiences and information in the light of their existing knowledge, their stage of cognitive development, their cultural background, their personal history, and so on. Learners use these factors to organise their experience and to select and transform new information. Knowledge is therefore actively constructed by the learner rather than passively absorbed; it is essentially dependent on the standpoint from which the learner approaches it.

What is learning?

Because knowledge is actively constructed, learning is defined as a process of active discovery. The role of the instructor is not to drill knowledge into learners through consistent repetition or to goad them into learning through carefully employed rewards and punishments. Rather, the role of the teacher is to facilitate discovery by providing the necessary resources and by guiding learners as they attempt to assimilate new knowledge to old and to modify the old to accommodate the new. Teachers must thus take into account the knowledge that the learner currently possesses when deciding how to construct the curriculum and how to present, sequence and structure new material.

How should you teach?

Constructivist teaching methods aim to assist learners in assimilating new information into existing knowledge, and to enable them to make the appropriate modifications to their existing intellectual frameworks to accommodate that information. Thus, although constructivists accept some use of 'skill and drill' exercises in the memorisation of facts, formulae and lists, and so on, they place much greater importance on strategies that help learners to actively assimilate and accommodate new material. For instance, asking learners to explain new material in their own words can help them to assimilate this material by forcing them to re-express the new ideas in their existing vocabulary. Similarly, providing pupils with sets of questions to structure their reading can make it easier for them to relate the ideas in the reading to previous material by highlighting certain aspects of the text. These questions can also help pupils to accommodate the new material by giving them a clear organisational structure of ideas. Pre-reading questions such as this are referred to by researchers into reading as 'advance organisers'.

Because learning is largely self-motivated in constructivist theory, a number of methods have also been suggested that require pupils to monitor their own learning. For instance, the regular use of check-up tests and study questions can enable pupils to monitor their own understanding of material. Other methods that have been suggested include the use of learning journals by pupils to monitor their progress and highlight any recurring difficulties.

Constructivists also tend to place a great deal of emphasis upon practical activity, involving the physical manipulation of objects, in teaching such subjects as mathematics and science. Challenging and pushing forward pupils' ideas is much more likely to happen with this kind of hands-on experience and is well expressed in the proverb much beloved of constructivist learning theorists: 'I hear, I forget; I see, I remember; I do, I understand'.

SOCIAL CONSTRUCTIVISM

Brief history

Social constructivism is a variety of constructivism that emphasises the collaborative nature of much learning. Social constructivism was developed by the Soviet psychologist, Lev Vygotsky. Vygotsky rejected the assumption made by constructivists such as Piaget that it was possible to separate learning from its social context. He argued that all cognitive functions originate in, and must therefore be explained as products of, social interactions, and that learning was not simply the assimilation and accommodation of new knowledge by learners: it was the process by which learners were integrated into a knowledge community. According to Vygotsky (1978; this date refers to the translation into English of Vygotsky's work, which was in fact published in the original Russian in the 1930s):

> Every function in the child's cultural development appears twice: first, on the social level and, later on, on the individual level; first, between people (interpsychological) and then inside the child (intrapsychological). This applies equally to voluntary attention, to logical memory, and to the formation of concepts. All the higher functions originate as actual relationships between individuals.
>
> (p. 57)

What is knowledge?

Constructivists saw knowledge as actively constructed by learners in response to interactions with environmental stimuli. Vygotsky emphasised the role of language and culture in cognitive development. According to Vygotsky, language and culture play essential roles both in human intellectual development and in how humans perceive the world. Humans' linguistic abilities enable them to overcome the natural limitations of their perceptions by imposing culturally defined meaning on the world. Language and culture are the frameworks through which humans experience, communicate and understand reality. Language and the conceptual schemes that are transmitted by means of language are essentially social phenomena. As a result, human cognitive structures are essentially socially constructed. Knowledge is not simply constructed, it is co-constructed.

What is learning?

Vygotsky accepted Piaget's claim that learners respond, not to external stimuli, but to their interpretation of those stimuli. However, he argued that constructivists such as Piaget had overlooked the essentially social nature of language. As a result, he claimed, they had failed to understand that learning is a collaborative process. Vygotsky distinguished between two developmental levels: the level of *actual development* is the level of development that the learner has already reached and is the level at which the learner is capable of solving problems independently. The level of *potential development* (the ZPD) is the level of development that the learner is capable of reaching under the guidance of teachers or in collaboration with peers. Learners are capable of solving problems and understanding material at this level that they are not capable of solving or understanding at their level of actual development. The level of potential development is the level in which learning takes place. It comprises cognitive structures that are still in the process of developing, but that can only develop under the guidance of, or in collaboration with, others.

How should you teach?

If learning is social, then it follows that teaching should ideally use collaborative learning methods. These require learners to develop teamwork skills and to see individual learning as essentially related to the success of group learning. This should be seen as a process of peer interaction that is mediated and structured by the teacher. Discussion can be promoted by the presentation of specific concepts or problems and guided by directed questions, the introduction and clarification of concepts and information, and references to previously learned material. More specific discussion of collaborative teaching and the linked strategies of modelling and scaffolding will be found in the following unit.

NEW APPROACHES TO LEARNING THEORY

Neuroscience

A fairly recent development in terms of our attempts to understand processes of learning has concerned the insights coming from neuroscience, that is, detailed study at a physical, biological level of the workings of the brain. Such study has begun to suggest some profitable areas to explore, and this is the most that the majority of researchers in the area would claim. However, there have also been a number of other purported outcomes from this research that are not well founded.

These claims have been labelled 'neuro-myths' (OECD, 2002) in the sense that their popularity has spread, not through close scrutiny of research evidence, but through their adoption by commercial teaching programmes. Some of the most widespread of these neuro-myths (or misguided beliefs about neuroscience) include the following claims:

• *The brain is static, unchanging, and its parameters and nature are fully set before children begin school.* Therefore, teachers need to find ways of understanding and characterising learners according to the perceived natures of their brains (see, for example, the left-brain/right-brain and learning styles neuro-myths below). In fact, one of the most widely accepted conclusions from research in neuroscience is that of neuroplasticity. Our brains grow, change and adapt all the way through our lives. Thus, all learners are capable of adaptation.

- *Some people are left-brained and some are right-brained.* This purported division has become a powerful metaphor for different ways of thinking – logical, focused and analytic versus broad-minded and creative, and it probably originated in the split-brain work of Nobel Prize-winner Roger Sperry, who noticed differences in the brain when he studied people whose left and right brains had been surgically disconnected. However, in healthy, normal brains, the two sides are very well connected, all parts working together very well.
- *We use only 10 per cent of our brains.* This is also untrue. In fact, brain imaging research has not yet found any evidence of inactive areas in healthy brains. We use all our brains – which does not mean we could not individually use them better!
- *Male and female brains are very different.* There seems to be absolutely no significant evidence to suggest that the genders learn or should be taught differently. Male and female students may have different *preferences* for what they study, but these are more likely to be culturally determined than brain-based.
- *Children's learning styles can be identified as either visual, auditory or kinaesthetic* (which, in some schools, means that children wear a badge labelled either V, A or K, showing their learning style so that all their teachers can teach them accordingly). The paper by Sharp, Bowker and Byrne (2008) gives a comprehensive rejection to the learning styles myth.
- *Commercial packages that focus upon teaching children a series of simple body movements will have the added advantage of improving the ways the brains of these children work.* 'Brain Gym' is the best known of these packages and claims to 'integrate all areas of the brain to enhance learning'. Unfortunately, there is no evidence whatsoever that such activities have any discernible impact upon children's learning.

Although many people in education accept claims such as these as established fact, they are in fact very dubiously rooted in research evidence.

Task 2.2.3 Looking at neuro-myths

Look at the fourteen statements related to the brain and learning on the Centre for Educational Neuroscience web page (www.educationalneuroscience.org.uk/neuromyth-or-neurofact/). Some of these are correct (neuro-hits) and some incorrect (neuro-myths). Make a prediction about each one before checking whether you were right.

Growth mindset

An approach to learning that has achieved some popularity recently is that known as 'mindset theory' (Dweck, 2012). Dweck contrasts learners according to their attitudes towards themselves and their learning. Some learners have, she argues, a 'fixed mindset' – a belief that their abilities are innate and fixed. Someone with a fixed mindset would look at a difficult mathematics problem and think, 'I can't do that, I'm not good at maths', and then simply give up. However, other learners have a belief that success is based on hard work and sticking at problems. Such a 'growth mindset' might convince them to approach the difficult mathematics problem with the thought that, 'I just haven't learned enough maths to do that; I'll learn some more and try again'.

This is not terribly revolutionary – everyone knows that sometimes learners try harder at problems than others, and teachers may even judge their children on whether they tend to give up or persist in the face of difficulties. What makes growth mindset into an influential theory is Dweck's evidence that teaching a growth mindset makes learners more likely to tackle difficult learning problems. In one much-quoted study (Mueller and Dweck, 1998), children were tested, then all told that they had scored highly. A third were then told, 'You must have worked hard at these problems', another third were told, 'You must be smart at these problems', and the rest were given no feedback (control). They were all then given a choice of extra tests to do: easy or hard. Children who had been praised as 'smart' opted for the easy tests, and children praised as hard-working chose the harder ones. It seemed that the kind of feedback received had influenced their mindsets, and those encouraged in a growth mindset ('you must have worked hard') tended to tackle and succeed at harder problems. Dweck's conclusion is that growth mindset can be taught and can raise achievement.

This has certainly been an influential finding, not just in education. Yet, questions have been raised, mainly because nobody else has yet been able to replicate Dweck's findings. The difficulties with the evidence base on growth mindset are well explored on the Buzzfeed website: (www.buzzfeed.com/tomchivers/what-is-your-mindset?utm_term=.dn6DNJJ2o#.wppxGoovE; accessed 17 October 2017). For the moment, we would have to say that the jury is still out on the benefits of this approach to learning.

SUMMARY

The point made at the beginning of this unit was that learning is such a familiar and everyday thing that it is somewhat surprising that defining it has caused such huge debate. But, understanding the main principles of these debates is absolutely crucial if you are to successfully plan for and implement effective learning in your classroom. Learning is what you are mainly there to bring about, so, clearly, what you think learning is makes a difference to the way you teach. It is unfortunately the case, however, that some teachers never really give this issue much thought. Learning is so obviously important that it becomes un-problematic. But, teachers like yourself, sufficiently interested to read books and units such as this, will know that our intentions as teachers, our *theories* about teaching and learning, do make a difference to how we act in classrooms.

In this unit, I have reviewed the main theoretical approaches to learning and tried to pull out their practical implications. In many ways, you can be an effective teacher if you view learning mainly from a behaviourist, constructivist or social constructivist viewpoint: it is not your choice of theory that makes the difference. What matters is that your strategies for teaching and your teaching actions match the theory you hold about learning. Coherence between your theories and your practices will be much more successful in enabling learning than thinking one thing but doing another.

ANNOTATED FURTHER READING

Donaldson, M. (1978) *Children's Minds*, London: Fontana.

> This was an immensely significant book when it was first published. It brought together recent research into children's learning that fundamentally challenged Piagetian views that learners were limited by the current conceptual development stage they were operating in.

Joyce, B., Calhoun, E. and Hopkins, D. (1997) *Models of Learning: Tools for Teaching*, Buckingham, UK: Open University Press.

> This is a very useful outline of different models of learning. The writers isolate four 'families' of teaching based on the types of learning they promote: information processing, social/building a learning community, personal and behavioural.

Bransford, J., Brown, A. and Cocking, R. (2000) *How People Learn: Brain, Mind, Experience, and School*, Washington, DC: National Academies Press.

> This is a very comprehensive and well-written account of the major research into the learning process. The section on *How children learn* is particularly useful as a review of the major learning theories. It is freely available from: www.nap.edu/openbook.php?isbn=0309070368 (accessed 17 October 2017).

 ## FURTHER READING TO SUPPORT M-LEVEL STUDY

Wood, D. (1988) *How Children Think and Learn*, Oxford, UK: Blackwell.

> This is one of the most comprehensive and readable introductions to the study of learning. Wood is very good at relating the theoretical notions he describes so well to their practical implications for teaching. He concludes by arguing that, 'for some time to come, I suspect that the most valuable resources within the classroom will be found in human form', by which he means you – the teacher.

Siemens, G. (2005) 'Connectivism: A learning theory for the digital age', *International Journal of Instructional Technology & Distance Learning*, 2(1): www.itdl.org/Journal/Jan_05/article01.htm (accessed 17 October 2017).

> Connectivism is not the same as constructivism. Siemens, in this seminal article, puts forward a theory of learning that he claims better fits with the online, network-based learning that characterises the twenty-first-century digital world. This new theory takes into account the importance of informal as well as formal learning and the ways we typically use modern technology to support our memories and interactions with others.

 ## RELEVANT WEBSITES

emTech Learning Theories: www.emtech.net/learning_theories.htm

> The emTech Learning Theories website contains probably the most comprehensive collection of links on the Internet on the topic of learning theories (and other aspects of education – www.emtech.net). Most of the links are to downloadable articles/papers on topics ranging from operant conditioning to cognitive dissonance.

Learning Theories: www.learning-theories.com

> The Learning Theories website provides a useful outline of the principal theories of learning. It also gives access to numerous links to academic and practical material, which will expand your understanding of theories of learning.

📖 REFERENCES

Donaldson, M. (1978) *Children's Minds*, London: Fontana.

Dweck, C. (2012) *Mindset: How You Can Fulfil Your Potential*, London: Constable & Robinson.

Mueller, C. and Dweck, C. (1998) 'Praise for intelligence can undermine children's motivation and performance', *Journal of Personality & Social Psychology*, 75(1): 33–52.

OECD. (2002) *Understanding the Brain: Towards a New Learning Science*, Paris: Organisation for Economic Co-operation and Development.

Sharp, J.G., Bowker, R. and Byrne, J. (2008) 'VAK or VAK-uous? Towards the trivialisation of learning and the death of scholarship', *Research Papers in Education*, 23(3): 293–314.

Skinner, B.F. (1957) *Verbal Behavior*, Acton, MA: Copley.

Skinner, B.F. (1976) *About Behaviourism*, New York: Vintage Books.

Vygotsky, L. (1978) *Mind in Society*, London: Harvard University Press.

FROM LEARNING TO TEACHING

David Wray

INTRODUCTION

In the previous unit, we examined theories of learning from behaviourism to social constructivism. It will probably have occurred to you that, in planning for the learning in your classroom, you are guided, not by a single theory of learning, but by elements of several. There are a number of important insights into learning that can be used to underpin approaches to teaching, and it is the purpose of this unit to outline these insights and to develop some principles for teaching from them.

OBJECTIVES

By the end of this unit, you should be able to:

- discuss some important insights into the nature of learning and recognise the implications of these for teaching;
- describe the basic elements of an apprenticeship approach to teaching, justify such an approach in terms of its foundation in research and theory, and suggest examples of the implementation of this approach.

INSIGHTS INTO LEARNING

Four basic insights into the nature of the learning process have come from research, each with important implications for teaching.

Learning is an interaction between what is known and what is to be learned

It has become clear that to learn new material we have to draw upon knowledge we already have about a topic. The more we know about the subject, the more likely it is that we shall learn any given piece of knowledge. Learning that does not make connections with our prior knowledge is learning at the level of rote only, and is soon forgotten once we stop deliberately attempting to remember it.

Learning has been defined as 'the expansion and modification of existing ways of conceiving the world in the light of alternative ways' (Wray and Medwell, 1991: 9). Such a constructivist approach places great emphasis upon the ways in which prior knowledge is structured in the learner's mind. Theories about this, generally known as schema theories as they see knowledge as stored in our minds in patterned ways (schemas), suggest that learning depends, first, upon the requisite prior knowledge being in the mind of the learner and, second, upon it being brought to the forefront of the learner's mind.

As an example of this, in the field of learning through reading, try the following task.

Task 2.3.1 Schemas and reading

Consider this sentence:

> Mary remembered her birthday money when she heard the ice-cream van coming.

Without trying too hard, you can supply a great deal of information to the meaning of this, chiefly to do with Mary's intentions and feelings, but also to do with the appearance of the van and its driver's intentions. You probably do not immediately suspect him as a potential child molester! Notice that most of this seems so obvious that we barely give it much conscious thought. Our schemas for everyday events are so familiar that we do not notice when they are activated.

Now, compare the picture you get from the following sentence:

> Mary remembered her birthday money when she heard the bus coming.

What difference does this make to your picture of Mary, beyond the difference in her probable intentions? Most people say that she now seems rather older. Notice that this difference in understanding comes, not so much from the words on the page, as from the complex network of ideas that these words make reference to. These networks have been referred to as schemas, and developments in our understanding of how they operate have had a great impact upon our ideas about the nature and teaching of reading comprehension.

Task 2.3.2 The impact of varying the schema

Try out the 'Mary' sentences above on some pupils (say between the ages of 6 and 11). Do they have the same responses to the sentences as you do? If not, this probably suggests that they have not yet developed the background schemas that you use in reading the sentences.

If they do make similar responses to you, you can extend the activity by using further variations on the original sentence. What schemas does the following activate, for example?

> Mary remembered her gun when she heard the ice-cream van coming.

Or the following?

> Mary remembered her stomach when she heard the ice-cream van coming.

Ask the pupils to think of their own variations and to explain the different impressions each leaves on the reader.

We have explored this issue through the example of reading, but the same interaction between the known and the new happens in any kind of learning. Many teachers have had the experience of asking a young child the apparently simple mathematical question:

What is the difference between 6 and 9?

The answer they receive might be 3, or 'one number is upside down', or 'my brother is 9 and he's older than me 'cos I'm 6', depending upon the schema that is activated by the word 'difference'.

Classroom Example

You may also have heard the story of the newly qualified teacher who began teaching a class of 5–6-year-olds in a rural school. She decided to begin her work with the class by using a topic she was reasonably confident they would be familiar with, so she showed them a picture of a cow.

She asked the class, 'Now, who can tell me what this is?', but, to her consternation, not one of them could give her an answer, all of them looking faintly puzzled by the picture. After several equally fruitless attempts to get an answer to this simple question, she eventually became exasperated. 'Surely *somebody* can tell me what this is? You see them every day.' Eventually, one little boy raised his hand, not to give her an answer but to ask if he could look more closely at the picture. Baffled by now, she allowed him to come closer. He studied the picture for several moments before announcing in a tentative voice, 'I *think* it's a Hereford Jersey cross heifer'.

In this case, the children actually possessed much more background knowledge – a richer schema – than the teacher. Their subsequent learning around this topic would be considerably different from that the teacher had planned.

Learning is a social process

Ideas about learning have moved away from Piaget's 'lone scientist' view of learners as acting upon their environments, observing the results and then modifying or fine-tuning their schemas concerning these environments. Today, we recognise the importance of interaction and see the learner as a social constructor of knowledge. In collaboration with others, learners establish:

- shared consciousness: a group working together can construct knowledge to a higher level than can the individuals in that group each working separately;
- borrowed consciousness: individuals working alongside more knowledgeable others can 'borrow' their understanding of tasks and ideas to enable them to work successfully.

From a social constructivist perspective, the most important tool for learning is discussion, or discourse. A lot of research has tried to understand the qualities of effective discourse. Raphael *et al.* (1992), for example, studied the discourse used by primary-aged pupils as they discussed the books they had read. A great deal was revealed about the role played by the constitution of the groups, the books they discussed and the writing activities they were asked to complete as a follow-up. For example, it was found that the books chosen needed to have the potential for controversy and the power to elicit emotional responses. Raphael's research identified some of the more useful roles the teacher could play in such book discussions, such as modelling ways in which they could articulate their personal responses to literature.

The crucial role that the teacher plays in promoting the co-construction of knowledge in classrooms was also shown by Forman *et al.* (1995), who studied the discussion of 11–12-year-old pupils and their teacher around mathematical problems. The classic pattern of classroom discussion has been found to consist largely of teachers initiating an exchange (usually by asking a question), a pupil responding (answering the question), and a teacher giving feedback on that response. This pattern is known as the initiation–response–feedback (IRF) exchange and has been shown to account for up to 75 per cent of normal classroom discussion. Forman, however, found pupils evaluating each other's contributions, with the teacher expanding upon their contributions to the discussion. Similar patterns of discourse have been found in the projects reported in Kumpulainen and Wray (2002) and suggest that group discussion, in changing the traditional patterns of classroom discourse, allows and encourages much greater involvement of pupils in learning.

Learning is a situated process

We learn everything in a context. That is not controversial. But modern learning theorists also suggest that what we learn *is* the context, as much as any skills and processes used within that context (Lave and Wenger, 1991). Psychologists have sought in vain for 'transferable skills', but we are familiar with the problems. Why is it that a child who spells ten words correctly in a spelling test is likely to spell several of these wrongly when writing a story? And why, to give an example from my teaching experience, can a 10-year-old boy, absolutely hopeless in class number work, maintain an extended, sensible discussion about horse-racing odds with peers in the playground. 'It's 9 to 4 on but it's going to soften.' Do *you* understand that statement? The learning of skills such as spelling and number knowledge is so bound up with the context of learning that it cannot easily be applied outside this context.

Traditionally, education has often assumed a separation between learning and the use of learning, treating knowledge as a self-sufficient substance, theoretically independent of the situations in which it is learned. The primary concern of schools has seemed to be the teaching of this substance, which comprised abstract, decontextualized, formal concepts. The activity and context in which learning took place were thus regarded as ancillary to learning – they were useful in terms of motivating the learners but not fundamental to the nature of the learning. Recent investigations into learning, however, challenge this separation. The activity in which knowledge is deployed is now seen as an integral part of what is learned. Learning and cognition, it is now argued, are fundamentally situated.

As an example of this, consider the work of Miller and Gildea (1987) on vocabulary teaching, in which they describe how children are taught words from dictionary definitions and a few exemplary sentences, and compare this method with the way vocabulary is normally learned outside school. People generally learn words in the context of ordinary communication. This process is startlingly fast and successful. Miller and Gildea note that, by listening, talking and reading, the average 18-year-old has learned vocabulary at a rate of about 5,000 words per year (13 per day) for more than 16 years. By contrast, learning words from abstract definitions and sentences taken out of the context of normal use, the way vocabulary has often been taught, is slow and generally unsuccessful. There is barely enough classroom time to teach more than 100–200 words per year. Moreover, much of what is taught turns out to be almost useless in practice. Miller and Gildea give the following examples of pupils' uses of vocabulary acquired in this way:

- Me and my parents correlate, because without them I wouldn't be here.
- Mrs Morrow stimulated the soup.

Given the method, such mistakes seem unavoidable. Teaching from dictionaries assumes that definitions and example sentences are self-contained 'pieces' of knowledge. But words and sentences are not self-contained in this way. Using language would be almost impossible without the extra help that the context of an utterance provides. Take all the words in English that directly refer to other words or elements of context – termed by linguists 'indexical' words. Words such as here, now, next, tomorrow, afterwards are not just context-sensitive: they are completely context-dependent. Even words that seem to carry content rather than point to other words – words such as 'word' – are situated. 'I give you my word that a word, unless it is the Word of God, means what I choose it to mean' is, in a word, context-dependent, each of these 'words' meaning something quite different.

Experienced readers implicitly understand that words are situated. They, therefore, ask for the rest of the sentence or the context before committing themselves to an interpretation of a word. And then they go to dictionaries with examples of the usage in mind. But the pupils who produced the sentences listed had no support from a normal communicative situation. In tasks such as theirs, dictionary definitions were assumed to be self-sufficient. The extra linguistic props that would structure, constrain and ultimately allow interpretation in normal communication were ignored.

All knowledge is like language. Its constituent parts refer to the world and so are inextricably a product of the contexts in which they are produced. A concept, for example, will continually evolve every time it is used, because new situations, negotiations and activities inevitably recast it in a slightly different form. So, a concept, like the meaning of a word, is always under construction. I remember being puzzled in one of my secondary school science lessons to be informed we were going to make a 'solution'. This sounded interesting: I envisaged science as being exactly that – finding solutions to the problems of the natural world. When making the solution turned out to be simply a matter of mixing some blue crystals with water and watching them disappear, I could not help asking the teacher what that was the solution to!

Learning is a metacognitive process

While reading some particularly densely written material before writing this unit, I noticed that it was becoming increasingly difficult for me to concentrate on what I was reading. My mind kept drifting to other, lighter, topics, and several times I came to with a jerk to realise that I had understood nothing of the paragraphs I thought I had 'read'. This was a metacognitive experience, and my comprehension monitoring had alternately lapsed and kicked into action. These terms are probably unfamiliar to many people, and yet the processes to which they refer have been increasingly demonstrated to be of special importance in learning and in the operation of many intellectual activities. What do they mean?

There are two stages in the development of knowledge: first, its automatic unconscious acquisition (we learn things, but do not know that we know these things) and, second, a gradual increase in active conscious control over that knowledge (we begin to know what we know and that there is more that we do not know). This distinction is essentially the difference between the cognitive and metacognitive aspects of knowledge and thought. The term *metacognition* is used to refer to cognition about cognition: thinking about your own thinking.

Metacognition can be differentiated into *metacognitive knowledge* and *metacognitive experience*. Metacognitive knowledge is the relatively stable information that we have about our own thinking processes. This knowledge may be about ourselves, about the tasks we are faced with and about possible strategies for tackling them. I may know, for example, that I have to read things at least twice before I will understand them, that it is much easier to understand texts if they are about a topic about which I already know something, or that it will help me remember information if I jot down key points as I read it.

Metacognitive experience refers to the mechanisms used by active learners as they regulate their own attempts to solve problems. These might include:

- checking the outcome of what has already been attempted;
- planning the next moves in response to a problem;
- monitoring the effectiveness of these attempted actions;
- testing, revising and evaluating strategies for learning.

Although it has been demonstrated that even quite young children can monitor their own activities when working on a simple problem, learners of any age are more likely to take active control of their own cognitive activities when they are faced with tasks of medium difficulty. This is not surprising, as it seems logical that with an easy task there is no need to devote too much attention to it, and with a task that is too hard there is a tendency to give up.

As an example of metacognition in action, we can consider the activity of reading. Most character-isations of the reading process include skills and activities that involve metacognition. Some of the metacognitive activities involved in reading are:

- clarifying your purposes for reading, that is, understanding the aim of a particular reading task;
- identifying the important aspects of a text;
- focusing attention on these aspects rather than on relatively trivial aspects;
- monitoring ongoing activities to determine whether comprehension is taking place;
- taking corrective action if and when failures in comprehension are detected.

Reading for meaning, therefore, inevitably involves the metacognitive activity of comprehension monitoring, which entails keeping track of the success with which your comprehension is proceeding, ensuring that the process continues smoothly and taking remedial action if necessary.

Although mature readers typically engage in these processes as they read for meaning, it is usually not a conscious experience. Skilled readers tend to proceed on automatic pilot until a triggering event alerts them to a failure or problem in their comprehension. When alerted in this way, they must slow down and devote extra effort in mental processing to the area that is causing the problem. The events that trigger such action may vary widely. One common triggering event is the realisation that an expectation held about a text has not been confirmed by actual experience of the text. For example, in reading a sentence such as '*The old man the boats*', the fourth and fifth words will probably cause a revision of your understanding and therefore take longer to process.

Realising that you have failed to understand is only part of comprehension monitoring: you also have to know what to do when such failures occur. This involves making a number of strategic decisions, such as:

- reading on: reading more of the text to see if more information can be gained;
- sounding out: examining letters and sounds carefully (this strategy is used most often by younger readers);
- making an inference: guessing a meaning on the basis of textual clues and previous knowledge;
- re-reading: reading the difficult section again;
- suspending judgement: waiting to see if the text provides more clues.

Numerous research studies have examined the operation of metacognition in children's reading, that is, their monitoring of their own comprehension. Overall, there has been a remarkable consistency in the findings of these studies, and it seems that young children and poor readers are less adept than older children/adults and good readers in engaging in planful activities to make cognitive progress or to monitor it and are less 'resourceful' in completing a variety of reading and studying tasks.

The above description has focused on reading, but this only parallels what we know about the importance of metacognition in all areas of learning. Self-awareness appears to be an essential ingredient in success in school, which poses a fundamental problem for young children: being much less aware of the operations of their own minds, and much less able to introspect to find out how their minds are working, they are thus less able to exert any conscious control over their own cognition. There is a strong implication that learning can be improved by increasing learners' awareness of their own mental processes.

PRINCIPLES FOR TEACHING

Arising from these insights, we can derive some clear principles for teaching:

- We need to ensure that learners have sufficient previous knowledge/understanding to enable them to learn new things, and to help them make explicit these links between what they already know and what they are learning.
- We need to make provision for group interaction and discussion, both in small, teacher-less groups and in groups working alongside experts.
- We need to ensure meaningful contexts for learning.
- We need to promote learners' knowledge and awareness of their own thinking and learning.

The year 2012 saw the publication of Hattie's *Visible Learning for Teachers* – a thorough account of his meta-analysis of the effects on student achievement of a host of teaching interventions. Hattie distils the results of evaluations of these interventions into what he refers to as 'effect sizes', that is, the size of the effect that the intervention had on learner achievement. An effect size that is bigger than zero means that achievement has been raised by the intervention. However, in many cases, achievement would have gone up anyway, just through such things as learners growing older and more mature, and so Hattie uses the figure of 0.4 as an effect size to take notice of. If an intervention has an effect size of 0.4 or higher, then it might be worth other teachers adopting it.

Hattie lists, in order of effect size, those interventions whose effects on achievement have been researched. The highest effect size (and thus, according to Hattie's argument, the most effective teaching intervention) is *Self-reported grades/Student expectations*, with an effect size of 1.44, which we might take to mean getting learners to grade their own achievements in particular tasks and set themselves targets for future tasks.

Interventions that relate to the insights discussed in this unit were found to have the effect sizes shown in Table 2.3.1.

Towards a model for teaching

Palincsar and Brown (1984) described a teaching procedure (reciprocal teaching – effect size 0.74, according to Hattie) that began from the principles outlined above and was based upon the Vygotskian idea that children first experience a particular cognitive activity in collaboration with expert practitioners. The child is first a spectator, as the majority of the cognitive work is done by the expert (parent or teacher), and then a novice, as he/she starts to take over some of the work under the close supervision of the expert. As the child grows in experience and capability of performing the task, the expert passes over greater and greater responsibility, but still acts as a guide, assisting the child at problematic points. Eventually, the child assumes full responsibility for the task, with the expert still present in the role of a supportive audience. Using this approach to teaching, children learn the task at their own pace, joining in only at a level at which they are capable – or perhaps a little beyond this level, so that the task continually provides sufficient challenge to be interesting. The approach is often referred to as an 'apprenticeship approach'. In the apprenticeship approach to reading, for example, the teacher and child begin by sharing a book together, with, at first, most of the actual reading being done by the teacher. As the child develops confidence through repeated sharings of the book, he or she gradually takes over the reading, until the teacher can withdraw entirely.

In mathematics learning, Taylor and Cox (1997) have researched the effects of such apprenticeship approaches. They developed what they termed a 'socially assisted learning approach', which involved teachers modelling the ways they solved mathematical word problems, then encouraging learners to engage in such problem-solving using several approaches, such as peer collaboration, reflective questioning, scaffolding and quizzes. The pupils experiencing this approach did significantly better on word-problem tests than a control group who just received their normal mathematics teaching. This approach to teaching has been termed a 'cognitive apprenticeship' (Collins, 2006), and there appear to be four stages to the teaching process implied by the model.

TABLE 2.3.1 Some effect sizes

Intervention	Effect size
Classroom discussion	0.82
Reciprocal teaching	0.74
Metacognitive strategies	0.69
Prior achievement and knowledge	0.65
Self-questioning	0.64
Comprehension programmes	0.60
Peer tutoring	0.55
Cooperative learning	0.54
Student-centred teaching	0.54

Demonstration

During this stage, the expert models the skilful behaviour being taught. There is some evidence that learning can be assisted if this modelling is accompanied by a commentary by the expert, thinking aloud about the activities being undertaken and giving learners access to the thought processes that accompany these activities.

Joint activity

The expert and the learner share the activity. This may begin with the expert retaining responsibility for the difficult parts, while the learner takes on the easy parts, whereas, in some teaching strategies, prior agreement is reached that participants will take turns at carrying out sections of the activity. The expert is always on hand to take full control if necessary.

Supported activity

The learner undertakes the activity alone, but under the watchful eye of the expert, who is always ready to step in if necessary. In my own work on the reading and writing of non-fiction (Wray, 2013), we found that teachers tended to move too rapidly from heavily supporting children's work to asking them to work without support. Consequently, this is the stage at which most of the practical teaching strategies arising from our work, such as writing frames, were aimed.

Individual activity

The learner assumes sole responsibility for the activity. Some learners will, of course, move much more rapidly to this stage than others, and the teacher needs to be sensitive to this.

SUMMARY

In this unit, I have outlined four major insights that can be derived from a study of learning:

1 Learning is a process of interaction between what is known and what is to be learned.
2 Learning is a social process.
3 Learning is a situated process.
4 Learning is a metacognitive process.

Using these insights, I have suggested four key principles for teaching:

1 We need to ensure that learners have sufficient previous knowledge/understanding to enable them to learn new things, and to help them make explicit these links between what they already know and what they are learning.
2 We need to make provision for group interaction and discussion as teaching strategies, both in small, teacher-less groups and in groups working alongside experts.
3 We need to ensure meaningful contexts for learning, particularly in what are often called basic skills.
4 We need to promote learners' knowledge and awareness of their own thinking and learning.

These principles are, I have argued, best exemplified by what can be termed an 'apprenticeship approach' to teaching.

ANNOTATED FURTHER READING

Hattie, J. (2012) *Visible Learning for Teachers*, London: Routledge.

> This is the key text for research-led information about teaching. It is hugely influential, and every teacher should be familiar with the Hattie argument, even if they might disagree about some of the details.

Lave, J. and Wenger, E. (1991) *Situated Learning: Legitimate Peripheral Participation*, Cambridge, UK: Cambridge University Press.

> This book contains an exploration of learning as participation in communities of practice. According to the authors, participation moves from the periphery to the 'centre'. Learning is, thus, not seen as the acquisition of knowledge by individuals so much as a process of *social* participation.

Mercer, N. and Hodgkinson, S. (eds) (2008) *Exploring Talk in School*, London: Sage.

> This book consists of a number of papers by leading international researchers who, drawing on the pioneering work of Douglas Barnes, consider ways of improving classroom talk.

 ## FURTHER READING TO SUPPORT M-LEVEL STUDY

Kovalainen, M. and Kumpulainen, K. (2005) 'The discursive practice of participation in an elementary classroom community', *Instructional Science*, 33: 213–50.

> This paper outlines and discusses the findings of a fine-grained study of the interactions between children during learning tasks in a primary classroom. It features such aspects as participation rights and their relations to knowledge construction, and the challenges for the teacher in maximising the learning potential of this classroom organisation pattern.

Edwards-Groves, C.J. and Hoare, R.L. (2012). '"Talking to learn": Focussing teacher education on dialogue as a core practice for teaching and learning', *Australian Journal of Teacher Education*, 37(8). http://dx.doi.org/10.14221/ajte.2012v37n8.8 (accessed 17 October 2017).

> This paper reports an investigation into the development of teachers' skills in classroom interaction. The findings suggest that teachers benefit from explicit study of classroom interactive practices, rather than relying on simply 'picking these up' in practice.

 ## RELEVANT WEBSITES

Teaching and Learning Toolkit: https://educationendowmentfoundation.org.uk/resources/teaching-learning-toolkit/

> This site, maintained by the Education Endowment Foundation, is a good place to start when trying to evaluate the effectiveness of various teaching approaches/strategies. It rates these against effectiveness (the months that pupils seem to gain in their learning from the use of the strategy), the quality of the evidence and the relative cost.

infed: www.infed.org/

> The encyclopaedia of informal education contains a veritable cornucopia of material related to teaching and learning. As well as article-length pieces on a variety of topics, it also has a comprehensive collection of links to take you further into the subject. If you consult no other information from the web about teaching and learning, do look at this site.

Companion website: www.routledge.com/textbooks/ltps2e

> Visit the companion website for additional questions and tasks for this unit and links to useful websites relevant to this unit.

REFERENCES

Collins, A. (2006) 'Cognitive apprenticeship', in R. Sawyer (ed.) *Cambridge Handbook of the Learning Sciences*, Cambridge, UK: Cambridge University Press, pp. 47–60.

Forman, E.A., Stein, M.K., Brown, C. and Larreamendy-Joerns, J. (1995) The socialization of mathematical thinking: The role of institutional, interpersonal, and discursive contexts. Paper presented at the 77th annual conference of the American Educational Research Association, San Francisco, CA.

Hattie, J. (2012) *Visible Learning for Teachers*, London: Routledge.

Kumpulainen, K. and Wray, D. (2002) *Classroom Interaction and Social Learning*, London: Routledge Falmer.

Lave, J. and Wenger, E. (1991) *Situated Learning*, Cambridge, UK: Cambridge University Press.

Miller, G.A. and Gildea, P.M. (1987) 'How children learn words', *Scientific American*, 257(3): 94–9.

Palincsar, A. and Brown, A. (1984) 'Reciprocal teaching of comprehension-fostering and comprehension-monitoring activities', *Cognition & Instruction*, 1(2): 117–75.

Raphael, T., McMahon, S.I., Goatley, V.J., Bentley, J.L. and Boyd, F.B. (1992) 'Research directions: Literature and discussion in the reading program', *Language Arts*, 69: 55–61.

Taylor, J. and Cox, B.D. (1997) 'Microgenetic analysis of group-based solution of complex two-step mathematical word problems by fourth graders', *Journal of Learning Science*, 6: 183–226.

Wray, D. (2013) 'Principles and practice in teaching extending literacy skills', *The Clearing House: A Journal of Educational Strategies, Issues and Ideas*, 86(1): 11–16.

Wray, D. and Medwell, J. (1991) *Literacy and Language in the Primary Years*, London: Routledge.

MOVING FROM NOVICE TOWARDS EXPERT TEACHER

Samantha Twiselton and Sally Elton-Chalcraft

INTRODUCTION

> Good teaching makes a difference. Excellent teaching can transform lives.
>
> (Alexander, 2010: 279)

Such a responsibility can be quite daunting to anyone contemplating the skills that might be needed for effective primary teaching. This unit will look at the skills and knowledge required for you to be able to create and support successful learning experiences that, ultimately, could transform lives. What you decide to do in the classroom can have a profound influence on the children you work with. In this unit, we unpack factors you need to consider when you plan for the children's learning, to help you move faster on your journey from novice towards becoming an expert teacher.

OBJECTIVES

By the end of this unit, you should be beginning to:

- understand that excellent teaching involves being aware of the underlying factors that underpin learning objectives (e.g., organisation of the curriculum; concepts of knowledge; a child's background, prior learning, aptitude, etc.);
- understand how knowledge is organised (connections);
- develop strategies to help your own decision-making in the classroom (creativity and knowledge, problem analysis).

KNOWLEDGE AND LEARNING – FOR THE PUPIL AND THE TEACHER

According to Bruner (1996) and many others, learning involves the search for pattern, regularity and predictability. We can only make sense out of the confusion of information continuously bombarding our senses if we can *relate* the pieces of information to each other in some way. If a young child is presented with some bricks and the task of building a tower, this is only likely to be possible if he or she has had some other similar experiences to draw on (e.g. experimenting with bricks and learning something about how they balance, building other simple structures, knowledge of what towers look like, etc.).

Input from a teacher should help children in the formation and discovery of the patterns and rules that are most likely to help them (1) make sense of the experience and (2) generalise it to other experiences. Complex tasks can be broken down into manageable smaller problems, so that the learner can detect patterns and regularities that could not be discovered alone. So, a task such as building a tower with bricks can be made possible by the presence of a teacher who helps the pupil through decisions and actions in small steps, while still holding 'the bigger picture' of the ultimate goal of the tower in mind.

The opening quotation is from the final report and recommendations of *Children, Their World, Their Education: Recommendations and Findings of the Cambridge Primary Review*, undertaken by a range of scholars and educationalists (Alexander, 2010). We would argue that, if you encompass the review's suggested principles and aims when designing your lessons, you will thus be engaging in excellent teaching. Alexander's aims (2010: 197) of primary teaching provide a framework that is consistent with (but goes beyond) the 2012 QTS standards. The first few aims call on you to nurture the qualities and capacities of the child, namely, well-being, engagement, empowerment and autonomy; the second group of aims relate to self, others and the world, namely encouraging respect and reciprocity, promoting independence and sustainability, empowering local, national and global citizenship, and celebrating culture and community (Alexander, 2010: 197-9). The third group of aims focus on what should be going on in the classroom, namely, exploring, knowing, understanding and making sense, fostering skill, exciting the imagination and enacting dialogue (Alexander, 2010: 197-9). Other units in Section 2 of this present volume discuss the philosophies and values underpinning the curriculum; here, we restrict our discussion to development of your teaching skills and the learning opportunities you provide. We would argue that teaching ought to be a research-led profession (Elton-Chalcraft, Hansen and Twiselton, 2008), and, in this unit, we show how increasing your own pedagogical knowledge (reading research about teaching and learning), coupled with increasing your own subject knowledge of curriculum areas, can provide an effective learning environment. We aim to support your development from novice towards becoming an expert teacher by encouraging you to:

1   think more deeply about *why* you have planned to do x, y and z with your learners;
2   evaluate more rigorously what effect your teaching has on your learners;
3   reflect more comprehensively on your practice and the progress of your learners.

Task 2.4.1 An evidence-led profession?

Access the Cambridge Primary Review website (www.primaryreview.org.uk) and read the booklet *Introducing the Cambridge Primary Review* (http://cprtrust.org.uk/wp-content/uploads/2013/10/CPR_revised_booklet.pdf). Consider the extent to which the thinking reflected in this introductory booklet is supported by your experience of what constitutes effective teaching and learning in school. It is also useful to reflect on the notion of teaching as an 'evidence-led profession'. Does M-level study as part of your ITE course have a role to play in this? To what extent do you draw on knowledge in the public domain (research papers, journal articles and books, professional journals, etc.) to enhance your planning and teaching?

An effective teacher will have an excellent grasp of these fundamental concepts and will be able to break down tasks in ways that will make them achievable, while still remaining consistent with the core ideas that underpin them. This means that core ideas are developed in nucleus as early as possible and are returned to with ever-increasing complexity and sophistication in a 'spiral curriculum', as children's experience and understanding make them ready for it.

The importance of underlying structures and the role of teachers in helping pupils to make connections is supported by the work of Medwell *et al.* (1998), in which they examined the work of teachers whose pupils made effective learning gains in literacy. In this, they claim that effective teachers are much more likely to embed their teaching in a wider context and to show how specific aspects of literacy relate to each other. They assert that such teachers tend to make connections, both explicitly and implicitly, and to put features of language use into the broader context of texts. Medwell *et al.* found that the effective teachers tended to have more coherent belief systems that led them to pursue an embedded approach, where the more technical aspects of literacy were taught within a broader framework of meaningful contexts. This theme is echoed by the parallel study into effective teachers of numeracy, undertaken by Askew *et al.*, (1997), who characterise effective numeracy teachers as being 'connectionist-oriented', which involves a conscious awareness of connections and relationships.

So what does this mean in terms of the knowledge base required by you as a teacher, and how this should be applied in the classroom? This can be a very alarming question for someone learning to be a primary school teacher, as there are so many different subjects in the primary curriculum, each having its own detailed requirements.

QUALITY VERSUS QUANTITY: ORGANISATION OF KNOWLEDGE

The answer to the problem of primary teaching's wide-ranging knowledge base may be helped by Sternberg and Horvath's (1995) attempt to define what is involved in teacher expertise. They comment that there are a number of studies (e.g. Larkin *et al.*, 1980; Chi, Feltovich and Glaser, 1981) that show that it is not so much the *amount* of knowledge that the expert possesses, but *how it is organised* in the memory. In general, experts are sensitive to the deep structures of the problems they solve – they are able to group problems together according to underlying principles. This supports Bruner's model (1996). It seems that the key to being able to teach, for example, history or mathematics is not so much your knowing endless information about the subject, as your understanding some of the key underlying principles and concepts that underpin it.

This is very much supported by the study by one of the authors (Twiselton and Webb, 1998; Twiselton, 2000, 2003, 2004, 2006, 2007) of the types of knowledge and understanding that primary student teachers develop as they go through their initial teacher education (ITE) programme.

TEACHER AS TASK MANAGER, CURRICULUM DELIVERER OR CONCEPT/SKILL BUILDER

Twiselton found that (partly dependent on how far through the programme they were) student teachers could be placed into one of three main categories (or points on a continuum) – task manager, curriculum deliverer or concept/skill builder. The task managers (who were likely to be near the beginning of ITE) viewed their role in the classroom in terms of task completion, order and business – without any explicit reference to children's learning. The curriculum deliverers did see themselves as there to support learning, but only as dictated by an external source – a scheme, curriculum or lesson plan – and they struggled to give a rationale for *why what was being taught mattered* in any other terms. In contrast, the concept/skill builders (likely to be at or near the end of ITE) were aware of the wider and deeper areas of understanding and skill needed by pupils that underpinned their learning objectives. Of the three types, the concept/skill builders were much more likely to be able to support learning at every stage of the learning experience, effectively, consistently and responsively. The most outstanding quality that separated the concept/skill builders from the other two categories was their ability to see the 'bigger picture' and give a rationale for what they were attempting to do in terms of key principles and concepts. This would appear to be particularly important at a time when policymakers in England swing from one end of the pendulum, a child-centred curriculum, to the other, a subject-focused one. Over the last few years, there has been a somewhat erratic, but nevertheless consistent, desire to make teaching an M-level profession, thus encouraging intending teachers to think beyond the current governmental directives, for example the Prevent Strategy and promoting fundamental British values (DfE, 2015; Elton-Chalcraft *et al.*, 2017).

Task 2.4.2 Lesson plans 1

- Choose the subject you feel most confident in – for example, (1) English, (2) science, (3) religious education.
- Choose a key area within it – for example, (1) poetry reading and writing; (2) solids, liquids and gases; (3) belief.
- Write the key area in the middle of a piece of paper and write words and phrases you associate with it around the edge – for example, (1) rhyme, rhythm, verses, language play, imagery; (2) evaporation and condensation, state, materials, properties; (3) beliefs, religious and secular food laws.
- In a different colour, write keywords and phrases for all the ways in which this area is important – for example, (1) it gives a pattern and meaning to chaotic experiences, it expresses emotion, it entertains, it communicates powerful ideas; (2) the changing properties of materials allow us to manipulate our environment; we can manufacture things using these changes; life on land requires the fresh water produced by evaporation and condensation; (3) beliefs and values can often affect action.
- Look at the words and phrases in the two different colours you have used. Is it possible to connect them? For example, (1) rhyme and rhythm help to entertain and impose pattern and meaning; imagery is an effective way of communicating powerful ideas; (2) evaporation and condensation are important examples of key processes we use to manipulate the environment; (3) the way we behave is often influenced by our beliefs and values. (The 'what' and the 'why' are connected – concept/skill builders do this.)
- Consider the implications for how these aspects of the subject should be taught to pupils. How can you ensure that they are presented with the 'why' sufficiently?

The next stage is to identify what other factors will be involved, and how this translates into classroom practice.

The need for teachers to develop a broad, rich curriculum is strongly promoted. This is set alongside a notion of a very individualised, highly child-centred approach to supporting learning and a strong emphasis on multi-agency working and the sharing of expertise and information. All of this implies a notion of the teacher that goes well beyond the technician who delivers a prescribed curriculum.

This broad, more flexible, child-centred view of the teacher is welcome, but is not without its challenges, particularly for those who are learning to teach. For a student teacher, it is very easy to become so enmeshed in the practicalities of simply 'surviving' in the classroom that it is difficult to focus on underpinning concepts or how to connect these meaningfully to the needs of individual learners. Task 2.4.3 is designed to lead you through a process that will help you to begin to do this in stages, away from the hurly burly of the classroom, and the lesson plans (Tables 2.4.1 and 2.4.2) with commentary should help you to make the link back to the classroom and your planning.

Task 2.4.3 Lesson plans 2: Moving from novice towards expert teacher

Take a recent lesson plan – ideally one that is your own and that you have already taught. Focus on the learning outcomes that you planned for this lesson. Attempt to answer the following questions:

- Why were these learning outcomes important for these children?
- What importance/usefulness would this learning have beyond this lesson?
- How was the above communicated to the children? Were they aware of why what they were learning mattered?

If you feel able to answer these questions with some confidence, the next step is to analyse the lesson chronologically to work out how well this was communicated at each stage. If possible, identify places where this could have been improved, and how.

If you don't feel able to answer the above questions with confidence, the next step is to replan the lesson, starting with the learning outcomes and rewriting them in a way that you feel can be justified in terms of their importance. You then need to go through the rest of the plan to amend it, to ensure this is clearly and meaningfully communicated to the children throughout the lesson.

This process will encourage you to move from novice towards expert teacher.

KNOWLEDGE AND CREATIVITY – DEEP LEARNING, NOT SURFACE LEARNING

Other sections later in this volume (Section 4, 'Approaches to the curriculum', and Section 7, 'Recent developments' - in particular Unit 7.4, 'Creativity and creative teaching and learning', by Cremin and Barnes) – discuss the 'what' and 'how' of teaching and learning in more detail; here, we are showing the link between the structural underpinning of lesson planning 'why' and the ways in which you can achieve this 'what and how'; (Elton-Chalcraft and Mills, 2013), together with the 'where and when' (Claxton, 2007).

Boden argues that knowledge and creativity are not opposing forces (2001: 95). For example, children need to know the rules of rhyme, or the tenets of belief, before they can playfully create new poems, or work out their own responses. It is important for teachers to support children's understanding of a curriculum area, but, as we have argued earlier, the organisation of this learning (how we teach) can lead either to mundane completion of tasks (task managers) or effective learning (concept/skill builders). Research in neuroscience tells us that knowledge is contextualised, and teachers need to support the child to make connections in the brain (Claxton, 1997; Heilman, 2005). If the curriculum is seen as a blueprint for learning, Copping (2011) argues, then tasks will not be meaningful. For example, task managers would happily ask children to complete a worksheet about Muslims fasting during Ramadan, perhaps filling in missing words. Concept builders, on the other hand, would have used the Internet/books/Muslim visitors to inform their own subject knowledge, thus enabling the children to explore reasons why many Muslims fast, yet other Muslims choose not to for particular reasons, why the children themselves eat or do not eat certain foods at particular times, and so on. Concept builders would make the links between the religious education lesson and the PSHE topic on healthy lifestyle, to discuss what foods the children eat and why, and how this relates to religious food laws (Elton-Chalcraft, 2015). Thus, task managers merely present knowledge – a blueprint – that the children learn, and the children have no interaction with that knowledge. Knowledge is a requisite, as Boden (2001) says, for creating new ideas and concepts and embedding learning in the child's own, personalised web of belief. Kuiper, Volman and Terwel (2009) show how children can be encouraged to use resources appropriately to ensure deep learning, using a 'healthy eating' topic. Elton-Chalcraft (2015: 12) describes how a teacher can engage learners in deep reflection on what they eat and the factors behind people's choice of foods – for example, allergies, texture, taste, appearance, moral or religious reasons, and so on. An effective teacher designs creative learning activities and provides creative learning environments that are not only fun but also challenge the children (Elton-Chalcraft and Mills, 2013). Claxton (2007) urges the teacher to engage in split-screen thinking – with a dual focus, on both the content of the lesson and the learning disposition of the child. In his compelling article, Claxton (2007) suggests teachers build children's 'learning capacity' and encourage children to strengthen their 'learning muscles'. All this requires pedagogical knowledge and understanding, which we outline below.

Task 2.4.4 Creativity and knowledge

Access Denis Hayes's (2011) *Guided Reader to Teaching and Learning*, extract 7, pp. 29–31, TASC (thinking actively in a social context), from Wallace *et al.* (2009). Hayes (2011: 31) asks in what ways are pupils seen as equal partners in learning? How is such a state of working attainable?

Read Cedric Cullingford's (2007) passionate article, 'Creativity and pupils' experience of school'. Is Cullingford convincing in his argument about 'children's preferred modes of thinking' (2007: 137)? How does this relate to our discussion of knowledge and concept/skill builders?

Read Claxton (2007), 'Expanding young people's capacity to learn'. What is your response to Claxton's argument that teachers should be concentrating on children's 'learning muscles', as well as teaching the topic? Do you think this approach is appropriate?

Gordon Stobart's (2014) *The Expert Learner: Challenging the Myth of Ability* discusses surface, strategic and deep/profound learning, with ideas taken from John West-Burnham (Stobart, 2014: 70, 71). To what extent do you help children to engage in deep, profound learning. Are there some times when strategic learning is necessary? Can children be challenged to understand that surface learning is to be avoided? Strategic learning might help them achieve the highest possible grades, but deep learning enables them to develop ideas for themselves, seek underlying patterns and become actively interested in their learning.

EXPERT AND NOVICE TEACHERS' USE OF KNOWLEDGE

Any attempt to define all the different kinds of teacher knowledge required in effective practice is bound to hit the problem that the list can be infinitely extended. However, it is worth noting that most people agree that, however you describe it, the knowledge base is wide-ranging and varied, and that different kinds of knowledge are required at different times. Tochon and Munby (1993) studied expert and novice teachers and found that a key characteristic that distinguished the experts was their ability to draw on a wide range of different kinds of knowledge (e.g. the subject, the plan, the individual pupil, the context, etc.) in making one teaching decision. The novices tended to think about one thing at a time and to stick quite rigidly to their plan, regardless of whether the pupil responses, the context, and so on, supported this.

Lee Shulman (1987) has classified the knowledge base of teaching in seven categories: content knowledge (better known to us as subject knowledge), general pedagogical knowledge, curriculum knowledge, pedagogical content knowledge, knowledge of learners and their characteristics, knowledge of educational contexts and knowledge of educational ends. The important thing for student teachers to note is not so much the items on the list (though these are useful), but the fact that they are so varied. It is the *drawing together and combining* of these varied factors that is important. For example, Devine, Fahie and McGillicuddy (2013: 83) investigate teacher effectiveness in terms of 'passion, reflection, planning, love for children' and the 'social and moral dimension' of what constitutes good teaching. They argue that, when discussing quality teaching, it is vital to consider sociocultural contexts such as gender, social class and ethnicity (Devine *et al.*, 2013).

The Medwell *et al.* (1998) study found that the subject knowledge of the effective literacy teachers was only fully identifiable when it was embedded within a teaching context:

> Our interpretation of what we have observed is that the effective teachers only knew their material by how they represented it to children . . . through experience of teaching it, their knowledge seemed to have been totally embedded in pedagogic practices.
>
> (p. 24)

They also found that the effective teachers tended to have more coherent belief systems linked to the importance of communication, composition and understanding. This links with Bruner's views about the key components that are the fundamentals of the subject.

In the parallel study of effective numeracy teachers, Askew *et al.* (1997) characterised effective numeracy teachers as being 'connectionist-oriented'. They claimed that the highly effective teachers believed that being numerate required having a rich network of connections between different mathematical ideas.

Beck (2013) discusses the 'knowledge of the powerful' and calls for teachers to be more politically aware. We encourage you to engage with the themes in this article in Task 2.4.4 to ensure development from novice teacher towards a well-informed, expert teacher.

KNOWING THE UNDERLYING PRINCIPLES, USING KNOWLEDGE EFFICIENTLY

In Sternberg and Horvath's (1995) study of teaching expertise, three key features are identified. The first is *knowledge*, and we have already considered their claim that the organisation of the knowledge around principles is the central factor. The second and third features are *efficiency* and *insight*. Efficiency is closely linked to experience, in that the claim is that experts are much faster at processing information and making well-informed decisions, partly because what is initially effortful and time-consuming becomes effortless and automatic with practice. This is obvious, and one of the most comforting pieces of advice that can be given to student teachers is that, as time goes on, many things that are difficult now become much easier. However, it is worth noting that Sternberg and Horvath (1995) also claim that experts typically spend a greater proportion of time trying to understand the problem, whereas novices spend more time actually trying out different solutions. Sometimes, deciding on the best response through more detailed analysis is a much more efficient way of dealing with problems than rushing in without clear judgement.

It can be argued that *insight*, Sternberg and Horvath's third feature of teacher expertise, involves a combination of the first two (knowledge and efficiency). Insight involves distinguishing information that is relevant to the problem solution from that which is irrelevant. This obviously provides the expert teacher with an insight into the situation, which will enable him or her to (1) make the most efficient use of the time available and (2) draw on the most useful areas of knowledge.

Twiselton's study of student teachers (mentioned above; Twiselton and Webb, 1998; Twiselton, 2000, 2003, 2004, 2006, 2007) also involved examining how expert teachers operate. She did this through watching them teach, making detailed notes of their actions and words and interviewing them closely afterwards about how they decided what to do. The observation notes on pages 96–7 are an example of the notes taken, and Task 2.4.5 helps with understanding how this can be analysed to show how effective teachers constantly assess the situation in order to make the most effective response.

Task 2.4.5 Observing other teachers

- Read through the Observation notes 1 on page 96 and use the 'Assessment/response' column to make a note of any points at which Teacher A appears to be making an assessment or acting on the basis of an assessment made.
- Repeat this with the Observation notes 2 on page 97 for Teacher B.
- What are the differences you notice between the two teachers?
- Which teacher is supporting the children's learning more effectively? Why?

The second set of observation notes were taken from a student teacher, Teacher B, during her first placement. The differences are notable. Teacher B assesses in a limited way and only uses a narrow range of strategies. The expert teacher, Teacher A, is constantly assessing and responding, and she uses a range of strategies in doing this. This supports Sternberg and Horvath's (1995) claims that effective teachers demonstrate knowledge, efficiency and insight through their ability to quickly process and analyse a learning experience and draw on a range of conceptual principles to make the best decisions for action.

Observation notes 1 for Task 2.4.5

Observation notes 1	Assessment/response
9.23 Teacher A is talking to child (C1) about her picture of a ladybird: 'Do you want to do some writing to tell everyone about this?' (C1 nods) 'What shall we write?' C1: The ladybird is sitting on a leaf. Teacher A : Excellent. Which side shall we start? C1: Over here. **9.25** Teacher A: You go ahead and write it and show me in a minute. Teacher A is explaining the spider's web pattern to a child (C2). **9.27** Teacher A: Can you make the lines go all along the web? It's very important you start at the left and finish on the right because we are practising for writing. Where's the left? Where will you start? (C2 shows her; she observes closely as C2 starts the web) Teacher A: Lovely, don't forget to keep your pencil on the line. Nice and slow. **9.30** Teacher A: What a lot of lovely writing. I can see some of the letters of your name. Where's the 'm'? C1: Here and here. Teacher A: You've done those beautifully. Can you read me your writing now? C1: The ladybird is sitting on the leaf. She has lots of children and they like flying. **9.32** Teacher A: Wow! You've added more to it! You told me earlier on that there was an 'l' at the beginning of ladybird. Where might the 'l' have gone here? (C1 points randomly and vaguely) Teacher A: Can you read it again and point to the words at the same time? (C1 moves her finger along the line from left to right, but there is no attempt to match up the writing with what she is saying) **9.34** Teacher A: Now I'll write my writing. Where shall I start? (C1 shows her; Teacher A writes the words and reads them as she does so) Teacher A: Let's read it again together. (They read it; Teacher A gently holds C1's finger and helps her to point to the words as they read)	

Observation notes 2 for Task 2.4.5

Observation notes 2	Assessment/response
10.10 Teacher B to C1: What does that say? (Points from left to right over the label) (No answer from C1) Teacher B: What does it start with? C1: It's a drink. Teacher B: Yes, but what does it start with? C1: Don't know. Teacher B: It's milk! 10.12 Teacher B to the whole group: Take it in turns to choose a card – see if you can match it. (C2 takes a card) Teacher B: What does that say? (C2 is looking at the picture) C2: Chocolate. Teacher B: Good girl! Put it in the right place. 10.14 (C3 takes a card with a sandwich label) Teacher B: What does that say? Have you got that? C3: It says pizza. Teacher B: It's not pizza. What does it say? It says sandwich! 10.17 (C1 takes a card) Teacher B: What does that card say? (No answer) Teacher B: W . . . C1: Watermelon. Teacher B: Brilliant! 10.19 (C2 takes a card) Teacher B: What does it say? C2: Ice-cream. Teacher B: Have you got ice-cream? (Teacher B points to game card) C2: No. 10.20 Teacher B: Well done!	

SUMMARY

It does not require a unit in a book to tell you that teaching is a very complicated business, and that effective teaching requires a wide range of types of knowledge and a large number of skills. In this unit, we have tried to elaborate on some of the more important components of teaching skills and to explore the implications of these for your teaching. It is important to close this unit with a reminder of the importance of quality over quantity. It is not the amount you know, or the number of teaching skills in which you have some competence, that is crucial. Your depth of knowledge and level of confidence in your skills are of much more importance. As you experience teaching, keep asking yourself the 'why' question and keep your eyes and ears open to children's responses. Deeper knowledge and surer confidence in your actions will follow if this becomes your natural mindset, and you will develop from novice into expert teacher.

 ANNOTATED FURTHER READING

Alexander, R. (2010) *Children, Their World, Their Education: Final Report and Recommendations of the Cambridge Primary Review*, London: Routledge.

    An impressive body of research underpins this volume, which covers most aspects of teaching and learning, philosophy and practice.

Boyd, P., Hymer, B. and Lockney, K. (2015) *Learning Teaching: Becoming an Inspirational Teacher*, Northwich, UK: Critical Publishing.

    A text for intending teachers who wish to move from novice towards expert teacher by recognising their own agency. The book includes critical exploration of metacognition and self-regulated learning, deep and surface learning and feedback.

Elton-Chalcraft, S., Hansen, A. and Twiselton, S. (2008) *Doing Classroom Research*, Milton Keynes, UK: Open University Press.

    This book has been designed to support those studying at Masters-level as part of their initial teacher education programme.

Graham-Matheson, L. (2014) 'How children learn', in *Essential Theory for Primary Teachers*, London: Routledge, chap. 6, pp. 128–53.

    Graham-Matheson analytically discusses theories of learning in an accessible format, with pointers to further reading.

 FURTHER READING TO SUPPORT M-LEVEL STUDY

Beck, J. (2013) 'Powerful knowledge, esoteric knowledge, curriculum knowledge', *Cambridge Journal of Education*, 43(2): 177–93.

    John Beck highlights three tensions that impede teachers' efforts to extend powerful learning to disadvantaged pupils. This clearly written but conceptually challenging article draws on sociological and philosophical ideas that can challenge a novice student teacher to move towards expert teacher. Beck discusses 'knowledge of the powerful' in terms of the ruling ideas (p. 180) that can lock working class children out of 'high culture'. Beck claims that education inflicts 'symbolic violence' on working-class children. He describes how the relatively accessible arts, as opposed to the conceptually challenging sciences, are still used as a benchmark for defining 'good taste'. The tensions that confront a teacher include, first, the problem of disciplinary knowledge being esoteric and accessible primarily for the initiated. The second tension, related to the first, is the breadth versus specialisation debate. The third tension is the cultural capital afforded to the ruling classes, which perpetuates hegemony.

Claxton, G. (2007) 'Expanding young people's capacity to learn', *British Journal of Educational Studies*, 55(2): 115-34.

> In this article, particularly useful for M-level students, Claxton expands his view that hesitancy and unclear knowing are vital aspects of intelligence, and that the teacher's role is to help children to become better learners – increase their 'learning capacity' – as opposed to supporting them to become conformist pupils, which, Claxton argues, can result in learned helplessness.

Cullingford, C. (2007) 'Creativity and pupil's experience of school', *Education 3-13*, 35(2): 133-42.

> Cullingford discusses children's preferred modes of thinking and how teachers can appropriately support children to learn more effectively. This journal article is ideal for M-level study concerning relevant curriculum design and appropriate teaching skills.

Devine, D., Fahie, D. and McGillicuddy, D. (2013) 'What is "good" teaching? Teacher beliefs and practices about their teaching', *Irish Educational Studies*, 32(1), Special Issue on Research in Education Related to Teacher Accountability.

> This journal article discusses the need for teachers to take into account the broader sociocultural context of the school and the needs of their learners, which will have an influence on the way they construct learning. M-level students will find this an engaging read to inform effective classroom practice.

RELEVANT WEBSITES

https://chartered.college/

> The Cambridge Primary Review website is located in that of the Chartered College of Teaching, an independent organisation run by teachers for teachers.

REFERENCES

Alexander, R. (2010) *Children, Their World, Their Education: Final Report and Recommendations of the Cambridge Primary Review*, London: Routledge.

Askew, M., Brown, M., Rhodes, V., William, D. and Johnson, D. (1997) *Effective Teachers of Numeracy*, London: Teacher Training Agency.

Beck, J. (2013) 'Powerful knowledge, esoteric knowledge, curriculum knowledge', *Cambridge Journal of Education*, 43(2): 177-93.

Boden (2001) 'Creativity and knowledge', in A. Craft, B. Jeffrey and M. Leibling (eds) *Creativity in Education*, London: Continuum, chap. 6.

Bruner, J.S. (1996) *The Culture of Education*, Cambridge, MA: Harvard University Press.

Chi, M.T.H., Feltovich, J.P. and Glaser, R. (1981) 'Categorization and representation of physics problems by experts and novices', *Cognitive Science*, 5(2): 121-52.

Claxton, G. (1997) *Hare Brain, Tortoise Mind: Why Intelligence Increases When You Think Less*, London: Fourth Estate.

Claxton, G. (2007) 'Expanding young people's capacity to learn', *British Journal of Educational Studies*, 55(2): 115-34.

Copping, A. (2011) 'Curriculum approaches', in A. Hansen, *Primary Professional Studies*, Exeter, UK: Learning Matters, pp. 23-43.

Cullingford, C. (2007) 'Creativity and pupils' experience of school', *Education 3-13*, 35(2): 133-42.

DfE. (2015) *Promoting Fundamental British Values*. Retrieved from www.gov.uk/government/publications/promoting-fundamental-british-values-through-smsc (accessed on 1 November 2016).

Devine, D., Fahie, D. and McGillicuddy, D. (2013) 'What is "good" teaching? Teacher beliefs and practices about their teaching', *Irish Educational Studies*, 32(1), Special Issue on Research in Education Related to Teacher Accountability.

Elton-Chalcraft, S. (2015) *Teaching Religious Education Creatively*, London: Routledge

Elton-Chalcraft, S., Hansen, A. and Twiselton, S. (eds) (2008) *Doing Classroom Research: A Step-By Step Guide for Student Teachers*, Maidenhead, UK: Open University Press.

Elton-Chalcraft,S., Lander, V., Revell, R.,Warner, D. and Whitworth, L. (2017) 'To promote, or not to promote fundamental British values? Teachers' standards, diversity and teacher education', *British Journal of Educational research*, 43(1): 29-48.

Elton-Chalcraft, S. and Mills, K. (2013) ' "It was the funnest week in the whole history of funnest weeks." Measuring challenge, fun and sterility on a "Phunometre" scale: A case study evaluating creative teaching and learning with PGCE student teachers and children in a sample of primary schools', *Education 3-13: International Journal of Primary, Elementary and Early Years Education*. http://dx.doi.org/10.1080/03004279.2013.822904.

Hayes, D. (2011) *Guided Reader to Teaching and Learning*, London: David Fulton.

Heilman, K. (2005) *Creativity and the Brain*, Hove, UK: Psychology Press.

Kuiper, E., Volman, M. and Terwel, J. (2009) 'Developing Web literacy in collaborative inquiry activities', *Computers & Education*, 52(3): 668-80,

Larkin, J., McDermott, J., Simon, D. and Simon, A. (1980) 'Expert and novice performance in solving physics problems', *Science*, 208: 1335-42.

Medwell, J., Wray, D., Poulson, L. and Fox, R. (1998) *Effective Teachers of Literacy*, London: Teacher Training Agency.

Shulman, L.S. (1987) 'Knowledge and teaching: Foundations of the new reform', *Harvard Educational Review*, 57(1): 1-22.

Sternberg, R. and Horvath, J. (1995) 'A prototype view of expert learning', *Education Research*, 24(6): 9-17.

Stobart, G. (2014) *The Expert Learner: Challenging the Myth of Ability*, Maidenhead, UK: McGraw-Hill/Open University Press.

Tochon, F. and Munby, H. (1993) 'Novice and expert teachers' time epistemology: A wave function from didactics to pedagogy', *Teaching & Teacher Education*, 2: 205-18.

Twiselton, S. (2000) 'Seeing the wood for the trees: The National Literacy Strategy and initial teacher education; pedagogical content knowledge and the structure of subjects', *Cambridge Journal of Education*, 30(3): 391-403.

Twiselton, S. (2003) 'Beyond the curriculum: Learning to teach primary literacy', in E. Bearne, H. Dombey and T. Grainger (eds) *Interactions in Language and Literacy in the Classroom*, Milton Keynes, UK: Open University Press, pp. 63-74.

Twiselton, S. (2004) 'The role of teacher identities in learning to teach primary literacy', *Education Review: Special Edition: Activity Theory*, 56(2): 88-96.

Twiselton, S. (2006) 'The problem with English: The exploration and development of student teachers' English subject knowledge in primary classrooms', *Literacy*, 40(2): 88-96.

Twiselton, S. (2007) 'Seeing the wood for the trees: Learning to teach beyond the curriculum. How can student teachers be helped to see beyond the National Literacy Strategy?', *Cambridge Journal of Education*, 37(4): 489-502.

Twiselton, S. and Webb, D. (1998) 'The trouble with English: The challenge of developing subject knowledge in school', in C. Richards, N. Simco and S. Twiselton (eds) *Primary Teacher Education: High Standards? High Status?* London: Falmer, pp. 155-168.

BUILDING ON FIRM FOUNDATIONS

Early years practice

Janet Rose, Sue Rogers and Elizabeth Carruthers

INTRODUCTION

The early years sector in the UK has seen an unprecedented period of development and change via major investment and attention from policymakers in the past 20 years, although this has diminished somewhat in recent years. The sociopolitical agenda to ameliorate the divisive and fragmented nature of early years provision in the UK was (and, arguably, still is) closely bound up with the desire to reduce child poverty and disadvantage and to encourage parents (and in particular mothers) back to work. These aspirations have required a major 'root and branch' approach to services for young children and their families (Anning, 2006), and central to this has been the dual aim to both increase the quantity, and improve the quality, of early education and childcare provision.

Within this context, our task in this unit is to challenge the popular conception that working with young children is easy and of less significance than formal schooling, and to convince you that, as primary school teachers, you need to understand how and in what ways children learn in the early years, and the range of diverse experiences they are likely to have had on arrival in the primary school. We offer also a cautionary note: we acknowledge that a key aim of early years education is to build firm foundations for future learning in the primary school and beyond. However, the purpose of early years education is not simply to achieve 'school readiness', as a preparation for future life or for later schooling: it is something that is important in its own right. Understanding this will enable you to build on the firm foundations established in the first 5 years and value the specific characteristics of young children as learners.

OBJECTIVES

This unit will help you to:

- highlight key issues you ought to know about in relation to the early years;
- eliminate any myths that may exist in your perspective of the early years;
- emphasise the importance of the early years and outline key policy initiatives;
- clarify the nature of early years practice.

EARLY YEARS POLICY

It is widely agreed that, from birth, children are powerful, creative and competent learners, and that early years provision should capitalise on this at a time when they are particularly receptive, developmentally, to exploratory, imaginative and social activity. Key questions about what an appropriate curriculum and pedagogy for young children might look like, and how, and in what ways, adults can support the learning and development of children in the early years, have been the major preoccupations of policymakers and early years educators alike. More recently, there has been a focus on the training and qualifications of the early years workforce.

The considerable recognition now afforded to the early years of education by policymakers is indicative also of a wider appreciation of the fundamental significance of this phase of childhood in lifelong learning, a view underpinned by a large and robust research literature. For example, there is compelling recent evidence from the neurosciences that testifies to the profound way in which children's earliest experiences affect their developing potential, with long-lasting implications (see, for example, Goswami, 2015; Gopnik, 2016).

The increasing complexity and demands of contemporary life mean that many children under the age of 5 will have had experiences in one or more different early years contexts, whether they have been cared for by a nanny or childminder, or have experienced group settings such as day nurseries, children's centres and/or preschool nurseries or playgroups. Each of these settings will have provided a range of diverse experiences, and, in turn, these will have affected the knowledge, skills and understanding that children bring with them to school. There has been a steady increase in early education provision for disadvantaged 2-year-olds since 2011. Coupled with the economic climate and sociopolitical trends, the likelihood of children spending time in settings other than the home is set to increase. It is, therefore, imperative that teachers, particularly those working in Key Stage 1, are fully cognisant of the potential range of provision and that they understand the types of experience these children will have had, in order to ease the transition process and be sensitive to the potential impact of these in helping young children to adapt and settle into the school environment. Indeed, the revised *Teachers' Standards* refer to the need for teachers to build on pupils' prior experiences and knowledge (DfE, 2013).

In Northern Ireland . . .

Controversially, Northern Ireland is the only country that legally obliges children aged 4 years to attend primary school. Compulsory school age is governed by Article 46 of the Education and Libraries Northern Ireland Order 1986. Children who have reached the age of 4 on or before 1 July will start primary school at the beginning of the September of that year. (Education Authority, 2017: 3).

Source: Education Authority Northern Ireland. (2017) *Starting School Age: A Guide for Parents*, Belfast, Education Authority. Retrieved from www.eani.org.uk/about-us/latest-news/school-starting-age-guidance-for-parents-is-published/ (accessed 18 October 2017).

> ## In Scotland . . .
>
> We know that most young children already come to ELCC settings as active, experienced learners with a natural curiosity. From the beginning, they are a person and a unique individual. At the earliest stage they are interested in themselves and their immediate environment. At times, some other children come to settings upset, vulnerable, from a difficult home environment, or have specific learning needs.
>
> (Scottish Government, 2014: 23)
>
> Source: Scottish Government. (2014) *Building the Ambition. National Practice Guidance on Early Learning and Childcare Children and Young People (Scotland) Act 2014*, Edinburgh: Scottish Government. Retrieved from www.gov.scot/Resource/0045/00458455.pdf (accessed 21 March 2016).

THE EARLY YEARS FOUNDATION STAGE

Educational provision for children under 5 in England is offered within a wide range of diverse settings, in both the maintained and private sectors. These settings include nursery classes, day nurseries, playgroups, childminders, children's centres and Reception classes of primary schools. All of these settings now fall within the Foundation Stage, a distinctive phase for children from birth to statutory school age, currently described as 'the term after a child's fifth birthday'.

In 2006, the Childcare Act provided the legal framework for the creation of the Early Years Foundation Stage (EYFS), implemented in 2008, replacing three earlier initiatives. Under the coalition government, a revised EYFS was developed that became statutory from September 2012 and was republished with some amendments in 2014 (DfE, 2014). Two main factors need to be taken into consideration in relation to the EYFS:

1   The EYFS is intended to create a holistic and coherent approach to the care and education (sometimes referred to as 'educare') of young children – this represents a considerable and welcome development within the early years sector in recognition that the care and education of young children are inseparable and inextricably linked.
2   The EYFS is a statutory framework, but it is not intended as a curriculum to be followed, as with the National Curriculum – rather, it is viewed as principles for practice across the early years sector.

The revised EYFS is based on the following principles:

*   every child is a *unique child*, who is constantly learning and can be resilient, capable, confident and self-assured;
*   children learn to be strong and independent through *positive relationships*;
*   children learn and develop well in *enabling environments*, in which their experiences respond to their individual needs and there is a strong partnership between practitioners and parents and/or carers; and
*   *children develop and learn in different ways and at different rates*; the framework covers the education and care of all children in early years provision, including children with special educational needs and disabilities.

Building on these principles, the revised EYFS places great emphasis on three key characteristics of effective learning:

1   Playing and exploring are the ways in which children engage with their learning – through finding out and exploring, playing with what they know and being willing to have a go.
2   Active learning is what motivates children – being involved and concentrating, keeping trying and enjoying achieving what they set out to do.
3   Creating and thinking critically – children need lots of opportunities to think, have their own ideas, make links and choose ways of doing things.

It is important to note that these characteristics are concerned with the process of how children learn and the context in which the early years curriculum should be offered. These apply equally to the indoor and outdoor environments.

Much of the old and new EYFS is based on a commitment to '*developmentally* appropriate practice', promoting activities that are in tune with the child's individual level of understanding and skills development. Though children are assessed individually, the significance of the sociocultural context on children's lives is also recognised, promoting *contextually* appropriate practice.

What is developmentally and contextually appropriate practice?

> Developmentally appropriate practice requires both meeting children where they are – which means that teachers must get to know them well – and enabling them to reach goals that are both challenging and achievable. All teaching practices should be appropriate to children's age and developmental status, attuned to them as unique individuals, and responsive to the social and cultural contexts in which they live.
>
> (National Association for the Education of Young Children, 2009)

Early years practice is commonly associated with the term 'developmentally appropriate practice' (DAP), a term that has particular currency in the USA, but has had a significant influence on early years education in the UK. The new research review by the Cambridge Primary Review Trust in the UK has reconfirmed the importance of a developmentally appropriate curriculum for young learners, such as the need for active experience, multisensory approaches and pretend play to promote cognitive development (Goswami, 2015).

Although DAP endorses a developmental perspective on children's education, we must be careful, however, not to over-emphasise the evidence from developmental psychology. Indeed, the new review by the Cambridge Primary Review Trust emphasises that Piagetian stage theory, which demarcates children's thinking into 'ages and stages', is no longer upheld by the evidence, particularly from neuroscience, and, instead, draws attention to the crucial parts played by social and motivational factors in children's learning (Goswami, 2015). Moreover, we need to consider that no framework or curriculum is 'value-free' or 'context-free' (Penn, 2008: 188). We therefore need to be conscious of the wide range of factors that may influence a child's experiences before entry into Key Stage 1, not just their apparent developmental levels, thereby implementing contextually appropriate practice to reflect how learning is socially and culturally mediated (Goswami, 2015).

'SCHOOL READINESS' AND STARTING SCHOOL

The issues related to developmentally and contextually appropriate practice are largely encapsulated in the debates surrounding school starting age and the notion of 'school readiness'. The notion of 'school readiness' is controversial among early years specialists. Usage of the term has increased within government discourse and is now explicitly stated in the revised EYFS, which is intended to promote:

teaching and learning to ensure children's 'school readiness' and gives children the broad range of knowledge and skills that provide the right foundation for good future progress through school and life.

(DfE, 2014: 5)

Recent Ofsted publications related to early years provision also make numerous references to the development of 'school readiness' (2014). Although the documents acknowledge the lack of a definition for, or shared understanding of, the concept of 'school readiness', they make it clear that ensuring young children's 'school readiness' is a requirement for early years providers.

The sociopolitical discourse, culture and policy of school improvement and school readiness has invariably led to features of a formal school curriculum percolating down to the teachers and children in the Reception class. Recent research has highlighted the pressures that are put on early years practitioners to create a more formalised learning environment in Reception classes (Rose and Rogers, 2012a; Roberts-Holmes, 2015). This process is compounded by the prevalence of children starting school at a younger age. In England, Scotland and Wales, the statutory school starting age is the term after a child's fifth birthday and, in Northern Ireland, it is the academic year following their fourth birthday. In England, changes to the School Admissions Code in 2011 meant that, in practice, most children enter school when they are just four. The stated rationale for this change to one intake per year is its perceived benefits for summer-born children, ensuring that children have sufficient time in school in order to be 'ready' for Key Stage 1 and the demands of the National Curriculum. The impact of this change is felt in Reception classes, where provision needs to be made for children who are likely to have different developmental demands owing to their immaturity.

Studies of Reception class pedagogy explicitly endorse a nursery-style provision for 4-year-olds and argue that there is no compelling evidence that starting school early has lasting educational benefits (Sharp, 2002; Rogers and Rose, 2007). Indeed, opponents of an early school starting age and 'school readiness' discourse warn that over-formal education, introduced too soon, may be detrimental to children's social well-being and long-term attitude to learning. Issues regarding formal instruction have been explored by Aubrey and Durmaz (2012). They report how international comparison studies create pressures for higher standards and the tensions this creates between a play-based pedagogy and a standards agenda, particularly in the light of the values and understanding practitioners bring to practice. These findings correlate with those from a study by Rose and Rogers (2012b) of newly qualified early years teachers in different parts of England who faced dissonance between their play-based pedagogical principles and the reality of the 'high-stakes' performativity culture and curriculum in schools. Other literature documents how Reception class children often experience a watered-down version of Key Stage 1 (Whitebread and Coltman, 2008; Brooker *et al.*, 2010).

The emphasis on skill acquisition in Reception classes can be to the detriment of children's motivation to learn, over-emphasis on formal reading skills being a classic example of this trend. The Cambridge Primary Review, for example, has noted that any gains have been 'at the expense of [pupils'] enjoyment of reading' (Whetton, Ruddock and Twist, 2007: 19). Young children's disposition to learning has been a critical factor identified in the literature for educational success (Katz, 1992), suggesting that the 'school-readiness' culture that permeates Reception classes may be counter-effective (Rogers, 2010). In reviewing the literature on school readiness, Whitehead and Bingham make the following pertinent points in relation to the school readiness debate (2012: 6; original emphasis):

> All children, at all ages, are 'ready to learn' and have been doing so since birth. Recent research . . . has established that many of our cognitive processes are fully functioning at birth, or mature very quickly during the first 4–5 years of life. So, the significant question is not *whether* a child is ready to learn but *what* a child is ready to learn and how adults can best support the *processes of learning*.

Task 2.5.1 Principles into practice

- Read the article by Rose and Rogers (2012b), 'Principles under pressure: Student teachers' perspectives on final teaching practice in early childhood classrooms'.
- Discuss whether the findings in the article echo your own experiences in placement.
- Outline your own principles of early years practice and consider possible challenges you might encounter when applying these principles in the classroom.

THE LEARNING ENVIRONMENT

The debate about what constitutes an appropriate learning environment in the early years inevitably draws into its sphere the role of play. In all countries of the UK, the early years curricula strongly endorse a play-based approach to learning in the early years (CCEA, 2007; SG, 2008; DfE, 2014; DfES, 2015). In practice, however, implementing a play-based approach can be challenging. Teachers often feel under pressure to ensure children are 'school ready', emphasising literacy and numeracy activities, presented in ways that may not reflect developmentally appropriate practice. We suggest here that being school ready also requires children to be socially and emotionally secure, and increasingly able to make choices, think critically and creatively, and plan ahead, skills that are well supported in play activities. Second, it is not always clear how much structure to provide in play. Do children need manufactured and elaborate resources to play, or open-ended materials and props that provoke imagination and conversation? Should play be tied to curriculum objectives, or are the outcomes of play determined by the children or in collaboration with adults? Third, what is the adult role in play? To what extent should adults intervene, and when does intervention become interference and overly directive? We suggest that children need a balance between activities that are child-initiated and those supported by adults who listen and tune into children.

Few would dispute the fact that one of the key ways in which children up to the age of 5 make human sense of the world around them is through their play (Donaldson, 1978). We can see this in the earliest sensorimotor play observed in babies and toddlers, involving mainly exploratory activity through the senses and through action on objects. You might be familiar with the tendency of babies to put things in their mouths and throw things. At this stage, children are interested in the properties of things. Take, for example, Sam, who is 10 months old. He is preoccupied with dropping objects from the top of the stairs, repeatedly. Though this behaviour may be difficult for adults to tolerate, it is a vital part of Sam's development in his efforts to make sense of the world around him. He is learning about his impact on the world and early scientific and mathematical concepts, such as gravity, cause and effect and trajectories. This exploratory play gradually changes as children approach their second birthday, when a profound and uniquely human capacity comes to the fore of children's activity. This is the ability to pretend, seen first in the simple imitations of toddlers and later in the highly sophisticated social pretend play or role-play of 4- and 5-year-olds. It is this social pretence that lays the foundations of many important life skills, such as problem-solving, creative activity and interpersonal relations, as well as being enjoyable and life-enhancing to children as they play.

In Scotland . . .

'There is a balance where we need to raise the profile of play and also to deepen an understanding for practitioners in supporting play experiences with children' (Scottish Government, 2014: 28).

Source: Scottish Government. (2014) *Building the Ambition. National Practice Guidance on Early Learning and Childcare Children and Young People (Scotland) Act 2014*, Edinburgh: Scottish Government. Retrieved from www.gov.scot/Resource/0045/00458455.pdf (accessed 21 March 2016).

In Wales . . .

In the Foundation Phase learning environment:

Children learn through first-hand experiential activities with the serious business of 'play' providing the vehicle. Through their play, children practise and consolidate their learning, play with ideas, experiment, take risks, solve problems, and make decisions individually, in small and in large groups. First-hand experiences allow children to develop an understanding of themselves and the world in which they live.

(Learning Wales, 2015: 3)

Source: Learning Wales. (2015) *Curriculum for Wales: Foundation Phase Framework*, Cardiff: Welsh Government (WG). Retrieved from http://learning.gov.wales/docs/learningwales/publications/150803-fp-framework-en.pdf (accessed 18 October 2017).

In Wales . . .

There must be a balance between structured learning through child-initiated activities and those directed by practitioners. A well-planned curriculum gives children opportunities to be creatively involved in their own learning which must build on what they already know and can do, their interests and what they understand. Active learning enhances and extends children's development.

(Learning Wales, 2015: 4)

Source: Learning Wales. (2015) *Curriculum for Wales: Foundation Phase Framework*, Cardiff: Welsh Government (WG). Retrieved from http://learning.gov.wales/docs/learningwales/publications/150803-fp-framework-en.pdf (accessed 18 October 2017).

Of particular interest to those of you working in Key Stage 1 classes is research that demonstrates that children aged 3-5 engage in more pretend play than any other kind of play (see, for example, Corsaro, 2005). Not only is it more prevalent than other kinds of play, but it also becomes highly complex, involving detailed planning and negotiation, and innovation. Developmentally speaking, there are good reasons for this. At around the age of 4, we see children's imaginative play become more complex, as they become more linguistically and socially expert. They have also discovered that other people have minds, and that what they think is not always what others think. This is the emergence of empathy, and theory of mind. All this is essential to successful pretend play and is also developed within it.

The prevalence of this kind of play occurs precisely at the point at which children enter Reception class settings in primary schools, and it continues to develop through to the role-play and other creative activities seen in primary school classrooms. In order to help children develop vivid imaginations, understand social relations and innovate (all transferable skills), it is essential that children are given ample opportunities to engage in social pretence with their peers at this age, and, furthermore, that these experiences are built upon in Key Stage 1 and beyond.

In recognition of the importance of all types of play across the early years phase, early years settings are developed around the concept of 'free-flow', continuous play provision, both indoors and outdoors. Classrooms are organised into resource areas to which children have access throughout the day. This approach presupposes choice and autonomy on the part of children, who will have regular and sustained opportunities to access resources independently. Remember that Einstein believed that 'play is research'.

Task 2.5.2 Child-initiated play

Read the following example of real-life practice and consider whether the teacher's aims fulfil her intention:

> A teacher of six year olds is planning an art activity to develop their creative skills. She decides the children will make pine-cone turkeys and collects the range of materials they will use. She sits with a group and demonstrates how they will make them and explains exactly how the materials fit together in particular places to create the turkey. She then supports them in making them, allowing each child to choose five coloured feathers, which she encourages them to count. The children then make the turkeys, but need help with the glueing, sticking and making the pipe-cleaner feet. The children mostly watch the teacher during the whole activity.
>
> (Woyke, 2001: 15)

How you could turn this adult-led activity into one that is child-initiated and allows the child to be more active, creative and independent in the process?

The outdoor environment

Of particular importance since the introduction of the EYFS is the recognition that young children need regular access to outdoor play to enhance their well-being and development in all areas: physical, emotional, social, cognitive and creative (Evangelou *et al.*, 2009). Outdoor spaces offer a range of different learning opportunities to children, not least the freedom to be more active, noisy and exploratory than is possible in indoor spaces. In addition to the obvious physical benefits of being in the outdoors, such activity offers young children a range of first-hand multisensory experiences, such as feeling the effects of the weather and related temperatures, and experiencing direct contact with the textures, smells and sounds of natural materials, such as wood, grass, ice, earth and water.

Research has shown that, not only do young children prefer to play outside, but they play in quite different ways in outdoor spaces (Rogers and Evans, 2008). Moreover, outdoor play, by its very nature, involves children taking risks that push them beyond their current capabilities and challenge them physically, socially and cognitively. For adults, managing risk is challenging too and may lead to anxieties about how far they can allow children to explore and push boundaries. Certain types of play can also pose a risk to adults' own boundaries about what is acceptable behaviour, particularly within the heavily regulated classroom (Rogers, 2013). As children develop, they move from a situation of dependence and adult-managed experiences to independence and self-management. Gill (2007) argues that there is growing evidence to suggest that, in the developed Western world, an increasingly regulated, risk-averse approach is severely limiting children's opportunities to practise some of the vital skills that would enable them to make this move and to exercise good judgement about what constitutes risk and danger. However, adults may hold an exaggerated view of what constitutes

FIGURE 2.5.1 Exploring and taking risks outdoors

a risk to young children, stemming from their own personal anxiety about potentially threatening situations, about the potential for disorder within the group and a genuine anxiety about litigation while *in loco parentis* (Waite, Evans and Rogers, 2011).

Redcliffe Nursery School and Children's Centre in inner-city Bristol has been pioneering more adventurous outdoor experiences for children (Carruthers, 2007; Hill, 2016). They have a vibrant forest experience for all the nursery children every week and have made their nursery garden more adventurous for the children. This includes providing tyres of all sizes, rope swings, large boxes to climb in and a huge, 4-feet-deep sand pit. A real motorbike is suspended from the canopy, and an innovative teacher decided to purchase second-hand aeroplane seats. There are many and varied climbing structures, as well as trees to climb. The children learn to be safe in this environment, practising balancing on a makeshift see-saw, climbing along ridges, and trying out all sorts of ladders. Through their time at nursery, they develop strong physical skills and grow in confidence in all areas of learning.

THE ROLE OF THE ADULT IN PLAY

It is not simply the material resources that make for a stimulating and effective learning environment for young children. Knowledgeable, skilled and caring adults will create an environment that creates, nurtures and sustains a positive learning ethos that matches the dispositions and characteristics of young children and acknowledges and values cultural diversity and equity. Earlier, we raised some of the dilemmas facing early years practitioners in relation to young children's play and some of the tensions that exist within different pedagogical approaches in terms of the amount or level of adult interaction or involvement in children's play activities – in other words, whether practitioners ought to 'develop a child or watch a child develop' (Alexander, 2010: 95). The EYFS compounds this debate by stipulating that, 'each area of learning and development must be implemented through planned, purposeful play and through a mix of adult-led and child-initiated activity' (DfE, 2014: 1.8).

In Northern Ireland . . .

Children need help to extend their play. Adults can contribute to the development of abstract thinking, for example, by adding resources and props, by asking open-ended questions and posing exciting challenges (Council for Curriculum, Examination and Assessment, 2003: 9).

Source: Early Years Inter-board Panel. (2003) *Learning Through Play in the Early Years: A Resource Book*, Belfast, CCEA Publications. Retrieved from www.nicurriculum.org.uk/docs/foundation_stage/learning_through_play_ey.pdf (accessed 16 October 2017).

One possible way forward is to reconsider the terms 'adult-led', 'adult-directed', 'child-initiated' and 'child-led' and replace these terms with just two: adult-initiated and child-initiated. Thus:

> By viewing all activities and exchanges as a process of initiation that immediately becomes an interconnected negotiation, rather than as an act of being led or directed by either the child or the adult, we can envisage the adult–child relationship as one that involves interchangeable processes of 'give-and-take' and mutual co-construction.
>
> (Rose and Rogers, 2012b: 9)

We have suggested that this might help early years teachers to 'understand the reciprocal nature of adult–child interactions and might help to diminish uncertainties regarding adult intervention' (Rose and Rogers, 2012b).

In Wales . . .

Foundation Phase practitioners should acknowledge prior learning and attainment, offer choices, challenge children with care and sensitivity, encourage them and move their learning along. The Foundation Phase curriculum should be flexible to allow practitioners working with children opportunities to plan and provide an appropriate curriculum for children who are at an early stage of their development and for those who are more able.

(Learning Wales, 2015: 4)

Source: Learning Wales. (2015) *Curriculum for Wales: Foundation Phase Framework*, Cardiff: Welsh Government (WG). Retrieved from http://learning.gov.wales/docs/learningwales/publications/150803-fp-framework-en.pdf (accessed 18 October 2017).

A recent research study by Rogers and Evans (2008) studied the role-play activity of 4- and 5-year-olds in Reception and Year 1 classes. They found that there was a mismatch between how children viewed their play and the way play was organised in the classroom. Typically, classrooms were set up with structured role-play areas around a particular theme or topic. For example, one classroom developed a shop, and another offered a café. Although these areas were resourced in elaborate and inviting ways, the children paid little attention to the theme, preferring instead to play games of their own choosing. In many instances, the play was difficult to contain and manage within the confines of the classroom. An alternative approach to role-play, well suited to children over the age of 4 and throughout the primary years, is open-ended play, with suggestive rather than pre-specified props.

For example, Kelvin and his friends built a 'ship' from large bricks. They 'sailed' to a 'cave' made from a sheet draped over some chairs. In the 'cave', there were some keys, which they used to lock up the baddies. This example of sustained role-play involving five children lasted for at least 20 minutes. Kelvin, a child with identified special needs, emerged as a 'master player', leading the group and utilising language rarely heard in formal teaching activities. Social relationships were explored, formed and re-formed in the course of the play, as children negotiated roles and planned the course of the play.

In this simple example of role-play, we see a wide range of important learning and potential assessment opportunities for the observant adult. McInnes *et al.* (2013) argue that children's performance is enhanced if they perceive an activity to be playful. Their research demonstrates learning is enhanced in settings that promote co-constructed play with shared adult–child interactions, open questions and more choice and control for children. Overall, research shows that adults need to:

- give children real choice about where, with whom, what and how they play;
- give children space (indoors and outdoors) and uninterrupted time to play, revisit, rebuild and recreate ideas with adults and children;

- show children we are interested in their play through co-construction, consultation and negotiation, observation and feedback;
- be knowledgeable others and advocates for play;
- develop outdoor spaces for playful learning where children can exercise greater choice over materials, location and playmates;
- develop open-ended resources and spaces, enabling children to create play contexts and content;
- provide time to play without unnecessary interruptions;
- develop a learner-inclusive environment that encourages children's participation and decision-making;
- encourage sustained shared thinking between adults and children and between children (adapted from Rogers and Evans, 2008).

Sustained shared thinking

Sustained shared thinking involves the adult being aware of the children's interests and understandings and the adult and children working together to develop an idea or skill. The adult shows genuine interest, offers encouragement, clarifies ideas and asks open questions. This supports and extends the children's thinking and helps children to make connections in learning (Sylva *et al.*, 2004).

The Effective Provision of Pre-school Education (EPPE) project findings (Siraj-Blatchford *et al.*, 2002; Sylva *et al.*, 2004) suggested that the potential for learning through play can be extended by what the researchers have termed 'sustained shared thinking'. This essentially involves adults 'getting involved' in children's thinking, interacting in a shared (verbal or nonverbal) dialogue. In this way, as Siraj-Blatchford explains, adults can act as co-constructors to 'solve a problem, clarify a concept, evaluate activities or extend narratives' (2004: 147). Sustained shared thinking builds on other research that demonstrates the importance of meaningful, child-initiated and supportive interactions, such as Bruner's (1986) work on scaffolding and learning as a communal activity, inspired by Vygotsky and by Schaffer's (1996) work on 'joint involvement episodes'.

Task 2.5.3 Sustained shared thinking

Read the following example of a real-life exchange between children and their teacher in a nursery. Evaluate the way in which the practitioner supported the children's thinking.

While playing outside, the children discovered a kitten (toy) stuck in the guttering of the barn area. The group was allowed time to discover the kitten and talk about how they thought it got there and how it could be rescued (*P* = practitioner).

Child B: Oh, poor kitty, I think she's stuck up there.
Child C: How did it get all the way up there?
P: Oh dear. How do you think the kitten got stuck up there in the first place?
Child A: He climbed up this pipe (pointing to the drainpipe), then went along here and got stuck in here.
Child C: He can't climb up there 'cos he's not real! I think he must have been 'throwded' up there.
P: Who do you think might have done that?
Child C: I don't know but it's not very kind is it? They might have done it on accident.

P:	Yes, they might have done it by accident. Well, I suppose we need to do some good thinking about what to do to help the kitten. How shall we do that do you think?
Child D:	I know, I know! We can, we can ask Charlotte to climb up all the way.
Child A:	Yeah, I seen Charlotte climb ladders to get that stuff off them tall shelves in the other room.
Child C:	Or we can get Jill to do the ladder.
Child B:	No, she 'don't' really like 'um' (meaning ladders).
Child C:	I know, we can find Graham, he's good with ladders and he fixes stuff.
P:	What do we need to ask Graham?
Child E:	Ask him to get the ladders and climb up there.
P:	Oh, I see.
Child D:	He can climb all the way up to that pipe thing and put it (the kitten) in his pocket.
Child B:	He 'don't' want to squash it though. That would hurt it, wouldn't it?
P:	Shall we decide what we think we should do then?
Group:	Yeah!
P:	Well, you had lots of thoughts and ideas; let's see if we can choose one idea to sort the problem out. You said we need to get a ladder, but who shall we ask to climb up it; you thought it could be Jill, Graham or Charlotte. Who do you think would be best to ask?
Child C:	Graham.
Children A and E:	Yeah, we can ask Graham.
P:	What makes you think Graham will be best for the job of getting the kitten down?
Child E:	He can climb ladders up really high.
Child D:	Yeah, I 'seen' him before on ladders. He can put it (kitten) in his pocket gently, can't he?
Child B:	He mustn't drop her or she'll have a headache and she might die!
P:	I hope she doesn't do that! Okay, so you think Graham can climb the ladder and put the kitten in his pocket gently and bring it back down again?
Child A:	Yeah, really gentle!
Child B:	And then the kitten will live happily ever after!

Source: Bowery (2008)

Apart from helping to develop children's learning, the adult needs to ensure that he or she is sensitive to the children's cues and levels of understanding, supporting them to make connections and transform their learning in a pleasurable and embedded way.

THE FOUNDATION STAGE PROFILE

The Foundation Stage Profile (FSP) is the precursor for the standard assessment tests (SATs) and is intended to provide a 'baseline assessment' of children starting school. In England, every government-funded setting, including schools, must complete an FSP for every child in the final term of the Reception year, or equivalent. In essence, it requires Reception class teachers to assess each child in relation to the seventeen Early Learning Goals, along with a brief commentary on the child's skills and abilities in relation to the three key characteristics of effective learning, and to share these assessments with parents and Year 1 teachers. The assessments need to indicate whether children

FIGURE 2.5.2 Creating towers with adult support

are meeting *expected* levels of development, or if they are *exceeding* expected levels, or not yet reaching expected levels ('*emerging*'; DfE, 2016; own emphasis) and should consider children's self-assessments. It is intended that Year 1 teachers use the summary profiles to help inform them of individual children's learning and development. The results from these profiles are moderated and collected by local authorities and published nationally. The Standards and Testing Agency has stipulated that these summative assessments should be derived from the ongoing observations of consistent and independent behaviour, undertaken largely in the context of spontaneous (self-initiated) activities and events.

It should be noted that many have criticised these summative and essentially numerical profiles and have questioned, among other things, their suitability, their effectiveness in feeding into teaching in Year 1, their oversimplification and the way in which they compartmentalise children's learning (Bradbury, 2014). There is an increasing call for more formative styles of assessment to take priority. The Researching Effective Pedagogy in the Early Years project has also shown that effective formative assessment directly impacts upon the quality of learning (Siraj-Blatchford *et al.*, 2002).

A formative form of assessment, namely 'Learning Journeys', has become common practice in early years settings. Indeed, the revised FSP uses Learning Journeys as exemplifications of the way in which practitioners might record children's achievements and use these as evidence for making summative assessments. Such Learning Journeys are largely derived from 'learning stories', developed in New Zealand, whereby early years practitioners carry out regular assessment of

FIGURE 2.5.3 A Learning Journey entry

children's natural activities, incorporating the observation, assessment and planning cycle within a framework of celebrating children's achievements. These are shared with both the children and parents, alongside discussion and decision-making among the children and staff to plan, enrich and progress children's learning. This style of assessment follows a sociocultural model. It is collaboratively and community based and reflects the learner's personal development rather than performance indicators. It is undoubtedly assessment *for* learning rather than assessment of learning.

TRANSITION FROM THE FOUNDATION STAGE TO KEY STAGE 1

Transition from one key stage to another inevitably presents children and practitioners with both challenges and opportunities. It involves unlearning and relearning, and the teacher's transition practice needs to take this into account. In conversation with Reception class children, Rogers and

Evans (2008) found that, for some, moving from the Foundation Stage to Key Stage 1 was an exciting prospect, signifying progress and achievement. For others, it was a source of anxiety, perceived as 'hard work', with fewer opportunities to play with friends.

Task 2.5.4 Supporting transition

Undertake an audit of Reception and Year 1 in a school from a child's perspective:

- What do the children see in the Year 1 classroom that is the same as the Reception classroom?
- What is different?
- What do the Reception children experience that is the same as the Year 1 children?
- What is different?

Now undertake an audit of transition procedures in the school:

- What does the school do to reinforce the similarities?
- What does the school do to accommodate the differences?

Evaluate your findings in terms of the suggestions made in this section about how teachers can support the transition process.

Research shows that educational transitions are highly significant to pupils and can be a 'critical factor in determining children's future progress and development' (Fabian, 2006: 4). Key Stage 1 teachers should be aware that some children may have experienced multiple transitions before starting school, and Smith (2011) highlights the emotional impact of transition on children's well-being and resilience, as they move from their 'comfort zone' into a new environment. With this in mind, it will be helpful to consider the following factors in order to ensure effective transition programmes:

- Children need ample opportunity to become familiar with the new situation through visits to the setting or class and contact with the teacher.
- Rules and rituals are significant issues in the transition process, and assumptions are often made by adults that children will automatically understand these and their complexities.
- Once the move has taken place, continuity of practice, where possible, is beneficial, with a gradual introduction to new and more formal activities (Smith, 2011).

SUMMARY

This unit has provided a brief review of government policy and statutory curricular requirements related to early years education, notably in England. The unit has looked at, and should have helped you formulate a view on, a number of issues: first, on the controversial topic of when children should start school and the notion of 'school readiness'; second, on the most effective ways for young children to learn, and why play is important in early learning; finally, on the nature of the adult role in early learning and the important part you can play in this, including easing the transition to KS1.

ANNOTATED FURTHER READING

Brodie, K. (2014) *Sustained Shared Thinking in the Early Years: Linking Theory to Practice*, London: David Fulton.
>This dedicated book on sustained shared thinking (SST) provides practitioners with an overview of SST and explores how it can be initiated, encouraged and facilitated in practice.

Rose, J. and Rogers, S. (2012a) *The Role of the Adult in Early Years Settings*, Maidenhead, UK: Open University Press.
>This book provides a helpful insight into the many different dimensions of the adult role in working with young children. It draws on a range of recent and classic theoretical perspectives and research that will help you to become an effective early years professional.

Moylett, H. (ed.) (2013) *Characteristics of Effective Early Learning: Helping Young Children Become Learners for Life*, Maidenhead, UK: Open University Press.
>This edited book provides a number of insightful chapters framed around the characterisitics of effective early learning enshrined in the EYFS, including a helpful chapter on transition to Key Stage 1.

FURTHER READING TO SUPPORT M-LEVEL STUDY

Siraj-Blatchford, I. and Manni, L. (2008) '"Would you like to tidy up now?" An analysis of adult questioning in the English Foundation Stage', *Early Years*, 28(1): 5-22.
>This study focuses attention on effective forms of questioning applied by early years practitioners and makes some significant points about the value of open-ended questions and the links to sustained shared thinking.

RELEVANT WEBSITES

Early Years Foundation Stage: www.gov.uk/early-years-foundation-stage
>This is the government site for the new Early Years Foundation Stage.

Early Years Foundation Stage Forum: http://eyfs.info/home
>This is a very useful support network and online community website for early years professionals.

REFERENCES

Alexander, R.J. (2010) *Children, Their World, Their Education*, London: Routledge.

Anning, A. (2006) 'Early years education: Mixed messages and conflicts', in D. Kassem, E. Mufti and J. Robinson (eds) *Education Studies: Issues and Critical Perspectives*, Maidenhead, UK: Open University Press/McGraw-Hill, pp. 5-11.

Aubrey, C. and Durmaz, D. (2012) 'Policy-to-practice contexts for early childhood mathematics in England', *International Journal of Early Years Education*, 20(1): 59-77.

Bowery, E. (2008) 'Is there a place for the discrete teaching of thinking skills and dispositions in a pre-school curriculum?' Unpublished dissertation, University of Gloucestershire, UK.

Bradbury, A. (2014) 'Early childhood assessment: Observation, teacher "knowledge" and the production of attainment data in early years settings', *Journal of Comparative Education*, 50(3): 322-39.

Brooker, E., Rogers, S., Robert-Holmes, G. and Hallett, E. (2010) *Practitioners Experiences of the Early Years Foundation Stage: A Research Report*, London: DCSF.

Bruner, J. (1986) *Actual Minds, Possible Worlds*, Cambridge, MA: Harvard University Press.

Carruthers, E. (2007) 'Children's outdoor experiences: A sense of adventure?', in J. Moyles (ed.) *Early Years Foundations: Meeting the Challenge*, Maidenhead, UK: Open University Press/ McGraw Hill.

Corsaro, W.A. (2005) *The Sociology of Childhood*, 2nd edn, London: Pine Forge Press.

Council for Curriculum, Examinations and Assessment (CCEA). (2007) *Understanding the Foundation Stage*, Belfast: CCEA Publications.

DfE. (2013) *Teachers' Standards*, London: DfE.

DfE. (2014) *Statutory Framework for the Early Years Foundation Stage: Setting the Standards for Learning, Development and Care for Children from Birth to Five*, London: DfE.

DfE. (2016) *Early Years Foundation Stage Profile 2017 Handbook*, London: DfE.

Department for Education and Skills (DfES). (2015) *Foundation Phase Framework*, Cardiff: Welsh Government.

Donaldson, M. (1978) *Children's Minds*, Glasgow, UK: Fontana.

Evangelou, M., Sylva, K., Kyriacou, M., Wild, M. and Glenny, G. (2009) *Early Years Learning and Development: Literature Review*, London: DCSF.

Fabian, H. (2006) 'Informing transitions', in A.-W. Dunlop and H. Fabian, *Informing Transitions in the Early Years*, Milton Keynes, UK: Open University Press, pp 3-20.

Gill, T. (2007) *No Fear: Growing Up in a Risk-Averse Society*, London: Calouste Gulbenkian Foundation.

Gopnik, A. (2016) *The Gardener and the Carpenter: What the New Science of Child Development Tells Us about the Relationship between Parents and Children*, London: Bodley Head.

Goswami, U. (2015) *Children's Cognitive Development and Learning* (CPRT Research Survey 3), York, UK: Cambridge Primary Review Trust.

Hill, J. (2016) 'Developing a challenging outdoor environment', *Nursery World*, 27 June.

Katz, L.G. (1992) 'What should young children be learning?', in *ERIC Digest*, Urbana, IL: ERIC Clearinghouse on Elementary and Early Childhood Education, ED 290 554.

McInnes, K., Howard, J., Crowley, K. and Miles, G. (2013) 'The nature of adult-child interaction in the early years classroom: Implications for children's perceptions of play and subsequent learning behaviour', *European Early Childhood Education Research Journal*, 21(2): 268-82.

National Association for the Education of Young Children (NAEYC). (2009) *Developmentally Appropriate Practice in Early Childhood Programs Serving Children from Birth through Age 8*, Position Statement, Washington, DC: NAEYC.

Ofsted (2014) *Are you Ready? Good Practice in School Readiness*, Manchester, UK: Ofsted.

Penn, H. (2008) *Understanding Early Childhood*, Maidenhead, UK: Open University Press.

Roberts-Holmes, G. (2015) 'The "datafication" of early years pedagogy', *Journal of Education Policy*, 30(3): 302-15.

Rogers, S. (2010) 'Play and pedagogy: A conflict of interests?', in S. Rogers (ed.) *Rethinking Play and Pedagogy: Contexts, Concepts and Cultures*, London: Routledge, pp. 5-18.

Rogers, S. (2013) 'Playing and exploring in the early years', in H. Moylett (ed.) *Characteristics of Effective Learning*, Maidenhead, UK: Open University.

Rogers, S. and Evans, J. (2008) *Inside Role-play in Early Education: Researching Children's Perspectives*, London: Routledge.

Rogers, S. and Rose, J. (2007) 'Ready for Reception? The advantages and disadvantages of single-point entry to school', *Early Years International Research Journal*, 27(1): 47-63.

Rose, J. and Rogers S. (2012a) *The Role of the Adult in Early Years Settings*, Maidenhead, UK: Open University Press.

Rose, J. and Rogers, S. (2012b) 'Principles under pressure: Student teachers' perspectives on final teaching practice in early childhood classroooms', *International Journal of Early Years Education*, 20(1): 43-58.

Schaffer, H.R. (1996) 'Joint involvement episodes as context for development', in H. Daniels (ed.) *An Introduction to Vygotsky*, London: Routledge, pp. 251-80.

Scottish Government (SG). (2008) *A Curriculum for Excellence: Building the Curriculum 3-18: Active learning in the early years (2007)*, Edinburgh: Scottish Executive, Education Scotland.

Sharp, C. (2002) *School Starting Age: European Policy and Recent Research*, conference paper, Slough, UK: NFER.

Siraj-Blatchford, I. (2004) 'Educational disadvantage in the early years: How do we overcome it? Some lessons from research', *European Early Childhood Education Research Journal*, 12(2): 5-20.

Siraj-Blatchford, I., Sylva, K., Muttock, S., Gilden, R. and Bell, D. (2002) *Researching Effective Pedagogy in the Early Years (REPEY)*, DfES Research Brief 356, London: DfES.

Smith, H. (2011) 'The emotional impact of transfer: What can be learned from early years practice', in A. Howe and V. Richards (eds) *Bridging the Transition from Primary to Secondary School*, London: Routledge, pp. 14-25.

Sylva, K., Melhuish, E.C., Sammons, P., Siraj-Blatchford, I. and Taggart, B. (2004) *The Effective Provision of Preschool Education (EPPE) Project: Technical Paper 12 - The Final Report: Effective pre-school education*, London: DfES/Institute of Education, University of London.

Waite, S., Evans, J. and Rogers, S. (2011) 'A time of change: Outdoor learning and pedagogies of transition between Foundation Stage and Year 1', in S. Waite (ed.) *Children Learning Outside the Classroom: From Birth to Eleven*, London: Sage, pp. 50-64.

Whetton, C., Ruddock, G. and Twist, L. (2007) *Standards in English Primary Education: The International Evidence (Cambridge Primary Review: Research Survey 4/2)*, Cambridge, UK: Cambridge University Press.

Whitehead, D. and Bingham, S. (2012) *School Readiness: A Critical Review of Evidence and Perspectives*, Occasional Paper 2, London: TACTYC.

Whitebread, D. and Coltman, P. (eds) (2008) *Teaching and Learning in the Early Years*, 3rd edn, London: Routledge.

Woyke, P.P. (2001) 'What does creativity look like in a developmentally appropriate preschool classroom?', *Earthworm*, 2(3): 15.

THE IMPORTANCE OF PLAY AND EXPLORATIVE LEARNING

Why bother with play?

Jo Trowsdale and Bernadette Duffy

INTRODUCTION

In this unit, we are looking at the role of explorative learning and play. These are stressed in the curriculum documentation for the early years, the *Early Years Foundation Stage* (EYFS) framework (DfE, 2014), and echoed again in the Ofsted report *Teaching and Play in the Early Years* (2015). However, as children get older and move through their primary education, these key elements for successful learning often receive far less attention than they deserve. This unit argues that it is vital to continue to promote a playful, explorative attitude to learning, which in turn promotes the essential learning capacities, such as independence, creative thinking, problem-solving and resilience, that children need for well-being and success, now and in the future. The best teachers use the ways of thinking encouraged by play and explorative learning to ensure that children are engaged and motivated to learn throughout the primary years and beyond.

This unit covers:

- what we mean by play and explorative learning;
- the importance of play and exploration in children's learning;
- play and exploration in the EYFS and National Curriculum;
- the role of the teacher in promoting children's play and exploration;
- using playfulness to enhance your teaching.

OBJECTIVES

By the end of this unit, you will be confident about:

- the importance and value of play and exploration in promoting learning;
- how to promote play and exploration throughout the primary years;
- how to use playfulness in your own teaching.

WHAT DO WE MEAN BY PLAY AND EXPLORATIVE LEARNING?

In Unit 7.4, Teresa Cremin and Jonathan Barnes make the case for creativity in primary education. Cecil *et al.* (1985) describe exploration and play as part of the creative process, and it is vital that teachers understand these elements if they are to promote effective learning and well-being.

FIGURE 2.6.1 KS1 boys in role as explorers, investigating water life

Explorative learning is about children learning through investigation, speculation, experiment and discovery, stimulated by their curiosity and wondering. It involves children exploring objects, events and ideas, playing with what might be possible, often using all their senses to gather information, observing and learning from others as part of the investigation. Through such explorations, children construct their own meanings and knowledge and find out what an idea or object is and what it can do, and, because they have been in control of the process, their learning is deeper than if they had simply been presented with the knowledge as a passive recipient (Bruner, 1986).

The phrase '*children learn through play*' is a much repeated in education, and, as it is used to cover a wide range of experiences, we need to be clear about what we mean by *play*. Although there are a number of theories of play relating to different views about degrees of structure (Bennett, Woods, and Rogers, 1997: 2), most agree that play is freely chosen by the children, controlled by them (Isaacs, 1971; Bruce, 2011) and characterised by spontaneity, often without clear final objectives. As there is little or no focus on a predetermined product, children are free to examine all kinds of detail during this period that they might have missed if they had been concentrating on the end product (Cecil *et al.*, 1985). It is also an opportunity to engage the imagination and for ideas from the unconscious to bubble up. As they play, children become aware of patterns and start to see possible connections (Duffy, 2006). Playfulness describes an attitude and readiness to explore and discover: to be open to the opportunities of an experience. It is a natural agency for learning that develops from young children's experience of play and, if fostered, can be utilised in a variety of learning contexts throughout the primary school.

As children get older, play is often contrasted with work. In organising the school day, we divide lesson time from playtime, suggesting play is something different from learning. Many educationalists share

Piaget's view that, 'play is the work of childhood' (Piaget, 1962). Indeed, recent, biologically founded research suggests that physical 'play' is a catalyst in shaping healthy brains (Brown and Vaughan, 2010). Carefully planned, adult-led experiences that enable children to learn specific skills and knowledge are important, but it is often through their play that children test, practise and consolidate the skills, knowledge and understandings they have acquired. Indeed, many would argue that, as accessing knowledge has become easy, our society increasingly values conceptual, original and creative thinking and behaviours more. Our role as educators, then, must be to resist over-direction and instead to focus on crafting our abilities to facilitate and harness play-based learning (Singer, Michnick Golinkoff and Hirsh-Pasek, 2006: 6).

These notions of play are not confined to children. Cultural anthropologists and theorists argue that the very same characteristics of play are significant to adults, in free and structured forms. Huizinga, for example, suggests that, 'civilization is, in its earliest phases, played. It does not come *from* play like a baby detaching itself from the womb: it arises *in* and *as* play, and never leaves it' (Huizinga, 1971: 171). In recent years, the study of neuroscience has enabled us to understand how cultural influences affect brain development. Research suggests that, if taught early enough, children can develop unexpected abilities, such as being able to see and breathe underwater (Music, 2011: 81) or speak another language, for example, if it is spoken at home. Likewise, the culture of the classroom, and the messages about the role of play, will affect the brain development of children and their capacities to imagine, empathise, collaborate and problem-solve, for example.

Task 2.6.1 What is play?

- Through reflecting upon this unit and following through reading, how would you define the role of play in the learning process?
- What are the key characteristics that make an activity play?
- What are the misconceptions and anxieties that teachers may have about using a playful approach?

As part of the creative process, exploration and play are about an attitude to life. They involve the ability to cope with uncertainty, explore new ideas, look at problems in a variety of ways, the lack of constraint, the existence of choice, creating and re-creating. Experiencing play thereby fosters adaptability and resilience in a changing world. Many creative processes in arts and business are founded upon the view that exploratory, playful behaviour is key to learning, discovering and making. So that, although an end product is typically a goal, its nature is not nor cannot be predetermined; in fact, it is defined and refined iteratively and responsively to source materials, ideas and context through explorative and experimental activity.

THE IMPORTANCE OF PLAY AND EXPLORATION IN CHILDREN'S LEARNING

Since Plowden (1967), the role of play in learning has been an influence in curriculum reform. In recent years, perhaps especially since international testing has developed (Mourshed, Chijioke and Barber, 2010), comparative studies seek to identify the factors and dynamics between factors that best affect learning. Setting curriculum aims, content and standards expected can affect the quality of pedagogy and learning. Yet, equally, research points towards the importance of linking across domains and of local, individualised processes being essential to ensuring the progress of individual learners (Barnes, 2015), to achieve a 'balanced and broadly based' curriculum (DfE, 2014) that promotes the 'spiritual, moral, cultural, mental and physical development of pupils'. Play can be a strong integrator here.

In Scotland . . .

What is important is that children and young people have the freedom to choose how and when they play. From the earliest days and months play helps children learn to move, share, negotiate, take on board others' points of view and cultivate many more skills. It remains equally important throughout infancy, childhood, the teenage years through adolescence, and beyond into adulthood and at all ages, stages and abilities.

(Scottish Government, 2013: 15)

Source: Scottish Government. (2013) *Play Strategy for Scotland: Our Vision*. Retrieved from www.gov.scot/resource/0042/00425722.pdf (accessed 21 March 2016).

We are born curious: play and exploration are the ways in which we express this and are vital to children's learning and development. Babies' brains are designed to enable them to make sense of the world around them. They think, draw conclusions, make predictions, experiment and look for explanations (Gopnik, Meltzoff and Kuhl, 2001). The skills developed through explorative learning provide the foundations for a playful approach to learning that promotes curiosity, initiative and resilience across the curriculum, throughout the primary years and beyond. Indeed, neuroscientists (Davidson, 2000) and evolutionary psychologists increasingly note the value of play in developing cognition and higher human intelligence.

Often, as children get older, play and exploration are sidelined in favour of highly structured activities with clear goals, inside and outside school. Curriculum demands can make it appear that the best solution is to try to pre-package children's learning to ensure that the whole curriculum is covered. But exploration at the outset can open up a learning area so that children can articulate, share and test their current ideas and, by playing with possibilities for next steps, suggest the most relevant and fertile way forward. Such approaches can feed the appetite to engage with more structured learning, enabling a teacher to recognise children's current knowledge and interests and thus teaching a teacher how to progress and adapt the planning for maximum learning (Dewey, 1916; Dale, 1954).

Task 2.6.2 How does play change over time?

- What are your memories of playing and exploring at 4 years old, 7 years old, 10 years old, and how do you play as an adult? How and what did/do you do?
- When did you change your play behaviours? What prompted such changes?
- Do colleagues/friends of different ages have similar recollections ? Do these reflect changes in society and our attitudes to play, inside and outside school?

Promoting imagination and thought

Vygotsky (1978) identified the crucial role of imaginative play in the development of the human mind. He saw the emergence of the imagination in the second year of life as connected with the frustrations children experienced when their desires were not immediately gratified. Whereas babies' needs are straightforward and either quickly gratified or forgotten, as children grow, their wishes and aspirations become more complex, less realisable and less capable of instant fulfilment. For example, they want to pour the tea out as adults do and become frustrated when, for safety reasons, they are not allowed to. Imaginative play develops when children experience this frustrating gap between their needs and the gratification of these needs. Such needs cannot be met in the real world, but can be satisfied in the imaginative world: they can pretend to pour the tea. Through imaginative play, children resolve the tensions of everyday life.

Objects may support the imaginative process as 'transitional objects' – these are used to represent a missing object and no longer have the meaning they have in the real world . For example, children may use stones to represent money while playing shops. The stones act as a prop or pivot to help them engage in the imaginative process (Vygotsky, 1978). Initially, transitional objects need to share many characteristics with the object being imagined. But, with practice, the need for physical similarity decreases. Eventually, children no longer require an actual object to support their imaginative play, but can pretend the object is there. As adults, we likewise suspend disbelief and enter the rules of imaginative play when watching theatre, accepting whatever mimed or symbolic use of props is suggested by the actors. When older children lose instinctive acceptance of imagined objects in play, the teacher can re-affirm the symbolic and representative role of objects through the practice of imaginative exploration in drama: a cardboard circle presented convincingly can symbolise a precious crown. Once children can separate objects and actions from their meaning in the real world and give them new meanings, they are no longer tied to the concrete world and start to think in an abstract way: beyond the moment and into possibilities.

In Scotland . . .

Creating an environment that provides rich play experiences is critical in meeting the needs of our children and young people. Offering them choices to develop the skills of expression, thought, curiosity, movement, problem solving and achievement provides a sound basis for fostering the development of useful skills and attributes which will serve them well throughout life.

(Scottish Government, 2013: 15)

Source: Scottish Government. (2013) *Play Strategy for Scotland: Our Vision*. Retrieved from www.gov.scot/resource/0042/00425722.pdf (accessed 21 March 2016).

Promoting well-being and relationships with others

Isaacs (1971) saw play as being essential for development and promoting mental well-being. Indeed, some scientific research argues play's importance for well-being throughout adulthood (Brown and Vaughan, 2010). Through playing and exploring with others, children develop the ability to see things from different perspectives. It is the ability to imagine that enables the child to empathise: to put themselves into the position of another person and understand that other people may have different perspectives, beliefs, intents, desires and knowledge than their own, often referred to as theory of mind (Goswami and Bryant, 2007). Through this ability, children develop their understanding of social and cultural expectation and important skills such as self regulation, negotiation and persuasion (Evangelou *et al.*, 2009). Many schools, either explicitly or in an embedded way, train children to develop skills for learning such as resourcefulness, self-management, collaboration and resilience (Goodbourn *et al.*, 2005, 2006; Gornall, Chambers and Claxton, 2005) and celebrate the mix of structure and play-like exploration required to hone such skills.

Promoting physical development

Movement is natural to children, and the importance of physical play should not be underestimated. Babies' first focus for exploration is their own bodies: how arms and legs move, and how to control that movement to achieve their own goals. For the youngest children, physical play will often be spontaneous *rough and tumble* activity, but, as they develop, physical play becomes more complex, involving rules and strategies. Through their physical play, children develop fine and gross motor skills and body confidence.

Recent research argues that, 'we think not just with our minds but with our brains and the rest of our bodies', and that opportunities to develop manual dexterity feed and shape mental agility (Claxton, Lucas and Webster, 2010: 13). Indeed, limiting movement has been shown to limit thinking, even when movement is routine, abstract or apparently unconnected to the task in hand (Goldin-Meadow and Wagner, 2005; Clark, 2008). Taking a physical or imaginative excursion from a task can feed thinking (Claxton, 2007), suggesting that the discipline of table-bound learning may be counter-productive to thinking and learning. Interest in brain gym within the classroom and in outdoor learning reflects increased recognition of learning as a whole-body experience.

Promoting language and literacy

Play and exploration with others offers meaningful contexts for children to develop their language and literacy. Negotiating roles, play scenarios and strategies for exploration, explaining ideas and listening to those of others all require good communication skills, and wanting to engage others is an excellent motivation to acquire and develop them.

Children develop their ability to create stories through their imaginative play. Although they start by imitating people around them, as they grow, their ability to imagine influences the scenarios they create, and children do not simply copy what they have seen but add their own ideas. As children become more skilled, the role of fantasy increases, and they develop scenarios that are no longer restricted to their first-hand experience of the world but include characters and events from stories and television. Sometimes, children's fantasy play is discouraged and seen as an avoidance of the real world or reinforcing stereotypical images. However, Paley (1988) presents a persuasive argument for supporting this type of play and using it to stimulate children's storytelling and interest in literacy. Holland (2003) explores this further and documents the work of practitioners who are actively addressing children's interests and finding ways to support them appropriately. Play also provides an important environment for experiential thinking and learning, for testing how effective (or ineffective) language might be for communicating, for recognising the significance of nonverbal communication in knowing and thus understanding the complexity of experience (Damasio, 2000; Music, 2011: 100).

Through their imaginative play, children develop and extend stories to create their own narratives, using ideas as well as props as stimulation or provocation. Being able to imagine also initiates the ability to empathise, and thus play feeds, not just creative writing, but also thinking, feeling and interpreting others' behaviour, in daily life and other literary and historical contexts. Through drama-based play at all ages, children can imaginatively behave 'as if' someone else. Teachers can develop their own and children's confidence to project themselves into, as yet unknown, experiences and practise thinking and feeling from another's perspective by working with them 'in role', collectively and supportively, using strategies such as 'conscience alley' or 'voices in the head' (see Farmer, 2011). Pair and small-group 'in role' preparation allows children to practise adapting language to role and thus extend their language repertoire within any curriculum. Such preparation for 'hot seating' enables children to imagine, rehearse and understand another character: how they might think, speak and feel. Children can recognise and practise new registers, expanding their understanding of language through imagined experience. Children are typically drawn into the imagined context, building their own belief and thus deepening engagement as they play with the role and hear their own voice reflected back to themselves. Teacher-supported drama here provides semi-structured play/play-based learning where children step in a structured and protected way into the shoes of another and try out thinking, feeling and speaking like them (Baldwin, 2008; Winston and Tandy, 2009; Woolland, 2009).

Promoting cross-curricular investigation skills

Through their explorations, children find out about the world around them and, as their skills and understanding develop during the primary years, they are able to deepen their knowledge and find out more. A playful approach motivates this exploration and ensures children are actively engaged. Play provides the opportunity to take risks and find out through trial and error (Isaacs, 1971).

As they explore, we can help children to:

* become aware of a problem, new idea or piece of information;
* start to tackle the problem by brainstorming ideas, using their existing knowledge to identify connections, similarities and differences;
* ponder and allow ideas to incubate; this may take place over a number of days or minutes;
* have an insight into the problem, a moment of illumination that helps them to understand the problem or the new piece of information;
* identify a new understanding or meaningful connection and become aware of a possible solution;
* test the solution or understanding of the idea for themselves or with others, which may lead them to modify their solution or understanding.

Example 1

Drawing on Heathcote's 'mantle of the expert' model, KS2 children from Coventry primary schools worked with their teachers and professional 'Imagineers' – artists, designers and engineers – to imagine, design and make an animated, moving vehicle as part of a performance event to take place in their city, about their city. To develop and refine ideas, they explored the stories of the city through drama. They discussed and negotiated which ideas and moments meant most to them and should be at the heart of their own design ideas. As they drew, talked, enacted ideas physically and made models, they were playing with the possibilities of how their ideas might be realised effectively in scientific, aesthetic and interactive ways to suit the performance event.

They kept 'imagineering journals' in which they sketched and noted ideas and responses to the stages and challenges of the project – sometimes as prompted by their teachers, but often in self-directed ways. In some schools, teachers allocated 'journal time' for children to reflect and develop ideas. Over time, children reflected in their journals the instinct to explore different media, using paints and collage to represent ideas. Sometimes, the same image idea was developed differently as children grew dissatisfied with an aspect and wanted to try another idea. At the end of the project, they could locate key pages in their thinking, and all children valued the ownership, feeling the process had given them confidence to explore, 'play' and have a go.

PLAY AND EXPLORATION IN THE EARLY YEARS FOUNDATION STAGE AND NATIONAL CURRICULUM

In the EYFS framework, play is described as 'essential for children's development, building their confidence as they learn to explore, to think about problems, and relate to others' (DfE, 2014: 1.8). The importance of exploration is stressed in the characteristics of effective teaching and learning. Playing and exploring are the first characteristics (DfE, 2014: 1.9), and opportunities to play and explore are seen as key to children's engagement. In the foundation stage, children need to:

*   *find out and explore*: show curiosity about objects, events, people, use senses to explore, engage in open-ended activity, show particular interests;
*   *play with what they know*: pretend objects are things, represent experiences in play, take on a role in play, act out experiences with others;
*   *be willing to 'have a go'*: initiate activities, seek challenge, show a 'can-do' attitude, take a risk, engage in new experiences, learn by trial and error (British Association for Early Education, 2012).

These characteristics are important throughout the primary years and should be as evident in Year 6 as they are in Reception. The Cambridge Primary Review recommended that the foundation years should be extended into primary schools until at least age 6 (Alexander, 2010: 172). Although the revised National Curriculum does not reflect this view (DfE, 2013), it does give schools more freedom over the curriculum by only specifying the essential knowledge that all children should acquire, freeing schools to design a wider school curriculum that best meets the needs of their pupils and decide how to teach this most effectively:

> The national curriculum is just one element in the education of every child. There is time and space in the school day and in each week, term and year to range beyond the national curriculum specifications. The national curriculum provides an outline of core knowledge around which teachers can develop exciting and stimulating lessons to promote the development of pupils' knowledge, understanding and skills as part of the wider school curriculum.
>
> (DfE, 2013, 3.2)

It is hoped that schools will be creative in using the revised National Curriculum to design a curriculum that includes play and exploration in each area of the curriculum and uses imaginative and authentic approaches to make connections between areas of the curriculum. A number of schools operate an 'enhanced' or 'creative' curriculum, where children's fortes and interests inform choices within the curriculum. Indeed, many such designed and locally developed curriculum models adopt the play-based roles of older learners proposed by Briggs and Hansen (2012), namely of autonomous and creative learners, investigators, problem-solvers, reflective and social learners. Such models also consider how to plan for and assess play-based learning across both key stages, using structures and examples (ibid.: 77–104). A curriculum that maximises the potential of play-based learning thus organises play through scaffolding (Bruner, 2006), where tasks are not totally structured, nor is play totally free, but rather organised in a way that allows a flexible facilitation of play to be directed to intended learning areas. One example of this, which has grown quite a following in the UK, is the 'mantle of the expert' – an approach developed by Dorothy Heathcote (Heathcote and Bolton, 1995; Heathcote, 2002) in which children are positioned within imagined, authentic contexts 'as if' they are the experts. The focus of the needs presented by a (planned) problem, in addition to the structure's expectation of expertise, can generate collaborative, motivating and purposeful contexts for learning. Any and multiple subject disciplines may come under scrutiny through such an approach. Complex learning happens as children engage in an imagined world and demonstrate an 'ability to plan, concentrate and self regulate as well as engage in complex interpersonal interaction' (Music, 2011: 128). The use of drama as strategy and medium for learning across the curriculum and how to plan for and assess it are documented in a number of teaching primary drama sources (Baldwin, 2008; Winston and Tandy, 2009; Woolland, 2009).

THE ROLE OF THE TEACHER IN PROMOTING CHILDREN'S PLAY AND EXPLORATION

Teachers must 'promote a love of learning and children's intellectual curiosity' and 'contribute to the design and provision of an engaging curriculum'(DfE, 2011). Successfully fulfilling this standard requires teachers to draw on approaches that recognise, feed and celebrate children's instinctive playfulness. To be engaged and motivated, children need to be curious and want to learn. Our role is to ensure that there are plenty of opportunities to actively explore in contexts that are meaningful to the children and stimulate intrinsic motivation. The teacher needs to be ready to set provocations for playful exploration and resist intervention, to absorb a child's fascination, to witness and watch their focus and challenge so that exploration is genuine. Ofsted emphasises the significance of teachers' 'interactions with children during planned and child-initiated play and activities: communicating and modelling language, showing, explaining, demonstrating, exploring ideas, encouraging, questioning, recalling, providing a narrative for what they are doing, facilitating and setting challenges' (Ofsted, 2015). Their interest can thus signal real value for the children's work, and their questioning can enable the children to work to communicate their ideas for themselves and thus deepen their own commitment to learning.

FIGURE 2.6.2 KS2 children and their teacher talking and developing ideas together

Dweck (2012) emphasises the importance of children developing a mastery orientation, whereby they see their intelligence as growable, rather than a learned helplessness, and teachers have a key role in this. To explore freely, children need to feel able to take risks, to try things out and experiment, but to do this they need to feel secure and trusted by their teacher. This is especially important when an idea or new connection doesn't work as predicted. It is at the point when children discover that something they thought would work does not, or that a guess was not correct, that they find out something they had not realised before, and learning deepens.

As teachers, we need to see the world through the children's eyes, offer secure relationships that allow curiosity to flourish and:

- enable children to find their own voice and style, not simply imitate others;
- provide experiences that emphasise exploration and active participation;
- set provocations to feed exploratory learning;
- value children's self-initiated activity by being available and interested;
- help children acquire new skills and identify possibilities;
- recognise that the process may sometimes be more important than the end result;
- resist intervention as a reflex and watch more; know when to be silent, when to encourage, when to inspire and when to help;
- work alongside children as a more experienced learner modelling learning together;
- establish with the children clear guiding principles, such as rules for use of materials and behaviour;
- extend learning by encouraging critical reflection;
- pause before speaking, giving children the opportunity to communicate their views first;
- offer constructive feedback and encouragement during an activity;
- craft appropriate questions to encourage the child to work to communicate their ideas for themselves and thus deepen their own commitment to learning;
- give children time to respond to our questions and comments.

The traditional classroom power balance between adult and child is disrupted in play-based learning, and this is at the root of many of the features identified above. Frameworks and guidance for teachers wishing to move from structured to more child-led learning suggest ways to situate a planned learning topic within a simulated/imagined real-world setting to enable playful yet thoughtful experiential learning – for example, learning French in a French café, estimating and measuring dinosaur prints/outlines positioned in the school grounds, designing toys to sell in a toy shop. Such changes may require some support and encouragement, but provide rewarding and more skilful teaching (Briggs and Hansen, 2012: 63–90; 72–4 for a case study example).

 Task 2.6.3 Preparing the environment to encourage play

Think about learning environments and contexts you have experienced as a child and student – how have these promoted or discouraged play and exploration?

Reflecting on these experiences, this unit and your further reading, how would you create an environment that encourages exploration and play for 4-year-olds, 7-year-olds and 10-year-olds. Think about: the physical environment, the kinds of object that might be offered to provoke and invite learning, routines that give time to play, and your interactions with the children.

USING PLAYFULNESS TO ENHANCE YOUR TEACHING

Artists often talk about playing with ideas and materials to discover and create; scientists emphasise the importance of experimenting and being open to the unexpected without a predetermined idea of outcome. Playfulness remains part of the creative process throughout life. Following Picasso's famous quote – 'Every child is an artist. The problem is how to remain an artist once we grow up' – the challenge to the teacher is to retain and foster imaginative ways of seeing to enable children to consider different and individual ways of approaching problems and finding solutions.

As teachers, we must be confident about drawing on our own playfulness in our work with children. A playful approach involves flexibility, spontaneity, problem-solving skills, creativity and a readiness to try out and risk 'failure' (Prentice, 1994). It also needs to shape our approach to assessment, so that we are recording 'what children know, understand and can do as well as tak[ing] account of their interests and dispositions to learning . . . and us[ing] this information to plan children's next steps in learning' (Ofsted, 2015: 11).

Example 2

Camden Early Years lesson study project

Early Years practitioners in Camden LA were keen to improve outcomes for children, especially in communication, language and literacy. They worked with Professor Sue Rogers, of UCL, to develop strategies based on a wide range of research about what really made a difference to children's learning and the value of playfulness in teaching . The group used the framework offered by the EYFS, *characteristics of effective learning*, to develop their practice through the lesson study approach. The programme involved small groups of practitioners across settings, observing, planning and assessing a group of target children's learning over a year.

The settings included an EYFS unit attached to a primary school. Practitioners in this setting were concerned about children's communication and language development, especially boys'. They set up a number of opportunities for play based on their observations of children's interests, which included dinosaurs and transport, and this encouraged the children to work together and devise their own solutions. Practitioners presented a range of resources and, although they had thought about how children might use them and how they might respond to extend learning, they were careful to ensure that children were free to use the materials in their own ways and develop their own ideas.

One of the most successful sessions involved the unit's much-loved teddy bear, who went missing overnight. The children tracked him down to the roof and spent the morning puzzling how he got there and how to get him down. They tried a range of strategies, including pushing the wall and building stairs using wooden blocks. Careful questions and comments by the practitioner helped them to express their ideas and thoughts and persist with the task. Eventually, after 2 hours' discussion and experimentation, they agreed that they needed a ladder and someone to climb up and called on the caretaker to help rescue teddy. During the session, children who had previously been described as hard to engage and lacking concentration demonstrated that, in a playful context, with a practitioner who was able to give them time, they were able to do both very successfully.

During the year, practice changed in all settings involved in the project. There was an increasing focus on open-ended experiences, leaving space for children to develop their ideas, and the practitioner's role was to facilitate learning rather than deliver lessons. At the end-of-year review, all practitioners saw significant improvements in children's learning.

Task 2.6.4 Setting the conditions to encourage play

What signals might a teacher give children to communicate that s/he values their playfulness and their exploratory possibility thinking? Consider how personal journals could help you as a teacher to develop children's confidence and opportunities to play with ideas and explore.

SUMMARY

In this unit, we have looked at the importance of play and exploration in children's learning. We have identified the key role of the teacher in providing the emotional and physical conditions to promote these key characteristics of effective learning and in pro-actively facilitating, modelling and engaging with playful behaviour.

The world is changing rapidly, and we do not know the challenges the children we are teaching now will face in their adult lives, but we do know that, if they have adopted a playful approach and are confident explorers, open to possibilities, they are more likely to be able to meet them.

ANNOTATED FURTHER READING

Briggs, M. and Hansen, A. (2012) *Play-based Learning in the Primary School*, London: Sage.
> A theoretically argued, practice-based account of why play-based learning matters, illustrated by examples and ideas for direct use by teachers. The book proposes types of play for older children, offering frameworks for planning and assessing.

Fisher, K., Hirsh-Pasek,K., Golinkoff, R., Singer, D. and Berk, L. (2011) 'Playing around in school: Implications for learning and educational policy', in A.D. Pellegrini (ed.) *The Oxford Handbook of the Development of Play*, New York: Oxford University Press.
> These authors argue that playful learning pedagogies not only promote important academic learning but also build the skills required for success in the twenty-first century. They review current educational trends, playful learning, free play and guided play, and how they promote learning and development.

Roopnarine, J.L., Patte, M.M., Johnson, J.E. and Kuschner, D. (eds) (2015) *International Perspectives on Children's Play*, Maidenhead, UK: Open University Press.
> This book offers an analysis of children's play across many different cultural communities around the globe and discusses children's play as an activity important for formal and informal education, mental health and childhood well-being, and children's hobbies and past-times.

FURTHER READING TO SUPPORT M-LEVEL STUDY

Jarvis, P., Newman, S. and Swiniarski, L. (2014) 'On "becoming social": the importance of collaborative free play in childhood', *International Journal of Play*, 3: 1.

> This article argues that decreased opportunities for collaborative peer free play and 'discovery' activities are having a detrimental effect on the mental health of the current generation.

Kuschner, D. (2012) 'Play is natural to childhood but school is not: The problem of integrating play into the curriculum', *International Journal of Play*, 1(3): 242–9.

> This article explores the innate tensions involved when integrating play into the school curriculum. It proposes that the term play should not be used when developing a play-based curriculum, but that self-directed play-based pedagogies should indeed be planned for.

 RELEVANT WEBSITES

National Association for the Education of Young Children: www.naeyc.org/play

> The National Association for the Education of Young Children has a useful website for research and resources related to play and play-based learning.

National Institute for Play: www.nifplay.org

> The National Institute for Play gathers research from a range of scientists and practitioners into the importance of play at all stages of life.

Mantle of the Expert: www.mantleoftheexpert.com/

> This offers guidance, resources and training for schools and teachers interested in developing the dramatic enquiry approach of Mantle of the Expert.

 REFERENCES

Alexander, R. (ed) (2010) *Children, Their World, Their Education, Final Report and Recommendations of the Cambridge Primary Review*, London: Routledge.

Baldwin, P. (2008) *The Primary Drama Handbook: An Introduction*, London: Sage.

Barnes, J. (2015) *Cross-curricular Learning 3–14*, London: Sage.

Bennett, N., Woods, L. and Rogers, S. (1997) *Teaching through Play: Teacher's Thinking and Classroom Practice*, Buckingham, UK: Open University Press.

Briggs, M. and Hansen, A. (2012) *Play-based Learning in the Primary School*, London: Sage.

British Association for Early Education. (2012) *Development Matters in the Early Years Foundation Stage*, London: Early Education.

Brown, S. and Vaughan, C. (2010). Play: How It Shapes the Brain, Opens the Imagination and Invigorates the Soul, New York/London: Penguin.

Bruce, T. (2011) *Learning Through Play*, London: Hodder Education.

Bruner, J. (1986) *Actual Minds, Possible Worlds*, Harvard, MA: Harvard University Press.

Bruner, J. (2006) *In Search of Pedagogy: The Selected Works of Jerome S. Bruner*, London: Routledge.

Cecil, L.M., Gray, M.M., Thornburg, K.R. and Ispa, J. (1985) 'Curiosity-exploration-play: The early childhood mosaic', *Early Child Development & Care*, 19: 199–217.

Clark, A. (2008) *Supersizing the Mind*, Oxford, UK: Oxford University Press.

Claxton, G. (2007) *Hare Brain, Tortoise Mind: Why Intelligence Increases when you Think Less*, London: Fourth Estate.

Claxton, G., Lucas, B. and Webster, R. (2010) *Bodies of Knowledge: How the Learning Sciences Could Transform Practical and Vocational Education*, London: The Edge Foundation.

Dale, E. (1954) *Audio-Visual Methods in Teaching,* revised edn, New York: Dryden Press.

Damasio, A. (2000) *The Feeling of What Happens*, London: Vintage.

Davidson, R.J. (2000) 'Cognitive neuroscience needs affective neuroscience (and vice versa)', *Brain & Cognition*, 42: 89–92.

Department for Education (DfE). (2011) *Teachers Standards*. Retrieved from https://www.gov.uk/government/uploads/system/uploads/attachment_data/file/283566/Teachers_standard_information.pdf (accessed 12 October 2017).

Department for Education (DfE) (2013) *The National Curriculum in England Key Stages 1 and 2 Framework Document*, London: DfE.

Department for Education (DfE) (2014) *Statutory Framework for the Early Years Foundation Stage*, London: DfE.

Dewey, J. (1916) *Democracy and Education. An Introduction to the Philosophy of Education*, 1966 edn, New York: Free Press.

Duffy. B (2006) *Supporting Creativity and Imagination in the Early Years*, Maidenhead, UK/New York: Open University Press.

Dweck, C. (2012) *Mindset: How You Can Fulfil Your Potential*, London: Robinson.

Evangelou, M., Sylva, K., Kyriacou, M.,Wild, M. and Glenny, G. (2009) *Early Years Learning and Development Literature Review*, London: DCSF.

Farmer, D. (2011) *Learning through Drama in the Primary Years*, Drama Resource.

Goldin-Meadow, S. and Wagner, S.M. (2005) 'How our hands help us learn', *Trends in Cognitive Sciences*, 9: 234–41.

Goodbourn, R., Higgins, S., Parsons. S. Wall, K. and Wright, J. (2005) *Learning to Learn for Life: Research and Practical Resources for Foundation and Key Stage 1* (Paperback). London: Continuum.

Goodbourn, R., Higgins, S., Parsons. S. Wall, K. and Wright, J. (2006) *Learning to Learn for Life: Research and Practical Resources for Foundation and Key Stage 2* (Paperback). London: Continuum.

Gopnik, A., Meltzoff, A. and Kuhl, P. (2001) *How Babies Think*, London: Phoenix.

Gornall, S., Chambers, M. and Claxton, G. (2005) *Building Learning Power in Action*, Bristol, UK: TLO.

Goswami, U. and Bryant, P. (2007) *Children's Cognitive development and Learning, The Primary Review*, University of Cambridge/Esmee Fairbairn.

Heathcote, D. (2002) Contexts for active learning – four models to forge links between schooling and society. Paper presented at the NATD conference.

Heathcote, D. and Bolton, G. (1995) *Drama for Learning: Dorothy Heathcote's Mantle of the Expert Approach to Education*, London: Heinemann.

Holland, P. (2003) *We Don't Play with Guns Here: War, Weapons and Superhero Play in the Early Years*. Milton Keynes, UK: Open University Press.

Huizinga, J. (1971) *Homo Ludens*. Boston, MA: Beacon Press.

Isaacs, S. (1971) *The Nursery Years: The Mind of the Child from Birth to Sixth Years*, London: Routledge.

Mourshed, M., Chijioke, C. and Barber, M. (2010) *How the Worlds Most Improved School Systems Keep Getting Better*, New York: McKinsey.

Music, G. (2011) *Nurturing Natures: Attachment and Children's Emotional, Sociocultural and Brain development*, Hove, UK/New York: Psychology Press.

Office for Standards in Education, Children's Services and Skills (Ofsted). (2015) *Teaching and Play in the Early Years – A Balancing Act*? Retrieved from www.gov.uk/government/publications/teaching-and-play-in-the-early-years-a-balancing-act (accessed 19 October 2017).

Paley,V.G. (1988) *Bad Guys Don't Have Birthdays*, Chicago, IL: University of Chicago Press.

Piaget, J. (1962) *Play, Dreams, and Imitation in Childhood*, New York: W.W. Norton.

Plowden. (1967) *Children and their Primary Schools- A Report of the Central Advisory Council for Education (England)*, London: HMSO.

Prentice, R. (1994) 'Experiential learning in play and art', in J. Moyles *The Excellence of Play*, Buckingham, UK: Open University Press.

Singer, D., Michnick Golinkoff, R. and Hirsh-Pasek, K. (eds) (2006) *Play = Learning: How Play Motivates and Enhances Children's Cognitive, Social and Emotional Growth*, Oxford, UK/NewYork: Oxford University Press.

Vygotsky, L. (1978) *Mind in Society*, Cambridge, MA: Harvard University Press.

Winston, J. and Tandy, M. (2009) *Beginning Drama 4-11*, 3rd edn, Abingdon, UK: David Fulton.

Woolland, B. (2009) *Teaching Primary Drama*, London: Longman

SECTION 3
PLANNING AND MANAGING LEARNING

BUILDING INCLUSIVE COMMUNITIES OF ENGAGED LEARNERS

Alison Peacock

INTRODUCTION

This unit focuses on how to establish a culture of irresistible learning for every single child within your class. Teaching is a brilliant and worthwhile role full of daily opportunities to make a difference to children's lives. I became a teacher because, in contrast with my own experience of being at school, I decided that I would like to create a classroom environment where no-one would feel overlooked, bored or uncomfortable. I was the head teacher of a primary school with nursery for over a decade. During that time, the school was transformed from being in 'special measures' to becoming an outstanding teaching school and educational research centre. Throughout my teaching career, I have been inspired by the principles of *Learning without Limits* (Hart *et al.*, 2004; Swann *et al.*, 2012; Peacock, 2016). When my school was studied for *Creating Learning without Limits* (Swann *et al.*, 2012), the research team uncovered seven key dispositions for leadership and learning. These dispositions enabled a culture of opportunity for everyone and refused to set a limit on what might be achieved. This ethos provided the background for pedagogy, curriculum and assessment in our school and enabled many children (and adults) to achieve much more than anyone could have expected. More recently *Assessment for Learning without Limits* (Peacock, 2016) documents ways that we can assess progress in classrooms without resorting to endless tick sheets and 'data drops'.

Within this unit, we will explore ways of ensuring that your classroom is somewhere that children are trusted, included and listened to. The key research studies that are drawn upon are the studies of Learning without Limits that took place at the University of Cambridge during the last decade.

OBJECTIVES

This unit will help you to:

- reflect on core dispositions that will support an inclusive community;
- introduce you to the principles of Learning without Limits;
- understand more about the impact of pedagogy free from labelling;
- provide practical ways of ensuring your classroom is inclusive.

PRINCIPLES OF AN INCLUSIVE CLASSROOM

The ethos of Learning without Limits (Hart *et al.*, 2004) is underpinned by core principles of:

1 *trust* (every child and adult is trusted to learn);
2 *co-agency* (children and teachers recognise the power of working together);
3 *inclusion* (every individual matters).

These principles apply equally to children and adults.

A Learning without Limits philosophy aligns with every child's natural, intrinsic motivation to explore, to find out and to connect. Children flourish within a class community if they know that they are trusted to learn and that they are able to challenge themselves (Whitebread and Coltman, 2015). If your classroom is going to be a place where no-one feels limited or labelled, then it follows that, as all children are different, there are going to be times when they will need opportunities to self-differentiate within and between tasks. From their earliest days in school, it is crucial that we actively listen to children and encourage them to talk about their learning (Whitebread and Coltman, 2015). All this should take place within a classroom where the teacher is knowledgeable and confident to teach in a manner that fosters a climate of ambition among all children to achieve a 'personal best' effort.

Dispositions for a Learning without Limits classroom

Every classroom is different, because it is a social organisation impacted by the leadership relationships that are established within and beyond the class. The culture you create within your classroom has the capacity to transform children's perception of themselves as learners. The dispositions described below illustrate the impact that we have upon others when we are able to resist notions that so-called 'ability' is fixed. The following dispositions for learning within your classroom will enable flourishing of a culture of opportunity for all.

The seven dispositions are divided into three areas or domains: intellectual, affective and social. They apply equally to adults and children. You may wish to reflect on your own experience of being a learner and note how each domain has relevance to your own learner identity. Each disposition relates to an approach to learning that resists labelling and does not set limits on what may be achieved. The dispositions apply to all areas of the curriculum and to the breadth of day-to-day experience that learners encounter, from the moment they enter the school grounds until they leave at the end of the day.

THE INTELLECTUAL DOMAIN

This domain encompasses the intellectual and academic approaches to learning and teaching within your classroom. Regardless of what you are setting out to teach, you are most likely to enable children to engage if they are learning within a culture of:

- openness
- questioning *and*
- inventiveness.

Openness

Openness to the art of the possible is fundamentally about the capacity to wonder. You will want to stimulate thinking and ideas among the children so that they become intrigued and motivated to engage. Openness from the teacher is the opposite to closed pedagogy that seeks one or maybe two answers (usually the one that the teacher has predetermined). Divergent thinkers will thrive in a learning environment where anything feels possible and where knowledge is not provided piecemeal. A teacher with an open mind is someone who can change and adapt planning to suit the needs of the children as they emerge. This is a particularly important quality in relation to supporting the learning of children with special educational needs or disability (SEND), as the typical ways of teaching or learning may not work. At this point, being open to 'finding a way through' for the child, as opposed to seeking to identify and address a deficit condition, enables the teacher to creatively seek ways of teaching that help the learner to achieve understanding.

Task 3.1.1 Openness

- If you spend time planning a lesson and a child tells you they already know about what you are going to cover, how do you respond?
- Are you open to the possibility that you may need to adapt your planning to accommodate this?
- Are you pleased by the knowledge of your pupil?
- How can you ensure that no child in your class is unintentionally limited by the confines of your plans?

Questioning

A classroom that celebrates questions and generates even more questions is a space that is vibrant and interesting. As a teacher, if you are able to keep questioning the impact of everything you set out to do, you will have a mindset that is open to change and free to respond to ideas. The opposite to a questioning learning environment is one where knowledge is neatly packaged and fixed. Robin Alexander (2008) coined the term 'dialogic pedagogy' to describe learning where children are given regular opportunities to explain and develop their thinking in dialogue with the teacher or with other learners. Dialogue that is open and valued within the classroom establishes a culture where ideas matter, and questioning of those ideas strengthens understanding. Children who may not necessarily be able to explain their thinking on paper may nonetheless have a great deal to contribute that should be valued.

Inventiveness

How inventive are you? How inventive do you hope the children in your class will be? A capacity for inventiveness is at the heart of creativity and enables learners to apply knowledge to new situations and contexts through making new connections. In an inventive classroom, everyone knows that the unexpected can happen, and that new ideas are celebrated and shared. This is highly motivating, as it means that, instead of a hierarchy led exclusively by the teacher, there is space for anyone in the room to share their thinking.

Task 3.1.2 Scaffolding play

Last week, Pria joined other children playing with percussion instruments in the Foundation Stage garden. She took control of the play and began to conduct her orchestra. The musicians responded, and this extended to an impromptu concert at carpet time, conducted by Pria, with fifteen children and the teacher delightedly following her lead.

Things to reflect upon

- What enabled Pria to extend her play?
- How did the teacher's response to Pria's play enable other children to become involved?

THE AFFECTIVE DOMAIN

It is necessary to create an emotionally secure experience for every child. Social development and interaction are fundamentally important in the primary years and are central to enabling every child to flourish. The dispositions of persistence and stability will be needed by you and any support staff you work with. You will need to remember that we can never give up on a child, and that consistently high expectations create an exciting learning environment. Through co-agency, if children and adults build trust and listen to each other within a dynamic environment, open to opportunity, amazing things happen.

Persistence

This disposition is a necessary quality to instil into young learners, but also applies to teachers. Observations of people in all areas of life who have achieved success show, almost without exception, that they have worked with dogged determination and practised for hours and hours to improve their skills, whether they are artists, scientists, entrepreneurs, writers, athletes – the list is endless. The idea, for example, that some people are naturally 'good' at mathematics and others are not is a limiting notion that provides an excuse rather than a motivation to apply effort towards achieving understanding. Within your classroom, you are going to want to encourage a climate that rewards effort and persistence, as this underpins a learning process that is ultimately hugely rewarding as what seemed unknowable or unachievable comes within reach.

Task 3.1.3 Practice

- How much opportunity do you provide for children in your class to practise their developing skills?
- Opportunities to practise enable children to build confidence. If we move on too quickly we risk losing learning that is almost (but not quite) embedded.

Stability

Children need stability to build certainty that they are safe. Once children know what you and the school expect of them and the routines that form the overall structure of the school day, they can use the spaces that exist to concentrate. All humans need stability, and to lose this is often to lose a sense of control. Children who feel out of control or emotionally threatened are unlikely to learn effectively and may even seek to disrupt or break out of the learning environment you are trying to create.

Task 3.1.4 Self-limiting behaviours

Jason in Year 4 says he is 'rubbish' at drawing and screws up his artwork, throwing it in the bin.

Things to reflect upon

- Have there been aspects of learning that you have found difficult? How have you tried to overcome these?
- How could you help children like Jason to experience success in art?
- How could you help Jason change his perception of himself as an artist?

THE SOCIAL DOMAIN

How do we help children to build relationships, to share and to understand the feelings of others? The importance of individuality, respect for every child and a good relationship between home and school is crucial. The social domain impacts on every child within your class. If you are building an inclusive culture of co-agency, where children know they can trust you and their peers, they will be in a place where they are safe to take risks with their learning.

Generosity

The disposition of generosity is crucial. If we believe that, essentially, people are good but may have difficulty in showing this, we need to offer a generous view that seeks to find positive ways forward. This quality is needed if we are to resist the temptation to label children. It can be much easier to point to deficit than to constantly strive to see flickering sparks of hope.

Empathy

The disposition of empathy is easily aspired to and more difficult to achieve. How will you know what it feels like to be a child in your classroom? How can you find out? When we show empathy, we enable others to see that we care about their perceptions and their concerns. Literature – especially picture books – can be a powerful means of building empathic skills among children and gives you valuable insight into children's responses to challenging ideas and situations. Ensure that you provide quality time every day to read with your class. Shared experience of story is a powerful way of building a community.

Task 3.1.5 Embracing difference

Mary, 9 years old, has a diagnosis of autism. She has a workstation at the back of the classroom and often has a teaching assistant working with her. She calls out sometimes during your teaching, but always in relation to what you are talking about. How do you react?

Things to reflect on

- Your response to Mary will be noted by every child in the class and will impact on the way she is valued (or not) by her peers.
- If you are able to acknowledge her contributions gently and with good humour, this is likely to set a positive tone for everyone.
- Are there ways you could draw her into the lesson more, before she calls out?

How can we be inclusive of every child?

Genuine inclusion is about understanding the individual needs of every child while enabling them to become highly valued members of the class. It is important that you get to know every child in your class really well, and that no child ever becomes defined by their special educational need. If you are working alongside a member of support staff, you need to remember that every child in your class is your responsibility, and this cannot be delegated. Ideally, you will have a good working relationship with other adults who join your classroom and allocated time when you can plan and assess together. A team approach to supporting individual children and groups is an effective way of ensuring that additional help is available for those who need it. Remember, every teacher is a teacher of special educational needs.

Task 3.1.6 How well do you know your class?

Think about your current class. Write down the name of every child as quickly as you can. Look at your list:

- Who came to mind first? Why?
- Which children were last on your list?
- Were there some children you struggled to remember?

Every child in your class would be able to bring you to mind immediately if asked about their teacher. There is only one of you for them to remember, and your relationship with every child is unique to them.

Finding a way through

The most important aspect of a Learning without Limits ethos is to take responsibility for 'finding a way through' for every child. If the child is finding any aspect of learning difficult, it is the school's collective responsibility to think about how everyone might help. Often this may take time, but there is always something that will become a breakthrough. One of our children with Down's syndrome began emergent writing and drawing in Year 1, but, at the beginning of Year 2, she found the transition to a new class very difficult and stopped writing. It took us a term and a half until we finally found a way to inspire Annie to begin writing again. How did we achieve this finally? One day, we decided to ask Annie if she would like a visit in school from Peggy the dog, a chocolate Labrador owned by one of our staff. The prospect of a visit by Peggy was the spur that Annie needed to begin writing again. She worked with Hannah, her teaching assistant, to compose an invitation, and the very next day, when Annie arrived in school, there was a written reply from Peggy's owner saying she would be in Year 2 that afternoon. From that exciting moment onwards, Annie began joining in with writing in class. There is no magic wand in these situations, but the learning dispositions outlined above clearly help us to resist giving up.

Seeking advice

If a child in your class is finding it difficult to learn, you will want to do everything possible to find out why. If the child has a specific learning difficulty or impairment, it is important to access specialist advice in order that you can provide as much help to support the child as you can. Every school is required to have a qualified special educational needs leader. This person should be able to help you give time to observe any children you are worried about and advise you of any external specialists that may be able to visit the classroom and give you suggestions of ways to help.

Working with parents and carers

The starting point for talking with families should always be that their child is precious and important. Make sure that you focus on all the positive aspects of their child's learning or behaviour and show the family that their child matters to you. They will be experts about their child and will be able to help you understand in greater depth how you may be able to teach the child. Sometimes, a family is under great stress, and a partnership approach between home and school can be of real benefit on both sides. It is unlikely that there will be any magic solutions, but providing a consistently caring, inclusive environment will reap rewards.

An irresistible curriculum

What is going to take place within your classroom and the school grounds that will mean children in your class cannot wait to come to school each day? For that matter, what will you be planning that means you cannot wait to get to school to teach it?

In our Year 6 class, in the week before Remembrance Sunday, the teacher, Sally Barker, planned an English lesson where she wanted the children to write a short, descriptive piece of prose. She booked a session in the school hall, talked to them about the experiences of soldiers in the trenches during the First World War and then played them sounds of the battlefield. The children engaged in a drama session where they enacted leaving the trench and going 'over the top' into the battlefield. The session in the hall was only for 15 minutes, and the children then returned immediately to their classroom, where they all wrote in respectful silence about their thoughts as they imagined that experience. The quality of writing that emerged from the lesson was very moving. Several children chose to read aloud their compositions during the Remembrance Day assembly later that week. Here is an extract from 10-year-old Frankie's writing:

> His legs shake, his hands wobble, his heart pounds. He is paralysed with fear. He thinks of his family, his lovely wife . . . Suddenly a whistle shrieks like an eagle in agony, reverberating across the ditches. The signal to attack.

Eleven-year-old Aathira writes:

> Karl rocked himself back and forth. Ears covered, eyes closed. Knees too shaky to stand. He fumbled in his coat pocket and muttered goodbye to his framed family. 'I'm not here, I'm not here' he prayed.

The experience offered to the children enabled their imaginations to inspire their writing. English is a curriculum subject that can readily be differentiated by outcome through shared tasks across the class that have a low threshold but high ceiling. In this lesson, every child in the class was able to participate in the drama and every child felt able to communicate their feelings afterwards through the written word.

The environment as enabler

The classroom environment, along with shared areas of the school such as the library and the outdoors, provides opportunities to extend learning and delight children. If you are fortunate enough to work in a school with a field or wooded area, there are huge benefits to providing 'forest school' lessons on a regular basis (Maynard, 2007). Some children behave very differently in the outdoors, as if the ceiling has literally been holding them back. One child in our school was an elective mute during the Foundation Stage and Year 1. He spoke his first ever words in school while playing in the woodland during a forest school lesson. Some time later, I heard chattering in assembly and stopped myself just in time before telling Benjamin to be quiet!

We encourage every adult in the Foundation Stage environment to see themselves as leaders of learning at all times, whether they are helping to build a den or reading a story. The environment in which we learn, both indoors and outdoors, reinforces and extends a culture of ideas and opportunity. Our Foundation Stage garden includes spaces for quiet, small-world fantasy play, woodland areas, tools for investigation and enquiry, room to run, leap and so much more. A well-organised environment supports growing independence and provides a constant supply of irresistible resources for play. Opportunities for children to make meaningful choices and decisions should be present throughout the primary phase. Too often, freedom may be replaced by compliance in primary classrooms, thereby unintentionally setting limits. It is very important to ensure that every child has sufficient challenge and opportunity to extend her thinking.

Beyond 'ability' groups

Think carefully about how you organise your classroom. Children seated in groups that are organised according to your perception of their capacity to learn will always know what the group labels actually mean. You may decide to seat children with learning partners (these may change each week) or in learning groups, where you judge that there will be a good balance of friendships. Choosing learning partners randomly with named lollipop sticks is a transparently fair way of organising who works with who. You may wish to ensure that any child who finds it difficult to make friends is chosen quickly from the pot!

In *Assessment for Learning without Limits* (Peacock, 2016), I describe classrooms in different types of school across England where teachers have decided not to prejudge what children may be able to achieve and have offered choices of tasks for the children to select from. Proponents of 'mastery' learning subscribe to the view that to differentiate automatically is to set limits. Seeing the classroom from the children's perspective means ensuring that you plan learning that offers what Mary Myatt (2016) describes as 'high challenge, low threat'. Children do not want to be bored, and you want them to achieve well. This means planning lessons with clear learning intentions in mind that will enable high-quality outcomes. Children who experience lessons where they are able to choose their own challenges and work collaboratively describe their experience as being liberated and trusted to extend their thinking (Craft *et al.*, 2014). This sense of agency that occurs when one feels inspired and trusted can be very empowering for learning.

Task 3.1.7 Overcoming a challenge

Think of a time when you know that you have found something difficult to learn.

- What helped you?
- Have you given up?
- Are you still learning about this?
- What are the factors that you can recall that have helped you along the way?
- Are you providing these or something similar for the children in your class?

How should I deploy my teaching assistant?

If you are fortunate enough to have a colleague within your classroom to support your teaching, you will want to plan how to ensure that the children gain maximum benefit from this. It may be that your teaching assistant will be able to lead the class for some of the time, thereby enabling you to spend time with an individual or small group to further support their learning. It is very important that the children in your class who find some aspects of learning challenging know that their teacher is there to help. Rob Webster and colleagues have researched the impact of teaching assistants and offer very helpful practical advice in their most recent book, *Maximising the Impact of Teaching Assistants* (Webster, Russell and Blatchford, 2016). Essentially, the key is to ensure high-quality communication between you and your team member, ideally with shared opportunities to plan and discuss lessons. You will want to ensure that your learning objectives for each lesson are fully understood by all adults working with you in your classroom. The aim should always be to build children's self-regulation and independence. It is important to recognise that a dependency on adult support can quickly build, thereby reducing a child's capacity to challenge him- or herself.

Assessment

There will doubtless be a comprehensive tracking system in place at your school. Tracking, however, is not assessment. Assessment is what you do every time you work with an individual, group or class of children. It is an intrinsic part of teaching and provides you with the feedback you need as you work with the class to help you gauge what children already know and need to learn next. As a general rule, it is helpful to think that planning for the next day should always be influenced by what the children engaged with and achieved the day before.

There are many ways of assessing learning. Within a Learning without Limits classroom, the point is not to assess in order to rank children in a hierarchy, but to hold the very highest expectations of everyone. Ideally, you will want to establish a culture of competition against self, where 'personal best' is the main aim, as opposed to high-stakes assessment. Within a class of thirty children with one teacher, there should be thirty-one assessors.

Instead of setting targets for children to assess themselves against, you may wish to consider encouraging children to record their individual next steps at the back of their exercise book. They may use feedback from the teacher or their peers, and also from marking, but the crucial aspect is that they recognise where they need to improve and how to achieve the improvement. Feedback that is specific enables the learner to move forward. Feedback that is a judgement (with or without grade) may unintentionally reinforce self-limiting behaviour.

Task 3.1.8 Assessment to inform teaching

James is planning a lesson on forces for his Year 5 class. What could he do to ensure that the children's misconceptions about forces are revealed, in order that he can pitch his teaching accordingly?

Things to reflect upon

Strategies to reveal children's thinking could include:

- providing a range of 'factual' statements around the room that children can review and choose to stand next to in agreement;
- opportunities for children to move again if they change their mind in the light of new evidence;
- silent debate, where up to six children add comments silently to an explanation – for example, 'Why do boats float?';
- exit tickets at the end of lessons with key learning points or facts.

Allowing children to surprise us

When we welcome children to a classroom where our expectation is that they will be able to surprise and delight us with what they may achieve, we offer an opportunity that is truly ambitious for all. This means focusing on providing learning opportunities that will enable every child to succeed. Activities that offer a 'low threshold and a high ceiling' allow children to take small steps initially, but do not set a limit on what may be achieved. Writing tasks are usually open-ended and allow for this kind of range in response. Mathematical investigations such as those on the NRICH website (www.nrich.maths.org) provide tasks that encourage depth of thinking. The more limitations we set within tasks, the less chance children have of revealing their knowledge and understanding.

SUMMARY

In this unit, we have discussed ways of creating a classroom where every individual child has the opportunity to thrive. We have considered seven dispositions for Learning without Limits and explored how these can impact on every aspect of classroom life. In considering the needs of a wide range of children within the class, we have recognised that the teacher has the opportunity to celebrate difference while maintaining an ambitious, open environment, where every child retains the capacity to surprise us.

ANNOTATED FURTHER READING

Hart, S., Drummond, M.J., Dixon, A. and McIntyre, D. (2004) *Learning without Limits*, Maidenhead, UK: Open University Press.

> Based on a University of Cambridge research project, this book provides a powerful critique of ability grouping and ability-focused teaching. It features nine case studies that document how teachers have developed alternative approaches.

Peacock, A. (2016) *Assessment for Learning without Limits*, London: McGraw-Hill.

> Following on from *Creating Learning without Limits*, this book explores how assessment can be used as a tool for improvement, rather than leading to the labelling of individuals or groups of children.

Swann, M., Peacock, A., Hart, S. and Drummond, M.J. (2012) *Creating Learning without Limits*, Maidenhead, UK: McGraw-Hill.

> A compelling account of how the Learning without Limits approach was implemented and developed in one primary school.

FURTHER READING TO SUPPORT M-LEVEL STUDY

Craft, A., Cremin,T., Hay, P. and Clack, J. (2014) 'Creative primary schools: Developing and maintaining pedagogy for creativity', *Ethnography & Education*, 9(1): 16-34.

> This explores characteristics of creative teaching and learning practices based on case studies of two primary schools.

Marks, R. (2013) 'The blue table means you don't have a clue: The persistence of fixed-ability thinking and practices in primary mathematics in English schools', *Forum for Promoting 3-19 Comprehensive Education*, 55(1): 31-44.

> This article draws on interviews and observation in two Year 4 classes, to critique the ways in which 'fixed ability thinking' can inform teaching in primary schools, as well as being significant to children's views of themselves as learners of mathematics.

RELEVANT WEBSITES

Learning without Limits: http://learningwithoutlimits.educ.cam.ac.uk/

> The Learning without Limits project website contains details of publications, events and other activities.

NRICH: www.nrich.maths.org

> This provides mathematical investigations that encourage depth of thinking.

REFERENCES

Alexander, R. (2008) *Essays on Pedagogy*, London: Routledge.

Craft, A., Cremin, T., Hay, P. and Clack, J. (2014) 'Creative primary schools: Developing and maintaining pedagogy for creativity', *Ethnography & Education*, 9(1): 16–34.

Hart, S., Drummond, M.J., Dixon, A. and McIntyre, D. (2004) *Learning without Limits*, Maidenhead, UK: Open University Press.

Maynard, T. (2007) 'Forest Schools in Great Britain: An initial exploration', *Contemporary Issues in Early Childhood*, 8(4): 320–31.

Myatt, M. (2016) *High Challenge, Low Threat*, Woodbridge, UK: John Catt.

Peacock, A. (2016) *Assessment for Learning without Limits*, London: McGraw-Hill.

Swann, M., Peacock, A., Hart, S. and Drummond, M.J. (2012) *Creating Learning without Limits*, Maidenhead, UK: McGraw-Hill.

Webster, R., Russell, A. and Blatchford, R. (2016) *Maximising the Impact of Teaching Assistants*, Abingdon, UK: Routledge.

Whitebread, D. and Coltman, P. (eds) (2015) *Teaching and Learning in the Early Years*, 4th edn, London: Routledge.

APPROACHING SHORT-TERM PLANNING

Jane Medwell

INTRODUCTION

The focus of this unit is short-term planning: the weekly and daily planning you will do to prepare your teaching across the curriculum. Planning at this level is one of your most onerous tasks during training, but it is one of your greatest learning experiences. As you build up your responsibility for planning, you will develop a real understanding of its central importance in teaching. This unit also refers to your use of ICT in teaching and underlines the importance of planning the use of ICT, for both yourself and for your pupils.

OBJECTIVES

By the end of this unit, you should:

- understand the difference between medium-term and short-term planning;
- understand the purposes of short-term planning;
- know the key features of short-term plans;
- be able to critically evaluate examples of short-term planning;
- feel more confident to write some of your plans during school experience.

THE IMPORTANCE OF SHORT-TERM PLANNING

All teachers undertake short-term planning for their teaching. They will do weekly and, sometimes, daily plans. As a trainee, you will do both weekly and daily plans. You will base these on the medium- or long-term plans available to you in schools during your placement or, later in your training, on medium-term plans you may have made yourself. A short-term plan is your tool for adapting the broad objectives of medium-term planning to the learning needs of your class. This means you may have to add or omit parts of the medium-term plan, rearrange the order in which work is done and plan the way you teach, in detail, so that all the children can learn.

The most obvious reason for planning your lessons carefully is to ensure that you offer children engaging and appropriate lessons. You have to ensure that your lessons address the teaching you have foreseen in medium-term plans in such a way that all the children in the class can understand and explore the issues. As each child is different, you have to plan lessons that present information in ways suitable for all. This is the role of differentiation.

The creation of short-term plans also has a formative role for you as a trainee and is a key training experience in itself. By writing a short-term plan, you are 'rehearsing' your lessons, anticipating challenges and working out exactly what you will do. By evaluating each short-term plan as the basis for the next, you are learning lessons from what you and the children have done. A cycle of planning, assessment, modification and more planning is the basis for children's learning. It is also the basis of yours!

Finally, short-term plans are also a way for you to be accountable, as a teacher and a trainee. Teachers write weekly plans so that they, or other teachers, can work from them and adapt them, but also so that head teachers, colleagues, inspectors and outside agencies can scrutinise and work with the plans. You will write plans so that your teacher and teaching assistants (TAs) can understand the plans and their roles in them. Teachers and mentors will be able to examine and advise you about these plans, and those assessing your performance can gain insights into your professional thinking. In inspections of initial teacher training (ITT), Ofsted expects outstanding trainees to 'demonstrate through their planning and teaching that their pupils, including those who are disabled and those who have special educational needs, make good progress' (Ofsted, 2012), and so, by doing this, you not only demonstrate your outstanding performance as a trainee, but also prepare for your future as a teacher.

PLANNING FORMATS

The format of your plans will depend on a number of factors, including the age group you are teaching, your course requirements and school practices where you are teaching. You will probably find that completing some sort of grid on the word processor is easiest, but it is not essential – clarity is the main issue. There is no single, perfect planning format, and you may find that you want to adapt your format to meet your training needs.

Teachers will usually have a weekly plan, at least for English and maths, but also for each subject, domain or area of learning at Key Stages (KSs) 1 and 2. Where there are strong links across the curriculum or an integrated topic approach, teachers may use a topic or integrated plan. Some of these may be based on commercial schemes, such as the International Primary Curriculum, but these will rarely be used unadapted to meet the needs of the children. In Early KS1 and the Foundation Key Stage, the weekly plan will usually be written by at least the teacher and TA. It may involve a larger team. It will address all the areas of development and will usually be planned around a theme. A good weekly planning format will include most, or all, of the following:

* weekly objectives related to daily tasks;
* references to the relevant curriculum documents;
* task objectives;
* texts, ICT and other resources to be used;
* a summary of each activity for each group, identifying differentiation;
* specific roles for TAs;
* key points for plenary sessions;
* assessment points, often linked to National Curriculum requirements.

Weekly plans will break down learning and teaching in such a way that the children can achieve the learning objectives. This is a difficult skill because, as well as knowing everything necessary for medium-term planning, to do weekly plans you need to know what the children have already done, know and can do; the pace the children work at; their individual needs; and the likely response of the children to what you are planning. You will 'predict' these elements of the teaching for the week, but will find that you have to change or amend these weekly plans in response to the children's learning. This is good practice and shows you are using assessments to inform your plans. It is a good idea to amend weekly plans by hand, so that observers can *see* that you are doing this.

Table 3.2.1 shows an example of a format suitable for planning a sequence of lessons. Annotations under the figure give further details about the kinds of material you might include in each section of the plan.

Experienced teachers may teach from their weekly plans, and, as you gain experience, you may too. When you start teaching, you will plan your early lessons and parts of lessons on the basis of the teacher's weekly plans. As your placement progresses, you will be required to write weekly plans (or sequences of lesson plans) for core subjects. You may do this as part of a teaching team, but you will be expected to make a significant contribution and to lead the planning at this level before you can achieve the standards for the award of QTS.

One very important aspect of planning that is best addressed through weekly plans is the issue of routine activities, such as guided group or individual reading and writing, storytelling, registration, distribution of maths games or books, story reading, book browsing, spelling tests, handwriting practice, tables practice, mark making, weather recording, show and tell, and action rhyme times. These routines are easy to overlook, but they are very important. Patterns of activity that are known to both child and adult are soothing, familiar and powerful learning activities. Your weekly plan needs to be checked to ensure these activities represent the balance you want and that they are planned.

LESSON PLANNING

On the basis of weekly plans, you can construct detailed daily plans. The format depends on the age of the children and what you are planning for. The key elements that you should include are:

- class/group taught;
- time and duration of lesson;
- objectives for the session or lesson;
- reference to the relevant curriculum documents;
- texts, ICT and other resources to be used;
- structure and timings of the lesson;
- summary of each activity for each group, identifying differentiation and what you expect teacher and children to do;
- specific roles for TAs and, usually, a plan for the TA;
- details of teacher and child activity;
- key vocabulary to be used;
- key questions to be asked;
- key teaching points;
- identified outcomes (how will you assess whether the children have achieved their learning objectives?);
- note of pupils' previous experience;
- cross-curricular links;
- identified health and safety issues (such as glue guns, the need to wear coats etc.);
- an evaluation section;
- key points for plenary sessions;
- assessment points (who are you assessing and what do you want to know?); and
- timings.

TABLE 3.2.1 An example format for planning a sequence of lessons

Term/Year:			Teaching group:		
Curriculum subject/Theme/Area(s) of learning:					
Broad learning objectives	Learning objectives	Key activities	Resources	Cross-curricular opportunities	Planned method of assessment

Notes: Broad learning objectives: Specific references to Early Learning Goals, National Curriculum

Learning objectives: stating anticipated achievement in one or more of the following:

- attitudes (show . . .);
- skills (be able to . . .);
- knowledge (know that . . .);
- understanding (develop concept of . . .).

These form the basis of assessment and are judged through planned outcomes.

Key activities should:

- enable learning objectives to be met;
- include a variety of experiences that progressively develop children's learning;
- recognise pupils' diverse needs (including pupils with special educational needs (SEN), more able and gifted pupils, and pupils with English as an additional language (EAL));
- take account of pupils' gender and ethnicity.

Resources should be:

- influenced by learning objectives;
- listed in detail;
- considered with health and safety in mind;
- related to displays where relevant.

Cross-curricular opportunities should develop significant and planned attitudes, skills, knowledge and understanding *across* the curriculum in, e.g.:

- English;
- ICT;
- PSHE/citizenship;
- other National Curriculum subjects/areas of learning where significant.

Planned method of assessment should include anticipated evidence to:

- demonstrate achievement of learning objectives, and to inform assessment and record keeping (may be observational, verbal, written or graphic evidence, depending on activity);
- reflect a *range* of assessment methods.

Task 3.2.1 Scrutinising weekly planning

To do this task, you will need a weekly plan and medium-term plan from your placement.

Ensure you know the following:

- Which parts of the medium-term plan does the weekly plan address?
- Which parts of the relevant curriculum documents does this refer to?
- How long will each lesson or session in the weekly plan be?

Focus on one part of the weekly plan, perhaps English, maths or science.

- What resources are needed for the lessons in the weekly plan?
- What is the balance of whole-class, group and individual work for this week?
- What are the class management challenges for this week?

Discuss your chosen element of weekly planning with your teacher. Possible topics for discussion include:

- How do you ensure that the learning is accessible to all the children in the class?
- How do you differentiate for children who have SEN or are on the gifted and talented register?
- What arrangements are made to include children with SEN?
- What role will a TA or other adult play in these lessons, and how will they know what to do?
- What do you do if the children do not make the predicted learning gains in one week?
- Will any of these sessions present particular management challenges?

What are the 'routine' activities in this week? Fill in the table and add other activities.

Activity	When	How long/ often	Resources	Content	Teacher action	Pupil response
Welcome/weather etc.						
Show and tell						
Action rhymes/poems						
Story time						
Spelling test						
Tables practice						
Register						
Handwriting						

You may begin your training by doing lesson plans for every session you teach and, later, when you have more experience, move to teach from your weekly plans. However, always do individual lesson plans when your lesson is being observed, because it helps the observer to see your thinking (and you to do it!). You should also do lesson plans when you are teaching new ideas, are unsure of yourself or the children, or have a specific training target in mind. For instance, if you find it hard to manage time in your lessons with KS2, you will find that planning your lessons in detail, writing predicted times on the plans and reviewing them afterwards can really help you to manage time.

PLANNING AN EFFECTIVE LESSON

The research about planning is varied. Brophy and Good (1986) stressed that effective teachers demanded productive engagement with the task, prepared well and matched the tasks to the abilities of the children. Effective lessons tend to be those with a clear structure and shared understandings about what is to be learned and why, where all children can do the activities and use the learning time effectively, and the teacher assesses progress and evaluates the lessons. All these elements of a successful lesson can be addressed through your planning by focusing on your: lesson structure, management, lesson objectives, differentiation for learning and use of evaluation of lesson plans. All these features will help you to make a lesson engaging and interesting.

Successful lessons have clear beginnings and strong conclusions, with a certain amount of 'academic press' – that is, impetus to complete tasks within the given time. Learning time can be divided up so that it is used productively for learning, and so that the parts of a lesson help children to progress through their tasks. However you structure your lesson, you should always make sure you have a strong, clear structure to a lesson, and that the children know what this is. In this way, the children can learn to use time effectively and experience 'academic press'.

Time spent learning, itself, is a significant factor in the effectiveness of lessons, with research suggesting that the most effective teachers are those who maximise learning time by reducing off-task chatter and managing the class effectively (Silcock, 1993). Transitions from whole-class to group work, effective distribution of resources, and strategies for behaviour management are all parts of lessons where time can be saved through effective planning, thereby maximising learning time for pupils.

Learning to manage the pace of your lessons, so that the teaching and learning are lively and challenging but not rushed, takes time. It is fairly well established that the efficiency of experienced teachers allows them to perform complex procedures in a fraction of the time taken by novices – this is why you need to plan things experienced teachers do not even think about! If you find it difficult to maintain the pace of a lesson, you may want to plan in 5-minute intervals and note down the times on your lesson plans.

Learning objectives are probably the most important points on a lesson plan. You should be absolutely clear about what you want the children to learn, understand or do as a result of your lesson. These lesson objectives must be reasonable and achievable. You may want to reference a National Curriculum area of work on your lesson plan, but phrase your lesson objective accurately, so that the children can achieve it. A single lesson may address or contribute to a unit of work or to the achievement of an Early Learning Goal, but no lesson will completely cover one of these big objectives.

Most importantly, you must make sure your lesson objectives are meaningful. This means they must make sense in terms of the curriculum, so that children are not simply learning a set of assorted skills and knowledge that may (or may not) make sense later. It also means that objectives must be clear to, and understood by, the children. A study of effective teachers of literacy (Wray *et al.*, 2001) found that these teachers made sure that even young children understood the wider role of tasks in their learning. You will undoubtedly write up lesson objectives somewhere in the class, such as on the interactive whiteboard (IWB), a sheet of paper or a chart, but, unless you discuss these objectives with the children and ensure they know what they are learning and why, written objectives are just additional wallpaper.

Task 3.2.2 Sharing lesson objectives?

Sharing lesson objectives with the children has become one of the accepted markers of good teaching and is certainly used by inspectors as a means of judging the effectiveness of a lesson. Yet its benefits are not universally accepted. Read the newspaper article on this topic by Philip Beadle (www.guardian.co.uk/education/2007/jan/16/schools.uk1). Beadle concludes his piece with the following:

> But why must children know what the objectives are at the beginning of the lesson? Why can't we ask them to guess what they are going to learn, or tell us what they learned at the end of the lesson? Why can't it be a surprise?

Try to compose *either* a reasoned rebuttal of Beadle's position, *or* a justification for his scepticism about the use of lesson objectives.

Your questioning is an important part of your teaching. The need to ask a range of open and closed questions has been well documented. Brophy and Good (1986) make recommendations from their review of research, which include the need to ensure that questions are clear, that all children are asked questions, that the pace of questioning is adjusted to the task, and that children are given sufficient wait time to answer. They also stress that it is important for questions to elicit correct answers, although, as new material is learned, the error rate will inevitably rise as a result of children being stretched. More recent characterisations of teaching have stressed the importance of teachers demonstrating, or modelling, the learner behaviour they wish to teach. This includes reading aloud to students, modelling comprehension strategies, modelling writing processes and thinking aloud as you solve mathematical problems. Plan the key points you want to make to the class, the key questions and main skills you want to model. In this way, you can make sure you teach what you intend to teach.

Questioning is only one approach to talk in class and one that may place too much focus on the child. Alexander (2008) emphasises the importance of talk as a tool for learning. This involves the teacher having detailed knowledge of the lesson content and possibilities, but guiding discussion in ways that challenge and develop children's learning. However, there is no magic formula, and different areas of learning may require different approaches to talk (Fisher, 2007).

Differentiation is the way you plan to meet the diverse learning needs of pupils. You will teach the knowledge, skills and understanding in ways that suit the pupils' abilities and previous experience. Differentiation is represented in different forms in your planning:

- *Presentation*: Plan to use a variety of media to present ideas or offer vocabulary or extra diagrams to those who need more support. You will find ICT particularly helpful in preparing different types of presentation on paper, audiotape, screens or IWBs.

- *Content*: Select appropriately so that there is content that suits most children, with additional content available to some. For instance: some children may do six calculations, where others complete ten. ICT, using the Internet, can offer you a range of content.
- *Resources*: Use resources that support pupils' needs, such as writing frames, language master word banks or Spellmaster machines for poor spellers. For children with EAL, you might need to ensure that target vocabulary is available in a written form.
- *Grouping*: Group pupils of similar ability for targeted support, or pair children with a more able pupil, TA or language support teacher.
- *Task*: Match tasks to pupils' abilities. This can mean different tasks for different pupils. It is sometimes a good idea to offer different tasks that address the same objectives to different pupils, so that they can achieve success.
- *Support*: Offer additional adult or peer assistance, from a TA, language support teacher or more experienced child.
- *Time*: Giving more or less time to complete a given task can make the task more suitable to the particular pupils.

Differentiation sounds simple, but it demands really good knowledge of the content, the children, resources and a range of teaching strategies. You will achieve appropriate differentiation by working closely with the teacher, so that you find out what strategies are available and work for these children. Key resources to plan into your lessons will be TAs, language support staff and the individual education plans written for children with special needs.

EVALUATION

Evaluation is a part of planning and also allows you to show you are able to improve your performance through self-evaluation. Evaluation means considering:

- how well the children achieved the learning objectives (assessment);
- how well you planned, taught and managed teaching in relation to your training targets.

Evaluations will usually be brief and will usually focus on two aspects: what you did and what the children learned. The most useful evaluations focus on particular aspects of your teaching and are the basis of your own training targets. You may be keen to record positive evaluations, but less keen to focus on improvement. However, you should develop your ability to analyse your teaching, especially when you can see an area for improvement. When your evaluation comment identifies work to be done, always say what you propose to do in response. The very best planning is that which clearly uses evidence from children's previous attainment and leads on to influence the planning and teaching of the next session or lesson. This sort of evidence may be the annotations to a lesson plan you make in response to previous evaluations.

BUILDING PLANNING EXPERIENCE

Your early plans on a teaching experience may not be for whole lessons but for short parts of lessons or sessions, such as a whole-class phonics game, a guided reading session for a small group of children or a mental/oral starter in a maths lesson. Planning these parts of lessons gives you the chance to pay attention to detail and really concentrate on some important aspects of using plans, such as:

- ensuring you make your key points clearly;
- maintaining a pace that is brisk and engaging, but not so fast that the children are lost;
- effective questioning and interactive teaching;
- using resources such as the IWB or phonics objects.

Task 3.2.3 Planning a mental/oral starter

Use the planner below to observe a mental/oral starter taught by your teacher. Then plan and evaluate a mental/oral starter or shared literacy session. This may be more detailed than you are used to, but using such detail will help you to construct the mental 'scripts' you need to manage this complex task.

Planner for a mental/oral starter, shared reading or shared writing session

Date	Group/class
Duration	NC/PNS reference
Resources	Key vocabulary

Activity

Questions

Less confident	Confident	More confident

Assessment

Less confident	Confident	More confident

Evaluation

Planning parts of lessons and teaching them makes a good start to building up responsibility for whole lessons.

PLANNING FOR OTHER ADULTS IN THE CLASS OR SETTING

The Class Size and Pupil-Adult Ratios Project investigated the role of TAs (Rubie-Davies *et al.*, 2010). This project established that, for TAs to make a real difference to pupil learning, teachers must ensure they are included in planning and assessment. TAs need to understand and support children to engage with the learning processes in the activities, and not just focus on pupils' achieving the task. Moreover, it is important that the teacher gets feedback from TAs and uses that information in planning.

TABLE 3.2.2 An example of a planning format for a TA

Date: .... Lesson focus:	
Activity (a brief account of the activity and the TA's role in any whole-class introduction, shared reading, mental/oral, etc.):	
Resources needed:	
Key vocabulary to use: • • •	Key questions to use: • • •
Objectives 1 2 3	

For completion by the TA after group work

Name		Can do	Needs help
	1		
	2		
	3		
	1		
	2		
	3		
	1		
	2		
	3		
	1		
	2		
	3		
	1		
	2		
	3		

To ensure you work effectively with TAs or other adults in class, you may use a set format to present clear expectations of what you would like the TA to do. This will usually include space for the TA to write assessment notes about how well the children achieved the objective. These notes may well affect your future planning.

Task 3.2.4 Involving a TA

Arrange a specific time to talk to the TA in your placement class about a lesson in which he/she has assisted. Find out the following:

- What does the TA think the objective of the session was?
- What did the TA understand his/her role to be?
- What key vocabulary did he/she use?
- What resources did he/she prepare?
- How did the TA know what to say and do?
- What additional information would he/she like about class tasks?

When you have this information, you will be able to use it to direct your communication with the TA in your lessons.

PLANNING AND ICT

ICT can assist you in your planning in two main ways. First, the computer is an invaluable tool for planning itself, because it can help with the process and content of planning. Word processing allows you to produce and amend your plans swiftly and effectively. (Alternatively, you can easily spend every evening colour-coding, cross-referencing and wasting time.) The Internet also offers you thousands of ready-made plans for almost any topic, especially on the *Times Educational Supplement* website. These will not be instant solutions to the problems posed by your next lesson, because they do not meet the needs of your particular class. However, they do present you with a spectacular range of ideas and formats. You need to use them, but not rely on them.

The second way that ICT can be useful is in planning for pupil activity. If you are planning to use an IWB or visualiser for your mental/oral starter in a maths lesson, you can make the lesson visually attractive (so that all eyes are attracted to it and are not distracted elsewhere). The content can be tailored to meet the whole range of abilities, and the children can come out and be fully involved in the learning. You might use your computer to produce worksheets for some groups of children, while others use calculators or tablets. To conclude the lesson, your plenary might include the IWB or a demonstration using a projected calculator. The ICT can make the lesson more effective, but only if you plan it carefully.

When you think of using ICT, do not concentrate only on the computer. Children can use audio or video recording to do speaking and listening, reading and writing activities. If children are presenting findings from group work, the visualiser might be the most accessible technology. Do not overlook the use of TV and radio materials. Like computer programs, they are produced specifically for schools, have helpful teaching guidance and can be very useful if planned carefully.

SUMMARY

An outstanding teacher, in Ofsted's terms, is one who has planning that is thorough and detailed, with clear subject and cross-curricular links. In the plan's assessment, opportunities are identified and annotated accordingly, to show you are using your assessments for planning subsequent teaching. An outstanding teacher's plans show links to speaking and listening, ICT and homework. These plans are what make sures every child learns successfully.

Planning is one of the most time-consuming processes you will engage in, but planning well will help you to become a successful teacher. All successful teaching relies on teachers producing lessons that engage and motivate the children. This is partly down to selecting the right content and partly down to the way the content is dealt with. These issues are planning issues. Use your plans to rehearse and evaluate your lessons and you can be confident, happy and interesting to your class of children.

 ## ANNOTATED FURTHER READING

Bearne, E. (2002) *Differentiation and Diversity*, London: Routledge.
> This looks at a set of case studies in a variety of areas of the curriculum, to meet a range of pupil needs.

Gipps, C., Hargreaves, E. and McCallum, B. (2000) *What Makes a Good Primary School Teacher?* London: RoutledgeFalmer.
> This accessible book offers an account of the range of teaching, assessing and feedback strategies used by individual 'expert' primary teachers, and how they know or decide which strategy to bring into play, and when.

 ## FURTHER READING TO SUPPORT M-LEVEL STUDY

Wray, D., Medwell, J., Poulson, L. and Fox, R. (2001) *Teaching Literacy Effectively*, London: RoutledgeFalmer.
> This books reports the findings of the Effective Teachers of Literacy project and includes several findings relating to the importance of good planning.

 ## RELEVANT WEBSITES

The *Times Educational Supplement* site: www.tes.co.uk/article.aspx?storycode=6081306&s_cid=Landing_Lesson Plans12
> This site offers access to thousands of lesson plans and has invaluable advice from other teachers about many aspects of planning.

REFERENCES

Alexander, R.J. (2008) *Towards Dialogic Teaching. Rethinking Classroom Talk*, 4th edn, York, UK: Dialogos.

Brophy, J. and Good, T. (1986) 'Teacher behaviour and student achievement', in M.C. Wittrock (ed.) *Handbook of Research on Teaching*, London: Collier Macmillan, pp. 328-75.

Fisher, R. (2007) 'Dialogic teaching: Developing thinking and metacognition through philosophical discussion', *Early Child Development & Care*, 177(6-7): 615-31.

Ofsted. (2012) *Initial Teacher Education Inspection Handbook*. Retrieved from www.gov.uk/government/publications/initial-teacher-education-inspection-handbook (accessed 10 November 2017).

Rubie-Davies, C.M., Blatchford, P., Webster, R., Koutsoubou, M. and Bassett, P. (2010) 'Enhancing learning? A comparison of teacher and teaching assistant interactions with pupils', *School Effectiveness and School Improvement*, 21(4): 429-449.

Silcock, P. (1993) 'Can we teach effective teaching?', *Educational Review*, 45(1): 13-19.

Wray, D., Medwell, J., Poulson, L. and Fox, R. (2001) *Teaching Literacy Effectively*, London: RoutledgeFalmer.

ORGANISING YOUR CLASSROOM FOR LEARNING

Peter Kelly

INTRODUCTION

In this unit, I link approaches to organising learning environments to views about how learning takes place, many of which have been discussed in earlier units. Learning is complex, and no one view can fully capture this complexity. However, each view of learning is helpful for understanding and planning for particular aspects of learning. I argue that a balanced approach to classroom organisation draws on each view of learning. Thus, we should use different approaches to promote different types of learning.

OBJECTIVES

By the end of this unit, you should be able to:

- recognise the link between views about how learning takes place and approaches to organising your classroom;
- know the key approaches to organising your classroom;
- recognise the scope and limitation of each of these approaches;
- be able to identify appropriate approaches for particular learning objectives.

ORGANISING LEARNING

How you organise your classroom says a great deal about how you view your children's learning. Colleagues, parents and, perhaps most importantly, children will read much about what you value from those features of classroom life for which you are responsible: the areas of the curriculum you choose to link and focus on; the lessons and activities you plan; the roles you ascribe to other adults in your classroom; how you group and seat the children; the decisions you allow children to take; the resources you provide and the ways in which you make them available; your use of display and of opportunities to learn outside the classroom and school; and so on.

Consider the range of options available to you in relation to just one of these: groupings. Children can be taught as a whole class, in groups or individually. In groups, they might work collaboratively or be provided with differentiated individual tasks. Such tasks might be differentiated in terms of the level of challenge of the task or the level of support the group receives, and so on. Such features are not simple alternatives; those you choose to use and the circumstances in which you choose to use them will say something about your beliefs as a teacher, even if these are largely tacit and the decisions you make are intuitive.

There is a lot of advice available on classroom organisation. This has not always been the case. It was not until the 1960s that the traditional model of teaching – that is, a teacher standing at the front of the classroom, with the children sat facing, working on the same task at the same time – was challenged. Progressive approaches, developed largely from the ideas of Jean Piaget (Brown and Desforges, 1979), suggested children should be free to work at different speeds and in different ways, learning from first-hand experiences through active exploration and personal discovery. However, traditionalists argued that such approaches were largely ineffective: there were things that children needed to be taught, such as spelling and grammar, which could not be discovered or left to chance. Thus began an enduring and polarised educational debate.

More recently, a loose consensus has prevailed that recognises that certain approaches favour certain kinds of learning, rather than one approach being best. Nevertheless, the range of approaches suggested can appear daunting. In fact, it is relatively straightforward, if you remain mindful of one thing: how you organise your classroom depends on how you believe children will learn in your classroom.

This unit considers classroom organisation in relation to four views of learning: basic skills acquisition, constructing understanding, learning together, and apprenticeship approaches.

Basic skills acquisition

Once a favourite of traditionalist knowledge-transmission approaches, direct teaching dominates approaches to basic skills teaching in schools as a result of a variety of government frameworks and strategies in the 1990s and 2000s. Originally conceived somewhat behaviouristically as teacher demonstration and student imitation, leading to a period of consolidation and practice, in these strategies direct teaching received a Vygotskian makeover, becoming an interactive approach where the importance of high-quality dialogue and discussion between teachers and pupils is emphasised. However, this was an issue with many teachers, who were less ready to move away from a teacher demonstration and student imitation model towards a more interactive one.

Learning as constructing understanding

Originating in the ideas of Jean Piaget (Brown and Desforges, 1979), constructivists see learners as theory builders, developing understandings to make sense of their observations and experiences and modifying these understandings in the light of subsequent observations and experiences, so that they become more generally useful and closer to accepted viewpoints. This perspective has had a huge impact on some curriculum areas, particularly science, where a cottage industry grew in the 1980s researching the alternative understandings and misunderstandings, termed 'alternative frameworks', that children have of the phenomena they encounter. Phil Adey and Michael Shayer's Cognitive Acceleration through Science Education (CASE) has adapted and extended the constructivist approach (Adey, Shayer and Yates, 2001). By challenging children's misunderstandings of phenomena, the CASE approach aims to develop the structure of their thinking.

Social learning

Social constructivists, such as Jerome Bruner (1986), cite the ideas of the Russian theorist Lev Vygotsky (1962) in positing a central role for talking and listening in learning. Making sense and developing understanding, they assert, are essentially social processes that take place through talk. In the early 1990s, the National Oracy Project, which was unfortunately overshadowed by developments in literacy and numeracy, identified a whole range of ways in which participation with others in activities involving discussion can improve learning: it supports learners in constructing new meanings and understandings as they explore them in words; it allows learners to test out and criticise claims and different points of view as they speak and listen to others; and, importantly, talk provides raw material for learners' own thinking, because, for Vygotsky, thought is an internal, personal dialogue.

Learning as an apprenticeship

The work of social anthropologists such as Jean Lave and Etienne Wenger (1991) has illuminated how people learn in everyday contexts. This has led them to reconsider school learning in sociocultural terms. Thus, there are many metaphors that we can adopt for our classrooms: the writer's workshop, the artist's studio, the scientist's laboratory, and so on. In each case, this view suggests, the children act as craft apprentices, engaging in the authentic activities of the community to which the metaphor pertains. So, for children to think as, for example, historians, they have to be helped to act like historians by doing what historians do. The same is, of course, true for scientists or practitioners in any other area of enquiry.

I will now turn to consider approaches relating to each of these views of learning.

Task 3.3.1a Looking for learning

Think back to one particular day during a previous school placement. Write down briefly each of the learning activities that the children engaged in during the day. Consider:

- which areas of the curriculum were addressed and linked;
- the planned lessons and activities;
- the role adopted by the teacher and other adults in the classroom;
- how the children were grouped and seated;
- the decisions that the children took;
- the resources provided;
- use of display;
- opportunities for learning outside the classroom.

CLASSROOM APPROACHES

Task 3.3.1b Looking for learning

Thinking about each of the learning activities identified in Task 3.3.1a, what does each suggest about how the teacher (whether it was you or the class teacher) views learning.

Task 3.3.2 Classroom culture

Culture can be described most simply as 'the way we do things round here'. Critically reflect on your answers from Task 3.3.1. How does each of these things contribute to the classroom culture? To help, consider the following questions:

- Is there a learning-centred culture or a working-centred one?
- Is there a teacher-led culture that emphasises pupils acquiring new knowledge and skills, or a student-led culture that emphasises pupils participating in developing new knowledge and skills?
- What metaphor best describes the classroom culture – a factory production line or perhaps a writer's study, an artist's studio or a scientist's laboratory?

You can explore these ideas further by reading Kelly (2005).

Basic skills and direct interactive teaching

As a whole-class approach, direct interactive teaching allows children to benefit from involvement with their teacher for sustained periods. However, direct teaching and interaction are also important during individual, paired and group work.

The role of dialogue is emphasised: children are expected to play an active part in discussion by asking questions, contributing ideas and explaining and demonstrating their thinking to the class. However, many studies have found that teachers spend the majority of their time either explaining or using tightly structured questions. Such questions are mainly factual or closed in nature, and so fail to encourage and extend child contributions or to promote interaction and thinking.

In recent years, new technologies have had a significant impact on direct interactive and whole-class teaching. These include interactive whiteboards, data projectors and remote devices such as infrared keyboards and graphics tablets.

Good direct interactive teaching is achieved by balancing different approaches:

- *directing and telling*: sharing teaching objectives with the class, ensuring that children know what to do, and drawing attention to points over which they should take particular care;
- *explaining and illustrating*: giving accurate, well-paced explanations and referring to previous work or methods;
- *demonstrating*: giving clear, well-structured demonstrations using appropriate resources and visual displays;
- *questioning and discussing*: ensuring all children take part; using open and closed questions; asking for explanations; giving time for children to think before answering; allowing children to talk about their answers in pairs before contributing them to the whole class; listening carefully to children's responses and responding constructively; and challenging children's assumptions to encourage thinking;
- *exploring and investigating*: asking children to pose problems or suggest a line of enquiry;
- *consolidating and embedding*: through a variety of activities in class and well-focused homework, opportunities are provided to practise and develop new learning; making use of this learning to tackle related problems and tasks;

- *reflecting and evaluating*: identifying children's errors and using them as positive teaching points by exploring them together; discussing children's reasons for choosing particular methods or resources; giving oral feedback on written work;
- *summarising and reminding*: reviewing, during and towards the end of a lesson, what has been taught and what children have learned; identifying and correcting misunderstandings; making links to other work; and giving children an insight into the next stage of their learning.

Direct interactive teaching approaches focus on knowledge and skills transmission and acquisition through active learning and interaction. In this, they leave little room for learners to construct their own understandings of phenomena. This is where the following approach is useful.

Constructing understanding

Constructivists believe learners build their understandings of the world from their experiences and observations. They suggest that children bring many misconceptions and misunderstandings to the classroom from their experiences of the world, and assert that the best way to change such misunderstandings is to challenge children to change them themselves through hands-on exploration. For example, in science, children may, from their experiences at home, have formed the misconception that clothes make you warmer. An investigation where chocolate is wrapped in fabric could be used to see if this causes the chocolate to melt. Such information might challenge the children's misconception, and the children would need to restructure their thinking to accommodate the new information that the chocolate is not warmed up; rather, it is prevented from cooling or warming as the outside temperature changes.

However, one of the problems here is that it is assumed children will recognise the need to change their thinking or even that they will want to do it. An approach that takes the constructivist approach further is CASE. This can be used to formalise the thinking and restructuring process, as it contains certain key elements that many teachers have adopted or adapted in their own classrooms:

- *Concrete preparation*: The problem is stated in terms that are understandable to the children – that is, so that they see it as a problem. For example, you might ask the children to talk to the person next to them and think about clothes they might choose to take with them on holiday to a very cold country, and why.
- *Cognitive conflict*: Children are encouraged to consider a range of possible explanations for causes and effects that may interact in complex ways with each other – for example, children investigating the effects of clothing (identifying features such as fabric type, thickness and shape) on its suitability for a cold location could consider which feature or combination of features is central.
- *Social construction*: Now the children work together on the challenging activity to construct new joint understandings. In this, although the teacher asks probing questions to focus debate, the children do most of the thinking. So, the children might share each others' discussions and try to come to a consensus.
- *Metacognition*: In this process, the children are helped to become conscious of their own reasoning in order to understand it. In putting pupils in charge of their own learning, it is important to enable them to articulate their own thinking and learning processes.
- *Bridging*: This is the conscious transfer of new ideas and understandings from the context in which they were generated to new, but related, contexts. So, the children could apply their new, shared understanding of clothing in cold countries to hot countries.

This approach focuses largely on the learning of the individual. Social learning approaches, which follow, focus more on what can be achieved by a group working together, with the view that what is done together the individual will eventually become able to do alone.

Social learning

Establishing ground rules

Before engaging in social learning approaches, a number of ground rules need to be established with children. Rules to stop interruptions of all those involved in group work, adults or children, should be negotiated first. Thus, children needing help might be encouraged to take greater responsibility for their learning by seeking support elsewhere, or by doing alternative work until support is available.

Such independent and self-directed learners can be referred to as *autonomous*. The American educationalist Susan Bobbit-Nolan (cited in Boud, 2015) considers three levels of autonomy. The first is when learners have autonomy or control over the strategies that they use to carry out a task without the guidance of their teacher. Thus, in mathematics, a teacher might teach a variety of strategies for children to undertake three-digit multiplication. The children can then choose which one to use in tackling a problem. Similarly, children might choose the form of recording to use for a science exploration, and so on. At the second level, learners have control over the content of the curriculum, the things to be studied and learned, the objectives of learning. Thus, children might decide to explore something in its own right, or set their own goals for their learning. They might choose an area or theme in history to research, an assignment to write, an experiment to do or a book to read. This is learning for pleasure, following tangents and satisfying curiosities. At the third level, learners are able to judge things for themselves, after taking evidence and various views into account. Thus, the children might make informed decisions about changes to school routines such as playtimes, spending money on new items for class or elections to the school council. They might tackle controversial issues in school and debate these, looking at the perspectives of different parties. This third level of autonomy goes beyond simple independence in accessing resources or completing the teachers' work and has been called 'intellectual autonomy'. Learners who have intellectual autonomy think for themselves, link their thinking to their experiences and open their minds to new ideas.

Discussions during group work should be democratic: everyone has the right to a say and for their contribution to be valued. This means that participants should:

- listen attentively to the contributions of others without interrupting;
- speak to each other, looking at the person to whom they are responding;
- take turns and allow everyone an equal opportunity to speak;
- be sensitive to each other's needs;
- try to see things from other people's points of view, even if they disagree with their position;
- give reasons for their views; and
- be prepared to change their viewpoint in the light of new information, and accept others doing the same.

Further, children should understand that it is disrespectful to others if they monopolise the talk or if they ridicule or are unkind about others or their views. Of course, it is often most effective when the children are allowed to come up with rules such as these themselves: with prompting, they can be encouraged to address the key areas. A good place to develop these, together with a regard for these democratic ways of working, is the school council.

Collaborative group work

Group tasks are most effective when children need to share their knowledge, skills and under-standings to a common end through some form of problem-solving or open-ended task, with one correct solution and many alternatives. In their activity, children's talk will centre initially on their actions, but should be moved towards their understandings.

Although research (Kutnick and Blatchford, 2014) suggests effective group work can take a number of forms, many believe the ideal size for groups engaging in collaborative work is four – pairs are too small to generate lots of ideas, threes tend to form a pair and exclude the third member, and groups bigger than four become harder for the children to manage, and so it is less likely that everyone will be fully included. Similarly, mixed-gender and mixed-ability groups tend to be more inclusive and focused and generate the widest range of viewpoints and ideas.

There are two basic forms of task organisation for collaborative work: 'jigsaw' and 'group investigation'. The former requires each group member to complete a subtask, which contributes to the whole group completing the assigned task. This might be the production of a picture, diagram or piece of writing about, say, Roman villas, for a group display on that topic. In the second, all of the group work together on the same task, with each member of the group being assigned a different role. So, the children might create a small, dramatic episode portraying life in a Roman villa. Each child would play a different character, and, in addition, one child might take on the role of director.

So, for example, a group might work together on a 'jigsaw task' to produce a leaflet welcoming newcomers and informing them about the school. Each child might survey a different group of children from across the school to find out what information newcomers would need and benefit from. Particular attention would be paid to the experiences of any newcomers to the school. Then, the group would make decisions together about which areas to address, in what format, and so on. Each child could then be allocated the task of developing an aspect of the leaflet, with these being finally brought together for the finished document.

Dialogical enquiry

Dialogical enquiries are discussions in which learners, through language and sometimes supported by written notes and prompts, jointly engage in:

- working towards a common understanding for all;
- asking questions and suggesting ideas relating to the evidence on which proposals are based;
- looking at issues and problems from as many different perspectives as possible;
- challenging ideas and perspectives in the light of contradictions and evidence, so as to move the discussion forwards.

Examples include book clubs or reading circles, where children discuss their reading and produce new books together. Similarly, writing conferences are extremely valuable, in which writers discuss their writing with their peers. Of course, having such shared dialogues about texts will improve participants' ability to engage in such dialogues alone.

Other opportunities exist in developing home–school learning partnerships in children's work. Thus, in one example, parents of a particular group of young children read the same book with their children at home one evening. During the shared reading, parents wrote down the children's responses to the stories on post-it notes and fixed them to the relevant pages. Next day, these notes became the starting points for discussion between the teacher and the group.

With older children, each child in a group reading the same book together might individually write, predicting the next stage of the story. This writing might provide the starting point for a group discussion about the evidence for each prediction, the likelihood and plausibility of each prediction and the group's preferred outcome. Such a discussion could equally be based on individual group members writing initially from the perspective of one of the characters of the story and providing that character's point of view. The discussion could then consider the story from this variety of perspectives.

In terms of interpretation of data, such discursive enquiries are important, because they can link the process of enquiry to the big ideas of the subject. So, for example, in science, following an investigation of the conditions in which plants grow best, rather than children simply describing the conditions that are most favourable to healthy plant growth, the discussion can focus on ideas about why this might be the case. Perhaps the children's text of the data collected can be compared in their discussion with other writing they have done that has attempted to explain findings.

Learning through apprenticeship

Apprenticeship models of learning require groups of children to engage in the actual or authentic activities of particular groups. So, for science, children work as scientists, engaging in an enquiry to which the answer is not already known, using the key ideas and tools of science and sometimes working in partnership with others from the local community. For example, Years 5 and 6 children might set up a weather station, or get involved in monitoring environmental changes in an environmental awareness campaign. In doing this, they might involve members of the wider community, contact experts at the Met Office for advice, and so on.

There are many other possibilities for authentic activities in schools. So, in mathematics, Years 1 and 2 children might conduct a traffic survey in order to provide evidence for a letter to the council for some form of traffic control outside school, and Years 5 and 6 children might be helped to cost and plan a residential visit, while children in Years 3 and 4 could run a school stationery shop – ordering, pricing and selling goods in order to make a small profit. Similarly, in geography, children in Key Stage 2 might survey and research the school population growth, using various indicators such as local birth rates, and could be encouraged to identify the implications of their findings. Finally, children from across the school could be involved in making a CD for sale, following their composition of various items for a particular event, such as a school anniversary.

Task 3.3.3 Planning for learning

Consider how you might plan a series of lessons in one subject area, so that a variety of the above approaches is used. For example, in science, looking at life processes in Years 1 and 2:

- Constructing understanding: Grow sunflowers from seed in class, exploring the conditions in which these grow best.
- Group work, discussion: Separate groups investigate the effects of one factor on plant growth, making hypotheses beforehand and discussing findings after.
- Authentic activity: Set up a garden centre in school, so that the children can grow a variety of plants to sell in time for the summer fair.
- Interactive direct teaching: The children are taught how to write clear instructions so that they can provide buyers at the summer fair with instructions for caring for their plants.

Try doing this for another area of learning, for example data handling in mathematics in Year 4.

Sometimes, it is important to look at particular areas of study in many different ways. For example, in an essentially historical study of the Battle of the Somme in 1916, older children could engage, not only in a historical enquiry-based approach, be it text- or computer-based or involving the examination of original artefacts, but also by looking at events through the eyes of poets and novelists, or through the eyes of geographers or scientists. As such, the work of others might be explored, and the children might engage in original work themselves, not only in writing and poetry, but also through the media of music, dance, drama and painting. This would provide the children with a very full and rich learning experience.

Task 3.3.4 Exploring approaches to group work

Try out some of the activities you have planned for Task 3.3.3 with children grouped in different ways, as suggested earlier and in some of the further reading. Closely observe the children taking part in two different activities that you have planned and try to answer the following:

- How does their participation differ, depending on the nature of the groups and tasks?
- Does one form of grouping or type of task appear to engage them more than others?

After the activities, talk to the children involved and try to answer the following:

- What did they think they had to do?
- Why did they think they were doing these activities?
- What did they think they learned?
- How much did they enjoy them?
- What did they remember most from the activity?

Now look at the work done by the children and critically reflect on this and the answers to the questions above. What does all this tell you about these children's learning?

The approaches described in this unit are summarised in Table 3.3.1.

SUMMARY

Learning is complex, so much so that no one view of learning can fully express this complexity. It is only by considering learning in a variety of ways that we can begin to gain a fuller understanding of its nature, and it is only by planning for such a variety of approaches to address learning as have been described in this unit that we can provide rich and inclusive classroom experiences for our children.

TABLE 3.3.1 Organising your classroom for learning

Approaches to organising your classroom	Learning focus	Broad learning objectives	Strengths	Challenges
Whole-class, small-group and individual teaching of literacy and numeracy	Basic skills acquisition	To teach fluency and confidence with reading and writing in literacy and with number and calculation in mathematics	An interactive approach where the importance of teacher modelling and high-quality dialogue between teachers and pupils is emphasised	Many teachers have had difficulty adopting fully interactive direct teaching; tendency to be used at whole-class levels rather than with individuals or groups; little emphasis on learners' own starting points
Constructive science investigations and explorations	Constructing understanding	To develop enquiry and investigative process skills; to develop children's own understandings of phenomena; to apply understandings to new contexts	Starts from children's ideas and perspectives, building on these using direct hands-on experience	Assumes children will notice experiences that don't fit their understandings, challenge their understandings and be able to restructure these to accommodate the new experiences
Group work; discussion; dialogical enquiry	Social learning	To develop collaborative and speaking and listening skills; to see things from different points of view; to develop critical and creative thinking; to develop children's own understandings of phenomena	Supports learners in constructing new meanings and understandings as they explore them together in words; allows learners to test out and criticise claims and different points of view as they speak and listen to others; and provides raw material for learners own thinking	Requires children to have certain basic skills and obey certain ground rules; sometimes difficult to organise; works best when children show areas of autonomous learning
Authentic activity and enquiry	Apprenticeship	To encourage children to act and see the world as scientists, historians, archaeologists, poets, and so on	Outward looking, considering learning as something that takes you outside the classroom; inspiring and motivating	Requires significant time to allow it to happen; often needs access to good quality resources; teachers need to feel confident and have some expertise in the area of activity or enquiry or be able to get in someone who has

ANNOTATED FURTHER READING

Adey, P. (2008) *Let's Think Handbook. A Guide to Cognitive Acceleration in the Primary School*, London: GL Assessment.

> The 'Let's Think' approach seeks to improve children's thinking processes. It focuses on questioning, collaborative work, problem-solving, independent learning, metacognition and challenge.

Baines, E., Blatchford, P. and Kutnick, P. (2016) *Promoting Effective Group Work in the Primary Classroom: A Handbook for Teachers and Practitioners (Improving Practice (TLRP))*, London: Routledge.

> This handbook is the outcome of a 4-year project funded by the Economic and Social Research Council.

Hayes, D. (ed.) (2007) *Joyful Teaching and Learning in the Primary School*, Exeter, UK: Learning Matters.

> This is an interesting take on teaching creatively that looks at a range of approaches to teaching, learning and organisation in different subject areas of the primary curriculum.

Kelly, P. (2005) *Using Thinking Skills in the Primary Classroom*, London: Sage.

> This gives a more detailed consideration of social learning and apprenticeship approaches, together with a wide range of examples and many suggestions for enhancing practice.

(M) FURTHER READING TO SUPPORT M-LEVEL STUDY

Baines, E., Rubie-Davies, C. and Blatchford, P. (2009) 'Improving pupil group work interaction and dialogue in primary classrooms: Results from a year-long intervention study', *Cambridge Journal of Education*, 39(1): 95-117.

> This is an interesting article that reports the findings of a study into the potential of group interaction to promote learning. The authors describe how they worked with teachers to develop strategies for enhancing pupil group work and dialogue, and to implement a pupil relational and group skills training programme.

Webb, N.M., Franke, M.L., De, T., Chan, A.G., Freund, D., Shein, P. and Melkonian, D.K. (2009) '"Explain to your partner": Teachers' instructional practices and students' dialogue in small groups', *Cambridge Journal of Education*, 39(1): 49-70.

> These researchers argue that collaborative group work has great potential to promote student learning, but that the role of the teacher in promoting effective group collaboration is often neglected.

RELEVANT WEBSITES

King's College, London: www.kcl.ac.uk/sspp/departments/education/research/Research-Centres/crestem/Research/Past-Projects/Cognaccel.aspx

> Research into cognitive acceleration approaches such as CASE has been carried out at King's College, London, and this site describes some of the work done.

Unicef Child Friendly Schools: www.unicef.org/cfs

> From a more global perspective, Unicef has developed an approach to education development that it calls 'Child-Friendly Schools' and that highlights issues of quality in classroom provision and organisation.

International Democratic Education Network: www.idenetwork.org/index.htm

> As an alternative to mainstream educational approaches, Democratic Schools use organisational approaches that seek to give children a say in their own learning, and this site gives an overview.

REFERENCES

Adey, P., Shayer, M. and Yates, C. (2001) *Thinking Science*, London: Nelson.

Boud, D. (2015) *Developing Student Autonomy in Learning*, London: Routledge.

Brown, G. and Desforges, C. (1979) *Piaget's Theory: A Psychological Critique*, London: Routledge.

Bruner, J. (1986) *Actual Minds, Possible Worlds*, Cambridge, MA: Harvard University Press.

Kelly, P. (2005) *Using Thinking Skills in the Primary Classroom*, London: Sage.

Kutnick, P. and Blatchford, P. (2014) *Effective Group Work in Primary School Classrooms: The SPRinG Approach*, London: Springer.

Lave, J. and Wenger, E. (1991) *Situated Learning: Legitimate Peripheral Participation*, Cambridge, UK: Cambridge University Press.

Vygotsky, L. (1962) *Thought and Language*, Cambridge MA: MIT Press.

MANAGING CLASSROOM BEHAVIOUR

Roland Chaplain

INTRODUCTION

Effective classroom management is concerned with both maximising pupil engagement with learning and developing appropriate social relationships. Although the Department for Education (DfE) has produced a list of basic behaviour management skill requirements for trainee teachers (DfE, 2016), there is no single approach that will work with all teachers in all contexts. The ultimate target of behaviour management should be to cultivate pupils' cognitive, socio-emotional and behavioural skills necessary to develop their self-control, self-regulation and social competence. As with academic development, pupils of the same age differ in their socio-emotional development. Some pupils (and classes) will arrive highly motivated to learn, be confident and cooperate with adults and peers – others will need more direction and support. This unit provides a framework for you to begin developing a personalised classroom management plan (CMP). It presents a practical, evidence-based approach highlighting the multilevel nature of behaviour management and emphasising *preventative* rather than *reactive* strategies.

OBJECTIVES

By the end of this unit, you should understand:

- how to manage your own behaviour;
- how to develop a personalised CMP;
- how to use a range of practical classroom management strategies effectively;
- how to cope with more challenging behaviour;
- how research-based evidence informs practice.

WHOLE-SCHOOL ORGANISATION AND CLASSROOM MANAGEMENT

Effective schools create 'a positive atmosphere based on a sense of community and shared values' (Elton Report, 1989). Achieving this requires attention to whole-school issues, classroom management and managing challenging individuals. Inconsistency between different levels offers pupils the opportunity to manipulate the system, generating ambiguity and stress for teachers and pupils.

Schools are required to produce a behaviour policy to support staff in managing behaviour (DfE, 2016). Behaviour policies *should* reflect the views and aspirations of *all* stakeholders in a school, including pupils, parents, staff and managers (for details, see Chaplain, 2016).

Working with a group in a classroom can create the impression that you are operating in isolation, but *your* classroom is one component of an interrelated whole-school system, which, through its policies and procedures, can facilitate or undermine your attempts to develop a positive classroom climate (ibid.). Schools differ in their aims, expectations and principles and the procedures adopted to care for, control and educate pupils. Similarly, structured schools, in the same area, can differ substantially in how they represent this.

TEACHER STRESS, PUPIL BEHAVIOUR AND CLASSROOM CONTROL

Teaching is one of the top three most stressful professions (Health and Safety Executive, 2000). Among the potential stressors in teaching, managing pupil behaviour has been consistently rated as the most stressful element for both trainee and experienced teachers (Chaplain, 1995, 2008; Berg and Cornell, 2016). Despite disruptive pupil behaviour being the most common stressor for teachers, many still report being very satisfied with their work (Klassen and Chiu, 2010). The main sources of satisfaction for teachers come from features inherent to the job, such as pupils' achievements and positive relationships with pupils (Chaplain, 1995; Veldman *et al.*, 2016). Hence, although pupil 'behaviour' is a primary source of stress, it is also a principal source of satisfaction.

Although teachers usually rate extreme behaviour (physical and verbal assault) as their biggest concern, it is relatively rare in the regular classroom. In contrast, low-level disruptive behaviours (e.g. talking out of turn, tapping pencils, swinging on chairs) are regularly experienced by many teachers (Elton Report, 1989; Office for Standards in Education, 2014), which cumulatively can be very stressful. These 'daily hassles' (Kanner *et al.*, 1981) are usually offset by 'daily uplifts' (e.g. positive feedback from pupils).

MANAGING YOURSELF

Effective classroom management requires attention to what you say and how you say it; checking you are being understood; looking and feeling confident; self-belief in your abilities; and communicating your authority and status as a teacher through verbal and nonverbal behaviour (NVB). Although NVBs are central to managing behaviour, they are not always under conscious control. You may plan to communicate something, but, under pressure, fail to do so because of lack of confidence or emotional interference (Chaplain, 2016).

You will have observed people's habits when anxious – for example, coughing, looking 'nervous' or tense. Overcoming such behaviours requires first becoming aware of them (e.g. by videoing yourself), then identifying and over-learning alternative behaviours when *not* under pressure (ibid., Chapter 4).

Task 3.4.1 Monitoring professional social skills

Video yourself (not your pupils) teaching one or more of your lessons. This can be done subtly using a laptop with an integral camera.

- Was your verbal and nonverbal behaviour as you believed it to be?
- Did you convey all the material that you planned?
- Did you reinforce required behaviour?
- Did you interact with the whole class?
- Were your instructions clear?
- Did you check for understanding?

Now plan what changes to make and practise them away from the classroom. Then video yourself again to monitor change.

Several psychological characteristics distinguish teachers who manage pupil behaviour effectively from those who do not. These include personality, emotional regulation and self-presentation. The next section will focus on two salient constructs – locus of control and self-efficacy.

Believing you can influence important events in your life ('locus of control'; Rotter, 1966) is central to effective coping. People who believe they *can* influence important events (internal locus) tend to cope far better than those who believe other people control important decisions for them (external locus). When making your CMP, you should differentiate between factors over which you have control and those over which you have no control. However, sometimes we miscalculate our ability to control situations. Trainee teachers are often reluctant to modify their classroom environment – for example, changing the seating layout – despite being aware that existing arrangements are creating management difficulties for them. Their reason for not making changes is usually because it is 'someone else's' classroom. However, most mentors (if asked) would not object to trainees changing the room settings to teach more effectively, provided the changes have a sound pedagogic rationale.

Teacher self-efficacy is 'a teacher's belief in his or her skills and abilities to be an effective teacher' (Swars, 2005: 139). It is concerned with the question, 'Can I do this?' High teacher efficacy is linked to teachers who persist when under pressure (Tschannen-Moran and Woolfolk Hoy, 2001), especially when dealing with challenging behaviour, and who generate more positive and orderly classroom climates. Teachers with positive self-beliefs use positive classroom management strategies and encourage pupil engagement with learning – even with regularly disruptive pupils (Chaplain, 2016).

Trainee teachers, unsure of their untested capabilities in managing behaviour, can experience self-doubt and anxiety (Ng, Nicholas and Alan, 2010), and 'it is difficult to achieve much while fighting self-doubt' (Bandura, 1993: 118).

Anxiety can make us feel physically tense, removing a valuable NVB – smiling. Make an effort to smile, write a prompt on your plan to remind you of a joke or something amusing. With difficult classes, it can be easy to slip into a negative mindset. It is best to meet such groups at the door. Smile and compliment them. Keep it light-hearted. *Do not* linger on the previous unpleasant lesson with a 'I do not want a repeat of the last lesson . . .'. Start each day with a blank slate.

However, being overly confident can lead to complacency. Weinstein (1988) found that trainee teachers had unrealistic optimism in thinking that the problems others experienced managing pupil behaviour would not happen to them. Furthermore, Emmer and Aussiker (1990) found that trainee teachers who had difficulty managing classes still had unrealistic beliefs about their ability to control behaviour, which McLaughlin (1991) attributed to the conflict between wanting to care for pupils and the need to control the class.

Being self- and context-aware, having realistic and achievable expectations of yourself and your pupils, being prepared to learn through accumulating knowledge from research, and developing your interpersonal skills lead to improved self-efficacy. This will be further enhanced should you find yourself placed with a knowledgeable mentor who is sufficiently experienced in training new teachers (Chaplain, 2008).

Self-monitoring is useful for determining how *all* your behaviours contribute to how you manage your class. Changing how you think, feel and behave is not easy and may feel uncomfortable; the benefits make it worthwhile, but it requires practice to overcome established ineffective habits (Chaplain, 2016).

DEVELOPING A CLASSROOM MANAGEMENT PLAN

A CMP is not dissimilar to your lesson plan, and specifies:

- how you will organise your classroom for different lessons, including seating arrangements that match the task;
- your planned classroom behaviour strategies – tactics to deter disruptive behaviour (preventative); responses to pupils who occasionally slip off task (reorientation); and responses to more persistent off-task behaviour (reactive; see Table 3.4.1);
- rewards and sanctions you will use (check they are compatible with your school systems);
- your verbal and nonverbal behaviour;
- contextual priorities (e.g. challenging behaviour).

Your CMP should be informed by, and *reflect*, the expectations of your school's behaviour policy.

MAKING AN EARLY IMPACT ON YOUR CLASS

We form impressions of other people in a few seconds, and these impressions often remain unchanged for long periods of time (see Chaplain, 2016, Chapter 3). Hence, the first part of your CMP should consider the type of impression you wish to make. In your early visits to the classroom you will be observing, which can feel uncomfortable, as pupils are inquisitive and will want to know all about you, weighing you up. You will want to settle in and learn the ropes, but do not be too friendly with the pupils, as you will eventually have to establish your authority with the whole class. This is not to suggest you should be standoffish or hostile – just remember to convey your status and authority as a teacher. Your early lessons may be relaxed, with pupils being quite passive, but at some point your behavioural limits will be tested, so make sure you are clear about your expectations and convey them to your pupils. It is essential to pay attention to detail.

Your CMP should detail how you will:

- establish your behavioural expectations;
- teach classroom routines;

- use verbal and nonverbal behaviour to control the class – especially at critical points in the lesson (see Table 3.4.1);
- reinforce required behaviour (see Table 3.4.2);
- respond to disruptive behaviour (see Table 3.4.2);
- organise the physical layout of the classroom.

These actions are not exclusive to early lessons, as they represent good professional practice. Adjust your learning plans and CMP over time, as your relationship with classes changes and you become more practised – experiment and rise to new challenges.

TABLE 3.4.1 Classroom behaviour strategies

Preventative tactics	Reorientation tactics	Reactive tactics
Make sure your lessons are interesting	Gaze – sustained eye contact to make pupils aware that you know what they are doing	Caution – inform what will happen should the unwanted behaviour persist
Teach and reinforce rules and routines	Posture and gesture – use to complement gaze, e.g. raised eyebrow, raised first finger, hands on hips	Remove privileges, e.g. ban from use of the computer or miss a trip
Teach explicitly the behaviour you expect from your pupils – reinforce and check for understanding	Space invasion – the closer you are to pupils, the more control you will have – the classroom is your domain to move around as you wish	Require pupil to complete extra work during break times
Be alert to changes in pupils' verbal and NVB (e.g. too quiet/too loud)	Restate rules – remind pupils about what is expected	Time out as arranged with colleague in advance – avoid having disruptive pupils wandering around the school
Scanning – make sure you can always easily see the whole class to detect potential disruption	Use individual encouragement to get pupils back on task – 'You have been doing really well so far . . .'	Contract – agree with pupil specific expectations and record successes – review and adjust as necessary
Prepare for possible disruption, e.g. new pupils, time of year, time of day	Name-dropping – mentioning a non-attentive pupil's name while you are talking will usually get their attention	Temporary removal from class – working elsewhere in school or with another class
Being enthusiastic even when you're not!	Reinforcing peers near someone off task to 'model' the required behaviour	Suspension from school
Manipulating classroom layout, e.g. matching seating arrangements to task	Humour – pupils like teachers with an appropriate sense of humour	Exclusion
Using appropriate reward systems for on-task behaviour	Maintain the flow of the lesson by carrying on teaching while moving around the room, using NVB and removing anything being played with (e.g. pens)	
Awareness of pupils' goals		
Getting lesson timings right		

Note: These are some examples of effective tactics, but you should modify them to suit your teaching styles and context

TABLE 3.4.2 Examples of hierarchical rewards and sanctions

Rewards	Example	Sanctions	Example
Verbal support, private	Quiet word, 'John that's excellent work'	Gesture	Raised first finger, thumbs down
Verbal support, public	Teacher and class applaud individual	Prolonged gaze	Hold eye contact (with frown)
Public display of positive behaviours	Star/points chart, postcard to parents	Rule reminder	'What do we do when we want to ask a question?'
Classroom awards	Certificates, badges or stickers	Physical proximity	Move closer to pupil – perhaps stand behind him/her – say nothing
Contact home (either for meeting points criteria or exceptionally positive behaviour)	Notes/cards/phone calls	Verbal reprimand	'I am very unhappy with your behaviour'
		Public display	Unhappy emoticons against name ☹
Special privileges	Helping around school, attending an event	Separate from group in class or keep back at playtime	Adjust length of time to suit needs/age of pupil
Tangible rewards	Book token, stickers, pens	Record name	Write name in report book
School award	Certificates, tokens	Removal from classroom	Teach outside normal teaching area
		Refer to SMT	Send to head/deputy (as per school policy)
		Contact parents	Letter/phone home
		Invite parents to school	For informal/formal discussion
		Behavioural contract	Short, focused on specific expectations
		Suspension	For an agreed period
		Review contract	As a basis for return
		Exclusion	Fixed/permanent

CONVEYING YOUR EXPECTATIONS: RULES AND ROUTINES

All lessons have similar patterns: for example, getting the attention of the class, conveying information, managing feedback, managing transitions, monitoring and responding to unwanted behaviour, and so on. Whether your teaching is enhanced or undermined by any or all the above depends on devising and applying appropriate, enforceable and effective rules and routines. Rules set the limits to pupils' behaviour (Charles, 1999). Whereas whole-school (core) rules are designed primarily to produce harmonious relationships among pupils, classroom rules have the added responsibility of maximising pupil engagement with learning. Effective rules provide pupils with a physically and psychologically safe, predictable environment and work in a preventative way to establish and keep order and maintain momentum through the lesson. To gain maximum effect, rules should be:

- *positively worded* – tell pupils what they *can do* rather than what they *cannot do*, for example, 'be polite', as opposed to 'don't be rude'; negatively framed rules are not effective long term (Becker, Englemann and Thomas, 1975);
- *few in number* – long lists of rules will not be remembered: focus on key concerns, for example, follow directions; keep hands, feet and objects to yourself; I would recommend having no more than five;
- *realistic* – have rules that are age-appropriate, enforceable and achievable by your pupils;
- *focused on key issues* – personal safety, safety of others, cooperation and facilitating learning;
- *applied consistently* – intermittent or selective reinforcement of rules will render them ineffective; for instance, if putting hands up to answer questions is a rule, and you respond positively to those pupils who shout out a *very* competent answer, then reprimand someone else for shouting out an unsophisticated answer, you are sending out mixed and unhelpful messages to pupils.

When taking over a class from another teacher, it is important to consider their expectations relative to your own, and whether this will affect the way in which you establish your rules. If you adopt the rules of the existing teacher, do not assume pupils will respond in the same way to you – they will not inevitably associate you with a particular rule – so teach the behaviour you require explicitly, even if it means repeating what they already know.

Display your rules prominently and keep reminding pupils about them subtly until they are established. Be creative, perhaps using cartoons or pictures to liven up your display.

Task 3.4.2 Rules and expectations

- Think of four or five rules that embody your behavioural expectations.
- Check the school behaviour policy – are your expectations similar?
- Discuss with your mentors how they established rules with the class.
- Do you feel confident applying them?
- What, if any, changes would you make?
- Justify your changes.

DEVELOPING ROUTINES

Classrooms operate through a series of established routines. Although rules provide the framework for the conduct of lessons, they are few in number, but frame many routines to link expectations to action. Routines are usually organised around times, places and contexts. Effective teachers spend considerable time in their early encounters with their classes teaching them routines (Emmer and Worsham, 2005), which, when practised, become automatic, leaving more time for teaching. Jones and Jones (1990) found that up to half of some lessons were lost to non-teaching routines – for example, getting out equipment and marking work – and so efficient routines provide a real learning bonus. The following paragraphs consider pivotal routines in more detail.

Entering the classroom

How pupils enter your classroom sets the scene for the lesson – charging noisily into a room is not the best way to start a lesson, so consider how you might control this initial movement. One way is to greet your pupils at the door, look pleased to see them and remind them what they are expected to do when they go into class. Have an engaging activity waiting for them that has a time limit and is, preferably, linked to a reward. Physically standing by the door reduces the likelihood of pupils charging in, but, if they do, call them back and make them repeat the procedure correctly.

Getting the attention of the class

This can be done by using verbal or other noises, silence or puppets.

- *Using noise*: for example, ring bells, tap the desk, clap, ask pupils to show their hands or sit up straight. Which method you choose depends on your personal style and school policy. However, make sure that you explain beforehand what the signal is and what you want pupils to do when they hear it. I witnessed one teacher, working with a 'lively' class, use a tambourine to gain attention part way through the lesson, but the teacher had omitted to let pupils know beforehand. Although it made everyone jump (including me!), it was not associated with any required behaviour. A more effective method would have been to tell the class in advance, 'Whenever I bang the tambourine I want you all to stop what you are doing and look at me'.
- *Using silence*: some teachers find they can gain attention using NVB – for example, folding their arms, raising their hands or frowning. These signals can be very powerful – indeed, the more you use NVB to manage behaviour the better, as it is less disruptive to the flow of your lesson. However, to be effective it requires you to feel confident about your presence, and to explicitly *teach* pupils to associate a specific behaviour with a particular stimulus.
- *Using puppets*: a puppet (see, for example, puppetsbypost.com) can be very effective in behaviour management. Introduce the puppet and say that it will only come out if everyone is quiet – because it is nervous. If the noise level gets too high, put the puppet away. 'Snail puppets' that only emerge if pupils are behaving as required are excellent. They can also be used as a reward: for example, the best-behaved group could have the puppet sitting at its table. Pupils are usually very attentive and empathetic towards puppets, and so they can be used to aid the pupils' socio-emotional development. We have had excellent results using them with pupils from Early Years to Year 6.

Briefing

Take time to ensure that pupils understand exactly what is required from them at each stage of the lesson – unless you want those pupils who find it hard to pay attention wasting time asking other pupils what they should be doing. Taking time to do this in your first lessons can be difficult if you are anxious about being in the spotlight – so, use prompts to remind yourself to speak slowly and carefully (writing 'SLOW' on your lesson plan). Write instructions, keywords and questions on the board to support your verbal inputs – *do so before the lesson*, so that you can maintain eye contact and scan the whole class while briefing them. You might also consider using consistent, colour-coded writing to differentiate instructions, keywords, questions, and so on, so that pupils recognise more easily what is expected of them.

Distributing equipment

Issuing equipment in advance can create a distraction, as pupils may fiddle with it while you are talking – whereas issuing it after you have finished talking can disrupt a settled group. Choosing which one to use depends on how the class responds to you and each other. If you issue equipment in advance, make sure you tell pupils beforehand not to touch the equipment, rather than having to correct afterwards. Always check all your equipment before the lesson – do not assume that people will have returned the electrical experiment kit complete with wires untangled, otherwise you may find yourself spending 20 minutes sorting it out, giving pupils the opportunity to misbehave.

Transitions

Often overlooked when planning lessons, keeping control of pupils on the move, both in and out of the classroom, requires careful planning if it is to be efficient and safe. Always specify in advance exactly what you require people to do (including supporting adults). If moving a class to a different location, think before the lesson about the group dynamics in the same way you would plan a learning activity. Plan where to position yourself in relation to the group to maintain your view of everyone you are responsible for. Reinforce those individuals who are behaving correctly to encourage the other pupils to copy them.

Checking for understanding

Throughout your lesson, check that pupils are clear about your expectations. Where appropriate, support your verbal instructions with written ones – especially when working with pupils who have attention difficulties. Avoid repeatedly asking the same child or group and encourage all pupils to ask relevant questions if in doubt.

Task 3.4.3 Planning classroom routines

List the routines you consider important in your classroom.

For each routine:

- Describe the behaviour you require. What behaviour is acceptable and what behaviour is not?
- How long should this routine take? Be specific.
- Are pupils allowed to speak during the routine? If so, what noise level is appropriate?
- Are pupils allowed to move around the room during the routine and, if so, for what purpose?
- What behaviour indicates successful completion?
- Can it be done quicker and more efficiently?

REWARDS AND SANCTIONS

The existence of rules and routines does not guarantee they will be followed. Establishing and maintaining them requires reinforcement. From a psychological perspective, a reinforcer is any consequence that strengthens the behaviour it follows. In contrast, a sanction (punishment) is any consequence that reduces or stops undesirable behaviour. Behaviour may be reinforced by a reward (e.g. praise or sticker), but may also be reinforced by what a *teacher* thinks is punishment. For example, telling a pupil off for persistent calling out in class provides the pupil with individual attention. Hence, it can be reinforcing and result in repetition of the behaviour to gain more attention. School

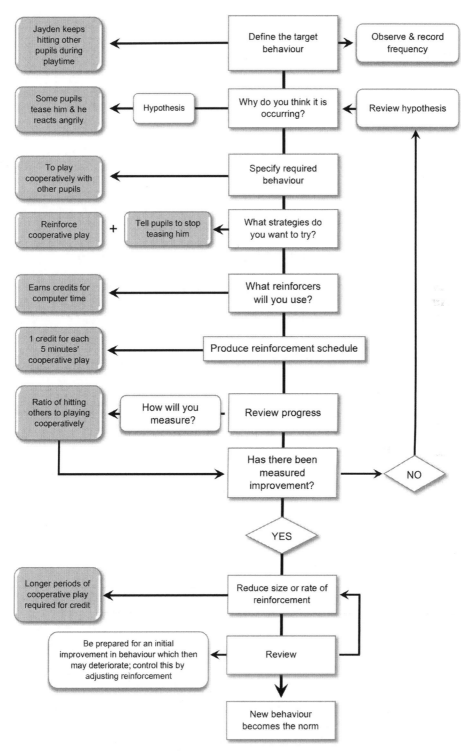

FIGURE 3.4.1 Behaviour change cycle

behaviour policies are required to specify what rewards and sanctions are acceptable (DfE, 2016). To be effective requires attention to detail – that is, following the principles of the behavioural approach (for details, see Chaplain, 2016).

Rewards and sanctions need to be fit for purpose – the reward must be something the pupils like, and the sanction(s) must be something they do not like. It is unwise to assume that *you* know what pupils like or do not like. One way of discovering what pupils value is to ask them to complete a simple 'All about me' questionnaire, in which they indicate their favourite subjects, lessons, hobbies, music, sports and learning styles (ibid.).

Reinforcing acceptable behaviour does not mean issuing rewards haphazardly; rather, they should be managed through a reinforcement schedule (ibid.). Initially, a tangible reinforcer, such as a sticker (accompanied by verbal support), could be given for every occurrence of the desired behaviour, but then, over time, given intermittently to maintain effectiveness (see Figure 3.4.1 for an outline of the process). Verbal support should be warm and natural, appropriate to a pupil's level of development, varied and given for specific behaviour. Any reward should be accessed by acquiring points, stars or raffle tickets. Raffle tickets are particularly effective and inclusive, as any pupil who earns at least one ticket has a chance of winning, unlike star-of-the-week systems, which lead some individuals to conclude that they can never win, so why bother? Whenever you issue a point, star or ticket, simultaneously reinforce the pupil's *specific* behaviour verbally. In that way, they will learn to associate the verbal comment with a rewarding experience, a process known as contiguity.

Always refer to the specific behaviour and *not* the pupil when issuing rewards or sanctions – for example, 'I am pleased to see everyone on this table has put all their equipment back in the correct place'. With difficult pupils, focus on catching them behaving as required, however rare that might be initially. When punishing unacceptable behaviour, do so in a way that suggests disappointment at having to do so, be emotionally objective. Encourage withdrawn pupils to contribute by building waiting time into your questions: 'I am going to be asking about X in five minutes, so start thinking about it now'. Teach more enthusiastic pupils to wait their turn, without disengaging them from learning: 'Thanks for putting your hand up all the time, Bella, but I am going to ask someone else to answer this one'.

List your planned sanctions and familiarise yourself with them; keep the list to hand as reference to avoid using higher-order sanctions prematurely, especially when you feel under pressure. Furthermore, when threatening sanctions, always offer the opportunity to respond positively. For example, 'Adam, you have left your seat again, despite being reminded of the rule. Now you can either sit down and stay there or stay in at break for two minutes'. Should Adam continue to ignore the rule say, 'Adam, you are already staying in for two minutes, now either sit down or you will be staying a further two minutes'. Whatever sanction you threaten, be sure to carry it through, otherwise a future repetition of the unwanted behaviour is more likely.

Start each new day on a positive note, whatever happened the day before – feeling negative in advance will focus your attention on negative behaviour, producing a negative cycle.

CLASSROOM LAYOUT

Seating arrangements are related to pupil behaviour (Steer, 2005). For example, sitting boys with girls tends to reduce disruption (Merrett, 1993), and children organised in rows tend to be less disruptive than when organised in groups (Wheldall and Lam, 1987). However, these findings need to be considered in relation to the learning task and the pupils' level of social functioning (Kutnick *et al.*, 2005).

Movement around the classroom should be free-flowing. Where this is not the case, there is potential for disruption. Some individuals will use every opportunity to push past, nudge or dislodge the chair or whiteboard of other pupils (Chaplain, 2016).

COPING WITH CHALLENGING BEHAVIOUR

Some pupils will persistently challenge your authority, with behaviour ranging from defiance and refusal to work to physical and verbal aggression, and may require specialist interventions.

When dealing with challenging behaviour, never take it personally or get angry – pupils seldom behave this way because they hate you. Do not become preoccupied with descriptive categories (e.g. ADHD) – focus on the behaviour itself and record what the pupil does, and when and where they do it, *including positive behaviour*, however infrequent. Recording positive behaviours not only provides an uplift when times are tense, but also provides insight into what motivates them to behave appropriately. A useful tool for observing challenging behaviour is the strengths and difficulties questionnaire available free from www.sdqinfo.com

Management of challenging pupils can require considerable effort and can be frustrating, which inhibits problem-solving and creativity. It is not uncommon for teachers to question their own ability and lower self-efficacy, which reflects in their behaviour – a change that pupils recognise and respond to negatively – making the situation worse. Finding humour in the situation can be sufficient to influence events positively (Molnar and Lindquist, 1989). Focus on controlling your emotions and on believing that the situation can be coped with, if not completely controlled. Even situations that are so awful that you have to grin and bear it won't last forever. Do not be afraid to ask for help with extreme pupils, especially where physical aggression is involved. If you anticipate an aversive reaction (e.g. aggressive outburst) to a particular event, arrange for a supportive colleague to be around in advance.

The DfE published guidelines on restraining aggressive pupils, and details can be found at www.gov.uk/government/publications/use-of-reasonable-force-in-schools. Fortunately, such occurrences are rare, and most common behaviours can be dealt with through you developing your knowledge of established interventions (see Chaplain and Smith, 2006).

Dealing with challenging behaviour requires attention to several issues, including the following:

- *Be consistent* with whatever approach you adopt. Challenging pupils are looking for structure and security and will repeatedly challenge you until they realise you mean business. They act like people playing slot machines and will keep pressing your buttons until they hit the jackpot (e.g. make you angry). Do not react – keep calm and focused.
- *Classroom organisation* – seating arrangements: Position challenging pupils near the front, so that there are no pupils between them and you to distract or provide an audience. This places you in close proximity while addressing the class, making monitoring and controlling their behaviour easier, for example through direct eye contact and using hand gestures.
- *Learning* – carefully organise their time and the sequencing/size of their learning tasks. If concentration is an issue, break down their learning into smaller, achievable, progressive units, vary the tasks, emphasise visual learning, use colours and shapes to help them organise their work and change their tasks frequently. Have a clock visible and indicate how long they are required to stay on task. Specify exactly what you want them to do and provide visual reminders of important instructions.
- *Support* – where you have a teaching assistant, plan in advance who will deal with a disruptive pupil and who will take responsibility for the rest of the class – this eliminates ambiguity and inconsistency.

- *Changing behaviour* – focus on observable behaviour and avoid describing a pupil as 'always badly behaved'. List the behaviours causing concern, then gather detailed observations of what triggers the unwanted behaviour (antecedent), the behaviour itself and what happens afterwards (consequence), along with when and how frequently it occurs.

Use your observations to determine what is causing the behaviour – that is, either the antecedent (e.g. classroom grouping) or the consequence (e.g. other pupils laughing at the misbehaviour). Use this information to decide what to change in order to modify the behaviour. (For detailed practical methods to help pupils develop self-control, see Chaplain and Smith, 2006; Chaplain, 2016.)

SUMMARY

This unit has outlined some key factors to consider when developing your CMP. It is essential to keep in mind that effective classroom behaviour management is strongly influenced by whole-school attitudes and practices, as well as your interpersonal skills and classroom organisation. Additional reading has been provided to assist you in extending your knowledge of the relevant areas, which is strongly recommended in order to advance your behaviour management skills.

 ## ANNOTATED FURTHER READING

Canter, L. (2009) *Assertive Discipline: Positive Behavior Management for Today's Classroom*, 4th edn, Los Angeles, CA: Canter.
> This text offers helpful guidance on developing a discipline plan and managing difficult behaviour.

Chaplain, R. (2016) *Teaching Without Disruption in the Primary School: A Practical Approach to Managing Pupil Behaviour*, 2nd edn, London: RoutledgeFalmer.
> A comprehensive account of the theory and practice of behaviour management, including whole-school issues, classroom management, coping with challenging behaviour, behaviour management theory and details of how to develop a CMP.

 ## FURTHER READING TO SUPPORT M-LEVEL STUDY

Clunies-Ross, P., Little, E. and Kienhuis, M. (2008) 'Self-reported and actual use of proactive and reactive classroom management strategies and their relationship with teacher stress and student behaviour', *Educational Psychology*, 28(6): 693-710.
> This article examines the relationship between stress and behaviour management strategies, comparing proactive and reactive strategies.

Sanson, A., Hemphill, S. and Smart, D. (2004) 'Connections between temperament and social development: A review', *Social Development*, 13: 142-70.
> Although sociocultural experiences affect social development, this paper highlights the role of temperament in children's social development. Temperament refers to elements of an individual's personality, regarded as innate rather than learned, and has implications for the development of behaviour problems in school.

RELEVANT WEBSITES

Department for Education – Behaviour and Discipline in Schools: www.gov.uk/government/publications/behaviour-and-discipline-in-schools
> This site contains advice and information for teachers (and heads and governors) on behaviour and discipline in schools.

Department for Education: www.gov.uk/government/publications/carter-review-of-initial-teacher-training
> The Carter Review of teacher training highlighted concerns about behaviour management.

REFERENCES

Bandura, A. (1993) 'Perceived self-efficacy in cognitive development and functioning', *Educational Psychologist*, 28: 117–48.

Becker, W.C., Englemann, S. and Thomas, D.R. (1975) *Classroom Management*, Henley-on-Thames, UK: Science Research Associates.

Berg, J.K. and Cornell, D. (2016) 'Authoritative school climate, aggression toward teachers, and teacher distress in middle school', *School Psychology Quarterly*, 31(1): 122–39.

Chaplain, R. (1995) 'Stress and job satisfaction: A study of English primary school teachers', *Educational Psychology: An International Journal of Experimental Educational Psychology*, 15(4): 473–91.

Chaplain, R. (2008) 'Stress and psychological distress among secondary trainee teachers', *Educational Psychology: An International Journal of Experimental Educational Psychology*, 28(2): 195–209.

Chaplain, R. (2016) *Teaching Without Disruption in the Primary School: A Practical Approach to Managing Pupil Behaviour*, 2nd edn, London: RoutledgeFalmer.

Chaplain, R. and Smith, S. (2006) *Challenging Behaviour*, Cambridge, UK: Pearson.

Charles, C.M. (1999) *Building Classroom Discipline: From Models to Practice*, 6th edn, New York: Longman.

Department for Education. (2016) *Behaviour and discipline in schools. Advice for Headteachers and School Staff*, London: The Stationery Office.

Elton Report. (1989) *Discipline in Schools: Report of the Committee Chaired by Lord Elton*, London: HMSO.

Emmer, E. and Aussiker, A. (1990) 'School and discipline problems: How well do they work?', in O. Moles (ed.) *Student Discipline Strategies: Research and Practice*, Albany, NY: SUNY Press.

Emmer, E.T. and Worsham, M.E. (2005) *Classroom Management for Middle and High School Teachers*, 7th edn, Boston, MA: Allyn & Bacon, Prentice Hall.

Health and Safety Executive (HSE). (2000) *The Scale of Occupational Stress: A Further Analysis of the Impact of Demographic Factors and Type of Job*, Contract Research Report 311/2000, London: HSE.

Jones, V.F. and Jones, L.S. (1990) *Comprehensive Classroom Management*, 3rd edn, Needham: Allyn & Bacon.

Kanner, A.D., Coyne, J.C., Schaever, C. and Lazarus, R.S. (1981) 'Comparison of two modes of stress measurement: Daily hassles and uplifts versus major life events', *Journal of Behavioural Medicine*, 4: 1–39.

Klassen, R.M. and Chiu, M.M. (2010) 'Effects on teachers' self-efficacy and job satisfaction: Teacher gender, years of experience, and job stress', *Journal of Educational Psychology*, 102(3): 741–56.

Kutnick, P., Sebba, J., Blatchford, P., Galton, M., Thorp, J., MacIntyre, H. and Berdondini, L. (2005) *The Effects of Pupil Grouping: Literature Review*, London: DfES.

McLaughlin, H.J. (1991) 'The reflection on the blackboard: Student teacher self-evaluation', *Alberta Journal of Educational Research*, 37: 141–59.

Merrett, F. (1993) *Encouragement Works Best*, London: David Fulton.

Molnar, A. and Lindquist, B. (1989) *Changing Problem Behaviour*, San Francisco, CA: Jossey-Bass.

Ng, W., Nicholas, H. and Alan, W. (2010) 'School experience influences on pre-service teachers' evolving beliefs about effective teaching', *Teaching & Teacher Education*, 26: 278–89.

Office for Standards in Education (Ofsted). (2014) *Below the Radar: Low-Level Disruption in the Country's Classrooms*, London: Ofsted.

Rotter, J.B. (1966) 'Generalised expectancies for internal versus external control of reinforcement', *Psychological Monographs*, 91: 482–97.

Steer, A. (2005) *Learning Behaviour: Lessons Learned* (Steer Report), London: DCSF/Institute of Education, University of London.

Swars, S.L. (2005) 'Examining perceptions of mathematics teaching effectiveness among elementary preservice teachers with differing levels of mathematics teacher efficacy', *Journal of Instructional Psychology*, 32(2): 139–47.

Tschannen-Moran, M. and Woolfolk Hoy, A. (2001) 'Teacher efficacy: Capturing an elusive construct', *Teaching & Teacher Education*, 17: 783–805.

Veldman, I., Admiraal, W., van Tartwijk, J., Mainhard, T. and Wubbels, T. (2016) 'Veteran teachers' job satisfaction as a function of personal demands and resources in the relationships with their students,' *Teachers & Teaching*, 22(8): 913–26.

Weinstein, C.S. (1988) 'Preservice teachers' expectations about the first year of teaching', *Teaching & Teacher Education*, 4(1): 31–40.

Wheldall, K. and Lam, Y.Y. (1987) 'Rows versus tables II: The effects of classroom seating arrangements on classroom disruption rate', *Educational Psychology*, 7(4): 303–12.

HANDLING DIFFICULTIES IN SOCIAL, EMOTIONAL AND BEHAVIOUR DEVELOPMENT

Janice Wearmouth and Louise Cunningham

INTRODUCTION

This unit focuses on difficulties experienced by children who demonstrate features of social, emotional and behavioural problems in schools, and ways to minimise the incidence of problematic behaviour. Schools play a critical part in shaping a young child's identity as a learner (Bruner, 1996). Use of the terms 'emotional and behavioural difficulties' (EBD) (DES, 1978), or 'social, emotional and behavioural difficulties' (SEBD), as a label for some students who behave inappropriately is not always helpful. Poulou and Norwich (2002: 112) conclude, from a review of international studies, that the more you, as a teacher, think student behaviour stems from problems within students themselves, such the 'child's innate personality', 'the more you may experience feelings of "stress" and even "helplessness"', and the less you may feel able to cope with difficult behaviour.

The new *Teachers' Standards for Qualified Teacher Status*, introduced from September 2012 (DfE, 2013a), require teachers to take responsibility for promoting good behaviour in classrooms and elsewhere, have high expectations and maintain good relationships with pupils. As a teacher, you can minimise the possibility of poor behaviour in your classroom if you recognise that appropriate behaviour can be taught (Rogers, 2013). Children can learn to make conscious choices about behaviour, even where it is associated with a genetic or neurological condition (Wearmouth, Glynn and Berryman, 2005).

OBJECTIVES

By the end of this unit, you should:

- be familiar with frames of reference commonly used in schools to research and understand social, emotional and behavioural difficulties, and form the basis for effective responses;
- be familiar with a range of effective responses in relation to these frames of reference;
- understand that learning environments that are designed to support children to engage with their learning will reduce the possibility of undesirable behaviour in the first place.

FRAMEWORKS FOR UNDERSTANDING DIFFICULT BEHAVIOUR

The frameworks for understanding problematic behaviour in schools really matter. Antisocial or challenging behaviour is sometimes explained as a problem that stems from the child him/herself and/or his/her family. This may be the case with some children. However, pupil behaviour does not occur in a vacuum (Watkins and Wagner, 2000). Behaviours can be interpreted as resulting from interactions between people and their environments or social events. We begin the discussion here with an outline of the principles of behavioural psychology, which is probably the most common theoretical framework underpinning behaviour management in schools. We continue by looking at social and emotional issues in childhood, biological and neurological explanations for difficult behaviour exemplified by Attention Deficit/Hyperactivity Disorder (AD/HD) and difficulties associated with autism. We conclude by examining bullying behaviour.

Behavioural methodologies

Behavioural methodologies hold that all (mis)behaviour is learned (Skinner, 1938; Baer, Wolf and Risley, 1968). There are two different ways of looking at this. First, research (Glynn, 2004) suggests that elements of a setting may exert powerful control over behaviour. It may be that something about a particular learning environment, for example the physical properties or behaviour of an adult, has provoked good, or alternatively poor, behaviour, and that the young people have come to associate good, or poor, behaviour with that setting. In behaviourist terms, we would consider that the setting has created 'antecedent conditions' for that behaviour to occur. As a teacher, therefore, if you can work out what these antecedent conditions are, you can modify (mis)behaviour through intervening and altering the setting in which the behaviour occurs. Second, particular behaviour can be learned if it is rewarded and thus reinforced, especially if this is done consistently. Many behaviourist principles were derived from work with laboratory animals. In a famous sequence of trial-and-error learning tasks related to the use of rewards, rats learned to press levers to find food (Skinner, 1938). Learning involved the formation of an action–response association in the rats' memory: pressing the lever resulted in a reward, finding food. If the reward was removed, the rats' behaviour would gradually cease through 'extinction'. Translating this interpretation into human terms, pupils can learn how to behave appropriately in response to positive reinforcement (rewards). Where children behave badly you might work out whatever it is that seems to be reinforcing (rewarding) this behaviour and remove the reward(s). Whenever they behave more appropriately, you might reward them in a way that recognises the greater acceptability of the new behaviour.

The opposite of positive reinforcement is negative reinforcement. From this view, you can reinforce compliance in classrooms by making rules and the consequences of unacceptable behaviour clear. Pupils may learn appropriate behaviour through avoiding punishment.

Practical applications of behaviourist principles for teaching appropriate behaviour and controlling what is unacceptable are discussed below.

Applying behaviourist principles to manage behaviour in schools

There is a lot of evidence to demonstrate that approaches derived from behavioural method-ologies are effective in establishing positive behaviour in schools and reducing incidents of disruption or challenging behaviour (Watkins and Wagner, 2000; Rogers, 2003, 2013). Antecedent conditions – in other words, the physical properties: for example, space, arrangement of desks, availability of resources around the school, including adults – may exert a powerful control over pupil behaviour. It is very important that you think about this, because, as a teacher, you are in a good position to make changes in the learning environment that can improve behaviour where required. The way in which you, as a teacher, reward behaviour, sometimes inadvertently, by your own actions can be a very strong reinforcer of good, or poor, behaviour (Sproson, 2004). Whatever you do, you need to know that changing pupil behaviour using this approach depends on you and your colleagues being very consistent in your own behaviour around children.

Establishing conditions that support appropriate behaviour in classrooms

Pupils will look towards you as the teacher for a sense of security and order, an opportunity to participate actively in the class and for it to be an interesting place (DfES, 2006). Establishing the right to feel safe, learn without disruption, and be respected and treated fairly is essential as the basis for instituting rules and routines (Rogers, 2013). Teachers who can control classes most effectively are those who can command respect and, often but not always, those whom pupils like (Elton, 1989; DfES, 2006). These teachers know how to get the best out of children.

Task 3.5.1 Reflecting on the qualities of effective classroom teachers

Note down what, in your experience, are the most important qualities of the classroom teachers who experience the least disruptive pupil behaviour. How do these teachers behave in the classroom?

How far do you measure up to your list of qualities?

How far do you agree with Elton (1989) that, to be effective, teachers should:

- have good subject knowledge;
- be able to plan and deliver lessons that are coherent and engage pupils' attention;
- be able to relate to young people and encourage good behaviour and learning;
- deal calmly and firmly with inappropriate behaviour;
- establish positive relationships with their classes, based on mutual respect;
- be able to create a classroom ethos in which pupils lose popularity and credibility with classmates by causing trouble;
- recognise potential disruptive incidents, choose an appropriate means to deal with them early on and prevent escalation;
- know what is going on around them;
- know how pupils react to each other and to teachers;
- be in full control of their own behaviour and model the good behaviour they expect of pupils?

The reverse of the effective teacher is the teacher who is ineffective in managing behaviour. Examples of teachers whose behaviour establishes conditions predisposing to poor pupil behaviour include:

> teachers who lack confidence in their own ability to deal with disruption and who see their classes as potentially hostile. They create a negative classroom atmosphere by frequent criticism and rare praise. They make use of loud public reprimands and threats. They are sometimes sarcastic.

They tend to react aggressively to minor incidents. Their methods increase the danger of a major confrontation not only with individual pupils but with the whole class.

(Elton, 1989: Chapter 3, paragraph 8)

Ways to reinforce positive behaviour and reduce incidence of disruption

In Rogers' (2013) view, a child's background is no excuse for poor behaviour. Behaviour learned most readily has consistent positive consequences: social attention, praise, recognition, access to favourite activities, and so on. It is really important that you inform parents about the good things their children are doing and their positive achievements, as well as your concerns.

Canter and Canter (1992) advocate that, as a teacher, you should be assertive in your approach to pupils and establish a classroom discipline plan with three parts: rules, positive recognition and consequences. You should provide a limited number of rules, with predictable, positive consequences. If children disrupt the lesson, they should take ownership of this, and you should remind them what the rules are: 'Jayson . . . you're calling out . . . Remember our class rules for asking questions, thanks' (Rogers, 2013: 238). You can give younger children a nonverbal cue to appropriate behaviour and show them clearly what is expected.

Students may imitate negative behaviour, and so, for example, the use of abusive or sarcastic language should be avoided at all costs. You should model ways of resolving conflict that respect the rights of students to learn and feel safe and:

- meet the needs of both parties, that is, provide win–win outcomes wherever possible;
- bring an end to the conflict, or at least reduce it;
- do not leave either party 'wounded'.

(Sproson, 2004: 319)

In your role as a teacher, it is important not to allow yourself to be drawn into a power struggle, which some pupils find rewarding. There are a number of techniques that can enable you to avoid power struggles:

- Some young people may take pleasure in not doing what they are asked immediately, especially if there is an audience of peers. In this situation, Rogers (2013: 240), among others, advocates that you build in a brief 'take-up' period for pupils to respond: 'Craig . . . Deon . . . you're chatting – it's whole-class teaching time'. Make the request, walk away so as to imply compliance, and acknowledge compliance when it happens. Many schools require pupils not to chew gum in classrooms. In the experience of Wearmouth, one of the current authors, children often ignore this. It is usually more positive, rather than beginning lessons on a negative note, to start by greeting everyone and walk round the room with a bin while talking.
- The 'broken record' approach (ibid.) also allows you, as the teacher, to repeat a request calmly without being drawn into an argument. As Sproson (2004: 320) exemplifies:

Teacher:	John, start your work, thanks.
John:	It's boring.
Teacher:	John, start your work, thanks.
John:	Didn't you hear what I said?
Teacher:	Start your work, thanks.
John:	This lesson's just so boring . . . (picking pen up – if you're lucky!)
Teacher:	Pleased to see you getting down to work – well done.

- Pupils engaging in inappropriate activities might be given what Rogers (2013: 242) calls 'directed choices'. Wearmouth's sister, a teacher, tells of a situation where teenage girls brought long sticks into her mathematics lesson – to test her out, as they later admitted. She responded by directing their choices: 'Shall I put them in this cupboard or that one? I'll keep them safe for you till the end of the day'. They never asked for them back.

- It is important for you to distinguish between the primary (target) behaviour that is of concern and secondary behaviours that are just intended to annoy. Secondary behaviours (sighs, looks, and so on) can be ignored, and take-up time to comply with the original request can be allowed.

- Finally, you may be able to address inappropriate and/or disruptive behaviour by defining behaviour that is incompatible with this, and modelling and reinforcing it with positive consequences. For example, as a new teacher, Wearmouth was once in a position where all the pupils had been told not to bring 'clacker balls' into school, because one child had broken her wrist playing with these. When she walked into her classroom the next day, every single pupil pulled out their clackers and began to play, 'clack', 'clack', 'clack'. For a moment she felt sheer panic, but then she turned round and, without saying anything, wrote on the whiteboard very clearly, 'Copy this into your books', and began to write the first few sentences of a story. Very soon, all the clacker balls had disappeared into bags, and there was quiet in the room while the children began to engage in their own storytelling. Clacking the balls together and writing could not be done simultaneously.

SOCIAL AND EMOTIONAL ISSUES IN CHILDHOOD

Some educators, for example Greenhalgh (2004), highlight the importance of an environment that fosters children's sense of safety, trust and acceptance of themselves as individuals so that they can develop and learn. The links between well-conceptualised provision for social and emotional aspects of learning in the primary curriculum, positive pupil behaviour and academic achievement have been accepted by central government (DfES, 2006).

SEAL

In the mid 1990s, the Department for Children, Schools and Families (DCSF) in England commissioned materials, *Social and Emotional Aspects of Learning (SEAL): Improving Behaviour, Improving Learning*, to be used as part of schools' personal, social and health curriculum. Primary SEAL has been available since 2005, based on a number of aspects of social and emotional aspects of learning: self-awareness, managing feelings, motivation, empathy and social skills. The underpinning assumption is that all children benefit from support to understand and manage their feelings, work cooperatively in groups, motivate themselves and develop resilience in the face of setbacks.

Circle Time

In primary schools, you may well come across the initiative 'Circle Time' (Mosley, 1996), which was designed to resolve disputes between pupils. In schools, Circle Time is a meeting following strict protocols of involving all participants in discussion. Both teachers and students are bound by rules that stipulate no one may put anyone down, no one may use any name negatively and, when individuals speak, everyone must listen. Everyone has a turn and a chance to speak. Members of the class team suggest ways of solving problems, and individuals can accept or politely refuse help (Wearmouth, Glynn and Berryman, 2005: 184). If a child breaks the protocol, a visual warning is given. If this persists, time away from the circle follows.

Importance of attachment for young children

One theory of human development that has influenced educational provision for young children whose behaviour is antisocial is attachment theory (Bowlby, 1952). Babies quickly attach themselves emotionally to their adult carers and progress through well-recognised stages towards maturity. Successful development depends on needs being adequately met at an earlier stage. If they are not, then children will persist in inappropriate attachment behaviour, being over-anxious, avoidant, aggressive or incapable of positive human relationships (Bennathan, 2000). Learning, personality and behaviour difficulties can result from inadequate early care and support from parents who struggle with poverty, damaged relationships and harsh, stressful living conditions (Boxall, 2002).

Establishing attachment to address antisocial behaviour

Attachment theory has influenced the development of 'nurture groups' in some infant schools, originally in the Inner London Education Authority in 1970-1 and, more recently, in other local authorities. The nurture group attempts to create the features of adequate parenting, with opportunities to develop trust, security and positive identity through attachment to an attentive, caring adult. Features include: easy physical contact between adult and child; warmth and a family atmosphere; good-humoured acceptance of children and their behaviour; familiar, regular routines; a focus on tidying up; provision of food in structured contexts; opportunities to play and appropriate adult participation; adults encouraging children's reflection on troublesome situations and their own feelings; and opportunities for children to develop increasing autonomy (Wearmouth, 2009).

If you teach in early years settings, you may well come across the *Boxall Profile* (Bennathan and Boxall, 2000). This is an observational tool, based on attachment theory and developed to identify children's developmental needs and the levels of skills they possess to access learning. It was originally standardised for children aged 3-8 years to support work in nurture groups.

Transactional analysis (TA)

An approach that is rather different from behaviourism is transactional analysis (TA), first developed in the 1950s by Eric Berne and now adopted in some schools. Clearly drawing on psychodynamic and humanistic theories, Berne devised a series of models to make sense of how people develop, view the world and communicate.

TA philosophy is based on three principles: 'the importance of positive unconditional regard, a common capacity to think and make decisions and a commitment to growth as a fundamental feature of human nature' (Barrow, 2015: 169).

TA is based on the theory that each person has three ego states: parent, adult and child. These are used together with other key concepts, tools and models to analyse how individuals communicate and identify what interaction is needed for a better outcome. Each ego state reflects a system of thought, feeling and behaviour and determines how individuals express themselves, interact and form relationships. These are:

- the 'child ego state', the set of thoughts, feelings and behaviours learned from childhood;
- the 'parent ego state', the set of thoughts, feelings and behaviours about how to be a parent that are learned from parents and significant others and become part of the developing personality; they can be supportive or critical;
- the 'adult ego state', the set of current responses not influenced by childhood experience.

When individuals communicate, their ego states interact to create 'transactions', that is, communication exchanges between people. If the ego states interact in a healthy way, transactions tend to be positive, but sometimes ego states can create a distorted view of the world. Understanding of these transactions and the states to which they refer is key to conflict resolution.

A powerful aspect of work in TA in schools is understanding how children give and receive positive and negative 'strokes', compliments, acceptance and recognition, or the opposite, which influence how children behave. Berne (1964) defined particular socially dysfunctional behaviour patterns as 'games' people play. These patterns are principally intended to obtain strokes, but instead they hide the direct expression of thoughts and emotions. Understanding these patterns can lead to changing unhealthy patterns of stroking in classrooms through 'redecision', the assumption that individuals have the potential to behave as they choose. The capability to make decisions is also the basis for mutual 'contracting' for change, child to teacher or vice versa, and child to child.

Educational TA has become recognised as a 'field of application in its own right' (Barrow, 2015: 178). It makes the assumption that successful behaviour management in the classroom relies on positive relationships being built between pupils and teachers, and that use of the concepts of TA can create 'win-win' situations. Drawing on her experience of using TA in her own school, Cunningham, one of the current authors, comments:

> A child that feels safe to learn and knows it is acceptable to make mistakes will thrive and a passionate teacher who builds positive relationships with pupils and with the subject can make all the difference to engage a 'distraught or upset' pupil within the lesson. As a teacher your response to pupil behaviour or disengagement makes the difference between motivation and willingness to learn.

NEUROLOGICAL AND BIOLOGICAL EXPLANATIONS OF BEHAVIOUR

Sometimes behaviour that you may experience as challenging to yourself as the teacher or to the welfare and academic progress of the children may relate to an underlying condition or dysfunction.

Attention Deficit/Hyperactivity Disorder

One such condition is Attention Deficit/Hyperactivity Disorder (AD/HD), 'characterised by chronic and pervasive (at home and school) problems of inattention, impulsiveness, and/or excessive motor activity which have seriously debilitating effects on individuals' social, emotional and educational development, and are sometimes disruptive to the home and/or school environment' (Norwich, Cooper and Maras, 2002: 182) .

A diagnosis of AD/HD may result in a prescription for psychostimulants:

> The medication stimulates areas of the brain regulating arousal and alertness and can result in immediate short-term improvements in concentration and impulse control. The precise mechanism is poorly understood and the specific locus of action within the central nervous system remains speculative.

> (BPS, 1996: 50-1)

Methylphenidate (Ritalin) is the most widely used stimulant, prescribed in the form of tablets to be taken regularly.

There are particular concerns about the use of such psychostimulants, including the effects and side effects of these drugs and ethical considerations about the lack of adequate monitoring of the day-to-day classroom learning and behavioural outcomes of medication (BPS, 1996: 51-2). Prescribing a drug may provide an insufficient response to supporting pupils in how to behave more appropriately.

'We have evidence that children given the diagnosis ADHD don't attend, don't wait and don't sit still. But just because they don't do all these things does not mean that they cannot do them' (BPS, 1996: 23). The use of psychostimulants is not the only response to AD/HD, as we discuss below.

Responding to AD/HD

The use of drugs is not, then, a complete answer to controlling the behaviour of children identified as having AD/HD. Children can also sometimes be taught alternative behaviours that offer a sense of belonging and increase self-control (Rogers, 2013). The British Psychological Society (1996: 47-8) identified a number of approaches that focus on the effects of consequences through positive reinforcement, training in the reduction of behaviour viewed as problematic, and response cost, that is mild punishment designed to make the undesirable, behaviour more difficult and more of an effort to perform. 'Several studies showed that behaviour management and medication were most effective when combined' (ibid.).

Behavioural methodology is a scientifically based technology, and so the first requirement is a clear definition of the target behaviour. For instance, if a child is thought to be 'hyperactive', an operational definition of behaviours, such as 'out of seat', will be required. Once the behaviour has been operationally defined, there should be systematic observational sampling across times of day, situations, nature of activity, person in charge, and so on. Once the baseline can be clearly seen, an analysis detailing the following three stages should be carried out: (1) the antecedent event(s), that is, whatever starts off or prompts the undesirable behaviour; (2) the observable behaviour; (3) the consequence(s). When a consequence seems to be reinforcing a behaviour, then that consequence should be removed. It may be that by telling the child off you are maintaining and reinforcing a child's 'attention-seeking', for example. If the positive reinforcement is removed, the occurrences of that behaviour should reduce. This is not always easy to achieve, of course, and it may be that you will need to work out alternative, incompatible behaviour as outlined above.

At the same time as making clear to pupils what behaviours are unacceptable, individualised behaviour management strategies should also provide opportunities for modelling, rehearsing and reinforcing behaviours that are acceptable (Rogers, 2013: 167-9). For example, a teacher might explain to the child what his/her current behaviour looks and sounds like, and how it affects the other students in the classroom: 'Do you mind if I show you what you do when . . .?' It is also important to model the desired behaviour to the student: 'Let me show you how I want you to . . .' The student might then be encouraged to copy this behaviour. In the classroom, the teacher should acknowledge any positive changes in the student's behaviour with positive verbal encouragement.

Potentially unsafe or abusive behaviour should be addressed very assertively: '[That language] is not a joke to me - it stops now', 'Kyle . . . put the scissors down, on the table - now' (Rogers, 2013: 243-4). If it is necessary to remove a student from a group of peers, this can be achieved 'by asking the other students to leave. It may be more appropriate, and safer, to bring other staff to the place where the student is, rather than the other way around' (Dunckley, 1999: 10).

Physical restraint is a last resort that should only be used to manage a dangerous situation. In a non-statutory advisory document on the use of 'reasonable' force in schools in England (DfE, 2013b: 4), school staff are advised that reasonable in this context means 'using no more force than is needed' to control or restrain young people.

Whatever you do, you should familiarise yourself with school policies that should indicate when restraint can be used.

Autism

It is highly likely that you will meet children in schools who have been diagnosed as having an autistic spectrum disorder (ASD). Autism is a condition generally thought to affect communication, cognition and learning. In 1943, Leo Kanner (Kanner, 1943) identified a small group of young children who faced a difficulty that seemed to centre around excessive focus on the self. He called it 'early infantile autism', from the Greek αυτος (*autos*) meaning 'self'. These children appeared unable to relate to people and social situations from early life, experienced profound 'aloneness', failure to use language fluently to communicate and an anxious and obsessive desire to maintain sameness. Some seemed to have a fascination for objects that are handled with skill in fine motor movements, a good rote memory, over-sensitivity to stimuli, and apparently good cognitive potential. Around the same time, Hans Asperger (1944/1991) used the term 'autistic' to denote a range of attributes bearing a similarity to that commented on by Kanner. This included extreme egocentricity and an inability to relate to others, speech and language peculiarities, repetitive routines, motor clumsiness, narrow interests and nonverbal communication problems (Wing, 1996). Additional features included unusual responses to some sensory experiences: auditory, visual, olfactory (smell), taste and touch. Asperger also noticed an uneven developmental profile, a good rote memory, very narrow special interests and motor coordination difficulties. Asperger Syndrome now commonly refers to a form of autism used to describe people at the higher end of the autistic spectrum (National Autistic Society, 2016). Delay in language development is not likely. One in ten people with ASD have what appear to be extremely well-developed skills in one specific area. These skills are often found in mathematical and calendrical calculations, and areas such as music and art. In autism, however, three-quarters of the population have difficulties in learning, some at a severe level.

Recently, Frederickson and Cline (2015: 283) have summarised the areas of difficulties often associated with autism as:

- social communication and social interaction;
- restricted, repetitive patterns of behaviour, interests or activities, including sensory difficulties.

Children experiencing difficulties in these areas are unlikely to understand unwritten social rules, recognise other's feelings, seek comfort from others or understand and interpret other people's feelings and actions. They may appear to behave 'strangely' or inappropriately, and may often prefer to be alone. Difficulties in social communication mean that children often find it hard to understand the meaning of gestures, facial expressions or tone of voice. They may also find it hard to plan for the future and cope in new or unfamiliar situations. This may result in restricted, obsessional or repetitive activities, and difficulties in developing the skills of playing with others. In addition to this dyad, repetitive behaviour patterns are often a notable feature, as well as a resistance to change in routine.

Responding to autistic spectrum disorders

Commonly, approaches to addressing difficulties associated with autism are based on behavioural principles. In a classroom, you might address the learning and behavioural needs of children on the autistic spectrum by, for example, paying close attention to clarity and order, reducing extraneous and unnecessary material in order that children know where their attention needs to be directed, and maintaining a predictable physical environment with very predictable and regular routines, ensuring that everything is kept in the same place. You might teach children agreed signals to be quiet or to call for attention. You might provide specific low-arousal work areas free from visual distractions and make headphones available to reduce sound. You might also provide a visual timetable, with clear symbols to represent the various activities for the day, and a simple visual timer with, for example, an arrow that is moved across a simple timeline to show how much time has passed or is left.

To develop greater understanding of personal emotions, you might teach children in a very deliberate way to name their feelings and relate these to their own experiences, predict how they are likely to feel at particular times and in particular circumstances, and recognise the signs of extreme emotions such as anger. A visual gauge showing graduated degrees of anger in different shades of colour might be helpful here. You might also teach pupils, in small steps, to identify and name others' feelings, link these to possible causes, and identify appropriate responses to others' emotions. They might keep a feelings diary in which they record times when they feel happy, sad or frightened, and what they can do about this. You might use art, drama and social stories to identify the different kinds of emotion and/or explore their physical aspects and/or talk through situations that need to be resolved. Above all, it is really important for you to get to know the pupil really well and to understand his/her individuality, strengths, weakness, likes and dislikes.

BULLYING BEHAVIOUR

You may find that bullying behaviour is a concern in your school.

Task 3.5.2 Personal reflection on the experience of 'bullying'

Take a few minutes to reflect on your own school experiences:

- Do you have experience of being bullied, or even of being a bully? Or perhaps you saw someone being bullied? How did this make you feel?
- How would you define what constitutes 'bullying' behaviour? How far do you think this behaviour was related to the characteristics of you as the victim or bully, and/or to the other person/people involved? How far was it related to the context in which it occurred?
- How did it start?
- Is it possible to identify the cycle of its development?
- Did you (or the victim) try to resist the bullying?
- What might have been done to stop this bullying behaviour?
- How did it all end?

How did you feel when you were carrying out this activity? Did you feel any of the same emotions that you did in your experience of bullying?

Government guidance in England (DfE, 2014a) advises that bullying means behaviour by an individual or group, repeated over time, that intentionally hurts another individual or group, physically or emotionally. Bullying can take many forms, including cyber-bullying. Bullying is often associated with an imbalance of power. Once the victim reacts to the bullying by showing signs of stress, bullies may experience pleasure from feelings of dominance. The cycle of bullying may continue and intensify.

The victim may fight back or find ways to avoid the bullying by hovering around teachers or staying at home. If the bullying is extremely serious, and the bully is over the age of 10, the bully could be prosecuted for a criminal offence, for example harassment. If the bully is under 10, it may be possible to take legal action for negligence against the school and the local authority for failure in their duty of care.

Under the Children Act 1989, bullying is a child protection concern when there is 'reasonable cause to suspect that a child is suffering, or is likely to suffer, significant harm'. If so, staff should report concerns to their local authority children's social care. Schools may need to consult a range of external services to support pupils who are bullied, or address underlying issues contributing to bullying behaviour (DfE, 2014a).

Interventions to address bullying behaviour in schools

Bullies trade in secrecy from adults. Breaking through this secrecy is crucial. There need to be clear, school-wide consequences for bullying, otherwise the bully will continue in the belief that s/he can continuity with impunity (Olweus, 1978).

State schools should have an anti-bullying policy (DfE, 2014a) that sets out the way that bullying should be dealt with in the school. This should include:

* bullying related to race, religion and culture;
* bullying pupils with disabilities or special educational needs;
* sexist bullying and harassment;
* bullying pupils because of their sexuality or perceived sexuality;
* cyber-bullying (the use of mobile phones and the Internet to bully pupils).

Task 3.5.3 Advice about cyber-bullying for head teachers and school staff

In England, government guidance about bullying for parents, pupils and teachers, *Preventing and Tackling Bullying*, is available from the Department for Education (DfE, 2014a) at: https://www.gov.uk/government/uploads/system/uploads/attachment_data/file/444862/Preventing_and_tackling_bullying_advice.pdf

The DfE has also issued a publication *Cyberbullying: Advice for Headteachers and School Staff* (DfE, 2014b), which includes sets of links to resources offering guidance to professionals and families who might be concerned about what to do in cases of suspected cyber-bullying. This is available at: https://www.gov.uk/government/uploads/system/uploads/attachment_data/file/374850/Cyberbullying_Advice_for_Headteachers_and_School_Staff_121114.pdf

You might like to access both these documents and the links that are embedded in them.

How useful and practical do you find the advice that is offered here?

SUMMARY

'Difficult' neighbourhoods tend to produce more 'difficult' children than neighbourhoods in more affluent circumstances (Watkins and Wagner, 2000), but economic impoverishment in the neighbourhood does not necessarily lead to disruptive behaviour in schools (Rutter *et al.*, 1979; Ofsted, 2001). Even in areas of disadvantage, good classroom management, as well as interventions with individual students, can make a difference to student behaviour, learning and future life chances. It is crucial for teachers to understand that belonging is a fundamental human need (Maslow, 1943). As Rogers (2003) notes, young people spend a third of their day at school, and so teachers are in a position to provide structured frameworks within which these young people can be taught alternatives to unacceptable behaviour that offer a sense of belonging and increase self-control.

ANNOTATED FURTHER READING

Rogers, B. (2015) *Classroom Behaviour. A Practical Guide to Effective Teaching, Behaviour Management and Colleague Support*, 4th edn, London: Sage.

> Bill Rogers, an Australian educator, has written a number of books and articles on addressing challenging behaviour in schools that may be interpreted as using the principles of behavioural psychology. This publication provides strategies to meet the challenges of controlling behaviour, as well as building positive relationships with both students and colleagues to enable productive learning environments.

Rogers, B. (2012) *You Know the Fair Rule: Strategies for Positive and Effective Behaviour Management and Discipline in Schools*, London: Pearson.

> This book is concerned with establishing good, effective classroom management strategies to prevent disruptive and difficult behaviour developing in the first place, planning behavioural interventions and resolving conflict in schools.

FURTHER READING TO SUPPORT M-LEVEL STUDY

Cooper, P. and Whitehead, D. (2007) 'The effectiveness of nurture groups on student progress', *Emotional & Behavioural Difficulties*, 12: 171-90.

> This is a national evaluation exploring the effectiveness of nurture groups (NGs). It set out to measure: the effects of NGs in promoting pupil improvement in the NGs; the extent to which these improvements generalised to mainstream settings; and the impact of NGs on whole schools. Statistically significant improvements were found for pupils who had attended NGs in terms of social, emotional and behavioural functioning.

Barrow, G. (2015) 'Transactional Analysis in the classroom, staffroom and beyond', *Pastoral Care in Education*, 33(3): 169-79.

> This article broadly considers the application of TA in education and its use in reducing conflict in the classroom and staffroom. TA offers essentially a psychodynamic perspective on aspects of teaching and learning associated with the nature of the relationships of child to teacher, child to child and teacher to teacher in schools. The author discusses concepts important to an understanding of TA: the ego-state model of personality, psychological game-playing and contracting.

RELEVANT WEBSITES

Responsibility for administering medication: www.medicalconditionsatschool.org.uk/documents/Legal-Situation-In-Schools.pdf

    It is really important that you are aware of statutory guidance in relation to responsibility for administering medication such as Ritalin to children, and this website has guidance for schools and colleges across the UK.

Resources for social and emotional aspects of learning: http://webarchive.nationalarchives.gov.uk/2011080 9101133/nsonline.org.uk/node/87009

    This has SEAL resources designed for schools who have identified the social and emotional aspects of learning as a key focus for their work.

Guidance on the use of 'reasonable force': www.gov.uk/government/uploads/system/uploads/attachment_data/file/444051/Use_of_reasonable_force_advice_Reviewed_July_2015.pdf

    This has advice for schools in England.

Guidance on the use of 'reasonable force': https://www.education-ni.gov.uk/sites/default/files/publications/de/Reg-policy-framework-reasonable-force.pdf

    This has the policy issued by the Department of Education in Northern Ireland.

Guidance on the use of visual supports for autistic children: www.autism.org.uk/about/strategies/visual-supports.aspx

    The National Autistic Society has made this information sheet available on the use of visual supports for autistic young people. If you are responsible in any way for the learning and progress of students with autism, you might like to have a look at this and consider how you might make use of the advice that is offered here.

Useful resources for TA in education: www.crackingbehaviour.com

    The Giles Barrow website has a useful set of downloads, articles and CPD links related to TA in education. A recent book in this area is *Educational Transactional Analysis – An International Guide to Theory and Practice*, by G. Barrow and T. Newton (eds; 2016, 1st edn, London: Routledge).

REFERENCES

Asperger, H. (1944/1991) '*Autism and Asperger Syndrome* [translation]', ed. U. Frith, Cambridge, UK: Cambridge University Press.

Baer, D.M., Wolf, M.M. and Risley, T.R. (1968) 'Some current dimensions of applied behavior analysis', *Journal of Applied Behavior Analysis*, 1(1): 91-7.

Barrow, G. (2015) 'Transactional Analysis in the classroom, staffroom and beyond', *Pastoral Care in Education*, 33(3): 169-79.

Bennathan, M. (2000) 'Children at risk of failure in primary schools', in M. Bennathan and M. Boxall, *Effective Intervention in Primary Schools: Nurture Groups*, 2nd edn, London: David Fulton, pp. 1-18.

Bennathan, M. and Boxall, M. (eds) (2000) *Effective Intervention in Primary Schools: Nurture Groups*, London: David Fulton.

Berne, E. (1964) *Games People Play*, London: Penguin.

Bowlby, J. (1952) 'A two-year-old goes to hospital', *Proceedings of the Royal Society of Medicine*, 46: 425-7.

Boxall, M. (2002) *Nurture Groups in School: Principles and Practice*, London: Paul Chapman.

British Psychological Society (BPS). (1996) *Attention Deficit Hyperactivity Disorder (ADHD): A Psychological Response to an Evolving Concept*, Leicester, UK: BPS.

Bruner, J. (1996) *The Culture of Education*, Boston, MA: Harvard University Press.

Canter, L. and Canter, M. (1992) *Assertive Discipline: Positive Behaviour Management for Today's Classroom*, Santa Monica, CA: Lee Canter.

Department for Education (DfE). (2013a) *Teachers' Standards for Qualified Teacher Status*, London: DfE.

Department for Education (DfE). (2013b) *Use of Reasonable Force. Advice for Headteachers, Staff and Governing Bodies*, London: DfE.

Department for Education (DfE) (2014a) *Preventing and Tackling Bullying: Advice for Head Teachers, Staff and Governing Boards*, London: DfE.

Department for Education (DfE) (2014b) *Cyberbullying: Advice for Headteachers and School Staff*, London: DfE.

Department for Education and Skills (DfES). (2006) *Learning Behaviour. Principles and Practice – What Works in Schools (Steer Report)*, London: DfES.

Department of Education and Science (DES). (1978) *Special Educational Needs, Report of the Committee of Enquiry into the Education of Handicapped Children and Young People*, (Warnock Report), London: HMSO.

Dunckley, I. (1999) *Managing Extreme Behaviour in Schools*, Wellington, New Zealand: Specialist Education Services.

Elton, Lord (1989) *Enquiry into Discipline in Schools*, London: DES.

Frederickson, N. and Cline, T. (2015) *Special Educational Needs, Inclusion and Diversity*, Maidenhead, UK: Open University Press.

Glynn, T. (2004) 'Antecedent control of behaviour in educational contexts', in J. Wearmouth, R.C. Richmond and T. Glynn (eds) *Understanding Pupil Behaviour in Schools: A Diversity of Approaches*, London: Fulton.

Greenhalgh, P. (2004) 'Emotional growth and learning', in J. Wearmouth, R.C. Richmond, T. Glynn and M. Berryman, *Understanding Pupil Behaviour in Schools*, London: David Fulton, chap. 10, pp. 151–61.

Kanner, L. (1943) 'Autistic disturbances of affective contact', *Nervous Child*, 2: 217–50.

Maslow, A. (1943) 'A theory of human motivation', *Psychological Review*, 50(4): 370–96.

Mosley, J. (1996) *Quality Circle Time in the Primary Classroom: Your Essential Guide to Enhancing Self-esteem, Self-discipline and Positive Relationships*, Cambridge, UK: LDA.

National Autistic Society. (2016) *What is Asperger Syndrome?* Retrieved from www.autism.org.uk/about/what-is/asperger.aspx (accessed 9 March 2016).

Norwich, B., Cooper, P. and Maras, P. (2002) 'Attentional and activity difficulties: Findings from a national study', *Support for Learning*, 17(4): 182–6.

Office for Standards in Education (Ofsted). (2001) *Improving Attendance and Behaviour in Secondary Schools*, London: Ofsted.

Olweus, D. (1978) *Aggression in the Schools: Bullies and Whipping Boys*, New York: Wiley.

Poulou, M. and Norwich, B. (2002) 'Cognitive, emotional and behavioural responses to students with emotional and behavioural difficulties: A model of decision-making', *British Educational Research Journal*, 28(1): 111–38.

Rogers, B. (2003) *Behaviour Recovery*, Melbourne, VIC: ACER Press.

Rogers, B. (2013) 'Communicating with children in the classroom', in T. Cole, H. Daniels and J. Visser, *The Routledge International Companion to Emotional and Behavioural Difficulties*, London: Routledge, chap. 26, pp. 237–45.

Rutter, M. Maughan, B., Mortimore, P., and Ouston, J. (1979) *Fifteen Thousand Hours: Secondary Schools and Their Effects on Children*, London, Open Books.

Skinner, B.F. (1938) *The Behaviour of Organisms*, New York: Appleton Century Crofts.

Sproson, B. (2004) 'Some do and some don't: Teacher effectiveness in managing behaviour', in J. Wearmouth, T. Glynn, R.C. Richmond and M. Berryman (eds) *Inclusion and Behaviour Management in Schools*, London: Fulton, chap. 18, pp. 311–21.

Watkins, C. and Wagner, P. (2000) *Improving School Behaviour*, London: Paul Chapman.

Wearmouth, J. (2009) *A Beginning Teacher's Guide to Special Educational Needs*, Buckingham, UK: Open University Press.

Wearmouth, J., Glynn, T. and Berryman, M. (2005) *Perspectives on Student Behaviour in Schools: Exploring Theory and Developing Practice*, London: Routledge.

Wing, L. (1996) *The Autistic Spectrum: A Guide for Parents and Professionals*, London: Constable.

ORGANISING EFFECTIVE CLASSROOM TALK

Lyn Dawes

Teachers must value the relationship between the talk they use for teaching, and the talk they hope to inspire their pupils to use for learning.

(Smith and Higgins, 2006: 500)

INTRODUCTION

Most children arrive at school able to talk. Their everyday talk skills are invaluable, but may not include ways to use talk to aid their own learning. Children are rarely taught how to use the essential tools of spoken language in the same way that they are taught key aspects of literacy and numeracy. Because of this, they may never learn how to share and negotiate a range of points of view, how to listen attentively to others, and how to evaluate what they hear and provide a considered response. Children who are not helped to understand these important skills have few resources when it comes to discussing ideas, collaborating or undertaking joint activities. They may instead use strategies such as talking over others, ignoring what is said or not talking at all. Children need to know how to talk to one another in order to solve problems and learn effectively. An inability to communicate with others through talk is a true deprivation, and it is unnecessary, because in classrooms we can readily teach children how to engage one another in discussion. This extension of their talk repertoire is not simply an added social skill, but fosters a crucial capacity and enables access to educational opportunity. Effective talk – 'talk for learning' – does not just happen in classrooms, but is a product of planning, teaching and organisation. We need to make sure that every child learns ways to share their ideas through talk. A focus on talk for learning is essential if all are to benefit from classroom activities.

OBJECTIVES

By the end of this unit, you should be able to:

- consider the crucial importance of classroom talk for learning;
- identify ways that teachers use talk for learning;
- understand when and how to move between different sorts of talk within lessons;
- raise children's awareness of their classroom talk and its impact on others.

THE CRUCIAL IMPORTANCE OF CLASSROOM TALK FOR LEARNING

Children learn, not just through experience, but by talking about what they are doing. Talk precipitates thought, as children share ideas and comment on what they observe. In this way, children help one another to generate new understanding while stimulating curiosity, imagination and interest. Children talking may articulate tentative or more firmly entrenched ideas, make suggestions or offer information. The chance to listen to children's talk allows useful insight into their thinking. In whole-class settings, talk with a teacher can provide children with new information. Even more importantly, children can hear and consider a range of alternative points of view. Classroom talk has the social function of helping the child to learn how effective communication goes on, as ideas are raised and negotiated. The 2014 Primary National Curriculum emphasises both the importance of children's talk, and the importance of direct teaching of the relevant skills:

Spoken language

6.2 Pupils should be taught to speak clearly and convey ideas confidently using Standard English. They should learn to justify ideas with reasons; ask questions to check understanding; develop vocabulary and build knowledge; negotiate; evaluate and build on the ideas of others; and select the appropriate register for effective communication. They should be taught to give well-structured descriptions and explanations and develop their understanding through speculating, hypothesising and exploring ideas. This will enable them to clarify their thinking as well as organise their ideas for writing.

(DfE, 2014)

We must teach children such skills, because they may not encounter them often, and so will not learn them indirectly. Within the classroom, we cannot be satisfied with casual conversation between children; we need to organise the sort of educationally effective talk that we know will help everyone to develop, think and learn. So it is that we need to organise talk for learning. To do so, we need to be able to say what *talk for learning* is, and be able to describe what it sounds like and achieves.

WHAT IS TALK FOR LEARNING?

We can start by saying what it is not. Every teacher is aware that children's talk is not so easily focused on learning. Children are marvellous beings: imaginative, funny, charming and inconsequential, but also anarchic and self-centred. Classrooms put children in a social setting in which much is expected of them in terms of behaviour and concentration. They can, and do, use language in ways we find difficult. They contradict one another, are unkind, insensitive or rude; they come up with irrelevant or oblique comments; they shout, laugh or don't speak at all; they make jokes and distract others; they talk but do not listen; their concentration wavers, and their thoughts drift off to their homes, games or friends. This is all fine – we want our children to be natural, chatty and confident. But we also want them to focus their minds on the educational task in hand. So we comment on talk in terms of behaviour: 'Everyone's being lovely and quiet'; 'Stop talking now please'; 'You need to listen, and no-one can listen if you're talking'.

Classes do need to learn how to be quiet and attentive. They also need to learn how and why to talk and listen to one another in ways that support everyone's learning.

Whole-class talk

Children's everyday experiences and their willingness to offer ideas for joint consideration by the class are invaluable resources. Children may rely on the teacher to tap into the minds of others on their behalf. To ensure access to this rich seam of imagination and information, teachers are required to establish a positive relationship with children, based on an understanding that everyone's ideas will be valued. Developing an environment in which every child has the confidence to be open is a slow process, but the process can be helped along by direct teaching of the knowledge, skills and understanding needed to contribute to whole-class talk.

Group talk

Children's expectations of their contribution to group talk differ enormously from what we optimistically imagine. The moment adult attention is withdrawn, a group left to work alone may find it very hard to focus on the artificial, complex and sometimes less than fascinating learning intentions that the curriculum demands. Again, direct tuition of talk skills and an understanding of why talk is so important for learning can help children to take part in effective discussions with one another in a small-group setting. The chance to hear a range of ideas or points of view can be truly motivating; children taught how to discuss things enjoy the experience and are better able to stay on task.

So what is talk for learning? Talk for learning is educationally effective talk; it is talk that is focused on the task in hand, is inclusive and equitable, and helps everyone to gain new understanding, or to articulate their inability to understand. Like everything else good that goes on in classrooms, it is unlikely to happen unless we organise it; we cannot leave this to chance. We can consider ways of organising talk for learning in two common classroom contexts:

- whole-class talk between teacher and class: *dialogic teaching*;
- children working in groups with their classmates: *exploratory talk*.

Much (though by no means all) talk for learning falls into these two contexts. A brief description of each follows, with references to further information and a summary of key points in Tables 3.6.1 and 3.6.2.

DIALOGIC TEACHING

Using dialogue as a way of thinking and learning has a long history in education (Alexander, 2006; Scott and Asoko, 2006). Dialogic teaching can be described as teaching in which the teacher is aware of the power of dialogue and creates everyday opportunities to engage children in dialogue. For example, during whole-class work, children are expected to contribute, not just brief answers, but more lengthy explanations in which they go into detail about what they do, or do not, know or understand. They listen attentively and are prepared to contribute. In this way, children work together to discuss, reflect on and modify their ideas. The teacher orchestrates the discussion to lead children through a line of thinking. Crucially, there is time to deliberate, elaborate and listen to tentative ideas. An effective lesson may contain dialogic episodes in addition to more authoritative episodes, in which the teacher sums up or clarifies the discussion and offers clear explanations.

What does dialogic teaching look and sound like?

During dialogic teaching, the class and teacher have the same aims for their learning and are engaged in pursuit of knowledge and understanding through talk. Dialogic teaching is characterised by purposeful listening, a willingness to offer ideas or make problems with learning explicit, and teacher contributions that keep the children talking. This might mean that one child is encouraged to hold the floor, or another to talk about problems with their work in a way that helps their classmates to identify solutions or strategies. Contributions are linked to generate an overall 'bigger picture' through

TABLE 3.6.1 Dialogic teaching: Talk between a teacher and a class of children

Purpose	Children summarise and share their thinking, express hypothetical ideas, admit to lack of understanding, listen to and reflect on other points of view, follow a line of reasoning
	Exploring children's thoughts
Organisation	Everyone can see and hear one another
During dialogic teaching . . .	Children pay attention to each other's words, take extended turns, ask one another questions or challenge ideas, follow up on what they hear
	The teacher chains responses into a coherent whole, orchestrates the talk, may speak very little themselves
Talk tools	What is your opinion/idea . . .? Could you say more? Have you considered . . .? Choose someone who might contribute next . . . What if . . .? Remember what * said . . .? Who would like to challenge that . . .? What is your question/idea . . .? That's helpful because . . .
Ground rules	Children are prepared to explain their thinking, ask questions, admit lack of understanding, reason, listen attentively and follow the discussion
	Teacher elicits contributions and maintains a focus on a line of thinking or reasoning
Outcomes	Shared understanding and developing knowledge; respect for ideas; awareness of the limits of understanding, leading to productive questioning and learning
Notes	Children may need input in active listening
	Some may have an unwillingness to contribute or take an extended turn, and need positive support
	There may be problems with admitting to lack of understanding
	Children need to know that their contributions are of value to others

which children can make connections with previous learning. A feature of dialogue is that questions are raised that, instead of leading to immediate, brief answers, lead to further questions, a discussion of detail or recognition that more information is required. Such talk fosters children's natural curiosity.

EXPLORATORY TALK

Exploratory talk is talk in which children engage one another in a good discussion. Children draw on what they have been taught about talk for learning. They are aware of the importance of their talk and take responsibility for their own learning and that of the others in their group. Each child is invited or encouraged to contribute. All information is shared. Opinions are backed up with reasons and discussed with respect. In addition, the talk may be hesitant, as half-formed ideas are tentatively suggested, or particular points may be taken up and elaborated in some detail. Children may not be aware that this is what we require when we ask them to work in a group; direct teaching of the essential skills and understanding is necessary (Mercer and Littleton, 2007).

Exploratory talk requires shared motivation and purpose; when it happens, it enables children in a group to achieve more than each child would alone, whatever their ability. Crucially, their talk with classmates enables the child to internalise the structures of reasoned discussion. By doing so they learn a powerful and indelible way to think as an individual.

TABLE 3.6.2 Exploratory talk: Talk between groups of children with no adult support

Purpose	Inclusive talk to enable joint problem-solving; sharing of ideas, opinions and reasons; negotiation
Organisation	Three children seated near one another, around a table
During exploratory talk . . .	All are invited to contribute; ideas and opinions are offered with reasons; information is shared; the group seeks to reach agreement; everyone listens; the group is on task
Talk tools	What do you think? Why do you think that? I agree because . . . I disagree because . . . What do we know about . . . ? I think . . . Shall we decide that . . . ? Wait a minute . . . But . . . Have we explained about . . . ? What is your reason?
Ground rules	Everyone is invited to speak by others; contributions are treated with respect; reasons are asked for, and given; ideas are considered fully before agreement is reached
Outcomes	Group agreement on a joint solution, idea or course of action. Group responsibility for decisions Children support one another's thinking
Notes	The task or activity must necessitate discussion Children need preparation; they must have an awareness of talk for learning, and have thought about and created a set of their own shared class ground rules for exploratory talk

What does exploratory talk look and sound like?

Children work closely in groups, using exploratory talk. They are able to use questions as talk tools – 'What do you think?', 'Why do you think that?' – and as prompts – 'Can you say what you know about . . . ?', 'Tell us what happened . . .', 'Please explain . . .'. They can be heard to offer hypothetical ideas – 'What if . . . ?', 'But . . .' – and to elaborate on ideas – 'Yes, but remember when we did this before, we . . .'. They listen attentively to one another, and their talk is courteous and purposeful, characterised by a degree of challenge and explicit reasoning. Every child in the group can give an account or summary of the discussion, having been fully engaged in it.

WHEN AND HOW TO MOVE BETWEEN TYPES OF TALK

We can plan talk for learning without being able to say precisely how the talk will proceed. We have to rely on our professional expertise to decide when and how to switch between types of talk. We can generalise a little to say that:

- *Whole-class introductory dialogue* requires authoritative input, such as clear instructions and information. We might use the sorts of question that simply check for items of knowledge: 'What did we do last week?', 'Remind us of the difference between an isosceles and equilateral triangle?', 'Where do herons lay their eggs?'. Some of these questions might be targeted at individuals and often have a behavioural function: the question 'Jason, what is your answer to this?' is a way of ensuring Jason's involvement without actually saying, 'Are you listening, Jason?'. After more than 5 minutes of such closed questions, children are not usually learning much. Some children always involve themselves with this particular sort of questioning; some do just the opposite. It is not motivating to think of answers to questions when you know that the questioner already knows the answer they require.

Introductions benefit from more complex dialogue, in which we ask genuine questions: 'What do you already know about . . . ?', 'Has anyone heard of anything about this that might help us . . . ?', 'What is your experience of this . . . ?'.

- *Group work* requires children to engage one another in exploratory talk. The teacher's role is, first, to ensure that the children have been taught the structures of exploratory talk and, second, to listen in, support the children's work and move on. We can model exploratory talk as we move around the groups: 'Could you give a reason please?', 'Does anyone have any more information we can think about?', 'Has everyone been asked for their ideas?'.

  A problem with exploratory talk is that a persuasive argument can sway a whole group into believing things that are not necessarily true. However, as the talk is part of an ongoing classroom dialogue, the group is subsequently able to hear other ideas from their classmates and can reconsider. Ideas established during discussion may not be firmly held until the child has had a chance to check them against practical experience and the ideas of others. Thinking about new ideas - 'weighing things up' and reflecting on how new ideas fit with one's own current thinking - is a learning process and an invaluable experience for a child. The chance to reject or accept an idea enables children to understand that they are responsible for their own learning and to create their own ideas as they speak, listen and think with others.

Task 3.6.1 Children's classroom talk

Listen carefully to children's classroom talk in two contexts – a whole class in discussion with a teacher, and a small-group discussion with no adult support. Ask yourself questions about the purpose, organisation and outcomes of the talk.

- *Purpose*: What is the purpose of the talk? Is everyone aware of this purpose? Is the talk fulfilling its purpose?
- *Organisation*: Who is organising the talk? How do people bid for turns? Who gets a turn and why? What happens to people who do not get a turn? Is any of the talk to do with behaviour management? Does the talk always stay on task?
- *Outcomes*: What are the outcomes of the talk? What have different individuals learned about (1) the topic under discussion, (2) their position in the classroom, (3) how to communicate effectively with others?

- *Whole-class closing plenary sessions* require dialogue that brings together the children's ideas from their group work. The teacher's role is to ensure that there is plenty of time for talk and to orchestrate the dialogue. In addition, there is often the necessity for some authoritative summary information. Dialogic teaching can be thought of as including episodes of exploratory talk and episodes of authoritative teacher input, which will later contribute to further dialogue. Plenary discussion should bring out children's thinking about new concepts and also about the quality of the talk that took place in their group work. You can ask children to suggest who offered ideas, listened carefully, asked an important question, and so on.

RAISING CHILDREN'S AWARENESS OF TALK FOR LEARNING

Organising effective talk involves raising children's awareness of the power of spoken language. Children need to know that they contribute to the learning of others through sharing their thoughts.

Some children may never have imagined that this is the case. Others may find it difficult to contribute orally in a classroom context.

The teacher is a powerful model for educationally effective talk. The phrases we use in whole-class talk, such as 'What do you think?', 'Can you explain your reason please?', 'Can you say a bit more about . . .?', are exactly what we want children to say to one another. Encouraging someone to keep talking, making links between contributions, rephrasing and summing up are all skills children learn from experience, especially if they happen often and are explicitly discussed as talk strategies.

If we are honest, we know that group work can go wrong. The classroom becomes too noisy, or little learning seems to be happening. When children are in discussion in small groups, the teacher cannot know what every child is saying. Children in a group may bicker or deliberately ignore one another; they may feel that helping others is not helping their own learning, or that others are 'cheating' if they want to talk about their answers. It is instructive to ask children what they think of group work.

However, we know that talk is essential for learning. This is a real paradox and a problem for every teacher. We want to ensure effective group talk because what is the alternative? We must insist on quiet. The command 'Please be quiet!' immediately confines each child to their own thoughts – sometimes, an uneasy silence reigns. Silence is a behaviour management strategy and not always conducive to developing minds. No doubt quiet has some value, but not if it is overused, and not when a child is trying to puzzle something out, explain something, use a recently heard word, ask a question or find out a missing piece of information. And silence cannot guarantee that children are thinking and learning about the topic in hand.

So, 'talk lessons' are necessary – that is, before you expect them to conduct a good discussion, children need direct teaching about exploratory talk. We need to make explicit the usually hidden 'ground rules' that keep a discussion on track (Dawes, 2008, 2011).

What talk skills are needed? In essence, the ground rules that children need are to:

- listen;
- stay on task;
- include everyone;
- know how to ask what others think and why;
- respect contributions;
- ask questions;
- elaborate and explain.

This list can be used to devise learning intentions for lessons that focus on each skill in turn. There are innumerable contexts for talk throughout the curriculum. After an activity in which groups have talked about their thinking, plenary discussion about the effectiveness of talk can help children to build up an awareness of their ability to contribute to one another's learning, and can help groups to establish an ethos of exploratory talk. Importantly, the child's own world of talk, that is their accent, bilingualism, vocabulary, dialect and indeed personality, is valued rather than diminished by learning exploratory talk as an extension to their talk repertoire.

So, we can discuss and model relevant talk skills during introductory sessions, identify them as learning intentions and review them during plenary sessions, and thus help children to experience and evaluate the difference good talk makes. Children need constant chances to reflect on what they have said and heard, in order to examine what they have learned, and how, and who from. They need opportunities to identify particular talk episodes that helped them to understand, or caught their imagination, or made them feel puzzled. They need to acknowledge who it is that has contributed orally. It has to be made clear to children that knowledge and understanding are not simply contained in the teacher, computers or books, but in the class as a whole, and that, by talking and thinking together, such understandings can be profitably shared. They can usefully learn the term 'interthinking' – thinking aloud together – as a description of the spoken mechanism for creating joint understanding (Littleton and Mercer, 2013). Children given a direct insight into the idea of interthinking, and taught the skills to take part in interthinking, can see how to find out what others think, and why. They can articulate their own ideas. They can include themselves in the everyday educational conversations of their classroom. For some children, this makes a huge difference to their engagement. For others, it overcomes barriers caused by wider social issues or their personal inhibitions. For all children, interthinking is a life skill.

Effective talk modelled by the teacher

Year 4: Talk for writing

The teacher identified two children who found writing especially difficult. Yasmin found it hard to put ideas on paper and tended to 'pretend' write, with her work under the table and her head down. Alfie took every opportunity to be distracted and was halted by the least difficulty in spelling, because he hated to write words inaccurately.

The teacher asked each child to specify a friend in the class and invited the friends to join the new writing activity. She asked, 'Why do you like your friend?' The children talked about this in a group of four, while the teacher modelled exploratory talk and jotted down key phrases and sentences. She then provided each pair with a copy of what she had written and asked them to read this together and to decide if it really said what they wanted it to; if not, they should make changes. Once this was done – with all children contributing some of the writing – she combined their ideas to create this poem:

Friends

> I like my friend because he's funny and he's strong.
> My friend is really pretty and she helps me all the time.
> She helps me carry things.
> My friend passes the ball to me,
> He is on my side in football.
> If he's not playing I'm not playing.
> I can ask my friend anything. And she asks me.
> My friend has time to give me.

This piece of writing was then available to be keyed in, handwritten, displayed, taken home, illustrated, read and re-read and used as a model for other pairs of friends writing in the class. In addition, there was a chance to concentrate on spelling specific words, such as 'friend', 'football', 'passes', and so on; and to look at capital letters and the use of commas and full stops to convey meaning.

Task 3.6.2 New vocabulary

Discuss with colleagues how they tackle teaching children new vocabulary. How frequently does this happen? How do they ensure new words are put to use? What links are there with reading and writing?

Children learn to talk by listening and using what they hear. New words and how to use them are learned at school – the more the better! The written symbols of the English language represent sounds, and reading is what happens when sounds are put back into texts. So, reading and speaking are inextricably linked, and a child's capacity to read is profoundly dependent on their capacity to speak and listen. New vocabulary should be a daily acquisition through spoken language.

Task 3.6.3 Children's rules for classroom talk

Work with a group of three or four children. Ask them to discuss their ideas with you.

- When they are working in a group with classmates, who do they like to work with and why? What do they like or dislike about working in a group with other children? Why do they think that teachers ask them to work in groups?
- Ask the children to suggest a list of five or six positive 'rules', which, if applied, would help a group to work well together. Compare their suggestions with the ground rules for exploratory talk in Table 3.6.2.
- Have the same discussion with the whole class. Collate ideas to establish a class set of ground rules for exploratory talk. Devise an activity that requires group discussion and ask the children to try to apply their rules. Did the rules help everyone to join in and share ideas? If not, can the class alter them?

PLANNING FOR EXPLORATORY TALK

Paired learning objectives can ensure exploratory talk. During planning, pair up a learning objective for talk with your curriculum learning objective. In this way, you can teach skills that are tailored to class or individual needs, practise their use, and reflect on their effectiveness in closing plenary discussions, within curriculum contexts. Include some time for discussion. Talk invariably takes longer than you would imagine, and there is a limit to time in any classroom situation. Unless you plan for discussion time, children will lose the chance to articulate, develop and reflect on their ideas, use new vocabulary and generally think things through properly.

Example 3.6.1 is a brief example of a lesson outline, with science as a context for the talk.

Suggestions for further work using talk for learning objectives

- Identify and use objectives for specific talk skills in curriculum lessons.
- Choose one particular talk objective, teach the skills directly and integrate throughout a week.
- Ask children to identify their particular problems with spoken language in class.
- Make the link between speaking, listening, thinking and learning explicit at all times.
- Encourage children to see that learning cannot happen unless certain sorts of talk go on – and unless voices are modulated, contributions are thoughtful, and everyone in the class is included in effective discussions.
- Create a 'speaking and listening for thinking and learning' display.

Example 3.6.1 Science and talk lesson

This lesson features paired learning objectives. The aim is to be able to:

- offer reasons and evidence for views, considering alternative opinions;
- identify some starting ideas about the topic of friction.

Introduction

Ask children to explain to one another what the words *reasons*, *evidence* and *alternative opinions* mean; then share with the class. Then think about friction to find out what everyone already knows.

Group work

Ask groups to discuss the following *Talking Points* (Dawes, 2012).

Talking points: Friction

True or false, or is your group unsure? Make sure you give reasons for what you say.

1 Grip is another word for friction.
2 Friction always happens when surfaces are moving against each other.
3 Friction is usually a nuisance.
4 Trainers have friction built into the soles.

Focus the children on active listening and ask them to try to remember something that they think is particularly interesting from their group talk.

Plenary

1 *Science*: Choose a talking point to discuss. Ask groups to contribute ideas about friction; what were contradictory opinions? Ask groups to explain their ideas and reasons. Sum up, or ask a child to sum up, the outcome of the discussion.
2 *Talk for learning*: Ask the class to suggest classmates who offered ideas, listened well, gave good reasons, summed up discussions and helped negotiation.

Ask children to reflect, recall and share examples of productive talk; who gave an *opinion* and what was their *reason*? This session would be followed by practical activity in which children have a chance to learn about friction through experience.

LISTENING

It can be useful to track a child during their school day. Who listens to them? Do they have a voice in the classroom? Some do; they are heard. They contribute. Others may not have the skills to be in this position. Every child should have a voice if the class is to learn well and as a whole. Listening to classmates is essential if all voices are to be heard. The skills of listening – such as attending, considering words and nonverbal messages, reflecting and responding – can be developed once they are made explicit. Listening for learning is a very active process and quite demanding, but ultimately truly satisfying and rewarding. Children need to experience such listening so that they can appreciate its rewards and take pride in their own skill. Whole books and websites are devoted to describing and explaining listening. Listening for learning is not innate and not something that just happens. A week at the start of every term might be usefully dedicated to taking part in listening activities, with the aim of ensuring that every child understands how to hear and process spoken language, how to reflect and respond appropriately, and thus how to enjoy their own learning.

SUMMARY

We cannot just leave classroom talk to chance. Children learn new ways to talk in school. Exploratory talk and effective listening require direct teaching. Talk is such an everyday medium that children may take it for granted, but they should be taught as much about talk as they are about reading and writing. Talk can be so bound up with classroom behaviour that its crucial function of stimulating and developing thinking may be unclear to children.

Dialogic teaching is a means to move whole classes through steps of reasoning, hypothesis and deduction, by valuing contributions and encouraging reflection. By employing a dialogic approach and simultaneously teaching children how to engage one another in exploratory talk, we offer them opportunities to work on their own thinking and that of others. Exploratory talk is educationally effective talk – talk for learning – and children need an awareness of what it is and why it's important. The everyday occurrence of talk for learning can only happen if we organise classrooms by planning time for talk and by using resources and activities that merit discussion. Effective teachers move between different types of talk as a lesson proceeds. Every child needs to know how and why to listen actively if they are to develop their thinking and make the most of learning opportunities.

Engaging children in talk for learning helps teachers to develop effective classroom relationships. Talking about what they are doing with their group helps to motivate children and focus their interest. The busy hum of a classroom in which children are discussing their work – a sure sign of a well-organised teacher – is a happy feature of effective primary schools. Teachers want to hear children talking: it is an indication of learning and a sign that children are practising the talk skills that will help develop their minds throughout their education.

 ## ANNOTATED FURTHER READING

Dawes, L. and Sams, C. (2017) *Talk Box: Activities for Teaching Oracy with Children aged 4–8*, 2nd edn, London: Routledge.

> This updated and fully revised version of *Talk Box* (2004) contains comprehensive activities to teach talk skills, encourage interthinking and ensure that every child starts by learning to understand the repertoire of talk that will enable them to make best progress in school. It has maths, science, stories, poems, cross-curricular activities and suggestions for a variety of 'Talk Boxes' to motivate, engage and teach throughout the school day.

FURTHER READING TO SUPPORT M-LEVEL STUDY

Rutter, R., Edwards, R. and Dean, P. (2016) 'Who's that talking in my class? What does research say about pupil to pupil exploratory talk that leads to learning?', *Teacher Education Advancement Network Journal*, 8(1): 22-32.

> A focus on secondary education but with great value for the primary teacher in its clear and concise review of literature relevant to both phases, its evaluation of types of classroom talk, its focus on exploratory talk and subsequent learning outcomes, and the breadth of its advice for teachers and school leaders.

Mercer, N. (2008) 'The seeds of time: Why classroom dialogue needs a temporal analysis', *Journal of the Learning Sciences*, 17(1): 33-59.

> 'The relationship between time, talk, and learning is intrinsically important to classroom education [. . .] The coherence of educational experience is dependent on talk' (p. 55).

Smith, H. and Higgins, S. (2006) 'Opening classroom interaction: The importance of feedback', *Cambridge Journal of Education*, 36(4): 485-502.

> 'It is arguable that it is neither the act of asking questions itself, nor, as we have argued, the types of questions teachers ask, which limits pupil response. Rather, it is the feedback given in reaction to pupil responses and the historical precedence of the perception of teacher intent this engenders, which either opens or restricts classroom interaction' (p. 500).

 RELEVANT WEBSITES

Thinking Together project: thinkingtogether.educ.cam.ac.uk

> A dialogue-based approach to thinking and learning in classrooms. This site offers links to classroom-based research and downloadable materials for classroom use.

The Communication Trust: www.thecommunicationtrust.org.uk/

> The Communication Trust (CT) is a coalition of more than fifty not-for-profit organisations. Working together, the CT supports everyone who works with children and young people in England to support their speech, language and communication.

Learning, Playing and Interacting: www.keap.org.uk/documents/LearningPlayingInteracting.pdf

> It may not always be clear how play and direct teaching work together - this useful document answers some difficult questions and stresses the value of talking with children.

 REFERENCES

Alexander, R. (2006) *Towards Dialogic Teaching*, York, UK: Dialogos.

Dawes, L. (2008) *The Essential Speaking and Listening: Talk for Learning at Key Stage 2*, London: Routledge.

Dawes, L. (2011) *Creating a Speaking and Listening Classroom: Integrating Talk for Learning at Key Stage 2*, London: Routledge.

Dawes, L. (2012) *Talking Points: Discussion Activities in the Primary Classroom*, London: Routledge.

Department for Education (DfE). (2014) *The National Curriculum*, DfE. Retrieved from www.gov.uk/national-curriculum (accessed 9 November 2017).

Littleton, K. and Mercer, N. (2013) *Interthinking: Putting Talk to Work*, London: Routledge.

Mercer, N. and Littleton, K. (2007) *Dialogue and the Development of Children's Thinking: A Sociocultural Approach*, London: Routledge.

Scott, P.H. and Asoko, H. (2006) 'Talk in science classrooms', in V. Wood-Robinson (ed.) *Association of Science Education Guide to Secondary Science Education*, Hatfield, UK: Association for Science Education (ASE).

Smith, H. and Higgins, S. (2006) 'Opening classroom interaction: The importance of feedback', *Cambridge Journal of Education*, 36(4): 485–502.

THE VALUE OF OUTDOOR LEARNING

Stephen Pickering

INTRODUCTION

For learning beyond the classroom's four walls to be truly valued, it needs to be considered by management, teachers, pupils and parents to be a fundamental element of every child's formal education. It should be seen to be as normal a part of school life as teaching indoors. Teaching outdoors can be fun, stimulating, exciting and rewarding, and it can be all of these things without being seen as a treat, a reward, or a special Welly Wednesday (Pickering, 2017). We all appreciate the importance of creating a vibrant environment within the school to aid the holistic development and progress of the children in our care. Working outside the classroom expands and enriches this learning environment.

Learning beyond the classroom is fully endorsed by the Early Years Foundation Stage (EYFS), where a strong emphasis is placed on the value of daily outdoor learning experiences for children's health, well-being and intellectual development (DfE, 2014: section 3.58, p. 28). It is also fully supported by the National Curriculum in England (DfE, 2013) across a range of subject areas and is included within the Ofsted inspection framework (Children, Schools and Families Committee, 2010). Beyond emphasising the need for a broad, balanced curriculum in a holistic sense, the National Curriculum in England (DfE, 2013) also states (in a number of areas), 'The national curriculum forms one part of the school curriculum' (DfE, 2014: Section 2.2, p. 5). Simply put, this means that, as well as teaching the National Curriculum through broad, balanced, safe environments, including the outdoor as well as the indoor environments, any school should develop its own school curriculum, of which the National Curriculum is a part. Every school has licence to develop a curriculum that reflects and develops understanding of local communities and beyond. So, if your school is in an urban environment, then explore that urban environment. If your school is very rural, then embrace the natural or farmed landscape as part of your curriculum. 'Education influences and reflects the values of society, and the kind of society we want to be' (DfEE/QCA, 1999).

In Northern Ireland . . .

> Young children's basic need for well-being and involvement, and their urge to explore and make sense of the world, is developed through high-quality play in an outdoor environment.
>
> (Council for Curriculum, Examination and Assessment, 2005: 16)

Source: Early Years Inter-board Panel (2005) *Learning Outdoors: In the Early Years*, Belfast: CCEA Publication. Retrieved from https://ccea.org.uk/sites/default/files/docs/curriculum/area_of_learning/fs_learning_outdoors_resource_book.pdf (accessed 25 October 2017).

OBJECTIVES

By the end of this unit, you should be able to:

- appreciate the value and benefits of children experiencing outdoor environments and of developing learning beyond the classroom;
- identify opportunities in your own planning and teaching to make effective and enjoyable use of outdoor spaces;
- plan to support the holistic development of children in your class through learning outdoors;
- help to provide the motivation and confidence to teach outside.

THE TEACHERS' STANDARDS

These objectives reflect the requirements in the Teachers' Standards for trainee teachers. Planning for learning and teaching outside involves meeting the standards for teaching, including, 'setting high expectations which inspire, motivate and challenge pupils' (Standard 1), planning and teaching 'well-structured lessons' (Standard 4) and 'managing behaviour effectively to ensure a good and safe learning environment' (Standard 7, DfE, 2012).

Task 3.7.1 Reflection

It is valuable to reflect upon your own understanding and experiences of learning and taking part in outdoor activities, not just as part of your schooling, but also through other outdoor activities such as Scouts and Guides, camps or adventurous pursuits and travel that you may have engaged in.

- For each of a range of outdoor experiences that you may have had, reflect on and note down how you felt and what you learned. Remember that learning is not just about knowledge gained, but also about challenges managed and experiences learned from.
- Could the learning, or the style of learning, you experienced in outdoor activities not associated with school be replicated through taking a class of children outdoors to learn?
- Discuss whether children should always be aware of the learning outcomes. And, if so, whether this is always possible. Should learning outcomes focus on the acquisition of knowledge alone?

THE VALUE OF LEARNING AND TEACHING OUTDOORS

The largest research on outdoor learning with school-aged children in England to date, the Natural Connections Demonstration project (Waite *et al.*, 2016), which involved 40,000 primary and secondary children, from 125 urban and rural schools, across a 4-year period, provides some over-whelmingly positive statistics, with more than 82 per cent of schools surveyed describing how outdoor learning improves social skills, pupils' health and well-being, and behaviour. Additionally, more than 69 per cent of teachers surveyed claimed that outdoor learning had a positive impact on their teaching, professional development and job satisfaction. With such positive results clamouring for more learning and teaching to take place in the outdoors, it is a shame that another large survey, conducted within the same time period, concluded that only '8 percent of children (aged 6–15) in England visited the natural environment with their schools in an average month during 2013–2015' (Cutler, 2016, reporting on Natural England, 2016). One of the principle reasons given for this low figure, set against such powerful statistics highlighting the potential benefits, is a lack of teacher confidence when teaching in outdoor environments.

The values of learning and teaching outdoors operate on a number of levels:

1   *Cognition*: Outdoor environments tend to be messy places, and, by messy, I do not necessarily mean that they are muddy, wet and dirty (although sometimes they are), but that they are disordered (Catling and Pickering, 2010). Forests, woodlands, playgrounds, beaches and urban areas are complex places and as such provide many opportunities for problem-solving, planning and enquiry-based work. Take, for example, den building. Children have a complex set of issues to manage and resolve when constructing and creating a den, large, safe and secure enough to house a group of children, with irregular materials, a short timescale and a variety of tools and resources at their disposal (Lamb, in Knight, 2011). There are clear links here to design and technology and mathematics, as well as science, and the questions that may well arise can also include history and geography as part of the learning curricula, too. More important for the learner, though, than the teacher's ability to monitor rich cross-curricular learning, is the fact that the children will be engaging in a wide range of thinking skills and a variety of learning processes. The outdoors can become an 'intellectually playful classroom' (Eyre and Staricoff, in Cremin and Arthur, 2011), where children are encouraged to reflect deeply, monitor progress and modify their approach until they achieve success. Even failure can be fun and is also a valid learning experience. Children will develop their own questioning skills as they learn to collaborate on the task. Children tend to work very happily and independently with the freedom that learning outside provides, but the learning skills and processes used by the children can be brought back into the classroom with some judicious plenary work by the teacher. Metacognition simply means becoming aware of your own thinking. If, as a teacher, you can help children to reflect on and understand the thinking skills that they used to build the den, then later, perhaps back in the classroom, you can help children to re-engage with such skills gained for other problem-solving exercises. So, for example, the child stuck on a maths problem in the classroom can be reminded that she achieved success with the den by sorting and categorising the sticks before using them and then planning how best to apply them. 'Can you do the same type of thing to solve this maths problem?'

2   *Health and well-being*: Every one of us, I think, has experienced the restorative effect of being outside to a certain extent. Just think about how our breathing often relaxes when we step outside, or about the feeling of having done something good, when we step back inside after a walk. We all have a sense that being outside is good. But just how good can it be, and can time spent outside with children during a school day be justified as an important part of their learning and development? Teachers, after all, face constant time pressure with a bulging curriculum. The 'biophilia hypothesis', first postulated by Wilson in 1984, suggests that the natural world has a positive influence on our emotional, cognitive and aesthetic development (Jordan, 2015). The notion of 'nature deficit disorder' (Louv, 2005), whereby symptoms of stress, anxiety and behaviour issues may correlate with a lack of engagement with natural spaces, is predated by Kaplan and Kaplan (Kaplan and Kaplan, 1989; Kaplan 1995) and 'Attention Restoration Theory', where the restorative effect of being outside and away from the multiple distractions that children face within the classroom environments helps them to learn to become better focused on tasks

in hand. Indeed, Reese and Myers (2012) cite a wealth of research-based literature to support the argument that regular time spent outdoors contributes to the health and well-being of individuals. As a teacher, I always found enormous – although not always immediately apparent – benefits in chatting to individual children while walking along the path that led to the school's Forest School site. There is an undeniable freedom that children enjoy when outside walking to something they love, and this is a super opportunity to let children open up about events and thoughts in their life: both positive and negative. This is precious time for teachers and children, and the space afforded by time outside helps children to relax into their lives, focus on something different and recharge their batteries during busy school weeks.

3   *Motivation and aspiration*: Children love creating things, experimenting and trying things out. They love to learn by doing. Experiential learning is motivational. There is neurological evidence (Goswami, 2008), but this can perhaps be described more simply as learning through a process of hand to heart to head. Children engage actively with a subject by touching and feeling, moving, building and working with tools and resources. The very texture of wood, or mud, or soft grass, or even bricks promotes some form of emotional response, and this is coupled with the satisfaction of achieving a task independently, or problem-solving, or working as a group. Learning fixes in the brain for longer if it passes through the brain's emotional receptors, and so this emotional response is crucial for developing learning and learning skills. And then, during the activity, and afterwards too, children will think and reflect. They will engage in reasoning skills, perhaps justifying why they completed the activity in a certain way, or synthesising a range of suggested ideas in order to complete the task. In other words, learning outdoors provides the opportunity for learning to pass through the hands to the heart to the head and, in so doing, become better fixed in the learning memory and more satisfying to complete. Success motivates children to achieve more, but actually failure can do so, too, if failure is seen as part of learning and is used as a platform from which to develop new skills, ideas and practices. This way of thinking is not new. Vygotsky's theories of learning and child development run deeper than a simplistic understanding of constructivism. Vygotsky described how social interaction is the cornerstone of learning, based within a cultural construct. Learners collaborate and learn as they participate, developing as they make sense of the 'goals, practices, and tools common to the activities of which they are a part' (Seaman and Gingo, in Smith and Knapp, 2011: 160). Seaman and Gingo describe how various studies (the Rogoff Study, 1995, the Seaman Study, 2007, and the Emo study, 2006) provide examples to show how learning experientially outdoors follows the same process of hand to heart to head to cement learning. Beyond the classroom walls, pupils tend to be free of the behaviourist – reward and sanction – classroom management practices that Vygotsky railed against in early twentieth-century Russia and that are still apparent in many classrooms today. Deep learning can develop through enjoyable, motivational activities in accord with constructivist processes of development.

4   *Responsibility and independence*: Forest School philosophy advocates pedagogies based on allowing children to experience and learn over a long period of time (www.forestschool association.org). I have known teachers to become frustrated with the repetitive nature of some children's activities while out on Forest School. Given the choice, for example, some children will head straight into den building every week. There is an argument that, although such practice may well be repetitive and thus limit new learning, it may actually serve a very important part of a child's development. In permitting children to develop their own learning experiences while offering a range of opportunities, responsibility and independent incremental learning are nurtured. Outdoor activities are very experience-based, and not just through the joy of exploring outdoor environments, but also through the social learning that can develop. Consider the montage of photos in Figure 3.7.1.

Robin was determined to set up a swing with some rope he had, but he couldn't reach the branch. When Robin wanted help in a classroom situation, he tended to put his hand up and wait for help to arrive. If it didn't arrive, then he would either just sit there, or go and confront the teacher or teaching assistant. On seeing that there was no help readily available, and being determined to succeed, he looked around, spied a log used for sitting on, rolled it until it was under the branch and then, through a process of trial and error, finally managed to stand on it and reach the branch. By this time, he had attracted a small audience and so he then proudly demonstrated how he could reach the branch and he helped his friends to do the same. This is a very simple example of the type of practice that occurs in Forest Schools and other similar outdoor provisions up and down the country on a daily basis, but within such simple steps taken there is a great deal of learning. The slow or 'eco pedagogical approach' (Payne and Wattchow, 2009) provides time for children to work things out for themselves. This is a clear demonstration of constructive, incremental learning: pausing to think about the resources to hand, reviewing and problem-solving. And there are the additional aspects of multisensory learning: the thrill of finally reaching up to grab the branch will remain with Robin and help to cement the thinking skills needed to achieve success again, coupled with the additional personal satisfaction of then helping others – learning is social!

5   *Collaboration and communication*: Froebel advocated the importance of play as a learning tool in the early nineteenth century, describing it as 'the serious business of childhood' (Froebel, in Carroll and McCullogh, 2014: 31). Play promotes the effective use of imagination and creativity, self-expression and the development of many skills (depending upon the type of play), such as language acquisition, emotional intelligence, social skills and, importantly, 'the capacity to act and to recognise that actions have consequences' (James and James, 2004: 24). There is an important element of playing outdoors that adds scope to the development of imagination. Within the classroom, children's play makes use of purpose-made resources: a toy car is a car, a plastic dinosaur is a plastic dinosaur. In a woodland, children have little more than twigs and leaves, mud and stones. But this fosters creativity and imagination. A stick can be a car, or a plane, a fairy home or a magic wand. The unconstructed and messy nature of natural resources provides greater freedom to develop imagination and imaginative play. And, because one child's entrance to a secret medieval kingdom may look like just a hole in a bush to another child, there is a natural development of communication skills: of talking and listening, describing and contributing, taking part and acceptance.

In Scotland . . .

The core values of *Curriculum for Excellence* resonate with long-standing key concepts of outdoor learning. Challenge, enjoyment, relevance, depth, development of the whole person and an adventurous approach to learning are at the core of outdoor pedagogy. The outdoor environment encourages staff and students to see each other in a different light, building positive relationships and improving self-awareness and understanding of others.

(Scottish Government, 2010: 7)

Source: Scottish Government. (2010) *Curriculum for Excellence through Outdoor Learning*. Retrieved from https://education.gov.scot/improvement/Documents/hwb24-cfe-through-outdoor-learning.pdf (accessed 25 October 2017).

FIGURE 3.7.1 Learning through independent play

ORGANISING AND MANAGING LEARNING AND TEACHING OUTDOORS

First, you must consider how the learning outcomes, and by this I mean all that you wish the children to gain academically, socially and in terms of developing further skills for learning, can best be served by activities outside or inside. When you are planning a lesson, clearly the whole lesson does not have to be in one set environment, so consider how the needs of the children are best met at each stage of the lesson. Part of these lesson-planning decisions involve looking at the bigger picture of children's learning, too. How would a lesson outside contribute to more than just the lesson itself, but as part of a whole programme of holistic education.

In Wales . . .

Planning and supporting a balance of child-initiated and adult-led tasks is as important outdoors as it is indoors. Without appropriate planning children may not have the opportunities to move on in their development and learning. Time spent outdoors must be purposeful if children are to gain skills and knowledge from playful experiences and make good progress. Children need to be supported outdoors by enthusiastic practitioners who provide and model good quality play so that they don't see it as an opportunity for disorganised playtime.

(Learning Wales, 2014: 4)

Source: Learning Wales. (2014) *Further Steps Outdoors: Guidance*, Cardiff: Welsh Assembly Government. Retrieved from http://learning.gov.wales/docs/learningwales/publications/141013-further-steps-outdoors-en.pdf (accessed 25 October 2017).

Task 3.7.2 Taking children out of the classroom

Use the Ofsted evaluation, *Learning outside the Classroom*, supplemented by recent case studies (accessible through www.gov.uk/search?q=outdoor&filter_organisations=ofsted) to review the benefits and challenges of taking children to work outside the classroom. Go to the Ofsted website (www.gov.uk/government/organisations/ofsted) to review recent subject reports, too. Once you have reviewed the benefits and barriers, you can apply the same processes to reviewing the potential for your school to develop outdoor learning.

CASE STUDY: A VEGETABLE GARDEN

As part of a class topic on food from around the world, the class teacher, Stephen, decided to engage the help of parents and children to create a vegetable garden. The children had to research, design and present their gardens in groups, and the best garden design – based on a range of criteria – was chosen. Local community help was enlisted, with parents wielding spades and a grandfather giving a talk about how to grow vegetables, to help the children design and create their vegetable garden. The topic area was food from around the world, and so children were given the task – after conducting favourite-food surveys in class – of finding out just where and how various fruit and vegetables grow best. The start of a school partnership with a school in the Gambia heralded a slight change of direction. Stephen realised that the children's knowledge of everyday Gambian life was scant, and that misconceptions were based on more general stories about Africa derived mainly from charity campaigns. So, he arranged for the children from the partnership schools to find out what was grown locally and to try growing each other's fruit and vegetables. An initial, striking, positive outcome was that, when the English and Gambian children discovered that they grew many of the same crops – such as onions and greens – there was a shift from considering the children as different to seeing each other as pretty much the same. A connection was made between the children, after which they learned all about science and design technology and geography and sustainability by trying to grow, for example, bananas in England and apples in the Gambia.

Planning a lesson using the outdoors requires the same degree of thought and care that a lesson indoors requires, but it is not simply the learning space that may change. Teaching outdoors requires a different management approach, a holistic set of learning objectives and, simply because it is a different environment, a different set of safety measures to have in place. Some teachers may be put off by a perception of additional safety and risk assessment that is required for outdoor teaching. In fact, the focus on risk assessment and safety is no different from inside a classroom. In both situations, the safety and well-being of the children in your care are paramount. The difference does not occur in the *focus* on safety, only in the types of risk you need to assess and plan to manage.

In Northern Ireland . . .

Learning outside can encourage better problem solving, critical thinking, inquiry skills and self-management in pupils. . . . It is important to frame your activity with the pupils before you leave the classroom. Giving the activity context and sharing the learning expectations with the pupils will help keep them more focused on the task outside.

(Eco-schools: 9)

Source: http://eco-schoolsni.org/eco-schoolsni/documents/007123.pdf (accessed 25 October 2017).

You would probably never consider walking straight into a classroom to teach without knowing how the tables were set out, what resources were available and how any technology worked, and so it is with an outdoor learning environment. It is vital to visit the place first and complete an assessment of resources and space and possible hazards or risks. Risk/benefit assessments can be quite daunting, as they appear to carry a burden of responsibility, but then you are always responsible for the children in your care, whether you are in or out, and the aim is simply to identify any risk so that it can be managed safely. You should complete your first risk/benefit assessments with a colleague who has experience of risk assessments and then get this checked and signed by the head teacher or designated safety officer for your school. Each school will have policies for teaching off-site and for health and safety. Additionally, every local authority will have a set of regulations. Many institutions, such as the Council for Learning Outside the Classroom (www.lotc.org.uk) and the Forest School Association (www.forestschoolassociation.org), offer support and advice. *Nothing Ventured* (Gill, 2010) is an excellent starting point. Figure 3.7.2 is an example of a risk/benefit assessment template provided by Bishops Wood Centre in Worcestershire (www.field-studies-council.org/centres/bishopswood.aspx)

a centre that specialises in providing excellent quality outdoor learning opportunities for local schools and community groups. It is worth looking to see who provides such support in your local area. A second consideration when assessing the risks associated with a different learning environment concerns any risks associated with the activities. Managing children in an outdoor environment, where there is clearly greater freedom of movement requires many eyes! Make sure you follow the school and local authority guidelines for adult:pupil ratio. These vary according to the age of the children and the nature of the tasks. You will also need to consider the type of clothing needed and to plan for any change in the weather. Planning what to do in the event of a sudden downpour of rain is not too dissimilar to knowing how to cope with a breakdown in technology in the classroom! Be prepared.

Task 3.7.3 Risk assessment

Use the school's risk assessment pro forma, or the one provided in Figure 3.7.2, to assess the risk of a lesson you normally teach indoors but could possibly teach outdoors. Complete the assessment for both indoor and outdoor learning, including an assessment of the site and also of the activities. In what ways do these two assessments vary?

Bishops Wood Centre
OCN accredited training for Forest School

Site Risk Benefit Assessment

Venue and postcode:	Location:	
Assessment carried out by:	Signature:	Date:
Review date		

Benefits of the site regarding play and learning opportunities that it affords.

© Bishops Wood Centre
01299 250513, e-mail: bishopswoodcourses@worcestershire.gov.uk

Page 1 of 3

FIGURE 3.7.2 Example of a risk/benefit assessment template

Site Checked for	Hazards	Risks	Level of Risk	Action Proposed	New Level of Risk
Canopy layer					
Shrub layer					
Field layer					
Ground layer					

Bishops Wood Centre
OCN accredited training for Forest School

Site Checked for	Hazards	Risks	Level of Risk	Action Proposed	New Level of Risk
Access to the site:					
Boundaries around the site:					
Other people using the site					
Structures					
Animals on site					
Other					

FIGURE 3.7.2 continued

SUMMARY

There are huge educational benefits to learning outside the classroom, and recent research has highlighted the value of learning and teaching outside. Indeed, it is an essential part of the curriculum with both the EYFS and the National Curriculum, and all subjects can benefit from making use of the outdoors as part of the learning environment. Learning outside can help with a child's holistic development, aiding cognitive development, health and well-being, their learning skills such as problem-solving and teamwork, and their personal development, through providing the means to work with motivating lesson activities.

Learning outdoors can take on many forms, from a quick trip out into the school grounds, to regular sessions in the outdoors, visits, residential visits and adventurous pursuits. Each has its own learning value and requires careful planning to ensure the learning is safe, effective and enjoyable. Learning outside the classroom embodies learning, in the sense of being in a place, of children engaging practically, cognitively and affectively, and in its experiential nature. Learning outdoors is memorable, and its impact goes far beyond the nature of the planned activities.

ANNOTATED FURTHER READING

Pickering, S. (ed.) (2017) *Teaching Outdoors Creatively*, London: Routledge.
> The authors explore the full range of opportunities for teaching outdoors, including teaching in urban and rural environments and from the calm to the adventurous. This book has a great range of practical activities and ideas grounded in current theory and research. It covers learning and teaching in early years settings as well as primary schools.

Waite, S. (ed.) (2017) *Children Learning Outside the Classroom,* 2nd edn, London: Sage.
> There are a super range of chapters that consider various aspects of learning outside the classroom, through subject areas as well as cross-curricular routes such as Forest Schools, residential centres and national parks. This book is grounded with theory and provides a strong argument for the benefits of learning and teaching outdoors.

FURTHER READING TO SUPPORT M-LEVEL STUDY

Reese, R. and Myers, J. (2010) 'EcoWellness: The missing factor in holistic wellness models', *Journal of Counseling & Development*, 90: 400-6.
> This article is of great interest for the way in which it uses a broad range of research on the benefits to the health and well-being of children who regularly attend learning sessions outdoors. It uses this research to provide an argument for 'EcoWellness' – a model to show the impact on the health and well-being of children and adults.

Bentsen, P. and Søndergaard Jenson, F. (2012) 'The nature of udeskole, outdoor learning theory and practice in Danish schools', *Journal of Adventure Education & Outdoor Learning*, 12(30): 199-219.
> This article examines the experience of outdoor practice in Danish schools and raises a number of questions, issues and possibilities that are pertinent to British outdoor learning practices.

RELEVANT WEBSITES

Council for Learning Outside the Classroom: www.lotc.org.uk
> This is a site that opens up a huge range of resources and opportunities for members and it also contains a lot of useful resources and guidance for non-members.

Forest School Association: www.forestschoolassociation.org
> Again, this site has more resources for its members, but nevertheless has support and guidance for non-members. Of particular interest are the principles of Forest Schools.

Ofsted: www.gov.uk/government/organisations/ofsted
> Many people think of Ofsted as the body that only completes reports on individual schools, and, although you can find some examples of excellent practice by looking at some of these school reports, it is also worth knowing that Ofsted completes significant research in different areas of learning.

The Geographical Association: www.geography.org.uk

Learning through Landscapes: www.ltl.org.uk

REFERENCES

Carroll, M. and McCullogh, M. (eds) (2014) *Understanding Teaching and Learning in Primary Education*, London: Sage.

Catling, S. and Pickering, S. (2010) 'Mess, mess, glorious mess', *Primary Geography*, 73: 16-17.

Children, Schools and Families Committee. (2010) *Transforming Education Outside the Classroom. Sixth Report of Session 2009-10*, London: The Stationery Office.

Cremin, T. and Arthur, J. (2011) *Learning to Teach in the Primary School*, 3rd edn, London: Routledge.

Cutler, M. (2016) *The Call of the Wild*, Cambridge Primary Review Trust blog, 30 September 2016. Retrieved from http://cprtrust.org.uk/cprt-blog/the-call-of-the-wild/ (accessed 30 September 2016).

Department for Education. (2012) *Teachers' Standards. Guidance for School Leaders, School Staff and Governing Bodies*, London: DfE.

Department for Education. (2013) *The National Curriculum in England Key Stages 1 and 2 Framework Document*, London: DfE.

Department for Education. (2014) *Statutory Framework for the Early Years Foundation Stage. Setting the Standards for Learning, Development and Care for Children from Birth to Five*, London: DfE.

Department for Education and Employment/QCA. (1999) *The National Curriculum. Handbook for Primary Teachers in England*, London: DfEE/QCA.

Gill, T. (2010) *Nothing Ventured . . . Balancing Risks and Benefits in the Outdoors*. Retrieved from www.englishoutdoorcouncil.org/wp-content/uploads/Nothing-Ventured.pdf, English Outdoor Council (accessed 28 March 2017).

Goswami, U. (2008) 'Principles of learning, implications for teaching: A cognitive neuroscience perspective', *Journal of Philosophy of Education*, 42(3-4): 381-99.

James, A. and James, A. (2004) *Constructing Childhood. Theory, Policy and Social Practice*, London: Palgrave.

Jordan, M. (2015) *Nature and Therapy. Understanding Counselling and Psychotherapy in Outdoor Spaces*, London: Routledge.

Kaplan, R. and Kaplan, S. (1989) *The Experience of Nature: A Psychological Perspective*, Cambridge, UK: Cambridge University Press.

Kaplan, S. (1995) 'The restorative benefits of nature: Towards an integrative framework', *Journal of Environmental Psychology*, 16: 169–82.

Knight, S. (2011) *Forest School for All*, London: Sage.

Louv, R. (2005) *Last Child in the Woods*, London: Atlantic Books.

Natural England. (2016) *Monitor of Engagement with the Natural Environment: A Pilot to Develop an Indicator of Visits to the Natural Environment by Children, Results from Years 1 and 2 (March 2013 to February 2015)*, Natural England Commissioned Report NECR208. Retrieved from https://www.gov.uk/government/uploads/system/uploads/attachment_data/file/498944/mene-childrens-report-years-1-2.pdf (accessed 25 October 2017).

Payne , P.G. and Wattchow, B.(2009) 'Phenomenological deconstruction, slow pedagogy, and the corporeal turn in wild environmental/outdoor education', *Canadian Journal of Environmental Education*, 14: 15–32.

Pickering, S. (ed.) (2017) *Teaching Outdoors Creatively*, London: Routledge.

Reese, R. and Myers, J. (2012) 'EcoWellness: The missing factor in holistic wellness models', *Journal of Counseling & Development*, 90(4): 400–6.

Smith, T.E. and Knapp, C.E. (2011) *The Source Book of Experiential Education. Key Thinkers and Their Contributions*, London: Routledge.

Waite, S., Passy, R., Gilchrist, M., Hunt, A. and Blackwell, I. (2016) *Natural Connections Demonstration Project, 2012–2016: Final Report*, Natural England Commissioned Reports, Number 215. Retrieved from http://publications.naturalengland.org.uk/publication/6636651036540928 (accessed 25 October 2017).

APPROACHES TO THE CURRICULUM

INVESTIGATING THE AIMS, VALUES AND PURPOSES OF PRIMARY EDUCATION

The case of the Cambridge Primary Review

Liz Chamberlain and Roger McDonald

INTRODUCTION

If I were in a classroom today, I wouldn't run it too differently from the way I ran it all those years ago [20 years]. I'd want it to be a stimulating place, filled with colour and interest. I'd want my pupils to enjoy coming to school. I'd want them to interact positively and sensitively, and to feel what they were doing was worthwhile. And I'd want every child to feel the excitement of acquiring knowledge and fulfilling whatever potential they have.

(Kent, 2006: 65)

These are the words of Mike Kent, a London head teacher with more than 40 years' experience. As you re-read his words, reflect on whether what he proposes is what you recognise to be the kind of learning experience you hope for for the children in your future classes. Is what he proposes what you envisage to be synonymous with the aims, values and purpose of primary education as a whole?

OBJECTIVES

In this unit, you will:

- be introduced to some key moments from the last two centuries of primary education;
- become aware that political, social, economic and cultural factors are always at play in any education system;
- consider and reflect on the aims, values and purpose of primary education;
- learn about the aims and principles underpinning the Cambridge Primary Review;
- be encouraged to define your own pedagogical approach for primary teaching and learning.

This unit starts by outlining a snapshot of some key moments in the history of primary education over the last 150 years, in order to illustrate how philosophical and practical questions about the purpose of the primary school and education have long been the subject of debate. It is beyond the remit of this unit to offer a full timeline of education policy and practices, but the unit will signpost you to a useful Internet source that explores the development of education, starting in the seventh century up to the present day (http://bit.ly/2qbWLag). The unit will use one case, that of the Cambridge Primary Review (CPR), to outline ways in which schools tackle the big questions about the purpose of primary education and how the choices schools make are reflected in practice. The remainder of the unit offers the reader an overview of the CPR's main aims and objectives, before looking at the legacy of the work.

In Wales . . .

We know that school effectiveness requires an ethos where children and young people are expected to succeed and achieve a personal standard of excellence. The ethos needs to reflect the values inherent in Wales, including the importance of the Welsh language within the context of a bilingual country with its unique culture and traditions. It needs to provide the right support to ensure all children and young people have equal opportunities to succeed.

(DCELLS, 2008: 8)

Source: Department for Children, Education, Lifelong Learning and Skills (DCELLS). (2008) *School Effectiveness Framework: Building Effective Communities Together*, Cardiff: Welsh Assembly Government. Retrieved from http://gov.wales/docs/dcells/publications/091020frameworken.pdf (accessed 25 October 2017).

A HISTORICAL PERSPECTIVE: THE GREAT EDUCATION DEBATES

The 1870 Elementary Education Act was committed to providing education on a national and 'mass' scale. Prior to the Act, there had been educational provision for some children in some areas in the form of voluntary schools, provided by churches or charities. It was later in 1876, and as an outcome of the Royal Commission on the Factory Acts, that the recommendation was made to make education compulsory in an attempt to halt child labour. At the end of the nineteenth century, education became compulsory for all children up until the age of 13, including those with additional needs. A restricted curriculum was on offer, focused on the 3 Rs: reading, writing and arithmetic, and in later years these core subjects were joined by additional subjects such as geography, history, grammar and needlework (for girls). As is ever the case with primary education, it was the findings of two Royal Commissions (1881 and 1884) on technical education that had the indirect effect of influencing and enriching elementary (or primary) education (Gillard, 2011).

In terms of the 'system' of schooling, prior to 1870, the role of infant schools was to separate what Matthew Arnold (a school inspector at the time) referred to as the 'babies' to prevent them distracting from the important job of teaching the older children. However, it was the Huxley Committee of 1871 (see Gillard, 2011) that stressed that infant schools also had a role, not only in protecting children from outside (and corrupting) influences, but also in providing foundational experiences to support children's later learning in the advanced schools.

Politicians have been concerned with curriculum since the time of the Elementary Education Act of 1870 (Gillard, 2011), when discussion and debate moved away from the early concerns of school buildings, teachers and resources. Before this time, the 'what' of what to teach was not the main consideration; interestingly, it was another 100 years before the 'way' in which children learn became the subject of political debate and disagreement. The early focus of nineteenth-century education was on preparing children for employment, and, in some areas, the turn of the twentieth century saw the establishment of 'day trade schools', which prepared (mainly) boys for entry into furniture- or cabinet-making. And, as is ever the case with education, you may notice echoes in the implementation of the modern-day apprenticeship schemes for 16+ pupils, as the school leaving age in England rose to 18 as a result of government policy in 2015.

There has always been a debate about what school is for; in those early days, it was about ensuring the next generation was ready for work, with the discussion shifting in the early twentieth century to consideration of how the aims and values of schools might mirror those of society. The 1931 Hadow Report suggested that, 'A good school . . . is not a place of compulsory instruction, but a community of old and young, engaged in learning by co-operative experiment' (Hadow, 1931: xvii). Later, the Plowden Report (CACE, 1967) posited that, 'all schools reflect the views of society, or of some section of society, about the way children should be brought up, whether or not these views are consciously held or defined' (p. 185). As you enter the teaching profession, you may wonder what the current education system says about the society we currently live in, or indeed the one we are preparing children for. For example, you may have heard mention of Year 5 pupils being prepared for jobs that as yet don't exist; there is no actual evidence that this is the case, especially as many of the jobs for young adults have existed for centuries – the healthcare profession, catering, jobs involving technology, and so on – but what is true is that the ways in which these jobs are carried out are changing.

What then is the role of school, the curriculum or the type of teacher you are, in ensuring that the children you come into contact with throughout your career will be prepared for the future challenges ahead? Maybe you disagree that the role of the primary school is to prepare children for employment, and at interview for your teaching course you may even have been asked, 'What is the purpose of primary education?' If your answer had been that it was to prepare children for secondary school, you wouldn't be reading this book now, as to have been accepted for your primary education course, you evidently recognised that primary schools have a special and different role in the education of young children. However, it is no surprise that some people can view primary education in quite simplified terms. It is not uncommon in political discourse or debate for 'education' to be used as a proxy for *secondary* education, which is where some consider that 'real' learning happens. For example, if you review any of the suggested initiatives by a previous education secretary, Michael Gove (2010-14), whether focused on changing school structures through academisation, or on overhauling traditional university-based teacher training through the introduction of 'on the job training', these initiatives have their origins in the secondary sector, with subsequent 'lite' versions abridged for the primary school.

Schools, both primary and secondary, are complex systems; learning and teaching are complex in the nature of their interdependence, and children are complex because they are different – they think differently, interpret your interpretation of policy differently and come to any learning experience with experience of prior learning, which the very best of teachers take account of and incorporate within their teaching approaches.

This unit argues that one of the unique features of primary education is the nature of the relationship between the teacher and learner. Although it is true that all teachers should focus on 'enabling children to learn' (Cullingford, 1997: 2), it is the teacher-pupil relationship within the primary setting that allows the teacher to take on the role of guide and to nurture the children in their charge. In the 1990s, Cullingford (1997) attributed the distinctive ethos of British primary schools to the teachers' role in supporting the social and emotional well-being of the children in their classes. Fast-forward 20 years, and teachers still take on this role, despite an ever-changing curriculum and the many political footballs played out in the media. In addition to the type of teacher–pupil relationship you begin to establish in school, the other unique feature of primary education, which you will begin to notice, is that schools and teachers, depending on the school context, can still exert autonomy (despite external pressures) over what they teach through the ways in which they interpret the statutory curriculum. The decisions that a school staff chooses to make will be due, in part, to what the school understands as to the purpose of primary education, which you are most likely to notice through how the school vision is communicated. Gammage (1996) challenges us to consider that 'Schooling and education are, of course, not necessarily synonymous' (p. 144). What he argues is that education should be viewed as a lifelong process where, through the experience of learning, we find out about ourselves and others and we learn how to negotiate our way in the world. On the other hand, schooling is a relatively short and systematic, compulsory process.

Task 4.1.1 Personal reflection on your own primary education experience

What was it that made your primary school experience different to what you may have experienced when you turned 11 and went up to 'big' school?

To help you reflect on how your primary experience was framed, spend some time browsing through Derek Gillard's excellent repository of documents, including education Acts, White Papers, reports and other key events (http://bit.ly/2qbWLag). The website provides a useful timeline of education since the seventh century.

As you read through the website, reflect on your own experience of primary school, with the policy/papers/Education Acts of the day, and compare your reflections with those of your peers. If you were educated in a different country, compare your experience with those of your UK counterparts to see what was the same/what was different.

You may find out, if you attended primary schools in the UK in the 1980s, that your education was framed partly by policies introduced by education secretaries, including Margaret Thatcher and Kenneth Baker; it was during this decade that the current INSET days were first introduced and called Baker Days (after Kenneth Baker). Or, you may remember, as a direct result of the 1988 Education Reform Act (HMSO, 1988), your teacher struggling with the ten A4 folders that heralded the introduction of the first National Curriculum for England, Wales and Northern Ireland. Or, if you're in your twenties, you will no doubt remember the curriculum being influenced by the national strategies for literacy and numeracy (DfEE, 1998), and in particular you may have hazy memories of the 'literacy hour clock' dominating your literacy learning.

Unit 4.2, Aims into practice: Understanding schools' aims and enacting your own, will explore how schools develop a curriculum, and Unit 4.3, Critical perspectives on the curriculum, will discuss current statutory curricula in more depth.

For the remainder of this unit, we will present just one way in which increasing numbers of schools have chosen to interpret and supplement their curricula, and that is by using the Cambridge Primary Review (CPR) to reflect their aims, purposes and values of primary education more broadly.

WHERE ARE WE NOW? THE CURRENT CONTEXT

The political culture within which modern English primary schooling is set remains in some respects as it was a century ago – deeply paternalistic, utilitarian and suspicious of change from within.

(Alexander, 2000: 128)

So, where does this leave primary education in the twenty-first century – where is the middle ground that keeps children and their learning at the heart, learning that is facilitated and taught by teachers grounded in subject knowledge and a definable pedagogy?

DEVELOPING A PRINCIPLED PEDAGOGY

In Northern Ireland . . .

The aim of the Northern Ireland Curriculum is to 'empower young people to develop their potential and to make informed and responsible choices and decisions throughout their lives' (CCEA, 2007: 4). The learning opportunities provided through the Northern Ireland Curriculum should help young people to develop as an individual, as a contributor to society, and as a contributor to the economy and the environment. Underpinning this is the aim to build desirable attitudes and dispositions, such as moral character, community spirit, tolerance, flexibility, self-belief, pragmatism, concern for others, personal responsibility and curiosity.

Source: Council for Curriculum, Examinations and Assessment (CCEA). (2007) *The Northern Ireland Curriculum: Primary*, Belfast: CCEA Publications. Retrieved from http://ccea.org.uk/sites/default/files/docs/curriculum/area_of_learning/fs_northern_ireland_curriculum_primary.pdf (accessed 25 October 2017).

Offering time to reflect on the pedagogical practices used within a school and within our classrooms may seem like a luxury considering the number of day-to-day processes, pressures and practicalities teachers and school leaders need to balance. With this in mind, it is understandable that finding space to examine the pedagogy employed in a school through triangulating practice, research and progress can, in some cases, be overtaken by the day-to-day routines within a school, possibly resulting in what Alexander (2010a) notes as the reduction of education to focus on skill acquisition. However, finding this space within the crowded life of the school community is paramount to developing teacher professionalism and teacher pedagogy. Indeed, Devine *et al.* (2010) remind us that, 'teacher professionalism emerges from teachers' capacity to cite evidence and pedagogical principles in the pursuit of teaching goals' (p. 816), therefore enabling the teacher to develop a principled approach to their teaching repertoire.

An increasing number of schools and centres of education have sought to carve out space for examining pedagogy through setting up their own continuing professional development (CPD) programmes, with the aim of developing practice. In some cases, these are developed internally and specifically respond to the needs of the school as identified by the senior leadership team. Other establishments have looked for external support and partnered with universities or subject associations such as the United Kingdom Literacy Association, the Mathematical Association and the Geographical Association in order to provide breadth, balance and challenge (see Units 9.2 and 9.3).

One organisation that has been highly influential in supporting the development of a principled pedagogy is the Cambridge Primary Review Trust (CPRT), which was formed following the culmination of the work from its predecessor, the CPR. One practical influence of the work of the CPRT has been the development of school-based reading forums. These forums offer colleagues time and space to debate, interact, discuss and ponder on their own practice, framed around the key priority areas resulting from the CPR.

THE CAMBRIDGE PRIMARY REVIEW

Published in 2010, as a result of 6 years of work, including more than 1,000 submissions, twenty-eight specially commissioned reviews, more than 3,000 published sources of evidence reviewed, and 237 meetings at regional and national level, the CPR was 'a comprehensive and independent enquiry into the condition and future of primary education in England' (Alexander, 2010a: 1), with the final report and research companion referencing more than 4,000 sources drawing on the work of thirteen contributing authors (Moss, 2010). The final report raised critical questions regarding the underlying philosophy and direction of primary education in England (Devine *et al.*, 2010) and sought to highlight an education that emphasised the importance, relevance and need for equity and empathy, challenge and relevancy, as well as exploration and freedom. Significantly, the Review focused on a number of salient questions, asking:

> What is primary education for? To what needs and purposes should it be chiefly directed over the coming decades? What core values and principles should it uphold and advance? Taking account of the country and the world in which our children are growing up, to what individual, social, cultural, economic and other circumstances and needs should it principally attend?
>
> (Alexander, 2010a: 174)

Supported by the Esmee Fairbairn Foundation, the final report was significant, as it was the first major scrutiny and systematic analysis of primary education for more than 30 years, since the Plowden enquiry from 1963-7. The report identified four phases of political interaction with education that took place in the intervening years, which Drummond (2010) outlined as the 'unchallenged' phase from 1967-76, the 'challenged' phase, which spanned 1967-87, the 'regulated' phase from 1987 to 1997 and then the 'dominated' phase, starting in 1997 and arguably continuing beyond 2016. The publication of the Review took place subsequent to the commissioning and publication of the government's own review of primary education in the form of the Rose Review (DCSF, 2009). This review had a more limited scope than that of the Cambridge Primary Review and did not challenge policy, pedagogy and practice in the same way or to the extent that Alexander (2010a) was able to do. Indeed, it was reported that the proposals identified in the Rose review 'would not run against the grain of existing policy' (Campbell, 2011: 344). In 2009, the commissioning government adopted the Rose proposals, but they were later abandoned in May 2010 by the incoming coalition government.

It was soon evident that the driving force of the coalition education reforms (2010-15), under the then Secretary of State for Education, Michael Gove, would be less far reaching than the principled pedagogy identified within the CPR. And, as the review had no political affiliation, in that it was an independent review of primary education, it became increasingly clear that the curriculum would remain centrally controlled. However, 7 years on, and three Secretaries of State for Education later, the principles and aims of the CPR remain as relevant and active as ever. Indeed, many schools have continued to adopt the aims and use them to shape or define their own approach to teaching and learning, reflected in the way they describe the curriculum and pedagogy of their school.

CPR AIMS AND PURPOSE FOR PRIMARY EDUCATION

Underpinning the review were three broad perspectives, ten themes and twelve aims for primary education in England. Chapter 12 of the final report ('What is primary education for?') highlighted the challenges involved in defining educational aims, which were borne out through the responses to the Review (evidence was gathered from parents, teachers, children, community leaders, international research and across a range of professional and third-sector organisations). The specific key questions were as follows:

- What is primary education for?
- To what needs and purposes should it be chiefly directed over the coming decades?
- What core values and principles should it uphold and advance?
- Taking account of the country and the world in which our children are growing up, to what individual, social, cultural, economic and other circumstances and needs should it principally attend?

In addition, at the core of the Review are three broad perspectives that provided the framework for the subsequent themes and questions. The perspectives, as outlined by Alexander *et al.* (2010), concerned 'children, the world in which they are growing up, and the education which mediates that world and prepares them for it' (Alexander *et al.*, 2010: 4) and can be summarised as:

- children and childhood;
- culture, society and the global context;
- primary education today and tomorrow.

The third perspective, which is concerned with primary education itself, was further subdivided into ten broad themes, which in turn have a set of questions each relating to the value, purpose, process, content and quality in England's primary schools. For a detailed overview of the themes and the subsequent questions, see http://cprtrust.org.uk/cpr/full-themes/

The twelve aims for primary education, the focus of this unit, are organised into three groups, which are reflected in the principles and the title of the final report, *Children, Their World, Their Education*: namely, the individual; self, others and the wider world; and learning, knowing and doing. A key priority for the CPRT was to encourage schools to adopt and pursue these aims, and, in order for them to do so, the aims should be acted upon as they 'will stand or fall by what teachers do with them' (Drummond, 2010: 12), and, if they fall, 'we shall be left the current dissonance of high ideas and expedient practice' (Alexander, 2010a: 262). The aims, organised into the three groups, are outlined below, but can also be found together with further explanation at: http://cprtrust.org.uk/about_cprt/aims/

The individual

- Well-being;
- engagement in learning;
- empowerment of pupils;
- autonomy and sense of self.

Self, others and the wider world

- Encouraging respect and reciprocity;
- promoting interdependence and sustainability;

- empowering local, national and global citizenship;
- celebrating culture and community.

Learning, knowing and doing

- Exploring, knowing, understanding and making sense;
- fostering skill;
- exciting the imagination;
- enacting dialogue.

Some notable critics (in addition to government officials) of the CPR were author and researcher Mary Jane Drummond (2010) and Emeritus Professor of Education R.J. Campbell (2011), with the latter describing the Review as 'backward-looking, cumbersome and partial' (p. 26). Such was the consternation that the Review was critiqued in such a way, other academics, including Michael Armstrong, wrote published articles in response (Armstrong, 2011). Apart from criticisms regarding areas considered partially covered, such as gifted and talented pupils, the private sector and the range of collected evidence (Campbell, 2011), it was also noted that the complexity of the principles, questions, themes and aims, together with the various subsidiary elements, could cause confusion and be impractical for teachers on a daily basis. It is certainly true that, as a new-to-teaching student, you may well be wondering why there is so much emphasis in this book on a Review that seemingly fell on deaf ears, and whose aims and priorities appear not to be reflected in current curriculum or policy documentation. However, what remains true of the Review and why it should matter to you as a trainee teacher is that, to be a successful teacher, you need to understand why you teach what you teach, how children learn from what you teach them, and from what and where your own values are derived.

One of the legacies of the CPRT is the access to the research reports and briefings that were commissioned to update and extend those originally published by the CPR. These reports, unrivalled for their educational evidence, vision and principle, are available to view on the CRPT website (http://cprtrust.org.uk/) and will also be available as a mainstay on the Chartered College of Teaching 'knowledge platform', available at www.collegeofteaching.org/

We would encourage you to have a look at some of the reports and reflect on how your own practice reflects the research. You may even want to set up a group within your school or university to share the findings from the reports and look at influencing and possibly shifting your own pedagogy through the research findings.

SHIFTING PEDAGOGY THROUGH POLICY

In many ways, teachers have been required to be flexible across the vast swathes of initiatives that have punctuated primary education during the last 30 years, all of which have arguably shifted pedagogical approaches adopted in the classroom. Such initiatives have included the National Literacy Strategy (DfEE, 1998) and the National Numeracy Strategy (DfEE, 1999), which were soon followed by the National Strategies (DfES, 2006). The strategies were implemented as short-term initiatives in a 'systematic attempt at a national level to drive improvements in standards through a focused programme of managing changes in the way that core subjects are taught in classrooms' (DfE, 2011: 4). It seems clear that there was a focused attempt to shift the pedagogy within the classroom to ensure that:

> Once a teacher has adopted the right approach – the system's pedagogical values – and has learned to manifest these in effective teaching practice, they become an invaluable asset to the school

system, which then often seeks to embed this expertise by promoting such teachers to new roles. As teachers progress along the professional path, they assume responsibilities as educators, mentoring and leading other teachers, as well as in developing new curricula of the system.

(Mourshed, Chijioke and Barber, 2010: 78)

This quote comes from a report into education, published by consultants McKinsey & Company, which analysed more than twenty school systems from around the world, in order to identify the factors that enable schools to demonstrate excellent performance. It was influential in the development of the English national numeracy and literacy strategies, which sought to ensure 'significant and urgent improvement' in primary education (DfE, 2011: 3), a clear example of the controlled approach adopted by the government of the day to enforce the *right approach*, which appeared to be synonymous with the *pedagogical values* prescribed by the system. The teachers who excelled in the agreed approaches to the teaching of literacy or numeracy were promoted to the status of leading literacy or numeracy teachers, and thus the virtuous circle of the *right approach* to a specific philosophy of teaching and learning was reinforced over the next decade.

It is difficult to identify within such a system as described above where the aims of the Cambridge Primary Review would sit, and what the role would be of creativity, choice and possibility thinking. Indeed, it has been argued that narrow initiatives have led to a restriction of creativity and imagination (Burke, 2011), where a 'professional culture of excitement, inventiveness and healthy scepticism has been supplanted by one of dependency, compliance and even fear' (Alexander, 2010b: 7). One of the resulting shifts in pedagogy has been a 'delivery' system of education (Cox, 2011), where pre-packaged knowledge is passed to the learner.

It is interesting to reflect on the different approaches highlighted so far. The CPR calls for a pedagogy of repertoire, whereas it could be argued that the influence of recent policies and practices has led to a pedagogy of recipe and delivery. However, given the diverse nature of schools and the number of still-principled school leaders who focus on the development of the whole child, the profession has become adept at weathering changes.

Task 4.1.2 Reflecting on pedagogical principles

From what you have read so far about the findings of the CPR and the possible pedagogical shifts in primary education, you could use the questions below to consider your own classroom practice and the influences on it. Make a subjective mark on each scale following the question. This will give you an indication of your current pedagogy.

To what degree:

1   Do children have ownership over the curriculum?

<————————————————————————————————>

2   Does the curriculum reflect the home lives of the children you teach?

<————————————————————————————————>

3   Is the curiosity of the children central to your planning?

<————————————————————————————————>

4 Is your class curriculum original and distinct from other classes?

<——>

5 Do you encourage play and exploration in open-ended contexts?

<——>

6 Do you develop children's opportunities and capacity for possibility thinking?

<——>

7 Do you afford the children time and space in their learning?

<——>

8 Is there a learning space developed in your classroom where teachers and children develop and learn together?

<——>

From the results above, consider forming two aims with relation to your own pedagogy. You may, for example, consider the question of curiosity and plan ways in which your classroom curriculum might better foster children's curiosity.

You may also be conscious of the need for children to have a sense of completion in their work and want to plan opportunities for children to revisit work they feel most connected with, in order for them to mould and shape it before finally presenting it.

THE AIMS OF THE PRIMARY CURRICULUM AND THE ROLE OF THE IMAGINATION

To highlight one of the many tensions in primary education, this next section considers how one of the twelve aims of CPR, 'exciting the imagination', can be fostered and become central to your classroom practice. Previously, recognition has been given to the place of creativity in the curriculum, with Sir Ken Robinson defining it as 'the process of having original ideas that have value' (Robinson, 2006), but less attention has been given to the role of the imagination, of both teachers and children. In the comprehensive *Handbook of Philosophy of Imagination* (edited by Kind, 2016), many authors note how fixing upon a definition has perplexed many researchers and academics, leading to the American philosopher Noel Carroll defining imagination as, 'the junkyard of the mind' (Kind, 2016: 1).

Alphen (2011) defines imagination as:

> a heightened form of cognition, capable of transforming the knowledge and skills to be learned into enhanced experiences. These experiences stimulate creativity in thinking and involve the emotions of the learners, through which a more meaningful relationship is established with the learning material.
>
> (p. 16)

It is easy to see how this concept supports the aims and purposes of the CPR, with its focus on the development, not only of skill acquisition, but on the identity of the individual child in their individual context. The Cambridge Primary Review encourages teachers and children to develop critical and imaginative thinking, in what Egan (2005) argues is 'the ability to think of things as possible – the source of flexibility and originality in human thinking' (p. 220). So how might a philosophy of imagination fit within the primary curriculum?

THE QUESTION OF AN IMAGINATIVE APPROACH TO THE CURRICULUM

The seminal text *Imagination* by Mary Warnock explores the tension between the aims of a primary curriculum that is overly concerned with the Standards agenda and the place of imagination. Warnock (1976) states that, 'I have also come very strongly to believe that it is the cultivation of imagination which should be the chief aim of education' (p. 9). However, the journey to imaginative learning is not straightforward or without its struggles; indeed, the detail of this central CPR aim highlights the 'pains' of imagining, while also stating that, 'entering into the imaginative worlds of others, is to become a more rounded and capable person' (Alexander, 2016: 5).

Warnock was writing almost 50 years ago, but the debates are just as prevalent today. An imaginative approach to the primary curriculum offers the opportunity for children and teachers to think freely and develop a *space for learning* within a class where contributions from the whole class community are encouraged to develop understanding, knowledge and skills. McKernan (2008) notes:

> by allowing students the opportunity to think freely for themselves we shed our being in authority and give this as a right to the student. This is what is emancipatory about education; it frees the student from the *patria potestas*, or the parental jurisdiction.
>
> (p. 23)

This freedom of thought can be difficult: we are no longer talking about elements of lessons and of learning that can be easily measured and assessed; instead, teaching and learning become a collaborative act, with teachers and children interacting together and creating learning in a shared space. Learning becomes real; it is happening in the present, and children and teachers can feel it.

In the case study below, Claire Williams, a Year 4 teacher at Saint Andrew's Church of England Primary School, discusses her approach to primary education and exemplifies, through her practice, how she prioritises the values of the CPR in order to provide a rich, broad, balanced and imaginative curriculum for her children.

CASE STUDY: YEAR 4 TEACHER

Position in school: Year 4 Class Teacher, Reading Coordinator, Outdoor Learning Coordinator, Forest School Leader and Mentor

Number of years teaching: 4

Route into teaching: Primary PGCE, University of Cambridge

What do you think the aims of primary education are?

In line with the core aims of the Cambridge Primary Review, I believe that primary education should have intrinsic value in itself rather than being seen solely as preparation for the future. A balance needs to be secured between attending to children's future fulfilment and to their needs and well-being in the here and now. A successful primary education should foster children's development as self-motivated, resilient learners, instil a lifelong love of learning and empower them with a sense of agency, autonomy and optimism for the future.

What do you consider to be your priorities as a teacher?

My priorities as a teacher give life to my values and view of the aims of primary education. As primary school teachers, we have a unique opportunity to influence children's learning dispositions and identities. Nurturing children's intrinsic motivation to learn and belief in themselves as learners is at the heart of my pedagogy, which is shaped by a commitment to the learning capacity of every child;

all children should have a positive view of what they can achieve and feel that their voice is valued. For example, committing time and space to finding out about individual children's reading preferences and home reading practices, through activities such as 'Rivers of Reading', enables me to develop reciprocal, interactive reader-to-reader relationships with the children and foster positive reading identities. By developing a dialogic pedagogy and listening to their perspectives, I hope to promote children's active engagement and foster their growth as autonomous learners. I strive to enable enjoyment, fun and laughter and, ultimately, nurture their happiness and well-being.

In what ways are your priorities evidenced in your practice?

These priorities are reflected in my classroom practice, which is principled and evidence-informed. By building positive, collaborative relationships with the children, I am able to make professional judgements to develop a broad, rich curriculum that balances policy requirements with their interests and needs. The 'Wonder Wall' in our classroom allows the children to share 'I wonder . . .'s and questions inspired by their learning, which then inform my planning, and as part of our creative, topic-based curriculum, the children choose and lead a topic for half a term. This year's child-led 'Cracking Contraptions' topic, which the children decided on collaboratively because they wanted to learn more about inventions and inventors, took a few 'uneggs-pected' yet 'eggs-citing' turns when one child highlighted the relevance of the picturebook *Egg Drop* by Mini Grey; this resulted in an 'Egg Drop Challenge' from Mini Grey herself and thirty-five unsuspecting eggs being parachuted from the school roof! Teaching creatively and for creativity across the curriculum excites the children's imagination and sparks their curiosity, which, in turn, fosters an enjoyment of learning.

I work hard to create a positive, safe classroom climate; together, we rise to challenges, take risks and celebrate each other's successes. As a way of encouraging the children to look for and recognise the positive in others, the display in our classroom that shows our school learning behaviours is interactive. When they 'see the sparkle' in another child, the children write them a star-shaped post-it note to stick on the display, recognising and sharing this; it could be anything from winning a cross country competition after putting in the hours of practice to showing resilience when faced with a challenge in maths.

Giving a high profile to a dialogic view of teaching, collaborative group work is a key part of my pedagogic repertoire. Collectively, we construct ground rules for high-quality discussion, which helps the children to engage in productive 'exploratory' talk. Opportunities to work collaboratively, think and reason together in this way are built in regularly; for example, at the beginning of a new teaching sequence in English, I plan in opportunities for the children to talk in groups about their reading of new texts, using Aidan Chambers' *Tell Me* approach.

As a reflective teacher, I am committed to continued and principled professional development, actively seeking out opportunities to use evidence to reflect on and improve my practice.

Claire responded to the following three key questions:

1   What do you think the aims of primary education are?
2   What do you consider to be your priorities as a teacher?
3   In what ways are your priorities evidenced in your practice?

These are three questions that you may wish to reflect on and to consider in the light of Claire's responses. Do you agree with her assertions about what good primary practice looks like? Are your experiences of primary education, either as a trainee or pupil, mirrored in Claire's reflections?

SUMMARY

As you reflect on this unit, consider what you have learned about some key moments in the history of primary education and how economic and social factors are always at play within any education system, and consider how your own ideas about the aims of primary education will be evidenced through your own day-to-day practice in the classroom. In the next unit, the authors will urge you to take the baton that is being handed to you and take things a step further by becoming a teacher with purpose, passion and empowerment.

ANNOTATED FURTHER READING

Cowley, S. (2017) *The Artful Educator: Creative, Imaginative and Innovative Approaches to Teaching*, Carmarthen, UK: Crown House.

> A familiar author for student teachers, in this easy-to-read book, Cowley likens teaching to art and teachers to artists, musicians and dancers. If you are looking to be more playful and creative in your teaching, the book's examples of practice provide a useful starting point.

Pollard, A., Black-Hawkins, K. and Cliff-Hodges, G. (2014) *Reflective Teaching in Schools*, London: Bloomsbury Academic.

> As director of the UK's Teaching and Learning Research Programme, Andrew Pollard, with contributors from the University of Cambridge, puts forward a range of examples of reflective teaching from diverse settings, underpinned by research and theory. It is easily accessible and useful for thinking more broadly about the principles and concepts that contribute to teacher expertise.

Taylor, K. and Woolley, R. (2013) *Values and Vision in Primary Education*, Oxford, UK: Open University Press.

> A practical book, easily accessible and with useful ideas student teachers can immediately put into practice. Key themes include curiosity, creativity and problem-solving, all of which are underpinned by sections covering the broader principles of values and vision.

M FURTHER READING TO SUPPORT M-LEVEL STUDY

Cox, S. (2011) *New Perspectives in Primary Education: Meaning and Purpose in Learning and Teaching*, Maidenhead, UK: Open University Press.

> In this excellent book, Sue Cox explores the changing landscape of primary education and tackles the perceived tension that exists between teachers as professionals and policy and procedures that, it could be argued, in some cases cause a shift in pedagogy within the classroom. Sue Cox revisits the meaning and purpose of learning and teaching and invites the reader to possibly reposition themselves as a result of reading the book and reflecting on their own practice.

Lefstein, A. and Snell, J. (2013) *Better than Best Practice: Developing Teaching and Learning through Dialogue*, London: Routledge.

> This book sets out to challenge current teaching approaches and to expose the meaning behind the phrase 'best practice'. Instead, the authors ask us to explore a pedagogy that is 'better than best practice' through highlighting the tensions that exist within any classroom and recognising the constant decision-making taking place, by both teachers and children. Using a range of case study material through a companion website, readers are able to view teachers as they develop learning in their classrooms through focusing on the dialogue taking place.

Alexander, R. (2000) *Culture and Pedagogy*, Oxford, UK: Blackwell.

> An extensive review of primary education across international borders, this combines policy discussion with offering fine-level thinking on schools and classrooms. Engaging with this seminal text, winner of the Outstanding Book Award (2002, AERA), will provide a firm understanding of the thinking behind the work of Robin Alexander and the CPRT.

 ## RELEVANT WEBSITES

Cambridge Primary Review Trust: http://cprtrust.org.uk/about_cprt/aims/

> A most comprehensive site outlining the principles, priorities and mission of the Cambridge Primary Review Trust.

Research Rich Pedagogies: https://researchrichpedagogies.org/

> A new website highlighting excellence in research showcasing projects from the Open University that offer inspiring and creative pedagogies. The website offers all teachers the opportunity to upload case studies from their own practice that highlight how children and young people are encouraged to explore their own ideas, use their imaginations and engage creatively.

Chartered College of Teaching: www.collegeofteaching.org/

> The college aims to create a knowledge-based community where good-practice examples can be shared, and it hopes to offer a collective voice for the profession. It invites you to join as a member, and for students what may be of most interest is the link to evidence-based research and the proposed 'pathway to professional development'.

 ## REFERENCES

Alphen, P. (2011) 'Imagination as a transformative tool in primary school education', *Research on Steiner Education*, 2(2): 16-34.

Alexander, R. (2000) *Culture and Pedagogy*, Oxford, UK: Blackwell.

Alexander, R.J. (ed.) (2010a) *Children, Their World, Their Education: Final Report and Recommendations of the Cambridge Primary Review*, Oxford, UK: Routledge.

Alexander, R. (2010b) 'The perils of policy success, amnesia and collateral damage in systematic educational reform', the C.J. Koh Lecture, National Institute of Education, Singapore, 18 March.

Alexander, R. (2016) 'What is education for?' Submission to the House of Commons Education Committee Inquiry. Retrieved from www.robinalexander.org.uk/wp-content/uploads/2016/01/HoC-Purposes-Inquiry-CPRT-logo-1.pdf (accessed 26 Oactober 2017).

Alexander, R.J., Doddington, C., Gray, J., Hargreaves, L. and Kershner, R. (eds) (2010) *The Cambridge Primary Review Research Surveys*, Abingdon, UK: Routledge.

Armstrong, M. (2011) 'Curriculum, pedagogy and the Cambridge Primary Review: A response to R.J. Campbell', *Education 3-13*, 39(4): 257-361.

Burke, W. (2011) 'Log jammed by standard assessment tests: How feedback can help writers', *Literacy*, 45(1): 19-24.

Campbell, R. (2011) 'State control, religious deference and cultural reproduction: Some problems with theorising curriculum and pedagogy in the Cambridge Primary Review', *Education 3-13*, 39(4): 343-55.

Central Advisory Council for Education (CACE). (1967) *The Plowden Report: Children and their Primary Schools*, London: HMSO.

Cullingford, C. (1997) 'Changes in primary education', in *The Politics of Primary Education*, Buckingham, UK: Open University Press, pp. 1-14.

Cox, S. (2011) *New Perspectives in Primary Education: Meaning and Purpose in Learning and Teaching*, Maidenhead, UK: Open University Press.

Department for Children, Schools and Families (DCSF). (2009) *Independent Review of the Primary Curriculum: Final Report*. Retrieved from http://webarchive.nationalarchives.gov.uk/20100202110005/http://www.dcsf.gov.uk/primarycurriculumreview/ (accessed 9 November 2017).

Department for Education (DfE). (2011) *The National Strategies 1997–2011. A Brief Summary of the Impact and Effectiveness of the National Strategies*. Retrieved from http://webarchive.nationalarchives.gov.uk/20110812093022/http://nsonline.org.uk/node/508779?uc=force_deep (accessed 9 November 2017).

Department for Education and Employment (DfEE). (1998) *The National Literacy Strategy: Framework for Teaching*, London: DfEE.

Department for Education and Employment (DfEE). (1999) *The National Numeracy Strategy*, London: DfEE.

Department for Education and Skills (DfES). (2006) *The Primary Framework for Literacy and Mathematics*, London: DfES.

Devine, D., Miriam, E., Menter, D. and Menter, I. (2010) 'Children, Their World, Their Education: Final report and recommendations of the Cambridge Primary Review', *British Journal of Sociology of Education*, 31(6): 813–26.

Drummond, M. (2010) 'BRAVO! and BUT . . .: Reading the Cambridge Primary Review', *FORUM*, 52(1): 9–16.

Egan, K. (2005) *An Imaginative Approach to Teaching*, San Francisco, CA: Jossey-Bass.

Gammage, P. (1996) 'What school is really for: Revisiting values', in A. Craft, *Primary Assessment: Assessing and Planning Learning*, London: Routledge.

Gillard, D. (2011) *Education in England: A Brief History*. Retrieved from www.educationengland.org.uk/history (accessed 28 December 2016).

Hadow (1931) *Infant and Nursery Schools, Report of the Consultative Committee*, London: HMSO.

Her Majesty's Stationery Office (HMSO). (1988) *Education Reform Act*, London: HMSO.

Kent, M. (2006) *The Rabbit's Laid An Egg, Miss*, Stoke-on-Trent, UK: Trentham.

Kind, A. (2016) *The Routledge Handbook of Philosophy of Imagination*, London: Routledge.

McKernan, J. (2008) *Curriculum and Imagination*, Abingdon, UK: Routledge.

Moss, G. (2010) 'Remaking primary education: Reading *Children, Their World, Their Education: Final Report and Recommendations of the Cambridge Primary Review*', *Literacy*, 44(3): 144–8.

Mourshed, M., Chijioke, C. and Barber, M. (2010). *How the World's Most Improved School Systems Keep Getting Better*, New York: McKinsey.

Robinson, K. (2006) 'Do Schools Kill Creativity?', Ted Talks. Retrieved from www.ted.com/talks/ken_robinson_says_schools_kill_creativity/transcript?language=en (accessed 6 May 2017).

Warnock, M. (1976) *Imagination*, Berkeley, CA: University of California Press.

AIMS INTO PRACTICE

Understanding schools' aims and enacting your own

Jo Evans and Emese Hall

INTRODUCTION

Who decides on the aims of primary education? We suggest that there are two answers here: other people and yourself. As a beginning teacher, you may feel uncertain about what your own aims should or could be. However, on a micro scale, you will be thinking about aims on a daily basis with regard to individual activities and lessons. Indeed, aims of one sort or another inform everything we do in schools.

According to many, the current government's aspiration to be at the top of international league tables is a limited, and potentially damaging, aim for primary education (e.g., Alexander, 2011; Adams, Monahan and Wills, 2015). We agree. At the heart of our unit is the argument that aims for primary education should be broader than a focus on academic outcomes. The teaching profession needs to have a clear view on not only what it *believes* to be best for children, but also what it *knows* to be best for children (Crossley, 2015). These aims should positively shape the learning environment and the learning taking place within it – that is, both the physical and social aspects of the primary school. In our unit, we will share some advice on understanding and enacting aims, illustrated by examples from Jo's practice.

OBJECTIVES

This unit's objectives are:

- to exemplify how aims for primary education are diverse and complex;
- to describe how to find and interpret the aims of primary schools;
- to highlight some essential aims, from our joint perspective;
- to support new teachers in enacting their own aims.

SOME SCENE SETTING

The White Paper *Educational Excellence Everywhere* (DfE, 2016) sets out the government's vision for education for the next 5 years. We cannot discuss every aspect of this document here, but the core mission is to: 'provide world-class education and care that allows every child and young person to reach his or her potential, regardless of background' (DfE, 2016: 124). This aspiration reflects an ethical stance that we fully support: that is, to challenge inequalities and offer an excellent school experience for all children. However, the focus on academic rigour – cautioned against above – is ever-present, and we are not fully convinced that this will serve to ensure all children benefit from and enjoy school, if it means a narrowing of the curriculum and an emphasis on testing (Alexander, 2010, 2011).

We are keen to promote the work of the Cambridge Primary Review Trust (CPRT), an organisation we were both involved with in different capacities.[1] The CPRT specifies twelve aims for primary education, underpinned by research, and groups these into three categories:

1 *the individual*: well-being, engagement, empowerment, autonomy;
2 *self, others and the wider world*: encouraging respect and reciprocity; promoting interdependence and sustainability; empowering local, national and global citizenship; celebrating culture and community;
3 *learning, knowing and doing*: exploring, knowing, understanding and making sense; fostering skill; exciting the imagination; enacting dialogue.

For us, this very usefully summarises the diverse elements that contribute to well-rounded primary education. It is notable that 'learning, knowing and doing' is listed as the third category, with 'the individual' as the first. This suggests to us that children's well-being, engagement, empowerment and autonomy should ultimately drive teachers' decisions about teaching and learning, rather than academic attainment. We should note that 'safety and wellbeing' also features as a goal of the Department for Education's current strategy (DfE, 2016), underlining how essential it is to meet the child's needs in this respect. However, as Maslow's (1954) famous *hierarchy of needs* theory clarifies, there is a great contrast between physical well-being and individual self-actualisation, which is much more about personal *interests*. This is one of the key differences between care and *education*.

Task 4.2.1 'The good old bad old days'

Educational aims are culturally and historically situated. Even within the last half-century, there have been some significant shifts in thinking in England and other European countries (Shuayb and O'Donnell, 2008). What is commonly agreed to be desirable or 'correct' practice in one time and place may be different in another time and place. Take, for example, the scene in Figure 4.2.1, which gives us a brief impression of teaching and learning some 500 years ago. It seems fair to say that the idea of an outdoor classroom is appealing, but imagining ourselves as the stern instructor wielding a stick is altogether a less agreeable thought. The title is telling – it is the teacher here who is important. This is not child-centred education.

FIGURE 4.2.1 Albrecht Dürer, *The School Teacher* (1510)
Source: National Gallery of Art (open access image)

We would like you to imagine how a lesson taking place outdoors in a twenty-first-century primary school might look different to the one from 1510 depicted by Dürer. Make a note of the aims you consider especially relevant (perhaps using the CPRT list to help you) and consider what these aims might look like in practice. You may well be able to draw on first-hand experience, but, if not, then the CPRT aims will act as useful prompts for your thinking.

We will now move on to sharing some insights into Jo's practice.

JO'S STORY

I began my career as an early years practitioner and, for the past 14 years, have been the head teacher of three very different schools. Each move has made me reconsider my beliefs in relation to different contexts (OECD, 2009), but some very fundamental principles have been constant, as follows (in no particular order):

- the valuing of each individual;
- the creation of purposeful and irresistibly engaging learning;
- an environment thriving on possibility.

In my schools, I sought to encourage both adults and children to be curious and – with support as needed – seek answers to their questions, thus enabling everyone to fulfil their learning potential. *The question is: what did these aims look like in practice?*

The section below draws upon a description of my work at Saint Leonard's Primary School in Exeter, which I wrote about in a blog post for the CPRT (Evans, 2015). The text in italics states the relevant CPRT priority areas: equity, voice, community, sustainability, aims, curriculum, pedagogy and assessment.

- *Principles pursued with confidence*: We strive for a principled approach not only to the curriculum but also to the whole experience we offer to children in our care. The CPRT's aims have been used as aspirational tools to remind us of what is important over and above government priorities. If you visit our website, you can see how we have made our educational philosophy explicit to parents and others. My previous school moved from being deemed inadequate by Ofsted to outstanding, and my experience of leading this process gave me the confidence to take responsibility for the independent path we have chosen to follow in my present school.
- *Planning informed by CPRT priorities*: While continuing to drive for improved progress and attainment in English and mathematics, we have incorporated CPRT priorities into the actions we take in relation to these goals and strategic planning more widely. Thus (1) we work to help pupils take greater responsibility for their own learning (*pupil voice, community*); (2) we ensure that assessment drives the progress and attainment of every pupil, rather than merely measures it (*equity, assessment*); and (3) keeping our aims firmly in mind, we use high-quality teaching to achieving the very best outcomes for all (*pedagogy, curriculum, aims*).
- *Practice informed by evidence*: To ensure that evidence continues to inform our practice, we operate a tiered approach to action research. This includes termly and half-termly, whole-school, classroom-based research projects, with shared foci, lesson study in cross-year/school groupings, and individual research projects. Following recent training as part of CPRT's South West Research Schools Network, we are now going one stage further and developing pupil-led research projects. All this in-school research activity links to the three strategic strands listed above and gives a

depth to our school's practice that it would not have if we merely followed government guidelines or requirements to the letter. Researching and discussing research are therefore no less fundamental to our approach to professional development and performance management and have enabled us to provide leadership for research and development in more than one teaching school.

- *Flexible curriculum, responsive teaching*: Keeping the curriculum meaningful and engaging is essential but also challenging, and we have developed a number of ways to monitor and refine it. Of these, the most obvious yet important is engaging pupils in frequent discussion about their learning. In addition, an assessment tool called Pupil Attitudes to Self and School (PASS)[2] provides quantitative whole-school data, and our home learning approach is pupil-driven: the more positive the response in the home learning to learning experiences in school, the more inspiring the topic. Our teachers are now used to adjusting the curriculum in line with evidence from these sources so that it is truly responsive to pupils and their world.
- *Values-based staff recruitment*: Being a church school, we recruit people who in the first instance can show how they will contribute to its distinctiveness. But, as a member of CPRT Schools Alliance, we also ask candidates to observe our children and teachers at work and identify how what they observe reflects the CPRT aims and priorities. This enables us to identify those who are genuinely receptive to the values and principles in which the school's teaching is embedded.
- *Revisiting core ideas*: In a period of increasing instability and sudden policy shifts, it's all too easy to be deflected from the long-term educational path one has mapped out. Re-reading the CPR final report and revisiting the CPRT aims and priorities reminds us why we are in teaching and provides the evidence and arguments to justify our belief that we can and must trust ourselves as professionals to provide for our pupils' development and learning.

The above will have given you a very good idea of the philosophies underpinning the practice in Saint Leonard's Primary School. The aims expressed by Jo might well correlate with your own beliefs. Equally, you are likely to have formulated many questions about what it must be like to teach in such a school.

Task 4.2.2 Does it all add up?

So, how do you find a school where you can enact and implement your philosophy, thus maximising the positive influence that you have on the learners in your care? One of our suggestions, as a useful starting point, is to closely look at the purported aims of a school and consider how these aims 'feel' to you. A school's website can offer a very useful 'window' on to its vision and aims. To take a negative example, one might find that a school's website features words such as 'excellence' and 'standards' and 'progress', but there may be very little evidence of what this looks like in practice. The question becomes: 'excellence', 'standards' and 'progress' in what exactly? Just in English and maths – or throughout all curriculum subjects and extracurricular activities, as well as in attitudes and behaviour? Further to this, Burnett (2016: 36) asks: 'How can we develop curriculum and pedagogy that are empowering to children now and for their future personal, social, economic and political lives?' – this is a question you can usefully reflect upon during this task.

In exploring a website, there are some key points to look for if you are seeking to work for an organisation that shares your same philosophy – even if your 'philosophy' does not feel fully formed. You could seek out the following:

- Vision statement/message to (prospective) parents from the head teacher: Do these two things align and give you a real sense of purpose in the school? What sorts of phrases are used? Is there a clarity in language use as well as ideas?
- Newsletters: Are these up-to-date and regular? Are alternative formats available to cater for a diverse community? Do these encourage families to participate in their children's learning?
- Photographs from classes and year groups: Is there a balance in the representation of different year groups? Is there a range of activity shown, reflecting the diversity of the children's experiences?
- Curriculum information: Do curriculum maps show evidence of a stimulating curriculum? What is the range of subjects mentioned? Do you think any essential ones have been overlooked? To what extent are cross-curricular links noted?

What we are suggesting is a critical appraisal of the above, guided by your own beliefs and values. It may help to print some of this information off, where possible, and annotate it with reflective notes. These are some areas worthy of investigation, but you may like to explore beyond this list. You could usefully refer back to the twelve CPRT aims in reflecting upon this task. As an alternative to focusing on specific schools, an Internet search on 'primary school vision and values' will yield numerous links for you to explore.

THE CLASSROOM ENVIRONMENT

The layout and organisation of a classroom can reveal much about how far aims are put into practice. The teacher who states that s/he believes every child learns in different ways, at different rates and through different interests must demonstrate this in the curriculum and also the physical environment. How do you envision your classroom space?

A personalised, democratic classroom is well organised, so that resources are clearly accessible to children. Children are able to make their own choices about materials they might need to use to support their learning and able to get them and put them away easily. This should be the case for learners whatever their age. The resources are varied and extensive, so – for example – there is not just one type of pen but a range from which to select. The room will have different kinds of learning space within it, perhaps a distraction-free zone, a creative space that invites you to think, somewhere for relaxed learning.

The evidence of learning in such a room will be equally varied. For instance, if the school uses working walls to support personalisation, these will demonstrate the range of ways a problem in maths might be solved, rather than indicate a particular method. Celebratory displays are likely to show the learning process from inception to outcome, exploring the ways that children approached the learning. The children's voices will be visible, perhaps through their writing but also through quotations that may have been transcribed from discussions.

CASE STUDY 1: THE IDENTICAL FISH

In looking around a school, you may well be impressed at beautifully presented displays, but taking a closer look can be revealing. What are these displays telling you about the aims for children's learning? A clear indicator of limited aspirations for learning is evident where walls are covered in near-matching examples of work:

The year one classroom was absolutely stunning: colourful and densely packed with wonderful artwork, clearly labelled and carefully double mounted. The theme was clear: Under the Sea; a great topic with so much opportunity for first-hand experience. A display of thirty colourful fish was highly decorative and bold, entitled 'The Aquarium', yet each fish was cut out of one of three photocopied templates. There was some evidence of children elaborating by drawing scale shapes or using a range of coloured pencils, but generally there was a homogeneous feel. When I asked a child about the display and why they had created the fish, the answer came back, 'to go on the wall, if they are good enough'. The children were not able to tell me what they were learning. The teacher too had difficulty in talking about the learning: 'We made the fish to make the topic more evident in the classroom. The children were developing their fine motor skills in colouring, keeping inside the lines and then cutting the fish out'.

What learning do you think took place as children coloured in and cut out fish? Consider ways that the activity could have been made into a richer, more personal learning experience. What might you put on display to show the learning process?

It's unfortunate that a 'factory-line' approach is sometimes taken to children's creative activities, when they are likely to have many exciting ideas to express in their own unique ways (Bresler, 1993). Can you see which of the twelve CPRT's aims connect to a less controlling approach?

FOSTERING CHILDREN'S CREATIVITY

Pupils' views offer the best source of whether worthwhile learning, which meets their requirements, is taking place. However, you will find that it is quite common for children to tell you about *how to* make something or *how to* complete a task, without any idea as to *what* they are learning, beyond, for example: 'about the Tudors'. When children are asked to follow a narrow set of instructions, this also narrows their thinking and learning. Unfortunately, design and technology activities, such as art and design (as shown in the case study above), seem to be a common source of limiting learning. For example, pupils are frequently asked to 'design' something, such as a torch, which they then are instructed to make in a particular way. In a truly open culture, the question would be, can you design and make something to bring light to the room? Suddenly, the parameters are lifted, and possibilities become endless, as children's creativity as 'possibility thinking' is activated; they can meaningfully ask: 'what is this?' and 'what can I do with this?' (Craft, 2001). Although, in making, we cannot always follow the direction in which children would like to go, if children have regularly experienced a personalised approach, they will be able to tell you about how they made a torch after being given some genuine choices in their learning.

CASE STUDY 2: ENGAGING OUTSIDE SPACES

We both argue for the importance of play in children's school experiences and learning (Wood and Attfield, 2005). Outdoor play provision at lunch and break times should reflect the principles described in this unit: the valuing of each individual; and purposeful and irresistibly engaging learning within an environment thriving on possibility. This view is in line with sociocultural learning theories, recognising that learning occurs via interaction with others, both in formal and informal learning spaces (e.g. Vygotsky, 1978).

At St Leonard's, pupils are enabled to learn at every opportunity. With this in mind, the 'outside' space – that is, any spaces external to the classrooms – provides opportunity to explore, take risks, be sociable or simply relax and play alone.

Inside spaces host games, mini world, for example, Lego, comics, things for drawing, all for self-selection, set amidst comfy sofas and chairs. Children are trusted to use the space and put things back. There is a 'wonder room' too, full of unusual objects and images that pupils can explore and wonder at.

Outside there are team-based games, led by an adult who ensures fair play and draws children into refereeing. There are pieces of large apparatus that spin alongside the more traditional climbing and adventure equipment. Long pieces of tree trunk (see Figure 4.2.2) and bits of old sheets and blankets are dotted around for shelter making.

Older pupils act as play leaders, facilitating positive interactions for younger pupils and those with additional needs.

Space is well used and pupils often come up with new ideas that are not just adopted but trialled, adjusted and reviewed. Mealtime assistants meet regularly with leadership team members and pupils. It's great to see them enjoying their work, often coming into school bringing their latest charity shop buys to incorporate into play.

Jo's example illustrates how well-considered spaces enable children to feel relaxed and confident. These spaces should offer stimulation and challenge, as well as reassurance. For example, the children in Figure 4.2.2 feel a sense of success in carrying the heavy trunk as a team, knowing that others, including adults, are nearby for assistance if needs be.

FIGURE 4.2.2 Teamwork in the outdoor environment

Source: J. Evans

Task 4.2.3 My dream playground!

Asking children to design their ideal playground is a popular learning activity in many schools. Sometimes, these designs actually inform real change, but even when they don't, it can be a useful opportunity for the teacher to learn what children think about their existing play provision and how it might be improved.

In this final task, we would like you to design your dream playground – a place in which you think children would relish spending time. You can either draw your ideas or make a 'mood board' using images from the Internet. Annotations could be helpful. The ideas should be physically realisable rather than fantastical, but you do not have the restraints of a budget. When you have completed your drawing or mood board, spend some time reflecting upon the aims that your vision fulfils. What new insights have you gained?

The purpose of this task is to further reinforce that children's experience of school – and their learning – is not confined to the classroom, but also that teachers need to exercise their imaginations as much as young learners and recognise the excitement of playtime.

THE IMPORTANCE OF BEING CURIOUS

Education should be about asking meaningful questions. We argue that inspiring children to hold on to and develop their love of learning should be a key priority. As Socrates said: *wisdom begins in wonder*. For example, watch any 3-year-old child exploring his or her environment, asking question after question; it is this curiosity and delight that needs to be nurtured, like the precious resource it is. Equally, a teacher's own curiosity and interest in how children learn are crucial ingredients in this nurture. This is why critical reflection on your teaching practice is useful for your professional development (Hatton and Smith, 1995), regardless of the stage of your career. What has been successful and why? What has surprised you? It can be particularly useful to discuss your reflections with colleagues.

A school, like a classroom, should foster the different interests and capabilities of its community, as well as catering for its needs. For teachers, this means that variation should be evident, alongside some consistency of practice. If everything is uniform, then this might not be a school where deviation from the script is permitted, thus potentially limiting both child and adult growth. Indeed, international research conducted with more than 2 million teachers highlighted that teachers' beliefs about the nature of teaching and learning directly influence classroom practice and pupil outcomes (OECD, 2009). Being aware of your personal educational beliefs and how you enact these is therefore essential.

If everyone is enabled to grow and flourish, then support staff should have the same opportunities as teachers to further their careers through access to professional development opportunities. Schools that value every member of staff are places where professional development takes place at all levels. Support staff will be able to tell you about the opportunities afforded to them, for example, starting with National Vocational Qualifications, into Foundation Degrees. They describe not only the difference it makes to them but the impact on their skill levels in working with pupils.

As a teacher, developing and understanding your own personal philosophy of education and what kind of learning experience you want children to have while in your classroom/care is more likely to have a greater impact on outcomes than any national education policy.

SUMMARY

In this unit, we have noted how the aims for primary education are wide-ranging and not universally agreed upon. There has been a look at recent policy and research, in order to contextualise our discussion. We have shared some advice on identifying, understanding, formulating and enacting aims. In particular, we have drawn your attention to the twelve aims for primary education identified by the research of the Cambridge Primary Review, which are now being operationalised through the work of its trust. Examples from Jo's practice have been shared in order to relate theory to practice. You will also have engaged in some activities to help you better understand various aspects of putting aims into practice.

Perhaps the strongest recommendation we can make to you is to be broad-minded and open to new ideas and developments. What you hold to be important now might well change with more experience. This is not a failing. It is testament to the fact that education, as a social endeavour, is constantly shifting and is context-dependent. Your professional development will be shaped by your experiences in schools, and your interactions with children and with colleagues will enrich your knowledge and understanding of what it means to be a primary teacher.

NOTES

1   Jo sat on the CPRT Board, representing the Schools Alliance. Emese was a regional CPRT coordinator.
2   See: www.gl-assessment.co.uk/products/pass-pupil-attitudes-self-and-school (accessed 26 October 2017).

ANNOTATED FURTHER READING

Egan, K. (n.d) *Competing Voices for the Curriculum*. Retrieved from www.sfu.ca/~egan/Competingvoices.html (accessed 26 October 2017).
> This think-piece provides a clear and informative discussion about educational aims, drawing on some seminal literature such as Rousseau's *Emile*. Egan identifies three main ideas that underpin education in its broadest sense and explains the incompatibilities between these, providing a useful introduction to some of the complex relationships between educational theory and practice.

FURTHER READING TO SUPPORT M-LEVEL STUDY

Alexander, R.J. (2010) *Children, Their World, Their Education: Final Report and Recommendations of the Cambridge Primary Review*, London: Routledge.
> We direct readers to this important text in order to fully understand the remit and research of the Cambridge Primary Review and how this informs the twelve CPRT aims referred to throughout our unit. With regard to aims, of particular relevance are Chapters 3, 10, 12 and 24.

Burnett, C. (2016) *The Digital Age and Its Implications for Learning and Teaching in the Primary School*, York, UK: Cambridge Primary Review Trust.

> We identify Burnett's research report as essential reading for twenty-first-century teachers. Whether or not digital literacy features high on your personal list of aims for primary education, one cannot deny that the (digital) world is changing at an unprecedented pace, and this has massive implications for teaching and learning.

Bates, A. (2014) '(Mis)Understanding strategy as a "spectacular intervention": A phenomenological reflection on the strategy orientations underpinning school improvement in England', *Studies in Philosophy & Education*, 33: 353-67.

> You may at first wonder at the relevance of this article to day-to-day classroom activities, but philosophies underpin all our actions as teachers – it's just we may not always recognise them. Bates's discussion is valuable reading, and she also explains complex ideas in accessible terms.

RELEVANT WEBSITES

Cambridge Primary Review Trust: http://cprtrust.org.uk/

> An excellent portal to a wide range of research evidence and contemporary debates about primary education from every imaginable angle. Sign up to the mailing list.

Teaching Schools Council: http://tscouncil.org.uk/

> This features insights from the 'self-improving school-led system' comprising more than 600 teaching schools nationwide. You can sign up to the mailing list for news.

New Schools Network: www.newschoolsnetwork.org/

> This organisation represents free schools – independent state-funded schools established by different interest groups. The website gives useful insights into their philosophies.

Whole Education: www.wholeeducation.org/

> In its own words: 'Whole Education facilitates shared learning and collaboration between innovative schools'. Well worth visiting for inspiration.

REFERENCES

Adams, K., Monahan, J. and Wills, R. (2015) 'Losing the whole child? A national survey of primary education training provision for spiritual, moral, social and cultural development', *European Journal of Teacher Education*, 38(2): 199-216.

Alexander, R.J. (2010) *Children, Their world, Their education: Final Report and Recommendations of the Cambridge Primary Review*, London: Routledge.

Alexander, R.J. (2011) 'Evidence, rhetoric and collateral damage: The problematic pursuit of "world class" standards', *Cambridge Journal of Education*, 41(3): 265-86.

Bresler, L. (1993) 'Three orientations to art in the primary grades: Implications for curriculum reform', *Arts Education Policy Review*, 94(6): 29-34.

Burnett, C. (2016) *The Digital Age and Its Implications for Learning and Teaching in the Primary School*, York, UK: Cambridge Primary Review Trust.

Craft, A. (2001) 'Little c Creativity', in A. Craft., B. Jeffrey and M. Leibling (eds) *Creativity in Education*, London: Continuum, pp. 45-61.

Crossley, D. (2015) 'An education worth having: The aspirations and the development of the Whole Education Network in England', *European Journal of Education*, 50(2): 184-95.

Department for Education (DfE). (2016) *Educational Excellence Everywhere*, London: HMSO.

Evans, J. (2015) *Living the CPRT Ideal* [blog]. Retrieved from http://cprtrust.org.uk/cprt-blog/living-the-cprt-ideal/ (accessed 11 October 2016).

Hatton, N. and Smith, D. (1995) 'Reflection in teacher education: Towards definition and implementation', *Teaching & Teacher Education*, 11(1): 33–49.

Maslow, A. (1954) *Motivation and Personality*, New York: Harper.

OECD. (2009) 'Teaching practices, teachers' beliefs and attitudes', in *Creating Effective Teaching and Learning Environments: First Results from TALIS* (Chapter 4). Retrieved from www.oecd.org/berlin/43541655.pdf (accessed 2 December 2016).

Shuayb, M. and O'Donnell, S. (2008) *Aims and Values in Primary Education: England and Other Countries*, Interim report summary. Retrieved from http://cprtrust.org.uk/wp-content/uploads/2014/06/research-survey-1-2.pdf (accessed 9 November 2017).

Vygotsky, L.S. (1978) *Mind and Society*, Cambridge, MA: Harvard University Press.

Wood, E. and Attfield, J. (2005) *Play, Learning and the Early Childhood Curriculum*, 2nd edn, London: Paul Chapman.

CRITICAL PERSPECTIVES ON THE CURRICULUM

Ayshea Craig and Dominic Wyse

INTRODUCTION

The idea that countries, or other jurisdictions, should have a national curriculum for primary (elementary) and secondary education is very common across the world. Over the last two decades, the attention paid by governments to national curricula has become more intense, not least because of the comparison of jurisdictions made in international testing and surveys such as PIRLS (Progress in International Reading Literacy Study), PISA (the Programme for International Student Assessment) and TIMSS (Trends in International Mathematics and Science Study). Responding to these international developments, the countries of the UK have also paid increased attention to their national curricula. At the same time, with increasing political devolution, the curricula of the different countries in the UK have diversified. As far as the National Curriculum in England is concerned, the rise of high-stakes national testing has had a significant impact on the curriculum children have access to in schools. And the diversification of primary schools in England, not all of which are now required to follow the 'National' Curriculum, has led to more variety, as some schools take up the opportunity to choose or design their own curriculum.

As part of the preparation for your school experience, you will have become more familiar with the idea of a national curriculum. There has not always been a national curriculum in the countries of the UK, and, as a result of political devolution, the national curricula of Northern Ireland, Scotland, England and Wales have developed important differences in their aims, structure and scope. In this unit, you will explore national curricula and reflect on differences between a curriculum document and the curriculum as enacted in the classroom. You will also be introduced to some of the broader pressures and influences on what is taught in primary schools, such as statutory testing, school inspections and school type.

OBJECTIVES

By the end of this unit, you should:

- be aware of debates about the aims of the primary curriculum;
- appreciate that the history of the curriculum is an important aspect of continuing debates;
- be starting to think about how teachers make professional decisions about the curriculum in the best interests of the children that they teach;
- be aware of the range of curricula in place in countries across the UK and in different types of school across England;
- have considered the influence of statutory testing on the taught curriculum.

When a national curriculum was first proposed by the British government, there was strong resistance to its introduction (Haviland, 1988). Previously, teachers, schools and school boards had a great deal of freedom to decide what would be taught in their classrooms. Resistance to the idea of a national curriculum was based in part on the perception that it threatened teachers' professionalism, by introducing political involvement into an area that had previously been under the control of the profession (ibid.). However, one of the arguments mounted in favour of a national curriculum was that pupils across England and Wales were receiving an uneven education, which could include considerable repetition of subject matter, a situation that was exacerbated if children moved areas to different schools. There were also claims that some groups of children, particularly minority ethnic ones, were subject to low expectations, enacted in the curricula that were delivered to them. A national curriculum was seen as a solution to these problems, because it would ensure that all children had an *entitlement* to a continuous and coherent curriculum (one of four *purposes* of the original National Curriculum). But, exposing children to the *same* curriculum does not necessarily lead to the fulfilment of their entitlement. The purpose of a national curriculum could be seen as to set out a minimum, shared entitlement, rather than putting a limit on what schools and teachers might aim for when designing their local curricula.

Despite the resistance to the National Curriculum evident in the public consultation, it was introduced in England, Northern Ireland and Wales in 1988. Following complaints that the 1988 National Curriculum was overburdening schools, it was revised in 1993, but the revisions did little to reduce the load.

Since then, control of education and of the curriculum has been devolved to the Northern Irish and Welsh assemblies, which now, along with Scotland, have their own national curricula. These curricula differ in significant ways. In spite of three significant reviews of the primary curriculum in 2009 (the government-commissioned report, Rose and DCSF, 2009; House of Commons Children, Schools and Families Committee, 2009; and the Cambridge Primary Review, e.g. Wyse, McCreery and Torrance, 2010), the National Curriculum in England remained very similar to the previous versions until 2014, when a new National Curriculum was introduced.

SOME INTERNATIONAL THEMES IN NATIONAL CURRICULA

There are two themes that are particularly prominent in the study of curricula: knowledge in the curriculum, and international comparison of national curricula. The idea that theories of knowledge are at the heart of thinking about curricula goes back many decades, for example to work by Hirst (1974) and Tyler (1949). More recently, the idea that knowledge in the curriculum had been neglected was aligned with a perceived need to 'bring knowledge back in' (Young, 2008). However, the nature of knowledge represented in England's 2014 National Curriculum for primary schools is a rather crude, 'knowledge-based' curriculum that does not reasonably reflect Young's complex ideas – for example, Young's proposition that curriculum *theory* had lost sight of its object of study, teaching and learning, and its distinctive role in education sciences (Young, 2013).

The differences between types of curriculum – for example, what are called 'process' curricula (Kelly, 2009) or 'aims-based curricula' (Reiss and White, 2013) and knowledge-based curricula – have been a long-standing point of contention. Our view of England's current 2014 National Curriculum for primary education, in comparison with other curricula internationally, is that it has a lack of emphasis on processes and aims in comparison with its focus on knowledge (see also Reiss and White, 2013). For example, the over-specification of the transcription elements of writing (such as grammar and spelling, including their emphasis in national testing) risks minimising the important processes of composition of writing. And the lack of attention to cross-curricula aims, such as the development of creativity, is a problem when the emphasis of the curriculum is so heavily subject-based and knowledge-based, particularly in the modern era when cross-curricula topics such as creativity are so highly valued (Wyse and Ferrari, 2014).

Another way to look at how knowledge is manifest in curricula is to compare the ways in which different countries structure their national curricula. International comparison has two quite different traditions. The first kind is exemplified in the tradition of in-depth understandings of small groups of different countries, taking due account of their different social and cultural contexts (e.g. Alexander, 2000). The second kind is exemplified by the pupil testing and surveys of teachers and head teachers that is typical of international comparative work, such as PISA, PIRLS and TIMSS (see www.oecd.org /pisa/ and https://timssandpirls.bc.edu/). In recent years, the political attention to these international surveys, including league tables of countries' performance published in the media, has grown, along with academic concern at what is called 'performativity' (Wyse, Hayward and Pandya, 2015). The idea of performativity draws attention to the consequences that arise when 'high-stakes' testing is used as an accountability measure (for schools and/or teachers), at national or international level.

With regard to curriculum policy development in England, a curious feature of its history has been governments' targeting of single countries round the world as exemplars, typically based on the kinds of international league table outlined above, rather than looking much closer to home at the four nations of the UK, an approach that has been called 'home-international comparison'.

In 2013, Wyse *et al*. published the first book-length home-international analysis comparing the national curricula in England, Northern Ireland, Scotland and Wales. The book explored the idea of national educational policy being influenced by transnational policy trends, and it includes historical perspectives on the development of a national curriculum, paying particular attention to the national curriculum texts and research evidence on the implementation of national policies. One of the findings of the work was to identify the increasingly stark differences between national curricula in England and national curricula in the other three nations as a result of political devolution. The policy in Scotland was particularly noteworthy. In Scotland, the Education (Scotland) Act 1980 very clearly gave power over the curriculum to local authorities: '(2) In any such school the education authority shall have *the sole power* of regulating the curriculum and of appointing teachers' (The Education (Scotland) Act 1980, Section 21, p. 13; emphasis added). This early legislation was an important feature of the greater democratic involvement of educators in their system. In spite of the roots in democratic involvement, the place of teacher agency was still uncertain (Priestly and Biesta, 2013).

In England, the Education Reform Act 1988 (HMSO, 1988) put the power to develop a national curriculum in the hands of the government through the Secretary of State for Education:

> Duty to establish the National Curriculum
> 4.–(1) It shall be the duty of the Secretary of State so to exercise the powers conferred by subsection (2) below as–
> (a) to establish a complete National Curriculum as soon as is reasonably practicable (taking first the core subjects and then the other foundation subjects); and
> (b) to revise that Curriculum whenever he considers it necessary or expedient to do so.
> (Chapter 40, section 4, p. 3)

Another difference between the curriculum in England and the curriculum in Scotland is that Scotland's *Curriculum for Excellence* (Scottish Government, 2011) is a through curriculum that covers birth to 18, rather than the position in England, with different curricula for different phases of the education system.

In Scotland . . .

Curriculum for Excellence allows for both professional autonomy and responsibility when planning and delivering the curriculum. There are no longer specific input requirements in terms of time allocations. The framework provides flexibility to organise, schedule and deliver the experiences and outcomes in ways that meet the needs of all learners, but also provides reassurance about consistency where necessary. Such flexibility will result in a more varied pattern of curriculum structures to reflect local needs and circumstances.

(Scottish Government, 2008: 11–12)

Source: Scottish Government. (2008) *Curriculum for Excellence. Building the Curriculum 3: A Framework for Learning and Teaching*. Retrieved from https://www.education.gov.scot/Documents/btc3.pdf (accessed 26 October 2017).

In order to understand the practical implications of the National Curriculum in Scotland, let us take one area, 'languages' (note this more appropriate title, as opposed to the National Curriculum subject title, 'English', in England). In the *experiences and outcomes* element of the curriculum, the five major sections in the language requirements are each divided into the *organisers* of: listening and talking, reading, and writing ('mode' might have been a more appropriate description in relation to language). The requirements are preceded by a list of aspects that pupils are expected to have opportunities to engage with. These include, 'engage with and create a wide range of texts' (p. 24). An interesting feature of the language of these aspects and the requirements more generally is the use of the personal pronoun 'I', implying that the curriculum is pupil-centred. For example, 'I develop and extend my literacy skills when I have opportunities to: communicate, collaborate and build relationships'(p. 24). Another interesting feature is the *enjoyment and choice* strand, which is the first column in the first section of the tables that are used to organise the requirements for each organiser. For the teaching of writing, the requirements in the primary education stages include, 'I enjoy creating texts of my choice and I regularly select subject, purpose, format and resources to suit the needs of my audience' (p. 33). This is indeed a powerful statement. The opportunity for pupils to choose what to write (in the fullest sense, including topic, form and ways of working) is something that has very rarely been seen in practice since the process approach to writing of the 1980s and early 1990s (Wyse, 1998). Like Northern Ireland, Scotland's National Curriculum texts include extensive descriptions of the rationales for the experiences and outcomes material and for its organisation.

In Scotland . . .

Curriculum areas are not structures for timetabling: establishments and partnerships have the freedom to think imaginatively about how the experiences and outcomes might be organised and planned for in creative ways which encourage deep, sustained learning and which meet the needs of their children and young people.

(Scottish Government, 2008: 11–12)

Source: Scottish Government. (2008) *Curriculum for Excellence. Building the Curriculum 3: A Framework for Learning and Teaching*. Retrieved from https://www.education.gov.scot/Documents/btc3.pdf (accessed 26 October 2017).

We need Scottish education to deliver both *excellence* in terms of ensuring children and young people acquire a broad range of skills and capacities at the highest levels, whilst also delivering *equity* so that every child and young person should thrive and have the best opportunity to succeed regardless of their social circumstances or additional needs.

(Scottish Government, 2016: 3)

Source: Scottish Government. (2016) *National Improvement Framework for Scottish Education; Achieving Excellence and Equity*. Retrieved from http://www.gov.scot/Resource/0049/00491758.pdf (accessed 21 March 2016).

Unlike Scotland's attempts over many years to fully engage society in developing a shared curriculum, in preparation for England's 2014 National Curriculum, ministers in England opted for an expert group to make recommendations to a dedicated group of civil servants in the Department for Education, and hence rejected the opportunity for a longer-term, considered and democratic process to build a national curriculum fit for the twenty-first century. However, even accepting many of the recommendations of the national curriculum expert group, appointed in 2010 by Education Minister Nick Gibb, proved impossible, and hence several members of the expert group resigned, as was clearly documented (see www.bera.ac.uk/promoting-educational-research/issues/background-to-michael-goves-response-to-the-report-of-the-expert-panel-for-the-national-curriculum-review-in-england (accessed 26 October 2017)).

As we have briefly outlined in this unit so far, there are strong arguments to suggest that primary-phase national curriculum development in England has suffered from a lack of rigour, understanding and coherence as a result of poor government interventions. The most serious of these are:

- insufficient attention to the range of relevant scholarship and research evidence;
- an undue emphasis on comparison with other countries in international league tables, as opposed to greater democratic involvement in curriculum development, including in development of curriculum aims;
- insufficiently rigorous attention to views expressed in public consultations (Wyse, 2013).

Task 4.3.1 Other national curricula

Examine a national curriculum from your own and one other UK country. Try to identify some similarities and differences and then identify two or three changes that you think would be of benefit to the national curriculum you will be expected to work with.

In Northern Ireland . . .

In 1992, the first Northern Ireland Curriculum was introduced. This was similar in structure to that in England and Wales, but with a few points of distinction in relation to subjects and cross-curricular themes. It was found, in practice, to be much too overloaded and, in 1996, was revised, with a significant amount of content removed but remaining unchanged in structure. In 1999, the then minister gave permission for the CCEA to undertake a fundamental review of the statutory requirements of the curriculum. Following a 5-year period of research, review and consultation, a new and quite different statutory curriculum was approved in 2004. Legislation was passed for the phased introduction of that curriculum over a 3-year period, beginning in September 2007. Among the changes introduced was a new Foundation Stage for the first 2 years of schooling. The revised curriculum, in each of its stages, is now almost devoid of statutory requirements relating to subject content. Instead, statutory requirements now mostly concern the skills and competences that children are expected to develop, such as, information management, thinking skills, problem-solving and creativity.

The result of these changes is that, from 2007, there has been much greater divergence between the statutory curriculum in Northern Ireland and that in England.

Source: www.bbc.co.uk/northernireland/schools/pdf/NIschools_curriculumOverview.pdf (accessed 26 October 2017).

In Wales . . .

A new curriculum is being developed for settings and schools in Wales. The aim is that it will be available by September 2018, and used throughout Wales by 2021.

The new curriculum will have more emphasis on equipping young people for life. It will build their ability to learn new skills and apply their subject knowledge more positively and creatively. As the world changes, they will be more able to adapt positively.

They will also get a deep understanding of how to thrive in an increasingly digital world. A new digital competence framework is now introducing digital skills across the curriculum, preparing them for the opportunities and risks that an online world presents.

The new curriculum will bring this about by making learning more experience-based and the assessment of progress more developmental, and by giving teachers the flexibility to deliver in more creative ways that suit the learners they teach.

This new approach was informed by Professor Graham Donaldson's independent review of curriculum and assessment arrangements in Wales, Successful Futures.

Source: http://gov.wales/topics/educationandskills/schoolshome/curriculuminwales/curriculum-for-wales-curriculum-for-life/?lang=en (accessed 26 October 2017).

THE JOURNEY FROM STATUTORY CURRICULUM TO THE CLASSROOM

In spite of the importance of statutory curricula, you may find that once you start your school experience the statutory requirements are rarely referred to. One reason for this is that schools' long-term and medium-term planning has often been discussed, agreed and written down over a considerable period of time. Once this thinking has been translated from a National Curriculum document into teaching plans, the official documents are not really needed so much. This can make it difficult for student teachers to appreciate the links between the National Curriculum documentation and school planning. Another area in which it is sometimes difficult to see the links with the statutory documents is the extent to which some of the important opening statements of national curricula are genuinely reflected in classroom practice. These opening statements, such as aims, principles and values, should be very important because, in theory, it is these that guide everything else in the documents. In practice, curricula vary in their internal coherence, and the values and aims implicit in the detailed curriculum can be very different from those espoused in the opening statements.

There is further room for variation in the move from planning, or the locally planned curriculum in a school, to the teaching that goes on in the classroom. This teaching can be thought of as the *enacted curriculum*, and there are many reasons why the curriculum enacted in the classroom may differ from statutory curricula and from locally planned curricula. An experienced teacher will adjust and adapt planning in response to the needs and attainment of their pupils, often as a lesson unfolds. There is a further leap to be made to consider the children and what they each learn through the experiences they have in the classroom (sometimes referred to as the *received curriculum*). Learning does not necessarily follow just because something has been taught, and it is important to recognise that 'covering the curriculum' does not in any way guarantee children's learning.

In England, the period from 2000 to the present has seen the development of an increasingly diversified school sector. Academies, first introduced in 2000 by a Labour government under Tony Blair, are state-funded schools that do not fall within the control of local authorities. Significantly, academies, free schools and private schools do not need to follow the National Curriculum. They are required to ensure that their curriculum is 'balanced and broadly based, and includes English, mathematics and science', but can make many of their own decisions about curriculum design. This means that, in 2016, the 'National' Curriculum in England applied as a statutory requirement to the education of only 76 per cent of primary-age children (calculated from figures in DfE, 2016b).[1] This is in contrast with Wales, Scotland and Northern Ireland, where the vast majority of primary-age children are educated in schools that are required to teach the same national curriculum, although there may also be a number of different school types and systems in place.

If the trend towards academisation of primary schools in England were to continue, we could expect to see a wider range of curricula in use and fewer teachers in schools required to teach the National Curriculum. Early evidence, however, suggests that the potential for curriculum innovation in these schools has not always been realised (Greany, 2016), and it may be that the opportunity to develop a different curriculum has led instead to a reduced curriculum, at least in the non-core subjects. It is in the provision of non-core subjects that English primary school head teachers have indicated they are most likely to deviate from the National Curriculum (Cirin, 2014), an area of entitlement once protected for all children by a statutory National Curriculum.

Although there are many local reasons for differences between statutory and enacted curricula, there are also some system-wide pressures, such as national testing and school inspection frameworks, which affect the curriculum in primary schools. As the range of curricula in use diversifies, the role of school inspections and statutory national assessments, with the associated dangers of performativity, in shaping the curriculum becomes even more evident. It has been argued that the high-stakes nature of statutory testing in mathematics and English in England at age 6 (the phonics screening check), 7, 11 (statutory assessments) and 16 (examinations and other qualifications) has narrowed and distorted the curriculum (Select Committee on Children, Schools and Families, 2008). This sort of high-stakes testing system is designed to hold schools and teachers to account in what is seen as one of their core purposes at primary level - to ensure that all pupils are supported to become literate and numerate. Many people remain unhappy about the nature of national testing of children in England and the effects on children's experiences in school.

One of the effects of the focus on English and mathematics in statutory tests (SATs) has been the narrowing of the primary curriculum (Boyle and Bragg, 2006), so that other subjects are squeezed out. The story of science provision in English primary schools helps illustrate this. When SATs were introduced, from 1991 onwards, science was tested alongside maths and English. When science testing was made non-compulsory and replaced by teacher assessment, this led to a significant reduction in the time spent teaching the subject (Boyle and Bragg, 2005). Since 2010, there have also been pressures on funding, as local authorities have reduced their provision of central services in areas such as music and instrument teaching, leaving provision varied.

It has been argued that the pressure on schools and teachers to raise test scores has affected the distribution of resources within schools, as well as affecting the overall balance of subjects taught, particularly in Years 2 and 6 when the SATs are held (Marks, 2014). This can be seen when additional support is diverted to those children identified as close to but not yet achieving the required standards and pedagogy, or where the style of teaching becomes distorted, with 'quick fixes' becoming tempting at the expense of working towards a deeper understanding of the subjects.

In mathematics, the use of formulaic 'word problems' rather than testing problem-solving skills has led to the teaching of potentially counter-productive techniques, such as looking out for keywords to identify which arithmetic operation to use (Ehren *et al.*, submitted). Some of these techniques can be detrimental to understanding when applied to achieve quick results; much, however, depends on how teachers use them. The revised SATs, first introduced in 2016 in England, had a new focus on 'reasoning', with pupils asked to provide verbal and/or diagrammatic justifications for the truth of mathematical statements. This is in keeping with an emphasis on reasoning in the overall aims of the mathematics curriculum. Some schools have responded by looking at how children's skills in reasoning can be developed across the primary school. In other schools, there is evidence of the coaching of children in techniques to answer this type of question - techniques that are unlikely to improve their ability to reason about mathematics.

Any high-stakes assessment or accountability system poses a danger that playing the game through shortcuts and quick fixes may be inadvertently rewarded over genuine improvements; thus the intended goal of raising standards can be lost. The pressures on organisations and individuals within these systems can be immense. In English primary schools, there has been resistance to the predictable but unintended effects of SATs, both from teaching unions and from parents. The negative effects of ranking and frequent testing on the emotional well-being of children have also been highlighted (Hutchings, 2015). These negative effects were well understood at the time of the House of Commons national curriculum inquiry in 2008, and unfortunately they were more pronounced at the time of another House of Commons inquiry, into national assessment and accountability, in 2017.

As we have seen, there are a range of factors at play affecting the curricula actually enacted in schools and classrooms, and these can represent both constraints and opportunities for the class teacher in planning. The National Curriculum is the starting point for understanding the curriculum in schools, but awareness of other factors, such as funding, diversification of school types and, in England, the effects of high-stakes testing, is key to making sense of what you see in classrooms.

Task 4.3.2 Thinking about national curricula

- What are your views about a subject-led curriculum?
- Do you think that the strong emphasis on English and maths in England since 1997 has been a reasonable one? What are the advantages and potential disadvantages?
- Which aspects of the national curriculum are you excited about teaching? Which ones are you less confident about? And what will you do to improve your confidence?

THE PRIMARY CURRICULUM IN ENGLAND TODAY

Between September 2014 and September 2016, a new national curriculum was introduced in England. Despite the wider influences on what is taught in school discussed in the previous section, changes in the statutory curriculum still matter. For example, the move to make modern foreign languages compulsory in KS2 in 2014 has had a big impact on provision, with an immediate increase in the number of schools teaching a language, although concerns remain about the quality of provision (Board and Tinsley, 2015).

We saw in the previous section that high-stakes testing can result in a narrowing of the curriculum to focus on the areas being tested. Schools have responded in a variety of often imaginative ways to resist or mitigate these potential effects. One example of this is a move to a more topic-based curriculum as one way to find more space for subjects such as the humanities and expressive arts in a squeezed timetable. The current challenge for schools and teachers is to create time for a rich curriculum with proper engagement with a wide range of subjects, whether they approach this through high-quality cross-curricular teaching or by maintaining separate subjects.

Primary computing has been introduced as a subject for the first time, replacing information and communication technology (ICT). The new curriculum has an increased emphasis on understanding how computers work and on computational thinking, applying this through the development of programming skills. The old ICT curriculum aimed more to ensure that children were competent users of technology, but without the emphasis on understanding and problem-solving. This goal of developing competent users has remained, but has been enhanced in the new computing curriculum. The computing curriculum has created an opportunity and a challenge for schools, as investment in high-quality continued professional development is required to ensure that teachers' subject knowledge and skills keep up with the demands of the curriculum.

Although academies and free schools have a great deal of freedom, in theory, to set their own curriculum, we have seen that the government has made some elements of the curriculum statutory, and these are specified in the funding agreements for these schools. Independent schools are subject to the Education (Independent School Standards) Regulations (2014), which set out some minimum requirements for the 'quality' of education provided. Through these different mechanisms, all schools in England are required to provide teaching in English, mathematics and sciences, and all have some commitment to providing a broader curriculum. The Office for Standards in Education, Children's Services and Skills (Ofsted) inspects schools and makes judgements about how well schools and school leadership perform against this requirement (Ofsted, 2015). The inspection framework (Ofsted, 2016), and schools' interpretations of this, is another important factor influencing the local curricula found in English schools.

In Northern Ireland . . .

Similarly, in Northern Ireland, the Education and Training Inspectorate (ETI), which is a 'unitary' inspectorate and part of the Department of Education (DENI), inspects schools on a risk-based schedule, so that schools that are causing concern will be inspected more frequently. Schools can be rated as outstanding, very good, good, satisfactory, inadequate or unsatisfactory. The ETI claim that their remit is to promote school improvement through supporting schools' self-evaluation processes.

Source: www.etini.gov.uk/site-topics/inspection (accessed 26 October 2017).

In Wales . . .

Estyn is the education and training inspectorate for Wales. All education and training providers in Wales are inspected at least once within a 7-year period from 1 September 2016, with 20 working days' written notice. The focus will be on five inspection areas: standards; well-being and attitudes to learning; teaching and learning experiences; care, support and guidance; and leadership. It will also focus on a thematic area, which will help inform Estyn's thematic reports, the chief inspector's annual report and advice to the Welsh government.

Source: www.estyn.gov.wales/inspection/inspection-explained (accessed 26 October 2017).

There is no national curriculum for religious education (RE) or personal, social and health education (PSHE) in England, but both areas are currently part of the 'basic curriculum' in maintained schools, meaning that they must be taught. In these schools, they are subject to some statutory requirements and non-statutory guidelines, which set out requirements such as promoting respect for others. In early 2017, the Education Secretary announced the intention to make relationships education and PSHE statutory in academies as well as maintained primary schools.

A key distinction here is between RE – that is, learning about religions and religious practice in general – and religious instruction in one particular religion. In some countries, the national curriculum is completely secular, and state schools are not seen as an appropriate setting for religious education or instruction. In the UK, the Church of England and the Catholic Church have a long history of involvement in the education system, and RE remains a requirement in most schools, whereas religious instruction is permitted in some and regulated against in others.

The guidance for RE is non-statutory and applies to local-authority maintained schools (which excludes independent schools, academies and free schools). Requirements for the nature of RE teaching provided in academies and free schools vary depending on their funding agreements and tend to reflect the history of the school and its 'religious character'. On the whole, they tend to have much less detail and to leave more to the schools to decide. One of the arguments for the value of RE is that, in a religiously diverse society, even where the majority of people do not actively practise any religion, knowledge of other religions is valuable for promoting mutual respect and understanding.

Respect for others is one of the few areas that is required teaching across all schools in England (not least as a result of the Equality Act 2010; see Wyse, Ford *et al.*, 2016). Independent schools are subject to the least detailed requirements, but must still ensure that any PSHE encourages 'respect for other people' (The Education (Independent School Standards) Regulations, 2014). Academies and free schools, although not required to provide PSHE, are required to actively promote what are described as 'fundamental British values of democracy, the rule of law, individual liberty, and mutual respect and tolerance of those with different faiths and beliefs' and 'principles that support equality of opportunity' (DfE, 2016a). Maintained schools are subject to the same requirements (DfE, 2014). These state school curriculum requirements have arisen in part as a government response to concerns about extremism and terrorism.

All state schools are subject to requirements to teach children about evolution, and academies and free schools must not 'allow any view or theory to be taught as evidence-based if it is contrary to established scientific or historical evidence and explanations' (DfE, 2016a). This is another example of a relatively isolated curriculum requirement created in response to concerns about how some schools have used the freedom to set their own curriculum.

Finally, academies, free schools and independent schools, like maintained schools, must 'prevent political indoctrination' in their teaching. Interestingly, it is also a requirement that, in academies and free schools, children 'learn the nature of marriage and its importance for family life and for bringing up children' (DfE, 2016a), demonstrating the ongoing influence of the Church in the education system.

The diversity of primary school types in England means that there are very few requirements that apply to all schools and, hence, to all children, apart from the teaching of English, maths and science. As we have seen above, the government has made exceptions for a small number of issues, such as evolution, 'British values' and respect for others. The issues that are selected tell us something interesting about the histories of these school types, as well as current government concerns and priorities.

Task 4.3.3 Statutory for all?

If you were setting the regulations, would you make some elements of the curriculum statutory for all? Look back through the areas that are currently required for most or all schools to teach in England.

- Do you agree that these areas should be included in statutory curricula?
- What else would you include?

SUMMARY

In this unit, we have discussed the nature of national curricula and have explored how teachers make professional decisions about the curriculum for their pupils. We have also looked at the range of influences on the curriculum as it is enacted in classrooms and in variations between national curricula in different countries in the UK. The key issue that faces pupils, teachers and policymakers is the nature of autonomy over the curriculum. In England, in spite of greater school diversification, the autonomy of teachers and pupils has been increasingly challenged by high-stakes testing and by the government's particular interpretation of knowledge in the curriculum. Despite this, teachers and schools continue to find spaces to innovate.

One of the most important things about curricula in the future is that they need to be relevant from the early years up to the end of schooling, and should genuinely prepare pupils for lifelong learning. The current model in England for early years education differs from the model for primary years. We propose the model in Figure 4.3.1 as a starting point for thinking about a through curriculum and end by using the elements of this model to explore what such a curriculum might foreground.

A curriculum model that reflects learning and teaching from birth to adulthood needs to put the individual person's motivation to learn and their interests foremost. The curriculum needs to encourage teaching that explicitly encourages pupils to find areas of thinking that motivate them, and to pursue these in depth, even at the very earliest stages of education. Children's rights to participate in all matters that affect them should not be an abstract item in the programmes of study for citizenship, but a daily reality in their lives. Role-play and drama will be a recurrent medium for reflecting on the self in relation to the social context. Physical development, including health, will be nurtured as part of this focus.

The environment in which learning takes place is vital to sustain the self. In spite of futuristic claims about learning electronically from home, a place called school will still be the main arena for learning, but it should be one that is not a grimy, damp, cold, boomy building: it should be architecturally inspiring. It should be a place where the crafts of life, such as the preparation and sharing of food and the performing of and listening to music, are centre stage. The social interaction provided by the home and community will form an integrated link with the social interaction provided by the school's curriculum. Sights, sounds and

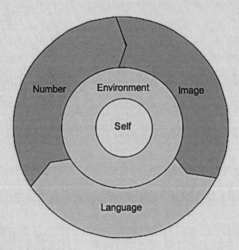

FIGURE 4.3.1 Proposed curriculum model

exploration of the world, beginning with the immediate surroundings, will form part of the environmental curriculum. Investigations will take place, problems will be solved, and things will be made. All of this will be set in the context of active participation in working towards a sustainable environmental future for the world.

Learning centred on image – both still and moving, icons, logos, signs, symbols – will no longer be neglected in view of the dominant role these things have in our daily lives, and have done for many years. The counting and categorisation of entities ultimately leading to the beautiful abstraction of mathematical symbols will remain a powerful focus for learning about number. Language in all its linguistic contexts, including text and talk, will also remain a powerful focus and one that unites all other aspects of this curriculum.

The introduction of computing as a subject in England from 2014 is interesting, but does it sufficiently represent the rapid developments in digital media? Digital technologies represent one of many realities of the modern world: a set of tools that paradoxically represent both the stability and change that are natural parts of the evolution of written language (Wyse, 2017). Digital technology and media should be present across the whole curriculum as appropriate, just as any other basic resource is. They should not be seen as the latest solution to educational problems, but rather, whenever appropriate, as means to enrich the possibilities for learning and teaching, and their influence will continue to grow organically.

The key elements addressed in this unit are most likely to be realised by a curriculum organised not by traditional subjects but by areas of learning. Is this suggestion that we abandon the current subject-dominated curriculum in England particularly radical? Not really. Well-tried examples include the Royal Society for the encouragement of Arts, Manufactures and Commerce (RSA)'s 'Opening Minds' curriculum, or the Helen Hamlyn Trust's *Open Futures* approach. Internationally, the primary curriculum developed by the International Baccalaureate Organization (IBO) organises its curriculum around six themes. Consider, also, higher education, which offers hundreds of subjects, and continues to add new ones, that combine a range of understanding and skills that would benefit from preparation by a different curriculum model in schools. However, the reason that these changes have not been made before, and why England's curriculum, we suggest, is still entrenched in the nineteenth century, is that it requires our political leaders to have the knowledge, understanding and courage to change legislation and revolutionise the primary education system in order to bring it into the twenty-first century.

NOTE

1   Based on 4.8 million primary-age children in England in January 2016, of whom 19.5 per cent were educated in academies or free schools (DfE, 2016b) and nearly 200,000, or about 4 per cent, were being educated in independent schools (figure taken from associated National Tables, table 1c, DfE, 2016b).

ANNOTATED FURTHER READING

Department for Education (DfE). (2011) *The Framework for the National Curriculum, A Report by the Expert Panel for the National Curriculum Review*, London: DfE.
> Thorough research-based review with recommendations based on a selection of evidence. Interesting to compare this with the National Curriculum produced.

Kelly, A.V. (2009) *The Curriculum: Theory and Practice*, 6th edn, London: Sage.
> An excellent overview of issues that combines comprehensive definitions with necessary political analysis. The comments about the increase in political interference with the curriculum, revealed through the author's reflections about the six editions of this book, are fascinating.

 FURTHER READING TO SUPPORT M-LEVEL STUDY

Wyse, D., Hayward, L. and Pandya, J. (2015) 'Introduction: Curriculum and its message systems: from crisis to rapprochement', in D. Wyse, L. Hayward and J. Pandya (eds) *The SAGE Handbook of Curriculum, Pedagogy and Assessment*, London: Sage, pp. 1-25.
> The introduction to a two-volume set of sixty-two chapters from experts on curriculum worldwide.

Young, M. (2014) 'What is a curriculum and what can it do?', *Curriculum Journal*, 25(1): 7-13.
> This is a response to the articles in a special issue of the BERA *Curriculum Journal*. The special issue was subsequently selected by Routledge to be published as a book called *Creating Curricula: Aims, Knowledge and Control*.

 RELEVANT WEBSITES

Cambridge Primary Review Trust: http://cprtrust.org.uk/
> This website contains links to the evidence for the Cambridge Primary Review, a large-scale, wide-ranging independent review of primary education headed by Robin Alexander and originally based at the University of Cambridge's Faculty of Education.

National Curriculum England: www.gov.uk/government/publications/national-curriculum-in-england-primary-curriculum
> This is the home of the Primary National Curriculum for England.

National Curriculum Scotland: https://education.gov.scot/scottish-education-system/policy-for-scottish-education/policy-drivers/cfe-(building-from-the-statement-appendix-incl-btc1-5)/What is Curriculum for Excellence?
> This is the homepage of the national curriculum for Scotland, Curriculum for Excellence.

 REFERENCES

Alexander, R.J. (2000) *Culture and Pedagogy: International Comparisons in Primary Education*, Oxford, UK: Blackwell.

Board, K. and Tinsley, T. (2015) *Language Trends 2014/15*, Reading, UK: CfBT Education Trust.

Boyle, B. and Bragg, J. (2005) 'No science today – the demise of primary science', *Curriculum Journal*, 16(4): 423–37.

Boyle, B. and Bragg, J. (2006) 'A curriculum without foundation', *British Education Research Journal*, 32(4): 569–82.

Cirin, R. (2014) *Do Academies Make Use of Their Autonomy? Research Report*, London: DfE.

Department for Education (DfE). (2014) *Promoting Fundamental British Values as part of SMSC in Schools*. Retrieved from www.gov.uk/government/publications/promoting-fundamental-british-values-through-smsc (accessed on 27 October 2017).

Department for Education (DfE). (2016a) *Mainstream Academy and Free School: Single Funding Agreement*. London: DfE.

Department for Education (DfE). (2016b) *Schools, Pupils and their Characteristics: January 2016*. Retrieved from https://www.gov.uk/government/uploads/system/uploads/attachment_data/file/552342/SFR20_2016_Main_Text.pdf (accessed on 27 October 2017).

The Education (Independent School Standards) Regulations. (2014) No. 3283. Retrieved from www.legislation.gov.uk/uksi/2014/3283/pdfs/uksi_20143283_en.pdf (accessed 21 January 2017).

The Education (Scotland) Act. (1980). Retrieved from www.legislation.gov.uk/ukpga/1980/44.

Ehren, M., Wollaston, N., Goodwin, J. and Newton, P. (submitted) 'Teachers' backward-mapping of patterns in high stakes math tests', *Assessment in Education: Principles, Policy & Practice*.

Greany, T. (2016) 'Innovation is possible, it's just not easy', *Educational Management Administration & Leadership*. Retrieved from http://journals.sagepub.com/doi/abs/10.1177/1741143216659297 (accessed 27 October 2017).

Haviland, J. (1988) *Take Care, Mr Baker!* London: Fourth Estate.

Her Majesty's Stationary Office (HMS). (1988) *Education Reform Act*, London: HMSO.

Hirst, P. (1974) *Knowledge and the Curriculum: A Collection of Philosophical Papers*, London: Routledge & K. Paul.

House of Commons Children, Schools and Families Committee. (2009) *National Curriculum. Fourth Report of Session 2008–09. Volume 1*, London: House of Commons.

Hutchings, M. (2015). *Exam Factories? The Impact of Accountability Measures on Children and Young People*, London: NUT.

Kelly, A. V. (2009) *The Curriculum: Theory and Practice*, 6th edn, London: Sage.

Marks, R. (2014) 'Educational triage and setting in primary mathematics: A case-study', *Research in Mathematics Education*, 16(1): 38–53.

Ofsted. (2015) *The Common Inspection Framework: Education, Skills and Early Years*. Retrieved from www.gov.uk/government/publications/common-inspection-framework-education-skills-and-early-years-from-september-2015 (accessed 27 October 2017).

Ofsted. (2016) School Inspection Handbook. Retrieved from www.gov.uk/government/publications/school-inspection-handbook-from-september-2015 (accessed 27 October 2017).

Priestly, M. and Biesta, G. (eds) (2013) *Reinventing the Curriculum: New Trends in Curriculum Policy and Practice*, London: Bloomsbury.

Reiss, M. and White, J. (2013) *An Aims-Based Curriculum: The Significance of Human Flourishing for Schools*, London: IOE Press.

Rose, J. and Department for Children, Schools and Families (DCSF). (2009) *The Independent Review of the Primary Curriculum: Final Report*, London: DCSF.

Scottish Government. (2011) *Curriculum for Excellence*. Retrieved from www.gov.scot/Publications/2011/02/16145741/0 (accessed 27 October 2017).

Select Committee on Children, Schools and Families. (2008) *Third Report*. Retrieved from www.publications.parliament.uk/pa/cm200708/cmselect/cmchilsch/169/16902.htm (accessed 27 October 2017).

Tyler, R. (1949) *Basic Principles of Curriculum and Instruction*, Chicago, IL: University of Chicago Press.

Wyse, D. (1998) *Primary Writing*, Buckingham, UK: Open University Press.

Wyse, D. (2013) *What Are Consultations For?* [IOE London Blog]. Retrieved from https://ioelondonblog.wordpress.com/2013/09/20/what-are-consultations-for/ (Accessed 9 February 2017).

Wyse, D. (2017) *How Writing Works*, Cambridge, UK: Cambridge University Press.

Wyse, D., Baumfield, V., Egan, D., Gallagher, C., Hayward, L., Hulme, M., Leitch, R., Livingston, K, Menter, I. and Lingard, B. (2013) *Creating the Curriculum*, London: Routledge.

Wyse, D. and Ferrari, A. (2014) 'Creativity and education: Comparing the national curricula of the states of the European Union with the United Kingdom', *British Educational Research Journal*, 41(1): 30–47.

Wyse, D., Ford, S., Hale, C. and Parker, C. (2016) 'Legal issues', in D. Wyse and S. Rogers (eds) *A Guide to Early Years and Primary Teaching*, London: Sage, pp. 301–20.

Wyse, D., Hayward, L. and Pandya, J. (2015) 'Introduction: Curriculum and its message systems: From crisis to rapprochement', in D. Wyse, L. Hayward and J. Pandya (eds) *The SAGE Handbook of Curriculum, Pedagogy and Assessment*, London: Sage, pp. 1–26.

Wyse, D., McCreery, E. and Torrance, H. (2010) 'The trajectory and impact of national reform: Curriculum and assessment in English primary schools', in R. Alexander, C. Doddington, J. Gray, L. Hargreaves and R. Kershner (eds) *The Cambridge Primary Review Research Surveys*, London: Routledge, pp. 792–817.

Young, M. (2008) *Bringing Knowledge Back In: From Social Constructivism to Social Realism in the Sociology of Education*, London: Routledge.

Young, M. (2013) 'Overcoming the crisis in curriculum theory: A knowledge-based approach', *Journal of Curriculum Studies*, 45(2): 101–18.

ASSESSMENT

ASSESSMENT FOR LEARNING

Formative approaches

*Eleanore Hargreaves, Caroline Gipps
and Alison Pickering*

INTRODUCTION

Assessment for learning (AfL) is a particular approach to assessment used by teachers in classrooms. It is not the same as the standardised tests or exams that you may give, but rather is a way of using informal assessment during ordinary classroom activities to improve learning. Here, assessment is seen as an integral part of the learning and teaching process, rather than being 'added on' for summative purposes. This approach brings with it a rather different relationship between teacher and learner than in traditional models of assessment, as the pupil needs to become involved in discussions about learning and assessment tasks, including learning objectives, the assessment criteria (success criteria), their performance and what they need to do to progress: the relationship is more of a partnership, with both pupil and teacher playing a role. We know that, with appropriate guidance, children as young as 5 can exercise considerable self-direction and benefit from doing so (Pramling, 1988).

Although there are many different interpretations of how AfL would ideally work, early defining sources were those of the Assessment Reform Group (ARG, 2002) and of Black and Wiliam (1998), who showed that improving children's learning through assessment depended on five, deceptively simple, key factors:

- the provision of effective feedback to pupils;
- the active involvement of pupils in their own learning;
- adjusting teaching to take account of the results of assessment;
- recognition of the profound influence assessment has on the motivation and self-esteem of pupils, both of which are crucial influences on learning;
- the need for pupils to be able to assess themselves and understand how to improve.

This unit will attempt to unpack two key issues: first, the nature of the feedback given to learners to help them understand the quality of their work and inspire them to consider how to progress in their learning; and, second, the active engagement of the learner, which is essential for promoting the learner's self-direction.

OBJECTIVES

By the end of the unit, you should be able to:

- understand the key factors associated with AfL;
- develop a range of strategies that will facilitate improved learning/teaching;
- recognise that pupils' self-direction in assessment is a powerful tool in raising achievement in the classroom.

AFL: FROM THEORY TO PRACTICE

The ten principles of AfL

AfL should be part of the effective planning of teaching and learning

A teacher's planning should provide opportunities for both learner and teacher to obtain and use information about progress towards learning goals. It also has to be flexible to respond to initial and emerging ideas and skills. Planning should include strategies to ensure that learners understand the goals they are pursuing, why they are pursuing them, and the criteria that could be applied in assessing their work against these. How learners will receive feedback, how they will take part in assessing their learning and how they will be helped to make further progress should also be planned, ideally in negotiation with the pupils themselves.

AfL should focus on how pupils learn

The process of learning has to be in the minds of both learner and teacher when assessment is planned and when the evidence is interpreted. Learners should become as aware of the 'how' of their learning as they are of the 'what'. Up-to-date research into how the learning process works needs to be recognised (see, for example, Hargreaves, 2012; Watkins, 2015).

AfL should be recognised as central to classroom practice

Much of what teachers and learners do in classrooms can be described as assessment. That is, tasks and questions prompt learners to demonstrate their knowledge, understanding and skills; what learners say and do is then observed and interpreted; and judgements are made about how learning can progress. These assessment processes are an essential part of everyday classroom practice and involve both teachers and learners in reflection, dialogue and decision-making. These definitions of assessment expand its meaning beyond tests to include all forms of enquiry into the learner's progress.

AfL should be regarded as a key professional skill for teachers

Teachers require the professional knowledge and skills to: plan for assessment, observe learning, analyse and interpret evidence of learning, give feedback to learners and support learners in self-assessment. Teachers should be supported in developing these skills through initial and continuing professional development. Today, there is research to indicate that continuing professional development can be most effective when it is continuous, inspired by teachers' own needs and aspirations, integrated into the school's agenda, collaborative, and supported by sources beyond the school too. One effective means of developing the skills of AfL has been the teacher learning community within the individual school, whereby a group of teachers meet together every 6 weeks

FIGURE 5.1.1 Assessment for learning should take account of the importance of learner motivation

and report back on AfL strategies with which they have experimented in the classroom (see Wiliam, 2008).

AfL should be sensitive and constructive because any assessment has an emotional impact

Teachers should be aware of the impact that comments, marks and grades can have on learners' confidence and enthusiasm and should be as constructive as possible in the feedback that they give. Comments that focus on the work rather than the person are more constructive for both learning and motivation. A student who is distracted by negative – or even positive – personal comments is less likely to be focusing on learning (see Torrance, 2012).

AfL should take account of the importance of learner motivation

Assessment that encourages learning fosters motivation by emphasising progress and achievement rather than failure. Comparison with others who have been more successful is unlikely to motivate learners. It can also lead to their withdrawing from the learning process in areas where they have been made to feel they are 'no good'. Motivation can be preserved and enhanced by assessment methods that protect the learner's autonomy, provide some choice and constructive feedback, and create opportunity for self-direction.

AfL should promote commitment to learning goals and a shared understanding of the criteria by which they are assessed

For effective learning to take place, learners need to understand what it is they are trying to achieve and why they are trying to achieve it – and they must also want to achieve it. Understanding and commitment follow when learners have some part in deciding goals and identifying criteria for assessing progress. Communicating assessment criteria involves discussing their importance and meaning with learners, using terms that they can understand, providing examples of how the criteria can be met in practice and engaging learners in peer and self-assessment.

Learners should receive constructive guidance about how to progress

Learners need support in order to plan the next phases of their learning. Teachers should:

- pinpoint the learner's strengths and advise on how to develop them;
- be clear and constructive about any weaknesses and how they might be addressed;
- provide opportunities for learners to improve upon their work.

AfL develops learners' capacity for self-assessment so that they can become reflective and self-managing

Reflective and self-managing (or self-directed) learners seek out and cultivate new skills, new knowledge and new understandings. They are able to engage in self-reflection and to identify how to progress in their learning. Teachers should support learners to take charge of their learning through developing the skills of reflection and self-assessment and allow pupils to take their own initiatives for progressing learning at times. The following case study illustrates the well-researched fact that pupils thrive on directing their own learning and having some choice. The following exchange occurred between Dave and his teacher during a metacognitive lesson in which the children wrote down their own responses to the experience of making wooden catapults:

> *Teacher to Dave*: Right, not just one word, we need it in a sentence, Dave. Exactly what we were just talking about. I said to you about – do you know what you're going to write about in the sentence, then, Dave?
> *Dave*: Concentrating on Wayne yelling in my ear.
> *Teacher*: Er, in a full sentence. 'Concentration would be hard with people distracting me.' Rather than 'yelling', we'll have maybe the word 'distracting'.

This dialogue was played back to Dave in interview. His body language and facial expression in interview indicated frustration with the fact that the teacher had told him what to write, using a different vocabulary. Later in interview, he told me that he had not in fact used the teacher's words, despite her instruction to do so. Dave told me her instruction made him feel like a postman, because the teacher's feedback concerned delivering, rather than authoring, the text. The interview ran as follows:

> *EH*: Okay. So do you wish [the teacher] hadn't given you an example?
> . . .
> *Dave*: If I ask for help, I need help, but most of the time I come up with stuff on my own.
> *EH*: Yes. So how does that make you feel when she does it for you?
> *Dave*: I'm not sure. Probably– I'm not sure what it's called, but someone has the idea, and you just write it down for them, it's weird.
> *EH*: You end up feeling like a–
> [Long pause]
> *Dave*: Postman.

EH: Postman?

Dave: Yeah, because they have to deliver letters.

(Hargreaves, 2013: 8)

AfL should recognise the full range of achievements of all learners

AfL should be used to enhance all learners' opportunities to learn in all areas of educational activity. It should enable all learners to achieve their best and to have their efforts recognised (adapted from ARG, 2002).

PLANNING FOR AFL

Effective planning enables you to provide learning opportunities that match the needs of all the children. It should include the following:

- objectives that focus on learning; the task then becomes the vehicle for the learning;
- strategies for finding out what the children already know, so that you can pitch the learning/ teaching at the appropriate level;
- an element of pupil choice;
- ways in which you can share the 'bigger picture' with the children, so that they know what they are aiming for;
- mini plenaries, so that the children can regularly reflect back on the bigger picture;
- opportunities for peer and self-assessment, with and without teacher support.

Sharing the bigger picture

From the start, discuss the success criteria with your pupils. Articulate exactly what it is you will be assessing. In writing, for example, a success criterion might be 'a descriptive piece of writing using a range of adjectives'. Teachers and pupils can create the success criteria together. Figure 5.1.2 shows a pupil self-assessment sheet for a history topic. You can display a large version on the wall and have an individual copy for each child. There are three levels of attainment here, which can be used for either pupil self-assessment or peer assessment.

What was it like to live here in the past?

Pupils must:
- understand that St Paul's School was different in the past;
- make comparisons between the school in the past and as it is today.

Pupils should:
- recognise features of the school building and know how it has changed over time;
- enquire about some of the people who have worked at the school (both pupils and staff) and understand differences in working conditions at different times;
- be able to use a range of historical sources in a variety of ways.

Pupils could:
- describe and compare features of the school and identify changes on a time line;
- select and combine information from different sources.

FIGURE 5.1.2 Pupil assessment sheet

Task 5.1.1 Pupil assessment sheet

Referring to Figure 5.1.2, choose another area of the curriculum and construct a similar sheet.

Discussion during the sessions and mini plenaries

Discussions take place before, during and after each lesson, as well as outside the classroom, so that the teacher can check the children's understanding and judge their progress. Discussion also provides a vehicle for a continued sharing of the learning objectives. Here are some strategies for doing this:

- Before the lesson, have discussions with the children to ascertain what they already know about the subject, in order that you can plan the work effectively to include different levels of understanding. Identify in your planning the children you wish to support in that lesson.
- Once you have identified children's misconceptions or unexpected responses, you can follow up your individual discussion during the session to clarify these.
- Monitor the children's progress throughout the lesson by asking them questions about the task and then sharing with them targets for the next steps in their learning.
- At intervals during the session, remind the children of the lesson objectives, then ask children to feed back to the class what they have found out so far, and what they still have to do to complete the task.
- Ask the children to evaluate their own progress against the success criteria given.

QUESTIONING

Effective questioning is the key to good teacher assessment, but make sure you know which questions to use and when you will use them. Teachers are always asking questions, but, in order to develop higher-order thinking skills, it is important to ask open-ended, provocative and child-centred questions (see Table 5.1.1). Harris and Williams have suggested that open-ended questions 'provoke speculation and extend the imagination' (2012: 375). The use of open questioning is critical in encouraging children to develop and then offer their own opinions. This occurs when the teacher acknowledges that these opinions are a valid response, rather than assessing whether they are 'right' or 'wrong'. This open-ended approach to questioning is much more productive than a closed questioning technique, where only one response is deemed 'correct' by the teacher, leaving the children guessing what the teacher wants to hear, rather than basing their response on their own ideas. Ask follow-up questions to make the children think more deeply. (For details of 'convergent' or 'divergent' questions, see Pryor and Crossouard, 2008; Harris and Williams, 2012.) Table 5.1.1 illustrates some questions designed to elicit higher-order thinking, which may be posed by either teacher or other pupils (King, 2002: 2).

Thinking time ('wait' time)

To encourage this process of high-level thinking, children must be given time to think more deeply before responding to questions. Once you have asked a question, allow the children 'thinking time' before listening to their responses. This has a twofold effect. First, it encourages pupils to think more

TABLE 5.1.1 How open-ended questions encourage thinking skills

Type of question	Responses
What do you notice about . . .?	Descriptive observations
What can you tell me about . . .?	Inviting recalled information but content chosen by the children
What does it remind you of?	Seeing patterns/analogies
Which things do you think belong together? Why do you think that?	Seeing patterns/classifying and creative explanations
What do you think will happen next?	Creative predictions
What happened after you did that?	Descriptive reasoning/cause and effect/conclusions
Why do you think that happened? I wonder why it did that?	Creative hypotheses/explanations
Do you think you could do it differently?	Evaluation/reflective analysis
I wonder what made you think that?	Reflective self-awareness/metacognition
Anything else? Or?	Neutral/inviting more of the responses listed above

deeply and fosters higher-order thinking skills, and, second, it builds the confidence of those pupils who take longer to respond. Teacher expectation is important here, expecting a response from every child. A useful technique for encouraging this is the use of 'discussion' or 'talk partners'. The child first shares their ideas with a partner, before some children are selected to share their response with the teacher and the class. This does require careful planning of partnerships to be effective, and frequent changes of partners can offer children exposure to a wider range of ideas. In this way, the children can test their ideas with their peers and perhaps adjust their thinking before offering a response, which in turn helps them feel more confident about voicing a response. During these peer discussions, the teacher has an opportunity to find out any misconceptions that the children may hold, or indeed areas of the topic that excite them. S/he may use a randomising method to choose who responds in front of the class each time – for example, using raffle tickets or lolly sticks with names on (sometimes known by pupils as the 'unlucky draw'). The information s/he gains from every child can be fed into planning, making it more personalised.

PEER AND SELF-ASSESSMENT

An increased awareness of the role of the learner in the assessment process has led to changes in approaches to teaching, involving more dialogue between pupils and teachers in the setting and adaptation of the assessment process. Learners are more aware, not only of what they learn, but how they learn and what helps them learn. Pupils can assess themselves and can learn from their own and others' assessments. This, in turn, leads them to reflect on how they learn. Children should be involved, not only in their own assessment, but also in peer assessment. This gives children a central role in learning and is a really important shift from the teacher having all the responsibility for assessment to a position of sharing goals, self-evaluation and setting their own targets (see Read and Hurford, 2010).

FIGURE 5.1.3 Peer and self-assessment

Task 5.1.2 Questioning to encourage thinking skills 1

- Table 5.1.1 shows a range of questions designed to help children think in sophisticated ways. Apply this technique to a specific curriculum area.
- Ask a colleague to observe your teaching session and comment on your inclusion of the following aspects of questioning – you could reciprocate by observing his or her teaching and then sharing your findings:
  - asking questions to assess the children's starting points in order to adapt learning and teaching;
  - asking a range of questions;
  - using thinking time and 'talk partners' to ensure all children are engaged in answering questions;
  - giving the children opportunities to ask questions before and after the session;
  - creating a question board related to a particular topic and encouraging children to 'post' on this;
  - having an agreed time to discuss the questions with the children.

Task 5.1.3 Questioning to encourage thinking skills 2

Reflect on how the information you obtained in Task 5.1.2 then impacted on your planning for this aspect of the curriculum.

This approach can be highly motivating, but must be endorsed by a supportive classroom ethos, which should include clear guidelines for the children in terms of supporting and guiding each other's learning. Some research has highlighted that peer assessment can be anxiety-provoking unless carefully guided (e.g. Hargreaves, 2015). There must, for example, be a clear focus and structure for the lesson. Children need a set of success criteria and assessment criteria (see 'Planning for AfL', above) by which to judge the success of their own and peers' learning, and avoiding marks or grades is essential. These criteria can be negotiated with the children. Consider some of the following methods of engaging your children in their own assessment. Notice that the final example is a class's assessment of its own learning strategies, not just focused on a particular curriculum domain.

(a) In Mr Zak's class, before starting any new topic of learning, the pupils describe what they already know about that topic and what they would like to know about that topic. Mr Zak then teaches the topic in accordance with what the pupils have told him. Sometimes he invites pupils to teach some parts if they have good knowledge about it.

(b) In Miss Sophie's class, each month pupils are asked to do 'self-assessments'. They look back at the work they have done over the past month, noticing progress made since the previous month, and write down in a Learning Log specific tasks they need to do in order to achieve the targets they have been set. Sometimes they work in collaboration with a peer assessor.

(c) Before the class does any work or project, teacher Mrs Han asks the class to suggest what features a good end product would include. For example, when writing a creative story, the children suggested that the story would be interesting to read. When all the criteria are agreed, they are written for everyone to see. At the end of the work or project, the pupils assess each other against these agreed criteria.

(d) Mr Nat's Year 5 class uses a system of peer assessment. When an assignment is finished, two peers read the assignment. The author of the assignment then assesses it against agreed criteria (making judgements about its value). The two peers then give *provocative* feedback, asking the author questions that will make the author think more deeply about the topic. No judgements are made by the peers, only by the author him/herself. The author may then rework the assignment.

(e) In Mrs Yasmina's class, there are two big noticeboards pinned up at the front of class. One is titled 'What helps our learning', and the other is titled 'What hinders our learning'. At the end of each day, the children reflect on their day's learning and contribute factors for each noticeboard. They then discuss how they can decrease the hindrances and increase the helping factors.

Task 5.1.4 Self-assessment

Support your pupils to assess themselves or their peers using one of the methods described above.

FEEDBACK

Effective feedback to children provides information to support self-assessment and suggests steps that will lead to progress. Feedback through written comments (if written text is easily accessible by your students) should refer back to the learning goals set at the beginning of the session and should be constructive. We know that many teachers focus on spelling, punctuation, grammar or the structure of the piece of work, often omitting to comment on children's learning of the specific lesson objective. It can help to keep the presentational factors as *separate but constantly important* criteria, but on *each individual occasion to emphasise comments that relate directly to the specific learning and assessment objectives* for that lesson.

A useful way of thinking about/describing feedback is whether it is evaluative, descriptive or provocative (Hargreaves, 2017). All too often, teachers provide evaluative feedback in the form of grades and short (usually non-specific) comments, praise or censure. This kind of feedback tells pupils whether they are doing well or not, but it offers little direction for moving their learning forward. Regular critical, evaluative feedback, without guidance for how to improve, can lower motivation and self-esteem. Descriptive feedback, however, relates to the task at hand, the learner's performance and what they might do to improve in relation to specified learning objectives. Provocative feedback, finally, is less directive and inspires the learner to think more deeply and engage further, or to extend their imagination in relation to learning goals.

The ideal situation is when the teacher can discuss and annotate work with the child present, so that progress can be negotiated together. Difficulties in accessing written text can this way be decreased. However, this is not always possible, and so the teacher writes comments for the child to read and then gives them time to consider the comments. Here, a Year 5 pupil, Esther, describes the teacher's feedback during a lesson on using adjectives. The feedback led Esther to reflect further about adjectives and additionally encouraged her to draw on her own resources for progress:

> [The teacher has told Esther not to use 'silly' as her adjective]
> *Interviewer:* Do you remember why [the teacher] said not to use 'silly'?
> *Esther:* Well, normally she says, because we're not 5, we're Year 5, and we can actually think of much better words than just 'silly' or 'stupid' or something like that. You can think of much better words, because you've got a big thesaurus in your brain.
> *Interviewer:* Indeed . . . All right, then [teacher] gave you some advice, not just about what you were doing today, but always – she said the word 'always'. She said, 'It always helps to read your work out loud.'

RECOGNISING AND CELEBRATING CHILDREN'S WORK

You need to consider how a child's successful learning is recognised. Build in time for reflection at the end of the day or the week. In an early years setting, good learning may be celebrated in a discussion at the end of each session, taking the opportunity to point out what makes it worthy of comment. Another method of highlighting good learning is by taking photographs, which can be displayed as a slide show on a computer screen, providing a permanent reminder for both child and teacher. Some teachers simply display a chosen piece of work on the wall or on a bookstand, so that everyone can share that pupil's success. In this case, a specific time needs to be allocated to focusing on the displayed work and why it has been chosen.

It is important to involve the class sometimes in pointing out the learning processes that are particularly appropriate and not to focus only on their products. Praise in the form of 'excellent' or a reward/high grade for completed work does little to direct learning processes and can encourage children to avoid risk-taking or asking questions in the future.

Task 5.1.5 Questions to ask yourself in relation to your planning for AfL

- Does the assessment allow children multiple ways to demonstrate their learning across the range of curriculum activities?
- Does it assess the ways in which learning has taken place?
- How do you ensure that feedback from assessments allows the children opportunities to develop and progress in their learning by linking your comments to agreed success criteria and indicating the next phase to encourage further learning?
- How do assessment outcomes influence session planning and modifications to future curriculum planning?
- How will you/should you keep track of this?

Task 5.1.6 Peer reflection

You have had an opportunity to evaluate your practice in relation to pupil self-assessment and questioning. Now ask one of your peers to observe another lesson and comment on another two of the principles of AfL identified by the ARG. You can then observe your peer's class and share your comments to help each other learn. Remember that your comments should focus only on the aspects requested by the colleague you observe: you are not assessing their competence, but rather helping them to learn.

SUMMARY

Assessment for learning as opposed to *assessment of learning* is part of ongoing learning and teaching, and is not a 'bolt-on'. Its aim is to assess all areas of the curriculum, and, in order to achieve this, it uses a wide range of strategies to secure a range of opportunities to find out about each child. It leads to a recognition of what a child can already do and the identification of progress they might now make in their learning, so that they can proceed at a pace, and in ways, appropriate for them. This is done by a mixture of teacher-led assessment and pupils sharing in the assessment process, so that they can eventually assess their own work and set appropriate targets. Although there is currently a national debate on the extent to which AfL strategies raise attainment, many teachers in England and especially Scotland, as well as in diverse countries across the world, have described AfL as transforming their children's learning and their own experiences of teaching. When this happens, it seems to involve the teacher and pupils in a whole new approach to learning and teaching in which the teacher–learner relationship is freshly negotiated, and pupils take a greater lead over directing their own learning.

ANNOTATED FURTHER READING

Dann, R. (2018) *Developing Feedback for Pupil Learning*, London: Routledge.

> *Developing Feedback for Pupil Learning* seeks to synthesise what we know about feedback and learning into more in-depth understandings of what influences both the structure of and changes to the learning gap. This research-informed but accessibly written enquiry is at the very heart of teaching, learning and assessment. It helps to support our understanding of what works (and what doesn't) for whom, and why. Split into three main parts, it covers:
> - feedback for learning in theory, policy and practice;
> - conceptualising the 'learning gap';
> - new futures for feedback.

Hargreaves, E. (2017) *Children's Experiences of Classrooms*, London: Sage.

> This book emphasises pupils' own experiences of learning, teaching and feedback in the classroom. Chapter 4 focuses exclusively on feedback, comparing traditional definitions of feedback as 'knowledge of results' with 'divergent', 'process-focused' and 'provocative' examples of teachers' feedback. It explores the dangers of feedback emphasising the pupil's character. It then provides extensive examples of pupils' responses to teachers' classroom feedback in a selection of primary classrooms.

FURTHER READING TO SUPPORT M-LEVEL STUDY

Stobart, G. (2008) 'Reasons to be cheerful: Assessment for learning', in G. Stobart, *Testing Times: The Uses and Abuses of Assessment*, London: RoutlegeFalmer, pp. 144–70.

> In this amusingly written chapter on AfL, Gordon Stobart provides a thorough survey of what AfL has been defined as, how this concept has developed in relation to learning theories, and what its implications are for classrooms. It is certainly useful as M-level reading and provides an insight into the ARG's thinking, as Stobart was a founder member of this. Stobart flags up the issue of teachers implementing the strategies of AfL without engaging with the 'spirit' of the strategies, that is, understanding how they might support learning most effectively. He gives considerable attention to classroom feedback, given its close relationship to enhanced learning.

Torrance, H. (2012) 'Formative assessment at the crossroads: Conformative, deformative and transformative assessment', *Oxford Review of Education*, 38(3): 323–42.

> This article is suitable for M-level reading, although more demanding than the three readings suggested above. In the article, Harry Torrance suggests that the theory and practice of formative assessment (AfL) seems to be at a crossroads, even an impasse. Different theoretical justifications for the development of formative assessment have been apparent for many years. However, practice, although quite widespread, is often limited in terms of its scope and its utilisation of the full range of possible approaches associated with formative assessment. The paper reviews the issue that the aim of AfL is, ostensibly, to develop independent and critical learners, whereas, in practice, highly conformative assessment procedures are being designed and developed. The paper argues that educators need to attend to the divergent possibilities inherent in formative assessment, if the full potential of AfL is to be realised as a transformative practice.

RELEVANT WEBSITES

Collaborative Group Learning: www.collaborativegrouplearning.com

> This website of Rob Gratton's is mainly about how to support children in working together in productive groups and will therefore help you with the difficult task of making peer assessment successful.

Chris Watkins: http://chriswatkins.net/

    Chris Watkins's website is mainly about learning and it should help teachers to clarify the difference between performance – that is, outcomes – and learning – that is, processes.

REFERENCES

Assessment Reform Group (ARG). (2002) *Assessment for Learning: 10 Research-based Principles to Guide Classroom Practice*. Retrieved from www.aaia.org.uk (accessed 27 October 2017).

Black, P. and Wiliam, D. (1998) 'Assessment and classroom learning', *Assessment in Education: Principles, Policy & Practice*, 5(1): 7–74.

Hargreaves, E. (2012) 'Teachers' classroom feedback: Still trying to get it right', *Pedagogies*, 7(1): 1–15.

Hargreaves, E. (2013) 'Inquiring into children's experiences of teacher feedback: Reconceptualising assessment for learning', *Oxford Review of Education*, 39(2): 229–46.

Hargreaves, E. (2015) '"I think it helps you better when you're not scared": Fear and learning in the primary classroom', *Curriculum, Pedagogy & Society*, 23(4): 617–38.

Hargreaves, E. (2017) *Children's Experiences of Classrooms: Talking about Being Pupils in the Classroom*, London: Sage.

Harris, D. and Williams, J. (2012) 'The association of classroom interactions, year group and social class', *British Educational Research Journal*, 38(3): 373–97.

King, A. (2002) 'Structuring peer interaction to promote high-level cognitive processing', *Theory into Practice*, 41(1): 33–9.

Pramling, I. (1988) 'Developing children's thinking about their own learning', *British Journal of Educational Psychology*, 58(3): 266–78.

Pryor, J. and Crossouard, B. (2008) 'A socio-cultural theorisation of formative assessment', *Oxford Review of Education*, 34(1): 1–20.

Read, A. and Hurford, D. (2010) '"I know how to read longer novels" – developing pupils' success criteria in the classroom', *Education 3–13*, 38(1): 87–100.

Torrance, H. (2012) 'Formative assessment at the crossroads: Conformative, deformative and transformative assessment', *Oxford Review of Education*, 38(3): 323–42.

Watkins, C. (2015) 'Meta-learning in classrooms', in D. Scott and E. Hargreaves (eds) *The Sage Handbook of Learning*, London: Sage, pp. 321–30.

Wiliam, D. (2008) 'Developing classroom practice: Meeting regularly in teacher learning communities is one of the best ways for teachers to develop their skill in using formative assessment', *Educational Leadership*, 65(4): 36–42.

ASSESSMENT AND LEARNING

Summative approaches

Kathy Hall and Kieron Sheehy

INTRODUCTION

In this unit, you will have the chance to reflect on what summative assessment is, its uses and its potential impact on learners. You will also be able to consider some aspects of current policy on assessment. We start by considering some basic questions about summative assessment and by linking it with formative assessment. We will go on to identify purposes of summative assessment, as well as sources of assessment evidence and we will explain what counts as good evidence of learning. We also describe current policy on assessment and reporting. We highlight some difficulties with 'high-stakes' assessment and we finish by inviting your views on current assessment policy and practice.

OBJECTIVES

By the end of this unit you should be able to:

- define summative assessment and relate it to formative assessment;
- explain why it is important to assess learners in a variety of contexts and know the kinds of assessment tasks that are effective in generating good evidence of learning;
- identify ways in which schools might use summative assessment information to feed back into teaching and learning;
- describe some aspects of the national policy on assessment and offer an informed opinion about the current emphasis on different assessment purposes and approaches.

WHAT IS ASSESSMENT AND WHY DO IT?

Assessment means different things in different contexts and it is carried out for different purposes. There is no simple answer to what it is or why we do it. Indeed, one of the most important messages that we would like you to take away from this unit is that assessment is not a simple or innocent term. Assessing learning is not a neutral or value-free activity – it is always bound up with attitudes, values, beliefs and sometimes prejudices on the part of those carrying out the assessment and on the part of those being assessed. When we make assessments of children's learning, we are always influenced by what we bring with us in terms of our previous experiences, personal views and histories.

Children's responses to assessment are influenced by what they bring with them - their previous experiences and their personal views.

Summative assessment sums up learning

Most recent sources on assessment refer to two important types. One is summative assessment, the other is formative assessment. Sometimes, summative assessment is termed 'assessment of learning' (AOL), and, in recent times, formative assessment has been associated with 'assessment for learning' (AfL). These newer terms are useful, as they give an insight into the purpose of assessment that is involved in each case. In the previous unit (5.1), the area of formative assessment is addressed in more detail.

As the term implies, summative assessment tries to sum up a child's attainment in a given area of the curriculum. Summative assessment is retrospective: it looks back at what has been achieved, perhaps over a term, year or key stage. Formative assessment, on the other hand, is prospective: it looks forward to the next steps of learning. However, debate continues over whether and how summative and formative assessment should be distinguished (Black and Wiliam, 2007; Torrance, 2012). As we explain in a moment, we consider that the use to which assessment information is put is also helpful in determining whether it is labelled summative or formative.

SOURCES OF ASSESSMENT EVIDENCE

Assessing learning is about collecting information or evidence about learners and making judgements about it. The evidence may be based on one or more of the following:

*   what learners say;
*   what learners do;
*   what learners produce.

The information or evidence may come from learners' responses to a test, such as a spelling test; a classroom activity, such as a science investigation; a game or a puzzle; or a standard assessment task or test such as the SATs. It may come from a task or activity that is collaborative, that is, one where several pupils work together on the same problem. It may come from a task that pupils do on their own, without interacting with other children.

We suspect that you will have observed children and made judgements about them in many of those settings, and you may have noted down some of your observations and/or shared them with the class teacher or tutor when you were on teaching practice.

PURPOSES OF SUMMATIVE ASSESSMENT

As a new teacher, you will be meeting children whom you have not taught or may not have even met previously. In these situations, you might wish to gain an overview of each pupil's progress. This is particularly so when children are transferring between different stages of schooling and the classwork is different. Summative assessment is used frequently in these contexts because obtaining a summary of what learners know or can do helps the teacher to decide what to teach next.

Summative assessment is carried out for several purposes. First, it provides you with a summary of learners' achievements that will inform your future teaching and, of course, your planning for future learning. (This is close to the notion of formative assessment described in Unit 5.1.) Second, it provides valid and accurate information that can be shared with parents about their children's progress.

And, third, summatively assessing learning can provide a numerical measurement that can be used in league tables – the purpose being to make schools accountable by allowing comparisons of achievement across schools.

In Scotland . . .

We need Scottish education to deliver both *excellence* in terms of ensuring children and young people acquire a broad range of skills and capacities at the highest levels, whilst also delivering *equity* so that every child and young person should thrive and have the best opportunity to succeed regardless of their social circumstances or additional needs.

(Scottish Government, 2016: 3)

Source: Scottish Government. (2016) *National Improvement Framework for Scottish Education; Achieving Excellence and Equity*. Retrieved from http://www.gov.scot/Resource/0049/00491758.pdf (accessed 21 March 2016).

Before reading on, try to put these purposes in order of importance for yourself as a classroom teacher.

We suspect this exercise is not that simple to do. Assessing learners for the purpose of helping you to plan your teaching can't easily be accommodated alongside assessing learners for the purpose of rendering the school or class accountable through the publication of league tables. League tables call for assessment methods that are reliable, in that they are comparable across all schools and across the country as a whole, and valid, in that they offer an account of what is considered important to know at various stages of schooling. As Black *et al.* (2003: 2) note, these are 'exacting requirements'. Reliability and comparability are not major issues if, on the other hand, you are seeking evidence to help you decide what to teach next.

For the purpose of generating league tables, as Black *et al.* (2003) note, the main assessment methods are formal tests (not devised by teachers). These are usually isolated from day-to-day teaching and learning, and they are often carried out at special times of the year. In contrast, assessments designed to inform your teaching are usually more informal, they may be integrated into your ongoing teaching, and they are likely to be carried out in different ways by different teachers. In the light of the previous sentence, you may well wonder what the difference is between summative and formative assessment, and indeed some research challenges the distinction in the first place (Threlfall, 2005). However, in line with the work of Black and Wiliam (1998), we are reluctant to label the latter as formative assessment.

As we see it, the salient feature of formative assessment is that learners themselves use the information deriving from the assessment to bridge the gap between what they know and what they need to know (see Hall and Burke, 2003, for a full discussion). Collecting information to inform your teaching is in itself no guarantee that learners will use this information to move forward in their learning.

PRODUCING GOOD EVIDENCE OF ACHIEVEMENT

It is important to appreciate that summative assessment can take a variety of forms – it need not, indeed should not, just be a written test. In addition, it is important for you as a teacher to try to anticipate how pupils might respond to the demands of an assessment task. In 1987, Desmond Nuttall wrote a paper describing the types of task or activity that are good for assessing learning. Such tasks, he says, should be concrete and within the experience of the individual, they should be presented clearly, and they should be perceived by the pupils as relevant to their current concerns.

Being able to respond to a task by using different methods - for example, making, doing, talking and writing - allows learners to demonstrate their learning in a variety of ways. The value of varied approaches to assessing learning is that they help learners really show what they know or can do. For example, a learner who is not a very skilled writer may be better able to demonstrate their historical knowledge through talk or through a combination of written work and oral work. Think about your own history as a pupil - do you feel that a written test enabled you to demonstrate what you really knew? Would other ways have been more appropriate for assessing your competence in different curriculum areas?

The use of a variety of ways of assessing learning (often referred to as 'multiple response modes') allows adults to have evidence of learning from a variety of contexts, and to avoid making judgements about learning based on single sources of evidence, such as, say, a pencil-and-paper test. This results in information that is more accurate and trustworthy than information deriving from just one assessment in just one situation. You could say that it is more valid and dependable. By looking across several instances in which a child uses, say, reading, the teacher and teaching assistant gain valuable information about that child as a reader.

Judgements based on the use of a variety of sources of assessment information are, of course, more demanding on time and resources. This means teachers and policymakers have to consider the appropriate balance to obtain between validity and trustworthiness of assessment evidence on the one hand, and manageability and cost on the other.

Tick sheets and portfolios

Some teachers use 'tick sheets' to summarise a child's achievements at a point in schooling. This type of assessment is also summative. What is your view of this approach in the light of the previous section about good assessment evidence?

The tick-sheet, yes/no approach might be manageable for very busy practitioners and could provide a useful overview of a child's learning. However, it is likely to be too crude to offer a really meaningful account of learning, and usually it offers no source of evidence or little evidence regarding the context in which the assessment took place. Mary Jane Drummond, an expert on early years education, says that a tick-sheet approach may hinder the production of a 'rich respectful account' (1999: 34) of a child's learning.

Portfolios offer a useful way of keeping evidence of learning. For example, your pupils may have an individual literacy portfolio into which they put lists of books read, written responses to stories, non-fiction writing, drawings or paintings in response to literature, and so on. They may include drafts of work, as well as finished pieces of writing. You might then use this evidence to write short summary accounts of your pupils, which in turn could be used as a basis of discussion at a parents' evening.

As well as individual portfolios, some schools keep 'class' or 'school' portfolios where they put samples of pupil work. They may annotate the samples with reference to context and the standards met. So, for example, contextual annotations might include the date, whether the piece of work was the result of pupils collaborating or an individual working alone, whether the teacher helped or whether it was done independently. Annotations about the standard met might include a grade or a score and a comment indicating how closely the work met a National Curriculum standard. This kind of portfolio sometimes acts as a vehicle for teachers to share their interpretation of standards and perhaps agreed targets, not just among themselves but also with parents and with pupils.

SUMMATIVE ASSESSMENT AND TEACHER ASSESSMENT

As well as the external testing regime of standard assessment tests (SATs), teachers assess and report on their pupils via teacher assessment – they are required to 'sum up' their pupils' attainments in relation to the National Curriculum. As we noted earlier, in order to offer defensible and trustworthy accounts of their attainment, you need to assess pupils in a variety of contexts and in a variety of ways. But, any assessment is only as good as the use to which it is put. An important question is: what happens to the assessment information once it is collected? This aspect of assessment is known as 'consequential validity', as it refers to the consequences of the assessment. Is the assessment information used to inform teaching, to enable the production of league tables or to summarise achievement for parents, or to pass on to the next teacher to support planning?

Changes across the UK over the past several years have given teachers more responsibility for summative assessment (Black *et al.*, 2011). Assessment information, including that obtained via SATs and, especially, teacher assessment, can be used in a way that supports teaching and learning. We will explain this with reference to the way some teachers use assessments in their schools. A study conducted in six different schools in six different local education authorities (LEAs) in the north of England sought to understand primary teachers' summative assessment practices (Hall and Harding, 2002). On the basis of many interviews, over 2 years, with teachers and LEA assessment advisers and observations of assessment meetings, two contrasting approaches by schools were identified. The approaches are described as *collaborative* and *individualistic*. To illustrate, we will describe two scenarios at either end of a continuum – highly collaborative and highly individualistic. One we call East Street and the other West Street, which show these contrasting tendencies. The purpose of presenting this here is not to make any statement about representative practice in schools today, but to offer you contrasting scenarios to enable you to think more constructively and critically about practices you might encounter. As you read the descriptions, consider your own experience of being in schools on teaching practice.

A collaborative approach

East Street School is a large inner-city primary school of more than 400 pupils, all but 5 per cent of whom are from ethnic minority backgrounds. East Street has an assessment community that is highly collaborative, with teachers, parents and pupils having many opportunities to talk about assessment and how and why it is done. The staff frequently meet to discuss the purposes of assessment in general and their ongoing teacher assessment in particular. They talk about what constitutes evidence of achievement in various areas of the curriculum and they compare their judgements of shared samples of pupil work. They use a range of tools, such as school portfolios and sample material from official websites, to help in their assessment tasks and to ensure that they are applying assessment criteria consistently. They strive to include pupils, parents and other teachers as part of that assessment community.

An individualistic approach

West Street School is a larger-than-average primary school serving a varied socio-economic area in a northern city. West Street reluctantly complies with the demands of national policy on assessment. Teachers here work largely in isolation from each other in interpreting and implementing assessment goals and, especially, in interpreting standards and criteria for assessment. Very little or no use is made of portfolios, and there is limited opportunity for staff to meet as a team to share their assessment practices and perspectives. There is no real attempt to involve interested groups, such as parents and pupils, in assessment discussions. The staff tend to view national testing as an unhelpful, arduous intrusion.

It is likely that, some 16 years after that study was conducted, schools are now much more collaborative in their approaches in general, and especially in relation to assessment.

Task 5.2.1 Assessment – different approaches

- Study Table 5.2.1, which summarises the assessment approach in the East Street and West Street schools.
- Suggest some reasons for the difference in approach in the two schools.
- Practice in most schools is probably somewhere in between these two. Make a note of which practices listed for East Street you are aware of from your experience in school recently.

TABLE 5.2.1 Assessment communities and assessment individuals

	Collaborative (East Street School)	Individualistic (West Street School)
Goals	Compliant and accepting	Reluctant compliance and resistance
Processes	Assessment seen as a requiring interpretation Interpretation is shared Portfolios in active use Exemplification materials used by teachers A mixture of school-devised and official website materials in use to support summative judgements Evidence – planned collection of evidence Variety of modes Assessment embedded in teaching and learning Emphasis on the process and not just the product Common language of assessment Commitment to moderation (cross-checking of interpretations of evidence) to ensure consistency and fairness	Limited emphasis on collaboration and sharing of assessment information Portfolios – dormant Exemplification materials not used Commercially produced materials used by some individuals No school-level policy on assessment Evidence – not used much Assessment often bolted on to learning and teaching Emphasis on products rather than processes Uncertainty/confusion about terms Weak or non-existent moderation or cross checking of assessment judgements
Personnel	Whole school; aspirations to enlarge the assessment community to include pupils, parents and other teachers	Teachers as individuals; no real grasp of the potential for enlarging the assessment community
Value system	Assessment seen as useful, necessary and integral to teaching and learning; made meaningful through collaboration	Assessment seen as 'imposed' and not meaningful at the level of the class teacher or the school

To become a collaborative assessment community, staff need time to develop their expertise. Teachers need time to talk about and share their practices in a culture that shares the expectation that adults too are valued learners.

SUMMATIVE ASSESSMENT AND REPORTING: CURRENT POLICY

Summative assessment does not just refer to the kinds of end of key stage assessment carried out in schools in England and known as SATs (there are no SATs in Wales, Scotland or Northern Ireland; see below). Although these external tasks and tests are indeed summative, they are not the only kind of summative assessment that goes on in schools. However, because of their 'high stakes' – that is, schools' ranking in league tables depends on them – they are accorded very high status in practice in schools, and people sometimes make the mistake of assuming that summative assessment means SATs.

This section offers a description of current assessment policy in the primary school.

Assessment and reporting of attainment

A new national curriculum (NC) was introduced into primary schools in September 2014, setting out the programmes of study for the various subjects. The NC sets out the expectations for the end of each key stage (KS), and schools are free to develop a curriculum relevant to their pupils that teaches that content. Schools are expected to have an assessment system that checks on what children have learned and the extent to which they are on track to meet the externally set expectations associated with the end of the relevant KS.

Attainment targets in the form of performance descriptors were introduced in the summer of 2016. These are described as frameworks to support teacher assessment and, alongside the external tests, are intended to provide evidence of learners' achievement. The descriptors are for indicating how a child is performing at the end of a KS and are in the form of three categories: 'working towards the national standard', 'working at the national standard' and 'working at greater depth within the national standard', from which one is selected to describe the child's performance. In the case, say, of writing at KS1, 'working at the national standard' incorporates twelve criteria that have to be demonstrated through a writing narrative that involves attention to a range of skills and knowledge in spelling, punctuation, grammar and handwriting.

Tests based on the NC for English, maths and science were implemented in the summer of 2016. The KS2 test results are reported as scaled scores, where the expected score is 100. The policy is that pupil progress will be measured in relation to the average progress made by children with the same baseline – that is, the same KS1 average point score. For 2016, the attainment component of the 'floor' target is set at 65 per cent of pupils in a school reaching that level. This is how 'floor standard' is defined:

> Schools will be above the floor if pupils make sufficient progress across all of reading, writing and mathmatics or more than 65 per cent of them achieve the national standard in reading, writing and mathematics. According to the Government's Association for Achievement and Improvement through Assessment (AAIA) website, schools will be above the floor if they meet either the progress or the attainment threshold.

(www.aaia.org.uk)

The attainment aspect is to be based on the proportion of pupils reaching the new expected standard in all of reading, writing and maths. They will need a scaled score of 100+ in reading and maths to have met the expected standard in writing. A school will be considered below the floor standard if two conditions apply: fewer than 65 per cent of pupils meet the expected attainment standard in reading, writing and maths combined (reading and maths assessed by external tests; writing via teacher assessment, or TA), and pupils have not made 'sufficient progress' in any one of reading, writing and maths.

There is no floor standard for the earliest years of formal primary schooling.

In Wales . . .

Foundation Phase requirements are that:

> Teachers and/or practitioners are required to assess children twice during the Foundation Phase – a baseline assessment, carried out within the first six weeks of a child entering Reception year, and an end of Foundation Phase assessment. There are currently no statutory requirements at the end of Nursery or Year 1; however leaders/ head teachers, where appropriate, should ensure that all teachers and/or practitioners gather evidence to inform judgements on each child's progress in all Areas of Learning. The Foundation Phase Profile can be used to support these assessments.
>
> (Learning Wales, 2016: 10)

Source: Learning Wales. (2016) *Statutory Assessment Arrangements for the Foundation Phase and End of Key Stages 2 and 3*, Cardiff: Welsh Government. Retrieved from http://learning.gov.wales/docs/ learningwales/publications/161011-statutory-assessment-arrangements-en.pdf (accessed 27 October 2017).

Performance tables remain central to accountability in England. The performance measures that are relevant for each primary school are all of the following:

- average progress in reading, writing and maths;
- percentage reaching the expected standard in reading, writing and maths at the end of KS2;
- average score of pupils in the end of KS2 assessments;
- percentage of pupils who achieve a high score (yet to be defined) in all areas at the end of KS2.

The above measures are described by the AAIA as 'headline' measures, and all schools are required to publish them in a consistent, standard format on their websites from 2016. Thus, each school must post on its website a profile of itself, telling parents about pupil performance, progress and other priorities (DCSF, 2008).

Schools are required to report to parents of pupils in Years 2 (at end of KS1, usually age 7) and 6 (end of KS2, usually age 11) the results of their teacher assessments (using the framework described above). In addition, schools are required to report the results of the KS2 externally set and marked tests. KS1 test results are not necessarily reported to the local education authority (LEA) or to the DfE or parents. School test results are published on their websites and in the form of league tables in the media and are commented upon extensively by journalists.

In Wales . . .

KS2 requirements are as follows:

> Teachers are required to make their statutory teacher assessments, at the end of the key stage, for each eligible learner in: English; Welsh (if the learner has followed the Welsh programme of study) or Welsh second language; mathematics; science.
>
> (Learning Wales, 2016: 2012)

Learning Wales. (2016) *Statutory assessment arrangements for the Foundation Phase and end of Key Stages 2 and 3*, Cardiff: Welsh Government. Retrieved from http://learning.gov.wales/docs/learningwales/publications/161011-statutory-assessment-arrangements-en.pdf (accessed 27 October 2017).

Parts of the UK compared

There are no standard assessment tests (SATs) in Scotland, but new assessments in literacy and numeracy are being planned and are due to commence in 2017. Scottish schools have access to a bank of materials to support assessment – the National Assessment Resource, which is an interactive computerised assessment system (InCAS). These resources align with the curriculum (see Education Scotland, 2016) and attempt to help teachers integrate their teaching and assessment. They also include moderation guides with examplars of children's assesed work, designed to help teachers interpret and cross-check their own assesssment of their pupils' work. Teachers and schools decide when to administer tests to their pupils. At the end of their primary schooling, a pupil profile is prepared for each pupil, summarising their achievements in the various curriculum areas, with a summative category indicating whether the achievement is 'developing', 'consolidated' or 'secure'. National standards in literacy and numeracy are monitored through representative sampling procedures. Thus, unlike England, individual schools are not held to account through comparative achievement data, and there are no league tables of performance.

In essence, the tests available to Scottish schools are not substantially different to those used in England, but, crucially, they are not 'high stakes', because there is not an emphasis on ranking and comparing. Performance tables are not compiled and published.

In Scotland . . .

> There is currently too much support material and guidance for practitioners. This is contributing to the growth of over-bureaucratic approaches to planning and assessment in many schools and classrooms across the country. Despite the recognition of these issues in the Tackling Bureaucracy report, progress has been far too slow. As a result we are taking action to significantly streamline all our support and guidance materials for the curriculum.
>
> (Education Scotland, 2016: 2)

Source: Education Scotland. (2016) *Education Scotland Curriculum for Excellence: A Statement for Practitioners from HMIE Chief Inspector of Education*. Retrieved from https://www.education.gov.scot/Documents/cfe-statement.pdf (accessed 27 October 2017).

Up until 1999, the English and Welsh school systems were aligned. Since then, Wales has opted for quite a different approach, especially in matters of assessment for accountability purposes. Wales ceased to externally assess 7-year-olds through SATs in 2006 and abandoned external testing for 11-year-olds in 2014, but teacher assessment is mandatory at the end of KS2 (age 11). There are changes occuring in relation to the introduction of reading and numeracy assessments from age 7 as part of the new national literacy and numeracy strategy. The situation in Wales is changing in the light of the review of its curriculum and assessment framework under Graham Donaldson (Learning Wales website (http://learning.gov.wales/); Donaldson, 2015). The recommendation from that review is that key stages should be removed in favour of a more coherent and holistic approach to assessment, where 'progression steps' or points of learning on a continuum should be viewed as a staging post for a child's development, not a judgement. The Welsh government does not publish primary performance data through which league tables can be compiled.

In Northern Ireland, literacy and numeracy tests are implemented in Years 4-7 via InCAS (see above in respect of Scotland). Teacher assessment is based on levels of achievement allocated for cross-curricular skills of communication, using and applying maths and using IT.

Unlike the situation in England, there is not a high-stakes culture in Wales, Scotland and Northern Ireland, compared with that in England.

In Northern Ireland . . .

The Education (Northern Ireland) Order (2006), in operation from 1 August 2006, provides the statutory base for the assessment arrangements in Northern Ireland. Teachers will assess each pupil in each component part of Communication (Talking and Listening, Reading, and Writing), Using Mathematics (the Requirements for the skill as well as the related Knowledge and Understanding) and Using ICT (Explore, Express, Exchange, Evaluate and Exhibit). Having assessed the pupils in these component parts of the Cross-Curricular Skills, teachers will use this information to decide the level that has been achieved by each pupil in each skill at the end of the key stage. Teachers' assessments of their pupils will be transferred electronically from schools to CCEA by electronic data interchange. Schools do not have to use CCEA assessment tasks within the assessment arrangements for end of key stage pupils (Years 4 and 7). However, these tasks can be used as a key element in support of teachers' assessment judgements. Tasks should not be regarded as 'tests', nor should they be used by teachers to determine their summative judgements. They should be regarded as one element of ongoing teacher assessment, alongside samples of work from across the curriculum, to support the summative judgements made. The use of tasks can also assist whole school internal standardisation processes.

Source: http://ccea.org.uk/curriculum/assess_progress/statutory_arrangements/assessment_arrangements/key_stages_1_and_2 (accessed 14 November 2017).

THE IMPACT OF 'HIGH-STAKES' ASSESSMENT ON PUPILS

Many researchers on assessment, including ourselves, have written about the impact on pupils of different assessment purposes and practices (Harlen and Deakin Crick, 2002). The research shows that schools feel under pressure to get more of their pupils achieving at higher levels in national tests. This pushes some teachers, especially those who have classes about to take national tests, to spend more time and energy on helping pupils to get good at doing those tests. This is often referred to as 'teaching to the test', and it means there is less time to actually develop pupils' skills and understanding in the various areas of a broad and balanced curriculum.

This is exactly what we found in a study of Year 6 pupils in urban areas of disadvantage (Hall *et al.*, 2004). The external pencil-and-paper tests, which are designed to offer evidence to the government about how schools are raising standards, received enormous attention in the daily life of pupils in the schools that were part of our study. Such is the perceived pressure in schools to do well in league tables that they sometimes feel unable to place sufficient emphasis on assessment designed to promote learning across the curriculum, or on assessing learning through a variety of modes. Summative assessment can even be seen as the goal of teaching: George W. Bush, a former president of the USA, visited an East London primary school. After listening to a story being read to the children, he commented on the importance of literacy to the teachers: 'You teach a child to read, and he or her (*sic*) will be able to pass a literacy test' (cited in Yandell, 2008).

In situations where passing a test is seen as the purpose of teaching, the children's learning experiences become focused towards this end. Yandell (2008) described how pupils, studying a play, were only given photocopies of the 'SATs' sections of the text and never read the play itself. Reviewing a range of evidence concerning the impact of high-stakes summative testing led Wyse and Torrance (2009: 224) to conclude that it can drive teaching in 'exactly the opposite direction to that which other research indicates will improve teaching, learning and attainment'.

There are many other potential consequences for pupils. High-stakes tests can lead teachers to adopt transmission styles of teaching and thus disadvantage pupils who prefer other, more creative ways of learning. Practice tests, when repeatedly undertaken, can have a negative impact on the self-esteem of lower-achieving pupils. Research from outside the UK suggests that pupils' expectations about the purpose of assessment reflects badly on summative approaches (Black, 2003) – for example, pupils believing that summative assessment was entirely for their school's and parents' benefit. Children who did less well in such assessments felt that their purpose was to make them work harder. It was a source of pressure that resulted in pupil anxiety and even fear.

Pupils used to a diet of summative assessments, based on written tests and on only a few curriculum areas (often numeracy and literacy), can take time adapting to more formative approaches. The same can be true for teachers. For example, in response to calls for formative assessment, many teachers produce formal summative tests that mimic the statutory tests. This again reflects the perceived importance of SATs. Weeden *et al.* (2002) make the point that the more important a quantitative measure becomes, 'the more it is likely to distort the processes it is supposed to monitor' (p. 34).

High-stakes testing might also influence the way you respond to and feel about the children in your class. 'How many teachers of young children are now able to listen attentively in a non-instrumental way without feeling guilty about the absence of criteria or the insistence of a target tugging at their sleeve' (Fielding, cited in Hill, 2007). There is clearly an emotional/affective factor that is often overlooked in seeking the objective viewpoint that summative assessments are seen as presenting. Robert Reinecke highlights this:

> Assessments, formal or informal, considered or casual, intentional or not, powerfully affect people, particularly students. The assessment climate that students experience is a crucial component of instruction and learning. Students' assessment experiences remain with them for a lifetime and substantially affect their capacity for future learning ... emotional charge is part of the character of assessment information.
>
> (1998: 7)

For any assessment to have a positive impact on children's learning, the way in which performance results are used and communicated is vitally important.

The phonics screening test for use in the early years classroom is intended to be a 'light-touch' assessment to confirm whether individual pupils have 'learnt phonic decoding to an appropriate standard' (www.gov.uk/guidance/2016-key-stage-1-assessment-and-reporting-arrangements-ara/section-7-phonics-screening-check; see also DfE, 2012). The check consists of twenty real words and twenty pseudo-words that a pupil reads aloud to the teacher. However 'light touch' it was intended to be, one can see how such a statutory test, whose results provide information at school, local authority and national level, could have a profound effect on classroom practice and pedagogy. Dombey (2011) argues that the assessment distorts the process of learning to read, and the United Kingdom Literacy Association (2012) questioned its usefulness as a summative assessment for all readers.

Task 5.2.2 Testing – what do you think?

- Note down some advantages and disadvantages of testing all children at various times in their primary schooling.
- Why do you think England, in particular, places such a strong emphasis on external testing for accountability purposes?

We would suggest that external testing in primary schools is part of a wider social preoccupation with measuring, league tables and auditing. If you consider other social services, for example the health service and the police service, you find a similar push towards accountability in the form of league tables. England has experienced all of this to a greater degree than other parts of the UK. Education in England seems to be more politicised than in other parts of the UK, and politicians in England are less inclined to be influenced by professional groups such as teachers and researchers. This means that, in turn, such groups have less power in educational decision-making in England than their counterparts have in Scotland, Wales and Northern Ireland.

A CRITIQUE OF ASSESSMENT APPROACHES

Dylan Wiliam, a researcher on assessment over many years, has expressed concern about the narrowing effect on the curriculum of teachers teaching to the test – a point we noted earlier in this unit. Here are some key questions he poses, which we believe will be helpful to you in critically reflecting on your own and others' practices and in examining national and school policies:

- Why are pupils tested as individuals, when the world of work requires people who can work well in a team?
- Why do we test memory, when in the real world engineers and scientists never rely on memory: if they're stuck, they look things up.
- Why do we use timed tests when it is usually far more important to get things done right than to get things done quickly?

He favours an approach that would support teachers' own judgements of pupil achievement and believes that this approach should replace all forms of testing, from the earliest stages through to GCSE and A-levels. He points out that this happens in Sweden. This is how he justifies his argument:

In place of the current vicious spiral, in which only those aspects of learning that are easily measured are regarded as important, I propose developing a system of summative assessment based on moderated teacher assessment. A separate system, relying on 'light sampling' of the performance of schools, would provide stable and robust information for the purposes of accountability and policy-formation.

(Wiliam, 2002: 61-2)

He goes on to say that his preferred approach 'would also be likely to tackle boys' underachievement, because the current "all or nothing" test at the end of a key stage encourages boys to believe that they can make up lost ground at the last minute' (pp. 61-2).

He envisages that there would be a large number of assessment tasks, but not all pupils would undertake the same task. These good-quality assessment tasks would cover the entire curriculum and they would be allocated randomly, he suggests. This would guard against teaching to the test or, as he puts it, 'the only way to teach to the test would be to teach the whole curriculum to every student' (p. 62). He suggests that schools that taught only a limited curriculum, or concentrated on, say, the most able pupils, would be shown up as ineffective in this scenario.

Task 5.2.3 What do you think?

- What do you think of Wiliam's ideas?
- Do you think his suggestions are more in line with what we know about learning and assessment, especially what we know about the impact of testing on pupils?
- Do you think his suggestions are feasible?
- How would these groups view his ideas: parents, pupils, teachers, politicians?

SUMMARY

In this unit, we have sought to define and describe summative assessment and ways of using it. We have also highlighted the (mostly negative) impact on learners of testing, especially high-stakes testing. Whatever the national policy on external testing, as a class teacher you will have a powerful influence over how you assess your pupils. In turn, how you assess your pupils will have considerable influence on how they perform, on how motivated they become as learners, and on how they feel about themselves as learners. You are likely to influence the kinds of lifelong learner they become.

To recap the major points of the unit, we suggest that you revisit the learning objectives we noted on the first page. As you do this, you might consider the different ways in which you could demonstrate your understanding and knowledge of the topic.

ANNOTATED FURTHER READING

Boon, S.I. (2015) 'The role of training in improving peer assessment skills amongst year six pupils in primary school writing: An action research enquiry', *Education 3–13*, 43: 6.

Fleer, M. (2015) 'Developing an *assessment pedagogy*: The tensions and struggles in re-theorising assessment from a cultural-historical perspective', *Assessment in Education*, 22: 2.

> The first article listed here describes an action research study where Year 6 students were trained in peer assessment skills and shows how learners' facility in assessment language can enhance their learning. The second article is about assessment in a broader sense and is highly relevant to formative and summative assessment alike. It invites us to ponder what assessment pedagogy is, and how our assumptions about assessment and pedagogy shape our practice.

(M) FURTHER READING TO SUPPORT M-LEVEL STUDY

Black, P., Harrison, C., Hodgen, J., Marshall, B. and Serret, N. (2011) 'Can teachers' summative assessments produce dependable results and also enhance classroom learning?', *Assessment in Education: Principles, Policy & Practice*, 18: 4.

> This research is based on a longitudinal study of teachers' opinions and practices and addresses the issue of how summative assessments might be used to positive effect within the classroom. Five key features of summative assessment practice are presented.

Elwood, J. and Murphy, P. (2015) 'Assessment systems as cultural scripts: A sociocultural theoretical lens on assessment practice and products', *Assessment in Education: Principles, Policy & Practice*, 22(2): 182–92.

> This editorial to a special issue on sociocultural perspectives on assessment, along with its accompanying articles, offers a challenging and theorised account of assessment research, policy and practice that is worth studying to sharpen your thinking and invite you to challenge some current practices.

Hondrich, A.L., Hertel, S., Adl-Amini, K. and Klieme, E. (2016) 'Implementing curriculum-embedded formative assessment in primary school science classrooms', *Assessment in Education: Principles, Policy & Practice*, 23(3): 353–76.

Nortvedt, G., Santos, L. and Pinto, J. (2016) 'Assessment for learning in Norway and Portugal: The case of primary school mathematics teaching', *Assessment in Education: Principles, Policy & Practice*, 23(3): 377–95.

> Both these articles show how local assessment practices, whether formative- or summative-oriented, are highly influenced by national policies, such as curriculum reforms, national professional development projects and teacher autonomy. Both these papers offer an interesting comparative lens through which one can evaluate one's own national context.

RELEVANT WEBSITES

Association for Achievement and Improvement through Assessment (AAIA): www.aaia.org.uk

Department for Education: www.education.gov.uk/

> A useful source for details of assessment initiatives mentioned in the unit and the results of statutory tests.

Phonics screening check: www.gov.uk/guidance/2016-key-stage-1-assessment-and-reporting-arrangements-ara/section-7-phonics-screening-check

> This has information on phonics assessment.

Northern Ireland Curriculum: www.nicurriculum.org.uk/
>This has information on Northern Ireland's curriculum and assessment arrangements.

Primary Assessment – Making Summative Assessment Work for You: www.teachers.tv/video/3360
>Professor Wynne Harlen, whose work is referred to in this unit, takes part in a discussion of teacher's summative assessments.

The companion website: www.routledge.com/textbooks/ltps2e
>Visit this for additional questions and tasks for this unit and links to useful websites relevant to this unit.

REFERENCES

Black, P. (2003) *Testing: Friend or Foe? Theory and Practice of Assessment and Testing*, London: RoutledgeFalmer.

Black, P., Harrison, C., Hodgen, J. and Serret, N. (2011). 'Can teachers' summative assessments produce dependable results and also enhance classroom learning?', *Assessment in Education: Principles, Policy & Practice*, 18(4): 451-69.

Black, P., Harrison, C., Lee, C., Marshall, B. and Wiliam, D. (2003) *Assessment for Learning: Putting it into Practice*, Buckingham, UK: Open University Press.

Black, P. and Wiliam, D. (1998) *Inside the Black Box*, London: King's College.

Black, P. and Wiliam, D. (2007) 'Large-scale assessment systems: Design principles drawn from international comparisons', *Measurement: Interdisciplinary Research & Perspectives*, 5(1): 1-53.

Department for Children, Schools and Families (DCSF). (2008) *Primary Framework for Literacy and Mathematics*, London: DfES.

Department for Education (2012) Statutory Phonics Screening Check. Retrieved from www.education.gov.uk/schools/teachingandlearning/pedagogy/a00198207/faqs-year-1-phonics-screening-check#faq2 (accessed December 2012).

Dombey, H. (2011) 'Distorting the process of learning to read: The "light touch" phonics test for six year olds', *Education Review*, 23(2): 23-33.

Donaldson, G. (2015) *Successful Futures: Independent Review of Curriculum and Assessment Arrangements in Wales*, Cardiff: Welsh Government.

Drummond, M.J. (1999) 'Baseline assessment: A case for civil disobedience?', in C. Conner (ed.) *Assessment in Action in the Primary School*, London: Falmer, pp. 3-49.

Education Scotland. (2016) *Achievement of Curriculum for Excellence Levels*. Retrieved from www.gov.scot/Publications/2016/12/3546/336271 (accessed 13 November 2017).

Hall, K. and Burke, W. (2003) *Making Formative Assessment Work: Effective Practice in the Primary Classroom*, Buckingham, UK: Open University Press.

Hall, K., Collins, J., Benjamin, S., Sheehy, K. and Nind, M. (2004) 'SATurated models of pupildom: Assessment and inclusion/exclusion', *British Educational Research Journal*, 30(6): 801-17.

Hall, K. and Harding, A. (2002) 'Level descriptions and teacher assessment: Towards a community of assessment practice', *Educational Research*, 40(1): 1-16.

Harlen, W. and Deakin Crick, R. (2002) 'A systematic review of the impact of summative assessment and tests on students' motivation for learning' (EPPI-Centre Review, version 1.1), in Research Evidence in Education Library, London: EPPI-Centre, Social Science Research Unit, Institute of Education.

Hill, D. (2007) 'Critical teacher education, New Labour in Britain, and the global project of neoliberal capital', *Policy Futures in Education*, 5(2): 204-25.

Nuttall, D. (1987) 'The validity of assessments', *European Journal of the Psychology of Education*, 11(2): 109-18.

Reinecke, R.A. (1998) *Challenging the Mind, Touching the Heart: Best Assessment Practice*, Thousand Oaks, CA: Corwin Oaks.

Threlfall, J. (2005) 'The formative use of assessment information in planning: The notion of contingent planning', *British Journal of Educational Studies*, 53(1): 54-65.

Torrance, H. (2012) 'Formative assessment at the crossroads: Conformative, deformative and transformative assessment', *Oxford Review of Education*, 38(3): 323-42.

United Kingdom Literacy Association. (2012) UKLA Analysis of Schools' response to the Year 1 Phonics Screening Check, (July), 1-5

Weeden, P., Winter, J. and Broadfoot, P. (2002) Assessment: What's In It For Schools?, London: RoutledgeFalmer.

Wiliam, D. (2002) 'What is wrong with our educational assessment and what can be done about it?', *Education Review*, 15(1): 57-62.

Wyse, D. and Torrance, H. (2009) 'The development and consequences of national curriculum assessment for primary education in England', *Educational Research*, 51(2): 213-28.

Yandell, J. (2008) 'Mind the gap: Investigating test literacy and classroom literacy', *English in Education*, 42(1): 70-87.

DIVERSITY AND INCLUSION

PROVIDING FOR DIFFERENTIATION

Eve Bearne and Rebecca Kennedy[1]

INTRODUCTION

Differentiation is one of those 'iceberg' terms in teaching – what you see on the surface covers something much bigger. But, not only does it have underlying complexities, it is also one of those concepts that teachers assume 'everyone knows' the meaning of. The DfE *Teachers' Standards* document states that a teacher must 'adapt teaching to respond to the strengths and needs of all pupils', knowing 'when and how to differentiate appropriately, using approaches which enable pupils to be taught effectively' (DfE, 2012: 8). This is all well and good, but there is no clear consensus about what the term means and implies. It is linked in many teachers' minds with 'mixed ability teaching', but there is still considerable debate about what it might look like in the classroom and just what 'ability' is. Some place greater emphasis on curriculum provision, whereas others see differentiation as more linked with individual progress. Most recently, differentiation has been linked with narrowing the gaps between the achievements of different groups of learners. The Ofsted common inspection framework points out that inspectors will evaluate, among other things, the extent to which leaders, managers and governors:

> actively promote equality and diversity, tackle bullying and discrimination and narrow any gaps in achievement between different groups of children and learners.

> (Ofsted, 2015: 12)

However, as well as seeing the progress of specific groups as important, this includes an awareness of individual pupils' needs. Inspection will check on how schools:

> plan appropriate teaching and learning strategies, including to identify children and learners who are falling behind in their learning or who need additional support, enabling children and learners to make good progress and achieve well.

> (ibid.: 13)

As with many classroom issues, the answer often lies in the combination of providing a suitable curriculum to ensure progression for all learners while catering for the needs and experiences of individuals.

OBJECTIVES

By the end of this unit, you should be able to:

- see the links between differentiation, diversity and difference;
- understand the importance of providing a differentiated approach to the curriculum for a diverse range of learners;
- understand the main approaches to differentiation;
- develop some practical strategies to provide differentiated approaches to learning.

DEFINING DIFFERENTIATION

When teachers were asked to define differentiation, one described it as 'making one thing accessible to all, through providing different learning experiences based on knowledge of individuals' skills and potential'. Another likened it to teaching children to swim: 'Differentiation is ensuring that every child can find their depth in every lesson but also challenging them to swim. If we don't support/encourage children to take chances, they will never leave the shallows'. The first teacher emphasises providing for the different qualities, knowledge and experiences of every learner, while aiming for common learning objectives for all; the second sees it as important to create an environment that allows learners to feel secure enough to push themselves further. These descriptions indicate the variations that experienced teachers may have in mind as they consider differentiation, although they share a concern to provide for individual differences within a common curriculum.

 Task 6.1.1 Describing differentiation

What does differentiation mean to you? Write a few words of explanation to describe differentiation. You might then compare your ideas with others in your group and discuss with your tutor the range of descriptions of differentiation gathered by the group. A group list would be a good starting point for a definition.

DIFFERENTIATION, DIFFERENCE AND DIVERSITY

In general terms, differentiation is about how far the curriculum is appropriate for groups of learners with particular needs. This does not only mean considering special educational needs (SEND), including the group sometimes described as gifted and talented, but takes into account the differences between what a young learner at the Foundation Stage may need in contrast to an appropriate curriculum for pupils at Key Stage 2. Such a general approach would also consider differences between schools, settings and their communities. For example, a school where there are many multilingual pupils will adjust its curriculum to make the most of its linguistic diversity; or a school where pupils have to travel long distances may adopt specific approaches to home-school liaison. In this general sense, differentiation means providing an appropriate curriculum, within national guidelines, for the particular school. In its more specific usage, differentiation refers to provision of learning opportunities and activities for individuals in particular classrooms. This often includes a concept of 'matching' the task or activity to the child's experience, knowledge and skills.

In Scotland . . .

Getting it right for every child is important for everyone who works with children and young people – as well as many people who work with adults who look after children. Practitioners need to work together to support families, and where appropriate, take early action at the first signs of any difficulty – rather than only getting involved when a situation has already reached crisis point.

(Scottish Government, 2012: 3)

Source: Scottish Government. (2012) *A Guide to Getting it Right For Every Child*. Retrieved from www.gov.scot/Resource/0045/00458341.pdf (accessed 27 October 2017).

Ofsted emphasises educational attainment and the need to provide for different groups of pupils to reach national standards, but it is worth being cautious about categorisations of the 'differences' between learners. Ainscow *et al.* (2007: 9) argue that 'differences are never neutral', as descriptions of learners are necessarily constructed according to prevailing educational values. Recently, for example, attention has been given to children who are seen as 'disadvantaged' (Ofsted, 2014), who attract the pupil premium to be paid to their schools. However, children defined in this way do not necessarily compose a 'group' in terms of provision for learning, as the pupil premium is paid for children who are entitled to free schools meals, looked-after children and children of service personnel who are eligible for the service child premium, any of whom might come from a range of backgrounds. Indeed, Ofsted identifies one of the key principles for using the pupil premium as ensuring that:

> The school never confuses eligibility for the pupil premium with low ability, and focuses on supporting our disadvantaged pupils to achieve the highest levels.
>
> (Ofsted, 2014)

Similarly, attention has been given to boys' 'underachievement' (see Unit 6.6) but again, neither 'boys' nor 'girls' compose undifferentiated groups.

There are, of course, links between differentiation and inclusion. The Ofsted common inspection framework includes a requirement to evaluate the extent to which 'equality of opportunity and recognition of diversity are promoted through teaching and learning' (Ofsted, 2015: 13). But, whereas inclusion is largely concerned with equity in terms of individual rights and curriculum entitlement, differentiation focuses on the management of teaching and learning, including:

- identifying pupils' knowledge, experience, skills and learning preferences;
- planning for a variety of ways into learning;
- classroom organisation for learning;
- using resources (material and human);
- response to the outcomes of activities or units of work and assessment of achievement in order to plan for future learning.

The Education Reform Act 1988 legislated for every pupil's entitlement to a curriculum that is broad, balanced, relevant and 'subtly' differentiated. In 1992, the National Curriculum Council referred to providing a curriculum suitable for 'differences in the abilities, aptitudes and needs of individual pupils' (NCC, 1992: 67). Twenty years later, Ofsted (2013) noted that the most effective lessons were characterised by, among other qualities, 'differentiation used effectively to ensure that activities and teaching were matched to pupils' specific learning needs' (Ofsted, 2013: 19). The DfE (2012) expects teachers to:

> have a clear understanding of the needs of all pupils, including those with special educational needs; those of high ability; those with English as an additional language; those with disabilities; and be able to use and evaluate distinctive teaching approaches to engage and support them.
>
> (DfE, 2012: Part 5)

In addition, a teacher must 'set goals that stretch and challenge pupils of all backgrounds, abilities and dispositions' (ibid.). However, taking account of difference and diversity is complex. In addition to acknowledging that learners may use a range of approaches according to the task/context and/or time of day, differentiation that genuinely allows for diversity needs to consider:

- differences in learning approaches, strategies or preferences;
- the time individuals take to complete tasks;
- particular strengths and difficulties in some areas of the curriculum;

- physical and medical differences;
- variations in fluency of English, which may not be the first or home language;
- the range of previous experiences brought to the classroom.

Providing for the needs of different learners means having some sense of where they are in their learning at any specific time. This in turn implies having some sense of where you want them to be. So, before planning for any unit of work or series of activities, the teacher will need to have a clear idea of learning objectives. This will need to be accompanied by useful pupil records of progress, so that the learning can be matched to individuals or groups. Grouping pupils is common classroom practice, but the reasons for grouping have to be clear. Some activities require grouping pupils according to their common achievements, for example in guided reading, where grouping is determined by a perceived common level of reading competence. At other times, teachers will opt for 'mixed ability' groups.

Grouping pupils can be trickier than it may at first appear, as, even if learners can be grouped according to common qualities, they may not form genuinely homogeneous groups. It is by no means a simple matter to group according to ability, because it begs the question, 'ability in what?'. There is a danger in making generalised judgements. It is all too easy to assume that someone who has difficulty with spelling or reading or mathematics is 'less able'. Such convenient definitions are best avoided; they are inaccurate and misleading and, in the end, give no help to either teacher or pupil. It is better to be precise and to describe the skills rather than the pupil – for example, 'less fluent in reading; confident in number calculations using addition and subtraction'.

Task 6.1.2 Reflecting on your own abilities

Think about your own 'abilities'. Are you good at everything? Some people are very good at spatial awareness in team sports, whereas others read music fluently. Some find mental calculations easy; some are good at constructing 3D objects; some express ideas elegantly through dance; others are successful at solving abstract problems.

- What are your strengths? What areas of your learning need, or have needed, support? Make a few notes, then compare your reflections with others in your group.
- How diverse are you as a group of learners? Discuss with your tutor the implications this diversity has for planning teaching and learning.

IDENTIFYING THE RANGE OF LEARNERS

Pupils' particular strengths and difficulties

Specific strengths or difficulties with learning can often be associated with pupils not making the expected progress or with a sense that more could be done to support or extend particular learners. One teacher describes the range of pupils who give her cause for concern:

- *Alex* struggles with writing. He often spends a lot of time thinking about what he has to write, and the result is that very little ends up on the paper. Sometimes it can take an hour to get one sentence on the paper. He is a sensitive boy with a vivid imagination and good memory. So, the ideas are there, but he seems to stumble with the writing and doesn't see the urgency of writing.

- *Rehan* is very hard-working, always completes homework, is reticent in class, but his written work is of a very high standard. He needs to be extended and challenged intellectually.
- *Jo* is an avid learner of facts – knows all the names, habits and habitats of birds – but does not have any friends in the class, and so it's difficult to set up collaborative activities. Also, although reading is fluent, I'm not sure how much reading between the lines goes on.
- *Kris* is bright and attentive and reads a lot, but written work is neat and 'safe'.

A 'special educational need' can mean catering for those who enjoy learning and excel, or who might be described as being gifted and talented in some aspects of learning, as well as those who struggle.

Identifying pupils who might be described as gifted and talented is an aspect of diversity that has come to prominence over the last few years. Unit 7.6 provides an overview, but, to ensure these pupils are not forgotten when you are thinking about differentiation, they are also noted here. Very able children often show outstanding potential or ability in one area or in several or all areas of the curriculum. This might not be in traditional academic learning, but could be in physical, creative, spatial, mechanical or technical learning. Pupils' abilities could be so well developed that they operate significantly in advance of their peers, or a pupil might show outstanding talent in just one area of learning, again outstripping others of their age. Whether their abilities are in a range of areas or just one, such pupils require extra learning experiences in order to support and extend the identified ability.

Generally, however, it is often the 'strugglers' who come to attention first in the classroom. You might have observed pupils who:

- have low self-esteem;
- are capable, but frustrated because they don't have the means, vocabulary, strategies or techniques to write what they want to say;
- do not yet speak English fluently;
- only skate on the surface of text when reading aloud and don't understand what they're reading;
- 'can't think what to write' because they are paralysed by fear of failure;
- have poor techniques;
- do not value their own experience;
- lack motivation;
- are restless – wanderers, diverters;
- can write with technical accuracy but do not seem to have their own voice;
- are naturally slow at working;
- have hearing loss/sight loss/difficulties with manual dexterity;
- are too proud to ask for help;
- have language or neurological disorders;
- have so many ideas they find it hard to follow one through.

Bilingual/multilingual pupils

As with other groups of learners, it is important to avoid generalisations. Bilingualism is perhaps best seen as a continuum of proficiency in speaking (and often writing) more than one language that varies according to the social contexts of language use: for example, with peers who speak the same language; with peers who don't; with older people or relatives; or at school, work or worship (see Unit 6.5). Everyone, including apparently monolingual people, uses a set of language variations, so it is worth trying to find out about:

- the languages/dialects used in school, in lessons, at break time with friends;
- the languages used in the home;
- any language classes attended out of school.

Gender

Issues of gender often focus on boys' underachievement, although concerns about boys' achievements in learning generally are not new. Although any underachievement is a proper concern for everyone involved in education – parents, teachers and pupils – it is wise not to take on generalised observations about boys, girls and learning without asking a few questions or gathering first-hand information (Bearne, 2007). Contexts differ, and pupils' attitudes, motivation and achievements will be influenced by a variety of home-, classroom- and school-based factors. Careful observation and monitoring are essential so that teaching approaches can be developed that will support boys' – and girls' – achievements (see Unit 6.6).

In Scotland . . .

All agencies in touch with children and young people must play their part in making sure that young people are healthy, achieving, nurtured, active, respected, responsible, included and, above all, safe.

(Scottish Government, 2012: 11)

Source: Scottish Government. (2012) *A Guide to Getting it Right For Every Child*. Retrieved from www.gov.scot/Resource/0045/00458341.pdf (accessed 27 October 2017).

Task 6.1.3 Focus on a specific group of pupils

This task requires you to work with colleagues in school. If you are not likely to be undertaking a school experience soon, you will need to consider this in relation to previous school experiences.

- Through discussion with a leader or class teacher, identify if the school has a group of pupils whose performance they are focusing on currently: for example, an under-performing group such as white British boys from low-income background; pupils whose first language is not English; looked-after children. This will be informed by data sources and will drive key aspects of the School Improvement Plan.
- Identify children belonging to this group in a chosen class and discuss with the teacher how they ensure that they provide challenge and support for these pupils. Explore examples of the teacher's planning – for example, English short-term plans – and consider how the plans demonstrate explicit guidance on how these pupils will be challenged and supported during lessons.
- Through observing teaching and learning, consider the effect of these plans on the children's learning outcomes. What is the impact of the approaches adopted by the teacher?

APPROACHES TO DIFFERENTIATION

Considering diversity involves looking, not only at the qualities and potential of different learners, but also at the provision that is made to support and build on that potential. Ainscow and Sandill (2010) argue that fostering inclusive education is fundamentally linked to the role of leadership in a school.

CASE STUDY – TIVERTON ACADEMY, BIRMINGHAM

The Tiverton Academy in Birmingham is a primary school whose website carries the slogan: 'One school – many talents'. This school welcomes and celebrates diversity. More than 80 per cent of pupils are from minority ethnic backgrounds, and half of the pupils speak English as an additional language. At the last Ofsted inspection, the inspectors commented:

> The curriculum is a real strength of the academy and is enriched by an extensive programme of art and sporting activities. The curriculum places a strong emphasis on values and this is the reason for pupils' outstanding spiritual, moral, social and cultural development. Consequently pupils are very well prepared for the next stage of their education and for life in modern Britain.
>
> (www.tiverton.bham.sch.uk/what-ofsted-say/)

They also note: 'The way the academy cares for pupils is exceptional, particularly for the large number of pupils that join and leave other than at the usual transition points'. This indicates the strengths of the school ethos and curriculum, as such turbulence in pupils coming and going can have a detrimental effect both on the progress of individuals and on the school's provision as a whole.

On the school website, the principal explains:

> We welcome all children into our school community and celebrate diversity. We firmly believe in 'Achievement for all'. Children who are part of our school community will be encouraged to be creative and active learners. Their journey with us will offer opportunities for them to discover and pursue individual talents and skills.

> Embedded into our curriculum and our ethos are twelve core values. We focus upon one of these every half term. Our values are: Courage, fairness, honesty, responsibility, respect, perseverance, loyalty, leadership, integrity, caring, citizenship and cooperation.

Even a brief visit to the school shows that diversity is a valued part of the everyday experience, as shown by the display of self-portraits (see Figure 6.1.1) and the display 'We are all different but together we are a masterpiece', where each child has drawn round their hand, cut it out and written on each finger something important about themselves.

The school's core principles are on display in the staff room, reminding all members of the school that the 'Journey from Outstanding to Inspiring' means:

- Inspiring pupils to discover their talents, interests and aptitudes.
- Providing a menu for success by helping them to develop transferable skills.
- Ensuring that when pupils leave us they have high aspirations by broadening pupils' social, moral, cultural and economic experiences.
- Building teachers' capacity to freely and confidently plan a rich and varied curriculum that deepens pupils' independence in learning.
- Becoming a model for other schools and learning from other schools.

But these are not just bland words. The principles are enacted throughout the school's life. The current half-term core value is Leadership. On the wall of one classroom, children have added their sticky notes in response to 'What are the qualities of a great leader?', including comments such as:

FIGURE 6.1.1 Self-portraits, Tiverton Academy

- A good leader is someone who cares abuot his group.
- A good leader is someone who treats people fairly.
- I was a leader when I was in my cub scout group.
- A good leader is someone who isn't bossy and who can enpower others.
- A good leader is someone who treats people fairly and dosn't turn back if they are scared [original spelling retained].

In another classroom, there is a sunburst display of a lion's head, where the mane is made up of children's advice to someone who is afraid: 'just do it', 'have courage', 'be strong', 'I would just take a deep breath' (see Figure 6.1.2).

Strong and enlightened leadership infuses all aspects of the curriculum and ethos of the school, ensuring that each child feels valued.

FIGURE 6.1.2 Advice to someone who is afraid, Tiverton Academy

PLANNING FOR DIFFERENTIATION

It is often assumed that intervention for learning is about teachers 'doing things' in the classroom. In fact, the most effective intervention happens before a teacher ever reaches the classroom – in the process of planning and organising activities and approaches.

Managing groups

Flexible planning for differentiation raises issues about how groups are constituted and how they might be varied. Strategies to organise groups may depend on social factors as well as learning objectives, so that pupils might be grouped according to:

- friendship patterns;
- expertise or aptitude relative to the task or subject;
- a mix of abilities relative to the task or subject;
- gender/gendered identity;
- home language;
- pupils' own choices;
- the content of the activity.

Whenever teachers plan for the management of learning there is an implicit question about classroom control. This is fundamental to successful group work, and so it is important to teach pupils to work productively in groups. This might mean:

- negotiating ground rules for turn-taking and dealing with disagreements;
- giving written prompts to guide discussion;
- developing ways of time-keeping for fair chances to contribute;
- using role-play and simulations;
- reviewing and evaluating with the pupils the ways in which they managed (or did not manage!) to work together.

(See Unit 3.5 for further support.)

Task 6.1.4 Observing group work

Either by observing during a day in your current school or by remembering a particular classroom, make notes about the ways in which work is organised:

- Is there a balance between whole-class teaching, group work, paired work and individual work?
- Are the pupils working *in* groups or *as* groups?
- Following one pupil, note the variations in groups that that child is involved in during the day.

Compare your observations with those of others in your group. From your discussions, make a list of the criteria used by the teachers to decide on how to group the pupils. Was it always by perceived ability? Discuss with your tutor the advantages and disadvantages of grouping according to any specific criterion.

All the observations you make in school will help you to think about how best to manage group work in your own teaching. (See also Unit 3.5.)

Provision – planning for input and activities

For certain activities, differentiation is unnecessary, although attention to diversity will be important. In drama work, for example, activities are likely to be 'open-access'; in PE, differentiation will be decided by criteria that will be different from those for maths. In long- and medium-term planning for classes and groups, teachers make decisions about learning objectives: the facts, concepts, strategies they want the class to learn in the course of a term or a year, as well as in the extended teaching sequences in each subject area; what experiences they want them to have; what attitudes they want them to develop (see Unit 3.1). In terms of input, decisions might be made about factual information, the concepts and the vocabulary that will be used to help learners grasp content and ideas. At this point, it is important to start with what the learners already know, in order to build on existing knowledge. At the same time, planning will identify what new information or concepts individuals and the group as a whole might now be introduced to (see Unit 5.1).

In shorter-term planning for specific learning outcomes (see Unit 3.2), teachers may differentiate by providing different tasks within an activity to cater for different levels of ability. In its worst manifestation, this version of differentiation is represented by three different worksheets: one with mostly pictures and few words; one with more words more densely packed and one picture; and a third with lots of words and no pictures. This kind of 'worst-case' practice gives very powerful negative impressions to all the learners in the classroom. It is more like division than differentiation. Although it can be recognised that these things are done with the best of intentions, in order to cater for the range of pupils, it is wrong to assume that ability is linked only with reading print text. Also, if differentiated tasks assume that certain individuals or groups will only be able to cope with a limited amount of new information, this can run the risk of excluding pupils who might be able to cope with more ambitious learning objectives. The challenge to the teacher is to find ways of framing tasks that, not only can genuinely stretch all the learners, but also might provide for the variety of approaches to learning.

These teachers describe their approaches to differentiated input and tasks:

> When I plan for a unit of work I make sure that I include visual stimuli and ICT, some activity-based and some writing tasks and some group and individual work.

> I try to vary the teaching approaches between and within lessons, scaffolding and extending where appropriate. When the children work in guided writing groups I might ask one child to write a paragraph about the setting, another to re-tell the story we'd read, and another to invent a story. In whole-class teaching I'll use a drama strategy for one activity and scaffold the learning, adjusting as I notice how individuals are doing.

> I use writing frames and word mats which have personal prompts including individual targets and success criteria linked to the learning objectives and perhaps key vocabulary matched to the child's ability. In maths I might give some children number squares if they need them (some might not) or give others particular apparatus.

Resources and support

Although it is important to identify a range of material resources to cater for the preferences of all learners – for example, digital texts, listening stations, audio equipment, pictures, photographs, maps, diagrams and print – it is also important to acknowledge and use the range of human resources available in the classroom, for example teaching assistants (TAs). In some schools, TAs are given responsibility for planning parts of the teaching, and the best practice is when practitioners and TAs plan jointly, particularly for group work. Although TAs are often used to support children who are experiencing difficulties, it can be just as effective, or even more effective, if the support is given to different groups, including those described as gifted and talented. The key lies in making sure that support time is carefully allocated according to the requirements of the curriculum and the children involved. (See Unit 8.2 for a full discussion of working with other adults in the classroom.) However, support need not only be seen in terms of the adults in the classroom, or peer support; it might also mean use of digital technology or other tools for learning – for example, prompts, scaffolds, texts, and so on. Perhaps the most critical element in considering this area of provision for diversity is to do with teacher time. There is never enough time to give the individual support that a teacher almost inevitably and continually wants to offer. Group and paired work, self- and peer-evaluation, support from adults or other pupils, collaborative revising and proofreading all help in offering differentiated support.

These teachers describe their approaches to differentiating by support:

> I find that I do differentiate by support, although with the older pupils I teach it has to be done subtly to avoid upsetting individuals. I tend to use paired work a lot, basing the pairs on different things – sometimes I suggest the pupils choose their own learning partners; at other times I select a more confident mathematician, for example, to work with someone who finds some of the concepts difficult. But I do think it's important to avoid making social divisions. In group work I'll sometimes select groups according to having someone who is more confident in literacy to take notes working with others who may not be quite so fluent and I also make the criteria for working in groups explicit so that everyone feels valued whatever role they take on.

> Of course, the TA is an important part of differentiated support but I don't really like the usual practice of putting her with the least able group – whatever that means. It's not good for her because it doesn't stretch her professionally and it means that I don't get to work with them and give them some focused support. We discuss things at the beginning of the week and sometimes she'll be working with the more able – she's particularly interested in science so I tend to ask her to work with the able scientists quite often. At other times I'll work with them and she'll work with other groups. She's also very good with ICT so she might work with individuals at certain times either to consolidate skills or to extend the exceptional pupils.

Outcome, response and assessment

Many teachers favour differentiation by outcome, but this can be seen as a less organised way to cater for the range. If differentiation by outcome is to be genuinely effective, it has to be allied with response to help move learners on, and that response has to be based on a clear view of the learning outcomes aimed for in a series of lessons or a unit of work. This teacher explains why she prefers to differentiate at this stage of the teaching process:

> I find individual feedback particularly powerful in moving learning forward. When I'm marking a pupil's work I identify strengths and areas for development. My feedback links to exactly what each pupil needs and what the next steps in learning are. Of course I focus on the learning objective but the development points are personal. I always identify part of the writing that could be improved and discuss or comment on how this might happen. After I've marked work I'll gather together pupils with the same needs and teach a guided session. For example, in guided writing I'd gather together the children who have been over-using adjectives or writing sentences that are too detailed. I also use the plenary to teach children to edit and improve their work. I might ask them to work in different pairs to find the most powerful use of language in their writing.

Then I ask them to underline the part that presents the reader with the image, for example. I use oral sentence stems to encourage them to explain their thinking to their partner like: *The most powerful sentence in my writing is . . . because it makes the reader . . .* This enables me to consolidate the learning, to make judgements on children's understanding and develop their ability to self-evaluate.

Outcomes can be both tangible and intangible. Tangible products (written or diagrammatic work, craft- or artwork, displays of physical activities or drama activities) provide obvious opportunities for assessment across a range of areas and kinds of ability. However, intangible outcomes are equally open to observation and assessment: increased confidence, the ability to carry out a particular operation or to present ideas orally, new-found enthusiasm or the articulation of concepts that have been understood, or the development of a vocabulary to talk about the subject or learning itself. Equally, feedback need not always be written. The end points of learning are often used to assess how well pupils have achieved, but, if assessment is to inform future teaching and learning, there may be a need for a diversity of kinds of assessment and variation in times when those assessments are carried out. Response to the outcomes of learning, by teachers and pupils, makes the process of learning explicit and acknowledges different abilities (see Units 5.1 and 5.2).

SUMMARY

Differentiation involves providing a curriculum that allows for the progress of all learners, but will specifically cater for the needs of different groups of pupils and the diverse strengths, needs and abilities of individual learners. It involves planning for teaching approaches that will build on the knowledge, concepts, skills and prior experiences of the pupils in the class. It also means balancing knowledge of the range of learners with the content of learning and managing and evaluating teaching and learning to try to move all learners on successfully. Judgements about lesson content, pace of learning, levels of challenge, management of groups in the classroom, use of support and response to individuals and groups for successful differentiation are part of the developed expertise of teachers. You are just starting on that professional journey; thoughtful observation and planning will help you to begin effective, supportive and stimulating differentiation.

NOTE

1   Our thanks to Joy Buttress, Shaun Holland, Ben Reave, Sara Tulk, Rowena Watts and children from primary schools in north Essex.

 ## ANNOTATED FURTHER READING

Ainscow, M., Booth, T. and Dyson, A. (2003) *Understanding and Developing Inclusive Practices in Schools*, Swindon, UK: ESRC.
This study, carried out by a research network that was part of the Economic and Social Research Council's Teaching and Learning Research Programme, highlights the relationship between externally imposed requirements to raise standards and a school-based commitment to inclusion and equity.

Brown, Z. (ed.) (2016) *Inclusive Education: Perspectives on Pedagogy, Policy and Practice*, Abingdon, UK: Routledge. Taking inclusion to refer to *all* learners, this book surveys the concept of inclusive practice in its broadest sense and examines its implementation in a variety of educational institutions, in the UK and abroad. Each chapter assesses key theories and concepts alongside a range of examples to encourage readers to think critically and reappraise their own experience as learners.

Special Children (magazine).

This magazine, published monthly by Questions Publishing, is a source of relevant articles. See http://specialchildren-magazine.com/ (accessed 29 October 2017).

 # FURTHER READING TO SUPPORT M-LEVEL STUDY

Kendall, L. (2016) '"The teacher said I'm thick!" Experiences of children with Attention Deficit Hyperactivity Disorder within a school setting', *Support for Learning*, 31(2): 122–37.

Using data drawn from a small-scale study, this article has sought to elicit the 'voice' of young people who have ADHD. The findings suggest the need for teachers to be better informed about the impact the condition may have on a pupil and the need to develop strategies to support these pupils in the classroom.

McPhillips, T., Shevlin, M. and Long, L. (2012) 'A right to be heard: Learning from learners with additional needs in literacy', in *Literacy*, 46(2): 59–65.

Pupils in Northern Ireland and the Republic of Ireland who have additional needs in literacy were consulted about how their learning experiences could be improved, revealing that they had a keen awareness of how their specific difficulties might be supported.

 # RELEVANT WEBSITES

Cambridge Primary Review Trust: http://cprtrust.org.uk/

The Cambridge Primary Review Trust has a range of research reports available online. Ainscow *et al.* (2007, 2016) report on the principles and operation of inclusive practices in schools, noting the barriers to provision as well as the possibilities for curriculum development.

See particularly:

Ainscow, M., Conteh, J., Dyson, A. and Gallanaugh, F. (2007) *Children in Primary Education: Demography, Culture, Diversity and Inclusion (Primary Review Research Survey 5/1)*, Cambridge, UK: University of Cambridge Faculty of Education. Retrieved from http://cprtrust.org.uk/wp-content/uploads/2014/06/research-survey-5-1.pdf (accessed 11 October 2016).

Ainscow, M., Dyson, A., Hopwood, L., and Thomson, S. (2016) *Primary Schools Responding to Diversity: Barriers and Possibilities*, York, UK: Cambridge Primary Review Trust. Retrieved from http://cprtrust.org.uk/wp-content/uploads/2016/05/Ainscow-report-160505.pdf (accessed 11 October 2016).

2020 Vision: Report of the Teaching and Learning 2020 Review Group: www.gov.uk/government/publications?departments%5B%5D=department-for-education and http://dera.ioe.ac.uk/6347/1/6856-DfES-Teaching%20and%20Learning.pdf

This report, commissioned by DfES and carried out by the Teaching and Learning in 2020 Review Group, argues that personalisation is a necessity if differences in children's prospects as learners are to be addressed.

National Association for Special Educational Needs: www.nasen.org.uk/resources/

This provides a variety of resources, case studies and information on inclusion.

Teachers TV: www.tes.co.uk/teaching-resource/Differentiation-in-Action-Primary-6084160/

Differentiation in Action shows how one teacher handles primary pupils of varying achievement in a school in Bethnal Green, London.

REFERENCES

Ainscow, M., Conteh, J., Dyson, A. and Gallanaugh, F. (2007) *Children in Primary Education: Demography, Culture, Diversity and Inclusion (Cambridge Primary Review: Research Survey 5/1)*, Cambridge, UK: University of Cambridge Faculty of Education. Retrieved from http://cprtrust.org.uk/wp-content/uploads/2014/06/research-survey-5-1.pdf (accessed 11 October 2016).

Ainscow, M. and Sandill, A. (2010) 'Developing inclusive education systems: The role of organisational cultures and leadership', *International Journal of Inclusive Education*, 14(4): 401-16.

Bearne, E. (2007) 'Boys (girls) and literacy: Towards an inclusive approach to teaching', in E. Bearne and J. Marsh (eds) *Literacy and Social Inclusion: Closing the Gap*, Stoke-on-Trent, UK: Trentham, pp. 27-40.

Department for Education (DfE). (2012) *Teachers Standards*. Retrieved from https://www.gov.uk/government/uploads/system/uploads/attachment_data/file/283566/Teachers_standard_information.pdf (accessed 20 September 2016).

National Curriculum Council (NCC). (1992) *Starting Out with the National Curriculum*, York, UK: NCC.

Ofsted. (2013) *Moving English Forward: Action to Raise Standards in English*. Retrieved from https://www.gov.uk/government/uploads/system/uploads/attachment_data/file/181204/110118.pdf (accessed 11 October 2016).

Ofsted. (2014) *The Pupil Premium: An Update*. Retrieved from https://www.gov.uk/government/uploads/system/uploads/attachment_data/file/379205/The_20pupil_20premium_20-_20an_20update.pdf (accessed 11 October 2016).

Ofsted. (2015) *The Common Inspection Framework: Education, Skills and Early Years*. Retrieved from https://www.gov.uk/government/uploads/system/uploads/attachment_data/file/461767/The_common_inspection_framework_education_skills_and_early_years.pdf (accessed 11 October 2106).

SPECIAL EDUCATIONAL NEEDS AND INCLUSION

Noel Purdy and Adam Boddison

INTRODUCTION

> Teachers are responsible and accountable for the progress and development of the pupils in their class, including where pupils access support from teaching assistants or specialist staff . . . Where a pupil is identified as having SEN, schools should take action to remove barriers to learning and put effective special educational provision in place.
>
> (DfE and DoH, 2015: sections 6.36, 6.44)

It is clear from many influential reports over recent years that much more is now expected of mainstream teachers than in the past in relation to meeting the needs of children and young people with special educational needs (SEN). For instance, the Bercow Report (DCSF, 2008) into children with speech, language and communication needs, the Lamb Report into parental confidence and SEN (DCSF, 2009) and the Cambridge Primary Review (2010) all made recommendations that teachers should be better equipped to meet the needs of pupils with a wide range of different SEN. The need for quality preparation for teachers is clear, given that census data for 2015-16 show that more than 14 per cent of pupils across all schools in England have SEN, and almost 49 per cent of children with a statement or Education, Health and Care Plan (EHCP) are educated in state-funded mainstream primary or secondary schools (DfE, 2016a)

OBJECTIVES

By the end of this unit, you should have:

- an awareness of the development policy context of SEN over recent years, across the UK;
- an understanding of current standards and expectations for primary teachers in relation to special educational needs;
- an understanding of the main principles involved in seeking to meet the needs of children with SEN in primary schools.

It is far beyond the scope of this introductory chapter to provide detailed practical guidance in relation to meeting the needs of children with specific SEN; however, student teachers are advised to follow the general principles at the end of the chapter and to consult the texts suggested in the Annotated Further Reading section.

THE DEVELOPMENT OF UK POLICY IN RELATION TO SEN

Perhaps the most significant report to date in relation to SEN in the UK was the *Report of the Committee of Enquiry into the Education of Handicapped Children and Young People* (DES, 1978), commonly referred to as the *Warnock Report*, after the chair of the committee, Professor Mary Warnock. This influential report led to legislation in the 1981 Education Act in England and led to the reconceptualisation of special education right across the UK by advocating a focus by teachers on children's 'special educational needs' (as a means to giving them access to learning), rather than on their 'handicap' or disability.

Prior to the changes in legislation resulting from the Warnock Report, there existed a rigid system of eleven categories of 'handicap', which dated back to the 1944 Education Act. The regulations at that time also prescribed that children who were blind, deaf, epileptic, had physical disabilities or were aphasic were 'seriously disabled' and *had* to be educated in special schools. They also stipulated that children with other disabilities might attend 'ordinary schools', but only if adequate provision for them was available. Before the 1970 Education Act, some children with severe disabilities had even been deemed 'ineducable'. In rejecting the medical model of disability (with its focus on a child's deficit), the Warnock Report advocated a new social model of disability that aimed to remove systemic obstacles to progress for children with SEN:

> The purpose of education for all children is the same; the goals are the same. But the help that individual children need in progressing towards them will be different. Whereas for some the road they have to travel towards the goals is smooth and easy, for others it is fraught with obstacles.

> (DES, 1978: section 1.4)

The Warnock Report not only coined the term 'special educational needs', but is important for a number of other reasons: it rejected once and for all the notion that some children with the most severe disabilities are 'ineducable' and asserted that 'education, as we conceive it, is a good, and a specifically human good, to which all human beings are entitled' (section 1.7); it suggested that 'up to one in five' (section 3.3) children will require a form of special educational provision at some stage during their school careers, thus broadening the term and removing the notion of a fixed or irreversible label; it endorsed the policy of 'integration' (now more commonly referred to as the 'inclusion') of children with SEN into mainstream schools; it introduced the principle that parents should be engaged in meaningful dialogue as 'equal partners' in the education of their children; and it safeguarded the educational provision for the small minority of children with more severe or complex needs by laying an obligation on local authorities to make special educational provision for any child judged to be in need of such provision, based on a multidisciplinary assessment of need (known as the 'statement').

There have been many subsequent policy developments, but perhaps the most significant was the introduction of the National Curriculum (HMSO, 1988), which established the notion that all children were entitled to have access to the same curriculum. However, this also marked the beginning of the standards and performance agendas in schools, which are often perceived to have had a negative impact on the inclusion of children with SEN.

In Wales . . .

Wales has produced an online pack for teachers: *Special Education Needs and Inclusion*. It has been put together to support teachers' practice and enhance knowledge and understanding of special education needs and inclusion:

> Current policy consultation is addressing the proposed reform of the legislative framework that guides practice in the field of SEN. The term 'additional need' is suggested to reflect the multi-disciplinary approach to supporting children and young people. In the continuing move towards collaborative practice and integrated planning and provision, practitioners from across the education, health and social care sectors may lead where appropriate.

Learning Wales. (2014) *Special Education Needs and Inclusion*. Cardiff: Welsh Assembly Government (WAG). Retrieved from http://learning.gov.wales/resources/learningpacks/mep/special-educational-needs-and-inclusion/impact-of-the-environment/?lang=en (accessed 30 October 2017).

Task 6.2.1 'Breaking down' special educational needs

Warnock (2005) argues that her own concept of SEN must be 'broken down' and that we must abandon the common practice of referring to children with SEN (or 'SEN pupils') as one homogeneous group. Think of three pupils you have come across who have SEN. To what extent are their needs and their barriers to learning the same/different? Why might a single label of SEN be unhelpful in planning to meet the needs of these children?

LEGAL DEFINITION OF SEN

The term 'special educational needs' was first defined in the Education Act 1981 (HMSO, 1981) and more recently in the Education Act 1996 (HMSO, 1996), and the Children and Families Act 2014 (HMSO, 2014):

When a child or young person has special educational needs

(1) A child or young person has special educational needs if he or she has a learning difficulty or disability which calls for special educational provision to be made for him or her.

(2) A child of compulsory school age or a young person has a learning difficulty or disability if he or she –
   (a) has a significantly greater difficulty in learning than the majority of others of the same age, or
   (b) has a disability which prevents or hinders him or her from making use of facilities of a kind generally provided for others of the same age in mainstream schools or mainstream post-16 institutions.

(3) A child under compulsory school age has a learning difficulty or disability if he or she is likely to be within subsection (2) when of compulsory school age (or would be likely, if no special educational provision were made).

(4) A child or young person does not have a learning difficulty or disability solely because the language (or form of language) in which he or she is or will be taught is different from a language (or form of language) which is or has been spoken at home.

(HMSO, 2014: 20)

A broader, more inclusive term of 'additional support needs' (ASN) has been introduced in recent years in Scotland (Scottish Government, 2004) and refers to any child or young person who, for whatever reason, requires additional support to benefit from their school education. This definition encompasses any factor that might relate to social, emotional, cognitive, linguistic, disability, or family and care circumstances.

THE INCLUSION DEBATE

There has been considerable focus in recent years on *where* children with SEN should be taught, whether wholly in mainstream classes or special schools or in dual placements where children can be integrated at certain times or for certain subjects, according to their individual needs. The polarity of opinion on this subject is often very evident. Some would argue (for instance Rustemier, 2002) that, although the UK has signed up to pro-inclusion international agreements, such as the *United Nations Convention on the Rights of the Child* (United Nations, 1989), the *Salamanca Statement* (UNESCO, 1994) and the *United Nations Convention on the Rights of Persons with Disabilities* (United Nations, 2006), financial and legislative support for separate special schooling continues as before. Others, including Mary Warnock herself, would contend that inclusion has not always worked and indeed can, at times, be experienced as a 'painful kind of exclusion' for some children (Warnock, 2005: 39), and that there remains a need for separate schooling for children with the most severe and complex needs.

Another perspective has proposed that the focus should rest, not on *where* children with SEN are taught, but rather on *how* they are taught. Frederickson and Cline (2009: 8), for instance, argue that the concept of SEN must be seen as 'the outcome of an interaction between the individual characteristics of learners and the educational environments in which they are learning', emphasising the degree to which the child has responded to their current learning environment and suggesting how the environment might be adapted to meet those learning needs more effectively. This is confirmed by Ofsted's survey report, *The Special Educational Needs and Disability Review* (Ofsted, 2010), which found that the most significant factor in promoting the best outcomes for pupils with learning difficulties and disabilities was not the *type* but the *quality* of provision. The review found, further, that pupil progress depended less on whether the placement was in a mainstream or special school or a combination of both, and more on the availability of high-quality teaching and learning, close monitoring of pupil progress and regular evaluation of the effectiveness of interventions.

The experiences of James (below) illustrate the difference that a supportive placement context can make to successful inclusion:

> James is eight and attends a mainstream primary school. He has hemiplegia (partial paralysis of one side of his body) and moderate learning difficulties. Two years ago his parents felt that they had no choice but to remove him from his previous school due to bullying by other pupils who mocked his disability which they did not understand ('You're just weird', 'You shouldn't be in this school'), resulting in severe anxiety and aggressive behaviour by James both at school and at home. In his new school James has made a fresh start with a very capable teacher, Mrs Thompson, who met James and his parents several times before the new school year, and has worked hard to differentiate her teaching, allowing James to be much more fully integrated into

all classroom lessons, including physical education. With his parents' permission, Mrs Thompson explained James' impairment to the other pupils in the class at the start of the year, which helped them to understand his disability and behaviours and has also led to much greater acceptance of him. Just a few weeks ago an increasingly confident and happy James volunteered to create and deliver a presentation to the rest of the class on hemiplegia.

Most recently, Tutt (2016) has argued that inclusion should be seen as a *process* by which children can be properly included in education to prepare them for life after school. She advocates a 'continuum of provision' so that all children can be included 'in a meaningful sense' in education, irrespective of the setting. For Tutt, 'equality is not about giving everyone the same experiences, but about recognising that, while everyone is different, they should be equally valued and educated in an environment where they feel they belong' (p. 10).

THE *CODE OF PRACTICE*

Needless to say, in working with children with SEN, teachers are often more interested in practical guidance rather than legal definitions. In this regard, students in England are referred to the most recent *Code of Practice* (DfE and DoH, 2015), which was a direct outcome of the Children and Families Act 2014. The *Code of Practice* sets out practical advice to local authorities, early years settings, schools and post-16 providers on how best to carry out their statutory duties in relation to provision for children with SEN, through the graduated approach of 'assess, plan, do and review' (DfE and DoH, 2015: 100-2). Although the *Code* itself is not a piece of legislation, all relevant education and health settings 'must have regard to [it]' and 'cannot ignore it' (DfE and DoH, 2015: 12). Nonetheless, the *Code of Practice* makes clear that there remains a duty on these bodies to decide what to do in each individual case, in light of the guidance provided. The *Code of Practice* provides guidance in areas such as the identification of SEN, the role of the Special Educational Needs Coordinator (SENCO), the central role of children and young people, EHCPs, and working with parents and other agencies. Such detailed guidance is, however, underpinned by a set of general principles (DfE and DoH, 2015: 19) that are designed to support:

- the participation of children, their parents and young people in decision-making;
- the early identification of children and young people's needs and early intervention to support them;
- greater choice and control for young people and parents over support;
- collaboration between education, health and social care services to provide support;
- high-quality provision to meet the needs of children and young people with SEN;
- a focus on inclusive practice and removing barriers to learning;
- successful preparation for adulthood, including independent living and employment.

In the spirit of the Warnock Report's recommendations, the *Code of Practice* acknowledges that, 'the purpose of identification is to work out what action a school needs to take, not to fit a pupil into a category' (DfE and DoH, 2015: 97). The spirit of the *Code of Practice* is clear that each child is unique, and that there is a wide spectrum of needs that are often interrelated. Nonetheless, the *Code of Practice* does indicate that children will have needs and requirements that may fall into at least one of four broad areas (see sections 6.28-6.35):

- communication and interaction;
- cognition and learning;
- social, emotional and mental health;
- sensory and/or physical needs.

> ### In Scotland . . .
>
> There is a wide range of factors which may lead to some children and young people having a need for additional support. These fall broadly into the four overlapping themes described below: learning environment, family circumstances, disability or health need, and social and emotional factors.
>
> (Scottish Government, 2010: 24)
>
> Source: Scottish Government. (2010) *Supporting Children's Learning Code of Practice (revised edition)*. Retrieved from www.gov.scot/Resource/Doc/348208/0116022.pdf (accessed 30 October 2017).

CHANGING POLICY AND SUPPORT IN MAINSTREAM PRIMARY SCHOOLS

Given the introduction of the Children and Families Act in 2014 and the *Code of Practice* in 2015, the focus in England is primarily on implementation rather than the development of new SEN policy. Nonetheless, the wider educational policy context remains turbulent and is likely to impact on children and young people with SEN and their provision. In 2016, the government published a white paper, *Educational Excellence Everywhere*, which outlined plans to convert all schools in England to academies and a further shift towards what is described as 'a school-led system' (DfE, 2016b: 6). With academy status comes an increased range of powers for schools, including greater control over admissions, finance and governance, all of which have important implications for pupils with SEN.

Looking ahead, the government has identified that changes are needed to the content of initial teacher education courses to ensure that students obtain sufficient knowledge and experience of effective SEN provision (DfE, 2016b: 12). Similarly, the government is committed to reviewing school funding (DfE, 2016b: 22) and has issued two consultations: *Fairer School Funding* (DfE, 2014) and *High Needs Funding* (DfE, 2016c). Currently, two children with similar needs may receive different levels of funding depending on which school they attend, and the aim of the funding reviews is to address this directly, although it is widely acknowledged that there are numerous historical and local complexities to be resolved.

Prior to the 2015 *Code of Practice*, there were three increasing levels of provision seeking to meet the needs of children with SEN in mainstream primary schools in England: School Action, School Action Plus and Statement of SEN. Since January 2015, School Action and School Action Plus have effectively merged to become SEN Support, and Statements of SEN have been replaced with EHCPs. Each of these two new levels of support will be considered in turn:

SEN support

SEN support refers to a level of support that can be met from within a school's existing resources. For each individual pupil, the school is required to keep a record of what SEN they have identified, the provision to be put in place to meet those needs, and the expected outcomes as a result of the provision. Although the overall responsibility for SEN provision lies with the SENCO, the *Code of Practice* is clear that the main class teacher is responsible for all the pupils they teach, including those with SEN:

> The class or subject teacher should remain responsible for working with the child on a daily basis. Where the interventions involve group or one-to-one teaching away from the main class or subject

teacher, they should still retain responsibility for the pupil. They should work closely with any teaching assistants or specialist staff involved, to plan and assess the impact of support and interventions and how they can be linked to classroom teaching.

(DfE and DoH, 2015: section 6.52)

Census data for 2015-16 show that almost 1 million pupils in England (11.6 per cent of the total pupil population) have been identified as requiring provision at the level of SEN Support to meet their needs (DfE, 2016a). Provision at the SEN Support level might typically include a personalised learning programme, additional help from a teacher or a teaching assistant or targeted educational interventions. At the heart of this level of provision is the principle that high-quality teaching and differentiation can remove barriers to learning so that children can 'achieve the best possible educational and other outcomes' (DfE and DoH, 2015: section 19d). Schools are required by the *Code of Practice* to publish an SEN Information Report on their website, which details their arrangements for providing a 'graduated response to children's SEN' (DfE and DoH, 2015: 69). This includes how schools will use the cyclic process of 'assess, plan, do, review' to meet the needs of children identified as needing SEN Support.

In Northern Ireland . . .

In 2016, Northern Ireland introduced a new Special Educational Needs Disability (SEND) Act. The SEND Act is the first building block in Northern Ireland's new SEN Framework. It received Royal Assent in March 2016. The Act places new duties on boards of governors, the education authority and health and social services authorities, and provides new rights for parents and children over compulsory school age.

Source: www.education-ni.gov.uk/articles/review-special-educational-needs-and-inclusion (accessed 30 October 2017).

EHCPs

If a school does not have the expertise or funding to meet the needs of a particular child, then an Education, Health and Care (EHC) needs assessment is undertaken by the local authority. This assessment is a full investigation of the child's needs and it must be completed within 16 weeks, with any final EHC plan issued within 20 weeks. The assessment should provide a holistic picture of the child, and, for primary school pupils, the following sections are legally required (DfE and DoH, 2015: 161-2):

- the views, interests and aspirations of the child and their parents;
- the child's special educational needs;
- the child's health care needs that relate to their SEN;
- the child's social care needs that relate to their SEN or disability;
- the outcomes sought for the child (including outcomes for life);
- the special educational provision required by the child;
- any health provision reasonably required by the learning difficulties or disabilities that result in the child having SEN;
- any social care provision that must be made for a child resulting from section 2 of the Chronically Sick and Disabled Persons Act 1970;

- any other social care provision reasonably required by the learning difficulties or disabilities that result in the child having SEN;
- the name and type of school that the child should attend;
- details of how any personal budget will support particular outcomes;
- any advice and information gathered/considered during the assessment process.

At the heart of this process are the wishes of the child and their parents, and both should be considered as equal partners in determining the provision required to meet the SEN. Once an EHCP is in place, the SENCO works with all of those organisations named to ensure that the provision detailed is delivered. EHCPs must be reviewed at least annually, and more regularly (every 3-6 months) for children under 5 years old. It should be made clear that, regardless of the complexity of the needs or the number of external agencies involved, the accountability for the educational progress and outcomes of the child remain firmly with the classroom teacher.

Census data for 2015-16 show that more than 235,000 pupils in England (2.8 per cent of the total pupil population) have been identified as requiring provision at the level of a Statement of SEN or an EHCP to meet their needs (DfE, 2016a). Any child who currently has a Statement of SEN is required to be assessed for an EHCP by the local authority, and the government target for completing all such transfers is April 2018.

In Scotland . . .

Where lead professionals are working with children or young people with additional support needs then, in addition to the points set out below, they also have a responsibility to be familiar with the Act and, in particular, to ensure that parents and young people themselves are aware of their rights when they have concerns or disagreements about the provisions being made under the Act.

(Scottish Government, 2010: 31)

Source: Scottish Government. (2010) *Supporting Children's Learning Code of Practice (revised edition)*. Retrieved from www.gov.scot/Resource/Doc/348208/0116022.pdf (accessed 30 October 2017).

TEACHERS' STANDARDS

The preamble of the current Teachers' Standards for England (DfE, 2011) makes it clear that teachers must 'make the education of their pupils their first concern'. Part One comprises the Standards for Teaching, which are set out under eight main objectives, each of which has several elements:

A teacher must:

1   set high expectations that inspire, motivate and challenge pupils;
2   promote good progress and outcomes by pupils;
3   demonstrate good subject and curriculum knowledge;
4   plan and teach well-structured lessons;
5   adapt teaching to respond to the strengths and needs of all pupils;
6   make accurate and productive use of assessment;
7   manage behaviour effectively to ensure a good and safe learning environment;
8   fulfil wider professional responsibilities.

Although *all* of the above standards are evidently relevant to the teaching of children with SEN, the fifth standard is of particular importance. Under this standard, in adapting their teaching to respond to the strengths and needs of all pupils, teachers must:

- know when and how to differentiate appropriately, using approaches that enable pupils to be taught effectively;
- have a secure understanding of how a range of factors can inhibit pupils' ability to learn, and how best to overcome these;
- demonstrate an awareness of the physical, social and intellectual development of children, and know how to adapt teaching to support pupils' education at different stages of development;
- have a clear understanding of the needs of all pupils, including those with special educational needs; those of high ability; those with English as an additional language; those with disabilities; and be able to use and evaluate distinctive teaching approaches to engage and support them.

Part Two of the Standards relates to teachers' personal and professional conduct. Here too it is important that, when working with children with SEN, teachers maintain high standards of ethics and behaviour by 'treating pupils with dignity, building relationships rooted in mutual respect' and 'having regard for the need to safeguard pupils' well-being' (DfE, 2011).

COLLABORATIVE SUPPORT

Student teachers can sometimes feel isolated and overwhelmed by the challenges of teaching children with SEN. Although this unit is unapologetic in arguing that 'all teachers are teachers of children with special educational needs', there is clearly a need for collaborative working with others, in particular the SENCO, teaching assistants and parents.

SENCO

The SENCO in a primary school has day-to-day responsibility for coordinating the specific SEN provision within a school. Although SENCO is the legal title, in recent years many alternative titles have emerged in England, such as director of inclusion, inclusion manager and head of learning support. In Wales, the title of ALNCO is used (additional learning needs coordinator), and, in Northern Ireland, the role is to be renamed 'learning support coordinator'. The new English *Code of Practice* (DfE and DoH, 2015; section 6.90) notes that the key responsibilities of the SENCO may include:

- overseeing the day-to-day operation of the school's SEN policy;
- coordinating provision for children with SEN;
- liaising with the relevant designated teacher where a looked-after pupil has SEN;
- advising on the graduated approach to providing SEN support;
- advising on the deployment of the school's delegated budget and other resources to meet pupils' needs effectively;
- liaising with parents of pupils with SEN;
- liaising with early years providers, other schools, educational psychologists, health and social care professionals, and independent or voluntary bodies;
- being a key point of contact with external agencies, especially the local authority and its support services;
- liaising with potential next providers of education to ensure a pupil and their parents are informed about options and a smooth transition is planned;

- working with the head teacher and school governors to ensure that the school meets its responsibilities under the Equality Act (2010) with regard to reasonable adjustments and access arrangements;
- ensuring that the school keeps the records of all pupils with SEN up to date.

The new *Code of Practice* (DfE and DoH, 2015) states that the SENCO must be a qualified teacher, and new SENCOs must achieve a National Award in Special Educational Needs Coordination within 3 years of appointment. The *Code* notes that the SENCO will be most effective in their role if they are part of the school leadership team. Smaller primary schools may share a SENCO across several schools, although the *Code* adds that such a SENCO should not normally have a heavy teaching commitment, and that this arrangement should be kept under regular review.

Teaching assistants

Student teachers also need to learn to manage teaching assistants (in NI, classroom/learning support assistants) effectively to support the learning of children with SEN. The role of teaching assistants has come under close scrutiny in recent years. In a primary phase-specific study of adult support for children with statements of SEN (for children with moderate learning difficulties and behavioural, emotional and social difficulties), Webster and Blatchford (2013) found that the role of teaching assistants could actually create a barrier between the child receiving support and the person with lead responsibility for her or his learning, the class teacher. Unfortunately, research findings have been wilfully misinterpreted by some commentators, who argue that they point to the need for schools to stop employing teaching assistants (Robertson, 2013). In fact, as Russell, Webster and Blatchford (2012) are careful to note, the real challenge is for school leaders, SENCOs and teachers to examine how best they can optimise the skills of teaching assistants, with a clear focus on teaching. Student teachers have a role to play, bringing new and fresh ideas of their own to discussions. However, they may also seek advice on teaching assistant deployment from SENCOs, other teachers with responsibility for this deployment and, of course, from experienced and effective teaching assistants themselves.

Parents and carers

Student teachers can sometimes feel daunted by the prospect of working 'in partnership' with parents/carers of children with SEN. This is not surprising, given that some parents/carers may, for a variety of reasons, have concerns about their child that might be expressed in terms of what can be perceived as blaming the teacher or school. Reading the Lamb Inquiry report on parental experiences of the special educational system in England (DCSF, 2009) helps to explain why some parents/carers can feel angry or upset about provision for their child, the lack of it or bureaucratic assessment procedures. It is also worth noting, however, that relatively straightforward approaches to honest communication can be used by teachers, SENCOs and head teachers to make a positive difference to the education of children with SEN, as Robertson (2010) and Laluvein (2010) make clear.

MEETING THE NEEDS OF CHILDREN WITH SEN: WHERE DO I BEGIN?

In learning to be a primary school teacher, students are often naturally apprehensive and indeed sometimes 'scared' at the prospect of teaching so many children with so many different types of SEN (see Richards, 2010), but, as the following student teacher's experience illustrates, these initial anxious moments are often quickly overcome:

My first experience of working with children with SEN was in 2011 when, aged 16, I began to volunteer for a local Special Olympics Club which is a sports organisation for children and adults with learning difficulties. At the start I was slightly apprehensive and unsure of what to expect as I had never worked with anyone with SEN before. But from that moment on, I had my heart set on working with these incredible individuals and I instantly knew that this was the career path I wanted to follow, so I applied to university to become a teacher. This year I got to complete my placement in a special school for pupils with severe learning difficulties – I couldn't have loved this placement more! If I was to give advice to a student teacher who was anxious about working with children with SEN, I would tell them first that it is only natural to feel anxious about a new experience. I would also advise them not to be afraid to ask questions, to learn from the expertise of more experienced professionals, and to get involved in volunteering. The prospect of teaching these remarkable pupils is extremely exciting and I cannot wait to see what the future of my teaching career in special education holds.

(Rachael Jess, final year student teacher, Belfast)

It would be foolish to make a selection of particular SEN in this unit and to offer 'teaching tips' as quick-fix solutions to complex individual situations. Instead, and in seeking to support a move from fear to confidence, the following additional advice is offered:

- Take advantage of the courses available during your ITE on the most common and challenging SEN (e.g. moderate learning difficulties; speech, language and communication difficulties; social, emotional and behavioural difficulties; autism; dyslexia), and thus try to develop your understanding of the particular learning needs of different children with SEN.
- Consider also the need to make adaptations to the learning environment, the task set and your teaching style, rather than focusing solely on the child's learning characteristics. The new English *Code of Practice* stresses the importance of high-quality differentiated teaching as the first step in responding to pupils with SEN and adds that, 'Additional intervention and support cannot compensate for a lack of good quality teaching' (DfE and DoH, 2015: section 6.37).
- Be aware of the particular targets set in a child's support plan and plan your teaching to facilitate the meeting of those targets. This necessitates knowledge and understanding of the particular child, their needs and the barriers to their learning, as well as the particular targets themselves. However, in your planning, you should also remember to take into account the whole-school provision, which might include, for instance, evidence-based group interventions for literacy, numeracy or social skills support.
- Realise that you are not alone: ask for advice and support from more experienced teachers, and especially from the school SENCO.
- Always seek the support of the child's parents/carers as 'equal partners', as they can offer unrivalled insights into the child's needs and also help to reinforce at home the strategies you are implementing in class.
- Try to keep abreast of the many changes to SEN policy across the UK that are already being implemented in England but are still incomplete in Wales and Northern Ireland.
- Take every opportunity to develop your own skills and understanding through professional development courses and/or membership of professional organisations (e.g. nasen – the National Association for Special Educational Needs).
- Remember that each child with SEN is unique. Although knowledge of key policy and legislation is a requirement, and although an understanding of key aspects of common SEN is very useful, it is crucial that you take time to get to know the individual strengths and needs of each individual child with SEN in your primary classroom, including an understanding of their lives outside school.

Task 6.2.2 What SEN knowledge do I need?

The *Cambridge Primary Review* (2010) concludes that expert teachers should possess knowledge of *children*, knowledge of *subject*, but also knowledge of children's *context* (recognising the importance of family and community). Think of two pupils with SEN. Explain the nature of the children's SEN, how the barriers to their learning depend on the curricular area in question (are the barriers different in mathematics, history, art and design?), and the extent of contact you or the school had with the pupils' families. If you have no knowledge of the children's context, how might you develop that in the future?

SUMMARY

In this unit, we have examined the current levels of SEN provision in schools and provided guidance on how planning should be used to support children with SEN in meeting learning targets. The policy context for SEN is changing rapidly, and in this unit we have considered the development of the concept of SEN, from its origins in the Warnock Report (DES, 1978) to the most recent policy changes across the four jurisdictions of the UK. Notwithstanding recent developments in SEN policy, we have concluded that nothing is more important than a teacher's willingness to engage with an individual child and to seek to meet their learning needs, while drawing on the support of parents, teachers and other professionals.

APPENDIX: ADDITIONAL MATERIAL ON REGIONAL VARIATIONS

Scotland

The Education (Additional Support for Learning) (Scotland) Act 2004 placed new duties on education authorities to provide for children with ASN, and this was updated in 2009 along with a revised version of the *Supporting Children's Learning: Code of Practice* (Education Scotland, 2010). In some respects, the Scottish *Code* shares many similarities with the English *Code* – for example, a four-stage process of 'assessment, planning, action and review' and a focus on preparation for adulthood. However, there are some clear differences between the two *Codes*. The Scottish focus on additional learning support needs is much broader than special educational needs and includes additional groups of children such as highly able children, children being bullied and those with English as an additional language. This, in turn, means that the terminology is somewhat different, with 'Additional Support Needs Coordinator' being used instead of SENCO and 'Coordinated Support Plan' instead of EHC plan. The 2010 *Code of Practice* states that ASN occur 'where, for whatever reason, the child or young person is, or is likely to be, unable without the provision of additional support to benefit from school education' (Education Scotland, 2010: 18). Looking ahead, the Scottish government has made broad commitments to inclusive education, but there are currently no specific plans in the public domain to further develop the 2010 *Code of Practice*.

Wales

Until 2002, provision for additional learning needs (ALN) in Wales followed a very similar pattern to that in England. Following devolution in Wales, at the time when the *Code of Practice* was being updated in England in 2002, Wales published its own *SEN Code of Practice* alongside a report, *Special Educational Needs: A Mainstream Issue* (Audit Commission, 2002). The Additional Learning Needs and Education Tribunal (Wales) Bill was introduced to the National Assembly for Wales in December 2016. The Bill replaces the term 'special educational needs' and learning difficulties and/or disabilities (LDD) with the term 'additional learning needs' (ALN) to encompass children and young people aged 0–25 across early years, schools and Further Education (FE) settings. The Bill replaces SEN statements (schools) and LDD plans (FE) with individual development plans (IDPs), and inter-agency collaboration will be enhanced through the introduction of Designated Educational Clinical Lead Officers in local health authorities. IDPs will cover those aged 0–25 years, with the emphasis on making provision that delivers tangible outcomes contributing to the fulfilment of the child/young person's potential.

Northern Ireland

The main legislation in Northern Ireland relating to special educational needs is contained in the Education (Northern Ireland) Order 1996 (DENI, 1996). A lengthy and at times contentious period of review began in August 2009, with the DE consultation on *The Way Forward for Special Educational Needs and Inclusion* (DENI, 2009), and has led recently to the passing of new legislation by the Northern Ireland Assembly (2016). The Special Educational Needs and Disability Act (Northern Ireland) 2016 means that the newly formed Education Authority (which replaced the five education and library boards on 1 April 2015) must publish a plan of its arrangements for special educational provision at least annually, boards of governors must appoint a learning support coordinator (a new role replacing the SENCO) with responsibility for coordinating provision, and each child with SEN must have a personal learning plan (replacing the previous individual education plan). In addition, a duty is now placed on the education authority to have regard to the views of the child when making decisions about their SEN, and a duty is placed on health and social care bodies to provide services identified by them as likely to be of benefit in addressing the child's SEN. In essence, the new Act provides the legislative changes necessary to support a new SEN framework. The passing of the new legislation was followed by a public consultation on new draft SEN regulations (February–May 2016) and will lead to the eagerly awaited revision of the *Code of Practice*, which has been operational in Northern Ireland since 1998.

 ANNOTATED FURTHER READING

Peer, L. and Reid, G. (eds) (2016) *Special Educational Needs – A Guide for Inclusive Practice*, 2nd edn, London: Sage.

>   The new edition of this edited volume contains chapters written by a range of experts on different SEN and includes many practical suggestions to promote the successful inclusion of children with SEN. The book sets out to represent the many different perspectives on SEN – research, policy, practice, parents and the children themselves. Discussion points, case studies and summaries help make this a highly accessible text.

Westwood, P. (2015) *Commonsense Methods for Children with Special Educational Needs*, 7th edn, London: Routledge.

> This seminal publication offers sound practical advice on assessment and intervention in relation to a wide range of SEN, embedded within a clear theoretical context supported by current research and classroom practice. This most recent edition features new material on the transition from school to employment for students with disabilities, lesson study, e-learning and computer-aided instruction.

 ## FURTHER READING TO SUPPORT M-LEVEL STUDY

Calder, I. and Grieve, A. (2004) 'Working with other adults: What teachers need to know', *Educational Studies*, 30(2): 113-26.

> This research article argues that teachers need to be much better prepared to manage effectively the growing number of other adults in their classrooms, including SEN classroom assistants. The article stresses the need for teachers to take the lead in managing, training, motivating and supervising assistants and in developing effective collaborative structures.

Richards, G. (2010) '"I was confident about teaching but SEN scared me": Preparing new teachers for including pupils with special educational needs', *Support for Learning*, 25(3): 108-15.

> This article is based on a small-scale research study carried out with a group of student teachers taking part in short, focused SEN placements in schools. The findings are very positive, with the students reporting higher levels of confidence and skills as a result of their experience.

 ## RELEVANT WEBSITES

2015 *Code of Practice*: www.gov.uk/government/publications/send-code-of-practice-0-to-25

> The 2015 *Code of Practice* provides statutory guidance for organisations in England that work with and support children and young people who have special educational needs or disabilities.

nasen: www.nasen.org.uk

> nasen is a leading national and international SEN membership organisation for education professionals, offering a wealth of publications, training and resources.

Mencap: www.mencap.org.uk/advice-and-support/children-and-young-people/education-support

> Mencap offer advice and support on children's rights in education, the new SEND system, SEN support, support for parents and carers, EHCPs, further education and how to challenge the support that children are receiving.

Anti-Bullying Alliance: www.anti-bullyingalliance.org.uk/tools-information/all-about-bullying/sen-disability

> The Anti-Bullying Alliance has produced a series of very useful resources to help schools address the bullying of children with SEN and/or disabilities.

 ## REFERENCES

Audit Commission. (2002) *Special Educational Needs: A Mainstream Issue*, London: Audit Commission.

Cambridge Primary Review. (2010) *Children, Their World, Their Education – Final Report and Recommendations of the Cambridge Primary Review* (ed. R. Alexander), London: Routledge.

Department for Children, Schools and Families (DCSF). (2008) *The Bercow Report: A Review of Services for Children and Young People (0-19) with Speech, Language and Communication Needs.* Retrieved from www.education.gov.uk/publications/eOrderingDownload/Bercow-Report.pdf (accessed 30 October 2017).

Department for Children, Schools and Families (DCSF). (2009) *Lamb Inquiry: Special educational needs and parental confidence.* Retrieved from www.education.gov.uk/publications/standard/publicationDetail/Page1/DCSF-01143-2009 (accessed 30 October 2017).

Department for Education (DfE). (2011) *Teachers' Standards.* Retrieved from www.gov.uk/government/uploads/system/uploads/attachment_data/file/283566/Teachers_standard_information.pdf (accessed 30 October 2017).

Department for Education (DfE). (2014) *Fairer Schools Funding in 2015-16.* Retrieved from https://www.gov.uk/government/uploads/system/uploads/attachment_data/file/293930/Fairer_school_funding_consultation.pdf (accessed 30 October 2017).

Department for Education (DfE). (2016a) *Statistics: Special Educational Needs in England: January 2016.* Retrieved from www.gov.uk/government/collections/statistics-special-educational-needs-sen (accessed 30 October 2017).

Department for Education (DfE). (2016b) *Educational Excellence Everywhere.* Retrieved from www.gov.uk/government/publications/educational-excellence-everywhere (accessed 30 October 2017).

Department for Education (DfE). (2016c) *High Needs Funding Formula and Other Reforms – Government Consultation.* Retrieved from https://consult.education.gov.uk/funding-policy-unit/high-needs-funding-reform/supporting_documents/HighNeedsFundingReform_Consultation.pdf (accessed 30 October 2017).

Department for Education (DfE) and Department of Health (DoH). (2015) *Special Educational Needs and Disability Code of Practice: 0-25 Years.* Retrieved from https://www.gov.uk/government/uploads/system/uploads/attachment_data/file/398815/SEND_Code_of_Practice_January_2015.pdf (accessed 30 October 2017).

Department of Education and Science (DES) (1978) *Report of the Committee of Enquiry into the Education of Handicapped Children and Young People (The Warnock Report),* London: HMSO.

Department of Education for Northern Ireland (DENI). (1996) Education (Northern Ireland) Order 1996, Bangor, NI: DENI.

Department of Education for Northern Ireland (DENI). (2009) *The Way Forward for Special Educational Needs and Inclusion.* Retrieved from www.education-ni.gov.uk/publications/every-school-good-school-way-forward-special-educational-needs-consultation-document (accessed 30 October 2017).

Education Scotland. (2010) *Supporting Children's Learning: Code of Practice.* Retrieved from www.gov.scot/Resource/Doc/348208/0116022.pdf (accessed 30 October 2017).

Frederickson, N. and Cline, T. (2009) *Special Educational Needs, Inclusion and Diversity,* 2nd edn, Maidenhead, UK: Open University Press.

Her Majesty's Stationary Office (HMS). (1944) Education Act, London: HMSO.

Her Majesty's Stationary Office (HMS). (1970) Education Act, London: HMSO.

Her Majesty's Stationary Office (HMS). (1981) Education Act, London: HMSO.

Her Majesty's Stationary Office (HMS). (1988) Education Reform Act, London: HMSO.

Her Majesty's Stationary Office (HMS). (1996) Education Act, London: HMSO.

Her Majesty's Stationary Office (HMS). (2014) Children and Families Act, London: HMSO.

Laluvein, J. (2010) 'Variations on a theme: parents and teachers talking', *Support for Learning,* 25(4): 194-9.

Northern Ireland Assembly. Special Educational Needs and Disability Act (Northern Ireland) 2016, London: TSO.

Ofsted. (2010) *The Special Educational Needs and Disability Review.* Retrieved from https://www.gov.uk/government/uploads/system/uploads/attachment_data/file/413814/Special_education_needs_and_disability_review.pdf (accessed 30 October 2017).

Richards, G. (2010) '"I was confident about teaching but SEN scared me": Preparing new teachers for including pupils with special educational needs', *Support for Learning,* 25(3): 108-15.

Robertson, C. (2010) 'Working in partnership with parents', in F. Hallett and G. Hallett (eds) *Transforming the Role of the SENCO: Achieving the National Award for SEN Coordination,* Maidenhead, UK: Open University Press, pp. 194-201.

Robertson, C. (2013) 'Future of teaching assistants: Let's wilfully misinterpret the evidence', *SENCO Update*, 147(July): 6.

Russell, A., Webster, R. and Blatchford, P. (2012) *Maximising the Impact of Teaching Assistants: Guidance for School Leaders and Teachers*, London: Routledge.

Rustemier, S. (2002) *Social and Educational Justice: The Human Rights Framework for Inclusion*, Bristol, UK: Centre for Studies in Inclusive Education.

Scottish Government. (2004) Education Additional Support for Learning Scotland Act, Edinburgh: Scottish Government.

Tutt, R. (2016) *Rona Tutt's Guide to SEND and Inclusion*, London: Sage.

United Nations. (1989) *The United Nations Convention on the Rights of the Child*. Retrieved from http://treaties.un.org/pages/viewdetails.aspx?src=treaty&mtdsg_no=iv-11&chapter=4&lang=en (accessed 30 October 2017).

United Nations. (2006) *Convention on the Rights of Persons with Disabilities*. Retrieved from www.un.org/development/desa/disabilities/convention-on-the-rights-of-persons-with-disabilities.html (accessed 30 October 2017).

United Nations Educational, Scientific and Cultural Organization (UNESCO). (1994) *The Salamanca Statement and Framework for Action*. Retrieved from www.unesco.org/education/pdf/SALAMA_E.PDF (accessed 30 October 2017).

Warnock, M. (2005) *Special Educational Needs: A New Look* (Impact 11), Salisbury, UK: Philosophy of Education Society of Great Britain.

Webster, R. and Blatchford, P. (2013) *The Making a Statement Project Final Report: A Study of the Teaching and Support Experienced by Pupils with a Statement of Special Educational Needs in Mainstream Primary Schools*, London: Institute of Education/Nuffield Foundation.

TEACHING FOR SOCIAL JUSTICE

Creating equity for pupils living in poverty and those from black and minority ethnic backgrounds

Hanneke Jones and Heather Smith

INTRODUCTION

The term 'social justice' has very different meanings for different people. Generally, the term is used to indicate a wish to 'change things for the better', or a desire to 'make a difference', which for many student teachers is a reason why they want to join the teaching profession.

Of course, it depends on your political standpoint exactly who or *what* needs to change: should people be helped to fit into society, or should society itself be changed to provide better opportunities for more people? Smith (2012) presents three different views of social justice: justice as *harmony* (a view that accepts as rightful that some have more opportunities than others); justice as *equality* (in which everyone is given the same opportunity, regardless of their background); and justice as *equity* (which aims to compensate for fundamentally unequal opportunities and to create equality of *outcomes*). We, the authors of this unit, are firmly aligned to the concept of justice as equity. We believe that we live in a deeply unequal and unjust society, in which many people are disadvantaged through, for example, poverty and race discrimination. These forms of disadvantage are, for a large part, created by the economic system in which we live and, to a large extent, exacerbated by what Althusser (1970) called the 'repressive and ideological state apparatuses' – that is, media, schooling, religion, courts, families, and so on. These disadvantages can, and do, have a huge bearing on educational success.

Although we believe that many of the causes of disadvantage are structural (and thus can't be changed easily by and for individuals), we also believe that there are forms of education and teacher behaviour that can empower pupils, break down elements of disadvantage, create more equity and, as part of wider struggle, contribute to a change in society. On the other hand, we also know that there are many forms of schooling and teacher behaviours that *increase* disadvantage. Teaching for social justice from this viewpoint involves having a clear commitment to maximising equity for your pupils, and having a clear understanding of both the positive changes we can make as teachers, and the risks of making things worse for some of the most disadvantaged pupils.

In the first section of this unit, we discuss issues in relation to poverty, and, in the second section, we discuss issues in relation to race and racism. Although these are distinct issues, it is important to remember your pupils may be disadvantaged by both. Finally, there are of course many other sources of potential disadvantage, such as disability, gender and sexuality, which you may want to explore further, but which we are not able to address here.

OBJECTIVES

By the end of this unit, you should:

- be aware of the ways in which education can increase inequalities;
- know how you can minimise these risks in your own practice;
- know how you can work towards greater equity in the classroom.

SUPPORTING PUPILS LIVING IN POVERTY

This section will start with some general background information about poverty and education. This is followed by a section describing what the life experiences of children living in poverty might be like, before we discuss some of the many challenges and misconceptions these children can face at school, and the effects these may have. Finally, we will discuss some ways to counter these injustices in school. Throughout, it is of course important to remember that, although we will make some generalisations, the lives of no two children living in poverty are the same.

Background

There are different ways of defining poverty, but, according to government figures for 2013-14 (DWP, 2015), a staggering 31 per cent of children in the UK were living in families with absolute low income after housing costs, and this figure is not expected to go down over the next few years. Children whose parents are entitled to a specific range of benefits are eligible for free school meals (FSM), and the percentage of children eligible for FSM is a common indicator of the level of material deprivation of the school population. In 2015-16, 14.5 per cent of primary pupils in the UK were eligible for, and claiming, FSM (DfE, 2016b). Although not all of the 31 per cent of UK children living in poverty attend school (this number includes, for example, children of pre-school age), the fact that only 14.5 per cent of primary pupils claim FSM means that large numbers of pupils living in poverty are either not entitled to, or do not claim, FSM. In other words, the number of pupils in your class who live in poverty may well be higher than that of the pupils who receive FSM.

In our exam-based education system, attainment in SATs and GCSE results is often seen as the main indicator of educational success. Although there are many children living in poverty who do well at school against these measures, socio-economic disadvantage remains the most important factor that determines statistical underachievement in schools in the UK (DfE, 2015; DfE, 2016a). To help to minimise this 'achievement gap' between children from poorer families and those from families that are more affluent, the coalition government introduced the pupil premium: at the time of writing, schools receive £1,320 for each child who has been eligible for FSM in the past 6 years, but they have to provide evidence of how this funding has benefitted specifically those pupils for whom the pupil premium was received. This can be very hard to demonstrate for two reasons: there is very rarely a direct link between the investment of specific resources and raised achievement, and, as Paul Gorski (Gorski, 2016) explains, the achievement gap is a symptom of economic injustice, which schools cannot be expected to solve. The pressure to 'prove' that the pupil premium has made a difference in test results can unfortunately lead schools and teachers to more or less publicly identify those pupils for whom the pupil premium is received, which can be detrimental to the children involved, owing to the very great stigma attached to being poor.

Additionally, too great a focus on the narrow curriculum measured in test results may have serious implications for children living in poverty: these pupils may miss out on the rich opportunities that a broad curriculum should provide them with, and a curriculum that is not engaging and meaningful can make it even harder for them to 'do well'.

Growing up in poverty

Many people who live in poverty would probably describe themselves as 'working class', but, as 14-year-old Naomi explains in *Breadline Kids* (Neumann, 2014): 'You could be rich at some point, then everything could go downhill and you might have to go to a food bank someday'. John Smyth and Terry Wrigley (2013) have described the chains of difficulties faced by families living in poverty. As many of these families have to choose between eating and heating, children's access to food supplies can be scarce, especially during holidays, when children don't receive FSM – and fresh food can be an unaffordable luxury. The Trussell Trust (2016) reports having supplied more than 400,000 foodbank parcels that were used to feed children in 2015-16 in the UK. Houses can be cold and damp, and worries about paying rent or mortgage and bills and ultimately homelessness can create a constant pressure for parents. Some 63 per cent of children living in poverty have parents who are in low-paid work, often carried out at unsociable hours, so that time itself can be a scarce commodity in these families. As a result of such factors, physical and mental health issues can affect members of the family, and ill health and disability can in themselves be causes of poverty. Transport can add extra pressures – many families living in poverty do not own a car, and public transport can be expensive and time-consuming. When it comes to weekends and holidays, it is clear that, in many families, there is no money for trips or holidays away, and there is simply no money to buy books, to attend out-of-school classes, have a home computer and access to the Internet. On the other hand, it is clear that many children growing up in poverty may have had life experiences that more privileged children have not. Many will have developed knowledge, problem-solving skills and resilience that put them far in advance of other children. However, these are skills that are acknowledged and celebrated in these children in very few schools.

Task 6.3.1 'Everything could go downhill'

Reflect on your own lifestyle. Imagine that some of the income you rely on was cut. What would you stop doing if you had to live on £200 a month less than you do now? What would you stop doing if you had to live on £500 a month less than you do now? What impact would this have on your life? If you have/had children, what impact would this have on theirs?

Exclusion within school

It is clear from the section above that there are many material challenges that may make it difficult for children from poorer backgrounds to do well at school. They may come to school hungry, tired and worried, they may not be able to do the homework as there is no Internet at home, or their parent(s) may not have had time to read their reading book with them last night. They may be worried about the state of their uniform, or worried that they might get bullied as a result of being poor, meaning that it is more difficult to concentrate on the curriculum. In addition, the language used in most schools is that of the 'middle classes' (Hatcher, 2012: 243), resources used tend to reflect life in affluent families, and it takes a very good teacher to make the current National Curriculum meaningful to pupils who live in the circumstances described above.

Gorski (2016) argues that another great disadvantage experienced by pupils living in poverty is the stereotyping by teachers. Such stereotyping, based on views frequently seen in sections of the media, might include the notion that families are in in poverty because of their own shortcomings, that all people living in poverty are somehow similar, that they lack aspiration and an interest in education, and that people who do well in education get their results by working harder than others. If teachers, consciously or less consciously, have such views, the resulting deficit view and low expectations of children living in poverty are therefore real barriers to the education of these children. In many classes, for example, children from poorer backgrounds will be seated at the same table and given less challenging work, which means they are not cognitively stimulated as much as other pupils and will fall further and further 'behind'. It is only by tackling our own conceptions of poverty that we can begin to counter the injustices that are continued in our education system.

Task 6.3.2 Class and values portrayed as 'normal' in school resources

Consider a range of educational materials, for example, textbooks, reading scheme books, test materials, and so on. What messages are given here of a 'normal' lifestyle? How might this come across to a child living in poverty? How would you introduce these materials to pupils from a poorer background? Would you make a difference in the way you would introduce them?

Countering inequality

In order to counter the inequality related to poverty in our schools, we thus need to start, at the personal and whole-school level, by looking at our own expectations and potential stigmatisation of poorer pupils. Merilyn Cochran-Smith (2004) has put forward six important principles of pedagogy to counter inequality: first, we must make sure to provide *all* pupils with challenging learning opportunities. Enquiry-based pedagogies such as Philosophy for Children and Mantle of the Expert (Taylor, 2016) can be particularly helpful, as students tend to feel very engaged by these approaches and experience the curriculum as meaningful. Second, we must challenge and expand the knowledge and interests of our pupils, while at the same time respecting their culture and language. If particular skills are lacking, we need to teach those. We must work with, rather than around, poorer pupils' families and communities. We must use diverse forms of assessment that are able to acknowledge the strengths of all pupils. Finally, Cochran-Smith (2004) suggests that we must make equity, power and activism part of the curriculum wherever relevant.

On a practical level, there is much that can be done to minimise stigmatisation. The charity Children North East, for example, provides a programme named Poverty-Proofing Education (Mazzoli Smith and Todd, 2016), which gives tailored advice to schools on lowering the marginalisation of children living in poverty. Poverty-Proofing is based on the views expressed by children living in disadvantage, that what they most wanted was an end to discrimination in school. Such measures can include a reorganisation of FSM so that it is not possible to detect whose meal is free, the provision of more access to computers and other facilities, a ban on brand items such as trainers, support with trips, and so on (see link below for further information).

Vignette about Mantle of the Expert

St John's Primary School is situated in a highly disadvantaged area in Newcastle, but is also one of its most successful schools. The head teacher ascribes this success to the school's use of the Mantle of the Expert, an approach that all members of staff have been trained in and build much of their teaching on, and which the pupils have taken to with enthusiasm. In Mantle of the Expert, drama is used through a process of imaginative enquiry to enable pupils (and teachers!) to experience new realities, take on the role of responsible experts and become completely immersed in deep learning across the curriculum, or, in Cochran-Smith's words (2004), 'in being challenged and having their knowledge and interests expanded'. For example, in a Mantle project about the First World War, a class of children experienced, through their imagination, the lives of many people who had lived through this. They wrote letters home from the Front and experienced, through Mantle, what it would have been like to receive these and make sense of them. They took on the roles of different people working in the (still) nearby arms factory, but also those of the War Cabinet making governmental decisions, and so on. Each of these perspectives or 'roles' took weeks of children's research and involvement and produced very large amounts of written work, artwork and understanding across the whole curriculum. By the end of the year, children in this class were disappointed that they would not be studying the First World War for another year! A deep engagement with social justice and the development of an understanding of different people's life histories, decisions and the impact of these on others (such as in the First World War example above) are also often apparent in the Mantle of the Expert, which makes it into a potentially transformative pedagogy.

RACE, RACISM AND EDUCATION

Background: Untangling an acronym

The teaching world is flooded with acronyms, so, before we begin our exploration of racism in education, let's begin by questioning the meaning of the acronym 'BME'.

Task 6.3.3 What does BME *mean*?

The following sketch represents the sort of typical conversation we, as teacher educators, often find ourselves holding with student teachers:

Teacher: What does BME *mean*?
Student 1:   Does it stand for British something?
Teacher: No it stands for black minority ethnic, but what does minority ethnic *mean*?
Student 1:   Does it mean not British?
Student 2:   No it means not white.
Teacher: But what does white mean?
Student 1:   Does it mean you're British? Like you speak English?

In other words, some student teachers conflate race, ethnicity, nationalism, language status and often religion too. This conflation is largely reflective of the current sociopolitical climate created by politicians and powerful media representations (Smith, 2016). And, as we shall see later, this imagining of some children as British and others as either not British or not quite British enough along the axes of race, ethnicity, religion and linguistic norms can have powerful consequences for teachers and pupils, not least because racism can be enacted through affiliated factors such as language, immigration status and culture (Kohli, 2009). But first, let's continue our investigation.

If black means not white (as in student 2 above), we are back to the question: what does white mean? If you are white, are you always white, everywhere? Is race a fixed, incontrovertible, biological truth? Although our eyes tell us that people look different, as phenotypic features vary, the scientific reality is that there are no sets of genetic markers that occur in everybody of any one specific race but in nobody of another race:

> There are no genetic characteristics possessed by all Blacks but not by non-Blacks; similarly, there is no gene or cluster of genes common to all Whites but not to non-Whites. . . . The data compiled by various scientists demonstrate, contrary to popular opinion, that intra-group differences [in genetic coding] exceed inter-group differences. That is, greater genetic variation exists *within* the populations typically labelled Black and White than *between* these populations. This finding refutes the supposition that racial divisions reflect fundamental genetic differences.
>
> (López, 2000: 166)

So how is race defined by social scientists? Gillborn (2008: 3) describes race as 'a system of socially constructed and enforced categories that are constantly recreated and modified through human interaction'. This has meant that sometimes people defined as white in one context are not quite so white in another. For example, there are echoes of the treatment of Irish immigrants to America in the early nineteenth century, by the white protestant elite, as an inferior race in today's sociopolitical representations of Eastern European immigrants to UK, particularly those from poorer countries such as Romania. Do you recall the removal of a blond-haired, blue-eyed 7-year-old girl from a Roma Gypsy family in Ireland in 2013, under the seeming suspicion that such a white-looking child could not possibly be Roma Gypsy (as reported in the *Daily Mail*, 22 October 2013)?

So, if race isn't real in a biological sense, why mention it at all? Colourblindness, or the putting aside of race in a focus on social inequities, although comfortable from a liberal perspective (many of us are taught that it's rude to even mention race), has not and will not lead to racial equality, including in education. As Mazzei (2008: 1130) so powerfully puts it:

> As progressive as she [the teacher] may be in her attitudes towards those from different backgrounds, what are the effects upon students when she 'doesn't see colour', or is silent as to the effects of colour and treats all students the same, thereby denying the fact that the students in her classroom are shaped and acted on by others because of their colour.

We would add that, so is the teacher him/herself.

In short, although race isn't real, racism is. Racism here does not refer solely to more obvious, crude acts of racial hatred, but to 'the more subtle and hidden operations of power that have the effect of disadvantaging one or more minority ethnic groups' (Gillborn, 2008: 27). Racism is also to be understood as a relational practice; it acts to disadvantage, but also to advantage, even when those benefitting from this are unaware of or do not seek advantages. This process of racial (dis)advantaging occurs through that which critical race theorists refer to as whiteness, which is defined 'not as an attribute of identity adhering to a white body, but as a process, a performance, or a constantly shifting location upon complex maps of social, economic, and political power' (Levine-Rasky, 2000: 287).

Although not fixed, 'whiteness has come to be associated with reproduction, dominance, normativity and privilege' (Solomon *et al.*, 2005: 159). So, if the practice of racism is real in all its forms, leading to certain advantages and disadvantages, what are the consequences for children's education? One way of investigating this is to refer to statistics.

A brief sojourn in statistics

Although it is beyond the scope of this unit to fully interrogate education statistics, even a cursory glance at the latest government report shows a complex web of intersectionality where race, gender and poverty impact together on children's exam success in school in UK. The African American Policy Forum (2013) describe intersectionality as:

> a concept that enables us to recognize the fact that perceived group membership can make people vulnerable to various forms of bias, yet because we are simultaneously members of many groups, our complex identities can shape the specific way we each experience that bias.

For example, Key Stage 2 SATs results in 2015 revealed that both white and black Caribbean boys eligible for FSM achieved below the national average for Level 4 in reading, writing and mathematics (21 and 17 percentage points behind, respectively). A report by the Equalities and Human Rights Commission (2016) showed black Caribbean and mixed heritage black Caribbean/white children had rates of permanent exclusion from schools about three times higher than the rate for all pupils. Now, unless we consider that some pupils are somehow *naturally* 'less able' or 'less well behaved', then we must continue to explore why such inequities exist. Let us do so from three perspectives: the effect of racism on pupils' lives; the effects of teacher stereotyping and resulting prejudiced and discriminatory behaviour; and education structures and systems.

Countering racial inequality

Perhaps it is easier to understand the effects of racism on pupils when considering overt acts of racism (verbal or physical). This is certainly the focus of many school policies and anti-discrimination materials (Rollock, 2012). However, for the purposes of this unit and in line with the definition of racism provided above, let us consider the impact of a particular manifestation of whiteness known as racial micro-aggressions, or 'brief and commonplace daily verbal, behavioural and environmental indignities, whether intentional or unintentional, that communicate hostile, derogatory, or negative racial slights and insults to the target person or group' (Sue *et al.*, 2009). The cumulative nature of such indignities is of most concern here. Let us illustrate this by considering an example that, on its own, may appear inconspicuous. How many times have you heard, or indeed have yourself used phrases such as, 'wow, that's a hard name to pronounce; it's so exotic compared to mine; is there a shorter version I can use?'? Kohli and Solórzano (2012) investigated the effect of the mispronunciation, change or disrespect of pupils' names by teachers in American high schools. Evidence suggested that when this happens to black minority ethnic pupils, coupled with numerous other daily micro-aggressions, pupils begin to hear a message that they don't belong, and, crucially, 'start to believe the message, and begin to doubt their place or cultural worth in . . . society. This can impact their aspirations, motivation, and love for their culture and themselves' (ibid.: 449). The resurgence of notions of Britishness and the intrusion of British values into education policies in England can only heighten prejudicial notions of belonging in the minds of both pupils and teachers (Smith, 2016).

If teachers hold damaging stereotypes of children (unconscious or not) based on associations relating to race, gender, assumed nationality and religion, then they are more likely to be perpetrators of such racialized micro-aggressions. This is because stereotypes, which abound in society and often remain unnoticed and unchallenged, are accompanied by prejudices (emotions) leading to discriminatory acts, however small and unconscious, such as micro-aggressions. For example, if a teacher believes purple people are devious (after all, the newspapers are full of stories of devious purple people), they are more likely to feel wary of the acts of purple people (a prejudice). When Peter (a purple boy) reports being called nasty names for being purple by some non-purple boys, rather than treating the incident as important, the teacher fails to believe Peter and tells him to stop telling tales and trying to get 'other' (i.e. non-purple) children into trouble (i.e. to stop playing the purple (race) card) – a discriminatory act against Peter and unhelpful too for the boys committing the racist bullying, who need an anti-racist education. This issue has led critical race theorists to argue that student teachers need to 'examine their overall understanding of their racial identity; the ideologies with which they enter the classroom; explore the impact of those ideologies on their teaching practices and their interactions with students' (Solomon *et al.*, 2005: 149).

But this is not just about individual acts by teachers or pupils, it is about the structures and systems of schooling in which teachers teach and in which pupils learn.

Here is an imagined sketch on how this might work, based on recent conversations we or others we know have been privy to. It takes place in a primary school with a higher than national average intake of black and working-class pupils:

> *Head teacher (to teacher)*: We must improve the SATs results this year or we will be faced with another visit from Ofsted.
> *Teacher*: Well we have to be realistic; there are a lot of challenging children in Year 6 this year.
> *Head teacher (later to deputy head teacher)*: I really don't want us to be forced to become an academy. We need to think of ways to change the student intake to improve results.

The word 'challenging' is a euphemism often used in education to signal, not just the reality of the challenging circumstances some children face, but a lack of belief that education can change anything for these children. The pressures on schools to raise results of ever-more-demanding tests, with real effects for schools (for example, the academisation agenda, where schools deemed by Ofsted to be failing are forced to become academies, even when this is not what parents of children in the school want or have requested), can act to shift the focus of school improvement away from providing a transformational education for the pupils in their school to, as in this case, a transformation of a school population itself.

CONCLUSION

In conclusion, we all need to be aware of, and then act to challenge, deeply ingrained prejudices in ourselves and in others, including our pupils. Prejudices related to poverty are often bound up with preconceptions related to ability and aspiration, whereas racial prejudices are often bound up with prejudices around nationalism, culture, religion and language status. We must be aware of the slippery and intersectional nature of these prejudices and their often covert operation to maintain hierarchies of power. We must understand such operations as acting from the level of interpersonal communication to systems and structures and, hence, we must educate ourselves and our students to resist them whenever and wherever they occur. However, we also need to understand that inequity is rooted in the historical, racial and socio-economic order of society and it therefore cannot be alleviated by schools and teachers alone. Encouraging children and young people to engage critically and actively with political matters within and beyond formal education remains vital to achieving a better world for all children.

SUMMARY

In this unit, we have discussed a number of challenges faced by pupils living in poverty or belonging to black minority ethnic groups, mindful of the fact that many pupils belong to both. For both groups, we have provided some statistical data highlighting the disadvantages faced particularly by white and black Caribbean boys who are eligible for FSM. We have explored these issues in relation to the effects of poverty and racism on pupils' lives, the impact of teacher stereotyping, and the education system as a whole. In relation to the latter, a number of suggestions have been made to maximise equity in the classroom.

In our conclusion we have highlighted the need to become aware of, and challenge, our own prejudices and those of others. We have also argued however, that many sources of inequality are structural and, therefore, less penetrable by individuals. Finally, we have suggested that teaching for equity involves questioning and challenging power structures in and outside school, and encouraging pupils to do the same.

ANNOTATED FURTHER READING

Smyth, J. and Wrigley, T. (2013) *Living on the Edge: Rethinking Poverty, Class and Schooling*, New York: Peter Lang.

> In this book, John Smyth and Terry Wrigley powerfully describe the chains of difficulties faced by families living in poverty, as well as the impact these can have on achievement in school. In the chapter 'Poor kids need rich teaching', the authors give examples of socially just pedagogical approaches, which you may wish to explore.

Pearce, S. (2005) *You Wouldn't Understand: White Teachers in Multiethnic Classrooms*, Stoke-on-Trent, UK: Trentham.

> Sarah Pearce kept a diary over the 5 years she taught in an inner-city multi-ethnic primary classroom in England. She began to trace how her own 'race' influenced her attitudes and relationships in the classroom.

FURTHER READING TO SUPPORT M-LEVEL STUDY

Reay, D. (2007) 'The zombie stalking English schools: Social class and educational inequality', *British Journal of Educational Studies*, 54(3): 208-307.

> The focus of this article is social class, rather than poverty. Although the educational landscape has changed since Diane Reay wrote this, many of the points she raises are at least as valid as they were in 2007.

Allard, A.C. and Santoro, N. (2006) 'Troubling identities: Teacher education students' constructions of class and ethnicity', *Cambridge Journal of Education*, 36(1): 115-29.

> Andrea Allard and Ninetta Santoro explore how Australian student teachers understand ethnicity and socio-economic status. They ponder the significance of this in the classroom and in teachers' relations with pupils.

RELEVANT WEBSITES

Some websites and videos on this topic which you may want to explore are as follows:

Poverty

Child Poverty Action Group: www.cpag.org.uk/
>
> The Child Poverty Action Group website is full of up-to-date facts and figures about child poverty and has a lot of information about campaigning and events.

Poverty Proofing the School Day: www.povertyproofing.co.uk/
>
> Find out how Children North East can help you to poverty proof the school day.

Race/racism

A Class Divided: www.pbs.org/wgbh/frontline/film/class-divided/
>
> This film shows the power of the teacher: watch as the teacher tells blue-eyed children they are better than brown-eyed pupils.

Britkid: http://cottenceau1.free.fr/activities/britkids/britkidsindex.htm
>
> This is a website about race and racism as seen through the eyes of a fictional group of young people from different backgrounds.

Project Implicit: https://implicit.harvard.edu/implicit/Study?tid=-1
>
> Test your racial biases with Harvard University's implicit association test.

REFERENCES

African American Policy Forum (AAPF). (2013) *Intersectionality*. Retrieved from www.aapf.org/2013/2013/01/intersectionality?rq=intersectionality (accessed 30 October 2017).

Althusser, L. (1970) *Ideology and Ideological State Apparatus*. Retrieved from www.marxists.org/reference/archive/althusser/1970/ideology.htm (accessed 30 October 2017).

Cochran-Smith, M. (2004) *Walking the Road – Race, Diversity and Social Justice in Teacher Education*, New York: Teachers College, Columbia University.

Department for Education (DfE). (2015) *National Curriculum Assessments at Key Stage 2 in England, 2015 (revised)*, London: DfE.

Department for Education (DfE). (2016a) *Revised GCSE and Equivalent Results in England: 2014 to 2015*, London: DfE.

Department for Education (DfE). (2016b) *Schools, Pupils and Their Characteristics: January 2016*, London: DfE.

Department for Work and Pensions (DWP). (2015) *Households Below Average Income: 1994/95 to 2013/14*, London: DWP.

Equalities and Human Rights Commission. (2016) *Healing a Divided Britain: The Need for A Comprehensive Race Equality Strategy*. Retrieved from www.equalityhumanrights.com/en/publication-download/healing-divided-britain-need-comprehensive-race-equality-strategy (accessed 14 November 2017).

Gillborn, D. (2008) *Racism and Education. Coincidence or Conspiracy?*, London: Routledge.

Gorski, P.C. (2016) 'Poverty and the ideological imperative: A call to unhook from defict and grit ideology and to strive for structural ideology in teacher education', *Journal of Education for Teaching*, 42(4): 378-86.

Hatcher, R. (2012) 'Social class and schooling – Differentiation or democracy?', in M. Cole (ed.) *Education, Equality and Human Rights – Issues of Gender, 'Race', Sexuality, Disability and Social Class*, London: Routledge, pp. 239-67.

Kohli, R. (2009) 'Critical race reflections: Valuing the experiences of teachers of color in teacher education', *Race Ethnicity & Education*, 12(2): 235-51.

Kohli, R. and Solórzano, D.G. (2012) 'Teachers, please learn our names! Racial microaggressions and the K-12 classroom', *Race Ethnicity & Education*, 15(4): 441-62.

Levine-Rasky, C. (2000). 'Framing Whiteness: Working through the tensions in introducing whiteness to educators'. *Race, Ethnicity and Education* 3(3), 271-292.

López, I.F.H. (2000) 'The social construction of race', in R. Delgado and J. Stefancic (eds) *Critical White Studies: Looking Behind the Mirror*, Philadelphia: Temple University Press, pp. 163-77.

Mazzei, L. (2008) 'Silence speaks: Whiteness revealed in the absence of voice', *Teaching & Teacher Education*, 24: 1125-36.

Mazzoli Smith, L. and Todd, L. (2016) *Poverty Proofing the School Day: Evaluation and Development Report*. Newcastle University, Newcastle, UK. Retrieved from www.researchgate.net/publication/305305247_Poverty_Proofing_the_School_Day_Evaluation_and_Development_Report (accessed 30 October 2017).

Neumann, J. (2014) *Breadline Kids*, London: True Vision.

Rollock, N. (2012) 'Unspoken rules of engagement: Navigating racial microaggressions in the academic terrain', *International Journal of Qualitative Studies in Education*, 25(5): 517-32.

Smith, E. (2012) *Key Issues in Education and Social Justice*, London: Sage.

Smith, H.J. (2016) 'Britishness as racist nativism: A case of the unnamed "other"', *Journal of Education for Teaching*, 42(3): 298-313.

Smyth, J. and Wrigley, T. (2013) *Living on the Edge: Rethinking Poverty, Class and Schooling*, New York: Peter Lang.

Solomon, R.P., Portelli, J.P., Daniel, B. and Campbell, A. (2005) 'The discourse of denial: How white teacher candidates construct race, racism and "white privilege"', *Race, Ethnicity & Education*, 8(2): 147-69.

Sue, D.W., Lin, A.I., Torino, G.C., Capodilupo, C.M. and Rivera, D.P. (2009) 'Racial microaggressions and difficult dialogues on race in the classroom', *Cultural Diversity & Ethnic Minority Psychology*, 15(2): 183-90.

Taylor, T. (2016) *A Beginner's Guide to Mantle of the Expert. A Transformative Approach to Education,* Norwich, UK: Singular Publishing

Trussell Trust. (2016) *Foodbank Use Remains at Record High*. Retrieved from www.trusselltrust.org/2016/04/15/foodbank-use-remains-record-high/ (accessed 30 October 2017).

RESPONDING TO CULTURAL DIVERSITY AND CITIZENSHIP

Pam Copeland and Des Bowden

INTRODUCTION

> Education for diversity is fundamental if the United Kingdom is to have a cohesive society in the twenty-first century.
>
> (Ajegbo, 2007)

This unit is for teachers who are hoping to develop an understanding of, and who are ready to implement a real commitment to, cultural diversity in their teaching. It explores the issues, challenges and opportunities that face schools, teachers and children in an ever-diverse, multicultural, twenty-first-century classroom.

OBJECTIVES

By the end of this unit, you will have understood:

- the issues surrounding diversity;
- entitlements to diversity;
- obstacles to entitlement to diversity;
- the value of diversity awareness;
- challenges in the classroom;
- teacher attitudes to diversity.

The population of the UK continues to be diverse in terms of ethnicity, religion, language and culture. This diversity was characterised in Professor Kwame Anthony Appiah's 2016 BBC Reith lectures as being by creed, country, colour and culture, to which might also be added community and indeed class (the four lectures are available on a podcast from the BBC website: http://www.bbc.co.uk/programmes/b081lkkj). The Census 2011 data showed that England and Wales have become more ethnically diverse, with increasing numbers of people identifying with minority ethnic groups. The white ethnic group has decreased in size; although it is still the majority, the trend is apparent: the white ethnic group accounted for 86.0 per cent of the usual resident population in 2011, a decrease from 91.3 per cent in 2001 and 94.1 per cent in 1991. Indeed, according to the 2011 Census, London has become so diverse that the white ethnic group is no longer in the majority: about 55 per cent of London's population is non-white. It is a clear sign of this great diversity that London claims some 300 languages are spoken throughout its streets (Johnson, 2012).

Religious affiliations are also changing. The 2011 Census reported a drop in the number of Christians from 71.7 per cent in 2001 to 59.3 per cent in 2011; at the same time, the number of Muslims increased from 3.0 per cent to 4.8 per cent, and those reporting no religion increased from 14.8 per cent to 25.1 per cent. The commonest non-UK countries of birth for usual residents of England and Wales in 2011 were India, Poland and Pakistan. Of the total population of some 4 million, between 2001 and 2011, some 2.9 million were foreign born, and these now make up 13 per cent of the total population. This diversity also has a great spatial and locality variation. For example, 94 per cent of the population in the north east are white, whereas, in Newham, 43.5 per cent of its population are Asian/Asian British, compared with 29 per cent white; in Harrow, 42.7 per cent are Asian/Asian British, and 42.3 per cent are white. The next full census will be in 2121, but annual school census data (e.g. Welsh Government, 2016) suggest that UK primary schools are becoming increasingly diverse in their ethnic composition, although there are variations in numbers at a national scale. The degree to which diverse populations should be integrated is often a matter of debate, but there are societal drivers that interact to encourage segregation. This is partly a cultural issue, but also controlled by social (e.g. language, housing allocation) and economic (e.g. job market) factors. Cantle and Kaufmann (2016) highlight that segregation has been linked to prejudice and intolerance of the 'other' owing to the lack of contact and interaction across social and cultural boundaries.

This cultural diversity is highlighted in Hall's recent study – 'Super-diverse streets' (2015). This research explored streets that are located in ethnically diverse and comparatively deprived urban places (streets in Leicester, Bristol, Manchester and Birmingham), where urban retail spaces shape and are shaped by migrant investments. Over time, integration does seem to occur more or less organically; for example, great concentrations of Jewish people in the East End of London and the central area of Birmingham are no longer clearly identifiable. These people have prospered, developed and moved out into wider society.

This unit investigates this diversity and develops strategies for use in school for identifying, sharing and working with this wealth of difference. It develops an understanding of the issues concerned with identities that children inhabit. It tries to promote an understanding of the different people in the UK today, and how children contribute to this diverse society. Teachers and schools have the difficult task of helping their children challenge and evaluate standpoints different from their own, and educating them to develop an informed view of diversity and, hopefully, become part of a more cohesive society.

Children in the UK can inhabit a range of identities that are as confusing as they are defining, not only for themselves, but also for others. It is for teachers to gain an understanding of these dilemmas and to devise appropriate learning episodes that contribute to a curriculum tailored to the individual needs of the children in their unique setting. This should be their entitlement for education for diversity.

There is much encouragement from government educational policies to work towards the goal of a more cohesive and united society. The Ajegbo (2007) Report, *Effective Leadership in Multi-Ethnic Schools* (National College for School Leadership, 2005) and Ofsted (2013a) are strong in their encouragement of understanding diversity and working towards a cohesive curriculum that reflects, understands and celebrates the values of today's multicultural society, and indeed there is a UNESCO convention on the protection and promotion of the diversity of cultural expressions (2005).

For schools, the current driver for ensuring pupils' spiritual, moral, social and cultural development comes, not so much from within the new primary curriculum, but rather from Ofsted (2013b). Spiritual, moral, social and cultural development is a significant focus in all lesson observations, as well as overall school effectiveness.

In Wales . . .

The Foundation Phase supports the cultural identity of all children, to celebrate different cultures and help children recognise and gain a positive awareness of their own and other cultures. Positive attitudes should be developed to enable children to become increasingly aware of, and appreciate the value of, the diversity of cultures and languages that exist in a multicultural Wales. They should become increasingly aware of the traditions and celebrations that are important aspects of the cultures within Wales.

(Learning Wales, 2015, p. 9)

Source: Learning Wales. (2015) *Curriculum for Wales: Foundation Phases Framework*, Cardiff: Welsh Government (WG). Retrieved from http://learning.gov.wales/docs/learningwales/publications/150803-fp-framework-en.pdf (accessed 30 October 2017).

In Wales . . .

Key Stage 2:

builds upon the Personal and Social Development, Well-Being and Cultural Diversity Area of Learning in the *Foundation Phase framework for children's learning for 3 to 7-year-olds in Wales* and progresses into the 14–19 Learning Core components that relate to PSE such as Personal, Social, Sustainability and Health Matters, Attitudes and Values, and Community Participation.

(DCELLS, 2008: 3)

Source: Department for Children, Education, Lifelong Learning and Skills (DCELLS). (2008) *Personal and Social Education Framework for 7 to 19-Year-Olds in Wales*. Cardiff: Welsh Assembly Government (WAG). Retrieved from http://learning.gov.wales/docs/learningwales/publications/130425-personal-and-social-education-framework-en.pdf (accessed 14 November 2017).

CASE STUDIES IN MODERN DIVERSITY

The following case studies demonstrate the challenges and benefits of living in a plural society on a range of scales. The example of Leicester shows the plurality of a modern British city. On a school level, the study of Gascoigne Primary School highlights the benefits and richness that a multicultural school can offer. The individual study of George Alagiah shows how people may have a range of identities, determined by racial, cultural, social and economic circumstances.

Case study 1: Urban diversity – Leicester

Based on the 2001 Census data and supplementary evidence, Leicester was likely to become the UK's first plural city. It was likely to become one of the first cities in England to have a majority of people with an ethnic minority background. This was owing to a range of factors, including higher birth rates among ethnic minority groups, increases in existing populations through family consolidations and increases in the numbers of new arrivals. If this trend continued, it was possible that Leicester would reach this milestone some time after 2011. The 2011 Census showed that 50.6 per cent of the population were classified as white, and 37.1 per cent were classed as Asian/Asian British. The Asian population is predominantly Indian, from either East Africa or from Gujarat in India. Other, much smaller Asian populations include Bangladeshis and Pakistanis. The black population in Leicester comprises two groups – those of Caribbean origin and those of African origin. This range of ethnic groups has led to the fact that 45 per cent of the pupils in Leicester schools say that English is not their preferred language (www.leicester.gov.uk/media/177367/2011-census-findings-diversity-and-migration.pdf).

Case study 2: School diversity

Gascoigne Primary School in Barking (East London) has been recognised as the largest primary school in the UK, with 160 staff and a challenging mix of some 1,200 pupils, ranging in age from 3 to 11 (www.gascoigneprimaryschool.co.uk). The diversity is evidenced by more than 60 different languages being spoken, and only 10 per cent of children have English as their first language. There is a high turnover, but the school is short of space for learning, teaching and play. It is located in one of Britain's most deprived areas (45 per cent of children qualify for Pupil Premium). It was the focus of a Channel 5 TV documentary series in the spring of 2015 (www.channel5.com/show/britains-biggest-primary-school).

Notwithstanding the challenges facing this school, it was judged 'good' at its last inspection (2013), and the inspectors noted the following:

- Children join the school with skills well below those expected for their age. Adults have very high expectations, so that routines for learning are established quickly. Children get on very well together, reflecting good development in their personal and social skills.
- Throughout the year, a significant number of pupils leave or join the school. Many of those joining are recent arrivals to this country or have additional learning and social needs. The school quickly identifies each pupil's needs and the support required, so that they achieve well.
- Nonetheless, from the moment pupils arrive, they settle in quickly and make good, and sometimes outstanding, progress.
- The school strives to establish close links with its community and celebrates its diversity. Albanian, Lithuanian and Portuguese groups use its facilities regularly. Pupils across the school benefit from a wide range of activities that engage their interest. These include external visits and in-school events – for example storytellers, theatre groups and Maasai warriors. Table 6.4.1 illustrates

TABLE 6.4.1 Diversity in action: The class names in the seven most spoken languages at Gascoigne Primary School

	English	Albanian	Bengali	Yoruba	Portuguese	Somali	French
Nursery	White	E bardhe					Blanc
Reception	Yellow	E verdhe	Holud	Ofeefee	Amarelo	Jaalle ah	Jaune
Year 1	Blue	Blu	Nil	Bulu	Azul	Buluug	Bleu
Year 2	Red	Kuq	Lal	Pupa	Vermelho	Cas	Rouge
Year 3	Purple	Vjollce	Benguni	Popu	Roxo	Iyo guduud	Violet
Year 4	Green	Gjelber	Shobuj	Awo Ewe	Verde	Cagaaran	Vert
Year 5	Orange	Portokalli	Komola	Osan	Laranja	Oranjo	Orange
Year 6	Gold	Ari	Shonali	Wura	Ouro	Dahab	Or

the diversity of the school population and the sensitivity of the school. As part of its action for diversity programmes, it developed strong links with many of the local communities, and yet it fully and sensitively implements the Prevent strategy (see Unit 2.1).

Case study 3: Personal identities – George Alagiah

George Alagiah was born in Colombo, Sri Lanka, on 22 November 1955, to Tamil parents. The Tamils were a minority group in Sri Lanka. His father was an engineer, and the family moved to Ghana in 1961, where George completed his primary education. They then moved to the UK and lived in Portsmouth, at a time when there was an unhappy intrusion of race into politics. After reading politics at Durham, he followed a career as a journalist and author, which led to him becoming a prominent BBC presenter. He married Frances Robathan, from a British family, with whom he has two sons. He writes of the gentle clash of cultures, as his mother wore a red sari, and his mother-in-law a floral patterned suit. He claims not to have found race an impediment: 'If you're hungry enough, you work that much harder'. But he recognises that multiculturism may not be the answer, as it results in almost ghetto-like communities of poor and isolated people (Alagiah, 2011). His is the kind of extended rainbow network of relationships, spanning countries and continents, that has become a conventional feature of the migrant experience.

ENTITLEMENT TO DIVERSITY EDUCATION

Multi-cultural education that celebrates diversity is an important part of responding to the kaleidoscope of cultural attributes in the school and the community. Children will be living in a more globalised world where the old barriers of geography will no longer be relevant. Children in all parts of UK (rural, inner-city, suburban) need to understand and respect a range of different cultural heritages. Minority ethnic children, like all children, are entitled to appropriate diversity education through their experiences in school, both in the overt curriculum and within the ethos of the school.

(Claire, 2006)

Schools are under a legal obligation to promote good race relations and provide full equality of opportunity for all children (Race Relations Amendment Act 2000). However, more recent policy statements have improved on these baseline requirements.

Ajegbo (2007) recommends that schools recognise the 'pupil voice' and have systems in place so these voices can be heard (such as school councils and other mechanisms for discussion). Head teachers and governors are required to meet statutory requirements for diversity. The National College for School Leadership ensures that training for diversity is an essential component of leadership. All schools are encouraged to audit their curriculum to establish their provision for diversity and multiple identities. There are many audit tools available for this process that help map the school's provision (for example, www.education-support.org.uk/teachers/ids/pre-school/4-what-next-the-school/). Schools should build active links between and across communities, with diversity understanding as the focus. Ajegbo further recommends the appointment of 'advanced skills teachers', with a responsibility for diversity training, and suggests that points on the pay scale be awarded to teachers taking special responsibility for diversity.

The *Every Child Matters* (ECM; Department for Education and Skills, 2004) agenda placed an emphasis on the needs and aspirations of each individual pupil, so that they can make the best possible progress in developing as responsible citizens and making a positive contribution to society. It placed learners at the heart of the curriculum, but recognised that all learners have a set of cultural diversity experiences that need to be understood and appreciated, so that learning can be more effective. Teachers were encouraged to be more flexible and to develop localised curricula relevant to the needs and aspirations of their children, their schools and their communities.

The former Qualifications and Curriculum Authority's (QCA) *Big Picture of the Curriculum* (2008), which was part of the government's *Children's Plan*, put identity and cultural diversity as one of its overarching themes, and this had a significance for individuals and society and provided relevant learning contexts.

The extensive Cambridge Primary Review (Alexander, 2009, 2010) was a major independent survey and analysis of primary school education that had been ongoing since 2004. Of its ten major themes, Theme 5 is diversity and inclusion. It warns that recognising diversity in school may not be a straightforward exercise:

> Differences between children are constructed rather than simply described, and ... the constructs embodied in official statistics and policy texts tend to dominate discourse in primary education currently. These constructions favour simplistic and evaluative categorisations which conceal as much as they reveal about diversity.
>
> (Ainscow *et al.*, in Alexander, 2010: 195)

This review went on to encourage individual schools to develop approaches to diversity that meet the needs of their children and the local community.

The Ofsted inspectors' handbook (2013b) states that evidence of pupils' spiritual, moral, social and cultural development can be found, for example, where pupils:

- are reflective about beliefs, values and more profound aspects of human experience, using their imagination and creativity, and developing curiosity in their learning;
- develop and apply an understanding of right and wrong in their school life and life outside school;
- take part in a range of activities requiring social skills;
- develop awareness of and respect for diversity in relation to, for example, gender, race, religion and belief, culture, sexual orientation and disability;
- gain a well-informed understanding of the options and challenges facing them as they move through the school and on to the next stage of their education and training;
- develop an appreciation of theatre, music, art and literature;
- develop the skills and attitudes to enable them to participate fully and positively in democratic modern Britain;

- respond positively to a range of artistic, sporting and other cultural opportunities;
- understand and appreciate the range of different cultures within school and further afield as an essential element of their preparation for life.

There are also developments that do not owe their origins to governmental initiatives. Some schools have formalized their commitment to diversity education through the Rights Respecting Schools Award, developed by UNICEF (see www.unicef.org.uk/rights-respecting-schools/). Schools can apply to register for this award, gathering evidence that demonstrates they have embedded children's rights in the practice and the ethos of the school.

Task 6.4.1 Provision for diversity

Use these questions to consider the provision for diversity in a school known to you:

- Do our primary schools attend fairly and effectively to the different learning needs and cultural backgrounds of all their pupils?
- Do all children have equal access to high-quality primary education?
- If not, how can this access be improved?
- How can a national system best respond to the wide diversity of cultures, faiths, languages and aspirations that is now a fact of British life?
- Of what is identity constituted in a highly plural culture, and what should be the role of primary education in fostering it?
- How can primary schools best meet the needs of children of widely varying abilities and interests?
- How can schools secure the engagement of those children and families who are hardest to reach?

Source: www.primaryreview.org.uk (accessed 31 October 2017).

OBSTACLES TO ENTITLEMENT TO DIVERSITY

Ajegbo (2007) recognises that the quality of education across the nation is uneven and suggests the following issues may prevent a coherent diversity curriculum being implemented:

- insufficient clarity about flexibility and customising the curriculum;
- lack of confidence in schools to engage in diversity issues;
- lack of diversity training opportunities;
- lack of proper consideration for the 'pupil voice';
- tenuous or non-existent links to the community.

Other challenges facing teachers wishing to develop diversity awareness in their school include:

- embedding it in a single subject, such as religious education, and not in others;
- lack of planning for integration of newcomers into the learning environment;
- concentration on famous British people;
- narrow selection of reading materials in the library;
- stereotypes in school displays;

- stereotypes in geography (e.g. all Africans are starving and live in mud huts);
- lack of empathy in questioning children who are different from the teacher;
- not recognising that some children do not have Christian names;
- exoticising minority children;
- tokenism;
- language;
- unwillingness to face controversial issues;
- unacknowledged racism.

VALUE OF DIVERSITY AWARENESS: BEYOND TOKENISM

Ajegbo (2007: 24) believes that 'education for diversity is crucial not just for the future well-being of our children and young people but for the survival of our society'.

If children are to develop as successful learners, confident individuals and responsible citizens, it is essential for them to understand and have respect for cultures, religions and identities.

The most successful teaching and learning for diversity occur when there is a whole-school commitment. This includes governors and staff, children, support staff and the local community, working together on the whole-school ethos, which includes the taught and learned curriculum as well as the hidden curriculum. Too many schools celebrate cultural diversity without really understanding the nature of that diversity.

In Northern Ireland . . .

Northern Ireland policy for responding to cultural diversity 'fits firmly within the emerging concept of "additional need", which recognises and encompasses the diversity within the classroom. That wider concept moves away from the in-child deficit model and recognises that many children at some time, and for a number of reasons, experience barriers to learning'. Importantly, the policy states 'that significant difficulty with the language of instruction presents a barrier to learning for newcomer pupils and seeks to develop the capacity of schools to respond' (Department of Education for Northern Ireland, 2011: 16).

Source: Department of Education for Northern Ireland (DENI). (2011) *Every School a Good School: Supporting Newcomer Pupils*, Bangor, NI: DENI.

FLEXIBILITY AND THE CURRICULUM

Ever since 2002, in the QCA's *Designing and Timetabling the Primary Curriculum* (Qualifications and Curriculum Authority, 2002), schools have been encouraged to adopt more flexible approaches to the curriculum by customising the basic entitlement to learning to create their own distinctive and unique curricula. Some schools have shown innovative ways to include this flexibility, by:

- using appropriate resources, such as artefacts and images, to show diversity within and between cultures and groups:
    - ensuring choice of examples provides balance;
- presenting a broad and balanced view of culture, identity and diversity:
    - giving learners accurate and objective views;

    -   avoiding presenting minority groups as problematic;
    -   looking for commonalities between groups.
- questioning commonly held opinions and stereotypes (e.g. migration in the UK is a recent occurrence):
    -   challenging media portrayal of different countries and peoples;
- creating an open climate (using ground rules and distancing techniques when dealing with controversial issues):
    -   encouraging learners to take pride in their identity and culture;
    -   encouraging learners to draw on their own experience.

DIVERSITY AND INCLUSION

TeacherNet produces a Community Cohesion Resource Pack, and Ofsted (2009) produces a booklet for inspecting community cohesion. *Who Do We Think We Are?* (www.wdwtwa.org.uk) is a readily available scheme of work designed to help teachers deliver diversity lessons at Key Stages 1 and 2.

Task 6.4.2 Racism

Consider the influence of such people on dispelling racialist myths:

- Mary Seacole – black nurse during the Crimea war;
- Nelson Mandela – anti-apartheid activist who eventually became president of South Africa;
- Anne Frank – Jewish refugee from Nazism;
- Anton Wilhelm Amo Afer – a Ghanian boy 'given' to the Duke of Brunswick-Wolfenbüttel in 1707, who became a professor of philosophy during the European Renaissance;
- Rosa Parkes – US activist against segregation who refused to give up her seat in a bus to a white passenger, galvanizing the Civil Rights Movement;
- Stephen Lawrence – victim of racist murder in London in 1993;
- Asquith Xavier – railway worker who challenged the colour bar on employment at Euston Station in 1966 (see Figure 6.4.1)

Develop a scheme of work to include activities that will enhance the learners' empathy.

FIGURE 6.4.1
Memorial plaque to Asquith Xavier, a railway guard who broke the colour bar on employment at Euston Station as recently as 1966

SCHOOL CONFIDENCE IN ADDRESSING DIVERSITY ISSUES

Many teachers feel that they do not have the experience or understanding to deal with diversity issues. At one level, it is treating individuals with politeness and respect, but this can be confounded by language difficulties. In some cases, female teachers may not be shown the same sort of respect as male teachers by certain minority groups. Schools need to develop their staff to feel confident in their approach to dealing with controversial issues. This could be through taking a certain viewpoint, or playing devil's advocate, or adopting a neutral stance. At the beginning of any teaching episode, every child needs to gain an understanding of which approach the teacher is adopting.

The children's voice

This is concerned with giving children a real say in what goes on in school. Most schools now have a school council. Some of these are strong and allow children to join in by making decisions on the nature of the school and its curriculum. Ajegbo (2007) reports that, in some schools, children are routinely asked for their feedback on all aspects of school life, being involved in staff selection processes and working with teachers on schemes of work. In these schools, children are seen as part of the solution, not part of the problem.

Developing community links

These may be addressed by engaging children, their parents and the wider community in the daily life of the school. The extended school day, with breakfast clubs and after-school activities, offers opportunities for more people to come into school and for the school to play a more important role in the community. Some schools, like Gascoigne, have developed successful strategies for involving the wider community in the life of their school. St Brigid's Catholic Primary School in Northfield, Birmingham, for example, has received a grant from the Awards for All scheme (National Lottery) and has been able to involve members of its diverse community in extracurricular school activities (www.stbrigid.bham.sch.uk).

CHALLENGES IN THE CLASSROOM

Teachers frequently encounter difficult classroom situations.

Various languages

Languages may be both barriers and bridges to learning. There are dangers that some teachers confuse not understanding a language with low ability. The child receiving language help and the other children need to be informed about the nature of the EAL support in the classroom (see Unit 6.5 for further information).

Transient populations

Some schools receive more or less transient children, such as those from a travellers' community, army children or the children of short-term migrants. Their inclusion in the classroom needs to be carefully managed, and their learning needs need to be catered for. As they move on, a teacher should supply a report on their progress and achievement.

Task 6.4.3 Watching children

Next time you are in school, take time to watch specific children who might be vulnerable, in the playground and on those occasions where children choose partners or group members. Isolation and marginalisation can be a signpost to more overt bullying away from teachers' eyes. Who is being left out? Who is hanging around on the sidelines?

- Can you find out why some children are popular and others are not?
- Does the school's equal opportunities policy have anything to say about bullying and name-calling? How is this monitored and dealt with?

Source: Adapted from Claire (2006)

BULLYING AND NAME-CALLING OF MINORITY ETHNIC GROUPS

Name-calling is probably one of the more frequently encountered expressions of racial hostility. Picking on individuals or small groups is also seen as bullying. Children need to be made aware that this type of behaviour is unacceptable – not only that, they need to understand why it is unacceptable. They may need to consider what their feelings might be if the situation were reversed. Moralising tends not to work in the face of opposing attitudes. Just to forbid such behaviour is controlling rather than educating. No Name-Calling Week runs annually in January and is a week of educational activities aimed at ending name-calling in school and providing schools with the tools and inspiration to launch a continuing dialogue about ways of eliminating bullying (www.nonamecallingweek.org).

It is hard to counter entrenched attitudes of racism, possibly learned from the family; nevertheless, racism is illegal, and children need to be made aware of their right not to be bullied. Teachers need to be vigilant about bullying in their school, and it may be a suitable topic for the school council to consider.

CONTROVERSIAL ISSUES

Teachers have to deal with controversial issues for many reasons, and sometimes they are unavoidable. They may result in exciting classroom learning and, indeed, reflect partly what it means to be human, and they may help children make connections between areas of learning. They will help children develop value positions.

The former QCA suggested that, 'Education should not attempt to shelter our nation's children from even the harsher controversies of adult life, but should prepare them to deal with such issues knowledgeably, sensibly, tolerantly and morally' (Qualifications and Curriculum Authority, 1998: 56).

A strategy for dealing with controversial issues is for the teacher to take a known stance and argue the issue with the children from there. The teacher may:

- be an impartial chairperson (procedural neutrality);
- speak from his or her viewpoint (stated commitment);
- present a wide variety of views (balanced approach);
- take an opposing position (devil's advocate).

Task 6.4.4 Tokenistic gestures or real understanding?

Consider these issues:

- Is learning a Caribbean song in music really improving diversity awareness?
- Does circle time raise awareness of difference?
- Are travellers' children ethnic minorities?
- Do all children in your school celebrate Christmas?
- Does making a curry make you more culturally aware?
- Does dressing up in native clothes improve understanding of other people?

TEACHER ATTITUDES

Sometimes, it is the teacher's attitude that is the concern in the classroom. Teachers need to acknowledge and decide how to deal with their own prejudices and viewpoints, and to consider how to represent their personal opinions in the classroom (see below). Low expectations of certain children and perceived typical behaviour problems are often associated with teachers' own stereotypical views.

Task 6.4.5 Teachers' viewpoint

Teachers should ask themselves:

- What are the different ways in which children at my school are categorised by others? (This might include categories such as ethnic groups, pupils with disabilities, new immigrants, residents of public housing, looked-after children.)
- What characteristics first come to mind when I think of each group?
- Where did these impressions come from (such as peers, media, family, religion)?
- How reliable are these sources and my impressions?
- Can I remember a time when someone made assumptions about me based on a group I belong to?
- How did that make me feel?

Source: After Ross (n.d.)

Task 6.4.6 Human rights

Use the European Convention on Human Rights (www.hrcr.org/docs/index.html) and the United Nations' Declaration of the Rights of the Child (www.unicef.org.uk/rights-respecting-schools/) to critically evaluate the level of equality in society.

SUMMARY

This unit has started to address the dialogue currently surrounding diversity in the classroom. It has considered the challenges posed and suggests some solutions to help combat what is seen by many teachers, children and schools as one of the major issues in school today.

Encouraging multicultural education to be an integral part of the school ethos and embedding it in the curriculum are the first stages towards real inclusion and equal opportunity for all children. It should be part of the whole-school ethos, embraced by all members of the school community. The unit highlights the need to be able to directly tackle racism and racial and other stereotyping, so that a relevant, meaningful and coherent curriculum can flourish. This curriculum needs to be designed to be appropriate for the whole school, in the local community. It should be challenging, exciting and inclusive, meeting the unique needs of the children and helping all concerned to develop a cohesive society, based on mutual understanding, tolerance and respect.

 ANNOTATED FURTHER READING

Centre for Studies on Inclusive Education. (2016) *Equality Making it Happen*, Bristol, UK: CSIE.
> A guide to help schools ensure everyone is safe, included and learning; a succinct and user-friendly guide to help schools address prejudice, reduce bullying and promote equality holistically. Created with schools for schools, the guide is sponsored by the NASUWT.

Claire, H. and Holden, C. (eds) (2008) *The Challenge of Teaching Controversial Issues*, Stoke-on-Trent, UK: Trentham.
> This is an authoritative book that offers much practical support in teaching controversial issues, including diversity, in the primary school. It helps teachers to understand their own role and be equipped with effective approaches to sensitive and complex issues.

Elton-Chalcraft, S. (2009) *It's Not Just About Black and White, Miss: Children's Awareness of Race*, Stoke-on-Trent, UK: Trentham.
> This book provides research-based evidence on what children themselves think about cultural diversity and about efforts to counter racism in their schools. It is empirical, child-centred research that tells educators what they need to know. It was conducted with a sample of Year 5 pupils in two predominantly white and two diverse schools, all of whom were themselves involved in the research process. The book offers the children's voices and their surprising and challenging ideas.

Richards, G. and Armstrong, F. (eds) (2016) *Teaching and Learning in Diverse and Inclusive Classrooms*, London: Routledge.
> This provides a guide for those teachers and other staff who are wanting to make their classrooms more inclusive spaces. The contributors consider how alienation may happen through ethnicity, gender and sexuality and suggest ways in which interaction and participation may take place.

FURTHER READING TO SUPPORT M-LEVEL STUDY

Mistry, M. and Sood, K. (2014) 'Permeating the social justice ideals of equality and equity within the context of Early Years: Challenges for leadership in multi-cultural and mono-cultural primary schools', *International Journal of Primary, Elementary & Early Years Education*, 43(5): 548–64.

> This paper explores the ideology of social justice through links between equality and equity within Early Years and what remain the challenges for leadership. It investigates the issues facing early year specialists working in mono- and multicultural settings.

Ford, R., Morrell, G. and Heath, A. (2012) '"Fewer but better"? Public views about immigration', in A. Park, E. Clery, J. Curtice, M. Phillips and D. Utting (eds) *British Social Attitudes: The 29th Report*, London: National Centre for Social Research. Retrieved from www.bsa-29.natcen.ac.uk (accessed 31 October 2017).

> This is a detailed investigation of the data collected on British attitudes to immigration. The evidence suggests the British public perhaps takes a more sophisticated and nuanced view of the issues pertaining to immigration, multiculturalism and integration than politicians seem to recognise at present, and, setting aside the current constraint, Britain would benefit from a policy response that reflected this nuance.

 RELEVANT WEBSITES

Equality and Human Rights Commission: www.equalityhumanrights.com/

> The website of the independent statutory body with the responsibility to encourage equality and diversity, eliminate unlawful discrimination and protect and promote the human rights of everyone in Britain. The Commission enforces equality legislation on age, disability, gender reassignment, marriage and civil partnership, pregnancy and maternity, race, religion or belief, sex and sexual orientation – these are known as protected characteristics.

No Name-Calling Week: www.nonamecallingweek.org

> See above.

Mixed Britannia: www.bbc.co.uk/programmes/b015skx4/episodes/guide

> Telling the story of mixed-race Britain, this is a BBC2 documentrary series (three programmes) hosted by George Alagiah (through BBC iPlayer).

Ofsted: *Creating a School Community that Celebrates Diversity*: www.gov.uk/government/publications/good-practice-resource-creating-a-school-community-that-celebrates-diversity

> A case study of Jenny Hammond Primary School, which demonstrates good practice with regard to developing a diverse but happy and tolerant school community.

UN: www.un.org/en/universal-declaration-human-rights/index.html

> The United Nations website detailing human rights.

 REFERENCES

Ainscow, M., Conteh, J., Dyson, A. and Gallanaugh, F. (2010) *Children in Primary Education: Demography, Culture, Diversity and Inclusion (Cambridge Primary Review: Research Survey 5/1)*, Cambridge, UK: University of Cambridge Faculty of Education.

Ajegbo, K. (2007) *Diversity and Citizenship in the Curriculum: Research Review*, London: DfES.

Alagiah, G. (2011) 'What it's like to be mixed-race in Britain', *BBC News Magazine*, 2 October. Retrieved from www.bbc.co.uk/news/magazine-15019672 (accessed 2 January 2014).

Alexander, R. (2009) *PISA 2012: Time to Grow Up?* Retrieved from www.primaryreview.org.uk (accessed 2 January 2014).

Alexander, R. (2010) *The Cambridge Primary Review Research Surveys*, London: Routledge.

Cantle, E. and Kaufmann, E. (2016) *Is Segregation on the Increase in the UK?* Retrieved from www.open democracy.net/wfd/ted-cantle-and-eric-kaufmann/is-segregation-on-increase-in-uk (accessed 31 October 2017).

Claire, H. (2006) 'Education for cultural diversity and social justice', in J. Arthur and T. Cremin (eds) *Learning to Teach in the Primary School*, London: Routledge, pp. 307–17.

Department for Education and Skills (DfES). (2004) *Every Child Matters: Change for Children*, Nottingham, UK: DfES.

Hall, S. (2015) 'Super-diverse street: A "trans-ethnography" across migrant localities', *Ethnic & Racial Studies*, themed issue on 'Cities, diversity, ethnicity', 38(1): 22–37.

Johnson, B. (2012) 'Let's not dwell on immigration but sow the seeds of integration', *Daily Telegraph*, 15 December.

National College for School Leadership. (2005) *Effective Leadership in Multi-ethnic Schools*. Retrieved from http://webarchive.nationalarchives.gov.uk/20101012162805/http://www.nationalcollege.org.uk/docinfo?id=1 7170&filename=effective-leadership-in-multi-ethnic-schools.pdf (accessed 9 November 2017).

Ofsted. (2009) *Inspecting Maintained Schools' Duty to Promote Community Cohesion: Guidance for Inspectors*, London: Ofsted.

Ofsted. (2013a) *Evaluating Pupils' Spiritual, Moral, Social and Cultural Development*, Subsidiary Guidance no. 110166, April, London: Ofsted.

Ofsted. (2013b) *Supporting the Inspection of Maintained Schools and Academies*, Subsidiary Guidance no. 110166, January, p. 30, para 126 and pp. 37–8, paras 37–8. Retrieved from www.ofsted.gov.uk/resources/subsidiary-guidance-supporting-inspection-of-maintained-schools-and-academies (accessed 31 October 2017).

Qualifications and Curriculum Authority (QCA). (1998) *Education for Citizenship and the Teaching of Democracy in Schools*, London: QCA.

Qualifications and Curriculum Authority (QCA). (2002) *Designing and Timetabling the Primary Curriculum*, London: QCA.

Qualifications and Curriculum Authority (QCA). (2008) *A Big Picture of the Curriculum*, London: QCA.

Race Relations Act. (2000) Retrieved from www.legislation.gov.uk/ukpga/2000/34/contents.

Ross, L. (n.d.) *Connect With Kids and Parents of Different Cultures*. Retrieved from www.scholastic.com/teachers/articles/teaching-content/connect-kids-and-parents-different-cultures-0/ (accessed 31 October 2017).

UNESCO. (2005) *Convention on the Protection and Promotion of the Diversity of Cultural Expressions*, Paris: UNESCO, 20 October.

Welsh Government. (2016) *Schools' Census Results*. Retrieved from www.gov.uk/government/statistics/schools-census-results-2016 (accessed 31 October 2017).

RESPONDING TO LINGUISTIC DIVERSITY

Virginia Bower

INTRODUCTION

The intention of this unit is to convey two key messages:

- that responding to linguistic diversity means far more than simply acknowledging and differentiating; rather, it involves celebrating, utilising and capitalising on this diversity to the benefit of all children in the setting;
- that bilingual learners should be seen as having something 'extra' in terms of the linguistic and cultural diversity they bring to the classroom, and not as being a burden in terms of support.

With these key messages in mind, the frequently observed tendency towards the 'deficit model', which perceives bilingual learners as 'lacking' something – that something being the English language – might be dispelled, in favour of appreciation of what bilingual children and their families can contribute to classroom life.

This unit will use the term 'bilingual learners' (in schools, they are often referred to as children and families with English as an additional language), in an attempt to further emphasise the linguistic power these learners possess. However, it is important to clarify what is meant, in this sense, by bilingual. It certainly does not mean that a child or adult is necessarily proficient and fluent in more than one language. Conteh and Brock's definition helps to clarify this when they refer to children who:

> live in two languages, who have access to, or need to use, two or more languages at home and at school. It does not mean that they have fluency in both languages or that they are competent and literate in both languages.

> (Conteh and Brock, 2011: 348)

Children might be fully literate in their first language, with very little knowledge of English. Others, such as very young children or children who have had no formal education, will have limited literacy in any language. Some children will be literate in their own language and can speak some/a great deal of English. Others will speak English in school and language 1 (L1) at home (Bialystok, 1991). Responding to linguistic diversity involves identifying these differences and ensuring that a classroom and school ethos is promoted that enables the creative use of pedagogies and practices to support all needs. This unit will examine these notions and will offer practical ideas and activities for everyday practice.

HISTORICAL BACKGROUND

An understanding of the historical, political and educational background underpinning current theories and practices relating to linguistic diversity is highly desirable if we are to comprehend the context in which we work. This section will provide an overview of the issues and perspectives that have emerged since the mid twentieth century, with reference to both policy and research.

Until the 1960s, it was suspected that learning more than one language was likely to have a detrimental effect on the brain, and that bilingual learners were likely to be confused and at a disadvantage. Fortunately, this perception has been the subject of radical change. From the late 1960s onwards, it was recognised that there were advantages to being bilingual, but that support would be needed for bilingual learners, and funding was provided for this. Until the mid 1980s, this support tended to take the form of out-of-class interventions, although, thanks to the Bullock Report (DES, 1975), it was recognised that allowing children to use their L1 in the classroom might be beneficial.

With the increase of research studies into bilingualism and supporting bilingual learners, different theories began to emerge. Some of these were related to what are known as 'cross-linguistic transfer' and 'contrastive analysis' (Melby-Lervag and Lervag, 2011), whereby bilingual learners are perceived to use what they know of L1 to support their development of the second language (L2). The notion of high- and low-status languages emerged, and this had an impact on bilingual learners in English educational settings, where the high-status language is inevitably English. The idea of additive and subtractive bilingualism developed, where additive bilingualism promotes the idea that bilingual learners develop the second language while maintaining and improving their L1, in contrast to subtractive bilingualism, which implies that L1 is gradually replaced by what is perceived as the dominant, high-status language (in the context of this book and our classroom experiences, English). It was later suggested by Conteh and Brock (2011) that 'transitional' bilingualism is what has actually evolved, where speaking L1 is perceived as an acceptable bridge to speaking good English, but, once English is established, a second language is not necessary.

The next milestone in terms of government policy relating to bilingual learners was the Swann Report (DES, 1985). This report advanced, in the most positive of terms, a respect for cultural diversity, the importance of language learning and the need for bilingual learners to be integrated into all aspects of classroom life, rather than excluded through interventions. Unfortunately, the Swann Report rejected the idea that minority languages should be taught or were useful to maintain. In fact, 'the promotion of biliteracy was seen as a threat to social cohesion' (Bower, 2016: 48), thus laying the foundations for a monolingual approach to teaching and learning in English primary schools that still, for the majority, holds true today.

From the 1990s, budgets were increasingly controlled by schools rather than local authorities, and this led to a reduction in funding for supporting bilingual learners. Schools had competing priorities, and bilingual support was rarely on the top of the list. Within a decade, the increasing centralisation of the education system, the introduction of the National Curriculum, statutory testing and the publication of league tables and parental choice over schools all had a profound effect on provision for bilingual learners. It has been suggested that children from diverse backgrounds who had English as a second language began to be perceived as having the potential to lower school test results, with the consequence that, 'it was no longer in a school's interest to welcome refugee children and other newcomers to England' (Rampton, Harris and Leung, 2002: no page).

Standard English was – and still is – held up as the only acceptable mode of oral and written communication in primary schools, with no acknowledgement of the benefits of promoting a bilingual approach. This monolingual philosophy was further embedded through the National Literacy Strategy (DfEE, 1998) and its accompanying Literacy Hour. Combined with this, the disbanding of specialist language support systems and the continued lack of funding in this area did nothing to promote a more positive approach to linguistic diversity in primary classrooms.

Encouragingly, however, research studies into bilingual learners – including research based on new technologies and neuro-imaging – continued to indicate the extensive benefits of being bilingual. These advantages include enhanced memory functioning and problem-solving; social, linguistic and cognitive flexibility; and high levels of reasoning. The conscious and deliberate nature of second-language learning means that bilingual learners often have a highly developed understanding of how they learn, and also of how languages work and connect. Advisory materials produced by the government in the last decade or so have, in some ways, recognised the benefits of being bilingual and offer sound advice in terms of supporting bilingual learners in the primary classroom. Among these, the Primary National Strategy materials (DfES, 2006), including *Excellence and Enjoyment: Learning and Teaching for Bilingual Children in the Primary Years*, explicitly promote the use of children's first language to support their learning and recognise the value of making links to the child's home culture and individual experiences. There is always the sense, however, that this support is all transitional; rather than capitalising on the diversity in English primary schools and using it to commit to a bilingual approach to the benefit of all children, the support is to ensure proficiency in English. Now, you might argue that this is surely part of joining the English education system, and that the children are being prepared for a life in England, learning English being key to this. This is certainly the case. With a monolingual curriculum and assessment system, an excellent grasp of English is essential. However, with all the research indicating the benefits of bilingualism, it seems a much wasted opportunity to use L1 merely as a bridge to English, rather than a pathway to a richer experience for all. Later in the unit, this bilingual approach will be discussed in more depth.

In Wales . . .

Wales' vision is:

> to have an education and training system that responds in a planned way to the growing demand for Welsh-medium education, reaches out to and reflects our diverse communities and enables an increase in the number of people of all ages and backgrounds who are fluent in Welsh and able to use the language with their families, in their communities and in the workplace.
>
> (DCELLS, 2010: 4)

Since this strategy was published in 2010, there has been an evaluation of it, 'to measure the effectiveness and impact of the Strategy, examining to what extent it has achieved its expected aims, objectives and outcomes'. All the documentation of this evaluation can be found at: http://gov.wales/statistics-and-research/welsh-medium-education-strategy/?lang=en (accessed 31 October 2017).

Source: Department for Children, Education, Lifelong Learning and Skills (DCELLS). (2010) *Welsh-medium Education Strategy*, Cardiff: Welsh Assembly Government. Retrieved from http://wales.gov.uk/docs/dcells/publications/100420welshmediumstrategyen.pdf (accessed 31 October 2017).

In Scotland . . .

Gaelic is a living language and part of a rich cultural tradition which belongs to the whole of Scotland. This Government has made its position very clear on this matter – we want to increase the number of people learning, speaking and using Gaelic. By working towards these aims, together we can ensure that Gaelic has a secure future in Scotland.

(Scottish Government, 2017: 3)

Source: Scottish Government (2017) *Gaelic Language Plan 2016-2021*. Retrieved from https://beta.gov.scot/publications/scottish-government-gaelic-language-plan-2016-2021/documents/00517453.pdf?inline=true (accessed 31 October 2017).

CHILDREN'S BACKGROUNDS

The preceding section examined the macro perspective, in terms of the historical and current context, hopefully setting the scene for this section, where the more local and personal in terms of children and families are explored. If we are to be successful in responding to linguistic diversity, an understanding is needed of children's backgrounds, so that we can recognise what they bring to the classroom and the areas in which they might need support. Imagine that a Nepalese child is enrolled in your class, and you are told they are from a military background, the family having recently been posted to England. Immediately, this provides you with useful context: the child may be accustomed to moving from country to country, school to school. It is likely that they can speak some English, and that their father will have at least a basic knowledge of the English language. A little more investigation might inform you that Nepalese families are often very keen on supporting their child's education and will be happy to engage with learning activities at home. You might discover that, although the child can switch between spoken languages with ease, they are not confident to write in either Nepali or English. It does not take much effort to find out useful details such as these, by speaking to family members or the military community, looking at any records that accompany the child, researching the culture, ethos and traditions of the Nepalese community or speaking with bilingual personnel within the school or local community. This information provides a starting point for planning, teaching and differentiating.

Without an awareness of children's backgrounds, assumptions might be made that are unhelpful in terms of capitalising on their existing knowledge and experience and providing effective support.

Below is a list of suggestions relating to how you might be proactive in terms of children's backgrounds:

- Find out what language/s is/are spoken at home and, if possible, if parents are literate/biliterate.
- Research aspects of the children's culture, traditions, language and so forth to help you avoid misunderstandings or actions that might prove to be disrespectful or alienating.
- Read any documentation that might have accompanied the child, so that you are aware of previous educational experiences.
- Investigate the education system in the child's home country and the prevalent pedagogies and practices – this can help you assess why a child might, for example, be reluctant to engage in a 'talk partners' activity or to raise their hand. I remember, in my first year of teaching, a girl in my class would stand up every time she answered a question. She soon realised that this was not expected within the English classroom culture, but, had I known this in advance, I could have talked to her about it and prevented potential embarrassment for her.
- Celebrate and take time to discuss different cultural practices and linguistic variances. Children will very soon realise if their language and culture are not valued in the classroom, and this can cause tensions for them between home and school: 'Children understand very quickly that the school is an English-only zone and they often internalise ambivalence and even shame in relation to their linguistic and cultural heritage' (Cummins, 2005: 590).

Task 6.5.1 Considering children's backgrounds

Look at the list below, which provides examples of possible backgrounds of bilingual learners. Consider how these diverse backgrounds might have an impact on the children's linguistic, cognitive and social development. Conduct a little research into the types of experience these children might already have encountered. List some ways by which you might ensure that the diversity they bring is acknowledged and celebrated, while their needs are met.

- Refugees
- Gypsy, Roma and Traveller children
- Children from well-established local communities
- Children of short-stay business families

LEARNING A SECOND LANGUAGE

If we are to respond successfully to linguistic diversity, some idea is needed of what learning a second language entails. In fact, not only this, but we also need to understand how it feels to learn to learn in a new language. Learning a second language has similarities and differences to learning our first language. The similarities include the following:

- learners need to realise that the way words are pronounced is crucial to meaning-making;
- the gradual accumulation of words enables ever more complex sentences to be created;
- connections between words (morphology);
- the need for grammatically correct sentences if meaning is to be conveyed;
- the realisation of the power of language in different contexts;
- there are recognisable stages and patterns in language learning.

The differences include:

- When learning a first language, a child is usually surrounded by others who speak that language and they are immersed in the sounds and cadences. If they are in an English primary school, they will certainly be immersed in English, but they might be the only individual who has a different L1.
- When children learn their first language, those interacting with them tend to adjust and simplify their language. In the classroom, bilingual learners are having to keep up with the pace of those who have English as their first language, and, more often than not, the language used is not modified.
- With a second language, the learner already possesses an understanding of how language works and some of the rules of spoken and written language.
- There is often a self-consciousness or embarrassment attached to speaking or writing in a second language, particularly if you are the only bilingual learner.

When learners begin familiarising themselves with a second language, they will usually initially recognise and utilise everyday words and phrases - what might be referred to as 'survival' language to enable them to negotiate the routines of life. These are sometimes referred to as basic interpersonal communication skills (BICs) (Cummins, 2001), which bilingual learners usually acquire within 2 years. Although this begins with straightforward words and phrases, interpersonal communication can of course become extremely complex, as often it includes the use of colloquial expressions, idioms and culturally based language, which can be difficult to master. Alongside BICs, bilingual learners in English primary schools are also obliged to learn to learn through the 'medium of a new language' (Kelly, 2010: 76). If they are to succeed within a monolingual assessment system, they need to rapidly acquire cognitive academic language proficiency (CALP) (Cummins, 2001), so that they are able to engage with the academic language of the curriculum. CALP can take from 5 to 7 years to achieve. Think about this in relation to the previous section, where children's backgrounds were discussed. If a child does not enter the English education system until they are 6 or 7, for example, they may be into their secondary school years before they are reaching a level of CALP. This, of course, depends on many factors, but it certainly should raise our awareness of the enormity of bilingual children's achievements.

Bilingual children will often be observed code-switching between L1 and L2, more often in spoken than written language. By this, we mean that they move from one language to another, sometimes within sentences or, at other times, to suit a particular context or situation. A more recent and potentially more useful term is used by Garcia (2009: 71), who refers to 'translanguaging'. This she describes as 'engaging in bilingual or multilingual discourse practices', whereby bilingual learners use language in the most effective ways at particular moments. For many families, translanguaging is a way of life, as some members might speak two or more languages, whereas others may be monolingual. Parents and children might be literate in more than one language, or they might be proficient with regards to BICs, but not with CALP. Sometimes, children are required to translate for their parents and switch between languages to ensure effective communication. One of my primary teacher colleagues once reported an instance at a parent consultation meeting where the child was translating for his mother. The news about the child's progress was not altogether positive, and yet the mother was smiling and seemed delighted. It was then that my colleague realised the translation might not be wholly accurate! Although this is a humorous anecdote, it emphasises the responsibility that is often on young children's shoulders.

Children might predominantly use L1 in play, but then switch to L2 for more formal classroom activities. Given the opportunity, children and adults will use the language most suited to them for particular situations and practices. They are never simply 'two monolinguals in one person' (Garcia, 2009: 48), meaning that it is not merely about learning one language and then adding another. Rather, it is about language use and need. Observing children playing and chatting in the classroom or the playground is vital so that we can assess the different ways they approach learning and their creative use of language. The following case study describes an observation of two 5-year-old Nepalese boys during a relaxed and informal whole-class activity. The children were all sitting on the carpet and, one at a time, were invited to the front to put a decoration on the Christmas tree. It was a very sociable event, and it is often during these less pressured situations that useful observations can be made relating to how children support each other with language and learning.

CASE STUDY

Suresh tapped the teaching assistant for attention and said 'Sujit said can he have his bottle?' She nodded, and he and Sujit went to their bottles and had long drinks and a little chat in Nepali. They lingered there for some time, patting their stomachs and clearly demonstrating the amount of water they were consuming by pushing out their stomachs as far as possible. There was quite a bit of very gentle contact between them. Then Sujit pointed at the Christmas decorations and said 'Star!' and Suresh pointed and said 'Wow!' They sat back down side by side and, for a few minutes, watched the other children decorating the tree. Then, whilst the tree was still being decorated, they rolled up their sleeves and compared muscles and pinched each other's muscles (in a friendly way!) in what looked like a macho contest. They started talking about red and white Ninjas very quietly, code-switching between Nepali and English. They had an extended conversation for over five minutes about who they were going to invite to play with them. Then they kissed each other on the shoulder and turned to me and started telling me about the rewards board they had in the classroom.

What is so significant for me about this incident is how the inherent sociability of the two boys enabled them to have one eye on the classroom activity, support each other linguistically and engage in conversation about their shared interests. Johnson (2006: 238) writes that our linguistic identity is 'constructed and reconstructed through human relationships', and this is apparent in the scenario above. First, Sujit recognises that Suresh might not have the confidence or linguistic competence to ask the assistant for his water bottle, so he does this for him, thus modelling the language needed. The boys then acknowledge the Christmas tree and decorations – using English – before engaging in several sociable interactions, moving between languages to suit their needs, which allows them to 'participate in the sociocultural activities of their community' (Rogoff, 1994: 209). Finally, the boys see me observing and engage me in conversation, in English, recognising that Nepali would not be appropriate. This whole incident was based on 'trust, reciprocity and playfulness' (Gregory, 2008: 97) and is an excellent model for our own responses to linguistic diversity. Allowing time for children to discuss and explore ideas, time where they can move between languages without anxiety or self-consciousness, is a step towards creating an ethos and educational climate that promote a bilingual approach. This is further explored in the following section.

Task 6.5.2 Capturing assessment evidence

Ongoing, formative assessment is an essential element of classroom practice, perhaps even more so in response to linguistic diversity. Children learning a second language will be acquiring vocabulary at an extraordinary rate and experimenting with grammatical structures, word order, spelling and much more. Effective ways need to be developed to enable you to capture this progress and plan and differentiate accordingly. In the case study above, observation of a short interaction provided a great deal of information about the linguistic, cognitive and social progress being made by the two boys. Think about how else you might capture assessment evidence and how you might design your classroom in certain ways to promote interaction and discussion between children.

A BILINGUAL APPROACH

In Northern Ireland . . .

Northern Ireland policy discusses 'the challenge of creating an inclusive primary school culture, which not only welcomes newcomer pupils but turns the linguistic, cultural and ethnic diversity to the educational advantage of all' (DENI, 2011: 21).

Source: Department of Education for Northern Ireland (DENI). (2011) *Every School a Good School: Supporting Newcomer Pupils*, Bangor, NI: DENI.

The key message in this section is very clear. Overt promotion of a bilingual approach to planning, teaching and resourcing will improve the educational experience of *all* the children in your class. By this, I do not mean that everything must be in two languages and that you have to learn the languages of the children in your class (although learning words and phrases will have a very positive effect on your relationships with children and families). It is more about examining how you might celebrate, promote and capitalise on the linguistic diversity in your classroom. Vygotsky (1962: 110) writes that a child needs 'to see his native language as one particular system among many', and this is true for all the children in the class. Early awareness and appreciation of different languages and cultures are fundamental to a society that has an authentic interest in and respect for human diversity.

The first recommendation for this is explicitly to encourage children to speak in their L1 where possible (obviously this will depend on whether there are other children/adults in the class with whom they can converse). This might be during group work – where children are being encouraged to discuss an idea or an investigation or a problem-solving activity – in the role play corner – where children can explore and chat in a safe environment – in the outside area – where particular resources might be provided to promote discussion – or to answer questions, if there is an adult or child in the classroom who might translate. It is not enough to 'allow' children to use L1. If it is not actively promoted, children will be very quick to realise that English is the only valued language, and that maintaining their L1 holds no material advantage.

Another way to promote a bilingual approach is explicitly to explore and teach children about language. The classroom environment 'needs to be planned in terms of language enhancement' (Elorza and Munoa, 2008: 94), and this includes planning, resources, displays, table layout, the grouping of children, and so forth. One very straightforward way of drawing children's attention to language is to have both a content and a language objective for as many lessons as possible. For example, in a science lesson focusing on materials, the content objective could be 'to identify a range of materials', and the language objective might be 'to use appropriate vocabulary to describe different materials'. Real objects and pictures/photographs could be used initially, enabling all learners to participate and identify the materials they are made from. The children could then do a matching activity, choosing the appropriate vocabulary to match the material – for example, the words 'shiny', 'smooth', 'soft' and 'silky' for the material satin. It would take very little extra effort to translate the nouns – satin, wool, cotton – and the associated adjectives to support bilingual learners. If there are many languages spoken in your class, this is not always manageable, but a resource such as this can be built up over time, with children and parents becoming increasingly involved with the translating.

Displays can be routinely produced to reflect the range of languages in the class. Most displays tend to have nouns identified, and these are relatively easy to translate. Small voice recorders can be attached to displays, and children could be encouraged to record themselves explaining an element of the display in their L1. For example, if several children have Polish as L1, they could contribute to a maths display on shape by naming the shape and describing it in Polish. These translation activities are beneficial in a number of ways. They raise the status of all languages spoken; they can potentially involve all children and their parents; they enable children to use and hear their L1, promoting a safe and stimulating, language-rich environment; and they enhance the linguistic experience of monolingual children, exposing them to the sounds and rhythms of different languages. Have a look at Figure 6.5.1. This was a display in a Reception class (children aged 4 and 5). Think about how you might improve this display by using a range of languages.

FIGURE 6.5.1 Display in a Reception class (children aged 4 and 5)

In a similar way, a bilingual approach can be promoted through the use of dual-language picture books. These are an invaluable resource – of enormous benefit to bilingual and monolingual learners. These texts demonstrate a respect for and interest in another language. They enable children to see their own language written down (even if they are not able to read it) and to share and delight in the shapes of the letters and words and explore the differences and similarities. In 2000, Edwards, Monaghan and Knight conducted research into the use of multimedia bilingual books, focusing on the effectiveness of these as tools for teaching. The teachers noticed a growth in metalinguistic awareness, not just for bilingual learners, but also for weaker, monolingual readers. Not only this, but the discussions held with the children after they had engaged with the bilingual texts were invaluable in terms of assessing their reading progress and their language comprehension.

One way of utilising dual-language texts might be to put children in pairs – one Bulgarian and one English, for example – and they could read to each other in their own languages. If they are not yet reading, they could look at the pictures and discuss what they think the story is about. Another possibility would be to encourage parents to come in and read books or poems aloud to the children in their first language. Free bilingual online texts are available at: www.trilingualmama.com/online-stories-for-children/

Task 6.5.3 Promoting a bilingual approach

Your task is to think of other ways through which a bilingual approach might be promoted. These do not need to be 'big' ideas that take a great deal of time and energy to implement. Instead, it is better to introduce small activities or resources more regularly, which will ultimately have a considerable impact on how you respond to and promote the linguistic diversity in your classroom. List some ideas and then try to incorporate one a week, building to one a day.

CELEBRATING AND CAPITALISING UPON LINGUISTIC DIVERSITY

Somehow, we need to nurture a sense of excitement about language within our schools. Having more than one language spoken in the classroom should heighten this excitement and enable us, as practitioners, to view our work with bilingual learners as a privilege rather than a burden. At first, this might seem daunting, particularly if you are unfamiliar with the languages spoken by the children and their families. Instead of being overwhelmed, however, think of ways in which the children can be encouraged to share their language with their peers, to the benefit of all. This can be as simple as learning 'good morning' in Slovakian, for example, and all the children answering the morning register in this language. This might extend to using different languages to give out instructions. Instructional vocabulary – using the imperative – tends to be short, sharp and easy to use and remember. If you, as the teacher, are able to learn from a pupil some brief instructions in one of the languages spoken in the class – 'Wash your hands', 'Fetch your coats', for example – you are leading the way in celebrating the linguistic diversity within the class, showing a respect for languages other than English and broadening the linguistic experience of all the children in your care.

If you have bilingual learners in the class who are confident and happy to speak in front of their peers, they could be encouraged to teach some words and phrases of their language. This does not need to be specifically planned for in a particular lesson. Instead, it is likely to be more powerful if it is spontaneous and authentic, responding to something that happens in a lesson. To give an example, you might be leading a class discussion about effective use of adverbs to enhance a piece of descriptive writing. The children might be offering examples, and you could ask for the equivalent words in another language, recording them in a useful word bank. The table below shows a very simple version of this, and, if you had this template set up, you could use it again and again for different lessons or in different contexts. In this way, the children begin to develop a bilingual mindset and they can make links between languages and note similarities and differences. In the example below, there is a very clear pattern with these particular words and a useful discussion could ensue, to the linguistic benefit of all.

English	Portuguese
quietly	silenciosamente
nervously	nervosamente
brightly	brilhantemente

When responding to linguistic diversity, it is vital to remember that children and families join the school and local community with a wealth of knowledge and understanding about the world, which can go unnoticed because of what might be seen as the language barrier. Without putting children under pressure, opportunities can be capitalised upon to encourage them to share this knowledge. Often, as we all know, children have a better understanding of certain topics than we do, and, if they come from another country with different cultures, traditions, education systems, and so forth, their knowledge base is bound to be very different to that of English children and teachers. The case study below describes a perfect example of this, where a very confident bilingual learner was able to take over my role as teacher!

CASE STUDY

Some years ago, a new boy arrived in my Year 6 class in October. His name was Petar and he was Bulgarian and spoke only a few words of English. Initially, he was, understandably, very anxious, shy and unwilling to speak. I sat him next to a kind, thoughtful girl who had a very good level of spoken and written English. Within a few days, Petar was looking much happier and was holding conversations with his peers. The other children were fascinated by his accent and the things he said and he soon became the class 'star', often referred to by the children as 'Professor Petar'!

On one occasion, several months later, I had planned a lesson on the oceans of the world and had a map displayed on the interactive whiteboard. I asked if anybody would like to come and write the ocean names where they thought they should be. Petar's hand was the first to rise and he raced to the board and confidently and correctly wrote all the names. He then pointed out where Bulgaria was on the map and the location of his hometown. Quite naturally, a discussion ensued, where the other children began asking him questions about his homeland and the type of town he had lived in; the clothes, shops, food and so on. Petar held forth for 10 or 15 minutes, making himself understood despite being far from fluent in English. The children were thoroughly engaged and learned a great deal more than if I had conducted the lesson according to my plan!

You may well read this case study and think, but what about the learning objectives? The success criteria? The planned activities? All the paraphernalia of a 'typical' lesson? In the example above, the main learning I had intended was for the children to identify the oceans of the world. Thanks to Petar, they learned the oceans and far, far more. Sometimes, it is about having the confidence to go with the flow, knowing that what is emerging is considerably more beneficial than what had originally been intended. This confidence often comes with time and experience, but always be on the lookout for this type of situation, where instinctively you know that you can capitalise on the diverse knowledge and understanding of the children in your class.

SUMMARY

If practitioners are effectively to respond to linguistic diversity, a recognition is needed that each child will arrive in school with useful and potentially transformative knowledge and experience. Within the confines of the curriculum, flexible and innovative approaches are required that provide a space for bilingual children to develop both L1 and L2 and work collaboratively to promote a rich learning environment for all. Rather than problematising children's bilingualism, it might be more appropriate to problematise our own monolingualism (Palmer and Martinez, 2013), and to seek ways by which to embrace and capitalise on linguistic diversity within our classrooms.

As teachers and learners in the twenty-first century, where language practices are 'multiple and ever adjusting to the multilingual multimodal terrain of the communicative act' (Garcia, 2009: 53), it is neither useful nor appropriate to adopt a monolingual approach. Instead, challenging ourselves to enhance the curriculum and support all learners through imaginative planning, teaching, resourcing and assessing will raise our own levels of practice, while enhancing the learning experience for all our pupils.

 ANNOTATED FURTHER READING

Garcia, O. (2009) *Bilingual Education in the 21st Century: A Global Perspective*, London: Wiley-Blackwell.
> This is a powerful text in which Garcia argues that a bilingual education is beneficial for all and has the power to reduce the inequalities caused by the status conferred on certain languages. The case studies used in the text are very useful, and the arguments put forward are wholly pertinent to both global and local issues, in and beyond the educational context.

Conteh, J. (2012) *Teaching Bilingual and EAL Learners in Primary Schools*, London: Sage.
> Jean Conteh has a wealth of experience working with and researching the lives of bilingual children and their families. In this text, she addresses beliefs and misconceptions relating to bilingual learners and provides ideas and strategies for supporting their needs. This is a very readable and engaging text that draws on a wide range of research within the field.

FURTHER READING TO SUPPORT M-LEVEL STUDY

Safford, K. and Drury, R. (2013) 'The "problem" of bilingual children in educational settings: Policy and research in England', *Language & Education*, 27(1): 70-81.

> This is a very readable article that includes a very useful timeline relating to how approaches to ethnic minority children have changed over the years. The authors promote the importance of understanding what bilingual children bring to the classroom, rather than seeing them as a problem.

Bialystok, E. (2011) 'Reshaping the mind: The benefits of bilingualism', *Canadian Journal of Experimental Psychology*, 65(4): 229-35.

> In this article, Bialystok provides explanations for the high levels of performance demonstrated by many bilingual children. Reading this article should convince you of the myriad advantages of promoting a bilingual approach.

RELEVANT WEBSITES

National Association for Language Development in the Curriculum: https://naldic.org.uk/

> This website has a wealth of information. Some of this is accessible without joining the association, but I would highly recommend joining. There is a very low subscription, and this then allows you access to all the online resources and the hard-copy journals.

EAL Teaching Strategies: www.eal-teaching-strategies.com

> This website has useful ideas, resources, readings, games, audio stories, and so on.

REFERENCES

Bower, V. (2016) 'Supporting Nepalese children with English as an additional language in the English primary school.' Unpublished PhD thesis, Canterbury Christ Church University, UK.

Bialystok, E. (ed.) (1991) *Language Processing in Bilingual Children*, Cambridge, UK: Cambridge University Press.

Conteh, J. and Brock, A. (2011) '"Safe spaces"? Sites of bilingualism for young learners in home, school and community', *International Journal of Bilingual Education & Bilingualism*, 14(3): 347-60.

Cummins, J. (2001) *Language, Power and Pedagogy*, Clevedon, UK: Multilingual Matters.

Cummins, J. (2005) 'A proposal for action: Strategies for recognising heritage language competence as a learning resource with the mainstream classroom', *The Modern Language Journal*, 898(4): 585-92.

Department of Education and Science (DES). (1975) *The Bullock Report: A Language for Life*, London: HMSO.

Department of Education and Science (DES). (1985) *Education for All: Report of the Committee of Inquiry into the Education of Children from Ethnic Minority Groups* (*Swann Report*), Cmnd. 9453, London: HMSO.

Department for Education and Employment (DfEE). (1998) *The National Literacy Strategy: Framework for Teaching*, London: DfEE.

Department for Education and Skills (DfES). (2006) *Primary National Strategy Excellence and Enjoyment: Learning and Teaching for Bilingual Children in the Primary Years*, London: DfES.

Edwards, V., Monaghan, F. and Knight, J. (2000) 'Books, pictures and conversations: Using bilingual multimedia storybooks to develop language awareness', *Language Awareness*, 9(3): 135-46.

Elorza, I. and Munoa, I. (2008) 'Promoting the minority language through integrated plurilingual language planning: The case of the Ikastolas language', *Culture & Curriculum*, 21(1): 85-101.

Garcia, O. (2009) *Bilingual Education in the 21st Century: A Global Perspective*, London: Wiley-Blackwell.

Gregory, E. (2008) *Learning to Read in a New Language*, London: Sage.

Johnson, K.E. (2006) 'The sociocultural turn and its challenges for second language teacher education', *TESOL Quarterly*, 40(1): 235-57.

Kelly, C. (2010) *Hidden Worlds*, Stoke-on-Trent, UK: Trentham.

Melby-Lervag, M. and Lervag, A. (2011) 'Cross-linguistic transfer of oral language, decoding, phonological awareness and reading comprehension: A meta-analysis of the correlational evidence', *Journal of Research in Reading*, 34(1): 114-35.

Palmer, D. and Martinez, R.A. (2013) 'Teacher agency in bilingual spaces: A fresh look at preparing teachers to educate Latina/o bilingual children', *Review of Research in Education*, 37: 269-97.

Rampton, B., Harris, R. and Leung, C. (2002) 'Education in England and speakers of languages other than English', *Working Papers in Urban Language and Literacies*, London: King's College London.

Rogoff, B. (1994) 'Developing understanding of the idea of communities of learners', *Mind, Culture & Activity*, 1(4): 209-29.

Vygotsky, L.S. (1962) *Thought and Language*, Cambridge, MA: MIT Press.

RESPONDING TO GENDER DIFFERENCES

Elaine Millard and Louise Wheatcroft
with Eve Bearne

INTRODUCTION

This unit discusses the influence of gender on attitudes to schooling in general and the development of literacy in particular. While working through it, you will be asked to think carefully about the way in which society conveys its messages about what it means to be a boy or a girl and some strategies that you might adopt for ensuring that all pupils are encouraged to develop effective learning skills, irrespective of their gender.

OBJECTIVES

By the end of this unit, you should:

* be clear about what is meant by gender, differentiating its role from that of sex and sexuality and considering its interaction with race and class;
* have an informed opinion of the role played by gendered cultural capital in determining school success and under-achievement;
* be able to identify some strategies that will support more gender-balanced classroom approaches;
* begin to connect children's experiences of home with their school learning.

BACKGROUND

In the 1970s and 1980s, girls' under-achievement in maths and science was a major concern. This was successfully addressed by a range of initiatives targeted particularly at increasing girls' access to these subjects, and girls began to match and, in some cases, outperform boys in all subjects. At the beginning of the twenty-first century, the concern for girls' education was replaced in most English-speaking countries with more strident debates about a perceived 'underperformance' by boys, fuelled by the results of international testing, although the concept has also been questioned on the grounds that panic over boys' achievements often oversimplifies what is a complex area of educational debate (Titus, 2004). The greatest concerns have been related to literacy. Major international surveys, PISA (OECD, 2010, 2016) and PIRLS (Twist *et al.*, 2012), show that girls outperform boys in reading across all the countries involved in the research. However, as with any study about gender, it is worth remembering that the children in the classroom may not conform to these international norms. In addition, it is worth noting that not all boys are underachieving or unmotivated readers and writers, nor do all girls achieve highly. There are also differences between boys and between girls that can be as wide as the differences between boys and girls.

Addressing the perceived gap in attainment between boys and girls is complex. It is not simply a matter of finding ways to motivate boys or to make learning more 'boy-friendly' (NLT, 2012). As someone preparing to teach, you will need to be both well informed in your judgements and have a well-thought-out strategy for supporting all pupils' learning, rather than a dependence on gender stereotypes or well-intentioned advice on managing boys' schooling.

DEFINITIONS

The first point to clarify is the definition of gender as it is employed in the debate, distinguishing it from sex. Whereas the term 'sex' is used to signify the biological differences between male and female, 'gender' designates the patterns of behaviour and attitude attributed to members of each sex that are an effect of experiences of education, culture and socialisation. Whereas sex is conventionally categorised by binary oppositions of male and female, gender has a less-determined division, embracing a spectrum of experiences and ways of self-presentation and identity markers, so that an individual may adopt a feminine gender without being biologically female, and vice versa. This means that both sexes respond either in accordance with, or in opposition to, what they take to be the gender role ascribed to their biological sex. These roles tend to emphasise differences between the sexes, rather than common patterns of similarity and correspondence. Put simply, sex is a biological given, but gender is socially and culturally constructed.

There is some disagreement about whether gender should include sexuality or whether sexuality should be a separate concept. Sexuality refers to one's preferred sexual orientation, but it is important not to assume that there are clear-cut behavioural differences between people who identify as LGBGTI and those who do not. Individuals will make choices about socially constructed gendered behaviours, including whether to hide sexual orientation or to make it public.

Gender regime

Gender regime refers to the accepted version(s) of masculinity or femininity as practised in a particular community or institution, such as the family, peer group, school or place of employment. It encompasses differences in patterns of behaviour, interests and relationships expected of boys and girls, men and women. In relation to schooling, Kessler *et al.* (1985) argued that young people were caught up in overlapping gender regimes, the most powerful influence of all being the peer group, which defines what is 'cool' for each sex, both in and out of a school context.

Habitus

Related to this concept of a 'regime' is the theory of *habitus* (Bourdieu, 1990). Bourdieu's term denotes taken-for-granted ways of thinking, which, although socially constructed, are so ingrained in an individual as a result of embodied action that they appear natural. What this implies is that human behaviour is often heavily influenced by dispositions of action, thought and attitude, created from previous experiences of both success and failure in contexts influenced by class, family, education and social groupings. Such behaviours are, therefore, neither entirely voluntary nor completely determined.

Cultural capital

This is another concept taken from the work of Bourdieu and his colleague Jean Passeron (1977/1970), which accounts for the cultural advantages bestowed on individuals from their own family and its position in society, rather than from mere economic power. It is used to understand and explain distinctions in cultural knowledge, taste and preference, which place individuals in positions of either social advantage or disadvantage in relation to dominant forms of education and experience. Cultural capital strongly influences educational opportunity and confers power and status on those whose capital is deemed to demonstrate their superiority. In terms of culture, men's activities often attract higher status than those practised by women (Millard, 1997).

Identity work

Sex and gender are key components of personal identity and upbringing, and social interactions all provide strong messages about what it is to be a man or a woman and how we should present ourselves and interact socially. Moss and Washbrook (2016), in a review of research into gender and literacy, point out that:

> Most studies consider that gender differences are shaped by the interaction between gendered expectations in the adult population and gendered expectations that children internalise and also construct independently with their peers.

> (Moss and Washbrook, 2016: 13)

Francis (2005) argues that gender policing impacts on gendered power relations and identities in both primary and secondary classrooms:

> This involves behaving in stereotypical ways to demonstrate their gender allegiance, but also in policing other children to ensure that they do the same.

> (Francis, 2005: 42)

EXPLANATIONS OF THE 'GENDER GAP'

In reviewing the research into gender and literacy, Moss and Washbrook (2016) categorise explanations of the gender gap as ranged along a continuum between *essentialist* or *sociocultural* explanations. Essentialist explanations see gender differences as hard-wired and incapable of change, whereas sociocultural perspectives argue that gender differences are socially constructed and so can be changed. Essentialist explanations do not consider differences within the category 'boys' (and there are possibly as many differences between boys as there are between boys and girls) but emphasise differences between the categories 'boys' and 'girls'. Narrowing the gap in performance between boys and girls is seen as a matter of responding to innate differences, for example, by developing 'boy-friendly' materials and approaches. Sociocultural explanations suggest that children's perceptions of what it means to be a 'boy' or a 'girl' vary according to the prevailing attitudes and beliefs in different social contexts. This means that, once differences in social norms are acknowledged and understood, strategies can be developed to change them – for example, open discussion of perceptions of gendered behaviour and opportunities to develop more 'gender-neutral' classroom practice. This large-scale study identified school, home and peer cultures as significant factors influencing gender differences in literacy attainment. Similarly, the Boys' Reading Commission (NLT, 2012) identified boys' underachievement in reading as related to the interplay of three factors: home, school and identity.

GENDER AND READING

It is in matters of literacy that most concern has been expressed about gender differences. Earliest attention to this difference focused on achievements in reading, and every survey of children's reading interests conducted since the seminal work of Whitehead *et al.* (1977) has shown that boys and girls have quite different reading tastes (Coles and Hall, 2002; Maynard, Mackay and Smyth, 2008). In general, girls are also far more committed readers (Sainsbury and Schagen, 2004; Clark, 2016). Research shows that children's enjoyment of reading is strongly linked to attainment, and that teachers often perceive boys as inherently less competent readers in contrast to girls (Hempel-Jorgensen *et al.*, 2017). The National Literacy Trust's annual literacy survey in 2015 (Clark, 2016) shows that, although the gap has narrowed slightly since 2011, boys still report that they do not enjoy reading as much as girls do; they are less likely to read outside school than girls; they are less likely to perceive themselves as readers than girls; they have different reading preferences to girls; and more boys than girls struggle with reading.

Socio-economic factors are often seen as significant in boys' perceived under-attainment in reading in relation to girls'. Clark (2016) reported that less than half of boys in receipt of free school meals (FSM) surveyed in English schools reported reading for pleasure, and were significantly underachieving educationally. In addition, classroom factors have a role in influencing boys' apparent disengagement with reading. Research by Hempel-Jorgensen *et al.* (2017) found that:

> a combination of teachers' perceptions of boys' in-school 'ability' labels, gender, ethnicity and social class, and the teaching practices for reading, caused some boys to become positioned as struggling readers who do not engage with volitional reading for pleasure. This impacted negatively on their orientations to, and level of engagement with, reading for pleasure.
>
> (Hempel-Jorgensen *et al.*, 2017: 2)

Figure 6.6.1 lists strategies that the *Raising Boys' Achievement project* (Younger *et al.*, 2005) identified as having the potential to make a difference to boys' (and girls') learning, motivation and engagement with reading, and consequently to raise levels of academic achievement.

Strategies that can enhance reading engagement include:

- enhanced and extended provision of books and other texts that invite boys (and girls) to express preferences for what might be bought;
- buddy systems, where older boys are trained to mentor younger readers (where possible, pairings should be matched according to home language);
- reading groups led by members of the school community who are not teachers where there is emphatically no overt 'teaching' but a general sharing of reading pleasures, based on all kinds of text;
- using reading journals on a regular but not routine basis as a reflective space to record, by choice, response to texts;
- explicit attention to teachers modelling ways of responding to the meaning and content of books, not just decoding the text;
- homework that specifically encourages students to read all kinds of text.

FIGURE 6.6.1 Strategies that can enhance reading engagement

Source: Chapter 6, 'Now I can read faster: Reading communities and partnerships', in Warrington, Younger and Bearne (2006)

Resources for both independent and whole-class reading need to include a wide and varied range of texts, including non-fiction, magazines and screen-based texts. Further, it is important to ensure that all pupils are able to experience a rich diet of well-crafted narratives and information texts and hear them read well. The experience of reading aloud and 'performing' powerful texts embeds an understanding of the rhythms as well as the language of both poetry and prose, and it is essential to create time for some texts to be read and re-read. Drama, poetry and fiction allow many opportunities for discussing important issues through considering the interrelationship of characters, experiences and events. The importance of developing empathy, a cornerstone of social and emotional aspects of learning, makes it important to share texts, with both boys and girls, that focus on character development and emotions, rather than always selecting for adventure, plot and action. It is also equally important to think about different cultures' responses to narrative and storytelling and weave other cultural interests into the classroom provision for reading.

A sustained research project conducted by Moss and Attar (1999) categorised reading events in particular schools: reading for proficiency, reading for choice and procedural reading. The observations indicated that the proficiency frame for reading creates most gender differentiation. Hempel-Jorgensen *et al.* similarly found that teaching is strongly driven by proficiency judgements by teachers related to the assessment agenda that drives current educational policy in England (Hempel-Jorgensen *et al.*, 2017). There needs to be some balance between aiming for proficiency and offering opportunities for choice. When catering for different tastes in individual reading, it is important that a focus on gender does not simply reinforce the differences in range and breadth of the texts that all pupils encounter, and that girls' preferences are not ignored when providing for boys' perceived interests. Asking for pupils' views about classroom and library reading provision can help to provide broad and diverse reading resources.

Task 6.6.1 Reviewing provision for reading

The first part of this task asks you to make some observations in school. If you are not likely to be making a school visit soon, you will need to complete the review by thinking back to a school that you are familiar with.

1 Note the school practices for each of the points in Figure 6.6.1. For example, how diverse was the reading provision, or how did the teacher model response to reading? Keep a note of any points that you don't have evidence for and focus on these on your next school placement.
2 Start to create a list of texts that you could use in the classroom that adequately reflect balanced and varied roles ascribed to men and women, boys and girls.

You might visit websites such as Just Imagine (http://justimaginestorycentre.co.uk/blogs/resources) or Books for Keeps (http://booksforkeeps.co.uk/).

GENDER AND WRITING

Differences in reading choices have been shown to have consequences, not only for children's reading in school, but also for developing their confidence as writers (Millard, 1997; Barrs and Cork, 2001). More of girls' writing shows evidence of traditional narrative influences and structures, whereas boys frequently draw on film or oral narrative structures, producing action-packed stories

(Marsh, 2003; Millard, 2005; Willett, 2005). This may make boys appear less competent writers in relation to narratives produced in response to school criteria.

Again, it is important to ensure that literacy activities from a wealth of different narratives, short stories, tales and children's novels are shared - not just a selection of excerpts to demonstrate specific language points. Digital and other multimodal texts, including the structure of computer games, can also afford interesting stimuli for writing (Bearne and Wolstencroft, 2007; Bearne and Reedy, 2018 forthcoming). A report on *Young People's Writing in 2011* for the NLT by Clark (2012) indicated that, in school, girls enjoy writing more than boys, and, although both boys and girls engage in reading and creating digital texts in their home literacy practices, girls also tend to write more in formats such as emails, text messages and messages on social-networking sites.

Millard's research (2005) found that boys often employed a wider range of vocabulary and used action verbs more effectively, whereas girls tended to spend more time developing the setting of a story or creating character. It is important to encourage boys and girls to reflect on their work and the work of others, sharing their work and understanding differences of language use in order to expand both groups' repertoires of image and vocabulary. Highlighting achievements can help children learn to analyse and comment on each other's work. Here are some comments made as part of the Castle of Fear Project (Millard, 2005) by Year 5 girls on stories that had been written by boys:

> My favourite part is where you find arrows firing across the room. I also liked the flame-pit room with a flaming fire. I think 'find a rope and swing for your life' is an original idea. I like the spiders and their sharp fangs. In fact I like everything.

Improvements in writing came when teachers:

- incorporated a range of spoken language opportunities in all learning;
- emphasised talk and time to reflect – finding ways to talk about learning and literacy;
- saw the importance of 'companionable' writing through using response partners and group work;
- were prepared to take risks in bringing more creativity to English sessions;
- wrote themselves, modelling writing and showing how it is constructed;
- used a variety of activities: at times, these might be short, specific-focused writing tasks; at other times they allowed opportunities to return to writing over a period of time;
- balanced attention to accuracy and neatness with a sense of writing purpose and knowing when it is important to 'get writing right';
- did not ask the children to do writing for the sake of it – just to prove they had read/ learned something – but required less writing – writing that mattered and was relevant to the learners;
- operated transparent assessment and marking, with targets shared and negotiated with the pupils;
- had some sense of how literacy is perceived and supported at home.

FIGURE 6.6.2 Strategies that can enhance attitudes and performance in writing

Source: Adapted from Warrington *et al.* (2006: 152–3)

I think your title is brilliant and so is your blurb. I like 'the mummy with gleaming eyes' and 'bubbly paper wrapped round it'. I like your pictures of the mummies. My favourite room is the dark chamber.

And a boy's comments on a girl's story:

I liked page two best. It has a brilliant description of the witch. I would have liked a picture of her though. The most interesting bit was where you discover the treasure. It was good how you could click your fingers to escape the magic.

The *Raising Boys' Achievement* project (Younger *et al.*, 2005) took a detailed look at boys' writing (as well as reading and spoken language). By the end of the project, improved attitudes and performance in writing were shown to develop when teachers adopted a range of practices (see Figure 6.6.2).

Task 6.6.2 Reviewing provision for writing

The first part of this task asks you to make some observations in school. If you are not likely to be making a school visit soon, you will need to complete the review by thinking back to a school that you are familiar with.

1 Note the school practices for each of the points in Figure 6.6.2. For example, how did the teacher use talk to support writing and model writing for the children? Keep a note of any points that you don't have evidence for and focus on these on your next school placement – for example, you may not have had a chance to discover what the teacher might know about the children's home experiences of literacy.

2 Thinking back to your last school experience, how did you vary the kinds of writing experience you provided for the class? For example, did they have a chance to write on screens as well as on paper? Did you plan for reading and writing a range of texts, including poetry, narrative, information, persuasion, and so on. Jot down a few ideas to use when planning to teach writing on your next placement.

Making a class collection of stories and poems can promote both better presentation skills and an opportunity for children to learn from each other's work. This could be stored online, and children could be encouraged to read work from the collection to children in other classes or to share with parents and school visitors, as well as each other. It is important that the children make the selection themselves, giving specific reasons for the choices they make, so that each pupil's writing strengths are identified and they can be drawn on for discussion in later writing sessions.

GENDER AND SPOKEN LANGUAGE

In spoken language work, girls can be placed at a disadvantage in both whole-class and mixed groupings. In whole-class settings, teachers have been found to direct more of their questions at boys, often for management of their behaviour, and, in all kinds of group work, assertive boys can dominate talk, even in small mixed groups, so that both girls and quiet boys may have problems in making themselves or their views heard. For successful group work, it is important, not only to make sure that the children will be able to work harmoniously together, but also to vary groupings from

Successful strategies for promoting spoken language include:

- *Modelling the language of texts and of learning*: This means, not only introducing specific terminology about texts, but consistently modelling ways of approaching texts or ideas – for example, when reading a poem or book: *I'm wondering why the author chose to use those words*; or, in discussing a problem in maths or science: *What might be a solution?*
- *Thinking aloud*: Teachers share their thought processes and give their own opinions – for example, *I think this is more effective because . . .* and *I can see that working . . . How might we sort this out?* These more speculative, tentative uses of language are particularly helpful models for group work.
- *Negotiating and collaborating*: The kinds of invitation teachers offer children in open discussion can be very powerful examples for paired or small-group exchanges – for example: *I think it might be helpful if we . . .*; *Would you like to . . . ?*; *Who might be the best person to do this?*
- *Asking questions – teachers*: Questions from teachers that are work-focused (rather than behaviour-focused) should vary between those requiring a precise response and those inviting reflection or speculation. This can be further supported by the teacher not expecting that everyone will have to answer all the time and providing chances for extended expression of opinion.
- *Asking questions – children*: There are gains in learning when children are encouraged to formulate their own questions about learning and opportunities are created for them to ask questions of each other and the teacher. Teacher questioning acts as a model for children's questions.

FIGURE 6.6.3 Teacher modelling of spoken language

Source: Chapter 7, 'I like the good words I used: Becoming writers', in Warrington *et al.* (2006)

time to time, to ensure that all children have experience of working in both mixed and single-sex groups. Homophobic attitudes can limit who speaks and what can be said in group work (Guasp, 2014). It is important to define roles carefully and set out clear and agreed strategies for cooperative work, so that ridiculing others' responses will not be tolerated. Encouraging children to draw up guidelines for good habits of working together for themselves contributes to productive group work. But, promoting gender equity is not just a matter of organising the classroom for talk. One of the main features of successfully balanced classrooms for boys' and girls' achievement is the way teachers include spoken language frequently and systematically in their teaching (Warrington *et al.*, 2006). The teacher's use of language is crucial (see Figure 6.6.3).

Talk is gaining increasing importance as an essential part of pupils' school experience, its value being emphasised by the Cambridge Primary Review (Alexander, 2010). Boys have been characterised as particularly enjoying argument, competition and disputation (Davies, 1998). These aspects of language can be built into many classroom activities, particularly through the use of role-play and simulations.

A ROLE FOR POPULAR CULTURE

Although English and language work in school concerns itself largely with what is judged by adults to be appropriate literature, out-of-school, pleasurable narratives are available in a much wider range of forms, including comics, magazines, television, film, videos, computer games, and so on. Many of these texts are interconnected, so that a film, a comic, a computer game and a popular book may share a common narrative source and main characters. These narratives have wide currency with all groups of children and are important in the development of friendships and peer groups (Dyson, 1997; Marsh, 2003; Marsh and Millard, 2003; Willett, 2005). As Marsh argues:

> Popular culture, media and new technologies offer a myriad of opportunities for deconstructing representations of gender and developing critical literacy skills, skills which are essential in order to challenge the stereotypes which perpetuate literacy myths, including those relating to underachievement.

> (Marsh, 2003: 73)

Marsh and Millard (2003) have examined the role that popular media can play in creating motivation, particularly among pupils who find conventional school work unappealing (more frequently boys). There are, however, disadvantages to popular texts, as they are often more marked by gendered interests than resources more commonly made available in school. Commercial interests deliberately frame them to appeal specifically either to boys or girls by reinforcing ideas of typical interests – for example, football and *Star Wars* for boys, home-making and Barbie dolls for girls. However, because of their wide circulation and the personal interest invested in them, they provide a very rich source of ideas for writing and discussion and can offer good opportunities for challenging stereotypes that limit expectations.

Task 6.6.3 Examining popular texts

Examine a range of popular texts for children that include paper-based and digital texts, such as comics, magazines and websites for children.

- How are gender stereotypes reinforced?
- How might you use popular texts in the classroom to challenge gender stereotypes?
- How might you use popular texts to engage and motivate pupils?

GENDER, ETHNICITY AND CLASS

Gender identity and its relationship to boys' schooling and achievement have now been on the agenda throughout the twenty-first century, and many individual strategies adopted have proved effective in particular contexts. However, the focus on boys' needs has taken place at the expense of a more thoughtful consideration of educational disadvantage and an understanding of the links with other markers of identity, such as ethnicity. As Gillborn and Mirza (2000) state in their report, *Educational Inequality*:

> Our data shows gender to be a less problematic issue than the significant disadvantage of 'race', and the even greater inequality of class. Our intention here is to contextualize these relative disadvantages: it is important not to fall into the trap of simply arguing between various

inequalities. All pupils have a gender, class and ethnic identity – the factors do not operate in isolation.

(Gillborn and Mirza, 2000: 23)

Claire (2004), in reflecting on Gillborn and Mirza's report, emphasises that:

No person is without class or gender, whatever their ethnicity, and through meticulous and systematic scrutiny of material which breaks down the broad categories of 'race', class or gender and takes into account the ways that they intersect, Gillborn and Mirza show how much more complex, and sometimes surprising, is the reality of lived experience.

(Claire, 2004: 16)

Task 6.6.4 Taking it further through research work

Those of you who are interested in conducting your own research in this area, whether as part of work towards an M-level qualification, or in order to address a specific need of your current context, may wish to consider working on a small project in your place of work. Here are some ideas you might choose to follow up:

- As recommended by Watson, Kehler and Martino (2010), widen the range of literacy materials that you use to engage pupils by investigating the current reading interests of the boys and girls in your class. Find out what types of text they are enjoying and explore ways to incorporate literacy materials from children's out-of-school experiences in your literacy lessons.
- Conduct a piece of action research. Identify a small group of children or individuals who are under-achieving and identify some approaches that would benefit both boys and girls in your class. Implement an approach and evaluate the effectiveness of the intervention.
- Observe boys and/or girls in the role-play area or in the writing area. What can you find out about how they enact and develop stories/narratives or about when and why they choose to write? How can this learning be used to inform your practice?

SUMMARY

Despite the many changes that have improved the position of both girls and women in society, Western culture is still saturated with notions of gender difference, often with an accompanying assumption that there are 'natural' attributes of the sexes that are best acknowledged as fixed. Questions of masculine identity have not been analysed with the same amount of scrutiny, even when stereotypical masculine responses result in poorer orientation to both schools and schooling. This unit stresses the importance of developing a pedagogy that is more likely to create a balanced approach to boys' and girls' learning rooted firmly in the sociocultural lives of children and is sensitive to their ethnicity, class and previous experiences.

ANNOTATED FURTHER READING

Millard, E. (1997) *Differently Literate: Boys, Girls and the Schooling of Literacy*, London: Falmer.

> Many of the main concepts on which this unit is based are found in this book. It also contains the research methodology useful in guiding you in how to find out about your classes' interests in reading and writing. In particular, it recommends collecting 'stories of reading' from all the children you teach, by asking them to write about their own journey into reading.

Moss, G. (2008) *Literacy and Gender: Researching Texts, Contexts and Readers*, London: Routledge.

> An excellent analysis of further research methodologies, including accounts of important findings from Moss's own research focusing on the structures of schooling and the 'literacy events' that shape children's perceptions of what is expected of them in the English curriculum. Her analysis of types of reader and their response to classroom tasks is particularly useful in helping understand how classroom organisation contributes to the construction of readers and their self-identity.

Warrington, M., Younger, M. with Bearne, E. (2006) *Raising Boys' Achievement in Primary Schools: Towards an Holistic Approach*, Buckingham, UK: Open University Press.

> Based on a 3-year research project, this book explores the gender debate throughout a range of curriculum areas, arguing for a pedagogy of inclusion and balance.

Watson, A., Kehler, M. and Martino, W. (2010) 'The problem of boys' literacy underachievement: Raising some questions', *Journal of Adolescent & Adult Literacy*, 53(5): 356-61.

> In this article, Watson, Kehler and Martino express concerns about the way in which boys and girls are often presented as competing victims. They suggest that the issue is oversimplified and should include consideration of a number of other factors, such as social class, race, ethnicity and sexuality, as well as gender. They argue that it would be more productive to challenge culturally and socially constructed understandings of masculinity.

FURTHER READING TO SUPPORT M-LEVEL STUDY

Moss, G. and Washbrook, L. (2016) *Understanding the Gender Gap in Literacy and Language Development*, Bristol Working Papers in Education no. 01/2016, Bristol, UK: Bristol University.

> In this summary review of research, Moss and Washbrook identify the scale of the gender gap, how it can best be explained, and what might make most difference to the gap in the early years (age 3-5), enabling boys and girls to read well by the end of primary schooling (age 11). It uses a range of research methods: a narrative review of the literature on gender, literacy and language development; statistical analyses of the Millennium Cohort Study; and a rapid evidence assessment of interventions relevant to the UK context and focused on the preschool age group.

Hempel-Jorgensen, A., Cremin, T., Harris, D. and Chamberlain, L. (2017) *Understanding Boys' (Dis)Engagement with Reading for Pleasure: Project Findings*, Open University. Retrieved from http://oro.open.ac.uk/49310/1/BA%20RfP%20report%20to%20funder.pdf (accessed 31 October 2017).

> This research project provides new evidence that how reading is taught in schools influences different boys' orientations to and engagement with reading for pleasure. It offers evidence that boys' (dis)engagement is not simply a gender issue, in that it involves teacher perceptions of other aspects of boys' social and learner identities, including 'ability', ethnicity and social class. The study explicitly focuses on how gender, ethnicity and social class intersect in producing different educational disadvantage among children.

RELEVANT WEBSITES

Gender and Education: The Evidence on Pupils in England: http://webarchive.nationalarchives.gov.uk/
20090108131525/http:/dcsf.gov.uk/research/data/uploadfiles/rtp01-07.pdf
> Although some of the data used for this Department of Education and Skills paper are drawn from
> 2007, it puts the gender debate in context by examining the extent of the gender gap and discussing
> the role of gender in education alongside the role of other pupil characteristics, particularly social
> class and ethnicity.

National Literacy Trust gender and literacy research pages: https://literacytrust.org.uk/resources/boy-meets-
world-addressing-gender-gap-research-summary/
> A very comprehensive research index that you can use to follow up specific issues in relation to
> literacy and gender.

Times Educational Supplement (*TES*): www.tes.co.uk

REFERENCES

Alexander, R. (2010) *Children, Their World, Their Education: Final Report and Recommendations of the Cambridge Primary Review*, London: Routledge.

Barrs, M. and Cork, V. (2001) *The Reader in the Writer*, London: CLPE.

Bearne, E. and Reedy, D. (2018 forthcoming) *Teaching Primary English*, Abingdon, UK: Routledge.

Bearne, E. and Wolstencroft, H. (2007) *Visual Approaches to Teaching Writing*, London: Sage.

Bourdieu, P. (1990) *The Logic of Practice*, Cambridge, UK: Polity Press.

Bourdieu, P. and Passeron, J. (1977/1970) *Reproduction in Education, Society and Culture* (trans. Richard Nice), London: Sage.

Claire, H. (ed.) (2004) *Gender in Education 3-19: A Fresh Approach*, London: Association of Teachers and Lecturers. Retrieved from https://www.atl.org.uk/Images/Gender%20in%20education%203-19.pdf (accessed 18 April 2017).

Clark, C. (2012) *Young People's Writing in 2011. Findings from the National Literacy Trust's Annual Literacy Survey*, London: National Literacy Trust.

Clark, C. (2016) *Children's and Young People's Reading Today. Findings from the 2015 National Literacy Trust's Annual Survey*, London: National Literacy Trust.

Coles M. and Hall, C. (2002) 'Gendered readings: Learning from children's reading choices', *Journal of Research in Reading*, 25(1): 96-108.

Davies, J. (1998) 'Taking risks or playing safe: Boys' and girls' talk', in E. Millard and A. Clark (eds) *Gender in the Secondary School Curriculum*, London: Routledge, pp. 11-26.

Dyson, A.H. (1997) *Writing Superheroes: Contemporary Childhood, Popular Culture, and Classroom Literacy*, New York: Teachers College Press.

Francis, B. (2005) 'Classroom interaction and access: Whose space is it?', in H. Claire (ed.) *Gender in Education 3-19: A Fresh Approach*, London: Association of Teachers and Lecturers. Retrieved from https://www.atl.org.uk/Images/Gender%20in%20education%203-19.pdf (accessed 18 April 2017).

Gillborn, D. and Mirza, H. (2000) *Educational Inequality: Mapping Race, Class and Gender* (HMI 232), London: Ofsted.

Guasp, A. (2014) *Homophobic Bullying in Britain's Schools: The Teachers' Report*. Retrieved from www.stonewall.org.uk/sites/default/files/teachers_report_2014.pdf (accessed 18 April 2017).

Hempel-Jorgensen, A., Cremin, T., Harris, D. and Chamberlain, L. (2017) *Understanding Boys' (Dis)Engagement with Reading for Pleasure: Project Findings*, Open University. Retrieved from http://oro.open.ac.uk/49310/1/BA%20RfP%20report%20to%20funder.pdf (accessed 31 October 2017).

Kessler, S., Ashden, D., Connell, R. and Dowsett, G. (1985) 'Gender relations in secondary schooling', *Sociology of Education*, 58(1): 34-48.

Marsh, J. (2003) 'Superhero stories: Literacy, gender and popular culture', in C. Skelton and B. Francis (eds) *Boys and Girls in the Primary School*, Buckingham: Open University Press, pp. 59-79.

Marsh, J. and Millard, E. (2003) *Literacy and Popular Culture in the Classroom*, Reading, UK: Reading and Language Centre Publications.

Maynard, S., Mackay, S. and Smyth, F. (2008) 'A survey of young people's reading in England: Borrowing and choosing books', *Journal of Librarianship & Information Science*, 40: 239-53.

Millard, E. (1997) *Differently Literate: Boys, Girls and the Schooling of Literacy*, London: Falmer.

Millard, E. (2005) 'Writing about heroes and villains: Fusing children's knowledge about popular fantasy texts with school-based literacy requirements', in J. Evans (ed.) *Literacy Moves On*, Portsmouth, NH: Heinemann, pp. 144-164.

Moss, G. and Attar, D. (1999) 'Boys and literacy: Gendering the reading curriculum', in J. Prosser (ed.) *School Cultures*, London: Chapman, pp. 133-44.

Moss, G. and Washbrook, L. (2016) *Understanding the Gender Gap in Literacy and Language Development*, Bristol Working Papers in Education no. 01/2016. Bristol, UK: Bristol University.

National Literacy Trust (NLT). (2012) *Boys' Reading Commission*, London: NLT. Retrieved from www.literacytrust.org.uk/assets/0001/4056/Boys_Commission_Report.pdf (accessed 18 April 2017).

OECD. (2010) *PISA 2009 Results: Executive Summary*. Retrieved from www.oecd.org/pisa/pisaproducts/46619703.pdf (accessed 3 December 2016).

OECD. (2016) *Results from PISA 2015. United Kingdom*. Retrieved from www.oecd.org/pisa/PISA-2015-United-Kingdom.pdf (accessed 31 October 2017).

Sainsbury, M. and Schagen, I. (2004) 'Attitudes to reading at ages nine and eleven', *Journal of Research in Reading*, 27(4): 373-86.

Titus, J.J. (2004) 'Boy trouble: Rhetorical framing of boys' underachievement', *Discourse: Studies in the Cultural Politics of Education*, 25(2): 145-69.

Twist, L., Sizmur, J., Bartlett, S. and Lynn, L. (2012) *PIRLS 2011: Reading Achievement in England*. Slough, UK: National Foundation for Educational Research. Retrieved from www.nfer.ac.uk/pirls (accessed 19 January 2017).

Warrington, M. and Younger M. with E. Bearne (2006) *Raising Boys' Achievements in Primary Schools: Towards an Holistic Approach*, Maidenhead, UK: Open University Press.

Watson, A., Kehler, M. and Martino, W. (2010) 'The problem of boys' literacy underachievement: Raising some questions', *Journal of Adolescent & Adult Literacy*, 53(5): 356-61.

Whitehead, F., Capey, A.C., Maddren, W. and Wellings, A. (1977) *Children and Their Books*, School's Council Research Studies, London: Macmillan.

Willett, R. (2005) 'Baddies in the classroom: Media education and narrative writing', *Literacy*, 39(3): 142-8.

Younger, M. and Warrington, M. with Gray, J., Rudduck, J., McLellan, R., Bearne, E., Kershner, R. and Bricheno, P. (2005) *Raising Boys' Achievement: Research Report No. 636*, London: Department for Education and Skills. Retrieved from http://webarchive.nationalarchives.gov.uk/20130402115731/https://www.education.gov.uk/publications/eOrderingDownload/RR636.pdf (accessed 18 April 2017).

RECENT DEVELOPMENTS

ENGAGING WITH PUPILS

Listening to the voices of children and young people

Carol Robinson

INTRODUCTION

Engaging with pupils involves listening to pupils about issues that matter to them and that affect their experiences in school. This unit focuses on outlining ways in which adults in schools can engage with pupils, and the benefits of this for both teachers and pupils. Within the unit we start by considering the terms used when referring to pupil engagement work, we consider the importance of building mutually respectful teacher-pupil relationships, and we identify ways in which teachers can engage with those they teach. We draw attention to how implementing strategies focused on engaging with pupils can make learning more meaningful for pupils and, as a result, improve the learning and experiences of children and young people in schools.

OBJECTIVES

By the end of this unit, you should:

- understand the terms 'pupil engagement', 'pupil voice' and 'pupil participation';
- be familiar with school practices that promote engagement with pupils;
- be aware of the benefits of engaging with pupils for both teachers and pupils;
- understand how to engage with pupils within your school, with a view to making lessons more meaningful and enhancing pupils' enjoyment of lessons.

PUPIL VOICE, PUPIL PARTICIPATION AND PUPIL ENGAGEMENT: WHAT DO THESE TERMS MEAN?

You are likely to come across the terms 'pupil engagement', 'student engagement' and 'learner engagement', as well as pupil, student and learner 'voice' and 'participation'. Each of these terms broadly relates to the move to consult pupils and provide opportunities for pupils to voice their opinions about matters that concern them and that affect their learning and other school experiences.

The term 'pupil voice', often used synonymously with the terms 'student voice' and 'learner voice' (Robinson and Taylor, 2007), refers to working with pupils to elicit their perspectives on matters relating to any aspect of school life. It is about teachers and other adults in schools wanting to learn from pupils about their experiences and providing opportunities for pupils to express their views. In extreme cases, if schools were to fully embrace pupil voice work, this would result in schools being run in a democratic way, with pupils' voices holding equal weight to those of the adults in the school. In such cases, staff and pupils would have a shared responsibility for the development of all practices and policies within their school.

According to Flutter and Rudduck (2004), 'pupil participation' implies the inclusion of pupils within a community in which they are respected contributors and have an active and direct involvement in school matters. The notion of participation can suggest that pupils are invited to contribute to decision-making processes, often as part of an institution-driven agenda, but they are not active participants in all school decision-making arenas. Other definitions of pupil participation strongly resonate with the above definition of pupil voice. For example, the Welsh Government's good-practice guide to pupil participation defines pupil participation as 'developing a culture in schools where all children and young people have a voice and have the opportunity to play an active role in decisions that affect their learning and well-being' (Welsh Government, 2011: 7).

The term 'pupil engagement' commonly has two meanings attributed to it. It can refer to the excitement and investment a pupil feels towards an aspect or issue that is of interest to them (Cheminais, 2008). However, it can also relate to pupils' being active partners in shaping their experiences of school. Similar to the notion of pupil voice work, pupil engagement in this latter sense is concerned with developing positive teacher–pupil relationships and with listening to individual and collective perspectives about matters that relate to pupils' experiences of school, including issues of teaching and learning – this work may be the outcome of institution-driven or pupil-driven agendas (Robinson, 2012).

For the purpose of our work in this unit, the term 'pupil engagement' will be used to relate to measures taken by teachers to develop positive teacher–pupil relationships; to increase awareness of the types of work and ways of working that interest, motivate and challenge pupils; and to encourage pupils to voice their opinions and become involved in school decision-making processes. We will focus in particular on the importance of engaging with pupils in relation to their experiences of learning and teaching in school.

LEGISLATION PROMPTING PUPIL ENGAGEMENT WORK IN SCHOOLS

The increasing importance placed on engaging with and listening to the voices of children and young people has stemmed from the United Nations Convention on the Rights of the Child (UNCRC; UN, 1989). In particular, Part 1 of Article 12 of the UNCRC states:

> States Parties shall assure to the child who is capable of forming his or her own views the right to express those views freely on all matters affecting the child, the views of the child being given due weight in accordance with the age and maturity of the child.

Part 1 of Article 12, therefore, comprises two key elements – the right for children and young people to (1) express their views and (2) have their views be given due weight (Lundy, 2007: 927). It gives children the right to freedom of opinion and the right to be heard and take part in decisions that affect them; this was a major factor that contributed to the positive recognition of practices that support listening to and engaging with pupils in schools.

Following the UNCRC, in 1991, Fullan posed the question, 'What would happen if we treated the student as someone whose opinion mattered?' (Fullan, 1991: 170). At this time, the notion of taking pupils' opinions into account was relatively new for most teachers; however, this idea, coupled with the implications of the UNCRC, served to open up spaces for consideration to be given to how the whole school community might benefit through listening to the voices of the pupils within it.

In recent years, although educational reforms within England have largely focused on raising pupils' measurable academic achievements and school performance, there have also been a number of Acts and reforms that have recognised and promoted the importance of engaging with pupils. For example, the 2002 Education Act (DfES, 2002) required that schools consult with pupils; the 2003 Department for Education and Skills (DfES) document *Working Together: Giving Children and Young People a Say* provided guidance on pupil participation; and the 2004 *Every Child Matters: Change for Children* legislation (DfES, 2004) provided a national framework for ways in which public services could work together to bring about improved outcomes for children, young people and families; central to this was the view that all children should have a say in decisions affecting their lives.

In 2007, the voices and views of children and young people informed the government's *Children's Plan* (DCSF, 2007); and, in 2008, *Working Together: Listening to the Voices of Children and Young People* (DCSF, 2008) made specific reference to the UNCRC and stated that schools should ensure the views of children and young people are 'heard and valued in the taking of decisions which affect them, and . . . are supported in making a positive contribution to their school and local community' (DCSF, 2008: 5). More recently, statutory guidance, *Listening to and Involving Children and Young People* (DfE, 2014), asserted that schools are 'strongly encouraged to pay due regard to the convention', and that local authorities and maintained schools should have regard to the guidance when 'considering how best to provide opportunities for pupils to be consulted on matters affecting them or contribute to decision-making in the school'.

In addition to these legislative documents, regulations relating to teachers' standards have implications for the extent to which teachers prioritise engaging with pupils. For example, teachers are more likely to engage with pupils if this is an aspect of their practice on which they are judged or graded. In September 2012, new *Teachers' Standards* (DfE, 2012) were introduced; these set a clear baseline of expectations for the professional practice and conduct of teachers from the point of qualification and apply to the vast majority of teachers, regardless of their career stage. These standards are used to assess all trainees working towards Qualified Teacher Status (QTS), teachers completing their statutory induction period, and the performance of all teachers, subject to the Education (School Teachers' Appraisal) (England) Regulations 2012.

Within these new *Teachers' Standards*, a teacher must 'Set high expectations which inspire, motivate and challenge pupils' (DfE, 2012: 7) and 'manage classes effectively, using approaches which are appropriate to pupils' needs in order to involve and motivate them' (DfE, 2012: 9). Therefore, implicit within these standards is the expectation that teachers will have built positive relationships with pupils, gained insights into individual pupils' interests, capabilities and preferred ways of learning, and be aware of, and understand, the sort of work and activities that are most likely to inspire, motivate and challenge pupils.

The recent Ofsted *Common Inspection Framework* (Ofsted, 2015) reinforces the requirement for teachers to understand the needs of pupils, and one of the areas on which school inspections now focus when evaluating the quality of teaching, learning and assessment is the extent to which teachers, practitioners and other staff 'have a secure understanding of the age group they are working with and have relevant subject knowledge that is detailed and communicated well to children and learners' (Ofsted, 2015: 13).

Task 7.1.1 Why is it so important to engage with pupils?

Imagine a classroom in which teachers teach only what they think learners ought to know, where there is no space for pupils to ask questions or voice opinions on areas of interest to them, where pupils are not encouraged to learn through discovery, where teacher–pupil relationships are not positive, and where pupils are simply passive recipients within a process. Alternatively, imagine a classroom in which teacher–pupil relationships are based on mutual respect, where pupils feel listened to and valued as individuals, where teachers want to know what interests and motivates the pupils, and where pupils feel confident about taking responsibility for aspects of their learning – a classroom in which pupils are encouraged to participate in assessing their work and setting future goals and where they feel a sense of belonging to the classroom and the wider school.

Of the two situations described above, in which of these would you expect pupils to thrive? Why?

HOW CAN ENGAGING WITH PUPILS BE OF BENEFIT TO THEM?

Children tend to enjoy school more when they are listened to and their views are taken seriously, when they are treated with respect and when they feel valued and included. Findings from research reported in the Cambridge Primary Review Research Report (Robinson, 2014: 5-6) indicate that positive pupil-teacher relationships are a significant factor in contributing to primary pupils' enjoyment of school, and, where such relationships dominate in schools, this contributes to pupils' feeling a sense of security within the school. DfE statutory guidance for schools (DfE, 2014) also outlines that the involvement of children and young people in school decision-making encourages pupils to become active participants in a democratic society, contributes to the achievement and attainment of pupils, promotes increased confidence, self-respect, competence and an improved sense of responsibility in pupils, and increases motivation and engagement with learning.

Flutter and Rudduck (2004: 7-8) report on findings from Jelly, Fuller and Byers (2000), who consulted pupils in a special needs school and found clear evidence that consulting pupils about their learning enhanced self-esteem and confidence, promoted stronger engagement and motivation to learn and encouraged pupils to become more active members of the school community. Similarly, Rudduck and McIntyre (2007: 152) found that pupil consultation tends to enhance pupils' commitment to, and capacity for, learning through strengthening self-esteem, enhancing attitudes towards school and learning, developing a strong sense of membership and developing new skills for learning. Furthermore, where pupils are actively involved in contributing to discussions and decisions about teaching and learning, this leads to them developing a deeper understanding of learning processes and promotes the development of higher-order thinking skills (Flutter and Rudduck, 2004).

ENGAGING WITH PUPILS: VIGNETTE 1

An experienced Year 4 class teacher in a primary school in the south west of England worked with a group of five pupils who she had identified as struggling with some aspects of learning in mathematics. The teacher invited these pupils to meet with her for 20-30 minutes over two lunchtimes and, rather than going over the aspects of mathematics these pupils found challenging and trying to reinforce learning, she engaged them in conversations that focused on their perspectives of what they considered would help their learning in mathematics. Pupils identified that, for them, learning was least likely to take place when teachers stood at the front of the class and described mathematical processes – 'It just doesn't sink in, I need someone to sit with me when I do it and show me how to do the bits I don't understand' (Year 4 pupil). Pupils also indicated that they were too embarrassed to say in front of the whole class that they didn't understand something, and that learning took place more readily when they had opportunities to work on a one-to-one basis with a teaching assistant or with competent older pupils. As a result of listening to pupils' views, the class teacher introduced a weekly lunchtime mathematics club. An open invitation was given to pupils in Years 5 and 6 to act as 'maths buddies', and those who volunteered tended to be some of the stronger mathematicians within these classes. The outcome was that the Year 4 pupils struggling with some aspects of mathematics made significant improvements in their confidence and achievement in mathematics. These pupils also commented that they felt valued by their teacher, as their suggestion about what would help their learning had been listened to and implemented.

HOW CAN ENGAGING WITH PUPILS BENEFIT TEACHERS?

Listening to pupils' views, considering their needs and interests, and involving them as active participants in their learning and other school activities can help schools to become learning communities, rather than knowledge factories, that serve the needs of the majority of the pupils within them (Busher, 2012).

Bragg and Fielding (2005) found that pupils can give valuable feedback to teachers in relation to their learning, and this in turn can inform teachers' future practice. Where pupils' views are heard on teaching and learning issues, teachers can gain an insight into pupils' perspectives on what helps and what hinders their learning. Finding out about pupils' perspectives of their school experiences, including learning, may take you outside your comfort zone in terms of the sort of dialogue you want to engage in with pupils. The outcomes, however, can be hugely beneficial through increasing your awareness of the learning needs of those you teach, and this can be of great help when analysing and reflecting on your own practices (Flutter and Rudduck, 2004). Rudduck and McIntyre (2007) found that consultations with pupils can lead to improved teacher awareness of pupils' capacities for learning, and can help teachers gain new perspectives and a renewed excitement about their teaching.

A further benefit of engaging with pupils is that a more collaborative relationship between teachers and pupils tends to develop, and, the better you are able to understand pupils, the more effective your teaching and their learning will be.

Creating listening classrooms can support teachers to identify factors that help pupils' learning and enjoyment of learning, as well as to identify factors that create barriers to learning and that lead to negative school experiences. Practices that support pupil engagement, therefore, have the potential to transform teacher–pupil relationships and lead to improvements in teachers' practices, through teachers learning from pupils about how they can make learning and other school experiences more meaningful for pupils.

ENGAGING WITH PUPILS: VIGNETTE 2

A Year 6 teacher from a primary school in the north of England shared her experience of how listening to comments from one pupil in her class changed the way she approached question-and-answer sessions with the class. This teacher quoted one Year 6 pupil to illustrate her point:

Miss, when you ask us questions, like what the answer to something is in maths or science, you ask different people until you get the right answer, and then you go on to the next question. But that doesn't really help us - just because someone has said the right answer that doesn't mean that the rest of us understand why it's the right answer, so we never actually learn that.

This simple comment by one pupil prompted this teacher to reflect on her teaching and to include more in-depth explanations in future lessons during question-and-answer activities.

WAYS OF ENGAGING WITH PUPILS IN SCHOOL

If schools are to develop an ethos in which it is the norm for staff to engage with pupils, and for staff and pupils to work together in a mutually respectful way, this requires staff to listen to pupils as part of their everyday practice. It involves teachers working with pupils to develop insights into pupils' needs, interests, likes and dislikes, and factors that motivate and demotivate pupils. Engaging with pupils also involves encouraging pupils to voice their opinions and providing opportunities for pupils to be active participants in their learning and in decision-making processes in school.

Schools vary in terms of the strategies they employ for listening to pupils; however, these may include setting up a school council or holding 'circle times' during which teachers listen to pupils' perspectives on particular issues. You, as the teacher, can pose simple questions to pupils during your day-to-day working with them in order to determine their perceptions of what motivates/demotivates them, what enhances/diminishes their enjoyment of lessons and what increases/reduces barriers to learners engaging in learning. For example, you might ask pupils: 'What activities help you to learn best? Why?'; 'Which activities do you enjoy the most? Why?'; 'What stops you from learning? Why?'; 'What would your ideal lesson be like? Why?'.

Pupil engagement can also take the form of pupils taking on roles as pupil governors and participating in management committees. As well as pupils being listened to verbally, they can also 'voice' their opinions through nonverbal means. For example, pupils can be encouraged to:

- draw, paint, take photos of, or role-play different situations - for example, situations that they either like or dislike in school;
- post their opinions in a postbox - this way pupils can remain anonymous if they wish;
- write a log about, for example, what aspects of lessons they enjoy and why;
- complete questionnaires, sentence-completion exercises or surveys on an aspect of their school experience; pupils could be involved in the writing and administering of these;
- take part in ballots and elections.

In order for 'listening schools' to be built, the development of positive working relationships between teachers and pupils is crucial; however, it takes time and perseverance by the whole school community to build such relationships. Constructing respectful cultures within schools is one of the key features of the UNICEF UK's Rights Respecting Schools Award (RRSA); taking on board the ideas of the RRSA may help schools in their endeavour to work towards building an ethos of respectful culture. The RRSA, which was developed in 2004, helps schools use the UNCRC as their values framework. More than 4,000 primary, secondary and special schools in England, Wales, Scotland and Northern Ireland are now registered for the award. A study involving schools registered on the RRSA found that, where schools adopted the principles of the RRSA, both adults and young people reported positive relationships between teachers and pupils, based on mutual respect and collaboration (Sebba and Robinson, 2010).

Task 7.1.2 Engaging with pupils in your classroom

- Define what you understand by the term 'engaging with pupils'. Identify factors you consider reflect high levels of positive engagement with pupils.
- Reflect on your experiences of engaging with pupils in your classroom. With which pupils do you have particularly high levels of engagement? In what ways do you engage with these pupils? Are there any pupils with whom you have lower levels of engagement? How could you address this issue?
- Identify one area of your work in the classroom in which you would like to develop more positive ways of engaging with pupils (this could relate to either a curriculum area or an aspect of your practice, such as assessment). What do you hope to achieve by such engagement? What steps will you take to ensure you engage with all pupils?

GUIDING PRINCIPLES FOR ENGAGING WITH PUPILS

Thomson points out that student representation is often tokenistic and seems more about students being *seen* to be involved in school processes, rather than being active partners in change (2011: 25). In order to avoid such tokenistic engagement with pupils, schools could develop a pupil engagement policy, taking into consideration the following principles:

- There should be a genuine desire by staff to engage with pupils.
- Pupils and staff should understand what is meant by 'pupil engagement', and staff should understand the benefits of this for individual pupils, for staff and for the whole school community.
- Pupils and staff should work together in ways that enable pupils to influence the conditions for their own learning.
- Teacher-pupil relationships should be based on mutual respect, and adults in the school should acknowledge that pupils have the right to express their views on matters affecting them.
- It should be acknowledged that there are as many voices as there are pupils, not just one unified voice.
- *All* pupils should be encouraged to have an active, rather than passive, involvement in discussions and decision-making.
- Pupils should feel confident that they can speak freely about what is on their mind, rather than feeling they ought to say what they think you or other adults want to hear, and alternative perspectives that do not align with the generally accepted school ethos should be listened to.
- Pupils need to know that if they express their views they will be taken seriously, and this won't be held against them, no matter how controversial their views are.
- It should be acknowledged that pupils may express their views through more than the spoken word.

LEVELS OF ENGAGING WITH PUPILS

Levels of engaging with pupils can be viewed along a continuum, with low levels of engagement at one end, reflecting minimal teacher-pupil engagement where teachers have little interest in pupils' opinions, and high levels of engagement at the opposite end, representing situations where teachers actively develop practices that interest, inspire, motivate and challenge pupils, and where teachers and pupils have mutually respectful relationships.

Task 7.1.3 Engaging with pupils to enhance the relevance of their learning

At what point on the continuum would you position yourself in relation to the class of pupils you most often teach? Why?

Identify ways in which you could use your knowledge of pupils in your class to support and challenge them within one curriculum area throughout (a) next term and (b) next year.

- Which pupils or groups of pupils do you think will be the most difficult to reach? What can you do to help reach these groups?
- What resources/training would be of help to you in order to facilitate taking the needs of individual pupils into account?
- Identify ways in which you could make your teaching more relevant to the needs of individual pupils in your class within one curriculum area, throughout (a) next term and (b) next year.
- Would you foresee any barriers to taking this work forward? If so, how might these be overcome?

As part of this work, you might also want to consider whether school practices affect levels of engagement with different groups of pupils and, if so, what you could do to address any issues you identify.

SUMMARY

This unit has provided an introduction to how you can engage with pupils within everyday classroom practices and has outlined that engaging with pupils and building an awareness of ways of working that interest, motivate and challenge pupils, individually and collectively, will help to motivate pupils and improve their learning and experiences of school. Levels of engaging with pupils are not static, with teachers engaging in different ways and at different levels, depending on the pupil and the situation. If teachers are to engage in genuine and meaningful ways with pupils, they need to develop appropriate ways of doing so, and there needs to be a recognition that one size may not fit all, and that different approaches will be needed for different pupils. However, once high levels of engaging with pupils become the norm, and mutually respectful teacher–pupil relationships are built, teachers will benefit from developing a better understanding of pupils' needs and interests, and pupils will benefit from feeling an enhanced sense of motivation and engagement with learning.

ANNOTATED FURTHER READING

John-Akinola, Y.O., Gavin, A., O'Higgins, S.E. and Gabhain, S.N. (2014) 'Taking part in school life: Views of children', *Health Education*, 1114(1): 20-42.

> This paper reports findings from research relating to the views of children about participation in school. The study involved 248 primary school pupils aged 9-13 years.

Robinson, C. (2014) *Children, Their Voices and Their Experiences of School: What Does the Evidence Tell Us?* York, UK: Cambridge Primary Review Trust.

> This report draws on evidence from empirical studies in the United Kingdom that explore pupils' own perspectives of their primary school experiences.

Sebba, J. and Robinson, C. (2010) *Evaluation of UNICEF UK's Rights Respecting Schools Award*, London: UNICEF UK.

> UNICEF UK's Rights Respecting Schools Award helps schools use the United Nations Convention on the Rights of the Child as their values framework. A major part of working towards the award involves schools listening to the voices of their pupils and developing a culture of respect in all aspects of school life, as well as developing a culture of respect in pupils outside of school.

FURTHER READING TO SUPPORT M-LEVEL STUDY

Busher, H. (2012) 'Students as expert witnesses of teaching and learning', *Management in Education*, 26(3): 113-19. Within this article, the author advocates that student voice is a key component in constructing discourse, empowerment and citizenship in schools, and that listening to and acting upon the views of students can lead to improvements in pedagogical and organisational practices. The article takes the position that students are expert observers of school life and teachers' practices, and draws on research with students in primary and secondary schools to explore students' perspectives in relation to such practices.

Robinson, C. and Taylor, C. (2007) 'Theorising student voice: Values and perspectives', *Improving Schools*, 10(1): 5-17.

> This article explores the core values that underpin and inform student voice work. The authors argue that student voice work is an inherently ethical and moral practice, and that at the heart of student voice work are four core values: a conception of communication as dialogue; the requirement for participation and democratic inclusivity; the recognition that power relations are unequal and problematic; and the possibility for change and transformation. Throughout the article, complexities that arise in theorising student voice work are highlighted.

RELEVANT WEBSITES

The Cambridge Primary Review Trust (CPRT): http://cprtrust.org.uk/

> The CPRT builds on the work of the Cambridge Primary Review to advance the cause of high-quality primary education for all children. The CPRT has, as one of its priorities, the development of a pedagogy for primary education of repertoire, rigour, evidence and principles, with a particular emphasis on fostering the high-quality classroom talk that children's development, learning and attainment require. The website provides details of the CPRT's mission, priorities, research evidence and publications.

Pupil Voice Wales: www.pupilvoicewales.org.uk/
> This site provides practical advice on how to involve children and young people in school activities and decision-making processes. The advice given is based on the premise that professionals working with young children must realise that every child has a right to be involved, and that children and young people of all ages and backgrounds have a valuable contribution to make, and suitable platforms should be provided to enable all children to contribute. The site gives separate advice for each of nursery, primary and secondary settings.

Department for Education (DfE) (2011) Teachers' Standards: www.gov.uk/government/publications/teachers-standards
> These new Teachers' Standards set a clear baseline of expectations for the professional practice and conduct of teachers, from the point of qualification, and will apply to the vast majority of teachers, regardless of their career stage.

REFERENCES

Bragg, S. and Fielding, M. (2005) '"It's an equal thing . . . it's about achieving together': Student voice and the possibility of radical collegiality', in H. Street and J. Temperley (eds) *Improving Schools through Collaborative Enquiry*, London: Continuum, pp. 105–34.

Busher, H. (2012) 'Students as expert witnesses of teaching and learning', *Management in Education*, 29(3): 113–19.

Cheminais, R. (2008) *Engaging Pupil Voice to ensure that Every Child Matters: A Practical Guide*, London and New York: Routledge.

Department for Children, Schools and Families (DCSF). (2007) *The Children's Plan: Building Brighter Futures: Summary*, Norwich, UK: The Stationery Office.

Department for Children, Schools and Families (DCSF). (2008) *Working Together: Listening to the Voices of Children and Young People*, DCSF-00410-2008, London: DCSF.

Department for Education (DfE). (2011) *Teachers' Standards*. Retrieved from www.gov.uk/government/publications/teachers-standards (accessed October 2016).

Department for Education (DfE). (2012) Teachers' Standards. Retrieved from http://webarchive.nationalarchives.gov.uk/20130404065617/https://www.education.gov.uk/publications/eOrderingDownload/teachers%20standards.pdf (accessed 9 November 2017).

Department for Education (DfE). (2014) *Listening to and Involving Children and Young People (Statutory Guidance)*, London: DFE. Retrieved from https://www.gov.uk/government/uploads/system/uploads/attachment_data/file/437241/Listening_to_and_involving_children_and_young_people.pdf (accessed October 2016).

Department for Education and Skills (DfES). (2002) *The Education Act Statutory Instrument 2002*, London: DfES.

Department for Education and Skills (DfES). (2003) *Working Together: Giving Children and Young People a Say*, DfES/0492/2003, Nottingham, UK: DfES.

Department for Education and Skills (DfES). (2004) *Every Child Matters: Change for Children*, DfES/1081/2004, Nottingham, UK: DfES.

Flutter, J. and Rudduck, J. (2004) *Consulting Pupils: What's in It for Schools?*, London: Routledge Falmer.

Fullan, M. (1991) *The New Meaning of Educational Change*, New York: Teachers College Press.

Jelly, M., Fuller, A. and Byers, R. (2000) *Involving Pupils in Practice: Promoting Partnership with Pupils with Special Educational Needs*, London: David Fulton.

Lundy, L. (2007) '"Voice" is not enough: Conceptualizing Article 12 of the United Nations Convention of the Rights of the Child', *British Educational Research Journal*, 33(6): 927–42.

Office for Standards in Education (Ofsted). (2015) *The Common Inspection Framework: Education, Skills and Early Years*, Manchester, UK: Ofsted. Retrieved from https://www.gov.uk/government/uploads/system/uploads/attachment_data/file/461767/The_common_inspection_framework_education_skills_and_early_years.pdf (accessed October 2016).

Robinson, C. (2012) 'Student engagement: What does this mean in practice in the context of higher education institutions?', *Journal of Applied Research in Higher Education*, 4(2): 94-108.

Robinson, C. (2014) *Children, Their Voices and Their Experiences of School: What Does the Evidence Tell Us?*, York, UK: Cambridge Primary Review Trust.

Robinson, C. and Taylor, C. (2007) 'Theorising student voice: Values and perspectives', *Improving Schools*, 10(1): 5-17.

Rudduck, J. and McIntyre, D. (2007) *Improving Learning through Consulting Pupils*, London: Routledge.

Sebba, J. and Robinson, C. (2010) *Evaluation of UNICEF UK's Rights Respecting Schools' Award, Final Report*, London: UNICEF UK.

Thomson, P. (2011) 'Coming to terms with "Voice"', in G. Czerniawski and W. Kidd (eds) *The Student Voice Handbook: Bridging the Academic/Practitioner Divide*, Bingley, UK: Emerald, pp. 19-30.

United Nations (UN). (1989) *UN Convention on the Rights of the Child: General Assembly Resolution 44/25*, New York: United Nations.

Welsh Government. (2011) *Pupil Participation - Good Practice Guide*. Retrieved from www.pupilvoicewales.org.uk/uploads/publications/540.pdf (accessed October 2016).

READING

Marrying word recognition with comprehension and pleasure

Angela Gill and David Waugh

INTRODUCTION

This unit takes a holistic view of reading. There is currently a preoccupation with early reading and, in particular, systematic synthetic phonics. However, we want to emphasise that, ultimately, reading is about comprehension and pleasure, and that the basics of learning to read can be taught in a lively, engaging way so that children see reading as more than just a skill and are not deterred from future reading.

By sharing texts with children and discussing vocabulary and content, we can help them to develop a love of as well as an understanding of language. In this unit, we look at the methods used to teach reading and explore ways in which these can be used to engage children with words and texts and encourage them to value and enjoy reading.

OBJECTIVES

By this end of this unit, you should have:

- an understanding of the importance of developing an understanding of words and their spellings and why this supports comprehension;
- an understanding of the importance of reading for pleasure;
- ideas about how you can develop reading comprehension alongside word recognition.

WHY DO WE READ?

Whenever educational standards are discussed, reading is at the forefront of discussions. Newspapers would have us believe that large numbers of children leave primary school unable to read, with headlines proclaiming that one in four children cannot read by the age of 11. The truth is, of course, rather different. Although around 75 per cent of children achieve at least level 4 in Y6 SATs tests, the remaining 25 per cent are not all illiterate: most simply haven't reached level 4 yet, and many may have English as an additional rather than a first, language (note that tests were made more challenging in 2016, resulting in a drop from 80 per cent to 66 per cent achieving level 4 or above;

DfE, 2016: 5). Nevertheless, children who cannot read at the required level will be disadvantaged in many ways and will find accessing the curriculum at secondary school challenging. Of equal concern is the fact that, although international comparisons show that children in England perform relatively well in reading, they also show that the gap between the best and weakest readers is wider than in some countries, and that children in England read for pleasure less often than those in many countries (Higgins, 2013).

Task 7.2.1 You as a reader

Consider the reading you have done in the last few days and ask yourself the following questions:

- What was the purpose of your reading?
- Did you read for pleasure?
- Did you read for information?
- Did you choose to read or did you have to read?
- Did you find any words difficult to read, and how did you decode them?
- Which texts did you find the most difficult to read?
- Which texts were easiest to read?

Now, consider children's reading, its purpose and the challenges they face.

WHAT DO CHILDREN NEED TO BE ABLE TO DO?

We all engage in reading for different reasons. It might be to find out something that we need to know, to understand something that we find challenging or to discover pleasure in a new or favourite book. Children need to understand that there is a purpose to reading, and that it is not just a task to be completed because they have been asked to do so by an adult. Children need to use strategies in order to recognise and read words. These might include phonic strategies – those that help children say phonemes, read graphemes and decode words. Writing uses visual symbols that signify sounds, and many argue that to be able to read we must first learn to decode these symbols. Willingham (2015) suggests that the idea with phonics is that you give children a code for reading that can be applied to any text. But, learning to read involves more than mastering visual symbols. Children must also learn that groups of symbols make a word. They need to develop the skills to blend phonemes to be able to read words fluently. Willingham (2015) notes that children need to know where one word ends and another begins. They need to understand that groups of words can make phrases and sentences, and the position of the words in the sentence is crucial in providing meaning.

The prominence of phonics as the preferred reading approach in primary schools in England came to the fore as a result of a government review of reading, the conclusions of which are summarised in the Rose Report (DfES, 2006). Rose states that a wide range of evidence was used, including the results of the 2004 Clackmannanshire Study into synthetic phonic approaches, in order to inform the findings. The report confirmed that the case for systematic synthetic phonics was 'overwhelming'. Many schools have been teaching phonics effectively through a variety of programmes, such as *Letters and Sounds* and *Read, Write, Inc.* However, much research has been conducted that contradicts this very definite conclusion. Davis (2013) agrees that phonics-based decoding plays a vital role in pupils' reading journeys, if offered in the context of reading for meaning, but he also argues that, when teaching phonics – by correlating letter combination with sounds and by blending those sounds – we are not in fact teaching children to read. He states that:

> Reading is a matter of grasping meaning conveyed by text. While sustained attention to letter-sound correspondences can be helpful to some novice readers, we should neither assume that it is helpful to all nor confuse mastery of such correspondences with the ability to read.
>
> (Davis, 2013: 3)

In addition, Wyse and Styles (2007), when drawing together several research sources that evaluate the evidence to support the Rose review's findings (DfES, 2006), concluded that the shift to the recommendation that phonics is taught in all primary schools as the preferred reading approach was not justified by research. Davis (2013) suggests that, rather than being taught to rely completely on phonic strategies through a 'universal imposition of phonics' in primary schools, children might also use other strategies in reading that don't rely on phonic ability, such as the whole language approach (Goodman, 1982) and 'real books' strategies (Smith, 1985). He argues that well-known children's authors, such as Michael Morpurgo, Michael Rosen and Philip Pullman, have stated their opposition to the policy of '*imposed*' phonics, and that it threatens children's reading motivation.

The above strategies are top-down approaches, focusing on language and reading as a whole, rather than the bottom-up approach of beginning with individual phonemes and their corresponding graphemes. Top-down approaches use whole-words strategies, and, as Wyse and Goswami (2008) report, the ability to recognise words instantly enables fluency. They maintain that English is a complex language and is different from many other alphabetic languages, owing to the complexity of syllable structure and inconsistent spelling systems. Wyse and Goswami (2008) also assert that the complexity of reading acquisition in English means that learning to read at levels other than the phoneme may be required, and that it is unlikely that one method of learning to read will be entirely effective. Willingham (2015) too notes that a whole-word approach removes the need for 'drilling' children in letters and means children can be engaged in reading that is pleasurable and authentic.

Children can be taught that, by using their phonic knowledge and semantic knowledge, they can often make sensible guesses about words by using other words in the sentence. They can use words that they already know to help them read unfamiliar ones. They can also use other clues, such as pictures and punctuation. In the Simple View of Reading, suggested by Gough and Tunmer (1986), the above strategies are thought of as word recognition processes, as seen in Figure 7.2.1. The Rose Report (DfES, 2006) adopted this as its model of reading. However, Davis (2013) asserts that reading is much more complex than this, and that the relationship between decoding and meaning is multifaceted and interactive.

The Simple View of Reading identifies the importance of language comprehension processes. Children need to know that they can find meaning in what they are reading, and that they can access the information that they need. The whole-language approaches, mentioned above, consider this to be a key strategy. Blevins (2006) notes that knowledge of alphabetic principles enriches phonemic awareness, but that this alone is not enough. He argues that children also need to develop knowledge-based competencies for developing comprehension skills. The UKLA (2005) states that the two components of word recognition and comprehension should not be developed in isolation. Oakhill, Cain and Bryant (2003) identified key factors that children need to develop in order to improve their comprehension skills: speed and efficiency of decoding skills, vocabulary development, syntactic development, identification of the main ideas, understanding text structure and learning to make inferences. They concluded that weaknesses in these skills may impede effective comprehension.

A more detailed view of what is involved in reading can be seen in Scarborough's 'Reading Rope'. Here, language comprehension and word recognition are subdivided into key elements (see Figure 7.2.2).

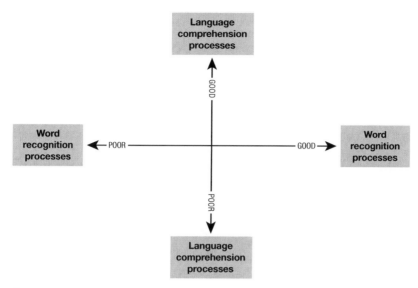

FIGURE 7.2.1 Simple view of reading model
Source: DfES (2006: 77)

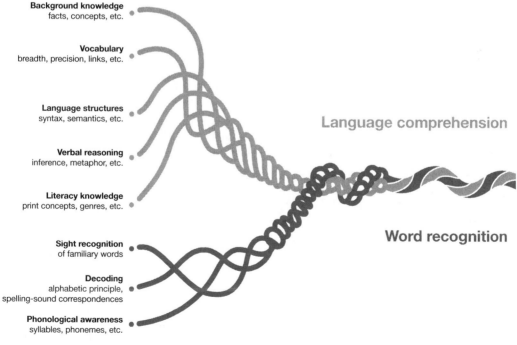

FIGURE 7.2.2 Scarborough Reading Rope
Source: Taken from EEF adaptation of rope (EEF, 2017)

The emphasis here is on a holistic view of reading in which aspects of language comprehension and word recognition come together to create a proficient reader. Although the means of achieving this may be the subject of debate, there is a universal view that it is important for children to read for pleasure.

In Wales . . .

Reading across the curriculum within the Literacy and Numeracy Framework focuses on two elements: locating, selecting and using information and responding to what has been read. Within this strand, word recognition is inherently linked with comprehension and pleasure.

Source: Welsh Assembly Government. *Language, Literacy and Communication Skills Area of Learning: Reading across the Curriculum*. See http://learning.gov.wales/docs/learningwales/publications/150717-nc-english-en-v3.pdf; http://learning.gov.wales/docs/learningwales/publications/150803-fp-framework-en.pdf; http://learning.gov.wales/docs/learningwales/publications/130415-lnf-guidance-en.pdf (accessed 1 November 2017).

READING FOR PLEASURE

Children need to know that reading can be a pleasurable experience. Attitude and motivation can significantly predict a child's performance level when reading (Medford and McGeown, 2012). Indirectly, a child will spend longer reading if their level of enjoyment is higher, and directly through an increase in cognitive engagement while reading. Indeed, Cremin (2010: 2) argued that, 'Enticing invitations need to be offered to hear, read, inhabit, explore and respond to potent texts; such invitations have the potential to increase learners' confidence and their interest in reading'.

Clark and Rumbold (2006) argued that the development of a love of reading was a key factor in determining educational success and personal development. Staff of Seven Stories (Waugh and Neaum, 2013: 103-4) maintain that there are four main areas that are developed through reading for pleasure:

- knowledge and understanding of the world;
- language acquisition and development;
- creativity and imaginative development;
- social and emotional development.

For many children, however, reading is regarded as a chore rather than a pleasure. This was evident in the PIRLS studies (2006 and 2011; see Mullis *et al.*, 2012), which showed that, although children in England performed relatively well in international studies, there has been a decline in the numbers stating that they read for pleasure. This may have resulted from a decline in reading to classes in the wake of the introduction of the first National Curriculum in 1998 and the subsequent highly prescriptive National Literacy Frameworks, which reduced the time available for what some teachers regarded as a luxury rather than a necessity.

Bowker (2012) found that, although 95 per cent of 3-4-year-olds have books read to them, with more than a third of parents (42 per cent) reading to them every day, this fell to around 33 per cent of 8-10-year-olds being read to regularly. The benefits of hearing reading include vocabulary development and experience of different sentence structures and language features, as well as exposure to stories and ideas. There are also considerable social benefits, with Cliff-Hodges (2011) maintaining that listening to reading provides a deep 'reciprocal social companionship from which there is something to be gained by both participants' (p. 20).

The 2014 National Curriculum (DfE, 2013) addresses and repeats for different age groups a key element of engagement with texts: book talk, using the phrase: 'participate in discussions about books that are read to them and those they can read for themselves'. There is very similar guidance on the importance of having books read to them for each stage - Years 1-2, Years 3-4, Years 5-6:

> Pupils should continue to have opportunities to listen frequently to stories, poems, non-fiction and other writing, including whole books and not just extracts, so that they build on what was taught previously. In this way, they also meet books and authors that they might not choose themselves.
>
> (DfE, 2013: 36)

Reading aloud to children gives access, not only to texts they might not *choose* to read independently, but also to those that they may not be *able* to read independently with ease. By performing reading skilfully, teachers can enable children to understand challenging material that might be lost on them if they read alone. You may have experienced something similar when studying a Shakespeare play at school. When you read the play, you may not have fully understood some of the language and the subtle nuances in the text. But, if you went to a performance of the play, these became much clearer. The expression and fluency that a skilled reader can bring to a text can open it up to an audience who might otherwise not be able to access it.

What we read and have read to us influences what we write. Children develop a wide, rich language through reading, which they can then use to enrich their writing. Waugh and Jolliffe (2016) suggest that children who have experienced a rich diet of literature in their early years are more likely to understand the purpose of writing and to know that we write to convey meaning.

We don't simply read traditional, paper-based, printed texts anymore. Levy (2009) suggests that the definitions of reading should be widened in order to embrace developments in technology and to acknowledge the fact that children access text in multimodal formats. She goes on to argue that we now live in a world where printed text is no longer the dominant format. We read the news on our devices, we check our email and we access text that is enhanced by images, sound and graphics. Children need to be able to read in different ways, using a variety of formats. Kress (2003) suggests that different texts demand different pathways to access meaning, and that we retrieve information from digital images differently than we do from the still images commonly used in books.

In Northern Ireland . . .

The Northern Ireland Curriculum states that children:

> should be given opportunities to read for different purposes, developing strategies for researching, understanding, managing and refining information from traditional and digital sources. They should be encouraged, through stimulating and fun activities, to read widely for enjoyment and information. Over time, with praise and encouragement, they should have opportunities to engage independently with more challenging and lengthy texts including those in digital format, whilst reflecting, analysing and discussing the meaning of the text.
>
> (Northern Ireland Curriculum, 2007: 51)

Source: Council for Curriculum, Examinations and Assessment (CCEA). (2007) *The Northern Ireland Curriculum*, Belfast, CCEA. Retrieved from http://ccea.org.uk/sites/default/files/docs/curriculum/area_of_ learning/fs_northern_ireland_curriculum_primary.pdf (accessed 1 November 2017).

TYPES OF TEXT

Eyres (2000) describes a text as a place where the symbols of language, meanings and the knowledge of speakers, listeners, readers and writers all come together. He maintains that a text is a connected spoken or written language that is capable of being discussed and analysed. Children encounter different types of text in their everyday lives, from the signs they pass as they walk down the street, to the stories they share with an adult and the graphics they see when using electronic devices. Although children may find that their early experiences of reading are based on fiction, their immediate environment is full of texts that provide information. There are many different texts that children are expected to engage with and read, and many of these genres have different conventions and characteristics that they must master.

To begin to understand the characteristics of different types of text, it is important that children hear them read aloud, frequently and by a skilled reader. Waugh and Jolliffe (2016) suggest that the teacher provides a model for expressive reading and indirectly demonstrates how to bring a text to life, while Cremin (2010: 6) maintained:

> In order to motivate young readers, teachers need to balance literacy instruction, which tends to focus upon decoding and comprehension, with a reading for pleasure pedagogy, which focuses more upon engagement and response.

However, we maintain that engagement is still possible when teaching word recognition and developing spelling skills, and that, when taught successfully, these skills have a significant impact upon children's comprehension skills.

CAN PHONICS BE FUN?

When children are introduced to phonics, they often begin with a small number of letters and learn the common sounds each letter makes. Typically, the letters might be s, a, t, p, i and n (or m in some programmes). Young children are used to finding meaning in their activities, but s and its sss sound carry little or no meaning, unless the sss sound is part of a name, place or person. A key element in phonics is making learning meaningful. Teachers use children's names and words they are familiar with to make phonics real. They might, for example, play sounds i-spy: 'I hear with my little ear someone's name beginning with sss', and so on.

Children in English primary schools spend a lot of time lining up or taking turns to move from tables to a carpeted area, and so forth. Such times can be problematic, as there is potential for disruption, noise and even accidents. However, a simple class management device can ensure calm movement and active learning: 'When I say the sound of the beginning of your name, please go and line up', or 'Everyone who has a jumper whose colour begins with /b/ can sit down', and so on.

VIVID EXAMPLE

To engage some older children with phonics, Benjamina felt that some of her Year 5 class were still unfamiliar with some grapheme-phoneme correspondences (GPCs), which they should have known by the end of Year 2. These children were often unable to use phonic strategies to read or spell unfamiliar words. Benjamina read about *Football Snap* and decided to try to arouse children's interest in GPCs through an activity that focused on one of their interests. She made cards with the names of football teams, such as the ones in the activity below, and then explained that members of the group could match teams that had phonemes in common, and that, if they did, they won a point and were able to read a football result, while emphasising a common phoneme that made a match possible. Thus, children came up with:

Leicester 4   Tottenham 2
Arsenal 1   Bradford City 3

Benjamina found that some children who had previously taken little interest in phonics and in developing their reading were more engaged and made good progress in developing their knowledge and understanding of GPCs.

Task 7.2.2 Football matches

Look at the teams below and see how many matches you can find. There are lots of possibilities!

Arsenal	Bradford City	Sunderland	Tottenham Hotspur
Doncaster Rovers	Leicester City	Hull City	Ipswich Town

This activity could also be done with children's names, names of TV programmes, places, pop stars and celebrities.

SPELLING

Accurate spelling is crucial to our understanding of texts. Without it, we can be confused about the meaning an author is trying to convey. English is full of *homophones* (words that sound the same but are spelled differently – for example, *their* and *there*, *see* and *sea*, *bold* and *bowled*); *homographs* (words that are written the same but pronounced differently – for example, a *lead* weight and a dog's *lead*); and *homonyms* (words that are spelled and pronounced the same but have different meanings – for example, a brown *bear* and to *bear* the pain). English spelling can be challenging, even for experienced readers and writers, but, for the inexperienced or those for whom English is a second language, it can be a major hurdle in their literacy development.

The English National Curriculum requires children to learn prescribed lists of words, but what strategies are available to help them to do this? A typical approach might be to learn spelling rules.

Task 7.2.3 Spelling rules, OK?

What do the following words have in common?

eight, either, foreign, forfeit, height, heir, neighbour, neither, science, seize, society, sovereign, veil, weight, weird

The answer is that all of the words are exceptions to the spelling 'rule' 'i before e except after c': a rule that most people cite when asked for an example, but this is probably because it rhymes and is easy to remember, rather than owing to the quality of the rule (it makes a little more sense if you make it 'i before e except after c – when the word rhymes with me', although there are still exceptions). Because 'i before e except after c' is not a very reliable rule, some people are sceptical about the value of learning rules. However, there are actually some very reliable rules and generalisations. Look at the following task and see if you can produce rules or generalisations.

Task 7.2.4 Spelling generalisations

- Which letters are not used to end English words?
- What do you do to make a noun ending with 'y' plural (for example, baby, monkey, boy, lady)?
- Which letter almost always follows 'q'?
- Do any English words begin with a double consonant, for example, 'bb', 'cc'?

Answers are given at the end of the unit.

There are many more generalisations that children can be taught and can discover through investigations. These can include learning how prefixes and suffixes are added to words to modify their meanings and how this affects spelling. As children gain a better understanding of how words are formed by combining morphemes (units of meaning), they will be better able to decode and understand what they are reading, as well as developing their spelling.

If the National Curriculum spellings (DfE, 2013) are taught well, it is possible to learn around five times the required number of spellings while developing strategies for reading and spelling new words. There can also be significant benefits for developing comprehension skills when children gain a deeper understanding of morphemes, their meaning and usage. Look, for example, at a word from the Y5-6 list: *accompany*. It can be modified with the addition of prefixes or suffixes (*affixes* or *bound morphemes*) to create several other words, including *accompanies, accompanied, accompanying, accompaniment, unaccompanied*.

By exploring words in this way, and using a dictionary or spell-checker to confirm that the derivatives actually exist and to check their meanings, we develop strategies for modifying other words that do not appear in the lists. This will enhance understanding of words and the way in which they can be segmented into morphemes to be read and spelled. This will also broaden vocabulary to support reading comprehension and writing. Just as teachers' engagement with and enthusiasm for texts can influence children (Cremin, 2010), their modelling of a range of simple but effective strategies and an interest in words will engage pupils' interest too.

BRINGING WORD RECOGNITION AND COMPREHENSION TOGETHER

Having considered aspects of comprehension and reading for pleasure, as well as word level reading, this unit concludes with an example of a teacher bringing these two key elements together.

VIVID EXAMPLE: INTERACTING WITH TEXTS

Wasim wanted his Year 4 class to enjoy and engage with the story he was reading to them. He felt that some children sometimes gave the impression that they were listening when he read to them, but were actually not sufficiently engaged that they were able to answer questions or take part effectively in associated activities such as hot-seating. Wasim felt that an issue for some was the inclusion in the story of some vocabulary with which they were unfamiliar. He decided to make vocabulary cards with names and other words from the story and to give these to each of five tables of children, one per child, before reading to them. He asked them to look at their words, read them to each other and discuss what they meant. He checked that everyone knew his or her word by asking each person to read it aloud, and then he told them that he would pause occasionally during the story to ask whose word had appeared.

small ball	playground	Chelsea	Lauren
Mrs Wright	Adam	Mark Langley	goalkeeper
stumbled	Grace Darling	baby sister	skipping
trot	bemused	pace	dribbling
hesitated	recovered	stunned	charged
goal	school field	chasing	huddled
focused	knee	expression	surrounded

Source: From Waugh (2015)

This worked very well, and Wasim discovered that children were able to use their words accurately when answering questions and could explain how the words fitted into the story. He was also able to use other forms of some words, for example *stumble, stumbled, stumbling* and *stumbles*, and discuss these when children mentioned them. He found that children's engagement and interest were such when he read the excerpt that they asked if they could have word cards next time the story was read to them.

Wasim's strategy could be extended to finding synonyms and antonyms or spotting and discussing phrases. It might also lead to writing activities in which children use their word or phrase cards as starting points for writing about a story. A focus on spelling might include looking at sound-symbol correspondences, as well as morphemes and etymology.

Task 7.2.5 Developing comprehension

Consider how the word and phrase card strategy might be extended to develop comprehension. How could it be used as a starting point for:

- retelling a story;
- hot-seating;
- summarising a story?

SUMMARY

Without an emphasis on reading for pleasure and meaning, there is little incentive for children to learn the word level elements. By placing a high value on reading and looking for opportunities to make word recognition and spelling engaging and interesting, we can help develop readers who are able to approach new texts with confidence and enthusiasm. This can lead to improved reading comprehension and stronger understanding of language.

ANSWERS FOR TASK 7.2.4

- Which letters are not used to end English words? *v*, *j* and *q*
- What do you do to make a noun ending with 'y' plural (for example, *baby, monkey, boy, lady*)? If a vowel precedes the *y*, add an *s*; if a consonant precedes the *y*, remove the *y* and add *-ies*, for example, *babies, monkeys, boys, ladies*.
- Which letter almost always follows 'q'? *u*
- Do any English words begin with a double consonant, for example, 'bb', 'cc'? No. Words such as *llama* come from other languages.

ANNOTATED FURTHER READING

Higgins, S. (2013) 'What can we learn from research?', in D. Waugh and S. Neaum (eds) *Beyond Early Reading*, London: Critical Publishing, pp. 4-17.

> Professor Steve Higgins, who has conducted meta-analyses on literacy development, sums up key findings in this chapter. He draws upon studies from around the world, as well as the Toolkit, to show what works well in schools. Given the depth of research behind the chapter, this is a good starting point for preparation for M-level studies in this area.

Gamble, N. (2012) *Exploring Children's Literature: Reading with Pleasure and Purpose*, London: Sage.

> See this book for ideas for using literature in the classroom and engaging children's interest, as well as developing reading for pleasure.

Waugh, D., Neaum, S. and Waugh, R. (2016) *Children's Literature in Primary Schools*, London: Sage.

> This book is useful for broad coverage of a range of aspects and genres of children's literature. It also includes chapters on developing a love of reading and sharing literature with children.

FURTHER READING TO SUPPORT M-LEVEL STUDY

Cremin, T., Mottram, M., Bearne, E. and Goodwin, P. (2008) 'Exploring teachers' knowledge of children's literature', *Cambridge Journal of Education*, 38(4): 449-64.

> There are several articles by Cremin *et al.* that discuss research teachers' knowledge of children's literature. This one may be particularly useful for those requiring background reading for M-level work.

RELEVANT WEBSITES

Research Rich Pedagogies: https://researchrichpedagogies.org/research/reading-for-pleasure

> A new Open Univerity research-informed website on reading for pleasure, with practical ideas, surveys to review practice and rich examples of classroom work written by teachers for teachers. An energising site to find ideas and to share your own development work.

My Read: www.myread.org/how.htm

> A wide range of literacy discussions and resources to support development of reading skills in the middle years can be found here.

Mr Thorne Does Phonics: www.mrthornenetwork.com/phonics

> See this website for practical ideas for teaching phonics, as well as excellent modelling of enunciation. It also encompasses wider literacy guidance.

Literacy Shed: www.literacyshed.com

> This is packed with ideas and resources, including images and films to use in lessons.

The UK Literacy Association: www.ukla.org

> The UKLA offers a range of resources, including *Building Communities of Readers*, a CPD booklet to help teachers develop as 'reading teachers' and to record children's attitudes.

The National Literacy Trust: www.literacytrust.org.uk

> The NLT provides a wealth of research and practice materials. Its *Literacy Guide for Primary Schools* and *Annual Literacy Review* both contain sections on reading for pleasure.

REFERENCES

Bowker®. (2012) *Understanding the Children's Book Consumer in the Digital Age*. Market research carried out by Bowker in the United States. Retrieved from www.bowker.com/news/2012/Young-Adult-Books-Attract-Growing-Numbers-of-Adult-Fans.html (accessed 10 January 2018).

Blevins, J. (2006) 'Word-based morphology', *Journal of Linguistics*, 42(3): 531–73.

Clark, C. and Rumbold, K. (2006) *Reading for Pleasure*, London: National Literacy Trust.

Cliff-Hodges, G. (2011) 'Textual drama: The value of reading aloud', *English Drama Media*, 19: 19–25.

Cremin, T. (2010) 'Motivating children to write with purpose and passion', in P. Goodwin (ed.) *The Literate Classroom*, 3rd edn, Abingdon, UK: Routledge, pp. 117–26.

Davis, A. (2013) *To Read or Not to Read: Decoding Synthetic Phonics* (Impact 20: Philosophical Perspectives on Education Policy), London: Philosophy of Education Society of Great Britain.

Department for Education (DfE). (2013) *The National Curriculum in England*, London: DfE.

Department for Education (DfE). (2016) *National Curriculum Assessments at Key Stage 2 in England (provisional)*, London: DfE.

Department for Education and Skills (DfES). (2006) *Independent Review of the Teaching of Early Reading, Final Report* (Rose Report), March, ed. J. Rose, 0201-2006DOC-EN, Nottingham, UK: DfES.

Education Endowment Foundation (EEF). (2017) *Improving Literacy in Key Stage Two*, London: Education Endowment Foundation.

Eyres, I. (2000) *Primary English*, London: Paul Chapman.

Goodman, K. (1982) *Language and Literacy*, Boston, MA: Routledge & Kegan.

Gough, P. and Tunmer, W. (1986) 'Decoding, reading, and reading disability', *Remedial and Special Education*, 7: 6–10.

Higgins, S. (2013) 'What can we learn from research?', in D. Waugh and S. Neaum (eds) *Beyond Early Reading*, Northwich, UK: Critical Publishing, pp. 4–17.

Kress, G. (2003) *Literacy in the New Media Age*, London: Taylor Francis.

Levy, R. (2009) 'Children's perceptions of reading and the use of reading schemes', *Cambridge Journal of Education*, 39(3): 361–77.

Medford, E. and McGeown, S. (2012) 'Cognitive and motivational factors for reading: The need for a domain specific approach to motivation', in J. Franco and A. Svensgaard (eds) *Psychology of Motivation: New Research*, New York: Nova Science, pp. 187–208.

Mullis, I.V.S., Martin, M.O., Foy, P. and Drucker, K.T. (2012) *The PIRLS 2011 International Results in Reading*, Chestnut Hill, MA: TIMSS and PIRLS International Study Center, Boston College. Retrieved from https://timssandpirls.bc.edu/pirls2011/downloads/P11_IR_FullBook.pdf (accessed 20 June 2012).

Oakhill, J., Cain, K. and Bryant, P. (2003) 'The dissociation of word reading and text comprehension: Evidence from component skills', *Language & Cognitive Processes*, 18: 443-68.

Smith, F. (1985) *Reading*, Cambridge, UK: Cambridge University Press.

United Kingdom Literacy Association (UKLA). (2005) *Submission to the Review of Best Practice in the Teaching of Early Reading*, Royston, UK: UKLA.

Waugh, D. (2015) *Girls Can't Play Football*, Bishop's Castle, UK: Constance Books.

Waugh, D. and Jolliffe, W. (2016) *English 5-11*, 3rd edn, London: Routledge.

Waugh, D. and Neaum, S. (eds) (2013) *Beyond Early Reading*, London: Critical Publishing.

Willingham, D. (2015) *Raising Kids Who Read: What Teachers and Parents Can Do*, San Francisco, CA: Jossey-Bass.

Wyse, D. and Goswami, U. (2008) 'Synthetic phonics and the teaching of reading', *British Education Research Journal*, 34(6): 691-710.

Wyse, D. and Styles, M. (2007) 'Synthetic phonics and the teaching of reading: The debate surrounding England's Rose Report', *Literacy*, 41(1): 35-42.

THE CREATIVE AND THE CRITICAL

Grammar and punctuation

Debra Myhill

INTRODUCTION

Grammar and punctuation are somewhat paradoxical aspects of the primary curriculum and certainly shrouded with controversy. On the one hand, all teachers would probably agree that grammar and punctuation are important; on the other hand, few teachers are excited by the prospect of teaching grammar and punctuation. In this unit, I hope to challenge this paradoxical ambivalence and inspire you to see grammar and punctuation as the lifeblood of being creative and critical readers and writers. Reflecting on the challenge of writing, children's author Tim Bowler observed:

> Why is writing so tricky? Because it requires mastery of two conflicting skills: a creative skill and a critical skill. The former is of the imagination, the latter of the intellect, and they come from different brain hemispheres. To write well, we have to employ both to maximum effect.
>
> (Bowler, 2002)

His comment draws attention to the complementarity of the creative and the critical in writing and is a salient reminder that the teaching of writing needs both to address the creative, imaginative engagement of writers and to help them hone their critical faculties. Grammar and punctuation are inextricably intertwined, and punctuation choices are strongly intertwined with grammatical choices, and they are key tools of this critical engagement.

Part of the problem is that grammar is often highly politicised, and everyone has an opinion! When I tell people that one strand of my research is grammar, I am nearly always treated to a diatribe on the parlous state of the nation's grammar and an account of that person's particular grammatical *bête noire*. Newspapers will take any research report on grammar, regardless of its actual findings, and present it as evidence of the nation's linguistic decline. All of this is highly regrettable, as it leads to reductive polemical debate, entrenched positions and ideological arguments. At the Centre for Research in Writing at the University of Exeter we have adopted a different position. Our research focus has been on writing and the teaching of writing, and, in addition to looking at children's composing processes and the relationship between talk and writing, we have conducted a substantial sequence of studies investigating grammar. Our fundamental goal has been to understand better the relationship between grammar and writing, not to prove an ideological point. This unit draws heavily on this body of research, all of which has been conducted in classrooms and has involved working closely with teachers. Our research challenges both conservative views that grammar is the remedial solution to the nation's literacy ills, and liberal views that grammar is unnecessary, stifling of creativity, and redundant.

OBJECTIVES

By the end of this unit, you should:

- understand the role of grammar in the curriculum;
- understand the relationship between grammar and meaning;
- understand the concept of grammar as choice;
- know how to plan purposefully to teach grammar and punctuation.

THE ROLE OF GRAMMAR IN THE CURRICULUM

The debate about whether we should teach grammar or not has been a source of controversy for more than 50 years. Curiously, this is a debate that has been confined to anglophone countries, particularly the UK, the USA, Australia and New Zealand. In many European and Asian countries, the teaching of grammar is routine and uncontested. But, in the 1960s, the Dartmouth Conference in the USA, which brought together teachers, teacher educators and researchers from anglophone countries across the world, made an influential decision that teaching grammar was not a relevant or useful aspect of a language curriculum. This decision was shaped by a view that being able to label and identify grammatical features made no difference to learners' proficiency as language users or, worse still, had a 'harmful effect on the improvement of writing' (Braddock, Lloyd-Jones and Schoer, 1963: 37). This view has been reinforced subsequently by reviews and research studies, all of which concluded that teaching grammar has no beneficial impact on students' writing (Hillocks and Smith, 1991; Andrews *et al.*, 2006; Graham and Perin, 2007).

What this debate reveals is a lack of clarity about why grammar might be included in a language curriculum and what knowing about grammar might achieve. Broadly speaking, a place for grammar in the curriculum might be described in one of three ways – to help learners:

- to avoid making mistakes in speaking and writing their own language;
- to understand the structure of their own language;
- to develop understanding about how texts work and make meaning.

The first of these focuses on grammar as a tool for error correction and thus has its focus on accuracy in written expression. This is, perhaps, Joe Public's view of what grammar is for, and both politicians and journalists tend to draw on this rationale for grammar teaching, frequently citing examples of grammatical 'abuses' that grammatical knowledge would resolve – for example, understanding subject and verb agreement. The second perspective focuses rather more on supporting learners in developing a body of knowledge about the grammar of their own language, just as, elsewhere in the curriculum, children learn about, for example, the solar system, the rain cycle or the Romans. It is knowledge for its own sake, rather than knowledge designed for real-world application. The final perspective is directed much more towards grammar as a resource that helps learners to develop greater knowledge about how language works and how texts make meaning: for example, understanding how the passive can hide the identity of who performs an action. These differing perspectives, of course, are not right or wrong but reflect different valorisations of grammar.

At the same time, underpinning these differing perspectives are contrasting theoretical views of grammar as prescriptive or descriptive. A *prescriptive* view of grammar sees grammar as a bench-mark or user manual outlining how we should speak or write. Traditionally, 'school grammar' has been prescriptive, a 'gold standard' that learners must work to acquire. The prescriptive theorisation of grammar is strongly aligned to a view of grammar in the curriculum as a tool to avoid making mistakes. In contrast, a *descriptive* view of grammar is more concerned with studying and analysing how language is used, rather than how it should be used. So, for example, descriptive linguists study, not only the grammar of formal writing, but also the grammar of spoken language, the grammar of texting and how grammar alters in different situational contexts, such as when writing formal letters or in advertising material. This theorisation of grammar aligns most strongly with the view that the place of grammar in the curriculum is to develop understanding about how texts work in context. In general, most modern linguists and education professionals tend towards a descriptive view of grammar, but it is important to recognise that there are times when all teachers are prescriptive because they need to be. For example, teachers will all be familiar with the very common error of writing 'should of' rather than 'should have' and, in correcting this in children's writing, teachers are adopting a prescriptive stance. Likewise, some punctuation decisions are right or wrong, although many more are a matter of choice.

So what role for grammar does the National Curriculum (DfE, 2014) present? No clear rationale for the inclusion of grammar is expressed at any point, but it is possible to trace each of the three perspectives above in the requirements set out in curriculum documentation. A prescriptivist, error-correction view of grammar is evident in the statement that, 'Pupils should be taught to control their speaking and writing consciously and to use Standard English' (DfE, 2014: 5), and an emphasis on knowing the structure of English is evident in the requirement that children 'should learn to recognise and use the terminology through discussion and practice' (DfE, 2014: 64). In the preamble to Appendix 2, which sets out the precise expectations for grammar and punctuation, a more descriptivist view is expressed, suggesting that learning grammar supports understanding of how language works, and noting the importance of learning in a context: 'Explicit knowledge of grammar is, however, very important, as it gives us more conscious control and choice in our language. Building this knowledge is best achieved through a focus on grammar within the teaching of reading, writing and speaking' (DfE, 2014: 64). However, as it stands, the National Curriculum is more noteworthy for outlining the content of grammar and punctuation that should be covered than for its clear articulation of a purpose for grammar in the curriculum.

In Northern Ireland . . .

The Northern Ireland Curriculum states that:

> Children should develop the ability to manage and communicate information effectively in their writing in order to produce more demanding, imaginative and factual texts including those in digital format. They should, over time, use a wider range of vocabulary choice, sentence structures and punctuation in their writing for a range of audiences. They should be helped to develop both the compositional and secretarial aspects of writing through planning, drafting, redrafting, presenting and evaluating their work.
>
> (CCEA, 2007: 51)

Source: Council for Curriculum, Examinations and Assessment (CCEA). (2007) *The Northern Ireland Curriculum*, Belfast, CCEA. Retrieved from http://ccea.org.uk/sites/default/files/docs/curriculum/area_of_learning/fs_northern_ireland_curriculum_primary.pdf (accessed 2 November 2011).

In Wales . . .

Writing across the curriculum is addressed in the Literacy and Numeracy Framework. See links below.

Source: Welsh Assembly Government. *Language, Literacy and Communication Skills Area of Learning: Reading across the Curriculum*.
http://learning.gov.wales/docs/learningwales/publications/150717-nc-english-en-v3.pdf
http://learning.gov.wales/docs/learningwales/publications/150803-fp-framework-en.pdf
http://learning.gov.wales/docs/learningwales/publications/130415-lnf-guidance-en.pdf
(all accessed 2 November 2017).

GRAMMAR AS CHOICE: A THEORETICAL RATIONALE FOR GRAMMAR IN THE CURRICULUM

It is important, then, as with all aspects of teaching, to approach the teaching of grammar and punctuation with a principled understanding of their role in the curriculum. Our research has been securely underpinned by a theoretical model that draws together different disciplinary perspectives on the teaching of writing and a functional approach to conceptualising grammar. Considering writing first, cognitive research on writing emphasises that writing is fundamentally an act of decision-making (Kellogg, 2008), from decisions about whether to write on paper or screen, to decisions about content and ideas, and decisions about structure, phrasing, imagery and word choices. These decisions are made within the process of writing, framed as three core activities: planning, generating text and reviewing (Alamargot and Chanquoy, 2001). Crucially, these three activities are not linear and chronological but recursive, and decision-making is a critical element in each of these, so that writers have to develop increasing accomplishment in making writerly decisions and choices. At the same time, writing is always a social process enacted within communities of writers (Prior, 2005). Writing classrooms are particular communities of writers where what is valued in writing is shaped by individual teachers' own values, by what the curriculum chooses to value (Dyson, 2008), and by children's own out-of-school writing experiences. Decision-making as a writer is, therefore, both a cognitive and a social process, shaped by the discourses of the classroom and by experiences of the world.

Grammatical decision-making is one element of this broader set of decisions that always surround the act of writing. Carter and McCarthy (2006) distinguish between two different, but equally valid, ways of thinking about grammar: grammar as structure, referring to the system of language and the labels we use to describe it, and the grammar of choice, referring to the way that grammatical choices we make are part of the way meanings are created and communicated. Just consider for a moment something as apparently straightforward as coordinating with 'and': in both *Mr Gumpy's Outing* by John Burningham and *The Very Hungry Caterpillar* by Eric Carle, there are two very long listing sentences, but Burningham chooses to use 'and' in his list, whereas Carle chooses to use commas:

> Then Mr Gumpy and the goat and the calf and the chickens and the sheep and the pig and the dog and the cat and the rabbit and the children all swam to the bank and climbed out to dry in the sun.

> On Saturday he ate through one piece of chocolate cake, one ice-cream cone, one pickle, one slice of Swiss cheese, one slice of salami, one lollipop, one piece of cherry pie, one sausage, one cupcake, and one slice of watermelon.

Both, of course, are grammatically correct, and both are effective sentences in the context of their respective stories, but that very tiny choice about whether to use 'and' or a comma subtly shifts the effect created by these two sentences. Arguably, Burningham's choice gives more emphasis to the accumulation of creatures that swam to the bank – it is less important which animals they were, but what is significant is that they all swam, children and animals. In contrast, Carle's comma choice means that the food itself is foregrounded, it is what the caterpillar eats that is interesting, as well as how much. This is the grammar of choice.

This conceptual view of grammar aligns very strongly to the functional view of grammar espoused by Halliday and the Sydney School. Halliday (1975, 2002) argues that grammar and grammar choices are at the heart of making meaning, and that, therefore, grammar is a rich resource for language users. When we express ourselves, *how* we say it is as important as *what* we say, as all commercial advertisers and public relations officers know well. A menu choice of 'Oven-roasted Devon Red Ruby Beef on a golden Yorkshire pudding with horseradish and peppercorn cream' communicates subtly different messages to a hungry customer than 'Beef on Yorkshire pud', and, when Tony Blair used to say, as he often did, 'What I would say to you is this', he was filling the space with words that said nothing, to give himself time to think of what he really wanted to say. So, these choices we make about the grammatical and syntactical shaping of sentences and texts are all key to how we communicate our ideas and how we manage our relationship with our readers. This is a long way from grammar as a tool for remediating the linguistic sins of the nation's children. In reflecting on Halliday's theoretical view of grammar, Derewianka and Jones (2010) make this distinction very clear: 'Whereas traditional approaches conceive of grammar as a set of structures which can be assessed as correct or incorrect, Halliday sees language as a resource, a meaning-making system through which we interactively shape and interpret our world and ourselves' (2010: 9).

PEDAGOGICAL PRINCIPLES

Our own research has taken this idea of grammar as choice and the importance of looking at how grammar creates meaning to develop a pedagogical approach that brings together grammar, reading and writing in a creative synergy. The evidence from this research is that it has a positive impact on students' writing outcomes (Myhill *et al.*, 2012). Although we recognise that there are times when we need to help young writers to be grammatically accurate, our view is that the most significant potency in understanding grammar goes beyond accuracy and helps writers to be more effective shapers of text. Accordingly, our pedagogy is more concerned with the rhetorical effects of language choices and how they construct meanings, and it is less concerned with the identification and naming of grammatical structures. Crucially, our goal is to open what we have called 'a repertoire of possibilities' (Myhill *et al.*, 2012: 148), not to teach only about correct ways of writing.

To support this approach, we adopt four key teaching principles that inform the design of teaching materials and classroom interactions. These are important because so often teachers are encouraged to seek quick-fix solutions or off-the-shelf material, but we believe that the most powerful learning occurs when teachers have a deep, embedded, principled understanding of what they are doing. Our four key teaching principles are:

- Make a link between the grammar being introduced and how it works in the writing being taught.
- Explain the grammar through examples, not lengthy explanations.
- Build in high-quality discussion about grammar and its effects.
- Use examples from authentic texts to link writers to the broader community of writers.

To help make clear what each of these principles mean, why they are important, and how they translate into classroom practice, I will take each one in turn and explore it in more detail.

Make a link between the grammar being introduced and how it works in the writing being taught

This principle supports learners in making connections between what they are learning grammatically and the choices they can make as a writer, and, at the same time, heightens their awareness of how language works. Being able to understand the relationship between a grammatical choice and its effect in a particular text is part of understanding the writer's craft and recognising the possibilities open to a writer. Moreover, considering how grammatical structures create meaning in specific contexts reinforces the importance of context and avoids students acquiring redundant learning, such as 'complex sentences are good sentences'.

One example of this kind of connection-making is embedded in a unit of work looking at writing like a scientist. There are many grammatical points you could explore, such as using topic-specific nouns and verbs (gestating, friction, lifecycle, etc.) or using a passive voice to foreground key information in a sentence, but one thing you might investigate is how well-chosen adverbials support writing with the precision of a scientist. In the example below, the adverbials are important in providing specific additional information about *how* the male kangaroos behave at breeding time and *why* they behave that way.

Writing focus	Writing a science text
Grammar focus	How adverbials are used to add precise detail in an information or explanation text
Real text example	Male kangaroos push, pull and wrestle *with their arms*, and may kick *out with their great feet, using their strong tail for support*. They are battling *for females at breeding time* (from *Children's A-Z Encyclopedia*, by Miles Kelley)

This exemplifies the first key teaching principle of making links, because the attention to the grammatical structure selected (adverbials) links explicitly with the learning about writing that the teacher is addressing (being precise when writing like a scientist).

Task 7.3.1 Exploring punctuation and meaning

Browse through some of the texts you read with children in your class and look closely at how they use punctuation. Using one or two examples from these texts, create an activity that would allow you to help children see a link between a writer's choice of how to punctuate a sentence and the meaning s/he wants to convey.

Explain the grammar through examples, not lengthy explanations

This principle avoids lessons becoming deflected into being grammar lessons but supports conceptual development of grammatical understanding. By using examples, children are able to see the grammatical structure and hear the grammatical terminology used to describe it – we learn best when we learn in context, rather than in decontextualized modes (consider how we learn vocabulary through encountering words used in context, both orally and in text). Crucially, it also means that children can access the structure and discuss its effect in a text, even when they cannot remember the grammatical name. Our research provides clear evidence that young writers often successfully integrate a grammatical structure that has been taught into their writing, but very few of them can confidently name the structure.

An example of this for younger children might be in the context of playing with the characters in *The Gruffalo*.

First, the class together thinks of a new forest animal that could be in the story, such as a bat, a frog or a mole. The teacher then gives children cards with the prepositional phrases in *The Gruffalo* printed on them and asks them to sort them into prepositional phrases about the Gruffalo and prepositional phrases about where the animals live. The teacher uses the term prepositional phrases and highlights that each one begins with a preposition, but no more than that. When the phrases are sorted, the class discusses how the prepositional phrases create the setting and tell us about the forest and where each animal lives. Together, the class creates prepositional phrases to describe where their new character lives and collaboratively composes a new section of the story involving that character.

Writing focus	Writing a narrative
Grammar focus	How prepositional phrases can establish the setting in a story
Real text example	*In a deep dark wood*; *in my logpile house*; *by the stream*; *over his back*; *in my treetop house*; *on the end of his nose*; *by this lake* . . . (from *The Gruffalo*, by Julia Donaldson)

This exemplifies the principle of using examples through the use of cards with prepositional phrases on them for children to sort and by giving children the opportunity to create their own.

Task 7.3.2 Teaching grammar through examples

Look back at some of your recent lessons teaching writing and consider whether you could have included more explicit grammar teaching that was relevant to your writing focus. Taking one of these, think of a way to explain the grammar through examples that does not use a card sort, as in the above example, but adopts a different strategy.

Build in high-quality discussion about grammar and its effects

As Britton famously said, 'learning floats on a sea of talk' (1983: 11), and this principle is underpinned by our understanding of the importance of talk for learning in general across the curriculum. In the context of grammar as choice, constructive exploratory talk enables young writers' learning about the choices available to them to develop. The teacher's input is very important in initiating learning and drawing attention to how a particular grammatical construction is working, but that learning cannot simply be transmitted from teacher to learner: it has to become independently understood by the learner. So, talk is key to moving students from superficial learning about grammar (e.g. add adjectives to create description) to deep learning (e.g. some adjectives are redundant because the noun is descriptive), and it is key to developing independent thinking about and taking ownership of the language choices they make. In particular, there are two focuses for talk about grammatical choices that are particularly constructive: First, extended talk about linguistic choices, which fosters discussion about choices, possibilities and effects, enables young writers to explore how language is working and to develop their own thinking about this. Second, talk allows for verbalising the effect a particular language choice has in the context of the text being considered, cementing the learning about choices and effects.

An example of an activity that is set up to foster high-quality discussion might be in the context of a unit on writing fictional narrative, where the teacher wants to support understanding of how to create and develop character. Using an extract from *Matilda* where the readers first meet Matilda's father, Mr Wormwood, the teacher leads a discussion about what kind of man we think Mr Wormwood is and what it is about Dahl's description that creates that impression. By looking closely at the noun phrase – 'a small ratty-looking man whose front teeth stuck out underneath a thin ratty moustache' – the teacher facilitates talk about each of these descriptive choices and explores how Dahl makes us infer what kind of man he is by showing us what he looks like. In pairs, children then play with changing these descriptions (e.g. 'a cuddly bear-like man') and discussing how these changes create different impressions.

Writing focus	Writing a fictional narrative
Grammar focus	How noun phrases can invite readers to infer character
Real text example	'Mr Wormwood was a small ratty-looking man whose front teeth stuck out underneath a thin ratty moustache' (from *Matilda*, by Roald Dahl)

Task 7.3.3 Planning high-quality dialogic talk

Taking the activity described above, plan in more detail how you would manage both the initial whole-class discussion and feedback from the paired discussion. Think about:

- what might be the key questions you would ask and in what order you would sequence them;
- how you will draw out discussion and extend student responses;
- how you will follow through and probe children's understanding;
- how you will avoid leading them to a predetermined right answer.

Use examples from authentic texts to link writers to the broader community of writers

The principle of using authentic texts has been exemplified in each of the three examples above, and it is important as the context for the three principles above. One reason for the importance of using authentic texts is that it avoids the pitfalls of examples that are created to exemplify a grammar point, as very often these are artificial and unauthentic. This includes texts written by teachers to support teaching points – a golden rule is that, if you can't find an authentic text that uses a construction you are teaching, perhaps you are teaching the wrong point! However, a more powerful reason for using authentic texts is that it highlights the relationship between being a reader and being a writer, and being within a community of writers. Using the many rich and creative texts written for children allows teachers to choose texts that will engage and motivate their students and that can be a source of shared enjoyment in their own right. It generates opportunities to explore and draw out what writers do and the choices they make, so that children are aware that they too have choices and possibilities when they write. By becoming more aware of writers' choices in texts being read, we help children to make more writerly choices themselves and to be more aware of the readers of their own writing.

Task 7.3.4 Reviewing your planning

Look at some of your existing planning for the teaching of writing and consider how you might adapt it to include a relevant focus on grammatical choice. Remember to think about the learning focus for writing and the learning needs of the children, and use the four key teaching principles to inform the design of your planning.

SUMMARY

This unit has outlined a way of thinking about grammar as choice and has illustrated what this might look like in classroom practice. We see this as a creative relationship between grammar and reading and writing that draws on rich and motivating texts as a source of exploring the choices writers make, and opening up for young writers a repertoire of infinite possibilities for writing. The teaching approach is underpinned by four pedagogical principles:

- Make a link between the grammar being introduced and how it works in the writing being taught.
- Explain the grammar through examples, not lengthy explanations.
- Build in high-quality discussion about grammar and its effects.
- Use examples from authentic texts to link writers to the broader community of writers.

Adopting these principles in your own teaching will enable you to provide explicit teaching of grammatical points that are relevant to children's learning about writing and to develop young writers' understanding of the language choices they can make in their writing, and how those choices shape meaning.

Our observations of many, many classrooms using this approach have highlighted that successful teaching of grammar as choice has three key characteristics. First, it does require teachers to have good grammatical subject knowledge, and so it is worth reflecting on your own grammar knowledge and considering whether it needs strengthening. There are some websites listed at the end of this unit that might help you. But, in addition, this approach requires the ability to notice how texts, both published texts and children's texts, are working and to be able to draw out relevant features to note. Finally, it requires the ability to plan purposefully, integrating an attention to grammar within teaching units at relevant points.

ANNOTATED FURTHER READING

Myhill, D.A., Jones, S.M., Watson, A. and Lines, H.E. (2016) *Essential Primary Grammar*, Maidenhead, UK: Open University Press.

> This is a practical text, based on research, that explains the grammar of the National Curriculum, links it to practical classroom activities and highlights typical misconceptions students may have.

Reedy, D. and Bearne, E. (2013) *Teaching Grammar Effectively in Primary Schools*, London: UKLA.

> Another practical text that is more about classroom activities rather than your own subject knowledge. It draws on our research to inform its 'REDM' approach.

FURTHER READING TO SUPPORT M-LEVEL STUDY

Myhill, D.A. and Watson, A. (2014) 'The role of grammar in the writing curriculum: A review', *Journal of Child Language Teaching & Therapy*, 30(1): 41-62.

> This article provides an overview of the historical debate about grammar teaching and theoretical thinking about grammar in the curriculum.

Myhill, D.A. and Newman, R. (2016) 'Metatalk: Enabling metalinguistic discussion about writing', *International Journal of Education Research*, 80: 177-87.

> This article explores in depth how teachers use talk to support, or not, children's developing understanding of the grammatical choices available to them.

RELEVANT WEBSITES

Cybergrammar: www.cybergrammar.co.uk/

Englicious: www.englicious.org/

> Both of the above are useful sites if you want to develop your grammatical knowledge - they are designed with teachers in mind.

Larry Trask's Guide to Punctuation: www.sussex.ac.uk/informatics/punctuation/

> This is an invaluable site if you want to brush up your understanding of punctuation and where there are rules and where it is a matter of choice.

REFERENCES

Alamargot, D. and Chanquoy, L. (2001) *Through the Models of Writing*, Dordrecht, Netherlands: Kluwer Academic.

Andrews, R., Torgerson, C., Beverton, S., Freeman, A., Locke, T., Low, G., Robinson, A. and Zhu, D. (2006) 'The effect of grammar teaching on writing development', *British Educational Research Journal*, 32(1): 39-55.

Bowler, T. (2002) 'Write off your plans and go with the flow', *Times Educational Supplement*, 16 August.

Braddock, R.R., Lloyd-Jones, R. and Schoer, L. (1963) *Research in Written Composition*, Urbana, IL: National Council of Teachers of English.

Britton, J. (1983) 'Writing and the story of the world', in B.M. Kroll and C.G. Wells (eds) *Explorations in the Development of Writing: Theory, Research, and Practice*, New York: Wiley, pp. 3-30.

Carter, R. and McCarthy, M. (2006) *Cambridge Grammar of English*, Cambridge, UK: Cambridge University Press.

Department for Education (DfE). (2014) *The National Curriculum in England: Framework Document–Grammar Annex*. Retrieved from https://www.gov.uk/government/uploads/system/uploads/attachment_data/file/210969/NC_framework_document_-_FINAL.pdf (accessed 17 August 2015).

Derewianka, B. and Jones, P. (2010) 'From traditional grammar to functional grammar: Bridging the divide', Special Issue of *NALDIC Quarterly*, 8(1): 6-15.

Dyson, A. (2008) 'Staying in the (curricular) lines: Practice constraints and possibilities in childhood writing', *Written Comunication*, 25: 119-59.

Graham, S. and Perin, D. (2007) 'A meta-analysis of writing instruction for adolescent students', *Journal of Educational Psychology*, 99(3): 445-76.

Halliday, M.A.K. (1975) *Learning How to Mean: Explorations in the Development of Language*, London: Edward Arnold.

Halliday, M.A.K. (2002) 'On grammar and grammatics', in J. Webster (ed.) *The Collected Works of M.A. K. Halliday*, vol. 3, London: Continuum, pp. 384-417.

Hillocks, G. and Smith, M. (1991) 'Grammar and usage', in J. Flood, J.M. Jensen, D. Lapp and J.R. Squire (eds) *Handbook of Research on Teaching the English Language Arts*, New York: Macmillan, pp. 591-603.

Kellogg, R. (2008) 'Training writing skills: A cognitive developmental perspective', *Journal of Writing Research*, 1(1): 1-26.

Myhill, D.A., Jones, S.M., Lines, H. and Watson, A. (2012) 'Re-thinking grammar: The impact of embedded grammar teaching on students' writing and students' metalinguistic understanding', *Research Papers in Education*, 27(2): 139-66.

Prior, P. (2005) 'A sociocultural theory of writing', in C.A. MacArthur, S. Graham and J. Fitzgerald (eds) *The Handbook of Writing Research*, New York: Guilford Press, pp. 54-66.

CREATIVITY AND CREATIVE TEACHING AND LEARNING

Teresa Cremin and Jonathan Barnes

INTRODUCTION

Nurturing learner creativity is a key aim for many schools. Teachers and school leaders continue to see the development of creativity as an essential part of their job. They recognise that an appropriate climate for creative thought and activity has to be established (Ofsted, 2006, 2009) and know that pressures to improve standards in 'the basics' can crowd creativity out of the curriculum.

In a world dominated by technological innovations and rapid change, creativity is a critical component; human skills and people's imaginative and innovative powers are key resources in a knowledge-driven economy (Robinson, 2009). As social structures and ideologies continue to change, the ability to live sustainably with uncertainty and deal with complexity is essential. So, organisations and governments all over the world are now more concerned than ever to promote creativity (Craft, 2011).

As primary professionals, it is our responsibility to steer the creative development of young people in our care. In the first decade of the twenty-first century, creativity was given a high profile in education policy and the media, and children were expected to think creatively, make connections and generate ideas, as well as problem-solve (Craft, 2011). In 2012, the EYFS (Department for Education) acknowledged that, alongside 'playing and exploring' and 'active learning', the third characteristic of effective learning is 'creating and thinking critically'. In relation to the current primary curriculum, however, explicit references to creativity are few. Nonetheless, there is professional recognition that developing the creativity of the young cannot be left to chance (e.g. Cremin, 2017).

Academic explorations of creative teaching and teaching for creativity continue to expand (e.g. Jeffrey and Woods, 2009; Cremin *et al.*, 2015; Cremin, 2017; Sawyer, 2011; Craft *et al.*, 2014), and teachers still seek innovative ways to shape the curriculum in response to children's needs. Creative teaching should not be placed in opposition to the teaching of essential knowledge, skills and understandings in the subject disciplines; neither does it imply lowered expectations of challenge or behaviour. Rather, creative teaching involves teaching the subjects in creative contexts that explicitly invite learners to engage imaginatively and that stretch their generative, evaluative and collaborative capacities.

However, many teachers still feel constrained by perceptions of a culture of accountability. You too may already be aware of the classroom impact of an assessment-led system. Such pressure can limit opportunities for creative endeavour and may tempt you to stay within the safe boundaries of the known. Recognising that tensions exist between the incessant drive to raise measurable standards and the impulse to teach more creatively is a good starting point, but finding the energy and enterprise to respond flexibly is a real challenge. In order to do so, you need to be convinced that creativity has an important role to play in education and believe that you can contribute, both personally and professionally. You may also need to widen your understanding of creativity and creative practice in order to teach creatively and teach for creativity.

OBJECTIVES

By the end of this unit, you should have:

- an increased understanding of the nature of creativity;
- an awareness of some of the features of creative primary teachers;
- a wider understanding of creative pedagogical practice;
- some understanding of how to plan for creative learning.

CREATIVE PRACTICE

A class of learners engage with interest as they collaborate to create three-dimensional representations of Egyptian gods to add to their classroom museum. Earlier that morning, at this Northamptonshire primary school, the 6–7-year-olds had generated and discussed their ideas and listened to others. Then, in groups, they sought to turn these ideas into action. Operating independently of their teacher, they found resources in their classroom and others, monitored their activities and talked about their work. A wide variety of representations were created, and new ideas were celebrated and appraised. Later, the children wrote instructions for making their images and added them to a huge class book, which contained DVDs of other cross-curricular activities. However, their ability to recall, explain and discuss the finer points of this carefully planned and executed project two terms later was an even richer testimony to the enjoyment and depth of creative learning involved.

In this school, as in many others, the staff had adopted a more creative approach to the curriculum, influenced in part by the significant achievements of what were then called 'creative schools' (Eames *et al.*, 2006; Ofsted, 2006). This trend was encouraged by many initiatives, including the report *Nurturing Creativity in Young People* (Roberts, 2006) and Creative Partnerships (2002–11), a government-funded initiative that encouraged schools to develop more innovative ways of teaching. It showed that creative and collaborative projects inspired and fostered creative skills and raised children's and young people's confidence and aspiration (Eames *et al.*, 2006).

The focus on creative learning has since shifted. Creativity in schools was overshadowed by what became known as the 'cultural offer' in 2008 (McMaster, 2008), and the Creative Partnerships programme ended in 2011. A 'cultural education' agenda took the former position of creative education, and creativity is currently barely mentioned in education policy documents. Nonetheless, creativity plays a key role economically, and, with increasing evidence of a close relationship between creativity and social and psychological well-being (Barnes, 2013), teachers continue to seek innovative ways of teaching to increase motivation and develop creative learning.

SO WHAT IS CREATIVITY?

Creativity is not confined to special people or to particular arts-based activities, nor is it undisciplined play. It is, however, notoriously difficult to define. It has been described as 'a state of mind in which all our intelligences are working together', involving 'seeing, thinking and innovating' (Craft, 2000: 38) and as 'imaginative activity fashioned so as to produce outcomes that are both original and of value' (NACCCE, 1999: 29). Creativity is possible wherever human intelligence is actively engaged and is an essential part of an effective education: it includes all areas of understanding and all children, teachers and others working in primary education. Indeed, it can be demonstrated by anyone in any aspect of life, throughout life.

It is useful to distinguish between high creativity and ordinary creativity, between 'big C creativity' (exemplified in some of Gardner's (1993) studies of highly creative individuals, such as Picasso, Einstein and Freud) and 'little c creativity', which Craft (2001) highlights. This latter form focuses on the individual agency and resourcefulness of ordinary people to innovate and take action. Csikszentmihalyi suggests that each of us is born with two contradictory sets of instructions – a conservative tendency and an expansive tendency, but warns us that, 'If too few opportunities for curiosity are available, if too many obstacles are put in the way of risk and exploration, the motivation to engage in creative behaviour is easily extinguished' (1996: 11).

In the classroom, developing opportunities for children to 'possibility think' their way forwards is, therefore, critical (Craft *et al.*, 2012; Cremin, Chappell and Craft, 2013). This will involve you in immersing the class in an issue or subject and helping them ask questions, be imaginative and playfully explore options, as well as innovate. At the core of such creative endeavour is the child's identity. Their sense of self-determination and agency and their understanding of themselves as unique thinkers able to solve life's problems are essential ingredients of their success, resilience and general health (Marmot, 2010). From this perspective, creativity is not seen as an event or a product (although it may involve either or both), but a process or a state of mind involving the serious play of ideas and possibilities. This generative, problem-finding/problem-solving process may involve rational and non-rational thought and may be fed by the intuitive, by daydreaming and pondering, as well as by the application of knowledge and skills. In order to be creative, children may need considerable knowledge in a domain, but 'creativity and knowledge are two sides of the same psychological coin, not opposing forces' (Boden, 2001: 102), and enrich each other.

Imaginative activity can take many forms; it draws on a more varied range of human functioning than linear, logical and rational patterns of behaviour (Claxton, 2006). It is essentially generative and may include physical, social, reflective, musical, aural or visual thinking, involving children in activities that produce new and unusual connections between ideas, domains, processes and materials. When children and their teachers step outside the boundaries of predictability and are physically engaged, this provides a balance to the sedentary and too often abstract nature of school education. Creative learning is often collaborative and uses mind and body, emotions, eyes, ears and all the senses, in an effort to face a challenge or solve a problem. In less-conventional contexts, new insights and connections may be made through analogy and metaphor, and teachers become the 'meddlers in the middle' (McWilliam, 2008), not the 'sage on the stage' of more transmissive modes of education. Modes of creative thinking, such as the 'imaginative-generative' mode, which produces outcomes, and the 'critical-evaluative' mode, which involves consideration of originality and value (NACCCE, 1999: 30), operate in close interrelationship and need to be consciously developed in the classroom.

The process of creativity, Claxton and Lucas (2010) suggest, involves the ability to move freely between the different layers of our memories to find solutions to problems. They propose a metaphor of the mind based on the concept of three layers of memory that impact upon our thinking: an upper layer or *habit map*, which is a map of repeated patterns of behaviour; an *inner layer*, comprised of individual conscious and unconscious memories; and an *archetypal layer*, laid down by our genes. Others see the creative mind as one that looks for unexpected likenesses and connections between disparate domains (Bronowski, 1978). Csikszentmihalyi (1996) wisely suggests, however, that creativity does not happen inside people's heads, but in the interaction between an individual's thoughts and the sociocultural context. When one considers examples of both big C and little c creativity, this explanation seems to make the most sense, as the social and cultural context of learning is highly influential.

In Wales . . .

A document for Foundation Phase pupils, age 3-7 years, sets out in its introduction that:

> Children should be continually developing their imagination and creativity across the curriculum. Their curiosity and disposition to learn should be stimulated by everyday sensory experiences, both indoors and outdoors. Children should engage in creative, imaginative and expressive activities in art, craft, design, music, dance and movement.
>
> (DCELLS, 2008: 4)

Source: Department for Children, Education, Lifelong Learning and Skills (DCELLS). (2008) *Creative Development*, Cardiff: Welsh Assembly Government (WAG). Retrieved from http://learning.gov.wales/docs/learningwales/publications/130423-creative-development-en.pdf (accessed 2 November 2017).

Task 7.4.1 Ownership of learning

Relevance, ownership and control of learning, as well as innovation, have all been identified as key issues in creative learning in children (Jeffrey and Woods, 2009). Imaginative approaches involve individuals and groups in initiating questions and lines of enquiry, so that they are more in charge of their work, and such collaboration and interaction help to develop a greater sense of autonomy in the events that unfold.

- To what extent have you observed children taking control of their learning, making choices and demonstrating ownership of their own learning? Think of some examples and share these in small groups.
- To what extent was the work also relevant to the children? Were they emotionally or imaginatively engaged, building on areas of interest, maintaining their individuality and sharing ideas with one another?
- If you have seen little evidence of these issues, consider how you could offer more opportunity for relevance, ownership and control of learning in the classroom.

It is clear, too, that creativity is not bound to particular subjects. At the cutting edge of every domain of learning, creativity is essential. It depends in part on interactions between feeling and thinking across boundaries and ideas. It also depends upon a climate of trust, respect and support, an environment in which individual agency and self-determination are fostered, and ideas and interests are valued, discussed and celebrated. Yet we have all experienced schools that fail to teach the pleasure and excitement to be found in science or mathematics, for example, or that let routines and timetables, subject boundaries and decontextualised knowledge dominate the daily diet of the young. In such sterile environments, when formulae for learning are relied upon, and curriculum packages are delivered, children's ability to make connections and to imagine alternatives is markedly reduced. So, too, is their capacity for curiosity, for enquiry and for creativity itself.

CREATIVE TEACHING AND TEACHING FOR CREATIVITY

The distinction between creative teaching and teaching for creativity is helpful in that it is possible to imagine a creative teacher who engages personally and creatively in the classroom, yet fails to provide for children's creative learning. Responsible creative professionals are not necessarily flamboyant performers, but teachers who use a range of approaches to create the conditions in which the creativity of others can flourish. Creative teachers also recognise and make use of their own creativity, not just to interest and engage the learners, but also to promote new thinking and learning. Their confidence in their own creativity enables them to offer the children stronger scaffolds and spaces for emotional and intellectual growth.

> ### In Northern Ireland . . .
>
> The importance of creativity, both in pedagogy and also as a theme that underpins the learning experiences of pupils, is regarded by educationalists as fundamental to the teaching and learning process. With this in mind, the competences have been designed to enhance professional autonomy, both at an individual and collective level, in a way that encourages creative and innovative approaches to teaching and which, in turn, develops in pupils the ability to think creatively. Indeed, the ability to think creatively, and the innovation it encourages, is central to any modern education system that strives to enhance the life chances of children and young people.
>
> (GTCNI, 2007: 8)
>
> General Teaching Council for Northern Ireland (GTCNI). (2007) *Teaching: The Reflective Profession*, Belfast, GTCNI. Retrieved from www.gtcni.org.uk/uploads/docs/GTCNI_Comp_Bmrk%20%20Aug%2007.pdf (acessed 2 November 2017).

Research undertaken in higher education, with tutors teaching music, geography and English, suggests that creative teaching is a complex art form – a veritable 'cocktail party' (Grainger, Barnes and Scoffman, 2004). The host gathers the ingredients (the session content) and mixes them playfully and skilfully (the teaching style), in order to facilitate a creative, enjoyable and worthwhile party (the learning experience). Although no formula was, or could be, established for creative teaching, some of the ingredients for mixing a creative cocktail were identified, albeit tentatively, from this work. The elements are not in themselves necessarily creative, but the action of shaking and stirring the ingredients and the individual experience of those attending are critical if the 'cocktail party' is to be successful. The intention to promote creative learning appeared to be an important element in this work.

The session content included placing current trends in a wider context and extensive use of metaphor, analogy and personal anecdotes to make connections. The teaching style included multimodal pedagogic practices, pace, humour, the confidence of the tutors and their ability to inspire and value the pupils. In relation to the learning experience, the themes included involving the pupils affectively and physically and challenging them to engage and reflect. Together, these represent some of the critical features of creative teachers and creative teaching that combine to support new thinking.

Task 7.4.2 Teaching as a cocktail party

- Consider the metaphor of teaching as a cocktail party for a moment. In what ways do you think it captures the vitality of teaching – the dynamic interplay between teachers, children and the resources available? Select one or two of the features, such as humour or personal anecdotes. Do you make extensive use of either? Remember, the research indicates that such features are employed with others at the 'cocktail party'.
- Consider your previous teachers. Which were the most creative? Did they create successful cocktail parties in which you felt valued and engaged, took risks, made connections and developed deep learning? How did they achieve this?

PERSONAL CHARACTERISTICS OF CREATIVE TEACHERS

It is difficult to identify with any certainty the personal characteristics of creative teachers. Research tends to offer lists of propensities that such teachers possess (e.g. Fryer, 1996; Beetlestone, 1998). Common elements noted in these various studies include:

- enthusiasm, passion and commitment;
- risk-taking;
- a deep curiosity or questioning stance;
- willingness to be intuitive and/or introspective;
- gregariousness and introspectiveness;
- a clear set of personal values;
- awareness of self as a creative being.

This list encompasses many of the personal qualities you might expect in any good teacher, except perhaps the last. Sternberg (1999) suggests that creative teachers are creative role models themselves – professionals who continue to be self-motivated learners, who value the creative dimensions of their own lives and who make connections between their personal responses to experience and their teaching. In addition, a clear set of values, reflecting fair-mindedness, openness to evidence, a desire for clarity and respect for others, are important and among the attitudinal qualities embedded in creative teaching. So, too, is a commitment to inclusion and a belief in human rights and equality. Such attitudes and values have a critical role in creative teaching and are, perhaps, best taught by example.

FEATURES OF A CREATIVE PEDAGOGICAL STANCE

The intention to promote creativity is fundamental. There are a number of features of a creative pedagogical stance that you may want to consider in relation to your teaching and observation of other creative professionals.

A learner-centred, agency-oriented ethos

Creative teachers tend to place the learners above the curriculum and combine a positive disposition towards creativity and person-centred teaching that actively promotes pupils who learn and think for themselves (Sawyer, 2011; Robinson, 2015). Relaxed, trusting educator–learner relationships exist in creative classrooms, and the role of the affect and children's feelings play a central role in learning in such contexts. Such relationships foster children's agency and autonomy as learners and enable, for example, children to respond to literature personally, imaginatively and affectively (Cremin *et al.*, 2014). A learner-oriented ethos will also involve you showing patience and openness, reinforcing children's creative behaviour, celebrating difference, diversity and innovation, as well as learning to tolerate mild or polite rebellion (Gardner, 1999). If you adopt such a person-centred orientation, you will be shaping the children's self-esteem and enhancing their intrinsic motivation and agency. You might, for example, explicitly plan for small groups to shape and plan for themselves how they might investigate melting, by giving them enormous 'ice eggs' (made from balloons filled with water and frozen) and telling an imaginary tale of how these came to be in your possession (see Craft *et al.*, 2012).

A questioning stance

Creativity involves asking and attempting to answer real questions; the creative teacher is seen by many as one who uses open questions and who promotes speculation in the classroom, encouraging deeper understanding and lateral thinking (Cremin, Barnes and Scoffham, 2009). In the context of creative teaching, both teachers and children need to be involved in this process of imaginative thinking, encompassing the generation of challenging and unusual questions and the creation of possible responses. The questioning stance of the teacher has been noted as central to children's possibility thinking, and the importance of question-posing and question-responding has been documented (Chappell *et al.*, 2008). You could, for example, play with the idea of 'book zips', new books that have invisible zips that prevent children opening them! (Zipped plastic bags or magical tales often help to extend the patience necessary!). Groups can generate questions about characters, plot and setting and respond to other groups' questions.

Creating space, time and freedom to make connections

Creativity requires space, time and a degree of freedom. Deep immersion in an area or activity allows options to remain open, and persistence and follow-through to develop. Conceptual space allows children to converse, challenge and negotiate meanings and possibilities together. For example, through employing both film and drama in extended units of work, teachers raised boys' standards and creativity in writing (Bearne, Grainger and Wolstencroft, 2004). Through adopting the role of 'Davis Jones', an archaeologist and the brother of Indiana Jones, you could, for example, trigger historical enquiry and exploration (see Cooper, 2013).

Employing multimodal, intuitive teaching approaches

A variety of multimodal teaching approaches and frequent switching between modes in a playlike and spontaneous manner appear to support creative learning (Cremin *et al.*, 2009). The diversity of pattern, rhythm and pace used by creative teachers is particularly marked, as is their use of informed intuition (Claxton, 1997). As you teach, opportunities will arise for you to use your intuition and move from the security of the known. Give yourself permission to go beyond the 'script' you have planned and allow the children to take the initiative and lead you, for such spontaneity will encourage you to seize the moment and foster deeper learning (Cremin, Craft and Burnard, 2006). In geography, for example, you might nurture creative play through opportunities for transforming and adapting places, making dens, yurts, shelters or tree houses perhaps (see Scoffham, 2015).

Prompting full engagement, ownership and ongoing reflection

In studying an area in depth, children should experience both explicit instruction and space for exploration and discovery. Try to provide opportunities for choice and be prepared to spend time developing their self-management skills so that they are able to operate independently. Their engagement can be prompted by appealing to their interests and passions, by involving them in imaginative experiences and by connecting learning to their lives (Cremin *et al.*, 2009). A semi-constant oscillation between engagement and reflection will become noticeable in the classroom as you work to refine, reshape and improve learning. The ability to give and receive criticism is also an essential part of creativity, and you will need to encourage evaluation through supportive and honest feedback (Jeffrey, 2006) – for example, in evaluating children's dramatic representations that convey mathematical concepts (see Pound and Lee, 2016).

Modelling risk-taking and enabling the children to take risks too

The ability to tolerate ambiguity is an example of the 'confident uncertainty' to which Claxton (1997) refers when discussing creative teachers - those who combine subject and pedagogical knowledge, but also leave space for uncertainty and the unknown. You will gain in confidence through increased subject knowledge, experience and reflection, but your assurance will also grow through taking risks and having a go at expressing yourself. Risk-taking is an integral element of creativity, and one that you will want to model and foster. The children, too, will need to feel supported as they take risks in safe, non-judgemental contexts.

To be a creative practitioner, you will need more than a working knowledge of creativity and the prescribed curriculum. You will need a clear idea of your values, a secure pedagogical understanding and a secure knowledge base, supported by a passionate belief in the potential of creative teaching to engage, inspire and educate. Such teaching depends, in the end, upon the human interaction between teachers and pupils and is also influenced by the teacher's state of mind. The creative teacher, it is proposed, is one who is aware of, and values, the human attribute of creativity in themselves and actively seeks to promote this in others. The creative teacher has a creative state of mind that is both exercised and developed through their creative practice and personal/professional curiosity, connection-making, originality and autonomy (Cremin *et al.*, 2009). Such practice is, of course, influenced by the physical, social, emotional and spiritual environments in which teachers and children work.

Task 7.4.3 Creative engagement

- Make a list of the times when you feel deeply engaged – in 'flow', as Csikszentmihalyi (1996) describes it, or in your 'element', as Robinson (2009) does. What are the characteristics of this engagement?
- How do these relate to the aspects of creative practice described above – are there parallels, and, if not, what might this reveal about the degree to which creative engagement can be prescribed or fostered?

CREATING ENVIRONMENTS OF POSSIBILITY

You may have been to a school where creativity is planned for and fostered, and where there is a clear sense of shared values and often a real buzz of purposeful and exciting activity. Such schools have a distinctive character that impacts upon behaviour, relationships, the physical and ethical environment and the curriculum. An ethos that values creativity will, according to most definitions, promote originality and the use of the imagination, as well as encourage an adventurous attitude to life and learning. In such environments of possibility, packed with ideas and experiences, resources and choices, as well as time for relaxation and rumination, physical, conceptual and emotional space is offered. Schools offering such spaces are, Robinson (2015) argues, revolutionising education from the ground up. They are not alone: there is considerable interest in such pedagogical practice internationally (Cremin, 2017).

The social and emotional environment

Taking creative risks and moving forward in learning are heavily dependent upon an atmosphere of acceptance and security. Children's well-being is widely recognised as important, in its own right and to support their creativity, but can only be fostered by a secure ethos. However, creative schools may display apparently contradictory characteristics. The ethos may be simultaneously:

*   highly active and relaxed;
*   supportive and challenging;
*   confident and speculative;
*   playful and serious;
*   focused and fuzzy;
*   individualistic and communal;
*   understood personally and owned by all;
*   non-competitive and ambitious.

Since Plato, many have argued that there are links between involvement in creative acts and a general sense of well-being. More recent research in cognitive neuroscience (Damasio, 2003) and positive psychology has suggested that the state of well-being promotes optimum conditions in mind and body, and ensures constructive and secure relationships. A perceived link between discovering one's own creativity and feeling a sense of well-being (Barnes, Hope and Scoffham, 2008) has led some to make arguments for revaluating curricula, in favour of educational programmes that offer frequent, planned and progressive creative opportunities across every discipline (Barnes, 2005).

The physical environment

The physical environment in a school that promotes creativity is likely to celebrate achievement and individuality and can be a valuable teaching resource. Children's views on this are important and deserve to be taken into account. Projects have shown how creative thinking in the context of focused work on improving the school building, grounds or local areas can achieve major citizenship objectives and high-level arts and literacy targets in an atmosphere of genuine support and community concern (Barnes, 2007, 2009).

Active modes of learning and problem-solving approaches that include independent investigation require accessible resources of various kinds, so that the richer and more multifaceted a range you can offer the better. This supports genuine choice, speculation and experimentation, happy accidents and flexibility. An environment of possibility in which individual agency and self-determination are fostered and children's ideas and interests are valued, shared and celebrated depends upon the presence of a climate of trust, respect and support in your classroom/school. Creativity can be developed when you are confident and secure in both your subject knowledge and your knowledge of creative pedagogical practice; then, you will seek to model the features of creativity *and* develop a culture of creative opportunities in school, although, in schools in socio-economically challenged contexts, a pedagogy of poverty that constrains learner agency has been documented (e.g. Hempel-Jorgensen, 2015). You cannot afford to be complacent.

PLANNING FOR CREATIVITY

Open-ended learning opportunities that offer space for autonomy and collaboration and have real-world relevance can be created through extended and creative units of work, encompassing multiple subjects. These can be enriched by regularly involving the expertise of partners from the creative and cultural sector; Galton (2015) argues such partnerships can enrich learning and raise children's expectations and achievements. Seek to plan coherent learning experiences in which 'school subjects [are seen as] resources in the construction of the curriculum, rather than determinants of its overall structure and emphasis' (Halpin, 2003: 114). In planning such creative units of work, you will want to build on insights from research. The following ten research-informed suggestions are worth considering:

1 Create a *positive, secure atmosphere* in which risks can be taken (Seltzer and Bentley, 1999).
2 Profile a *questioning stance* and frame the work around children's interests and questions (Chappell *et al.*, 2008).
3 Ensure a range of *practical and analytical, open-ended* activities (Craft *et al.*, 2014).
4 Emphasise *learner agency* and individual and cooperative thinking and learning (Hempel-Jorgensen, 2015).
5 Agree *clear goals*, some of which are set and owned by the learners (Jeffrey and Woods, 2009).
6 Build *emotionally relevant links* to the children's lives, offering opportunities for *engagement and enjoyment* (Barnes, 2007).
7 Integrate a manageable number of *relevant subjects/areas of learning* (Barnes, 2007).
8 Involve developmentally appropriate *progression* in skills, knowledge and understanding.
9 Set the work in a wider framework that includes *concepts, content and attitudes* (Cremin, 2009).
10 Provide supportive *assessment* procedures that build security and include time and tools for reflection (Adey and Shayer, 2002).

CREATIVE CURRICULA IN ACTION

Two examples bring such a curriculum, centred upon creative learning, to life. A whole-school community from Tower Hamlets made a winter visit to Canary Wharf, less than 500 metres from the school gates. Many pupils had never been there. The event was grasped as an opportunity to collect as much information as possible. None of the collected impressions could have been gathered from websites or written sources, and so the visit was a genuine investigation, involving every age group – traffic surveys, rubbings, observations of people walking, collections of geometric shapes, still images framed by 'key' describing words, moving images, sensory descriptions of sights, sounds and smells, intricate 360° drawings, mosaics or trees imprisoned in stainless steel, stone and scaffolded containers. Every moment, morning or afternoon, was fully used in information-gathering. Children and adult supporters collected digital, drawn, listed, tallied, acted and heard data from a variety of contrasting sites around the wharf.

The library of collected and remembered objects, images and sensations was brought back to school and formed the basis of the curriculum for the next few weeks. Creating responses from these disparate sources involved very different paths in each class, from Nursery to Year 6. One Year 2 class made a 'sound journey' using mapping and musical skills and knowledge. Groups of five or six composed music to capture different places on their journey and linked them with other compositions of 'walking music'. Separate teams then mapped their journeys using techniques learned in the previous term, and the resultant maps were used as graphic musical scores. A mixed group created large and imaginative abstract constructions from bamboo and tissue and applied decoration from rubbings and drawings, expressing their experience of the towering buildings at the wharf.

Children, along with their co-learning teachers, presented their compositions, artworks, mathematical investigations, stories and dramas to the rest of the school in a series of assemblies. These were especially appreciated across the school, because everyone had shared in the same initial experience. The whole project was evaluated through a continuous blog kept by children, teachers, artists and teaching assistants. Their challenge, like yours, is to take account of individual differences in learning, help each child become a self-regulated learner, and ensure appropriate coverage of the areas of learning and their attendant knowledge bases.

In another context, a class from a rural school decided, through discussion, to concentrate on the value of community in a 2-day project for the website Engaging Places (www.engagingplaces. org.uk/home). They divided into teams of five and went on walks up and down the street in which the school stood. Each group decided upon a sub-theme: improving the community, describing the community now and the community in the future, problems in the community, or litter and the community. After this first decision, the children used the walk as a data-gathering opportunity. The description group used cameras and viewfinders to record the different ages and materials of houses in the street, but also used sound recorders to collect the vastly different sounds at either end of the street. In class on their return, they combined the sound-based and visually based impressions on a street map, which they constructed with great enthusiasm. Bursts of creativity occurred as pairs decided how to represent the street and the sounds and images they had collected. Eventually, the group decided on a 3D street map, with press-button recordings of different sounds in four different parts of the street. The litter group arrived at a double focus. They decided to design and make attractive dustbins and an anti-littering video. This involved storyboarding, rehearsals, acting, filming and editing. The wild and wacky litter bins were planned in detail and made in model form for a presentation in the school and at a national launch of Engaging Places. Evaluation was crucial at every stage of these activities.

Careful planning for such creative learning experiences is important and perhaps best done in collaboration with others. Some will last a term, others just a few days, but all will seek to involve the children in real, purposeful and imaginatively engaging experiences.

SUMMARY

Creative teaching is a collaborative enterprise that capitalises on the unexpected and variously involves engagement, reflection and transformation, patterned at such a rate as to invite and encourage a questioning stance and motivate self-directed learning. Creative learning involves asking questions, exploring options and generating and appraising ideas, as the learner take risks and imaginatively thinks their way forwards, making new or innovative connections in the process. New thinking happens at the meeting places of different ideas and approaches, and it also takes place when new links occur between people. Many of the examples in this unit show both adults and children involved in thinking and learning together, which can be a key generator of creativity. We hope you will choose to teach creatively and promote creativity through your planning, and will build in choice and autonomy, relevance and purpose in engaging environments of possibility – environments both inside and outside the classroom.

For more ideas on teaching creatively across the curriculum, see the series that accompanies this handbook. Edited by Cremin, it includes books on *Teaching – English* (Cremin, 2015), *Mathematics* (Pound and Lee, 2016), *Science* (Davies, 2015), *History* (Cooper, 2013), *Geography* (Scoffham, 2015), *Music* (Burnard and Murphy, 2013), *Physical Education* (Pickard and Maude, 2014), *Religious Education* (Elton-Chalcraft, 2015) *Outdoors* (Pickering, 2017), *Design and Technology* (Benson and Lawson, 2017). Forthcoming is *Applying Cross Curricula Approaches Creatively* (Barnes, 2018).

ANNOTATED FURTHER READING

Cremin, T. (ed.) (2017) *Creativity and Creative Pedagogies in the Early and Primary Years*, Abingdon, UK: Routledge.
> This edited international collection reveals the possibilities and complexities of creative pedagogies in different cultural contexts and offers practical evidence of creative practice from around the world.

Sawyer, R. (ed.) (2011) *Structure and Improvisation in Creative Teaching*, New York: Cambridge.
> This US collection provides practical advice for teachers wishing to become creative professionals. It highlights the need for teachers to respond artfully to curricula and the unexpected demands of classroom interactions.

FURTHER READING TO SUPPORT M-LEVEL STUDY

Craft, A., Cremin, T., Hay, P. and Clack, J. (2013) 'Creative primary schools: Developing and maintaining pedagogy for creativity', *Ethnography & Education*, 9(1): 16–34.
> This paper comprises a case study of three schools; it documents their creative practice and the tenets underpinning this.

Cremin, T., Glauert, E., Craft, A., Compton, A. and Stylianidou, F. (2015) 'Creative little scientists', *Education 3-13, International Journal of Primary, Elementary & Early Years Education*, 43(4): 404–19.
> This paper, drawing on an EU-wide project with nine partner countries, explores key pedagogical connections between enquiry-based science and creative approaches.

RELEVANT WEBSITES

NACCCE report, *All Our Futures: Creativity, Culture and Education*: www.cypni.org.uk/downloads/allourfutures.pdf

Creative Little Scientists: www.creative-little-scientists.eu/
> This offers the materials from the research and is complemented by Creativity in Early Years Science Education, which includes rich examples of practice and support for teachers and teacher educators: www.ceys-project.eu/content/about

Research rich pedagogies: https://researchrichpedagogies.org/

> This Open University website seeks to foster creative and innovative pedagogies. It examines evidence from learners and teachers to distil key research messages and propose new approaches and includes a section devoted to reading for pleasure, with myriad examples of classroom practice.

 # REFERENCES

Adey, P. and Shayer, M. (2002) *Learning Intelligence: Cognitive Acceleration from 5 to 15 Years*, London: Open University Press.

Barnes, J. (2005) '"You could see it on their faces . . .': The importance of provoking smiles in schools', *Health Education*, 105(5): 392–400.

Barnes, J. (2007) *Cross-Curricular Learning 3–14*, London: Sage.

Barnes, J. (2009) 'The integration of music with other subjects, particularly in art forms', in J. Evans and C. Philpott (eds) *A Practical Guide to Teaching Music in the Secondary School*, London: Routledge.

Barnes, J. (2013) 'Drama to promote social and personal well-being in six-and seven-year-olds with communication difficulties: The Speech Bubbles project', *Perspectives in Public Health*, 134(2): 101–9.

Barnes, J., Hope, G. and Scoffham, S. (2008) 'A conversation about creative teaching and learning', in A. Craft, T. Cremin and P. Burnard (eds) *Creative Learning 3–11 and How We Document It*, London: Trentham, pp. 125–34.

Bearne, E., Grainger, T. and Wolstencroft, H. (2004) *Raising Boys' Achievements in Writing*, Leicester, UK: UKLS and PNS.

Beetlestone, F. (1998) *Creative Children, Imaginative Teaching*, Buckingham, UK: Open University Press.

Boden, M. (2001) 'Creativity and knowledge', in A. Craft, B. Jeffrey and M. Liebling (eds) *Creativity in Education*, London: Continuum, pp. 95–102.

Bronowski, J. (1978) *The Origins of Knowledge and Imagination*, New Haven, CT: Yale University Press.

Burnard, P. and Murphy, R. (2013) *Teaching Music Creatively*, London: Routledge.

Chappell, K., Craft, A., Burnard, P. and Cremin, T. (2008) 'Question-posing and question-responding: At the heart of possibility thinking in the early years', *Early Years: An International Journal of Research & Development*, 28(3): 267–86.

Claxton, G. (1997) *Hare Brain, Tortoise Mind: Why Intelligence Increases When You Think Less*, London: Fourth Estate.

Claxton, G. (2006) 'Mindfulness, learning and the brain', *Journal of Rational Emotive & Cognitive Behaviour Therapy*, 23: 301–14.

Claxton, G. and Lucas, B. (2010) *New Kinds of Smart*, Milton Keynes, UK: Open University Press.

Cooper, H. (2013) *Teaching History Creatively*, London: Routledge.

Craft, A. (2000) *Creativity across the Primary Curriculum: Framing and Developing Practice*, London: RoutledgeFalmer.

Craft, A. (2001) 'Little c creativity', in A. Craft, B. Jeffrey and M. Liebling (eds) *Creativity in Education*, London: Continuum, pp. 45–61.

Craft, A. (2011) *Creativity and Education Futures: Learning in a Digital Age*, London: Trentham.

Craft, A., Cremin, T., Burnard, P., Dragovic, T. and Chappell, K. (2012) 'Possibility thinking: An evidence-based concept driving creativity?', *Education 3–13*: 1–19.

Craft, A., Cremin, T., Hay, P. and Clack, J. (2014) 'Creative primary schools: Developing and maintaining pedagogy for creativity', *Ethnography & Education*, 9(1): 16–34.

Cremin, T. (2009) 'Creative teaching and creative teachers', in A. Wilson (ed.) *Creativity in Primary Practice*, Exeter, UK: Learning Matters, pp. 36–46.

Cremin, T. (2015) *Teaching English Creatively*, 2nd edn, London: Routledge.

Cremin, T. (ed.) (2017) *Creativity and Creative Pedagogies in the Early and Primary Years*, Abingdon, UK: Routledge.

Cremin, T., Barnes, J. and Scoffham, S. (2009) *Creative Teaching for Tomorrow*, Margate, UK: Future Creative.

Cremin, T., Chappell, K. and Craft, A. (2013) 'Reciprocity between narrative, questioning and imagination in the early and primary years: Examining the role of narrative in possibility thinking', *Thinking Skills & Creativity*, 9: 135–51.

Cremin, T., Craft, A. and Burnard, P. (2006) 'Pedagogy and possibility thinking in the Early Years', *Journal of Thinking Skills & Creativity*, 1(2): 108–19.

Cremin, T., Glauert, E., Craft, A., Compton, A. and Stylianidou, F. (2015) 'Creative little scientists: Exploring pedagogical synergies between inquiry-based and creative approaches in Early Years science', *Education 3-13, International Journal of Primary, Elementary & Early Years Education*, Special Issue on Creative Pedagogies, 43(4): 404–19.

Cremin, T. Mottram, M. Powell, S., Collins, R. and Safford, K. (2014) *Building Communities of Engaged Readers: Reading for Pleasure*, London and New York: Routledge.

Csikszentmihalyi, M. (1996) *Creativity: Flow and the Psychology of Discovery and Invention*, New York: Harper.

Damasio, A. (2003) *Looking for Spinoza: Joy, Sorrow and the Feeling Brain*, Orlando, FL: Harcourt.

Davies, D. (2015) *Teaching Science Creatively*, 2nd edn, London: Routledge.

Department for Education (DFE). (2012) *Statutory Framework for the Early Years Foundation Stage*, London: DFE.

Eames, A., Benton, T., Sharp, C. and Kendall, L. (2006) *The Impact of Creative Partnerships on the Attainment of Young People*, Slough, UK: NFER.

Elton-Chalcraft, S. (ed.) (2015) *Teaching RE Creatively*, London: Routledge.

Fryer, M. (1996) *Creative Teaching and Learning*, London: Paul Chapman.

Galton, M. (2015) 'It's a real journey: A life changing experience', *Education 3-13*, 43(4): 433–44.

Gardner, H. (1993) *Frames of Mind: The Theory of Multiple Intelligences*, London: Fontana Press.

Gardner, H. (1999) *The Disciplined Mind*, New York: Simon & Schuster.

Grainger, T., Barnes, J. and Scoffman, S. (2004) 'Creative teaching: A creative cocktail', *Journal of Education & Teaching*, 38(3): 243–53.

Halpin, D. (2003) *Hope and Education*, London: Routledge.

Hempel-Jorgensen, A. (2015). 'Learner agency and social justice: What can creative pedagogy contribute to socially just pedagogies?', *Pedagogy, Culture & Society*, 23(4): 531–54.

Jeffrey, B. (ed.) (2006) *Creative Learning Practices: European Experiences*, London: Tufnell Press.

Jeffrey, B. and Woods, P. (2009) *Creative Learning in the Primary School*, London: Routledge.

McMaster, M. (2008) *Supporting Excellence in the Arts: From Measurement to Judgement*, London: DCSF.

McWilliam, E. (2008) 'Unlearning how to teach', *Innovations in Education & Teaching International*, 45(3): 263–9.

Marmot, M. (2010) *The Marmot Review: Fair Society Healthy Lives*, London: Marmot Review. Retrieved from http://www.ucl.ac.uk/impact/case-study-repository/marmot-review (accessed 2 November 2017).

National Advisory Committee on Creative and Cultural Education (NACCE). (1999) *All Our Futures: The Report of the NACCE*, London: DfEE/DCMS.

Ofsted. (2006) *Creative Partnerships: Initiative and Impact*, London: Ofsted.

Ofsted (2009) *Twenty Outstanding Primary Schools: Excelling against the Odds*, Manchester, UK: Ofsted.

Pickard, A. and Maude, T. (2014) *Teaching Physical Education Creatively*, London: Routledge.

Pound, L. and Lee, T. (2016) *Teaching Mathematics Creatively*, 2nd edn, Abingdon, UK: Routledge.

Roberts, P. (2006) *Nurturing Creativity in Young People: A Report to Government to Inform Future Policy*, London: DCMS.

Robinson, K. (2009) *The Element: How Finding Your Passion Changes Everything*, London: Allen Lane.

Robinson, K. (2015) *Creative Schools*, New York: Allen Lane.

Sawyer, R. (ed.) (2011) *Structure and Improvisation in Creative Teaching*, New York: Cambridge.

Scoffham, S. (ed.) (2015) *Teaching Geography Creatively*, 2nd ed, London: Routledge.

Seltzer, K. and Bentley, T. (1999) *The Creative Age: Knowledge and Skills for the New Economy*, London: Demos.

Sternberg, R. (ed.) (1999) *The Handbook of Creativity*, Cambridge, UK: Cambridge University Press.

THINKING SKILLS

Robert Fisher

INTRODUCTION

> We need to think better if we are to become better people.
>
> (Paul, aged 10)

In recent years, there has been growing interest across the world in ways of developing children's thinking and learning skills (Fisher, 2005). This interest has been fed by new knowledge about how the brain works and how people learn, and evidence that specific interventions can improve children's thinking and intelligence. The particular ways in which people apply their minds to solving problems are called *thinking skills*. Many researchers suggest that thinking skills are essential to effective learning, although not all agree on the definition of this term (Moseley *et al.*, 2005). If thinking is how children make sense of learning, developing their thinking skills will help them get more out of learning and life. This unit looks at the implications of research into ways to develop thinking children, thinking classrooms and thinking schools.

OBJECTIVES

By the end of this unit, you should be able to:

- inform your understanding of 'thinking skills' and their role in learning;
- understand some key principles that emerge from research into teaching thinking;
- identify the main approaches to developing children's thinking;
- see how you might integrate a 'thinking skills' approach into classroom teaching and research.

WHAT ARE THINKING SKILLS?

Thinking skills are not mysterious entities existing somewhere in the mind. Nor are they like mental muscles that have a physical presence in the brain. What the term refers to is the human capacity to think in conscious ways to achieve certain purposes. Such processes include remembering, questioning, forming concepts, planning, reasoning, imagining, solving problems, making decisions and judgements, translating thoughts into words, and so on. Thinking skills are ways in which humans exercise the *sapiens* part of being *Homo sapiens*.

Some critics claim that there are no general thinking skills, and that all thinking must be about specific aspects of knowledge or linked to a particular subject in the school curriculum. However, different fields of learning can have shared aspects, and, although a subject such as history may have a particular content, this does not mean it has no links to thinking in other subjects – for example, in the need to give reasons and analyse evidence.

Nor does a focus on thinking mean ignoring the role of knowledge. Knowledge is necessary, but simply knowing a lot of things is not sufficient, if children are to be taught to think for themselves. Children need knowledge, but they also need to know how to acquire it and use it. 'Knowledge comes from other people', said Leo, aged 11, 'but thinking comes from yourself . . . or should do.'

It is true that thinking must be about something, but people can do it more or less effectively. The capacity, for example, to assess reasons, formulate hypotheses, make conceptual links or ask critical questions is relevant to many areas of learning. As Gemma, age 10, put it: 'To be a good learner you need to practice training your mind'.

We usually refer to skills in particular contexts, such as being 'good at cooking', but 'skills' can also refer to general capacities in cognitive performance, such as having a logical mind, a good memory, being creative or analytical, and so on. A thinking skill is a practical ability to think in ways that are judged to be more or less effective or skilled. However, learning a skill is not enough, for we want children to use their skills on a regular basis and get into the habit of thinking critically, creatively and with care. Good thinking requires that cognitive skills become habits of intelligent behaviour learned through practice, and children tend to become better at, for example, giving reasons or asking questions, the more they practise doing so.

Psychologists and philosophers have helped to extend our understanding of the term 'thinking' by emphasising the importance of *dispositions*, such as attention and motivation, commonly associated with thinking. This has prompted a move away from a simple model of 'thinking skills' as isolated cognitive capacities, to a view of thinking as inextricably connected to emotions and dispositions, including 'emotional intelligence', which is our ability to understand our own emotions and the emotions of others (Goleman, 2006), or what Lipman, founder of Philosophy for Children, describes as 'caring thinking'.

The curriculum is no longer seen simply as subject knowledge, but also as the skills of lifelong learning. Good teaching is about achieving curriculum objectives, but is also about developing general capacities to think, remember and learn. The last 50 years have seen a burgeoning of research across the world into the teaching of thinking, developing 'teaching for thinking' approaches in new directions, integrating them into everyday teaching to create 'thinking classrooms', and developing whole-school policies to create 'thinking schools'.

If thinking skills are the mental capacities we use to investigate the world, to solve problems and make judgements, to identify every such skill would be to enumerate all the capacities of the human mind, and the list would be endless. Many researchers have attempted to identify the key skills in human thinking, and the most famous of these is Bloom's taxonomy (Bloom and Krathwohl, 1956). Bloom's taxonomy of thinking skills (what he called 'the cognitive goals of education') has been widely used by teachers in planning their teaching. He identifies a number of basic, or 'lower-order', cognitive skills – knowledge, comprehension and application – and a number of 'higher-order' skills – analysis, synthesis and evaluation. Table 7.5.1 shows the various categories identified by Bloom and the processes involved in the various thinking levels.

Bloom's taxonomy built on earlier research by Piaget and Vygotsky that suggested that thinking skills and capacities are developed by *cognitive challenge*. Teachers need to challenge children to think more deeply and more widely and in more systematic and sustained ways. Or, as Tom, aged 10, put it: 'A good teacher makes you think . . . even when you don't want to'. One way in which you, as a good teacher, can do this is by asking questions that challenge children's thinking.

TABLE 7.5.1 Bloom's taxonomy

Cognitive goal	Thinking cues
1 Knowledge (knowing and remembering)	Say what you know, or remember, describe, repeat, define, identify, tell who, when, which, where, what
2 Comprehension (interpreting and understanding)	Describe in your own words, tell how you feel about it, what it means, explain, compare, relate
3 Application (applying, making use of)	How can you use it, where does it lead, apply what you know, use it to solve problems, demonstrate
4 Analysis (taking apart, being critical)	What are the parts, the order, the reasons why, the causes/problems/solutions/consequences
5 Synthesis (connecting, being creative)	How might it be different, how else, what if, suppose, putting together, develop, improve, create in your own way
6 Evaluation (judging and assessing)	How would you judge it, does it succeed, will it work, what would you prefer, why you think so

Task 7.5.1 Questions for thinking

Choose a story, poem, text or topic that you would like to use with children as a stimulus for their thinking. Using Bloom's taxonomy, create a series of questions to think about and discuss after you have shared the stimulus with them. List your questions under Bloom's six categories: knowledge, comprehension, application, analysis, synthesis and evaluation.

WHY ARE THINKING SKILLS IMPORTANT?

Thinking skills are important because mastery of the 'basics' in education (literacy, maths, science, etc.), however well taught, is not sufficient to fulfil human potential, nor to meet the demands of the labour market or of active citizenship. Countries across the world are recognising that a broad range of competencies is needed to prepare children for an unpredictable future. These higher-order thinking skills are required, in addition to basic skills, because individuals cannot 'store' sufficient knowledge in their memories for future use. Information is expanding at such a rate that individuals require transferable skills to enable them to address different problems, in different contexts, at different times, throughout their lives. The complexity of modern jobs requires people who can comprehend, judge and participate in generating new knowledge and processes. Modern, democratic societies require citizens to assimilate information from multiple sources, determine its truth and use it to make sound judgements.

The challenge is to develop educational programmes that enable all individuals, not just an elite, to become effective thinkers, because these competencies are now required of everyone. A 'thinking skills' approach suggests that learners must develop awareness of themselves as thinkers and learners, practise strategies for effective thinking and develop the habits of intelligent behaviour that are needed for lifelong learning. As Paul, aged 10, said: 'We need to think better if we are to become better people'.

WHAT DOES RESEARCH TELL US ABOUT THINKING?

Research in cognitive science and psychology is providing a clearer picture of the brain and the processes associated with thinking (Smith, 2004). This brain research has some important implications for teachers. For example, we now know that most of the growth in the human brain occurs in early childhood: by the age of 6, the brain in most children is approximately 90 per cent of its adult size. This implies that intervention, while the brain is still growing, may be more effective than waiting until the brain is fully developed. Cognitive challenge is important at all stages, but especially in the early years of education.

Dialogue is the primary means for developing intelligence in the human species. The large human brain evolved to enable individuals to negotiate, through dialogue, the complexities of social living. The capacity for dialogue is central to human thinking. Human consciousness originates in a motivation to share emotions, experience and activities with others. This 'dialogic' capacity is more fundamental than writing or tool use. It is through dialogue that children develop consciousness, learn control over their internal mental processes and develop the conceptual tools for thinking (Fisher, 2009). No wonder recent research emphasises that teacher–pupil interaction is the key to improving standards of teaching and learning (Alexander, 2006; Hattie, 2008; Higgins, Kokotsaki and Coe, 2011).

Psychologists and philosophers have helped to extend our understanding of the term 'thinking' by emphasising the importance of *dispositions*, such as attention and motivation, commonly associated with thinking (Claxton, 2002). This has prompted a move away from a simple model of 'thinking skills' as isolated cognitive capacities to a view of thinking as inextricably connected to emotions and dispositions, including 'emotional intelligence', which is our ability to understand our own emotions and the emotions of others (Goleman, 2006).

THE IMPORTANCE OF METACOGNITION

We need not only to teach cognitive skills and strategies, but also to develop the higher 'metacognitive' functions involved in metacognition. *Metacognition* involves thinking about one's own thinking. It includes knowledge of oneself: for example, what one knows, what one has learned, what one can and cannot do, and ways to improve one's learning or achievement.

Metacognition involves two levels of reflection:

1   knowledge of thinking: includes awareness of self, task and strategy;
2   self-regulated thinking: includes ability to self-evaluate, and self-manage learning.

Metacognition is promoted by helping pupils to reflect on their thinking and decision-making processes. It is developed when pupils are helped to be strategic in organising their activities and are encouraged to reflect before, during and after problem-solving processes. The implication is that you need to plan time for debriefing and review in lessons, to encourage children to think about their learning and how to improve it. This can be done through discussion in a plenary session, or by finding time for reflective writing in their own thinking or learning logs.

In practice, we prompt metacognitive discussion by asking metacognitive questions at different levels of cognitive challenge. First is the level of *cognitive description*, when we ask children to describe what they have been thinking and learning, as when we ask: 'What have you read/learned?'. We then seek *cognitive extension*, by probing their thinking more deeply, as when we ask: 'What does . . . mean?'. We should also encourage their *cognitive regulation* by asking them, for example, 'What does a good learner/reader/writer do?'. Other metacognitive questions to ask children include:

*   *Before a task*: How will you do this? What might help? What strategy could you use?
*   *During a task*: Is it working? What is difficult? Is there another way, what could you try?

- *After a task*: What went well? What have you learned? What do you need to remember for next time?

The human mind is made up of many faculties or capacities that enable learning to take place. Our general capacity for understanding or *intelligence* was once thought to be innate and unmodifiable. As a child once put it: 'Either you've got it or you haven't'. The notion of inborn intelligence that dominated educational practice until the mid twentieth century was challenged by Vygotsky, Piaget and others, who developed a constructivist psychology based on a view of learners as active creators of their own knowledge. Some researchers argue that intelligence is not one generic capacity, but is made up of multiple intelligences (Gardner, 1999). Howard Gardner's multiple-intelligence theory has had a growing influence, in recent years, on educational theory and practice, although not all are convinced of its claims. Whether intelligence is viewed as one general capacity or many, what researchers are agreed upon is that it is modifiable and can be developed.

In teaching for metacognition, we want to strengthen children's belief that their intelligence and ability to learn can improve, and teach them to set goals, plan, monitor and evaluate their own learning and, as far as possible, to be self-directed in their thinking and learning.

KEY PRINCIPLES IN TEACHING FOR THINKING

Key principles that emerge from this research include the need for teachers and carers to provide:

- *cognitive challenge*: challenging children's thinking from the earliest years;
- *collaborative learning*: extending thinking through working with others;
- *metacognitive discussion*: reviewing what children think and how they learn.

This research and the pioneering work of Reuven Feuerstein, who created a programme called Instrumental Enrichment, Matthew Lipman, who founded Philosophy for Children, and other leading figures, such as Edward de Bono, creator of 'lateral thinking', have inspired a wide range of curriculum and programme developments (Fisher, 2005). These include a range of teaching approaches that you could use, including 'cognitive acceleration', 'brain-based' approaches (such as 'accelerated learning') and 'philosophical' approaches that aim at developing the moral and emotional, as well as intellectual, aspects of thinking – caring and collaborative, as well as critical and creative thinking.

SHOULD THINKING BE TAUGHT IN SEPARATE LESSONS OR ACROSS THE CURRICULUM?

Research suggests that one-off 'thinking' lessons are less effective than teaching thinking and learning strategies that can be applied in subjects (such as CASE; see page 448) or as dialogic strategies across the curriculum. McGuinness (1999) points out that the most successful interventions are associated with a 'strong theoretical underpinning, well-designed and contextualised materials, explicit pedagogy and teacher support'.

TABLE 7.5.2 Thinking skills linked to Bloom's taxonomy

Thinking skills	Bloom's taxonomy
Information processing	Knowledge, comprehension
Enquiry	Application
Reasoning	Analysis
Creative thinking	Synthesis
Evaluation	Evaluation

Task 7.5.2 Identifying thinking skills

Identify, in a lesson plan or observation of a classroom lesson, the thinking skills that are being developed as general learning objectives. Look for evidence that the children are engaged in information processing, reasoning, enquiry, creative thinking and evaluation.

The following pro forma could be used for recording the evidence.

HOW DO WE TEACH THINKING IN THE CLASSROOM?

Researchers have identified a number of teaching strategies you can use to help stimulate children's thinking in the classroom. These approaches to teaching thinking can be summarised as:

- cognitive acceleration;
- brain-based techniques;
- philosophy for children;
- teaching strategies across the curriculum.

Cognitive acceleration

CASE

Adey and Shayer developed Cognitive Acceleration through Science Education (CASE) by applying the theories of Piaget on 'cognitive conflict' to Key Stage 3 science. Their work now extends into other subjects and to all age groups (Shayer and Adey, 2002).

The following format of a CASE lesson for thinking builds in time for cognitive and metacognitive discussion:

1   *concrete preparation*: stimulus to thinking, introducing the terms of the problem;
2   *cognitive conflict*: creates a challenge for the mind;
3   *social construction*: dialogue with others, discussion that extends thinking;
4   *metacognition*: reflection on how we tackled the problem;
5   *bridging*: reviewing where else we can use this thinking and learning.

CASE lessons have also been developed for young children under the title 'Let's Think!' and aim to raise achievement by developing Year 1 pupils' general thinking patterns and teachers' understanding of children's thinking.

Children are given a challenge and are required to work collaboratively, in order to plan and evaluate their own and others' thinking strategies. As in other discussion-based approaches, children are encouraged to state whether they agree or disagree with each other by giving a reason. For example, they are taught to say, 'I think . . . because . . .' or 'I disagree with you because . . .'. Activities are designed as problems to be solved, thus creating a context for developing thinking.

The teacher then gets the children to think about their thinking (metacognition) through asking such questions as, 'What do you think we are going to have to think about?' and 'How did you get your answer?', rather than, 'Is your answer correct?'. Of course, you do not need the Let's Think! materials to apply this teaching strategy to any area of the curriculum.

'Thinking maths' lessons for primary children are part of a related project called Cognitive Acceleration in Mathematics Education (CAME). These lessons involve discussion-based tasks in maths that aim to develop children's conceptual thinking, rather than the mechanics of doing the maths. The activities are planned to generate group and whole-class discussion, rather than written work, with an emphasis on 'How did you get your answer?' rather than 'What is the answer?'. As the CAME approach suggests, if your emphasis in teaching is, 'How did you get your answer?' rather than 'Is your answer correct?', it is a far more productive way of generating children's thinking and learning.

Brain-based techniques

Accelerated learning

Many educationalists are influenced by recent research into how the human brain works and draw on some of the implications of this research for teachers and schools. Accelerated learning and multiple-intelligence approaches all draw on these broad ideas, together with research into learning styles. The common feature is the reliance on brain research to inspire teaching techniques in the classroom.

There are many theories of learning styles. They are rooted in a classification of psychological types and the fact that individuals tend to process information differently. Different researchers propose different sets of learning style characteristics, but many remain unconvinced by their claims that children learn best through using one preferred style (Coffield *et al.*, 2004).

Accelerated learning approaches include applying VAK learning styles to teaching. VAK stands for:

*   *visual* – learning best through pictures, charts, diagrams, video, ICT, and so on;
*   *auditory* – learning best through listening;
*   *kinaesthetic* – learning best through being physically engaged in a task.

For example, in teaching a class to spell a word, a teacher might show them how to chunk the word into three pieces and emphasise this by using different colours for each section of the word and asking them to visualise it in their heads. The teacher might also ask them to write the word in the air with their fingers. Accelerated learning emphasises the importance of including a range of learning experiences – visual, verbal and physical – in your teaching, so that children are challenged to think in different ways. (For more on Alistair Smith's approach to accelerated learning, see: www.alite.co.uk)

These and other 'brain-based' teaching strategies, such as 'Brain Gym' (which uses simple but challenging aerobic exercises to focus the mind and stimulate the brain), offer much scope for research in the classroom (see www.braingym.org.uk).

De Bono

According to Edward de Bono, we tend to think in restricted and predictable ways. To become better thinkers, we need to learn new habits. His teaching strategy, known as 'thinking hats', helps learners try different approaches to thinking. Each 'thinking hat' represents a different way to think about a problem or issue. Children are encouraged to try on the different 'hats' or approaches to a problem to go beyond their usual thinking habits (de Bono, 2000). The 'hats', together with questions you might ask, are as follows:

*   White hat = information: *What do we know?*
*   Red hat = feelings: *What do we feel?*
*   Purple hat = problems: *What are the drawbacks?*
*   Yellow hat = positives: *What are the benefits?*

- Green hat = creativity: *What ideas have we got?*
- Blue hat = control: *What are our aims?*

De Bono claims that the technique is widely used in management, but little research has been published on its use in education. Some teachers have found it a useful technique for encouraging children to look at a problem or topic from a variety of perspectives. It encourages us, and our children, to think creatively about any topic and to ask: 'Is there another way of thinking about this?'.

Philosophy for children

A pioneer of the 'critical thinking' movement in America is the philosopher Matthew Lipman. Originally a university philosophy professor, Lipman was unhappy at what he saw as poor thinking in his students. They seemed to have been encouraged to learn facts and to accept authoritative opinions, but not to think for themselves. He became convinced that something was wrong with the way they had been taught in school when they were younger. He, therefore, founded the Institute for the Advancement of Philosophy for Children and developed, with colleagues, a programme called Philosophy for Children, used in more than forty countries around the world (see www.montclair.edu/cehs/academics/centers-and-institutes/iapc/). Lipman believes that children are natural philosophers, because they view the world with curiosity and wonder (Lipman, 2003). It is children's own questions, stimulated by specially written philosophical stories, that form the starting point for enquiry or discussion.

Stories for Thinking

Many resources have been developed that adapt Matthew Lipman's approach to Philosophy for Children to the needs of children and teachers in the UK. 'Stories for Thinking' is one such approach (Fisher, 1996). The aim, through using stories and other kinds of stimulus for philosophical discussion, is to create a *community of enquiry* in the classroom (see www.sapere.org.uk). Encouraging children to question and discuss what they do not understand is fundamental to this teaching method. Researchers have reported striking cognitive gains through this approach in the classroom, including enhanced verbal reasoning, self-esteem and dialogic skills (Topping and Trickey, 2007).

Teachers note that, in Stories for Thinking lessons, in which they may also use poems, pictures, objects or other texts for thinking, the children have become more thoughtful, better at speaking and listening to each other, better at questioning and using the language of reasoning, more confident in posing creative ideas and in judging what they and others think and do, and more confident about applying their thinking to fresh challenges in learning and in life (Fisher, 2013).

What stories or other forms of stimulus could you use to really engage your children in thinking? How could you create an enquiring classroom?

Task 7.5.3 Creating a thinking classroom

What would a thinking classroom look like?

- Collect words to describe what a thinking classroom might look like. These might include some reference to the teacher's behaviour, children's behaviour, classroom environment or kinds of activity that help children to think and learn well.
- Sort your ideas into small groups and give each group a heading that you think appropriate.
- Choose one idea from each group and consider how you could develop this in your classroom.

Teaching strategies across the curriculum

A growing number of programmes and strategies aim to help teachers develop children's thinking and learning across the curriculum, such as Thinking Actively in a Social Context (TASC) and Activating Children's Thinking Skills (ACTS). It is difficult to evaluate the success of these and other interventions because of the many variables involved in the teaching situation. There is much scope here for your own research into teaching strategies in the classroom and for developing new strategies.

A number of specific teaching strategies have been identified to help stimulate children's thinking in different subject areas. For example, 'Odd One Out' is a teaching technique to identify pupils' understanding of key concepts in different subjects. A teacher might, in a numeracy lesson, put three numbers on the board, such as 9, 5 and 10; or, in science, three materials; or, in English, three characters to compare and contrast – then ask the children to choose the 'odd one out' and to give a reason. Teachers who use this strategy claim it can reveal gaps in the knowledge taught and the knowledge and vocabulary that the children are then able to use. The children think of it as a game and are used to thinking up examples and ideas that show their thinking in different curriculum subjects. This approach encourages creative thinking and reasoning (Higgins, Baumfield and Leat, 2001). Can you think of three things and give reasons why one, two or each of them might be the odd one out?

Task 7.5.4 What do good teachers do to stimulate thinking?

Investigate and record what good teachers do to stimulate children's thinking in the classroom, and link this to what good learners do.

Think what stimulating children's thinking and learning looks like in the classroom. Record in the chart below what good teachers do to stimulate thinking and what good learners do.

What do good teachers do?	What do good learners do?
•	•
•	•
•	•
•	•
•	•

Collect data by observing teachers in the classroom and record examples of how they stimulate children's thinking. Interview teachers and children to discover what answers they would give to the questions above. Find out what others think through reading and Internet research.

After collecting ideas and data, summarise and evaluate what you find and draw conclusions about what you have learned from this investigation. Think in what ways your teaching practice might be modified by your research.

Mind mapping

Many approaches include the use of thinking diagrams – 'mind maps' or 'concept maps' – as aids to making thinking visual and explicit.

Concept mapping is an information-processing technique with a long history. Tony Buzan developed this technique into a version he calls 'mind mapping' (Buzan, 2006). Concept maps are tools that help make thinking visible and involve writing down, or more commonly drawing, a central idea and thinking up new and related ideas that radiate out from the centre. Children, by focusing on key ideas written down in their own words and then looking for branches out and connections between the ideas, are mapping knowledge in a manner that can help them understand and remember new information. A simple concept map might be used to map out the connections between characters in a story. Children might also draw maps from memory, to test what they remember or know. Teachers have found concept maps helpful in finding out or revising what children know, and the technique is especially popular when used in pairs or groups. Children can learn the technique from an early age, and many find it motivating. As one young child put it: 'Concept mapping gets you to think and try more'. Concept mapping is a useful teaching and revision technique for extending thinking and making it visually memorable.

When you are planning your next topic or activity with children, think of ways of making your own or your children's thinking visible, for example by creating a 'mind map' of a story, a process or collection of ideas.

Computers and thinking

Research shows that there are several ways in which ICT could particularly enhance information-processing skills. ICT enables multiple and complex representations of information, for example allowing learners to think with a richer knowledge base. As James, aged 8, said: 'I didn't know there was so much to know!'.

Educational software can act like a teacher to prompt and direct enquiry through asking questions, giving clues and suggesting avenues of investigation. It can also act as a resource while learners discuss and explore ideas, for example prompting reflection around a simulation. Networks via the Internet, including video conferencing, can allow children to engage directly in collaborative learning and knowledge-sharing with others who are not physically present.

Computers can help develop children's thinking skills when used as part of a larger dialogue about thinking and learning (Wegerif, 2002). The challenge for you as a teacher is to find ways to use the computer to encourage thinking with, and discussion between, children.

Recent test results show that standards in schools are rising – but slowly. Could the teaching of thinking provide a key to raising achievement? The experience of many teachers suggests that, when pupils are taught the habits of effective thinking, they grow in confidence, their learning is enriched, and they are better prepared to face the challenges of the future. Children think so too – as Arran, aged 9, put it: 'When you get out in the real world you have to think for yourself; that's why we need to practise it in school'. Research suggests that the most successful approaches to teaching thinking are dialogic teaching methods (such as Philosophy for Children), Piagetian approaches (such as CASE) and assessment for learning (AfL; Hattie, 2008; see also Unit 5.1 of this volume). *Toolkit of Strategies to Improve Learning*, published by the Sutton Trust (Higgins *et al.*, 2011), a research summary into cost-effective teaching strategies, identified 'effective feedback' and teaching for 'metacognition and self-regulation' as having the greatest impact on improving learning and attainment (see website on page 454).

Though AfL and teaching thinking grew from different theoretical and research bases, they share a common concern about the quality of thinking and learning. It is not surprising, therefore, that they share many common strategies for classroom practices, and many teachers and schools seek to pursue both simultaneously in their classrooms. For example, the Welsh Assembly Government funded a 5-year project on integrating both approaches, *How to Develop Thinking and Assessment for Learning in the Classroom* (see website). There will, however, be other approaches, not so well supported by research, that teachers may find useful in developing children's thinking and learning in any subject area, or across the curriculum, that could provide a good focus for their own research. Good teaching is about helping children to think for themselves, which is why it is both a challenge and an adventure.

In Wales . . .

How to Develop Thinking and Assessment for Learning in the Classroom

This document draws together a wide range of strategies and tools for practical classroom use. It has a range of suggested tools to support classroom practice and learning and is illustrated by helpful cross-curricular examples.

Source: http://learning.gov.wales/docs/learningwales/publications/130429how-to-develop-thinking-en.pdf (accessed 2 November 2017).

Introduction to Thinking Skills

Wales has put together a set of training modules for teachers to develop an understanding of thinking skills in the context of PISA. This link takes you to the first of those modules.

Source: http://learning.gov.wales/resources/learningpacks/pisa/understanding-classroom-experiences-as-a-newly-qualified-teacher/?lang=en (accessed 2 November 2017).

SUMMARY

In recent years, there has been much research into ways of developing children's thinking and learning skills. This has been informed by growing knowledge about how the brain works, how people learn, and how teaching approaches can help improve children's ability to think and learn. The phrase 'thinking skills' refers to many of the capacities involved in thinking and learning, skills fundamental to lifelong learning, active citizenship and emotional intelligence. Research shows that the key to raising standards in education is through teaching that promotes cognitive challenge, interactive dialogue with and between children and metacognitive review. These and other teaching strategies can help raise standards of achievement and create thinking children, thinking classrooms and thinking schools.

ANNOTATED FURTHER READING

Fisher, R. (2005) *Teaching Children to Think*, 2nd edn, Cheltenham, UK: Stanley Thornes.
>   This book discusses the nature of thinking and thinking skills and explores the development of thinking skills programmes and how they can be implemented in the classroom.

Fisher, R. (2009) *Creative Dialogue: Talk for Thinking*, London: Routledge.
>   This is a guide to dialogic learning, presenting practical, research-based ways of teaching children to be more thoughtful and creative and to learn more effectively through talk for thinking in the classroom. It includes advice on using dialogue to support AfL and ideas for developing listening skills and concentration.

Fisher R. (2013) *Teaching Thinking: Philosophical Enquiry in the Classroom*, 4th edn, London: Continuum.
>   A guide to using philosophical discussion in the classroom to develop children's thinking, learning and literacy skills.

Hattie, J. (2008) *Visible Learning: A Synthesis of Over 800 Meta-analyses Relating to Achievement*, London: Routledge.
>   This, the largest-ever overview of education research, suggests that raising the quality of teacher–pupil interaction is the key to improving education. Encouraging pupils to question their teachers on what they do and do not understand is identified as the single most effective teaching method. Other effective approaches identified include Piagetian programmes (such as CASE) and AfL.

(M) FURTHER READING TO SUPPORT M-LEVEL STUDY

Burke, L.A. and Williams, J.M. (2009) 'Developmental changes in children's understandings of intelligence and thinking skills', *Early Child Development & Care*, 179(7): 949–68.
>   This study extends previous research on the development of children's concepts of intelligence and produces new data on children's understandings of effective thinking and thinking skills.

Swartz, R. and McGuiness, C. (2014) *Developing and Assessing Thinking Skills Project Final Report Part 1: Literature Review and Evaluation Framework*, The International Baccalaureate Organisation.
>   Part 1 of this report presents a literature review of research identifying important and teachable kinds of thinking, how they can *be taught*, and how they can *be assessed*, including key thinking objectives for a thinking curriculum, and principles and practices for teaching thinking, by two of the most respected researchers in the field. The report is available at www.ibo.org/globalassets/publications/ib-research/continuum/student-thinking-skills-report-part-1.pdf (accessed 2 November 2017).

RELEVANT WEBSITES

Society for Advancing Philosophical Enquiry and Reflection in Education (SAPERE): www.sapere.org.uk/
>   This site promotes philosophy for children throughout the UK.

The Sutton Trust Toolkit: www.cem.org/attachments/1toolkit-summary-final-r-2-.pdf
>   The *Toolkit of Strategies to Improve Learning* evaluates teaching strategies, including teaching for metacognition.

G. Taggart *et al.* (2005) *Thinking Skills in the early Years: A Literature Review*, NFER: https://www.nfer.ac.uk/publications/TSK01/TSK01.pdf

Thinking Skills and Creativity: www.journals.elsevier.com/thinking-skills-and-creativity/
> *Thinking Skills and Creativity* is a journal of peer-reviewed articles on teaching for thinking and creativity.

Welsh Assembly Government: http://learning.gov.wales/docs/learningwales/publications/130429how-to-develop-thinking-en.pdf
> This Welsh Assembly Government site has *How to Develop Thinking and Assessment for Learning in the Classroom.*

REFERENCES

Alexander, R. (2006) *Towards Dialogic Teaching: Rethinking Classroom Talk,* 3rd edn, Cambridge, UK: Dialogos.

Bloom, B. and Krathwohl, D.R. (1956) *Taxonomy of Educational Objectives, Handbook 1: Cognitive Domain,* New York: David McKay.

Buzan, T. (2006) *The Mind Map Book,* London: BBC Active Publications. See also: https://imindmap.com/ (accessed 02 November 2017).

Claxton, G. (2002) *Building Learning Power: Helping Young People Become Better Learners,* Bristol, UK: TLO.

Coffield, F., Moseley, D., Hall, E. and Ecclestone, K. (2004) *Should We Be Using Learning Styles: What Research Has to Say to Practice,* London: Learning Skills and Development Agency.

de Bono, E. (2000) *Six Thinking Hats,* 2nd edn, London: Penguin.

Fisher, R. (1996) *Stories for Thinking,* Oxford, UK: Nash Pollock.

Fisher, R. (2005) *Teaching Children to Think,* 2nd edn, Cheltenham, UK: Stanley Thornes.

Fisher, R. (2009) *Creative Dialogue: Talk for Thinking,* London: Routledge.

Fisher, R. (2013) *Teaching Thinking: Philosophical Enquiry in the Classroom,* 4th edn, London: Continuum.

Gardner, H. (1999) *Intelligence Reframed: Multiple Intelligences for the 21st Century,* New York: Basic Books.

Goleman, D. (2006) *Social Intelligence,* New York: Bantam.

Hattie, J. (2008) *Visible Learning: A Synthesis of Over 800 Meta-analyses Relating to Achievement,* London: Routledge. See also Visible Learning website: http://visible-learning.org/

Higgins, S., Baumfield, V. and Leat, D. (2001) *Thinking Through Primary Teaching,* Cambridge, UK: Chris Kington.

Higgins, S., Kokotsaki, D. and Coe, R.J. (2011) *Toolkit of Strategies to Improve Learning: Summary for Schools Spending the Pupil Premium,* Sutton Trust. Retrieved from http://dro.dur.ac.uk/11453/3/11453S.pdf?DDD45+DDD29+DDO128+ded4ss+cqjd36 (accessed 2 November 2017).

Lipman, M. (2003) *Thinking in Education,* 2nd edn, Cambridge, UK: Cambridge University Press.

McGuinness, C. (1999) *From Thinking Skills to Thinking Classrooms: A Review and Evaluation of Approaches for Developing Pupils' Thinking,* Research Report RR115, London: DfEE.

Moseley, D., Baumfield, V., Elliott, J., Higgins, S., Miller, J. and Newton, D.P. (2005) *Frameworks for Thinking: A Handbook for Teaching and Learning,* Cambridge, UK: Cambridge University Press.

Shayer, M. and Adey, P. (2002) *Learning Intelligence,* Buckingham, UK: Open University Press.

Smith, A. (2004) *The Brain's Behind It: New Knowledge about the Brain and Learning,* London: Continuum.

Topping, K.J. and Trickey, S. (2007) 'Impact of philosophical enquiry on school students' interactive behaviour', *International Journal of Thinking Skills & Creativity,* 2(2): 73–84.

Wegerif, R. (2002) *Literature Review in Thinking Skills, Technology and Learning.* Retrieved from www.nfer.ac.uk/publications/FUTL75 (accessed 2 November 2017).

UNDERSTANDING MASTERY IN PRIMARY MATHEMATICS

Mark Boylan and Vivien Townsend

INTRODUCTION

Since 2010, there has been increasing talk of mastery in primary education. The 2014 PE, art and English curriculums refer to mastery of movement, art and design techniques and language, respectively. However, interest in mastery is most notable in mathematics, and this is the main focus of this unit.

This unit provides a background as to why mastery is being promoted in England, reviews mastery initiatives and discusses the different meanings of mastery. It then introduces some ideas from Shanghai and Singapore that are sometimes described as teaching for mastery and looks at examples of how mastery is enacted in practice in mathematics lessons in English classrooms, using short examples from teachers who are adopting mastery approaches.

OBJECTIVES

By the end of this unit, you should:

- understand reasons why mastery is being promoted in England by government and others;
- understand different meanings of mastery, and the meaning of key terms and ideas used in relation to mastery;
- know about key aspects of Singapore and Shanghai mathematics teaching;
- know some of the ways that teachers are implementing mastery in English classrooms.

BACKGROUND

For some time, there have been concerns about the mathematics teaching in primary schools in England. In 1999, the National Numeracy Strategy (NNS) was introduced, drawing on examples of local initiatives in England as well as lessons from other countries. One important aspect of the NNS approach was to promote structured lessons, typically in three parts: a mental or oral starter activity, a main activity and an end-of-lesson plenary. Differentiated lesson objectives were encouraged, and the pace at which content was covered was often emphasised.

In its first few years, the NNS led to increases in KS2 test performance; however, this was not sustained. In 2008, a major government-sponsored report – the Williams Review – on mathematics teaching in the primary and early years was published (Williams, 2008). It reported that there were examples of excellent practice in primary teaching, but there was a lot of variability, a finding also supported by Ofsted (2011). The Williams Review also found that many primary teachers needed support to develop their confidence and practice in teaching mathematics.

Since the introduction of the NNS, governments around the world have become interested in transnational comparison of educational outcomes. The Programme for International Student Assessment (PISA) is an international study of 15-year-old school pupils' performance in mathematics, science and reading. In mathematics, an equivalent test is used in lots of different countries, and pupil performance is compared. Results in England, on average, are lower than in the highest-performing countries, although the difference is often exaggerated in the media (Askew *et al.*, 2010). The desire to improve England's ranking led to an interest in the mathematics education systems of higher-performing jurisdictions – in particular, what have been referred to as, the teaching for mastery approaches found in Singapore and Shanghai.

In 2014, a new primary mathematics curriculum was published. There are three changes introduced in the new curriculum that are particularly important in relation to mastery. The first is that the curriculum was designed to be more comparable in terms of difficulty to curricula in high-performing educational systems. Second, the programme of study states that the 'expectation is that the majority of pupils will move through the programmes of study at broadly the same pace' (DfE, 2014). This is sometimes referred to as 'the mastery statement'. This is very different from what was common practice in many primary classrooms in England of sitting pupils in groups based on their 'ability'. These different groups would be given different tasks and treated differently by teachers (Marks, 2014). The third change is the removal of national curriculum levels. Previously, the focus was on progress through sublevels of the old national curriculum, from different starting points and to different destinations. Now, the focus is on all pupils achieving age-related expectations, with teachers planning extra support for those who need it and challenging those who meet expectations to deepen their understanding, rather than moving them on to content from later years.

To move away from accelerating children into the content of the year above, we began by exploring ideas for taking the children deeper within the same objective. We found lots of useful low-threshold high-ceiling activities on the NRICH website and began experimenting with mixed-ability grouping. We found that when all of the children are working on the same objective, even if it is at different depths, mixed-ability groups work surprisingly well. Interestingly, it is the previously higher attaining children who have found the change in approach most challenging as they are now expected to explain, prove and justify rather than just produce a correct answer. It has shown us that their depth of learning was not as we believed it was.

(Claire Duncan, World's End Junior School, Birmingham)

Task 7.6.1 The different ways the word 'mastery' is used

Before reading the next section, reflect on how you have heard the term 'mastery' being used, in schools or in your initial teacher education.

MEANINGS OF MASTERY

In this section, different meanings of mastery are discussed. Putting aside the gendered origins of the term 'master', mastery is one of those words, like 'community' and 'participation', that seem to be obviously good ideas. However, there is no universal agreement on the definition of the terms 'master' or 'mastery' (Askew *et al.*, 2015; ATM/MA Primary working group, 2016; NAMA, 2016). This makes it all the more important that you develop your ability to unpick different ways in which the words are used. This can support you to engage as a critical thinker with the mastery agenda.

In recent years, there have been various initiatives, groups and organisations in England promoting mastery. The National Centre for Excellence in the Teaching of Mathematics (NCETM) is tasked by the government with promoting mastery in England and coordinating the national network of Maths Hubs. Each Maths Hub is led by a school or college, working with other schools and mathematics education professionals. The hubs promote teaching for mastery alongside other projects and initiatives to enhance mathematics teaching in their local areas. The NCETM has developed the Primary Mathematics Teaching for Mastery Specialist programme. This professional development programme develops mastery specialists who can lead the introduction of mastery approaches in their own and others' schools. Many of the participants in this programme also take part in the Mathematics Teacher Exchange (MTE) programme, which involves teachers visiting Shanghai and hosting Shanghai teachers in England. The NCETM, with the Maths Hubs, coordinated a national textbook project that enquired into and encouraged the use of East Asian-inspired textbooks in primary schools.

As well as the MTE programme, there are other initiatives that are largely independent of, though encouraged by, government. Two prominent Singapore-inspired initiatives are: Mathematics Mastery, which offers programmes of study, lesson materials and professional development opportunities following a mastery approach (see Drury, 2014; Jerrim and Vignoles, 2016); and Maths – No Problem and Inspire Maths, based on translations of Singaporean textbooks with accompanying professional development activities. Many other publishers have also begun to produce resources that claim to either follow a mastery approach or be influenced by practices in Singapore or Shanghai.

It is important to be aware that the term mastery has been around for some time in Western education. Benjamin Bloom wrote an article in 1968 called 'Learning for mastery', in which he set out his belief that, given sufficient opportunity to learn, and enough engagement in learning, the vast majority of pupils could meet an expected level of understanding (Ellis, 2014). Bloom's mastery learning focuses on regular formative assessments, followed by re-teaching where necessary and providing enough curriculum materials and other resources for this to happen: a form of personalised learning. As well as mastery learning, mastery is also used to describe teaching. For example, NCETM – and others – describes some of the approaches to mathematics teaching in East Asia as teaching for mastery (NCETM, 2016). However, an important difference between learning for mastery and teaching for mastery is that advocates of the latter argue for particular ways of teaching that they believe help to ensure that everyone is successful. The basis of this approach is that pupils are taught through whole-class interactive teaching focused on the same lesson content for everyone. Later in this unit, this approach is described in more detail. So mastery can also refer to an approach to *teaching and learning*.

Central to learning and teaching for mastery approaches is the *belief* that everyone can be successful. This is also a view shared by more recent advocates of 'teaching for mastery' (NCETM, 2016). This belief underpins the current primary mathematics curriculum, which is why it is sometimes described as a *mastery curriculum*; it is a single curriculum for everyone to follow together, as opposed to the differentiated learning of the recent past (Askew *et al.*, 2015). Learning for mastery or teaching for mastery approaches are also reliant on pupils' motivation to learn. Thus, mastery also has links to the idea of learner *mindsets*. Carol Dweck describes a growth (or mastery) mindset as a belief that success is primarily due to effort. This is contrasted with a fixed mindset, where success is viewed as primarily due to an inborn or natural ability that cannot be easily changed (Dweck, 2006).

In our school we felt it was important to establish a shared understanding of the 'mindset' needed for working towards mastery. We have been working hard to develop an attitude of 'I can try my best' rather than 'I can't' which has not always been easy as some pupils have already developed a notion that they are not 'smart at maths'. With a lot of teacher modelling, the children finally believe in themselves as mathematicians and even if they can't get the right answer, they will always try their best.

(Martyn Yeo, Whitestone Infant School, Warwickshire)

Task 7.6.2 Mastery mindsets

How far do you believe that everyone can be successful at mathematics, or do you think some people have a natural ability for the subject?

Read Rachel Marks's article:

Marks, R. (2013) '"The blue table means you don't have a clue": The persistence of fixed-ability thinking and practices in primary mathematics in English schools', *Forum: For Promoting 3–19 Comprehensive Education*, 55(1): 31–44.

Consider how you might organise pupils into groups and teach in a way that would avoid reinforcing fixed-ability thinking.

A further meaning of mastery is related to the idea of mastering mathematics and so defines a particular a type of *mathematical capability*.

A mathematical concept or skill has been mastered when, through exploration, clarification, practice and application over time, a person can represent it in multiple ways, has the mathematical language to be able to communicate related ideas, and can think mathematically with the concept so that they can independently apply it to a totally new problem in an unfamiliar situation.

(Drury, 2014: 9)

This type of learning is sometimes referred to as deep learning.

In an early draft of National Curriculum performance descriptors (DfE, 2013), the government described performance above the expected 'National Standard' as 'Mastery Standard' (it was later replaced with 'Greater depth within the National Standard'), and consequently, in some schools, 'mastery' is used to describe the highest level of performance; it is synonymous with 'gifted and talented'. This use of 'mastery' is inconsistent with the uses described above.

In Northern Ireland . . .

We can change our mindset, and the strategies in AfL contribute to the development of mastery orientated, resilient and resourceful learners. Having a growth or mastery mindset is about being resilient in the face of frustration and failure, and having the ability to respond well to challenges, believing that effort can lead to success.

(CCEA, 2008: 9)

Source: http://ccea.org.uk/sites/default/files/docs/curriculum/assessment/assessment_for_learning/afl_practical_guide.pdf (accessed 3 November 2017).

Task 7.6.3 What does it mean to 'master' mathematics?

This task focuses on knowledge of multiplication tables in Year 3. However, you could adapt the activity to another year group that you are teaching. In Year 3, pupils are expected to recall and use multiplication and division facts for the 3, 4 and 8 multiplication tables (building on previous knowledge of working with 2, 5 and 10).

The NCETM has produced a series of booklets that focus on how assessment can take account of deep learning (see www.ncetm.org.uk/resources/46689). Download the booklet for Year 3 and read pages 16–18. These give examples of what mastery might mean in this context. Develop further examples of mastery using the following activities:

- different ways of representing multiplication using objects, areas, a variety of images and number lines;
- multiplication and division word problems;
- the relationship between multiplication and division;
- using multiplication and division facts in in other areas of mathematics;
- patterns and relationships comparing the 2, 3, 4, 5, 8 and 10 times tables.

TABLE 7.6.1 Different ways the term 'mastery' is used

Beliefs about learners	Curriculum	Mindset	Teaching and learning	Mathematical capability
The vast majority can be successful	Same curriculum for all	Growth (or mastery) mindset	Learning for mastery Teaching for mastery	Deep learning

Table 7.6.1 summarises these different meanings. Remember that, although these meanings are connected, they may not all be part of how people understand 'mastery' for themselves.

The next two sections focus on teaching for mastery as found in Shanghai and Singapore.

SHANGHAI

Shanghai's education system is organisationally separate from the rest of China and has its own curriculum. Practices in Shanghai are different in lots of ways from those found in England (for a comparison, see Boylan *et al.*, 2016: 17-18). In Shanghai, lessons are shorter – typically 35 minutes in primary schools, with most practice work being done as daily homework. Mathematics is taught using whole-class interactive teaching, with lots of questioning, and mini-plenaries. There is an emphasis on the use of correct mathematical language by pupils. Each lesson focuses on one specific element of the curriculum, which is then tackled in small incremental steps, so that learning builds gradually. This approach ensures that mastery of a concept or procedure has been achieved by the whole class before they move on. Pupils are taught in all-attainment classes of 40–50 pupils, and differentiation is through extension or deepening of understanding. Progression through the curriculum is encapsulated in textbooks that are used in every school. Shanghai teachers spend less time in class, which means that they have more time to mark daily homework; prepare lessons in great depth; collaborate with colleagues; and work with any pupils needing additional support, to ensure gaps do not open up in their understanding of mathematics.

At my school, we were interested in the shorter mathematics lessons in China that last a maximum of 35 minutes. So we decided to experiment with 'split lessons' where the traditional one hour lesson is separated into two half hours, with playtime and assembly in between.

During the first session children work with a partner initially, then independently, using carefully chosen practical resources as the teacher leads back and forth interaction, including questioning, repetition of sentence stems, short tasks, explanations, demonstration, and discussion. The children go out to play with a maths question to think about – sometimes with a designated 'maths buddy' – and return to the classroom eager to show their learning. In the second part of the lesson, pupils record their learning in journals, or complete practice exercises in workbooks.

The split lesson allows time for new learning to 'settle' in pupils' thoughts and gives teachers time to exchange observations with teaching assistants. If there are a small number of children who at the end of a lesson have not grasped the new learning, they spend 20 minutes that afternoon working with their teacher. It has been important that teachers do not pre-judge who will be in this group! This 'same day catch up' has been great for keeping classes working together and for helping us identify what needs to feature in future lessons or what support individuals need.

(Helen Hackett, Parkfield Community School, Birmingham)

In the remainder of this section, we will focus on ways in which Shanghai teachers aim to develop conceptual understanding and procedural fluency. One way that these different approaches have been summarised is in terms of teaching through *variation* (Gu, Haung and Marton, 2004). Variation theory supposes that an important aspect of developing understanding of a concept is through considering how that concept varies or is different from others, and a key role of the teacher is to provide mathematical contexts or problems in order to draw learners' attention to these differences. In Shanghai, two different sorts of variation are found: conceptual and procedural.

Understanding of a concept can be gained through familiarity with multiple representations or *models* of the mathematical concept - conceptual variation.

What does that look like in practice? Taking as an example, addition of 14 + 25, in a Shanghai-style lesson, this problem might be shown by:

- representing the numbers using base 10/Dienes materials;
- representing the numbers on tens/unit abaci;
- sets of counters organised into rows of 10, with an incomplete row for the 4 or 5;
- a picture of children sitting on chairs in 2 rows of 10, with part rows with 4 and 5 children;
- representing each of the numbers on a number line.

In England, although different models or representations might be used, often they would not be used in the same lesson. In Shanghai, these multiple representations would be the starting point for thinking about how to solve the addition and result in a solution represented in many different ways. Using these different representations together focuses attention on the mathematical relationships and the process of partitioning numbers, rather than the particular ways these are modelled with the different materials.

Procedural variation helps both to strengthen conceptual understanding and to support the development of fluency. The NCETM has promoted the idea of 'intelligent practice' as a way of distinguishing between rote learning - working through very similar, repetitive exercises - and the completion of carefully chosen practice examples. When a practice exercise is carefully constructed in this way, it becomes a rich task that develops mathematical thinking (Watson and Mason, 2006).

Here is an example:

Do these two sets of calculations arranged in columns. What do you notice? Can you predict the next two answers in each column?

$$
\begin{array}{ll}
19 - 9 = & 78 - 9 = \\
18 - 9 = & 68 - 9 = \\
17 - 9 = & 58 - 9 = \\
16 - 9 = & 48 - 9 = \\
15 - 9 = & 38 - 9 =
\end{array}
$$

Task 7.6.4 Variation and multiplication

To complete this task you will need to register with the NCETM.

In the mastery section of the NCETM site, there are a series of videos. This task focuses on a Year 3 lesson on multiplication: www.ncetm.org.uk/resources/48211

Watch the four segments of the lesson, as well as the clip on same-day intervention and intelligent practice. Make a note of:

- all the different representations of numbers and multiplication facts used in the lesson;
- all the different types of activity that the children engage in during the lesson.

Download the practice worksheet used in the lesson. Add to the list you made of different representations.

Plan a similar lesson focused on a different multiplication table, including practice questions. Think about ensuring that there is appropriate challenge in the practice questions for the year group you have in mind.

SINGAPORE

There is much in Singaporean mathematics education that is similar to teaching for mastery in Shanghai. This includes high expectations of all learners; a cumulative curriculum that emphasises depth over coverage and gives time for every child to develop concepts, skills and deep understanding; an emphasis on the importance of mathematical models; and high-quality mathematical talk and promotion of mathematical thinking (Drury, 2014). Problem-solving is central to the Singapore curriculum.

We begin each lesson with an 'anchor task'. This is a problem which draws on a familiar context, and gets pupils actively engaged in the lesson right from the start. The children sit in mixed-ability groupings and discuss the mathematics as they use carefully chosen practical resources to work through the problem together. The pupils have needed to learn how to work like this but it has been worth the effort. There is a strict time limit and the teacher observes and listens to what the children are doing during this time. The rest of the lesson builds on the anchor task and the teacher may explicitly refer back to the pupils' discussions later on.

(Helen Hackett, Parkfield Community School, Birmingham)

Singaporean mathematics education was developed in a way that systematically drew on educational and psychological research. One important idea taken up in Singapore is an application of Jerome Bruner's (1966) theory of the importance of the enactive, iconic and symbolic representations in mathematics learning. In Singapore, these ideas have been developed and adapted as the concrete–pictorial–abstract sequence (Hoong, Kin and Pien, 2015). An example of such a sequence in relation to subtraction of a two-digit number from a two-digit number might be to use base ten equipment to carry out calculations, then consider a pictorial representation of such equipment, before working with a formal written (symbolic) method.

Our school has made a significant investment in resources such as Dienes, Cuisenaire, bead strings and place value counters and these are now being used in lessons across the school supporting children to understand and explain the 'why' of their learning. In my classroom, the resources give all children – not just lower attaining pupils – models that allow them to explain their thinking and gain a deeper understanding of number concepts.

(Trisha Henley, Michael Drayton Junior School, Warwickshire)

In Singapore mathematics, a key pictorial representation is the bar model. The bar model can be used to represent a wide variety of mathematical problems: addition and subtraction, multiplication and division, and fraction and proportional reasoning problems. It is very flexible, so that, for example, both simple addition relationships of numbers less than 10 can be represented, as can problems with larger quantities.

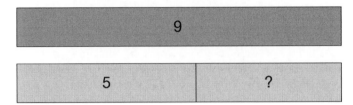

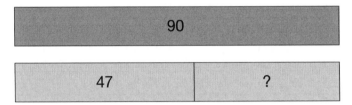

FIGURE 7.6.1 Bar model for subtraction of single-digit numbers

FIGURE 7.6.2 Bar model for subtraction of two-digit numbers

Task 7.6.5 Using bar models with fraction problems

The figure shows a bar model that could be used to solve this fractions question.

In a game, a player starts with a number of tokens that are used to buy objects. Julie has used up one-sixth of her tokens and has 20 tokens left. How many tokens did she have to start with?

Plan a lesson that:

- gives opportunities for exploration of this problem with concrete materials.
- includes questions that would help the class to work together to develop this bar model or a similar one;
- introduces symbolic representation at an appropriate point.

Task 7.6.6 Teaching for mastery

To complete this task, you will need to register with the NCETM, if you have not already done so (www.ncetm.org.uk).

- Familiarise yourself with materials on the section of the site focused on mastery.
- Locate and read the short summary document – 'The essence of mathematics teaching for mastery' (https://www.ncetm.org.uk/files/37086535/The+Essence+of+Maths+Teaching+for+Mastery+june+2016.pdf).
- Create a glossary of key terms. Make a note of words or terms in the document that you are unfamiliar with or are unsure what they mean and add to your glossary as you work through the unit.
- Reflect on your own experience of learning mathematics in primary and secondary school. How far is the approach promoted in the NCETM summary similar to and different from your own experience of learning mathematics? How is this similar and different to how mastery is talked about in schools you are teaching in?

MASTERY ACROSS THE CURRICULUM

Mastery learning (Ellis, 2014) was originally developed to apply to all curriculum subjects. In Table 7.6.1, above, different meanings of mastery were summarised. It is easy to see how most of these, such as a belief that all can learn together, can apply to any subject. However, applying teaching for mastery to other subjects appears more complex.

Up to now, in England, teaching for mastery has focused mainly on mathematics. However, many of the features of this approach are also used in other subject areas in East Asia. It is perhaps easier to see what teaching for mastery could mean in science, given the parallels between the structure of mathematical knowledge and scientific knowledge. Both subjects can be seen as a network of connected concepts and ideas; focusing on problem-solving and enquiry; and having an emphasis on the importance of developing models to aid understanding.

More generally, teaching for mastery could be viewed as similar to other approaches in which interaction between teacher and learner is considered important and that emphasise high-quality classroom talk. One example is dialogic teaching (Alexander, 2008), which draws on similar learning theories.

However, what mastering a subject might mean in different areas of the curriculum is open to debate, particularly, in those subjects where there is less emphasis on learning a body of pre-existing knowledge.

Task 7.6.7 'Teaching for mastery' of English?

Reflect on what mastery in English might mean. What might 'deep learning' look like? How can it be fostered?

Reflect on the meaning of teaching for mastery – you might re-read the NCETM's *Essentials of Mastery* document.

To what extent do the three different approaches to teaching English in Year 5 (described below) accord with a teaching for mastery pedagogy? Which might help to develop mastery of English and why?

1 Mainly working with extracts from a variety of texts identified in a mastery scheme that allow work on specific areas of spelling, punctuation and grammar in a step-by-step way and developing writing skills by revising and editing texts provided.
2 Working with a wide variety of texts around a particular topic – fiction and non-fiction, formal and informal texts (e.g. from the Internet) – at least some of these texts having been identified and selected by the students; students develop their own texts on the theme producing them in a variety of media.
3 Mastery lessons that are focused on the whole class reading the same, often classic, texts together, with teaching and learning of spelling, punctuation and grammar embedded in the work on the text.

ENGAGING WITH MASTERY

Dylan Wiliam is an educator who has been important in promoting assessment for learning. He argues, 'everything works somewhere and nothing works everywhere' (Wiliam, 2013). Adopting the attitude that 'everything works somewhere' can lead us to being able to reflect on different ideas and approaches to teaching, being open to trying out different strategies, experimenting in the classroom and coming to a judgement about what to do. Alternatively, focusing on the idea that 'nothing works everywhere' can lead to continuing with what is familiar. For beginning primary teachers, this can often be to teach in the way that they themselves were taught.

> The mastery approach has given me 'permission' to spend longer on each mathematical topic. Previously I followed the cyclical model of teaching as promoted by NNS, but this meant that many of my children were not secure in a particular area before I felt forced to move on. Now it is a joy to have the time to explore areas of mathematics more deeply, ensuring that every child's learning is secure.
>
> (Trisha Henley, Michael Drayton Junior School, Warwickshire)

It is important to recognise that there are many reasons why adopting a mastery approach is challenging, not least because there may be tensions between a mastery approach and existing practice. As a beginning teacher, your opportunities for engaging with teaching for mastery will depend on the school or schools you work in. However, there are many ideas in this unit that can be considered by any teacher in any mathematics classroom.

If nothing else, current discussions of mastery have created rich opportunities for debate about how children learn mathematics and have brought important ideas such as the role of problem-solving, talk, representation and all-attainment teaching to the fore.

SUMMARY

Mastery is being promoted in England, especially in mathematics. Teaching for mastery emphasises depth of understanding rather than speed of curriculum coverage and uses carefully chosen representations, problems and questions in order to achieve this. Both conceptual understanding and procedural fluency are promoted. There are challenges to extending teaching for mastery to other curriculum subjects. Engaging with teaching for mastery can stimulate teachers to think about and develop their practice.

 ## ANNOTATED FURTHER READING

Askew, M. (2015) *Transforming Primary Mathematics: Understanding Classroom Tasks, Tools and Talk*, Routledge: London.
> A number of chapters in this book are very relevant to understanding mastery, including those on variation theory and on promoting mathematical talk.

Drury, H. (2014) *Mastering Mathematics: Teaching to Transform Achievement*, Oxford, UK: Oxford University Press.
> This is written by the founder of the Mathematics Mastery programme. It outlines many of the principles that underpin that programme, both for the classroom teacher and also advice for whole-school implementation.

Haylock D. (2010) *Mathematics Explained for Primary Teachers*, 4th edn, London: Sage.
> Teacher subject knowledge is important to teaching for mastery. This book explains key concepts in primary mathematics. If you feel that you learned how to get maths right without really understanding what you were doing, this book is an excellent resource.

 ## FURTHER READING TO SUPPORT M-LEVEL STUDY

Askew, M., Hodgen, J., Hossain, S. and Bretscher, N. (2010) *Values and Variables: Mathematics Education in High-Performing Countries*, London: Nuffield.
> This is a review that summarises what is known about mathematics education in countries that do well in international tests.

Boylan, M., Wolstenholme, C., Maxwell, B., Jay, T., Stevens, A. and Demack, S. (2016) *The Longitudinal Evaluation of the Mathematics Teacher Exchange: China–England, Interim Research Report*, July, DfE. Retrieved from www.gov.uk/government/uploads/system/uploads/attachment_data/file/536003/Mathematics_Teacher_Exchange_Interim_Report_FINAL_040716.pdf (accessed 3 November 2017).
> This is a report on the evaluation of the exchange programme with Shanghai. Annexe 1 draws on research to compare various elements of Shanghai and English primary mathematics education.

Gu, L., Huang, R. and Marton, F. (2004) 'Teaching with variation: A Chinese way of promoting effective mathematics learning', in L. Fan, N.-Y. Wong, J. Cai and S. Li. (eds) *How Chinese Learn Mathematics: Perspectives from Insiders*, vol. 1, River Edge, NJ: World Scientific, pp. 309–47.

> This is an in-depth look at variation theory and its relationship to the theories of Piaget, Vygotsky, Dienes, Bruner and Marton. It discusses the many forms of variation and goes beyond the simplified version we have provided in this unit.

Merttens, R. (2012) 'The concrete-pictorial-abstract heuristic', *Mathematics Teaching*, May: 33–8.

> This short article challenges how Bruner's theory of representation is sometimes applied, including in Singapore's concrete-pictorial-abstract formulation. Reading this article should encourage you to reflect that much in mathematics education is open to debate.

RELEVANT WEBSITES

National Centre for Excellence in Mathematics Education (NCETM): www.ncetm.org.uk

> The NCETM aims to raise levels of achievement and engagement in mathematics through ensuring that all teachers of maths, including primary teachers, have access to high-quality maths-specific CPD. The NCETM site has a microsite focused on mastery, as well as links to many other resources. By registering on the site you will get access to regular primary mathematics updates.

Maths Hubs: www.mathshubs.org.uk/

> Maths Hubs are regional networks promoting mastery. Find your hub and register with it to be kept informed about activities in your local area.

Association of Teachers of Mathematics (ATM): www.atm.org.uk

Mathematical Association (MA): www.m-a.org.uk

> The ATM and MA are both organisations of teachers and mathematics educators that support members to be creative and effective mathematics teachers. They offer a variety of magazines and publications aimed at teachers and arrange events nationally and in local areas. They offer various offers for student teachers and NQTs.

REFERENCES

Alexander, R.J. (2008) *Towards Dialogic Teaching: Rethinking Classroom Talk*, 4th edn, York, UK: Dialogos.

Askew, A., Bishop, S., Christie, C., Eaton, S., Griffin, P. and Morgan, D. (2015) *Teaching for Mastery: Questions, Tasks and Activities to Support Assessment*, Open University Press. Retrieved from www.ncetm.org.uk/resources/46689 (accessed 3 November 2017).

Askew, M., Hodgen, J., Hossain, S. and Bretscher, N. (2010) *Values and Variables: Mathematics Education in High-Performing Countries*, London: Nuffield.

ATM/MA Primary Working Group. (2016) 'What does "mastery" mean to me?', *Mathematics Teaching*, April: 28–9.

Boylan, M., Wolstenholme, C., Maxwell, B., Jay, T., Stevens, A. and Demack, S. (2016) *The Longitudinal Evaluation of the Mathematics Teacher Exchange: China-England, Interim Research Report*, July, DfE. Retrieved from www.gov.uk/government/uploads/system/uploads/attachment_data/file/536003/Mathematics_Teacher_Exchange_Interim_Report_FINAL_040716.pdf (accessed 3 November 2017).

Bruner, J.S. (1966) *Toward a Theory of Instruction*, Cambridge, MA: Harvard University Press.

Department for Education (DfE). (2013) *Primary Assessment and Accountability under the New National Curriculum (Consultation)*, July, Crown Copyright.

Department for Education (DfE). (2014) *Mathematics Programmes of Study: Key Stages 1 and 2*, London: DfE. Retrieved from https://www.gov.uk/government/uploads/system/uploads/attachment_data/file/335158/PRIMARY_national_curriculum_-_Mathematics_220714.pdf (accessed October 2014).

Drury, H. (2014) *Mastering Mathematics*, Oxford, UK: Oxford University Press.

Dweck, C.S. (2006) *Mindset: The New Psychology of Success*, New York: Random House.

Ellis, A.K. (2014) *Research on Educational Innovations*, New York and Abingdon, UK: Routledge.

Gu, L., Huang, R. and Marton, F. (2004) 'Teaching with variation: A Chinese way of promoting effective mathematics learning', in L. Fan, N.Y. Wong, J. Cai and S. Li (eds) *How Chinese Learn Mathematics: Perspectives from Insiders*, Singapore: World Scientific Publishing.

Hoong, L.Y., Kin, H.W. and Pien, C.L. (2015) 'Concrete-pictorial-abstract: Surveying its origins and charting its future', *The Mathematics Educator*, 16(1): 1-19.

Jerrim, J. and Vignoles, A. (2016) 'The link between East Asian "mastery" teaching methods and English children's mathematics skills', *Economics of Education Review*, 50: 29-44.

Marks, R. (2014) 'Educational triage and ability-grouping in primary mathematics: A case-study of the impacts on low-attaining pupils', *Research in Mathematics Education*, 16(1): 38-53.

National Association of Mathematics Advisors (NAMA). (2016) 'Five myths of mastery in mathematics', *Mathematics Teaching*, April: 20-3.

National Centre for Excellence in the Teaching of Mathematics (NCETM). (2016) *The Essence of Mathematics Teaching for Mastery*. Retrieved from https://www.ncetm.org.uk/files/37086535/The+Essence+of+Maths+Teaching+for+Mastery+june+2016.pdf (accessed 3 November 2017).

Ofsted. (2011) *Good Practice in Primary Mathematics: Evidence from 20 Successful Schools*, London: Ofsted.

Watson, A. and Mason, J. (2006) 'Seeing an exercise as a single mathematical object: Using variation to structure sense-making', *Mathematical Thinking & Learning*, 8(2): 91-111.

Wiliam, D. (2013) 'Assessment: The bridge between teaching and learning', *Voices from the Middle*, 21(2): 15.

Williams, P. (2008) *Independent Review of Mathematics Teaching in Early Years Settings and Primary Schools: Final Report*, London: DCSF.

PRIMARY EDUCATION IN A DIGITAL AGE

John Potter

INTRODUCTION

One of the key debates in primary education is around the location and nature of its work in the digital age. This debate, held in the press, on TV, in schools, on social media and in teacher education, takes in a vast range of issues and responsibilities. These range from the statutory obligation to teach the computing curriculum through to attempts to link other subject areas, such as literacy, with digital practices, such as film-making, animation, video games and social media. It is further complicated by the messy and problematic issues of both safety and access, with some schools taking a pragmatic position and encouraging a wider integration with the online world and wider, popular media culture, and others taking the view that children need to be protected at all costs from the inherent risks of digital activity. A further connected range of issues concern the extent to which 'big data' are used or misused in the context of schools, with so much information collected about children from the minute they enter formal education. Indeed, there are widely differing views about whether or not the reductive nature of a curriculum based on testing is being manipulated at some level in the various algorithms and datasets, to produce policy outcomes over learning gains for our children (Selwyn and Facer, 2013). Thinking about education in the digital age means also, therefore, thinking about the relationship of home to school, of knowledge to information and of what counts as 'learning' in an age in which so much is available on-screen to discover. It also asks us to think about the spaces in which we learn and how many of these are in school, how many out of school, in a 'third space' of an after-school club or other space between educational settings and home. These aspects have all been highlighted in a report for the Cambridge Primary Review exploring the implications of the digital for primary schools, which states that:

> The digital age has implications for curriculum, pedagogy and schools' wider role in supporting children's emotional and social life, and indeed raises questions about the purpose and nature of schools themselves, and how schools' work relates to the wider political, economic and commercial context.
>
> (Burnett, 2016: 3)

Around the world, 'digital education' is an area that is addressed in many different ways. Sometimes, this is directly in policy documents, in the way a country will set out its message for parents, carers, children and educators, as a set of policy requirements, expectations or simply aspirations. Sometimes, as for other age groups, this is referred to as learning for the twenty-first century, with a set of skills presented that are assumed to be the goal of any digitally or technologically enhanced education system. Indeed, the degree to which technology actually enhances any educational outcomes is the subject of much debate, with the most frequent conclusion being that it *can* work in the right context, with the right amount of support and the appropriate pedagogy. There will be changes to education as a result of these seismic shifts in the ways in which we do things, though a surprising amount will remain the same, not least in societies in which assessment, often in highly traditional forms, plays such a huge part in determining both the curriculum and its outcomes.

It is worth stating at the outset that it is no longer tenable to think of the 'digital' as synonymous with 'technology'. The 'digital' connects us to themes and approaches that are cultural in nature. When we think of 'the digital', we need to think of more than just 'technology' and its associated artefacts; we need to think about its use in the world, the media that get made and distributed on it and the ways in which we use it. In doing this, we will begin to think more widely about what it means to be literate in the digital age. We may also begin to think of ways in which children can be enabled to think of themselves as makers, learning by being active and by crafting all kinds of media (Cannon, 2016).

One issue that will come up at some stage in your work with children is the notion that all young people are essentially 'native' to the digital world, and all adults are 'immigrants'. Teachers are out of touch with these millennial young people. This is a very popular and contagious pattern of thought about children and young people, derived from writing by Marc Prensky (2005). Once you start working with children and young people and talking to other adults in the school setting, you will discover that life is more complex than this, and that the issues are not so easily divided into generational differences. This argument is not tenable in the face of digital economic divides, nor the great differences between people's circumstances and lived experience. The children you teach and the adults you work with will all have varying experiences of life online and digital competence of various kinds that are not age-dependent, and much more to do with their habitus in the world and their experience in the various online spaces in which they live and spend huge amounts of time, or very little. Dave White and Alison Le Cornu (2011) have a much more nuanced way of looking at this issue that positions all learners and teachers in digital environments as either 'visitors' or 'residents'; either you are, every day, navigating your Instagram, Facebook and Twitter feeds, or you are using them sparingly, occasionally or just for work, or just for home. And these are subtle variations that reflect more accurately the world in which the children you teach will be living. The important thing to remember is that digital media are part of everyday, material and virtual culture and have complexity, depth and richness in people's lives.

OBJECTIVES

By the end of this unit, we will have:

- explored how we define digital and/or media literacy, broadening the definition beyond print literacy;
- considered social media and how this can be used, and how it impacts on primary school life in a range of ways, before considering aspects of safety and daily use of technology;
- addressed the biggest official curriculum change in relation to primary education and the digital, which has come in the form of the computing curriculum, and we will devote a substantial section to this towards the end of the unit;
- reviewed some further reading and sources of help in navigating teaching with technology and media, and with 'digital education'.

DIGITAL TEXTS AND MEDIA LITERACY

Children, their carers, parents and teachers are living in a world in which media generally, and digital still and moving images in particular, are the dominant modes of communication and meaning making. And yet, in schools in England, there is no formal requirement to study media in primary schools as a separate subject, to explore the codes and conventions of moving image literacy. This is not the case in other parts of the world, where there are developed, or developing, media literacy curricula, some of them based on a synthesis of ideas produced for UNESCO (Wilson *et al.*, 2011). In England, the use of media in the form of moving image texts has a tradition of being integrated into subject areas, although, in the most recent version (DfE, 2013a), reference to it has been removed from the English curriculum, where it had long resided as a way of looking at different kinds of narrative and of exploring links between popular culture and writing. Instead, there is a vestigial presence in the computing curriculum, which sets out that children should become:

> responsible, competent, confident and creative users of information and communication technology . . . [and] . . . able to use, and express themselves and develop their ideas through information and communication technology – at a level suitable for the future workplace and as active participants in a digital world.
>
> (DfE, 2013a: 178)

The implication at least is that children should become competent at reading and understanding media, as well as producing it (echoing Buckingham, 2003). Without a space in a crowded curriculum, it can be all too easy to forget or leave out these encounters with digital media and the opportunities to make and interpret moving image texts together. And yet, many teachers and researchers find that even the simplest activities around film-making and animation can bring many curriculum subjects alive and open a portal on to the lived experience and popular culture of children and young people, on to their funds of knowledge and cultural experience, which, in turn, produce huge benefits in terms of motivation, engagement and learning (Buckingham, 2003; Burn and Durran, 2007; Marsh, 2009; Bazalgette, Parry and Potter, 2011; Potter, 2012; Parry, 2013). This is not something that detracts from their experience of the literacy 'basics', but something that suggests a rather more ambitious curriculum experience that both enhances and produces contexts for learning the reading and writing of print.

Recent research connected the use of touchscreen devices in a primary school after-school club with learning about film-making (Potter and Bryer, 2016). Here, working with a device that is at the heart of everyday practices around technology was most important to its success. The work, with Year 5 students aged around 10 years, was based around the idea that the reading of images that children had been engaged with all their life could be productively analysed and turned into production quite rapidly on touchscreen devices. It was not unproblematic, owing to the constraints around file handling and other issues, but, compared with forays into this kind of work in previous years, involving cameras and cables, it was a far less technically intimidating experience for those teaching it, and for the children exploring it. Children moved through the experiences of reviewing clips, making short practice exercises, learning about shaping moving image stories and more into making them in an iterative way. The touchscreen devices, in this case iPad minis, enabled a shorter time frame between such activities and allowed the children to engage directly with shaping and crafting the scenes that they shot. This way of working is encouraged in the frameworks for screen literacy produced by the European Film Literacy Advisory Group (FLAG, 2014), which connects the creative to the cultural and the critical. It is also the basis for some of the innovative practices in moving image education undertaken by the British Film Institute Education department, Into Film and the Film Space, all of which have resources and contacts to support teachers in primary schools, but perhaps, more importantly, all have accounts, complete with films, of the kinds of work it is possible to do (Cannon and Reid, 2010; Into Film, 2015; BFI, 2016; The Film Space, 2016).

There are other projects that link media with more traditional forms of print literacy, such as Persistence of Vision, which connected animation to non-narrative poetry work in Year 1, for children aged around 6 years. Over the course of a year, the schools, in three geographically distributed areas of rural England, arranged for work to take place that matched stop-frame animation activities with webcams with working on features of poetry. A social media video-sharing site connected the schools, and children were able to critique each other's work. The researchers reported that:

> It became clear in many schools that the features of poetry which were being explored, such as rhythm, metre, tone and imagery, found corollaries in the time-based texts of animation where such understanding, particularly of timing, is critical to the successful construction of the form. Children were encouraged to plan for movements through time, calculating the numbers of frames needed to create convincing movements. In post-production in one school, children were observed working painstakingly and with great concentration adding the voiceovers for previously animated poems. Matching line length to image, movement and scene was by no means straightforward. Many of the films used no words, however, and one animator provided schools with 'poetic sounds' to stimulate production ideas. The recursive nature of the project allowed learning to be carried forward from one project to the next.

> (Bazalgette *et al.*, 2011)

In other animation work in primary schools, it has been shown to be possible to connect learning science concepts with the use of simple, short films made by children (Hoban, Nielsen and Shepherd, 2015). In these cases, and in Persistence of Vision, there is an inherent tension between media being the enabler of learning in different subject areas and, at the same time, being something that is valuable to learn about in and of itself. Media literacy and working with digital texts have equal parts to play in shaping such learning experiences, but there are judgements to be made the whole time in 'justifying' their inclusion in a curriculum diet for children and young people. However, the computing curriculum's third main element of working with digital texts does introduce the possibility of making a wider connection between digital making of all kinds, whether it is creating a short procedure in Scratch or constructing a piece of digital animation or a film sequence. All depend on creative collaboration, the ability to work iteratively to debug something that is not working while in progress, and all produce digital texts and, sometimes, action in the world (Burnett, 2016; Potter and McDougall, 2017). Sometimes, the ways in which digital making is described in the work appear to focus exclusively on making and writing procedures for the computing side of the curriculum. However, many people now promote and recognise the wider and more inclusive way of thinking about *all* digital making: animation, video, music, alongside programming procedures and making the more obviously digital text (Berry, 2013; Quinlan, 2015; Cannon, 2016; Turvey, Potter and Burton, 2016, especially Chapter 13).

Task 7.7.1 A short film describing a mood or emotion (no longer than 10 seconds)

Working with a friend or two and using your mobile phone, or a tablet device, or one you can borrow from a friend, open the camera app and switch to video. Take three shots, one of which must be a close-up of a face, the other two of which must show an encounter between two people. The way that you frame the shots or move the camera must describe an emotion that a viewer can take away from watching it. Negative emotions or attributes tend to be easier to work with in this kind of activity – for example, jealousy, fear, embarrassment or hate. Positive emotions are harder to represent, but include: feelings of friendship, kindness, empathy. Watch the sequences back. Which work? How much of each do you need to show? Open the shots in an editor on your phone or tablet device and cut them to improve the impact. What did you need to know to do this? Consult a source of advice on shooting for education online (such as learnaboutfilm.com – see the end of the unit).

SOCIAL MEDIA AND EDUCATION

We've looked earlier in this unit at some examples of digital making, drawn from the worlds of computing, media production and more. Throughout, we have tried to illustrate that these facets of life in digital culture are a central part of lived experience and cannot be excluded from a curriculum vision for the digital age. The world of social media, in the form of micro-blogging sites, blogging and wiki authoring and sharing of digital material, is a further realm in which children, even those as young as primary age, are immersed, like many of their adult carers and teachers. There is an argument that the flow of self-publishing online and exhibiting aspects of identity in social and other media is like a form of 'curation' of the self (Potter, 2012), a new literacy practice with digital media in which children and parents are engaged, either individually or in groups and communities (Potter and McDougall, 2017: Chapter 4). Even younger children are aware of these activities having, for example, taken selfies or seen older siblings, friends and family doing this and posting online or having shared media that they are excited by and find interesting, which they know will reflect their representation of themselves: pictures of toys, cats and family members, and so on.

Exploring these areas with children has the potential to provide contexts for a vast array of learning opportunities. Martin Waller's experience with Twitter in his class of Year 1 children a few years ago provided some insight into how the social practice of communication in micro-blogs can lift and frame writing and identity (Waller, 2013). In other projects that are worth following up online, collaborative writing in the form of blogging is something that has been shown to lift learning to write in important ways for younger learners (Barrs and Horrocks, 2014; Hawley, 2016). And, although there are important safety concerns associated with these forms of work in the digital age, there is no shortage of ways of modelling how to integrate social media sensitively and safely into a programme for teaching and learning in the digital age that can be accessed using the links and references at the end of the unit.

A NOTE ON SAFETY

Teachers bear considerable responsibility for promoting safe practices around technology, with the most usually cited aspect being preventing the unauthorised sharing or distribution of images of children. This is recognised in the National Curriculum document in the requirement to ensure that children:

> use technology safely, respectfully and responsibly; recognise acceptable/unacceptable behaviour; identify a range of ways to report concerns about content and contact.
>
> (DfE, 2013a: 179)

This is something that can appear daunting to parents, carers, teachers and beginner teachers, particularly in a culture whose media outlets encourage panic, outrage and blame, rather than considered thinking in this area. Nevertheless, schools are expected to provide guidance to children and their carers, and are at risk themselves if they do not have a policy about digital safety that is part of lived practice and experience, and not simply something that is covered by written statute and regulation alone. Indeed, there are significant projects, resources and spaces that are dedicated to advising on this issue, along with guidance in the form of policies, research and teaching about it (Livingstone, 2009; UK Safer Internet Centre, 2016), and no beginner teacher should feel that they are alone in dealing with potential issues such as access to inappropriate images or cyber-bullying and more.

That said, the process of both educating about digital media and safeguarding children can be made to work by application of the principles we have tried to establish throughout the unit of recognising that digital education is part of lived experience and material, everyday culture. It is not something that stands apart from everyday life; it is bound up in everyday social practices. With this in mind, conversations that establish a safe space in which to exchange information and support are important; simple, regular, short dialogues that bring the everyday into the classroom, rather than separate, large-scale interventions, are likely to inculcate positive and autonomous strategies and dispositions towards safety online. Examples of such conversations might include talking about: when and where pictures are shared and by whom; things that children might have seen online that make them feel uncomfortable in some way; feeling bullied or harassed in an online space; and so on.

Task 7.7.2 Social media reflections

Reflect on any time you have posted in an online social media space, either in print or in text, on a blog or a micro-blog, and felt uncomfortable over any consequences. What happened? Was an image shared without your consent? Did someone miss the point or get angry as a result of something you wrote? How did you handle it? What techniques or tools did you use? Did you defuse the situation with humour? Did you find a way to block the person from your social media space? If you are not currently a user of social media, find someone who is and interview them about these aspects of life online. How does this translate into dealing with such issues in school? Are adults better or worse at dealing with social media?

THE COMPUTING CURRICULUM

Although so far in the unit we have established that we will consider the wider picture of the digital in relation to primary school teaching, children's formal engagement with the digital within the school curriculum is prescribed by the subject orders for computing (DFE, 2013b). There is a long history to the ways in which this document came to represent statutory educational provision that has its origin in information and communication technology (ICT), which, if you are interested, you can follow up by reading Peter Twining's account online (2013). Lobbyists and multinational computing companies approached the UK government directly about the lack of coding and programming skills being developed in our schools. Essentially, they won the argument that the subject of ICT had become a kind of reductive, simple, unthinking training in the use of applications for office use, instead of creative and skilful work with programming and making things. As a result of this and with pressure from other directions (such as the British Computer Society), there was a big refocusing towards computing itself, as opposed to the applications we use every day. In school and out of school, from 2013, there was a concerted effort to take on board these arguments, not least, outside the school day, in the creation of many coding clubs (Sefton-Green, 2013; Dredge, 2014; Quinlan, 2015).

In everyday practice, we should ask: what is actually different about the computing curriculum, and what does it mean for teaching and learning in schools in the digital age? First, it is worth noting that, although the computing subject document is minimal in form and runs only to a few pages inside the larger curriculum document (DFE, 2013a), its implications are *potentially* revolutionary in the ways in which it positions children, and teachers to an extent, as people who can experiment, try things out and even make things in an educational context. The word *potentially* is important here, because the computing curriculum, like any other subject, could be taught badly and become a set of reductive exercises, arid, instrumentalist and devoid of connection to the world. In the most positive and agentive interpretations of the computing curriculum, with an imaginative and playful approach, children can become expert in *computational thinking*, a way of looking at the world as a place in which actions can be predicated on knowing a few lines of code, in order to solve particular, real or imagined situations.

One of the key advisers to the government on the computing curriculum helpfully identifies three components in a freely available guide for primary school teachers (Berry, 2013). These are: *computer science*, *information technology* and *digital literacy*, separated out as follows:

> The core of computing is *computer science*, in which pupils are taught the principles of information and computation, how digital systems work and how to put this knowledge to use through programming. Building on this knowledge and understanding, pupils are equipped to use *information technology* to create programs, systems and a range of content. Computing also ensures that pupils become *digitally literate* – able to use, and express themselves and develop their ideas through, information and communication technology – at a level suitable for the future workplace and as active participants in a digital world.
>
> (Berry, 2013: 5)

The emphasis on activity and action on the world comes through in the document in the choice of words such as 'building', 'develop' 'use' and, ultimately, 'active' itself. It is not intended as a rote-learning curriculum, and, if the curriculum itself is short on detail, documents such as Berry's guide, and the many supplementary websites to which it refers, offer opportunities to provide rich experiences in very accessible language, for both teachers and children.

In Northern Ireland . . .

CCEA is currently creating a framework to integrate digital skills across the different stages of the Northern Ireland education system, building thinking skills into the process of learning about digital devices and creating qualifications that are unique to Northern Ireland. The CCEA framework addresses all the statutory requirements for using ICT in Foundation Stage, Key Stage 1 and Key Stage 2, through a new, optional digital skills curriculum for primary schools. This curriculum is delivered through three strands and will be supported by the publication of teaching and learning resources for different types of ICT and a progression of skills appropriate for each key stage in primary. The strands are called:

- Becoming a Digital Citizen
- Becoming a Digital Worker
- Becoming a Digital Maker

Source: http://ccea.org.uk/digitalskills/primary (accessed 14 November 2017).

In Wales . . .

The new Digital Competence Framework (DCF) in Wales was published in September 2016, and digital competence is one of three cross-curricular responsibilities, alongside literacy and numeracy. It focuses on developing digital skills that can be applied to a wide range of subjects and scenarios. The framework has been developed by practitioners from pioneer schools, supported by external experts.

The link takes you to all the information and resources if you need more detail. http://learning.gov.wales/resources/browse-all/digital-competence-framework/?lang=en (accessed 3 November 2017).

One of the key concepts that underpins the computing curriculum is that of creating opportunities to develop children's 'computational thinking'. This is broadly defined as ways of thinking that people use when they systematically set out to solve problems in the world by experimentation, learning from feedback, working iteratively, and so on. This way of thinking may or may not involve computer software or hardware at all, but will involve developing the skills and dispositions that involve experimenting and playful activity, breaking down problems or routines in the world into smaller steps and reasoning the ways to undertake tasks, from the most commonplace to the most complex (see Turvey *et al.*, 2016: Chapter 8). Examples of these frequently used in primary classrooms involve looking procedurally at simple sets of instructions for tasks as a kind of programming, breaking down into simple steps such things as recipes (jam sandwiches) and tasks (making tea, programming central heating or TV recording). The point is to switch the view from the mundane to the micro level of instruction, to get back to the sequences of steps necessary to make things happen.

It is worth noting that the curriculum statement is a set of aspirations that state-controlled schools need to meet and that academies, trusts and free schools need to address at least as well in their own provision. For some teachers, this has proved to be really daunting, and there have been grave concerns over the numbers of generalist primary school teachers who are equipped to teach the subject at all. This does explain why many schools have turned to after-school expertise and the rise of organisations dedicated to supporting this initiative, and it may explain any variations in practice that you encounter when you go into different schools.

What do you need to know in order to teach this area of the curriculum? What do you need to know and do in order to look beyond what you see and play with every day, to gain an understanding of how it works and to have the opportunity to make things? Teachers could be forgiven for imagining that all children are somehow innately gifted in this regard and regularly exposed to the world of making things at home and in the wider world. And yet, although there is a vast and growing community of younger users of software and associated online spaces, such as Minecraft and Scratch (MIT, 2016), it would be wrong to assume that all children we teach are developing as sophisticated programmers beyond the classroom. Part of the role of the primary school teacher in this respect is to try and develop these skills, by finding out and building on what children already know and can do. This means learning some new skills and taking on unfamiliar activities as teachers, drawing on the wide range of support available (of which more later).

The computing curriculum encourages children to ask 'what if' questions, to experiment and to speculate on outcomes that they have helped to create. For example, it asks at Key Stage 1 that children should be taught to:

- understand what algorithms are; how they are implemented as programs on digital devices; and that programs execute by following precise and unambiguous instructions

- create and debug simple programs
- use technology purposefully to create, organise, store, manipulate and retrieve digital content
- recognise common uses of information technology beyond school
- use technology safely and respectfully, keeping personal information private; identify where to go for help and support when they have concerns about content or contact on the internet or other online technologies.

(DfE, 2013a: 179)

Clearly, there is an issue with such a range of expectations, and the list may appear daunting to anyone beginning teaching. It's important to remember that much of the work we do with children of that age in schools is to do with presenting them with a context or with finding ways of locating their experience within frames of reference that help them towards greater understanding. If the list is daunting, the actual realisation of the work may not turn out to be so, particularly if we can think of ways of situating the learning within the playful and the known, at least to start with. This includes working with what we know about it, not only as teachers, but also as people alive in the digital age, with its dramatic pace of change and development.

Algorithms, for example, are essentially rules by which artefacts and devices perform tasks or are controlled. Many teachers begin with playful ways to illustrate this, well away from the computer screen, around games and stories that have procedures and sets of occurrences that are logical and expected, because they are rigorously applied.

Grounding these activities in the world of the child has important benefits for their deeper conceptual understanding. So, some classroom discussion of devices in the home that are programmed and controlled usually precedes wider exploration at this point: TV remotes, phones, heating, and so on. The difference between such rule sets in a computing sense is that they can be altered, by user programming, to change the outcome. Making these rule creations and changes explicit means, to an extent, making them concrete and realisable by the very young, and there are a number of programmable toys that are available that work really well at Key Stage 1 to do this, such as the Bee-Bot, a small but attractive floor or table-top robot that children can programme to move. It's also extremely powerful for younger learners to take control of their learning of an aspect of the curriculum in this way. There are further connections here to other parts of the curriculum, not least maths, as has been pointed out:

> to operate these toys children, use the arrow keys and numerical values to input simple instructions . . . [they] can help to establish and develop some important mathematical concepts in young children such as an understanding of rotation or turning, and the development of estimation of distance.

(Turvey *et al.*, 2016: 124)

Although this connection to other subjects is important, it is also important not to lose sight of the computing curriculum itself, the fact that the sequence in which the instructions are entered, the timing of them and the values they give are all connected to what actually happens, and therefore to a developing understanding of what it means to programme something. Teachers make use of all kinds of props to scaffold this development, including PE lessons based on movement described by rules, cards with instructions and written records of their procedures. They also make it part of classroom talk and encourage speculation of the 'what if' kind. Guiding a programmable toy, such as a Roamer or Bee-Bot, around a track by means of simple, restricted instruction is one way in which children can learn the underlying concepts of programming in a playful way that invites them to speculate and to experiment. In some ways, it is closest at this stage to the playful elements of the

Foundation Stage, on whose principles rest some of the most successful and developmentally appropriate ways for children to learn: as autonomous, self-directed, experimental, problem-solving and playful learners.

This playfulness and experimentation can be successfully moved to the screen and its momentum maintained through the computing curriculum by connecting the work to wider popular culture, to computer games, and so on. This can be done through the use of specific software that takes the children into simple instructional procedures on screen, such as Scratch (MIT, 2016) or its earlier incarnation as Logo, developed by Seymour Papert and Christine Solomon and based on theories of learning that embrace the notion of the individual as interpreter and creator of their own learning through exploration of restricted codes of language (Papert, 1993). Building simple shapes or patterns, drawing the initial letters of their names, responding to challenges to draw on screen but only using the language of the program to do it, all promote an iterative understanding of instruction-giving and algorithms. In every case, the talk around the screen is of equal importance to what happens on the screen. We have known since 1996, from the work of Charles Crook, that this is so in the case of Logo, where children scaffold each other's conversations as they work together to solve problems and play on screen (Crook, 1996). You will see this in the ways that children gather round on-screen programming screens, wherever they have the opportunity, whether on a touchscreen or in a computer lab or on a phone.

The more modern and recent equivalents of these earlier developments come in the form of the social media around Scratch (see link at MIT, 2016), online environments for procedures in which children come to talk with each other about the things that they are making and sharing. At the interface between the worlds of gaming and programming lies the world of Minecraft, the globally successful phenomenon in which children play games, build or do both, using online software or working offline. Recent research has positioned this not simply as on-screen, virtual work: it has sought to describe the classrooms and after-school places involved in playing and learning in this way as assemblages of social actors and artefacts, bodies, and spaces in time. Work in the UK and Australia has used such conceptual frameworks to describe what happens in this fluid and hybrid space, where teachers and children work in, around and with Minecraft or similar world-building software (Burnett and Bailey, 2014; Dezunni et al., 2015).

Older primary school children, between the ages of 7 and 11, are expected to build on the curriculum statements shown for Key Stage 1 above, and to, for example:

- design, write and debug programs that accomplish specific goals, including controlling or simulating physical systems; solve problems by decomposing them into smaller parts
- use sequence, selection, and repetition in programs; work with variables and various forms of input and output
- use logical reasoning to explain how some simple algorithms work and to detect and correct errors in algorithms and programs.

(DfE, 2013a: 179)

There is a degree of similarity here with Key Stage 1, but with an increasing degree of abstraction. The principles for teaching and learning, however, remain essentially the same, foregrounding play, conversation, experimenting and connecting to popular culture.

In a study of a computing summer school, conducted as part of a wider evaluation of an after-school club, with older primary- and younger secondary-aged children building a game using the Scratch software, we noted high levels of engagement throughout, not least because of the opportunity to connect storying to gaming, via the medium of programming. The children were asked to construct stories first that would guide the creation of on-screen games, thinking about gameplay, characters, narrative, and so on. They made a series of racing and maze-based games that could be played by others and that were subsequently uploaded to the social media spaces of Scratch. This provoked many discussions about gaming and play outside school. This rich connection to outside culture has been noted in many places, including in the Playtimes project on children's playground games in the digital age (Burn and Richards, 2014) and in the work of other significant researchers in the field, going back a number of years (Marsh, 2004; Willett *et al.*, 2013). Examples include children designing websites to inform the world about playground games (Potter, 2014) and young people making games in projects that connected outside cultures to in-school activity (Burn, 2015).

VIGNETTE: SCRATCH 'GAMES FROM STORIES' PROJECT

This is an extract from field notes taken when observing the young game authors working with Scratch:

> Ab. enjoyed listening to music on the headphones as she worked and on Day 4, she spent time choosing music on YouTube – to listen to and to accompany her game. On Day 5 she seemed more determined and focused and sat near the wall, next to her brother Z. (both with their headphones on) and managed to make a maze game with 6 levels. During the final sharing, I played her game and she expressed her frustration that it was not set up to allow me to move beyond Level 2. She then enlisted the help of L. and E. and added transitions up to Level 6. In the final interview, Ab. said that her best moment was when V. had played the game (a few minutes before hand) and the transitions between the levels had worked. After our interview she rushed back in (as everyone was packing up), and L. helped her to 'change the broadcast so that Level 6 comes on afterwards and says you win' (23/8/13) – completing the game to her satisfaction.
>
> (Potter and Bryer, 2013)

From the notes, it is possible to revisit some of the dynamism and excitement that accompanied much of the experience, along with the features we have alluded to all along: the talk, collaboration, problem-solving and engagement. This is not to deny or to write out of the picture the occasional frustration and lack of progress that happen from time to time. But, the ways in which the children overcame the odds with help from each other, as well as from adults, were highly significant. In carrying out this work, they developed further their understanding of how programming works, what it does, what a set of instructions looks like when it goes wrong, and how it can be debugged to make it go right.

For the younger children in our schools, an important breakthrough with programming occurs when they understand what a program can be. Marion Whitehead has pointed out (2002) that, when children learn how writing can stand for them when they are no longer present, they make a huge developmental breakthrough. For computing, programming and coding activities, the breakthrough is when children realise that those texts, those lines of code, not only stand for them but perform some action on the world, whether they are present or not, an experience that is not unlike their first steps with writing (Whitehead, 2002; Potter and McDougall, 2017). It's a powerful lesson to learn and, potentially, therefore, one of the most exciting areas of the curriculum, particularly when connected to the wider world of children's popular culture and experience.

Task 7.7.3 Building patterns of shapes with Scratch (from scratch!)

Download Scratch in the format appropriate for your computer – or use the online version. Design a simple procedure for building a shape – let's say a rectangle. Rotate it through 90°, draw again and repeat in different colours four times, to create a repeating pattern. As you go through this process, note down the different concepts you have had to take on board. These should include: learning about the subroutines needed to build a shape and learning how to repeat these routines and nest them inside others. Where did you look for help in completing the task? How many times did you have to review and debug the program because it didn't work? What kinds of skill and disposition would young children need to exhibit to succeed in this? How did it make you feel? What impact would this have on the way you approach teaching with Scratch?

SUMMARY

Finally, as Burnett observes: 'Responding to the digital age involves more than just skills' and 'Digital practices vary, linked to social, emotional, cultural, economic and political circumstances' (2016: 9). As we ponder the ways in which we should work with children in the primary years in the context of digital education, we should be mindful of the fact that technology itself is neither fixed nor stable, and the meanings that are made in media created by users with that technology are always contingent and based in specific contexts, whether these are programs and procedures, films or animation, or more. As in other areas of the curriculum, we should begin by finding out where our children are starting from, in terms of their abilities, knowledge, skills and dispositions. We should work with the funds of knowledge they bring with them, but develop them further along the lines suggested by the curriculum and by the many examples of creative work available to support that work.

ANNOTATED FURTHER READING

Burnett, C. (2016) *The Digital Age and Its Implications for Learning and Teaching in the Primary School*, York, UK: Cambridge Primary Review Trust.
>   This gives a critical perspective and a wide-ranging review of the literature and research into primary education in the digital age.

Turvey, K., Potter, J. and Burton, J. (2016) *Primary Computing and Digital Technologies*, 7th edn, London: Sage.
>   This has detailed worked examples of classroom practice, research and digital education in primary schools.

Berry, M. (2015) *Quick Start Computing: A CPD Toolkit for Primary Teachers*, Swindon, UK: BCS.
>   See this for guidance on computing and computational thinking specifically, a toolkit for learning for teachers by one of the people behind the curriculum orders.

FURTHER READING TO SUPPORT M-LEVEL STUDY

Lynch, J. and Redpath, T. (2014) '"Smart" technologies in early years education: A meta-narrative of paradigmatic tensions in iPad use in an Australian preparatory classroom', *Journal of Early Childhood Literacy*, 14(2): 147–74.

> This article explores some of the issues and contradictions teachers face when integrating digital technologies within classrooms.

Selwyn, N. (2015) 'Data entry: Towards the critical study of digital data and education', *Learning, Media & Technology*, 40(1): 64–82.

> This is a discussion of the complex debates surrounding the role of digital data in education.

RELEVANT WEBSITES

Learn about Film: learnaboutfilm.com

> A very helpful resource for all kinds of hands-on work making moving image media with children.

BFI Education: www.bfi.org.uk/education

> A source of project links from moving-image education work throughout the UK.

MIT Scratch Project: scratch.mit.edu/about

> One of the most widely used resources for teaching programming, with freely downloadable materials.

Computing at School: www.computingatschool.org.uk

> The home of many excellent resources to support teachers and children in learning programming.

The Safer Internet Centre: www.saferinternet.org.uk

> Essential advice on safety issues around using the Internet with children and families.

REFERENCES

Barrs, M. and Horrocks, S. (2014) *Educational Blogs and Their Effects on Pupil's Writing*, London: CFBT.

Bazalgette, C., Parry, B. and Potter, J. (2011) Creative, cultural and critical: Media literacy theory in the primary school classroom. Creative Engagements 7, Mansfield College, Oxford University, Oxford, UK.

Berry, M. (2013) *Computing in the National Curriculum: A Guide for Primary School Teachers*. Retrieved from www.computingatschool.org.uk/data/uploads/CASPrimaryComputing.pdf (accessed 5 November 2017).

BFI. (2016) BFI Education website [Online]. Available at: www.bfi.org.uk/education (accessed 19 November 2016).

Buckingham, D. (2003) *Media Education: Literacy, Learning and Contemporary Culture*, Cambridge, UK: Polity.

Burn, A. (2015) *Playing Beowulf: Gaming the Library*. Retrieved from https://darecollaborative.net/2015/03/11/playing-beowulf-gaming-the-library/ (accessed 5 November 2017).

Burn, A. and Durran, J. (2007) *Media Literacy in Schools*, London: Paul Chapman.

Burn, A. and Richards, C. (eds) (2014) *Children's Games in the New Media Age: Childlore, Media and the Playground*, Farnham, UK: Ashgate.

Burnett, C. (2016) *The Digital Age and Its Implications for Learning and Teaching in the Primary School*, York, UK: Cambridge Primary Review Trust.

Burnett, C. and Bailey, C. (2014) 'Conceptualising collaboration in hyrbid sites: Playing Minecraft together and apart in a primary classroom', in C. Burnett, J. Davies, G. Merchant and J. Rowsell (eds) *New Literacies Around the Globe: Policy and Pedagogy*, Abingdon, UK: Routledge, pp. 50–71.

Cannon, M. (2016) 'Media-making matters: Exploring literacy with young learners as media crafting, critique and artistry.' PhD thesis, Bournemouth University, Bournemouth, UK.

Cannon, M. and Reid, M. (2010) BFI/Cinémathèque Blog [Online]. Retrieved from http://markreid1895.wordpress.com/ (accessed 12 July 2012).

Crook C. (1996) *Computers and the Collaborative Experience of Learning: A Psychological Perspective* (International Library of Psychology), London: Routledge.

Department for Education (DfE). (2013a) *National Curriculum Programmes of Study*, London: DfE.

Department for Education (DfE). (2013b) *Computing Programmes of Study for Key Stages 1 and 2*, London: DfE.

Dezuanni, M., O'Mara, J. and Beavis, C. (2015) '"Redstone is like electricity": Children's performative representations in and around Minecraft', *E-Learning and Digital Media*, 12(2): 147–163.

Dredge, S. (2014) 'Google backs Code Club Pro scheme to boost UK teachers' computing skills', *The Guardian*. Retrieved from www.theguardian.com/technology/2014/feb/07/google-code-club-pro-teachers (accessed 5 November 2017).

Film Literacy Action Group (FLAG). (2014) *A Framework for Film Education*, London: British Film Institute.

Hawley, S. (2016) Presentation: The sociomateriality of literacy. Language, Literacy and Identity Conference, Educational Studies, Sheffield University, Sheffield UK.

Hoban, G., Nielsen, W. and Shepherd, A. (eds) (2015) *Student-Generated Digital Media in Science Learning*, London: Routledge.

Into Film. (2015) Into Film: FAQs [Online]. Retrieved from: www.intofilm.org/faqs (accessed 19 November 2016).

Livingstone, S. (2009) *Children and the Internet*, Cambridge, UK: Polity.

Marsh, J. (ed.) (2004) *Popular Culture, New Media and Digital Literacy in Early Childhood*, London: Routledge.

Marsh, J. (2009) 'Productive pedagogies: Play, creativity and digital cultures in the classroom', in R. Willett, M. Robinson and J. Marsh (eds) *Play, Creativity and Digital Cultures*, New York: Routledge, pp. 200–18.

MIT. (2016) About Scratch [Online]. Retrieved from https://scratch.mit.edu/about (accessed 21 September 2016).

Papert, S. (1993) *Mindstorms*, 2nd edn, Hemel Hempstead, UK: Harvester Wheatsheaf.

Parry, B. (2013) *Children, Film and Literacy*, London: Palgrave MacMillan.

Potter, J. (2012) *Digital Media and Learner Identity: The New Curatorship*, New York: Palgrave MacMillan.

Potter, J. (2014) 'Co-curating children's play cultures', in A. Burn and C. Richards (eds) *Children's Games in the New Media Age: Childlore, Media and the Playground*, London: Palgrave, pp. 187–206.

Potter, J. and Bryer, T. (2013) *Field Notes for 'Games From Stories': The Roundhouse Summer School Project 2013*, London: Ministry of Stories/IOE.

Potter, J. and Bryer, T. (2016) '"Finger flowment" and moving image language: Learning filmmaking with tablet devices', in B. Parry, C. Burnett and G. Merchant (eds) *Literacy, Media, Technology: Past, Present and Future*, London: Bloomsbury, pp. 111–28.

Potter, J. and McDougall, J. (2017) *Digital Media, Culture and Education: Theorising Third Space Literacies*, London: Palgrave Macmillan/Springer.

Prensky, M. (2005) 'Listen to the natives', *Educational Leadership*, 63(4): 8–13.

Quinlan, O. (2015) *Young Digital Makers*. Retrieved from https://www.nesta.org.uk/sites/default/files/young-digital-makers-summary.pdf (accessed 5 November 2017).

Sefton-Green, J. (2013) *Mapping Digital Makers*. Retrieved from www.nominettrust.org.uk/knowledge-centre/articles/mapping-digital-makers (accessed 5 November 2017).

Selwyn, N. and Facer, K. (eds) (2013) *The Politics of Education and Technology: Conflicts, Controversies and Connections*, London: Palgrave MacMillan.

The Film Space. (2016) www.thefilmspace.org (accessed 20 October 2016).

Turvey, K., Potter, J. and Burton, J. (2016) *Primary Computing and Digital Technologies*, 7th edn, London: Sage.

Twining, P. (2013) *Peter T's Bliki.* Retrieved from http://edfutures.net/PeterT's_bliki (accessed 5 November 2017).

UK Safer Internet Centre. (2016) UK Safer Internet Centre: Page for Teachers and Education Professionals (Online). Childnet International/Internet Watch Foundation/European Union Connecting Europe. Retrieved from www.saferinternet.org.uk/advice-centre/teachers-and-professionals (accessed 20 November 2016).

Waller, M. (2013) 'More than tweets: Developing the "new" and "old" through online social networking', in G. Merchant, J. Gillen, J. Marsh and J. Davies (eds) *Virtual Literacies: Interactive Spaces for Children and Young People*, Abingdon, UK: Routledge, pp. 126–41.

White, D. and Le Cornu, A. (2011) 'Visitors and residents: A new typology for online engagement', *First Monday*, 16(9). Retrieved from http://firstmonday.org/article/view/3171/3049 (accessed 15 May 2014).

Whitehead, M. (2002) *Developing Language and Literacy with Young Children*, 2nd ed, London: Paul Chapman.

Willett, R., Richards, C., Marsh, J., Burn, A. and Bishop, J.C. (2013) *Children, Media and Playground Cultures: Ethnographic Studies of School Playtimes*, London: Palgrave.

Wilson, C., Grizzle, A., Tuazon, R., Akyempong, K. and Cheung C.-K. (2011) *Media and Information Literacy Curriculum for Teachers*, Paris: UNESCO.

PARTNERSHIP IN PRACTICE

WORKING WITH TEACHING ASSISTANTS

Andreas O. Kyriakides and Jenny Houssart

INTRODUCTION

A common feature of contemporary primary classrooms is the presence of other adults employed to work alongside the teacher. Such adults are known by different names; we will generally use the phrase teaching assistant (TA) here. They present a considerable opportunity for both teachers and pupils, but making the most of them is not straightforward. Current and recent guidance for initial teacher education stresses that teachers need to communicate and work effectively with others, recognising their contributions and showing a commitment to collaborative working. These themes also occur throughout the literature and in our research data, which we draw on here.

We start by considering the growth in TA numbers and the debate about their effectiveness. Next, we discuss TAs with a general role, followed by those assigned to individuals. Finally, we consider issues related to TA training and development. We draw on our own interviews with and about TAs, first, in sections called 'Viewpoints', where we give a range of perspectives, and, second, in 'Examples' sections, where we present examples of practice.

OBJECTIVES

By the end of this unit, you should have started to:

- be aware of some key research findings related to TAs' roles;
- consider the opportunities and potential challenges arising from the presence of other adults in primary classrooms;
- develop strategies for working collaboratively with TAs.

THE WHY AND WHO OF SUPPORT STAFF

The majority of primary teachers no longer work alone in classrooms. The large increase in the number of adults other than teachers working in schools is due to three main factors:

- increased opportunities for children considered to have special educational needs to attend mainstream schools;
- changed approaches to teaching English and mathematics
- changes in workload management, brought about by the 'National agreement'.

These factors apply to different degrees across the United Kingdom; the first has had impact worldwide. A range of research examines the changing role and impact of support staff.

Research round-up 1: The evolving role of support staff

Butt and Lance (2009) consider how workforce reforms in the UK have impacted the role of TAs and conclude that TAs are now more closely involved with children's learning. Issues raised include ambiguity with job descriptions. The changing roles of support staff are also a key theme of research by Barkham (2008), who identifies the introduction of the Literacy and Numeracy Strategies as a factor in increasing the involvement of TAs with learning. Concerns raised include lack of time for teachers and TAs to plan together and TAs' poor pay and conditions.

A large-scale study, with an emphasis on quantitative data, was the Deployment and Impact of Support Staff (DISS) project, carried out in England and Wales. One article reporting on this project (Blatchford *et al.*, 2011) explores the 'Positive approaches to learning' (PAL) and academic progress of pupils who work with support staff. Results on PAL are often positive. Results on academic progress suggest that pupils working with support staff make less progress than others; the authors claim this is not explained by the characteristics of these pupils. One suggestion in the paper is that this is because pupils who receive such support have less contact with the teacher and the curriculum as a result. There is general agreement in the research that TAs have increasing involvement in teaching and learning. However, the research is inconclusive about their impact, particularly if seen in terms of pupil progress.

Research has also considered the changing profile of support staff. Kerry (2005) outlines the change in attitudes and practices from the time when TAs were often associated with routine practical tasks and goes on to offer a typology for conceptualising the roles of TAs, which includes the categories carer/mentor, behaviour manager, curriculum supporter and mobile paraprofessional (p. 377).

Changes in the role of TAs are confirmed by a study from an industrial-relations perspective (Bach, Kessler and Heron, 2006), which comments on the growing diversity of the TA workforce, as well as changes in TA roles. They note the ethnic diversity of the TA workforce in some areas, as well as TAs with differing career aspirations. A large study by Russell *et al.* (2005: 180) also notes the range of TA qualifications, with those in their study ranging from having no qualifications to degrees or higher degrees, with the majority having their highest qualification at either GCSE or A-level. There is agreement in the literature that TAs are now a more diverse group, engaged in a wider range of tasks. They possess a range of skills and qualities, as the following extracts from interviews with TAs illustrate.

Viewpoints 1: Background and experience

Yes. I was an interior designer for about twenty years and I have my own business and things . . . And I'd started going into my son's primary school to read . . . and that's what got me started . . . And it sounds a bit clichéd, but it's a bit more meaningful than worrying about people's curtains and cushions and things, so that's really what got me started. So I went along for the interview with various odd dressing-up pictures, really, that I made with my son . . . I thought, 'Well, I've got to show I know *something* about kids'.

(Audrey)

I did a training . . . years ago. Mediation for youth offenders . . . I was trained to be . . . a mediator that goes to young offenders' homes . . . But I think that's been useful. Elements of that have stayed with me. And I know that when I'm speaking to children . . . I do use the skills that I know.

I have worked voluntarily in settings with young children . . . Just helping to run playgroups and things like that. Or maybe just being a big kid yourself helps, you know [*Laughter*].

(Charlene)

I know how to teach these things because I have a child of my own in primary school . . . I know what to ask, what to expect from the child . . . If you can't teach it, if you can't explain it yourself to the child he will not be able to understand it. I'm seeing this from my own perspective as a mother . . . I believe that the way you explain something to a child is very important.

(Diana)

Task 8.1.1 TA experience

- How would you make the most of the skills and experience of each of the assistants considered above?
- Have a conversation with a TA in the school you work in to find out their experience and consider how this might be used.

Examples 1: Drawing on individual strengths

The examples below, drawn from our research, show how some schools try to make the most of the expertise that individual TAs bring.

- Several of the TAs we interviewed reported that schools make use of the experience they gained from their *previous employment*, or voluntary work. For example, Tony, who had worked as a chef, started a cookery club and worked with the teacher to develop activities related to taste tests as part of a topic on chocolate.
- Some TAs had experience of children and adults with *particular needs* that schools could draw on, sometimes by assigning the TA to work with an individual child, sometimes by involving the TA in discussions about meeting the needs of various children. For example, Kate, who supported a child in a wheelchair, came from a family where children had particular physical needs.
- For some, living in the *local community* was important in helping them to understand the children. For Obi, her voluntary work teaching Swahili at a Saturday school contributed to her informal role in supporting children from East African communities, both in praising their progress in Swahili and in discussing with them the differing expectations in different school systems.

TEACHING ASSISTANTS AS PART OF A CLASSROOM TEAM

TAs work in a range of ways, and schools will often take the strengths and experiences of individual assistants into account when making decisions about this. However, the two basic alternatives are for them to be assigned to one or more learners with special educational needs, or to be assigned to a class or classes, with their particular role within the class decided in conjunction with the class teacher. We consider this sort of general TA next.

Research round-up 2: General classroom support

Several research projects have focused on TAs assigned to work with a particular class. An example is a project in Scotland reported by Woolfson and Truswell (2005), in which additional assistants were placed in primary schools in disadvantaged areas. Each assistant was placed in a class to work under the direction of, and in partnership with, the class teacher. The aims of the project were to improve the quality of learning, impact positively on pupils' personal and social development and encourage parental involvement. Evaluation of the project suggests that these aims were met, with particular success in the first two. The authors also suggest that assistants are more likely to be effective when they work closely with the class teacher, and their effectiveness can be enhanced by the provision of more opportunities for liaison between class teachers and assistants.

A detailed consideration of ways in which teachers and TAs might work together is presented by Cremin, Thomas and Vincett (2005). They used an intervention strategy to develop three classroom models: *room management*, involving assigning specific roles to each adult; *zoning*, where responsibilities are divided according to classroom geography; and *reflective teamwork*, where adults develop integrated ways of working together, based on thorough discussion. Each model was introduced to two schools for use in literacy lessons. They reported increased pupil engagement in all cases. All three models stressed enhanced teamwork and role clarity, and the findings suggest that these are the key features, rather than the details of the models, which can all be seen as having advantages and disadvantages.

Task 8.1.2 TA and teacher role agreement

- Consider the three models presented by Cremin *et al*. (2005). What do you consider the advantages and disadvantages of each model? Can you suggest other ways of agreeing roles?
- Think about the class you work in, or one you are familiar with. How does the agreement of roles between the TA and teacher in this class match those suggested by Cremin *et al*. (2005).?

Recent guidance on working with TAs also stresses the importance of liaison and the need to find time for this (Sharples, Webster and Blatchford 2015). The same guidance asserts that TAs should add value to what teachers do, not replace them. In the examples that follow, we show how the TAs in our research and the teachers they work with sought to address these issues.

Examples 2: Agreeing roles and responsibilities

- Some TAs have a role in *assessing children's learning*. For Marion, this happens at the start of a lesson, when the teacher introduces a topic to the whole class. The teacher indicates particular learners he would like Marion to observe in the introduction, making judgements about their understanding and providing support if necessary. When Margaret works with groups of learners, her support includes marking their work during the lesson and explaining what she is writing to the children, a process agreed with the class teacher. Pria also has a role in marking work and received specific training from the deputy head about the school's marking policy before she was asked to do this.
- When TAs are assigned to a group of children for the middle part of the lesson, they may have a role in *adapting work*, sometimes to assist children with difficulties. Jan listens to the teacher's introduction to work, so that, if she has to repeat the instructions later, she uses the same words and ideas, possibly in simplified form. Margaret has developed strategies for breaking down and

going over ideas, using whiteboards and practical equipment. Crucially, Jan and Margaret see their role as supporting children to enable them to do the work, not as doing the work for them. Rita works in a classroom where extension activities are planned by the teacher, and Rita can decide when children would benefit from these.

- Finding time to *liaise with teachers* can be challenging. Sheena is allowed some planning time with the teacher out of the classroom. Others use short periods of time inventively. Tony works with older primary children who do some work in sets. The children organise themselves to return from sets to classes, and Tony uses this short time every day to feed back information to the teacher about children he has supported during sets. Pauline writes brief information about children's responses to tasks and how much help they needed on post-its, which she gives to the teacher. Lola has a short pro forma that she completes at the end of sessions supporting groups, to give the teacher an outline of how the session progressed and how the children responded.

Viewpoints 2: Teachers' perspectives

As part of a focus-group discussion, experienced primary teachers, drawn from different schools, were asked to comment on the scenarios above and compare them with their own experience. The discussion included the following points:

- All were positive about involving the TAs they worked with in teaching and learning, but pointed to the need for TAs to be prepared for and supported in this role.
- There was very mixed reaction to the idea of TAs marking children's work as introduced in the scenarios above, with this being seen as standard practice in some schools and out of the question in others.
- There was agreement that TAs and teachers do not and should not have the same role, but differing views on what this might mean in detail.

SUPPORTING INDIVIDUALS

In many countries, TAs have been used increasingly to support individual children with special needs and to enable them to attend mainstream school. In the research round-up below, we draw on literature discussing this practice in England, Cyprus and the USA. Other countries using this system include Scotland (Woolfson and Truswell, 2005) and Northern Ireland (Abbott, McConkey and Dobbins, 2011). A strength of this system is that the TA may work alongside one child for several years, getting to know them well. Such TAs are sometimes linked to a unit within the school for children with a particular need, or have attended specialist training or liaised with external experts who visit the school. They sometimes form a relationship with the child's parents.

Despite the advantages, potential drawbacks exist. A key issue can be misunderstanding about who is responsible for the child's education. Role clarity is important here, and teachers should also understand the contribution TAs responsible for individuals can make.

Research round-up 3: TAs' support for individuals

Considerable international research and debate exist concerning the use of TAs assigned to support individual children. A study carried out in two schools in Cyprus (Angelides, Constantinou and Leigh, 2009) identified a range of practices across the schools, leading the authors to conclude that the role of 'companions' (a direct translation of their Greek title) in relation to inclusion was contradictory. They found instances where the presence of the 'companion' increased the child's participation in the learning process and encouraged relations with other children. However, they also give examples where the companions hindered inclusion, by reducing interaction between the pupil and the teacher or by completing work for the pupil. Sometimes, dependence on the companion appeared to be encouraged, and time spent with the companion was at the expense of time spent with other students. Teachers interviewed as part of this study had different expectations of companions. Some expected them to take much responsibility for teaching the child, whereas others felt they, as teachers, should retain that responsibility. Similar findings have arisen in studies in other countries.

Giangreco (2013) summarises research in this area and puts forward a range of practices that should be present when TAs support individuals. These include ensuring that teachers have main responsibility for planning work, and assistants are appropriately supported and monitored. The author also suggests that overuse or misuse of TAs is a symptom rather than a cause of issues related to inclusive education.

Although a TA may be assigned to a named child, they may be deployed in a more integrated way to meet the child's needs. Such practices were found by Rose (2000) in a case study of a school in England with a high proportion of pupils with special educational needs. The assistants had a wider role than working with the individuals they were assigned to; the implication is that this is the school's policy. Points are made about the importance of teamwork and effective communication.

Examples 3: Supporting individuals

The examples below are drawn from an interview with Nicki, an occupational therapist with extensive experience of visiting schools to offer advice to those who support children with particular needs:

- Max is in Y2 and has a hearing impairment that makes it difficult for him to follow whole-class introductions to lessons, as a result of which his behaviour can become challenging. The class is working on subtraction, but records from the previous year suggest Max is unlikely to be able to cope with the work prepared for the rest of the class. A TA who knows Max well is available to work alongside him.
- Angela is in KS2 and has a diagnosis of cerebral palsy. She is supported by a TA who has worked alongside her for 4 years. Angela's new teacher has no experience of working with children with cerebral palsy and does not regard herself as knowledgeable about this or other special needs.
- Alex has severe mobility difficulties, and two professionals are visiting the school to discuss specialist equipment he might be provided with. The TA who supports Alex is expecting to meet the professionals when they visit, though the teacher is likely to be working with the rest of the class at the time. The TA suggests that if another adult is needed to meet the professionals, then it should be Alex's mother or grandmother.

Task 8.1.3 Support scenarios

What would you do if you were the teacher in each of the scenarios above?

Viewpoints 3: Supporting individuals

During her interview, Nicki was asked what advice she would give to trainees or new teachers preparing to work with a TA assigned to an individual child. Here is her response:

> First of all, I believe that the teacher must be informed about the child's disability . . . Even if a teacher had in the past another student with the same disability, the two children will never

be the same, we speak about two different human beings. A learning plan must be designed from the beginning about the particular student and then the TA will supervise the child under the guidance of the classroom teacher, not by herself. The TA can't take the place of the teacher.

TAS' TRAINING AND DEVELOPMENT

We have hinted above at the variation in training and development available to TAs and how that is likely to affect the support they can offer. We now turn explicitly to this issue.

Research round-up 4: TAs' training and development

In the UK and many other countries, no formal training or qualifications are required to be a TA. Lack of training is raised as an issue by many studies (e.g. Butt and Lance, 2009). However, TAs increasingly have qualifications and specific training for the job, although many – including some TAs – see this as inadequate or patchy. Abbott *et al.* (2011), in Northern Ireland, focused on the training needs of support staff who worked with pupils with different special needs. The assistants consulted overwhelmingly said they would like more training, including training aimed at giving them a deeper understanding of the various syndromes and conditions they dealt with. Given the increasing role of TAs in numeracy and literacy, they are increasingly likely to receive training in these areas.

Mistry, Burton and Brundrett (2004) report on a case study from a school for 4–9-year-olds in England that examines the role of support staff. Recommendations include a need for training for support staff, to support their work, and for teachers, in order to enable them to manage adults more effectively. This reflects the fact that, traditionally, teachers received no such training, and many started their careers expecting that they would work alone in the classroom. Current and recent requirements, however, are that teachers will begin their careers aware of ways of working alongside support staff.

More recently, there have been attempts to establish standards for all TAs in England, though changes in government meant that no statutory requirements were published. Nevertheless, advisory recommendations were produced by an independent panel, designed to form the basis of constructive conversations between TAs and those they work alongside. The recommendations consider TAs' professional development under four themes (UNISON *et al.*, 2016: 6):

1   personal and professional conduct;
2   knowledge and understanding;
3   teaching and learning;
4   working with others.

Viewpoints 4: Training and development

Here is what some of the TAs in our research said about education and training:

> We have training . . . it's in my contract. Not all of us are contracted into joining INSET, . . . But it's cool. I want to. It's important, I think. I find them really useful, actually . . . those TAs who perhaps don't really feel that they want to move on don't have to attend.
>
> (Dorian)

> I actually found out about it (Aspergers) in my foundation degree . . . because I was actually doing a few modules where they spoke about autism, and I thought, 'Okay, I work with a boy, that rings a few bells'.
>
> (Salma)

Certainly, it would have been useful if I attended some seminars with regard to subject matter. Because you will offer much more to the children.

(Hara)

It depends on the level of the child. With this child I am working with, I don't need anything because he doesn't understand anything. But if I worked with a different child who understood and I was always next to him I would want to help him.

(Dorothy)

There's no need to attend any seminars about how to help children understand mathematics because then you get into the teacher's job.

(Mary)

Task 8.1.4 Views of the TAs

- What do you think about the differing views of the TAs quoted in Viewpoints 4 about the need for training or development related to subject matter? Do you agree with Dorothy's assertion that this is not required if the children supported are working on simple (to adults) tasks?
- How do the views and experiences of the TAs in your school compare with those expressed in Viewpoints 4?
- Discuss the implications of the aforementioned views.

Examples 4: Training and development

The examples below show the preparation some TAs in our research received for their role.

- For many TAs, part of their role involves working with individuals or groups considered to need additional support on intervention programmes in English and mathematics. These normally consist of pre-prepared materials and instructions and are ideally accompanied by appropriate training. For example, Tony attended training for catch-up literacy, and, in line with the programme's expectations, the deputy head with responsibility for literacy also attended, so that there was a member of staff with overall responsibility with whom the TA could discuss issues. In Jodie's school, training for TAs working on intervention programmes was led by the deputy head, who carried out some activities with a group of children, observed by TAs.
- Several TAs received training and guidance relevant to the specific needs of individuals they support. Pauline had attended several courses outside the school on supporting children on the autistic spectrum. Sometimes, outside agencies visit the schools and share expertise with TAs and teachers. For example, a speech and language specialist visited Jan's school to deliver sessions to a small group of children while Jan watched. After 6 weeks, Jan took over the sessions, while the specialist watched and supported. After that, the specialist made occasional visits. Sometimes, a special unit or department exists inside the school, and the department staff share their expertise with TAs; Jodie received support on working with hearing-impaired children from specialists within her school.
- Some TAs are involved in training in their schools alongside the teachers. Dorian's contract states that attending INSET within the schools is part of her job, and she is positive about sessions she has attended, for example about boys and writing. In Barbara's school, TAs attend staff meetings

concerned with literacy training and materials used for teaching mathematics. Thus, teachers are aware of the training the TAs have had and can make the most of it. This is only usually possible when training is provided during the working day, or when TAs work and are paid for sufficient hours to attend meetings after school.

SUMMARY

This unit offers strong examples of positive practice in primary classrooms where teachers work alongside other adults. When TAs have a general supporting role in the classroom, there is a range of models for agreeing the respective roles of the teacher and TA. Whichever model is used, it is clarity of roles that enhances the experience of both adults and children. When TAs work mainly or entirely with individual learners with particular needs, the teacher still has overall responsibility for learning, but should recognise, value and utilise the knowledge and expertise brought by the TA. The TA workforce varies from those with no qualifications to graduates, and some may have studied on work-based foundation degrees or attained higher-level teaching assistant status. All will bring with them tacit knowledge acquired in a range of contexts, and many will have expertise related to the particular needs of learners they support. If TAs and teacher work as a team to develop effective practice, they are better placed to meet the needs of all learners.

 ## ANNOTATED FURTHER READING

Blatchford, P., Russell, A. and Webster, R. (2012) *Reassessing the Impact of Teaching Assistants: How Research Challenges Practice and Policy*, London: Routledge.
> This is a book based on findings from the DISS project, including discussion of implications and recommendations for practice.

Bosanquet, P., Radford, J. and Webster, R. (2016) *The Teaching Assistant's Guide to Effective Interaction: How to Maximize Your Practice*, London: Routledge.
> This book suggests a range of strategies that TAs can use to enhance their interaction with pupils.

 ## FURTHER READING TO SUPPORT M-LEVEL STUDY

Kyriakides, A.O. and Houssart, J. (2016) 'Paraprofessionals in Cyprus and England: Perceptions of their role in supporting primary mathematics', *Research in Mathematics Education*, 18(3): 249–66.
> This paper considers TAs' roles in mathematics lessons in relation to children, teachers and mathematical processes.

Rubie-Davies, C., Blatchford, P., Webster, R. Koutsoubou, M. and Bassett, P. (2010) 'Enhancing learning? A comparison of teacher and teaching assistant interactions with pupils', *School Effectiveness & School Improvement*, 21(4): 429–49.
> This paper is based on detailed analysis of talk in English and mathematics lessons.

RELEVANT WEBSITES

Professor Michael Giangreco: www.uvm.edu/~cdci/archives/mgiangre/
    The website of Professor Michael Giangreco, who has carried out extensive research on TAs and inclusion, includes links to articles and project websites.

MITA: http://maximisingtas.co.uk/
    The website of the MITA project (Maximising the Impact of Teaching Assistants) includes a range of resources and summaries of research.

Teaching Assistants - Stars in our Classroom: www.youtube.com/watch?v=C6EFUInRHDs
    This has video clips of TAs talking about their role.

REFERENCES

Abbott, L., McConkey, R. and Dobbins, M. (2011) 'Key players in inclusion: Are we meeting the professional needs of learning support assistants for pupils with complex needs?', *European Journal of Special Needs Education*, 26(2): 215-31.

Angelides, P., Constantinou, C. and Leigh, J. (2009) 'The role of paraprofessionals in developing inclusive education in Cyprus', *European Journal of Special Needs Education*, 24(1): 75-89.

Bach, S., Kessler, I. and Heron, P. (2006) 'Changing job boundaries and workforce reform: The case of teaching assistants', *Industrial Relations Journal*, 37(1): 2-21.

Barkham, J. (2008) 'Suitable work for women? Roles, relationships and changing identities of "other adults" in the early years classroom', *British Educational Research Journal*, 34(6): 839-53.

Blatchford, P., Bassett, P., Brown, P., Martin, C., Russell, A. and Webster, R. (2011) 'The impact of support staff on pupils' "positive approaches to learning" and their academic progress', *British Educational Research Journal*, 37(3): 443-64.

Butt, G. and Lance, A. (2009) '"I am *not* the teacher!": Some effects of remodelling the roles of teaching assistants in English primary schools', *Education 3-13*, 37(3): 219-31.

Cremin, H., Thomas, G. and Vincett, K. (2005) 'Working with teaching assistants: Three models evaluated', *Research Papers in Education*, 20(4): 413-32.

Giangreco, M. (2013) 'Teacher assistant supports in inclusive schools: Resarch, practices and alternatives', *Australian Journal of Special Education*, 37(2): 93-106.

Kerry, T. (2005) 'Towards a typology for conceptualizing the roles of teaching assistants', *Educational Review*, 57(3): 373-84.

Mistry, M., Burton, N. and Brundrett, M. (2004) 'Managing LSAs: An evaluation of the use of learning support assistants in an urban primary school', *School Leadership & Management*, 24(2): 125-37.

Rose, R. (2000) 'Using classroom support in a primary school: A single school case study', *British Journal of Special Education*, 27(4): 191-6.

Russell, A., Blatchford, P., Bassett, P., Brown, P. and Martin, C. (2005) 'The views of teaching assistants in English key stage 2 classes on their role, training and job satisfaction', *Educational Research*, 47(2): 175-89.

Sharples, J., Webster, R. and Blatchford, P. (2015) *Making Best Use of Teaching Assistants, Guidance Report*, London: Education Endowment Foundation.

UNISON, NAHT, NET, MITA and RTSA. (2016) *Professional Standards for Teaching Assistants: Advice for Headteachers, Teachers, Teaching Assistants, Governing Boards and Employers*, June. Retrieved from http://maximisingtas.co.uk/assets/content/ta-standards-final-june2016-1.pdf (accessed 5 October 2016).

Woolfson, R. and Truswell, E. (2005) 'Do classroom assistants work?', *Educational Research*, 47(1): 63-75.

PARTNERSHIPS WITH PARENTS

John Ryan and Stephen Griffin

INTRODUCTION

This unit focuses on building effective, purposeful and long-lasting relationships with parents/carers. For the purposes of this unit, the term 'parents' should be taken to include carers also - single parents, grandparents, foster carers or older siblings, acting *in loco parentis*. After the Education Acts 1988 and 1992, parents have been increasingly described as 'partners' in their children's education. Coupled with the move towards greater parental choice in terms of the schools parents can send their children to, such as academy primary schools, there has also been an increased transparency of school performance data, via Ofsted reports, league tables and the publication of exam results; parents are viewed as key stakeholders in the educational process and, more recently, the choice of schools. Historically, in England, the home and the school have been two distinct and separate realms of a child's life. The role that parents have as educators has, therefore, been underdeveloped in the past. Indeed, the Hadow Report (1931) highlighted the importance of a child-centred curriculum, but it was not until the Plowden Report (DES, 1967) that recognition was attributed to the vital role that parents can play in their child's education: 'One of the essentials for educational advance is a closer partnership between the two parties (i.e. schools and parents) to every child's education' (DES, 1967: 102). The power of parental involvement should not be underestimated - in 2012, PISA studies highlighted the impact of positive parental involvement in children's education in terms of pupil educational outcomes (OECD, 2012; PISA, 2012). Therefore, it is evident that greater collaboration with parents needs to be a key aim in improving educational outcomes for children and as such should be a priority for all primary school teachers.

OBJECTIVES

By the end of this unit, you should:

- have an understanding of the need to ensure that you develop secure relationships with the parents of pupils in your class, during school placement, the first year of teaching and subsequent years of teaching;
- recognise and understand the importance of purposeful and structured working relationships with parents;
- know of effective ways of liaising and communicating with parents;
- have an appreciation of the need for trust and understanding as the foundation for successful relationships between parents and school;
- begin to have some strategies as a trainee teacher or newly qualified teacher (NQT) and begin to establish sound home–school links.

PROFESSIONAL REQUIREMENTS

It is important to recognise that, not only is parental involvement desirable in achieving positive educational outcomes, but it is also a professional requirement of all teachers, as detailed in the *Professional Standards* published in 2012.

The Qualified Teacher Status (QTS) standards are divided into three sections:

- professional attributes;
- professional knowledge and understanding;
- professional skills.

The implementation of a concise set of standards, which apply to teachers at the point of entry to the profession, as well as to experienced practitioners, will, according to the government, enable the following: 'an overarching set of standards establishes a platform for the coherent approach to Initial Teacher Education (ITE), induction and continuing professional development (CPD) that the profession aspires to' (TDA, 2007). Running through all these standards is a theme of being respectful towards all learners and considerate and committed to raising their achievement. The standards are organised as separate headings, numbered 1–8. Under each section, there are bullets and subheadings. These subheadings should not be referenced as separate standards and should be used advisedly. For example, under Section 8, we see the introduction of the role of parents for the first time. Despite the government's acknowledgement of the importance of schools working effectively with parents, the standards have only one reference to parental engagement. However, included in Standard Q8 is an emphasis on the need for all teachers to ensure the importance of working alongside parents:

- Communicate effectively with parents with regard to pupils' achievements and well-being, young people, colleagues, parents and carers.

(TDA, 2007: Q8)

Under the successive governments, there has been increasing concern regarding the teaching of reading and basic mathematic strategies. These now form an integral part of Ofsted inspections and ITE provision. As such, parents' understanding of pedagogical approaches in primary school, such as the teaching of synthetic phonics as the preferred method for teaching reading and a move towards an instrumental approach for the teaching of mathematics, has now increased.

ADVANTAGES OF SECURE RELATIONSHIPS WITH PARENTS

Research (Bastiani, 2003; Desforges and Abouchaar, 2003; DCSF, 2008; Ofsted, 2011; Carroll and Alexander, 2016; Robinson, Bingle and Howard, 2016) has shown that involving parents in their children's education can help remove barriers to learning, raise attainment and improve attitudes and behaviour. It is widely believed that primary schools, working in partnership with parents to support their children's learning and development, can expect significant and lasting benefits. Among these are improved, as well as consistent, levels of attainment, coupled with a more positive attitude towards behaviour and attendance.

O'Hara (2008: 14) highlights the importance of communicating with parents and suggests six practical ways to ensure that teachers and parents have effective dialogue:

1 regular parent–teacher contact (such as PTA);
2 joint teaching/work in the classroom;
3 home visits;
4 whole-school events;

5   school handbooks/prospectuses;
6   letters, notices and circulars.

As well as highlighting parental involvement, he also suggested strategies as to how this could be implemented, the most significant being Parent Teacher Associations (PTAs) – a common feature of our schools today. More recently, Desforges and Abouchaar discussed the obvious link between input from home and attainment in school: 'Parental involvement has a significant effect on children's achievement and adjustment even after all other factors (such as social class, maternal education and poverty) have been taken out of the equation' (2003: 9.2.2).

In a survey by Lewis *et al.* (2007: 2), primary head teachers were asked what were the most effective ways of involving parents in their child's education. The findings indicated that more than 90 per cent of primary schools used the following:

*   school newsletters;
*   special events for parents (e.g. information/discussion evenings);
*   gathering parents' views as part of school self-evaluation;
*   encouraging parents to contact/or visit the school.

As teachers, you need to ensure that such opportunities are constructively built upon and you have a secure understanding of pupils' cultural capital (Bourdieu, 1986). This can be understood as the set of dispositions that enable certain groups of pupils to succeed more readily at school than others; that is, they receive linguistic ability from their parents and have access to certain forms of culture, such as the theatre and the 'arts', which are reflected heavily in the school curriculum. Furthermore Corsaro and Fingerson (2006) and Hart and Risely (1995) outline that parents who engage children in their learning and talk to their children about learning before their children begin school ensure that their children are actually ready for school. It is these predisposed skills that give them the advantage, whereas pupils from less privileged backgrounds, or with parents who do not ensure their children are ready to begin school, may struggle to access the curriculum for this very reason.

When considering the behaviour of pupils in the classroom, Rogers (2000) contends that there are some behavioural issues outside the school or classroom environment that teachers or the school cannot influence. Similarly, Charlton and David (1993: 207) state that, 'much behaviour at school seems to be independent of home influences'. It could, therefore, be argued that some children's lives are split into two distinct parts: home and school. Thus, it is vital that, in order to provide a consistent and effective approach to the education of children in primary-phase education, both academically and socially, parents and teachers cooperate and form what Cooper and Olson (1996) term a healthy 'alliance'. The Steer Report (2005) and Ofsted (2011) placed similar emphasis on this crucial relationship, asserting that good, as well as effective, communication between the school and home is essential for appropriate behaviour.

Research by Miller and Rollnick (2002) outlined that many teachers have rather a negative view of parents of children in their class. This chimes with findings from the Elton Report (1989: 133), which concluded: 'our evidence suggests that teachers' picture of parents is generally very negative. Many teachers feel that parents are to blame for much misbehaviour in schools'. Yet the value of healthy parent-teacher relations has been strongly emphasised within the behavioural discourse (Cooper and Olson, 1996; Barnard, 2004; Addi-Raccah and Ainhoren, 2009; Robinson *et al.*, 2016), and Selwyn (2011a, 2011b) observes that, 'the notion of the "engaged parent" has become a key element of governmental policy efforts to improve educational standards and reduce inequalities' (Selwyn *et al.*, 2011: 314). Despite this, these potential relationships are not always fully utilised and realised, and, as a teacher new to the profession, it could be advantageous for you to be proactive in forming appropriate and effective relationships with parents.

The survey also described how the majority of primary schools actively sought strategies to involve their PTAs. However, the survey highlighted that socio-economic factors influenced the amount of involvement from the PTA or even whether the school had a PTA. Whether before or after qualifying as a teacher, you need to ensure that you know the strategies employed by the school to ensure that parents are involved in their child's education. Recently, online communication and virtual learning environments (VLEs) have been used increasingly to involve parents in school life. This is going to have an impact on your daily routine, and you may be requested to contribute to such forums, so you need a confident and capable approach to ICT. Lewis *et al.*'s (2007: 3) survey also outlines other strategies that head teachers feel they use to actively involve parents in primary education:

- parents' forums/focus groups;
- online communication/VLEs;
- family learning/parent-child workshops;
- as parent governors.

FIRST IMPRESSIONS

Recent initiatives at both a national and local level have encouraged greater collaboration between the two (schools and parents). For example, many schools now offer parents the opportunity to observe lessons and to discuss the new teaching methods employed.

To this end, it is essential that you seek out opportunities to forge meaningful and appropriate links with parents of the children in your class. Outside formal meetings such as parents' evenings, this can be done effectively by taking the opportunity to be 'seen' at key times. It is often the case that many home-school partnerships never reach their potential because the school is seen as being remote and distant from the home. When you also consider that there may be significant numbers of parents whose own experience of schooling was negative, it is not surprising that they are reticent to 'cross the threshold' and approach teachers comfortably. For these parents, school may still represent an unhappy and less-than-productive period of their lives. Also, demands on parents, who may work full time or look after younger children, may mean that they are less active than they would like to be regarding the teaching and learning of their children. Therefore, it is your duty as teachers to reach out and open up the possibilities of home-school partnerships.

A key time to achieve this aim is at the beginning and end of the school day. Although you need to be mindful of ensuring a prompt start to lessons, if you are visible and welcoming in the morning, it sends a clear message to parents and children alike. This is especially important at the beginning of a new school year. Both the parents and the children will be keen to meet the new teacher, and your presence will ensure that you have a positive influence throughout the year. As formal parents' meetings may not take place until later in the school year, a quick personal introduction is an effective means of establishing a relationship sooner.

Task 8.2.1 Relationships with parents

- *Action point*: Introduce yourself to parents at either the beginning or end of the school day – make a point of remarking positively on an achievement each child has made.
- *Task*: During your non-contact time (or NQT time), visit other schools (or compare approaches while on school placements) to research how they ensure that parents are involved with their children's education. Report your findings to your mentor, line manager or tutor.

DEALING WITH DIFFICULT SITUATIONS

As discussed previously, as teachers we are aware of the benefits that supportive parents have for the achievement of their children. Research (Edwards and Warin, 1999; Desforges and Abouchaar, 2003; Corsaro and Fingerson 2006; Robinson *et al.*, 2016) also highlights the enormous benefits that parents can bring to school when the values and ethos are shared between home and school. However, we need to be aware of the problematic nature of school when this is not the case. The work of Edwards and Warin (1999) raises many issues concerning the assumptions that schools make considering adequate and appropriate support from parents. They reached the conclusion that many schools were keen to utilise parents as 'long arms' for the schools' own purposes, and not as equal partners. They concluded that the ways in which schools enhance parental involvement is rather one-sided. This can be problematic if parents and the school have opposing views and values. As an NQT, you may find that not all parents are as supportive as you would hope.

A shared language concerning the nature of school is vital, and staff in primary schools have to be aware that this may not be the case for the majority of parents, so that schools have to take steps to ameliorate the feeling of failure, the feeling that education is of little or no value, and that school represents a legitimate target for verbal and physical abuse. It is vital that, if you are abused physically or verbally, your line manager or a senior teacher is informed immediately. It is against this background that your role as an NQT or trainee teacher may sit. When you are appointed, you will need local knowledge of the school and an understanding of the issues that families may bring: domestic violence, child protection, alcohol and substance abuse, teenage pregnancies, joblessness, and so on. Despite this, it is important to state that, as an NQT (or indeed any teacher), you should not make assumptions about parents and families that are unfounded.

You will also need a working knowledge of agencies and training opportunities for parents. The role of any NQT in a whole-school context is that of supporting families and children. This is crucial in building and developing a shared vision, where the outcomes ensure that every day matters for every child, and where parents and staff are given the tools, knowledge and understanding to enable this.

Task 8.2.2 Managing parent helpers

How would you respond to the following?
- A parent helper begins to discuss their child with you during a science lesson.
- A parent helper has led a design technology task (e.g. making puppets) with a group of children, but it has come to your attention that the children merely observed the process, rather than becoming actively involved in the activity.
- At the end of the school day, an agitated parent approaches you stating that their child is being bullied and that you have failed to deal with it.

Discuss these with an NQT or your school mentor or tutor and decide upon a clear, structured course of action.

One of the most challenging, yet rewarding, aspects of your NQT year, after teaching and learning, is the relationship between yourself and parents. Research (Bastiani, 2003; Desforges and Abouchaar, 2003; Robinson *et al.*, 2016) shows that, where the partnership between home and school is supportive, with shared values and expectations, this contributes greatly to the outcomes for the child. In order for this to happen, there needs to be a good relationship between home and school that facilitates open and honest communication. This does not just mean 'talking' to parents when there are concerns about the pupil, but taking the time to celebrate the child's achievements on a day-to-day basis, so that, when the difficult conversations have to take place, they do so against a background of 'perceived fairness'. It is imperative, therefore, that all school policies are consistently adhered to by all staff. Such policies may include the following, which you should find and read:

*   behaviour policy;
*   SEN policy;
*   teaching and learning policy;
*   whole-school policy;
*   assessment policy;
*   emotional literacy policy;
*   homework policy.

All policies should be followed with transparency, so that parents are kept informed about their children's behaviour and attainment at every stage.

All primary schools need to work hard to develop positive relationships with parents. This can be a challenge. It is, therefore, important that, as part of the induction process or while on placement, you as an NQT or trainee teacher have the opportunity to sit in at both formal and informal parent discussions. This will provide you with an opportunity to observe how such a meeting is structured, to observe the body language and the language used by the teacher, and to see how any issues are resolved. It is suggested that, should an NQT need to have a 'difficult conversation' with a parent, they discuss it with their mentor or line manager first, in order to 'rehearse' the points, and that the mentor or line manager should also be at the meeting with the NQT, whether this is formal or informal. There should be some reflection following the meeting, to critically analyse your responses and set common agreements after such meetings.

If appropriate, it would be extremely useful for NQTs to attend any parents' coffee mornings (or similar activities) from time to time. This allows parents to get to know the NQT in a different setting and also provides NQTs with the opportunity to observe the other staff's relationships with parents. Experienced staff may know the parents very well and may well have information about the whole family that the NQT needs to be aware of, on a need-to-know basis, before seeing the parents. You should be careful of making generalisations or labelling parents unduly.

PARENTS' EVENINGS

Parents' evenings form part of a teacher's statutory duties (DfES, 2009) and are an important fixture of the school year. Many schools will operate a termly parents' evening, where parents are invited in to discuss their child's progress. It is also worth mentioning that parents' evenings may vary in their nature. Pastoral parents' evenings are often held at the start of the academic year to allow discussion around specific issues of transition and settling into a new class. These meetings may well be held with the acknowledgement that it is too early to discuss academic progress, and, as such, the discussion will centre on the happiness and disposition of the child and friendship groupings. It may also be an opportunity for the teacher to share information regarding the curriculum. As was mentioned previously, these early meetings are particularly useful as a means of building purposeful relationships.

As with other aspects of school life, parents' evenings require careful planning to ensure success. Obviously, parents will expect to see their children's work marked effectively, with purposeful, formative comments. Also, it will help to make a few notes about each child prior to the meeting and be prepared to make notes during the meeting, should the need arise. Often, parents may use the meeting to air particular concerns about their child that you may not be able to respond to immediately without some investigation (e.g. a bullying issue). In this case, it is important that you offer the parents a particular time to meet at a later stage, when you have more information at hand.

It is always worth opening the meeting by asking the parents whether they have any particular concerns that they wish to discuss. This will allow for an open and frank dialogue. You must also be mindful that parents themselves are useful sources of information, as the Cambridge Primary Review (Alexander, 2009) suggests: 'Teachers need to establish more fruitful links between home and school which build on the support for children's learning that already exists in the home and community'. This highlights the need for the partnership between teachers and parents to be a two-way process.

Remember that the purpose of the meeting with parents is to report on the child's progress, but it is also an opportunity to enhance pupil learning by empowering the parents with knowledge that will help them support their child. Therefore, you will need to communicate pupil targets clearly and make suggestions as to how these can be supported at home. As these meetings operate (for the most part) on scheduled appointments, it is necessary to keep an eye on the time. It is inevitable that you will, on occasion, run over time, but, in the interests of all parents, it is important to keep an eye on the clock. If you find that a particular issue requires more time, you may have to arrange to meet at a later date.

Task 8.2.3 Parents' evenings

Case study

During your first parents' evening as an NQT you have ensured that all of the children's work has been placed out on their desks for parents to look at. This is normal school practice, and you speak to parents individually at your desk at allocated times. While talking to a parent, you notice that another parent is looking at his daughter's work and is now comparing her work with other children on her table. He then proceeds to look at the work of other children in the class on different tables.

- How do you deal with this situation?
- How could this situation have been avoided?
- What will you do to avoid a similar situation in the future?

Discuss these with your mentor or tutor.

PARENTAL EXPERTISE

Another strategy to encourage closer relationships between parents and schools is to maximise on the expertise of parents and other members of the community. Contributions to the development of the curriculum by support from outside agencies and parents has become increasingly common over recent years. The willingness of parents to share their experiences with a group of children can provide a renewed vigour and inspiration to an existing unit or scheme of work. Parents who are, for example, nurses, postal workers, police officers, community artists, technicians or workers for the fire service may be willing to support schools to enhance learning. Parents with particular interests or hobbies, or who have visited places of interest, or who have lived in different countries, could also be involved by being invited to the class (or a small group of children, if the whole class is too daunting) as visiting speakers.

It is vital that, if you are going to use the suggestions above, you arrange a meeting before any planned activities, in order to ensure that the work or talk that any visitor is going to lead is appropriate for the children in your class. You will also need to refer to the school's policy on Disclosure and Barring Service checks, to ensure that the correct protocols for adult visitors in class are followed. It is also important that follow-up work is planned for, and shared with, such parents, in order to celebrate the impact that their expertise may have had on a group of children. This work does not necessarily have to be in written form, thus encouraging all children to express their engagement with the visiting speakers.

Such an approach could ensure that you value as well as respect parents' contributions, and the children in your class will notice that you have a two-way relationship with parents.

Task 8.2.4 Using parents' expertise

Read the case study and discuss the questions with a peer or mentor.

Case study

Yasmin's father is a staff nurse at the local hospital, and the newly appointed class teacher, working in Year 5, is keen to use his expertise. Yasmin's father is invited to come and speak to the Year 5 class, and the class teacher tells him to prepare 'something about healthy eating'. On arriving in school, Yasmin's father shares with the class a PowerPoint presentation of thirty-three slides (with mostly words) that he has used on a recent INSET day. He also talks to the children for 30 minutes on nutrition and dietetics. Throughout the talk, advanced scientific vocabulary and terminology are used. At the end of the talk, the children and class teacher cannot think of any questions to ask, and there is a long, rather embarrassing pause, until the teacher asks the class to thank Yasmin's father by giving him a round of applause.

- How could the class teacher have avoided this situation?
- What should the class teacher have done prior to Yasmin's father visiting the class or school?
- How could the class teacher have maximised the parent's expertise?
- What follow-up activities could have been planned, if the presentation had been pitched at the appropriate level?
- Why is it important to liaise clearly and in advance with any visitors?

SUMMARY

In this unit, we have endeavoured to highlight the importance of purposeful, open and structured relationships with parents as a means of ensuring the best possible education for the children in school. At the heart of this is the acknowledgement that parents are partners in their children's education and, as such, are key educators themselves. The need to develop effective professional relationships is vital for all primary school teachers. We have suggested that there are many ways in which these partnerships can be developed and supported in school, and the tasks are a good starting point for this. We have established that, if links between parents and the school are strong, then children achieve more, both academically and in terms of behaviour. We have outlined that, when working with parents, you need to adopt a professional and understanding approach. It is our view that establishing strong home–school links is essential when it comes to ensuring that the individual potential of pupils is realised.

ANNOTATED FURTHER READING

PISA. (2012) *The Role of Families in Shaping Students' Engagement, Drive and Self-Beliefs*. Retrieved from www.keepeek.com/Digital-Asset-Management/oecd/education/pisa-2012-results-ready-to-learn-volume-iii/the-role-of-families-in-shaping-students-engagement-drive-and-self-beliefs_9789264201170-10-en#page1 (accessed 6 November 2017).

> This report from PISA 2012 provides a helpful insight into the impact that families have on pupils' engagement with their education. From considerations of the significance of the home environment, parental behaviour and involvement with their childrens' education, this report gives an overview of the relationship between educational achievement and parental expectation and support. It is helpful in particular to consider the key themes that emerge here from the data and the role that the school and teachers can play in promoting positive home–school relationships.

Hampden-Thompson, G. and Galindo, C. (2017) 'School–family relationships, school satisfaction and the academic achievement of young people', *Educational Review*, 69(2): 248–65.

> Drawing upon data from more than 10,000 students in England, this journal article examines the role of home–school relationships and the impact that these have on educational achievement. The data suggest, unsurprisingly, that positive school–family relationships are a 'predictor of achievement', but that the degree of parental satisfaction with the school has a significant role to play also. In particular, this highlights the importance of schools actively considering how they can enhance parental satisfaction in order to facilitate poistive working relationships and increase educational achievement.

FURTHER READING TO SUPPORT M-LEVEL STUDY

Abdullah, A.G.K, Seedee, R., Alzaidiyeen, N.J., Al-Shabatat, A., Alzeydeen, H.K. and Al-Awabdeh, A.H. (2011) 'An investigation of teachers' attitudes towards parental involvement', *Educational Research*, 2(8): 1402–8.

> This journal article discusses teachers' attitudes towards parents and their involvement in their children's education in Jordan, and whether individual teacher characteristics (such as age, qualifications and experience) have an impact upon these relationships. It will be useful for you to analyse the findings of the research and consider whether we might find parallels in England. What cultural differences might impact upon the teacher–parent relationship?

Selwyn, N., Banaji, S., Hadjithoma-Garstka, C. and Clark, W. (2011) 'Providing a platform for parents? Exploring the nature of parental engagement with school learning platforms', *Journal of Computer Assisted Learning*, 27(4): 314-23.

> This journal article considers how the utilisation of digital platforms can further support parental involvement in children's education. It will be useful for you to consider carefully just how such technologies might provide a support for parents. The report suggests that most learning technologies used for this purpose provide mostly 'one way traffic' from the school to the home. What might the barriers to engagement be? How might these be overcome?

RELEVANT WEBSITES

Department for Education: www.education.gov.uk
> Type 'parent support advisers' into the search box and follow the links.

Department For Education Teaching Agency: www.education.gov.uk/get-into-teaching
> This merged with the National College for School Leadership from 1 April 2013.

REFERENCES

Addi-Raccah, A. and Ainhoren, R. (2009) 'School governance and teachers' attitudes to parents' involvement in schools', *Teaching & Teacher Education*, 25(6): 805-13.

Alexander, R. (ed.) (2009) *Children, Their World, Their Education: Final Report and Recommendations of the Cambridge Primary Review*, London: Routledge.

Barnard, W. (2004) 'Parent involvement in elementary school and educational attainment', *Children & Youth Service Review*, 26(1): 39-62.

Bastiani, J. (2003) *Materials for Schools: Involving Parents, Raising Achievement*, London: DfES.

Bourdieu, P. (1986) 'The forms of capital', in J.G. Richardson (ed.) *Handbook of Theory and Research for the Sociology of Education*, Santa Barbara, CA: Greenwood Press, pp. 241-58.

Carroll, J. and Alexander, G. (2016) *The Teachers' Standards in Primary Schools*, London: Sage.

Charlton, T. and David, K. (1993) *Managing Misbehaviour in Schools*, New York: Routledge.

Cooper, K. and Olson, M. (1996) 'The multiple "I's" of teacher identity', in M. Kompf, T. Boak, W.R. Bond and D. Dworet (eds) *Changing Research and Practice: Teachers' Professionalism, Identities and Knowledge*, London: Falmer Press, pp. 78-89.

Corsaro, W. and Fingerson, L. (2006) 'Development and socialisation in childhood', in J. DeLamter, *Handbook of Social Psychology*, New York: Kluwer Academic/Plenum, pp. 125-55.

Department for Children, Schools and Families (DCSF). (2008) *The Impact of Parental Involvement in Children's Education*, Nottingham, UK: DCSF.

Department for Education and Skills (DfES). (2009) *School Teachers' Pay and Conditions Document 2009*, London: DfES.

Department of Education and Science (DES). (1967) *Children and Their Primary Schools* (Plowden Report), London: HMSO.

Desforges, C. and Abouchaar, A. (2003) *The Impact of Parental Involvement, Parental Support and Family Education on Pupil Achievement and Adjustment: A Literature Review* (Research Report RR433), London: DfES.

Edwards, A. and Warin, J. (1999) 'Parental involvement in raising the achievement of primary school pupils: Why bother?', *Oxford Review of Education*, 25(3): 325-41.

Elton, R. (1989) *Discipline in Schools*, London: HM Stationery Office.

Hadow, W.H. (1931) *Report of the Consultative Committee on The Primary School*, London: HM Stationery Office.

Hart, B. and Risley, T. (1995) *Meaningful Differences in the Everyday Experience of Young American Children*, Baltimore, MD: Paul H. Brookes.

Lewis, K., Chamberlain, T., Riggall, A., Gagg, K. and Rudd, P. (2007) *How Are Schools Involving Parents in School Life? Annual Survey of Trends in Education 2007: Schools' Concerns and their Implications for Local Authorities* (LGA Research Report 4/07), Slough, UK: NFER.

Miller, W.R. and Rollnick, S. (2002) *Motivational Interviewing: Preparing People for Change*, 2nd edn, New York: Guilford Press.

OECD. (2012) *Parental Involvement in Selected PISA Countries and Economies*, OECD Education Working Paper no. 73. Retrieved from www.oecd.org/officialdocuments/publicdisplaydocumentpdf/?cote=EDU/WKP (2012)10&docLanguage=En (accessed 6 November 2017).

Ofsted. (2011) *Schools and Parents*. Retrieved from https://www.gov.uk/government/uploads/system/uploads/attachment_data/file/413696/Schools_and_parents.pdf (accessed 6 November 2017).

O'Hara, M. (2008) *Teaching 3-8 (Reaching the Standard)*, 3rd edn, London: Continuum.

PISA (2012) *PISA 2012 Results*. Retrieved from www.oecd.org/pisa/keyfindings/pisa-2012-results.htm (accessed 6 November 2017).

Robinson, C., Bingle, B. and Howard, C. (2016) *Surviving & Thriving as a Primary NQT*. Northwich, UK: Critical Publishing.

Rogers, B. (2000) *Behaviour Management: A Whole-School Approach*, Thousand Oaks, CA: Sage.

Selwyn, N. (2011a) *Education and Technology: Key Issues and Debates*, London: Continuum.

Selwyn, N. (2011b) *Schools and Schooling in the Digital Age: A Critical Perspective*, London: Routledge.

Selwyn, N., Banaji, S., Hadjithoma-Garstka, C. and Clark, W. (2011) 'Providing a platform for parents? Exploring the nature of parental engagement with school learning platforms', *Journal of Computer Assisted Learning*, 27: 314-23.

Steer, A. (2005) *Learning Behaviour: The Report of the Practitioners' Group on School Behaviour and Discipline*, Nottingham, UK: DfES.

Training and Development Agency for Schools (TDA). (2007) *Professional Standards for Teachers: Qualified Teacher Status*, London: TDA.

UNDERSTANDING THE TEACHER'S PASTORAL ROLE

Helen Childerhouse

INTRODUCTION

> Children want to be respected, their views to be heard, to have stable relationships built on trust and for consistent support provided for their individual needs. . . . Anyone working with children should see and speak to the child; listen to what they say; take their views seriously; and work with them collaboratively when deciding how to support their needs.
>
> (HM Government, 2015: 9)

This unit explores the pastoral role of the teacher. It recognises the important links between a child's social and emotional well-being and their academic progress. As a teacher, you will need to be aware of the challenges some children face and how this can have an impact on how well they can access the teaching and learning in school. By developing an understanding of these challenges, you will be able to shape your teaching approaches and strategies.

The current focus of the National Curriculum (DfE, 2013), in particular, is subject-specific. This knowledge-based curriculum provides a breadth of opportunities for children to develop their skills and understanding. However, the pastoral element of learning, which promotes well-being and personal development, is not as explicit in Department for Education guidance. In this unit, you will be able to reflect on what you can do to incorporate experiences for children that address areas such as safeguarding and emotional and social well-being. An overview of expectations of, and guidance for, teachers identified in legislation will be discussed. Case studies will be used to demonstrate how personal issues can impact on a child's school life and what the teacher needs to consider, and do, to support the child through challenging circumstances.

OBJECTIVES

By the end of this unit, you will:

- understand how children's personal, social and emotional needs can have an impact on their learning;
- understand the legal framework associated with pastoral provision in schools;
- begin to identify the strategies and practices for developing pastoral provision in your teaching.

WHAT IS THE TEACHER'S PASTORAL ROLE, AND WHY IS IT IMPORTANT FOR EFFECTIVE TEACHING?

Throughout the school year, the teacher builds a good rapport with the children in the class. They will come to learn about the children's likes, dislikes, preferred ways of learning, and their home lives. They recognise when children are happy, healthy, and enthusiastic and engaged in their learning. They must also be able to spot any changes to their usual ways of behaving and demeanours. Through noticing these changes, such as a child becoming quiet, withdrawn, unusually emotional or exhibiting excessive and challenging behaviours, the teacher can be alerted to possible problems and the need for them to intervene to find out what is wrong.

The pastoral needs of children may arise from relationships with other children in the class or school, events at home, or social and emotional issues, which may be related to special educational needs or disability. Some children may become involved with bullying, or be affected by problems faced within the family, such as poverty, illness or domestic violence. Pastoral needs may also arise following minor events that occur during the school day, and these may lead to more serious concerns if a child is at risk owing to their general health and well-being or because of relationships with others, adults or children. By having a good understanding of the children in your class, you will be an important adult in their lives who can ensure that they receive any support they need.

TRANSITION THROUGH SCHOOL

Typical times in school when children can find it difficult and may need more reassurance and support can be during periods of transition (O'Connor, 2013; Symonds, 2015). Moving into a new class or new school can be daunting for some children, and one aspect of your role is to ensure that children are well prepared for moving out of, or into, your class. This can be achieved by good preparation and information-sharing about what to expect; you will need to be available to address any questions or concerns the children may have. Similarly, children can become worried or feel uncomfortable during the school day, when in transition between different lessons or at break times. It may be helpful to introduce a visual timetable in your class; examples of these, together with tools for creating your own, can be found at www.twinkl.co.uk/resources/visual-timetable. This will help children to know what is happening at each point in the day and can enable them to prepare for what is to happen next. You need to be aware that, for some children, lunchtimes or break times can be difficult, and you can support them by ensuring they can seek peer support to help them feel more socially and emotionally confident during these times. One way of implementing peer support is to establish a 'buddy system' in your class (Collins, 2005). It is useful for the children to be able to identify another child who they can approach at break times when they are feeling lonely or nervous or simply need someone to be with.

LOOKED-AFTER CHILDREN

There may be children in your school who are regarded as 'looked after', whereby they are currently living with a new family, owing to foster care or adoption. These children will have been allocated a professional from a social services team who has a responsibility for 'looked-after children'. There will also be a member of staff in the school who oversees the provision for these children. If you have a 'looked-after child' in your class, you will be expected to liaise with these people to ensure that the child is receiving the necessary support. You need to be aware of any issues the child may be experiencing to ensure you are sensitive in your expectations of them. An example of this could be in setting homework or when reading particular stories. It might be difficult for a child to read or write about relationships with their parents if they have recently been moved into foster care, or if they have experienced difficult relationships in the home. Many children who have moved into foster homes may have to travel into school by taxi, and so it helps to be aware that their arrival and departure from school will be shaped by this. This might prevent them from taking part in after-school activities and from building out-of-school friendships with their peers. You could address this by helping them to establish a group of friends to be with during the day.

Task 8.3.1 How do you know if the children in your class are happy?

Drawing on your experience of working with children in schools, consider the social and emotional needs of the children:

- How do you know if the children are happy, confident and able to learn?
- How might children behave if they do not feel happy and confident?
- Can you identify possible reasons for why children's social and emotional well-being may be affected?

THE DEVELOPMENT OF UK POLICY IN RELATION TO PASTORAL PROVISION IN SCHOOLS

Every teacher must be aware of the legislation and policy that have been implemented to ensure children are safe, happy and well. The current Teachers' Standards (DfE, 2011: 11-14) make it clear that teachers must:

- have a secure understanding of how a range of factors can inhibit pupils' ability to learn, and of how best to overcome these;
- demonstrate an awareness of the physical, social and intellectual development of children;
- safeguard pupils' well-being.

Every teacher must take responsibility for identifying any child whose welfare and personal development are affected or at risk. The non-statutory guidance in the Personal, Social, Health and Economic section of the *National Curriculum* (DfE, 2013) identifies the importance of 'drug education, financial education, sex and relationship education (SRE) and the importance of physical activity and diet for a healthy lifestyle' (n.p.). These elements will be incorporated into teaching and planning and are usually delivered alongside other curriculum subjects and lessons. However, it is important that the teacher also considers the broader holistic elements of welfare and well-being. Such elements require the teacher to be vigilant. The teacher's pastoral role requires them to be able to recognise when a child is unhappy, insecure and needs additional social or emotional support.

In Wales . . .

In the Foundation Phase, it is stated that:

> Personal and Social Development, Well-being and Cultural Diversity are at the heart of the Foundation Phase and children's skills are developed across all Areas of Learning through participation in experiential learning activities indoors and outdoors. Children

learn about themselves, their relationships with other children and adults both within and beyond the family. They are encouraged to develop their self-esteem, their personal beliefs and moral values. They develop an understanding that others have differing needs, abilities, beliefs and views.

(Learning Wales, 2015: 9)

Source: Learning Wales. (2015) *Curriculum for Wales: Foundation Phase Framework*, Cardiff: Welsh Government. Retrieved from http://learning.gov.wales/docs/learningwales/publications/150803-fp-framework-en.pdf (accessed 6 November 2017).

In Northern Ireland . . .

As well as their statutory responsibilities in relation to pupils' learning, schools have a pastoral responsibility towards their pupils and should recognise that the children and young people in their charge have a fundamental right to be protected from harm. In particular, schools are expected to do whatever is reasonable, in all the circumstances of the case, to safeguard or promote their pupils' safety and well-being. Children cannot learn effectively or develop unless they feel secure.

(DENI, 2015: 5)

Source: Department of Education for Northern Ireland (DENI). (2015) *99/10 Guidance Pastoral Care in Schools: Child Protection*, Belfast: DENI. Retrieved from www.welbni.org/uploads/file/pdf/DENI%2099-10%20Guidance%20Pastoral%20Care%20in%20Schools-%20Child%20Protection_045026.pdf (accessed 6 November 2017).

SAFEGUARDING

Ensuring that children are safe from harm is one of the most important elements of your role. Table 8.3.1 shows the key government legislation that has been issued to ensure all teachers know and understand the role they play. The expectations outlined within it identify how children could be vulnerable and how teachers must respond in order to address concerns.

Your immediate responsibility is to ensure that you know which member of staff to refer to if you have any concerns. You must read and understand the school's safeguarding and child-protection policies as soon as you begin working in any school, and it is your duty to liaise with this member of staff if there is anything you do not understand.

Although instances of abuse and risk are thankfully rare, you may find that a child in your class confides in you. Children who are living in difficult circumstances and who have not developed supportive relationships with their parents may see you as being the reliable, constant and trustworthy adult in their lives. They may choose to share their questions, personal thoughts and worries with you, and, as their advocate, you will be expected to share such confidences with the colleague in school responsible for safeguarding.

TABLE 8.3.1 Key legislation and documentation for safeguarding in schools

Document	Key points
Children and Families Act (HM Government, 2014)	This legislation focuses on adoption, special educational needs and disabilities, child care in the early years, and statutory rights for parents and carers. It identifies the support and guidance that parents and carers are entitled to from education, health and social services
Special Educational Needs and Disability Code of Practice (DfE and DoH, 2015)	This document outlines the education, care and support that 0–25-year-olds identified with special educational needs and disabilities are entitled to. It addresses areas including identification of needs, barriers to learning, working together with parents, carers and other professionals, and the statutory assessment process
Supporting the Attainment of Disadvantaged Pupils (DfE, 2015a)	This research report commissioned by the government describes the practices and strategies that schools use to improve pupil achievement and outlines the barriers that teachers describe when working with children and young people who are considered to be disadvantaged. The report identifies pupils from ethnic minority groups, those who have special educational needs and disabilities, those who live in socially and economically impoverished environments, and those who have low levels of school attendance as being vulnerable or disadvantaged
Working Together to Safeguard Children (HM Government, 2015)	This statutory guidance identifies the need for safeguarding children and young people. It describes the role and support available from the Local Safeguarding Children Boards and calls for effective multi-agency working of professionals involved in education, health and social services, and also those working within the police and housing services
Keeping Children Safe in Education (DfE, 2016)	This provides specific guidance for schools in terms of safeguarding and specifies the duties of staff in relation to recruitment, management of safeguarding strategy and policy, how to deal with allegations and the role of the 'safeguarding lead' member of staff
The Prevent Duty (DfE, 2015b)	This non-statutory guidance outlines the possible risks that children in schools may face in relation to terrorism and radicalisation. Further information and discussion regarding *Prevent* and safeguarding can be found in Unit 1.2

In Wales . . .

On child protection and safeguarding, the Welsh government state that this is a key priority.

> Safeguarding is about protecting children and adults from abuse or neglect and educating those around them to recognise the signs and dangers. The Social Services and Well-being (Wales) Act introduces a strengthened, robust and effective partnership approach to safeguarding. One of the most important principles of safeguarding is that it is everyone's responsibility. Each professional and organisation must do everything they can, to ensure that children and adults at risk are protected from abuse.
>
> (Welsh Government, n.d.)

Source: Welsh Government. (n.d.) *Safeguarding*. Retrieved from http://gov.wales/topics/health/socialcare/safeguarding/?lang=en (accessed 6 November 2017).

E-SAFETY

Access to the Internet during lessons in schools is a common element of teaching. Teachers use digital media to support their teaching, and children are increasingly familiar with using computers and mobile phones to support their learning. Guidance such as *Keeping Children Safe in Education* (DfE, 2016) has been issued; it recognises that children may be at risk when accessing the Internet owing to the availability of websites that provide content purely for adults. The school will have a policy outlining how they prevent children from accessing such sites, and you are responsible for ensuring these are followed in your class.

Issues such as cyber-bullying, which Pyzalski (2012) describes as 'electronic aggression' (p. 305), and the grooming of children through social network sites may put children at risk. Even though there are age restrictions for some social network sites, it is possible for children to claim they are older than they are, or to access them anyway. The more knowledge and understanding a teacher has about the possible risks, the more they can put measures into place to avoid children using such websites. You may find *Children, Risk and Safety on the Internet* (Livingstone, Haddon and Görzig, 2012) a useful text for raising your awareness of the concerns and for identifying strategies that you could put into place, such as working with parents to monitor, advise and support children as they use social networking.

ATTENDANCE

Children's attendance at school also relates to the teacher's pastoral role. *School Attendance* (DfE, 2014) provides guidance for schools and school governing bodies. This provides the statutory expectations for attendance at schools and outlines the measures schools can take to ensure that children do not miss their education. The document states that teachers must take two registers during the day, one in the morning and one in the afternoon. They must use the correct coding (identified within the document mentioned above) to mark children's attendance, absence or if they arrive late. This information is included in the school's census, which is collated by the Department for Education. You must ensure that you understand your role for registering pupils. In addition, if you have any concerns regarding a child's attendance, then it is your duty to bring this information to the member of staff responsible. Continued absences may indicate that the child is unwell or failing to attend owing to problems inside or outside school, and if you share this information, the situation can be investigated.

Task 8.3.2 Safeguarding children: Your role

Ensure you are aware of the legislative documentation regarding safeguarding children in schools.

- Reflect on the Teachers' Standards (2011), which outline your responsibilities. Make a list of specific activities and tasks that you can put into practice to help you to meet the expectations.
- Read the *Working Together to Safeguard Children* document (HM Government, 2015). What are your role and responsibilities as a teacher in relation to each of the sections?
- Read the school's e-safety policy. What role do you play in implementing this policy? How can you ensure that the strategies you put into place meet the policy requirements?

SCENARIO 1[1]

Molly, a 10-year-old who is in your Year 5 class, is normally happy and cheerful and eager to take part in the lessons. She arrives one morning looking tired and refuses to answer the register. She does not want to work with the other children in her group, and you see that she is standing by herself in the playground and refusing to play with the others when asked. During a lesson, another child comes over to you and says that Molly is crying. You go over and ask her if she is all right, but she wipes her eyes and says that she is fine and that she has something in her eye. Later in the day, the same thing happens, but again Molly says she is fine. Molly is usually met at the school gate by mum, a single parent with three other, younger children in the school. You look out for her at home time so that you can check everything is OK, but a neighbour collects Molly and her siblings on that day. The following day, Molly arrives late. She is not in uniform and has not brought her lunch box with her. When you ask her what she is going to eat for lunch, she cries. Molly settles down after you reassure her that she can have a school lunch. For the rest of the day, she remains quiet and withdrawn but rebuffs your efforts to talk. That afternoon, you receive a phone call from Molly's aunt, her mum's sister, who informs you that mum has been diagnosed with an aggressive form of breast cancer. She explains that Molly knows her mum is poorly, but does not know why or that the diagnosis is that she is terminally ill. Over the next few days, Molly's work deteriorates, she is often late and goes into the playground for the younger children to find her younger siblings each day. She is obviously very tired, increasingly dishevelled and has mentioned that she is now 'in charge' of her sisters and brother. During the register on the Friday afternoon, Molly blurts out in front of the class that her mum is dying.

Task 8.3.3 Identifying approaches to support specific needs in Scenario 1

- Reflect how Molly's situation will impact on her social, emotional, physical and academic well-being. Make a list of these possible impacts and consider her immediate needs.
- Consider who you need to liaise with in school to make sure everyone who needs to know is aware of the situation.
- You know that Molly's outburst has upset some of the other children. What can you do to support them?
- It is important that school remains a constant and reassuring environment for Molly. Reflect on the school day and consider how you can retain this consistency while maintaining support for Molly.

In this scenario, Molly's teacher identified her needs, and support was put into place to help her through the school day. She was allocated a teaching assistant (TA) who met her and her siblings at the school gate each morning, and she and the TA took each child to their classrooms and ensured they were settled. The teachers were kept informed of events regarding the mother's health and the children's experiences at home. The member of staff responsible for safeguarding was notified, and additional support focusing on the children's social and emotional needs was put into place. Each of the children was provided with tea and toast during the morning registration period, and they sat together with the TA so they could talk about their concerns if they needed to. A meeting with mum's sister was arranged, and she was appointed as the point of contact with the school. As Molly's mum became more ill, the social services support team was notified, and a multi-agency team (Cheminais, 2009), including the teacher for safeguarding, worked together to support the family. Molly's teacher ensured that she was provided with a buddy during the school day; she maintained consistency in her teaching and expectations to ensure that there were no additional changes to her life; she was sensitive to her emotional needs; and established a set time during each day when she and Molly could talk, if Molly wanted to. In addition to this, her teacher provided a time for the rest of the class to share their concerns and ask any questions they had. This was arranged with the permission of Molly, her mum and her aunt, and was done while Molly was out of the classroom. The children were not given specific details, but understood that Molly's mum was ill and were asked to be sensitive in their conversations with Molly and to include her in their groups and games.

SCENARIO 2

Tom is 6 years old and is in your Year 2 class. He lives with his grandma, because his mum and her new partner do not want him living with them. He lives on the same street as his mum. His mum and partner have recently had a baby, and Tom has seen them sitting in their garden playing with the baby. Tom is desperate for mum's attention, but mum is verbally abusive towards him and tells him to go back to his grandma's house and keep away. Tom finds it difficult to form attachments with adults and does not have a good rapport with his class teacher. He is rude, uses offensive language and is physically aggressive towards the other children. He has been temporarily excluded on two previous occasions owing to violent behaviour. The class teacher is concerned that the generic behaviour management strategies used for the whole class are not effective and is increasingly nervous about teaching Tom. Tom's grandma arrives at the school gate after the half-term holiday and comes to your classroom. She tells you that she cannot cope with him any more, and that she does not know what to do. She says that as she is now 75 years old she finds his challenging behaviour too difficult to manage. She explains that mum wants nothing to do with him, and that there is no one else to take him.

Task 8.3.4 Identifying approaches to support specific needs in Scenario 2

- As you see it from your perspective as a teacher, what do you feel are the main concerns and challenges you would face in teaching Tom and his peers?
- Write down the situation as you see it from Tom's perspective. What do you think Tom's needs are?
- What approaches do you feel you need to consider to help Tom cope with his emotional and behavioural outbursts? What additional strategies could you use in class to support Tom?

In this scenario, the class teacher worked closely with the teacher responsible for behaviour management in the school. Together, they devised a system for Tom that focused on rewards for positive behaviour, which included a 'time out' card. Tom could show this card when he felt that he needed to leave the class to calm down or talk to a member of the behaviour support team in school. A meeting was arranged by the head teacher, and professionals from the social services team, grandma and mum were invited. This 'Team Around the Child' meeting (Siraj-Blatchford, Clarke and Needham, 2007) identified the needs of all those involved, and a long-term support plan was put in place. Tom's specific needs were shared with his class teacher, and social, emotional and behavioural areas for development were identified. The head teacher worked closely with the teacher to put strategies in place to support Tom as the situation was resolved. He continued to live with his grandma, but with the additional intervention of a family support worker, provided by the social services team.

STRATEGIES TO SUPPORT THE TEACHER'S PASTORAL ROLE

From your own experiences and the example in Scenario 2, you can see how behaviour management systems and policy within school can help children to develop effective ways to behave. Establishing such systems, if part of your pastoral role, provides consistency of expectations and boundaries for all children. If children are aware of what is expected of them, then they are more likely to feel confident about how they act, talk and interact during the school day. Establishing and sharing expectations with the children at the beginning of the school year form an important part of your pastoral role. You need to ensure that you review and revisit these expectations throughout the weeks and year with your class.

There are also additional practices you can implement to enhance the pastoral provision in your class. Creating a safe and stimulating learning environment will provide a feeling of security for the children. Ensure that you: display a visual timetable; share the e-safety rules and procedures with the children; establish a support system so that the children feel able to ask for help; and make sure you are available and responsive to their concerns or questions. You will need to establish good relationships with children, so that they feel confident that you are going to listen carefully to what they tell you and are more likely to regard you as approachable.

You will also need to set up a system to record and monitor the welfare and needs of the children in your class. Most schools encourage teachers to use a journal or diary to record issues or concerns. The entries in a journal could identify when a child is late, if they share any worries with you, ask you unusual questions, or if they appear unkempt, hungry or upset. A journal is very useful in helping the teacher to recognise ongoing issues. An example of this would be in identifying issues relating to neglect. Individual entries in the journal that record that the child has arrived at school without having breakfast may not seem serious on one occasion, but when this is recorded many times over weeks or months, the teacher can recognise a pattern that may indicate concern about care and well-being. Every teacher is strongly advised to keep a journal or diary in which to log such incidences. This must be kept on the school premises in a locked, secure cupboard or drawer and shared with the teacher responsible for safeguarding regularly.

WHOLE-SCHOOL STRATEGIES TO SUPPORT THE TEACHER'S PASTORAL ROLE

There are a range of strategies that many schools use to support teachers with their pastoral role. Table 8.3.2 lists of some of the additional support that schools often provide. It provides information about their aims and purposes and gives websites that you may want to access to find out more about them.

TABLE 8.3.2 School strategies for supporting your pastoral role

Provision	Aims and purpose	Additional information
School councils	To listen to the voices of the children in schools. Designed to ascertain the opinions of all children in each class and provide a forum for these views to be shared with school staff. Children are also able to suggest and implement fundraising events	School Councils UK provides guidance, training and resources to help schools set up their own council. Further guidance and examples from other schools are available at www.schoolcouncils.org/
Circle Time	Circle Time is used in many schools. It gives children the opportunities to talk and be heard. Children share their thoughts and ideas about a specific focus and can choose to contribute or not. This gives the class teacher an opportunity to address concerns and to identify any children they feel may need further support at another time	Circle Time, devised by Jenny Mosely, has a designated website for further information. It provides guidance, training and ideas for use in schools: www.circle-time.co.uk/
Lunchtime or after-school groups	For all children, or for those identified as needing social support at particular times during the day. Examples include Lego, science, book games or craft clubs	
Small-group or one-to-one support groups	To provide support for children identified as having difficulties in their classrooms. This may include behavioural, social or emotional needs. These are often provided by TAs or specialist support staff	
Diary entries or video rooms and suggestion or worry boxes	Accessible to all children. They can leave comments, notes or small videos to inform staff of their concerns. The messages are confidential	
Nurture groups	Identifies the importance for children to experience effective attachments, good communication and a safe place during their early years. Nurture groups are designed to address possible developmental 'gaps' due to poor experiences in early childhood. First established by Boxall in 1960s (Boxall and Lucas, 2010). Children with social and emotional difficulties are usually recommended by their teachers for inclusion in the nurture group	Nurture Group Network provides further information and training: www.nurturegroups.org/

SUMMARY

In this unit, the teacher's pastoral role has been considered on two levels: generic daily practice and responses to specific children's needs. Strategies and suggestions have been provided that can be used by all teachers in their classrooms. The importance of a safe and stimulating learning environment has also been discussed; a teacher with an effective pastoral provision will establish an ethos in which children feel comfortable and confident to share their views, and in which they know that they will be listened to. Specific examples of times when additional pastoral support may be needed have also been provided in order to emphasise the importance of providing safeguarding and ensuring the well-being of children experiencing difficult circumstances or relationships. Every teacher has a duty to know how children could be at risk and how they must respond to the concerns they have.

By ensuring that you know every child in the class, you can be confident that your pastoral teaching will be enhanced. Your planning and teaching will be more personalised and responsive because of the knowledge you have of each child. This will mean that you can include their social and emotional needs, which will have a positive impact on their holistic development.

NOTE

1   The author would like to thank Sean Woolley for the scenarios and his general contribution to this unit.

 ## ANNOTATED FURTHER READING

Goepel, J., Sharpe, S. and Childerhouse, H. (2015) *Inclusive Primary Teaching*, 2nd edn, Northwich, UK: Critical Publishing.

> This text is written for trainee and recently qualified teachers and focuses on special educational needs and disability. However, it identifies good practice for supporting all learners, and many of the scenarios and suggestions are applicable to the teacher developing a pastoral role. The chapters 'Understanding learners who are vulnerable' and 'Working with children' are particularly useful and relevant.

Boddington, N., King, A. and McWhirter, J. (2014) *Understanding Personal, Social, Health and Economic Education in Primary Schools*, London: Sage.

> There are many useful and informative chapters in this book that develop and elaborate on the points made in this unit. It provides guidance on establishing effective practice within a supportive learning environment to ensure children's safety and well-being.

Dowling, M. (2010) *Young Children's Personal, Social and Emotional Development*, 3rd edn, London: Sage.

> Although this book is written with learners in the early years in mind, it is useful for providing an in-depth understanding of the holistic needs of children. By developing knowledge about their social, emotional, physical and cognitive growth and skills, the teacher will have a sound understanding of how this can impact on their long-term well-being.

FURTHER READING TO SUPPORT M-LEVEL STUDY

Clark, A. and Moss, P. (2011) *Listening to Young Children: The Mosaic Approach*, 2nd edn, London: NCB.

> The focus of this text is research with children. At M-level study, you may choose to develop your knowledge of the views and feelings of the children in your class so that you can enhance pastoral provision. The authors provide guidance and suggestions for how you can give children a 'voice' that can inform your understanding and improve your practice.

Harris, B. (2008) 'Befriending the two-headed monster: Personal, social and emotional development in schools in challenging times', *British Journal of Guidance & Counselling*, 36(4): 367–83.

> Harris reflects on the challenges faced by teachers of meeting the pastoral needs of the children in their classrooms while also achieving the levels of academic achievement and progress defined in policy. She argues that emotional well-being within a nurturing environment is more important than ever to support teachers and children in schools. Reflect on your experiences of teaching and learning in schools and consider your and your colleagues' provision. Do you consider academic and pastoral teaching to be different aspects of your role? How do you feel you can develop a balance between the two?

RELEVANT WEBSITES

National Association for the Pastoral Care of Education: www.napce.org.uk/

> This is an excellent website that provides guidance and suggestions relating to many issues, such as bullying, peer counselling, relationships and vulnerability.

EU Kids Online: www.lse.ac.uk/media@lse/research/EUKidsOnline/Home.aspx

> EU Kids Online provides guidance, research findings and recommendations for policy with regards to children's use of the Internet.

NSPCC: www.nspcc.org.uk/services-and-resources/working-with-schools/

> The NSPCC provides guidance and resources for schools to help teachers provide support for children who may need pastoral support or who may be considered vulnerable.

Nurture Group Network: www.nurturegroups.org

> The Nurture Group Network supports provision, training and resources in many schools. The principles for supporting social and emotional development will support the teacher's understanding of how he or she can enhance the pastoral learning in the classroom.

Looked-after Children: www.gov.uk/topic/schools-colleges-childrens-services/looked-after-children

> This government website provides further information and guidance regarding the care and education of 'looked-after children'.

REFERENCES

Boxall, M. and Lucas, S. (2010) *Nurture Groups in Schools: Principles and Practice*, 2nd edn, London: Sage.

Cheminais, R. (2009) *Effective Multi-Agency Partnerships: Putting Every Child Matters into Practice*, London: Sage.

Collins, M. (2005) *Young Buddies: Teaching Peer Support Skills to Children Aged 6–11*, London: Lucky Duck/Paul Chapman/Sage.

Department for Education (DfE). (2011) *Teachers' Standards*. Retrieved from www.gov.uk/government/uploads/system/uploads/attachment_data/file/283566/Teachers_standard_information.pdf (accessed 6 November 2017).

Department for Education (DfE). (2013) *National Curriculum*, including *Personal, Social, Health and Economic Curriculum Guidance*. Retrieved from www.gov.uk/government/publications/personal-social-health-and-economic-education-pshe/personal-social-health-and-economic-pshe-education (accessed 6 November 2017).

Department for Education (DfE). (2014) *School Attendance*. Retrieved from https://www.gov.uk/government/uploads/system/uploads/attachment_data/file/518586/Advice_on_school_attendance.pdf (accessed 6 November 2017).

Department for Education (DfE). (2015a) *Supporting the Attainment of Disadvantaged Children*. Retrieved from https://www.gov.uk/government/uploads/system/uploads/attachment_data/file/473974/DFE-RR411_Supporting_the_attainment_of_disadvantaged_pupils.pdf (accessed 6 November 2017).

Department for Education (DfE). (2015b) *The Prevent Duty*. Retrieved from https://www.gov.uk/government/uploads/system/uploads/attachment_data/file/439598/prevent-duty-departmental-advice-v6.pdf (accessed 6 November 2017).

Department for Education (DfE). (2016) *Keeping Children Safe in Education*. Retrieved from https://www.gov.uk/government/uploads/system/uploads/attachment_data/file/550511/Keeping_children_safe_in_education.pdf (accessed 6 November 2017).

Department for Education (DfE) and Department of Health (DoH). (2015) *Special Educational Needs and Disability: Code of Practice 0 to 25 years*. Retrieved from https://www.gov.uk/government/uploads/system/uploads/attachment_data/file/398815/SEND_Code_of_Practice_January_2015.pdf (accessed 6 November 2017).

HM Government. (2014) *Children and Families Act*. Retrieved from www.legislation.gov.uk/ukpga/2014/6/contents/enacted (accessed 6 November 2017).

HM Government. (2015) *Working Together to Safeguard Children*. Retrieved from https://www.gov.uk/government/uploads/system/uploads/attachment_data/file/419595/Working_Together_to_Safeguard_Children.pdf (accessed 6 November 2017).

Livingstone, S., Haddon, L. and Görzig, A. (eds) (2012) *Children, Risk and Safety on the Internet: Research and Policy Challenges in Comparative Perspective*, Bristol, UK: Policy Press.

O'Connor, A. (2013) *Understanding Transitions in the Early Years*, Abingdon, UK: Routledge.

Pyzalski, J. (2012) 'From cyberbullying to electronic aggression: Typology of the phenomenon', *Emotional & Behavioural Difficultie*s, 17(3–4): 305–17.

Siraj-Blatchford, I., Clarke, K. and Needham, M. (eds) (2007) *The Team Around the Child: Multiagency Working in the Early Years*, Stoke-on-Trent, UK: Trentham Books.

Symonds, J. (2015) *Understanding School Transition: What Happens to Children and How to Help Them*, Abingdon, UK: Routledge.

YOUR PROFESSIONAL DEVELOPMENT

APPLYING FOR JOBS AND PREPARING FOR YOUR INDUCTION YEAR

Jane Medwell

INTRODUCTION

Your ITT provider will make a recommendation to the National College for Teaching and Leadership concerning the award of QTS, which is the first step in your career. Gaining QTS is rather like passing your driving test - you will be safe to teach a class, but will still have plenty to learn about teaching. The next step comes during your year as a newly qualified teacher (NQT), when induction acts as a bridge between ITT and a career in teaching. Induction should provide a personalised programme that supports you in moving towards an assessment of your performance against the relevant teaching standards. After passing induction, you can be employed as a teacher in a maintained school. You only get one chance to pass induction, and so it is important you find the right job to do it in. Towards the end of your training, you will devote considerable energy to finding the right job for you. This is a job that you feel happy in and one that offers you the professional development you need to become a better teacher. By preparing your goals for the induction year thoughtfully, you can ensure you get the support you need in your NQT year. This unit should help you.

OBJECTIVES

By the end of this unit, you should:

- understand the role of the NQT year;
- know how to look for a teaching post;
- be able to begin to write job applications;
- be able to start work on objectives for your NQT year;

APPLYING FOR A TEACHING JOB

During your training, you may start to apply for jobs. This will necessitate some personal decisions about the area in which you aim to work, your preferred type of school, how far your domestic commitments allow you to commute each day, and whether you want a full-time post. This is the time to be realistic, because your first teaching post is so important. It is no use finding the perfect post if you have to leave for work at 5 a.m. every day to get there, or doing your NQT year in a school that does not suit you and your educational beliefs. Deciding where to apply is a crucial step.

Jobs suited to NQTs (starting in September) are advertised at any time from the previous October to the June or July before you start. If you have a target area, you must not miss the job advertisements for that area. Teaching posts are usually advertised by individual schools or by 'pools', whereby groups of schools recruit together. You must make sure you check the systems in place in your target areas – it is not uncommon for schools to advertise individually and be part of a cluster that recruits for a group of schools. Look at the websites for the academy groups/trusts or teaching school alliances (TSAs) you are interested in. This will tell you where they advertise teaching posts. Jobs are often advertised in the *Times Educational Supplement* (*TES*; Friday) and/or local newspapers, as well as on Internet sites such as e-teach.

In Northern Ireland . . .

In Northern Ireland, teachers in the controlled sector are employed by one or other of the five education and library boards. Application forms are obtained from and returned to the individual boards. Teachers in the maintained sector are employed by the Council for Catholic Maintained Schools (CCMS), which was brought into existence by the Education Reform (Northern Ireland) Order 1989. Application forms are obtained from and returned to CCMS.

Source: www.eani.org.uk/schools/beginning-teachers/beginning-teachers-induction-and-early-professional-development/ (accessed 14 November 2017).

In Wales . . .

All providers must ensure that all those who are assessed as meeting the QTS Standards receive and are supported in completing a Career Entry and Development Profile, are informed about the statutory arrangements for the induction of newly qualified teachers and have been helped to prepare for these.

(DCELLS, 2009: 157)

Source: Department for Children, Education, Lifelong Learning and Skills (DCELLS). (2009) *Becoming a Qualified Teacher: Handbook of Guidance (2009)*, Cardiff: Welsh Assembly Government (WAG). Retrieved from http://gov.wales/docs/dcells/publications/090915becomingateacheren.pdf (accessed 7 November 2017).

USING YOUR EXPERIENCE POSITIVELY IN YOUR APPLICATION

It is important that your application includes insights from your ITT course and placements and shows that you can learn from your experiences. The details about a teaching post will usually include a person specification. This may be general, simply listing a number of attributes sought, such as ability to plan, deliver, monitor and evaluate children's learning, and so on. Alternatively, there may be some very specific requirements. As an NQT, you should not be expected to coordinate a curriculum area in your induction year, but the school may well be seeking staff with particular areas of expertise.

Complete application forms neatly and accurately and demonstrate your enthusiasm. The usual rules for form filling apply: read the instructions carefully and follow them; write a draft first (and keep it for future reference); do not leave gaps, but write N/A (not applicable); check all your dates and have all your information to hand; make sure your writing is neat, spell correctly and make sure your personal statement (or letter) is effective. Plan plenty of time to fill in your application and ensure you have done a thorough review of your record of professional development or training plan.

Task 9.1.1 Reviewing your progress towards the Teachers' Standards

You review your progress throughout your training, but we suggest you conduct a thorough review just before you complete an application. This helps you to:

- remember and revisit all the training tasks you have done – assignments, school tasks and even visits, some of which may have been a while ago;
- identify progress you have made towards demonstrating the Teachers' Standards;
- decide what constitutes evidence of this progress and store this appropriately;
- prepare a portfolio of work in preparation for a job interview;
- begin to formulate your areas of interest, strength and weakness for your NQT year.

Go through your record of professional development (or training plan), reviewing your placement reports and academic work against the Teachers' Standards. Identify four areas where you have made progress and four areas in which you would like to improve.

You will be required to write either a supporting statement or a letter of application as part of an application form. The first thing you should do to prepare this is to examine thoroughly the job description, to work out what they are looking for. Then, read the instructions for completing the form or letter very carefully. Filling in this form is a chore, but it is your chance to market your skills. Do not be too modest or make impossible, exaggerated claims. The completed form will be slightly embarrassing, because it spells out your achievements and qualities, but it should not be untruthful. Mentors, personal tutors and teachers will help you to prepare your application, and you should discuss a draft of your letter of application, supporting statement or CV with them.

There are many ways of writing your letter of application or supporting statement, but there are some key points you should bear in mind. Give a brief overview of your training and mention your degree and any relevant projects, experiences or previous work. It is important to identify why you are the candidate who would suit this particular post, and why you are applying. Include any local links, faith issues or visits to the school.

Your teaching placements during training are very important, so include when you did the placement, what year groups you taught and the level of responsibility you took, but do not use up all your space by repeating what you have put on the form. Refer to special features of a placement - for example, open-plan classrooms or team teaching. You could also use placements to illustrate an aspect of your learning or an enthusiasm you have developed - for example, how you plan, teach and evaluate learning outcomes, behaviour management strategies, work with parents, and so on.

Write a little about your vision for education and the principles that underpin your practice. This might include beliefs about how children learn, classroom management and teaching styles. Illustrate with an example of how you have learned this on your course or school placement. This will give the school a flavour of you as a teacher.

Another part of your letter will include details of your personal experiences, leisure activities, interests or involvement with children. Make these relevant to your work as a teacher and be explicit about what skills you have.

One of the easier ways to organise this information is to identify a number of subheadings taken from the job description, such as:

- teaching experiences (placements);
- commitment to teaching;
- knowledge, skills and aptitudes;
- planning and organisation;
- strengths and interests;
- personal qualities.

Organise your information under these headings. You can then remove your subheadings and have a well-organised letter to discuss with your mentor or tutor. Write in the first person, check your grammar and use interesting adverbs and adjectives to lift the text. Ask someone else to proof-read your letter!

THE CURRICULUM VITAE

In applying for your first teaching post, you may find yourself writing a CV for the first time. This sets out important information about you on two sides of A4. Preparing for this is similar to preparing to fill in a form, but you will need to print it out on good-quality white paper. As with the letter, prepare a general CV well in advance, but adapt it for each application, so that it matches the job specification.

There are some things you should omit from a CV, such as your date of birth, age, marital status or ethnic origin. Photographs of yourself are also not necessary. Do not include failures on your CV – aim to keep it focused on what you have achieved and why you match the school's needs. You should also leave out previous salary information or reasons for changing jobs.

The following should be included on your CV:

- contact details: make sure that these are guaranteed routes to reach you; ideally, include your postal address, any telephone numbers you have (landline and mobile), and email addresses – *not* Twitter, Facebook details, and so on – these may create the impression that you do not know where to draw professional boundaries;
- your gender, if not obvious from your name;
- a short skills summary or supporting statement (see below);
- your work experience and placement experiences – most recent first;
- your education: best organised as follows: primary, secondary, further, higher;
- your qualifications, listed with the most recent first, including results;
- interests: only real and genuine ones – for example, any sports in which you actively participate; include any non-teaching qualifications that may have arisen from your hobbies or interests;
- membership of professional associations (not including unions);
- nationality, National Insurance number and referee details can be included at the end of your CV.

A skills summary need only be about 200 words, but can still cover a lot of ground. Write in the first person. Every word must have a use, and grammar should be immaculate. Do not just repeat your experience – your achievements and competence are more important. The reader will want to see that you have strong communication skills and, perhaps, even leadership potential. When writing a skills summary, some people prefer to include a short bulleted list of about six key skills.

With only two sides of A4, the layout of a CV is important, and you need to be economical with space. Although the page should not look cluttered, excess space will look messy and ill thought through.

- Present your contact details across the top of the first page (like a letterhead) to preserve space.
- Use a clear, standard font such as Times New Roman or Arial.
- Avoid abbreviations unless they are universally understood.

If you really cannot fit everything on to two sides of A4, try reducing the font size slightly. This will mean the print is still large enough to read, but will give you a little more room to play with. There really is not too much difference between 12 and 11 point text in terms of readability.

When you have designed your CV on screen, print off a draft version and try to view it through fresh eyes. Is it likely to grab the attention of a reader within a few seconds? Is it visually pleasing? Are there any errors? It is a good idea to ask someone else to cast an eye over it, as it is easy to miss typos on documents you have been working on yourself.

Writing a CV is not a one-off task. Once you have completed your CV (see the example in Figure 9.1.1), you will need to keep it up to date and make sure it is tailored to each application you use it for. It is not enough to send out a standard CV.

REFEREES

You will usually be asked to supply the names, positions and contact details of two referees. The first should be a senior member of staff in your ITT provider. Check carefully who this should be. It is common for universities to use the name of the head of department, even though your tutor will probably actually write the reference. It is essential to get this name right, for two reasons. If you do not get a first reference from your ITT provider, the job advertiser will usually assume you have something to hide. Second, the reference system in a large ITT provider will be geared up for a swift response, but it will only work if you get the right name. The wrong name will slow down your reference and may put you at a disadvantage.

Your second referee should usually be from your placement school – your mentor, class teacher or head teacher. Ask whether the mentor or head teacher is prepared to offer you a reference. In most cases, this is offered gladly. Professionals will not write a bad reference for anyone, but would decline to offer a reference if they could not truthfully recommend you.

Be clear who you intend to name as a referee and discuss this with your mentor or head, so that you get the best reference. Will you name the mentor him/herself, or the head teacher? Check that you know the full name, title and professional position of your referee and make sure he/she has your contact details and that you have theirs. You should contact them to let them know when you use their name as a referee in any application. Be clear about anything you would like your referee to mention (such as participation in out-of-school events) or avoid mentioning, such as a disability or illness. Say when you expect to be applying for jobs and whether these will be exclusively teaching jobs or will include things such as vacation jobs or voluntary work. Give your referee a copy of your CV and a summary of your strengths as part of the process of asking for a reference. Potential employers may ring your second referee for an informal reference, particularly if you are applying for a job locally. You want your referee to be prepared for this and to speak warmly about you, rather than be surprised and feel caught out.

Paula Grey
Eastleigh Cottage, 35 Thornton Hill, Cardiff CF21 9DE
Telephone: 0128 213 3567, mobile: 07337 632077, email: Paulie@yahoo.com

I am a newly qualified teacher trained to teach across the curriculum with the 5–11 age group. My previous work experience as an accountant has enabled me to develop an understanding of management in a large multinational corporation as well as demonstrable communication skills. Part of my role was the delivery of internal training for new staff. During my initial teacher training I taught in an inner-city Key Stage 1 class and in two Key Stage 2 classes in a school with a large multiracial population. In addition to my teaching, I ran a successful 'Get Into Reading' after-school workshop for parents, which crossed age and cultural boundaries and was recognised by the head and governors as a constructive addition to the wider school culture.

Education

Primary:	1984–1990 Abbey Primary School, Cardiff
Secondary:	1990–1995 Newport High School for Girls, Newport
Further:	1995–1997 Newport Sixth Form College, Newport
Higher:	1997–1999 University of Reading BA
	1999–2007 Membership of the Society of Chartered Accountants
	2008–2009 Institute of Education, University of London PGCE

Qualifications

PGCE:	Primary
Degree:	Archaeology and Statistics 2.1
A levels:	Mathematics A, Statistics A, Physics B, General studies B
GCSEs:	Mathematics A, English literature A, English language B, Physics B, History A, ICT A, Art B, Geography B, French A, Biology B

Professional development

During my initial teacher training I completed an LA-run 'Levelling Mathematics' course and attended a 'Developing Storysacks' training day.

Work experience

2004–2005:	ITT placements: High Five School, Camden and Nelson Mandela Primary School, Westminster
1999–2004:	British International Bank, London, Accountant
1997–1999:	Vacation positions with Marks and Spencer and Dillons, Cwmbran

Interests

I have run a local Brownies group for some years. I also run to keep fit and have completed the London marathon.

Additional qualifications

Full, clean driving licence

South Glamorgan County Junior Football Coaching

Nationality

British

National Insurance number

TY123456B

References

Referees available on request

FIGURE 9.1.1 A sample CV

VISITS AND INTERVIEWS DURING YOUR TRAINING

When you are considering applying for a job, you may ask or be invited to look around the school. Some schools schedule specific times and take a large number of applicants around the school together. This can be a good way to find out about a school and whether it will suit you. However, it does take time out of your training programme, especially if you are applying for posts some distance away. Consider the impact of absence from school or university on your training and the cumulative impact of multiple visits, particularly as this is often a time when you are on school placement. You have to complete a certain amount of placement time in school, and a large number of visits could affect the outcome of your placement, as well as the way your commitment to your placement school is seen. It may be better to try to visit schools after the end of the school day, or to explain to schools that your placement commitments prevent you from visiting informally.

On interview day, you will usually get a tour of the school prior to interview, and you have the opportunity to withdraw from the interview after this if you did not think the school would suit you. If you apply for a job through a teaching pool, you will usually go for an interview for the pool first and may then be invited to look around schools that have jobs available. This is a different sort of school visit from the informal, pre-interview visit, because you will be looking at a school to see whether you would take a job there. You should go on these visits, but again be aware of the time consideration.

When you have applied for a post and are invited to interview during training time, you should ask your tutor/mentor for permission to attend, thus missing the taught sessions or school placement that day. In practice, this is a courtesy, and you will always be given permission to attend interviews. It is a good idea to ask your mentor, tutor or class teacher to help you to prepare for interview, and such preparation might take a number of forms:

- Discuss 'hot' topics in the educational press or recent initiatives in school with a colleague, tutor or teacher. This will help you to explore the issues from another perspective.
- Role-play a 'mock' interview with your tutor, mentor, teacher or another trainee. This can help you to conquer nerves and prepare your interview manner. Practise framing your replies at interview – a pause to think, for example, rather than rushing in and babbling. What sort of body language do you want to exhibit – or avoid?

Your interview may include a task such as teaching a class or group, planning a lesson or making a presentation to the interview panel. If a letter of invitation states (or hints) that you will be asked to teach, do not be afraid to telephone the school to ask for details of the year group, subject required, technology available and time parameters of the task. Many schools leave the details vague and expect you to enquire.

Ask a tutor or teacher to help you to plan any teaching you are asked to do, but make sure you go to them with plenty of ideas and suggestions. You will not be able to prepare a perfect lesson, because you do not know the children, but you can still use a lesson plan to show that you know the relevant curricula, have good ideas, know a range of teaching strategies, are aware of a range of resources and have a good manner with children. Your tutor or mentor may be able to spot obvious faux pas or overambitious plans if you ask to discuss them.

Always re-read a copy of your application before you go to interview and prepare some questions to ask the panel at the end of the interview. It is perfectly acceptable to find that all your questions have been answered in the recruitment process (say so), but not to seem clueless.

INTERVIEWS AND PORTFOLIOS

As a trainee, you will be maintaining a training plan or record of professional development that contains evidence to demonstrate your achievement of the Teachers' Standards. You may use this to compile a portfolio for interview. Even if you are not asked to bring a portfolio, you may want to do so. You can offer this to your interviewers – they do not have to spend much time looking at it, but it does indicate you are well prepared and professional.

An interview portfolio can be a substantial document, but is, more usually, a slim document containing some of the following:

- title and contents page, preferably with a photo of you in a teaching situation;
- concise CV;
- placement assessment reports (one or more);
- a really good lesson plan or two, some examples of the work associated with the lesson and the lesson evaluation;
- an example of your assessment;
- a mentor, tutor or class teacher observation of a lesson that picks out a strength;.
- a sample mentor meeting summary (to show you are focused and organised);
- an example of a piece of your written work (and the marking sheet), if relevant;
- a few well-chosen photos of you teaching; generally, you might choose one photo of you 'at the front' teaching a class, one of you looking sensitive with a group and, ideally, one of you teaching elsewhere – perhaps on a school visit or outside; remember to choose photos to suit that job: if the school is very ICT-conscious, make sure there is a picture of you using ICT; if the school is keen to improve its physical education, a photo of your gym session would not go amiss! Make sure you follow your placement school policy on photo use, and that the school, teachers and children are not identifiable;
- one or two photos of displays, school visits you have been on, after-school clubs or assemblies you have led;
- any evidence of your special interests – coaching certificates, first aid, cookery, and so on.

When you are interviewed for a teaching post, the panel will usually include the head teacher and governors, as well as group representatives or other school staff. They will have agreed the questions to be asked of all candidates before the interview. When you answer questions, it is perfectly appropriate to pause and think before replying, and you should not feel under pressure to rush in and say the first thing you think of. Schools are concerned with 'safe recruitment' and may ask questions about your relationships with pupils or that deal with issues of e-safety, such as, 'A pupil contacts you on Facebook. How do you respond?'. These are important questions, so consider responses carefully. (A pupil should not be able to contact you on Facebook, nor should a primary child be using it.)

In addition to your interview with the panel, you may also be interviewed by pupils who are representatives of the school council. They, too, will have agreed on the areas they want to ask candidates about. Think about what the pupils are looking for – usually consistency, fun and warmth. It is a good idea to ensure you have an appropriate joke ready, in case you are asked!

INDUCTION FOR NEWLY QUALIFIED TEACHERS

Induction for NQTs is compulsory, follows ITT and is the foundation for CPD throughout your career. The induction period must be undertaken by NQTs who wish to work in maintained schools and non-maintained special schools, but is not necessary for academies, independent schools or free schools.

The induction period can be done in independent schools, academies and free schools, but not all of them offer this. You can usually complete induction part time, but it will take longer than the usual year. Check when you apply for a job, as failure to do a recognised induction period will mean you cannot be employed as a qualified teacher in maintained schools. You do not have to complete your induction period immediately after your ITT, and there is currently no time limit, but this changes, and so you should check this on the Department for Education website. In the same way, supply work of less than a term does count towards the induction period, but check this, as it may change.

In Wales . . .

All NQTs must successfully complete Induction to continue teaching in a maintained school or non-maintained special school. As with ITT, NQTs should play an active role in their Induction.

(DCELLS, 2009: 158)

Source: Department for Children, Education, Lifelong Learning and Skills (DCELLS). (2009) *Becoming a Qualified Teacher: Handbook of Guidance (2009)*, Cardiff: Welsh Assembly Government. Retrieved from http://wales.gov.uk/docs/dcells/publications/090915becomingateacheren.pdf (accessed 7 November 2017).

During induction, you have to demonstrate you can meet the Teachers' Standards over a sustained period. You will have an individualised programme of support from a designated induction tutor in your school. This includes observations of your teaching, your observing more experienced teachers and a formal review of progress three times during the induction year. You will also have the opportunity to attend school-centred, in-service provision and, often, external courses. During your induction year, you will not teach more than 90 per cent of a normal timetable to allow your induction to take place.

PLANNING AND MONITORING YOUR INDUCTION YEAR

At the end of your ITT, you should prepare for your induction year and evaluate, monitor and seek the appropriate experiences to ensure you can meet the Teachers' Standards consistently. During your induction year, there are clear induction responsibilities for the head teacher, the induction tutor and you, the NQT.

Your head teacher will register you with an appropriate induction body and will ensure you have an appropriate timetable and induction tutor. He/she will eventually report your assessments to the appropriate body and monitor your induction. However, the day-to-day support will come from your induction tutor, who will offer you the guidance, coaching and mentoring you need and arrange for you to observe good practice. The induction tutor will observe your teaching and discuss the observations with you. During the induction year, the induction tutor will make and report three formal assessments of your ability to meet the Teachers' Standards. This will be based on observations of your teaching and discussions with you. You will have copies of all the assessment forms, and it is your duty to keep those forms, seek the help you need and raise any concerns about your induction support.

NQT induction is all about you, and your role in your induction is central. You should see it as an opportunity to demonstrate your strengths and seek the training you need to develop as a teacher.

You will discuss with your induction tutor how to use your reduced timetable to meet your own professional targets, and it will be up to you to demonstrate and provide evidence against the relevant standards at each assessment meeting. This should sound familiar – it is very similar to the process of continuous reflection, evaluation and action you undertook during your ITT.

The starting point of your induction year are the targets you set for yourself as you complete your ITT. These will give you a basis for discussion at your first meeting with your induction tutor and help you to appear professional and focused on your professional development in a new setting. The same Teachers' Standards apply, not only to your ITT, but also to your induction year, and the difference in assessment of ITT and induction is that your induction year gives you the chance to demonstrate an ability to meet the Teachers' Standards consistently.

As you come to the end of your ITT programme, you should think about how far you have come in your professional development. This is likely to be a natural part of your ITT programme. Your ITT provider will also help you to understand your own role in your induction and will help you to think about your experience from before, during and outside your formal training programme, including your placements, and to identify your key achievements and aspirations in relation to teaching. You should aim to set targets that:

- reflect and build on the strengths in your practice;
- develop aspects of the teacher's role in which you are particularly interested;
- provide more experience, or build up your expertise, in areas where you have developed to a more limited extent so far.

Task 9.1.2 Preparing your targets for induction

- At this stage, which aspect(s) of teaching do you find most interesting and rewarding? What has led to your interest in these areas? How would you like to develop these?
- What do you consider to be your main strengths and achievements as a teacher? Why do you think this? What examples do you have of your achievements in these areas?
- In which aspects of teaching would you value further experience in the future? For example:
    - aspects of teaching about which you feel less confident, or where you have had limited opportunities to gain experience;
    - areas of particular strength or interest on which you want to build further.
- At the moment, which of these areas do you particularly hope to develop during your induction period?
- As you look ahead to your career in teaching, you may be thinking about your longer-term professional aspirations and goals. Do you have any thoughts at this stage about how you would like to see your career develop?

Record your responses to these questions for discussion with your induction tutor at the start of the induction year. Word-process your answers and include evidence. This shows your induction tutor, not only your IT skills, but also your professional approach.

The targets and evaluation you make at the end of your ITT will enable the school that employs you to:

* understand your strengths and experiences;
* support your professional development through your NQT year;
* support constructive dialogue with your induction tutor;
* make links between induction, CPD and performance management.

At your meeting with your induction tutor, you will identify your targets and actions for the beginning of your induction, based on this evaluation.

SUMMARY

This unit gives you a broad overview of moving on in your professional development and training. You will need to allocate a substantial amount of attention to securing the right first teaching post, but, when you have, you have real opportunities to develop as a professional. To do this, you must carry out a realistic review of your achievements and further professional development needs and put these into your targets for induction.

* When applying for jobs, enlist the support of your mentor or tutor. They can look at applications and offer you mock interviews.
* Start considering applications early and allow plenty of time.
* Prepare each job application carefully, making sure you use the application format they want and set out your abilities and skills appropriately.
* Ensure you name the appropriate referees and that you have asked them if you may use them as referees.
* Use evidence from your training plan (or record of professional development) to prepare an interview portfolio. Make sure it presents the image you want for each job.
* The induction year has its own standards for induction, and setting targets for these is a final task of ITT.
* Ensure you know about your strengths and targets as an NQT before you meet your induction tutor. Use your records and your final meeting with your ITT tutor to prepare.

 ## ANNOTATED FURTHER READING

Department for Education (DfE). (2016) *Induction for Newly Qualified Teachers (England)*. Retrieved from: www.gov.uk/government/publications/induction-for-newly-qualified-teachers-nqts (accessed 7 November 2017).
    This site also provides detailed guidance about induction and links to the Teachers' Standards.

FURTHER READING TO SUPPORT M-LEVEL STUDY

Cordingley, P. and Bell, M. (2012) *Understanding What Enables High Quality Professional Learning – A Report on the Research Evidence*, Coventry, UK: CUREE. Retrieved from www.curee.co.uk/files/publication/%5Bsite-timestamp%5D/CUREE-Report.pdf (accessed 7 November 2017).

> This report reviews a range of research to try to answer the question: 'What are the characteristics of high-quality professional learning for teachers?'. It will repay study as you plan for your own professional development beyond your NQT induction year.

Totterdell, M., Woodroffe, L., Bubb, S. and Hanrahan, K. (2004) *The Impact of NQT Induction Programmes on the Enhancement of Teacher Expertise, Professional Development, Job Satisfaction or Retention Rates: A Systematic Review of Research on Induction*, Research Evidence in Education Library, London: EPPICentre, Institute of Education. Retrieved from http://eppi.ioe.ac.uk/cms/Default.aspx?tabid=307 (accessed 7 November 2017).

> This report identifies studies that shed light on the impact of induction programmes for NQTs on teacher performance, career development and retention rates.

RELEVANT WEBSITES

Independent Schools Council Information Service (ISCIS): www.iscis.uk.net

The Independent Association of Prep Schools (IAPS): www.iaps.co.uk

> The above two websites offer general information about teaching in the private sector.

Eteach: www.eteach.com

Prospects: www.prospects.ac.uk

> Other useful online resources for finding a teaching post are available on these sites.

UNDERSTANDING AND PLANNING YOUR CONTINUING PROFESSIONAL DEVELOPMENT

Alison Fox

INTRODUCTION

In this unit, we consider how continuing professional development (CPD) is currently provided, reflect on what it could and should be and highlight a teacher's role in their own development. Since the closure of the Teacher Development Agency for Schools (TDA) in 2012, no national body has held responsibility for guiding CPD within the teaching profession. This is despite conclusions reached by the 'Schools and CPD in England – State of the Nation' review of a 'lost promise' to teachers due to a lack of: (a) strategic planning, (b) clear links between CPD and performance management; (c) appropriate opportunities (especially for early career teachers); and (d) the most effective forms of collaborative and evidence-informed CPD approaches (Pedder, Storey and Opfer, 2008; Pedder *et al.*, 2010). Grass-root providers, such as the Teacher Development Trust, note that little has improved recently:

> There is a huge amount of teacher PD that is concerned with imparting 'effective techniques' for teachers ... The sad part is that there is very little evidence that, by itself, simply demonstrating or even practising a technique outside of the classroom will actually improve student outcomes.

> (Weston, 2015)

This situation is despite an international call for schools to become increasingly innovative to enable them to prepare pupils for the twenty-first century (Schleicher, 2012, 2015). Confident teachers are needed, supported by challenging CPD opportunities. The UK's response, led by David Hargreaves and the UK National College for Teaching and Leadership (NCTL), has been to advocate a 'bottom-up' self-improving system based on 'disciplined innovation', led by a network of national teaching schools (TSs; Hargreaves, 2012). Disciplined innovation sees teachers developing evidence-informed practices through collaborative working. Examples of these are explored both in this unit and the next.

OBJECTIVES

By the end of this unit, you should:

- understand what CPD can and should encompass;
- recognise the links between CPD, teacher standards and performance management/appraisal;
- understand how reflective practice can be developed into sustainable CPD;
- appreciate the role of enquiry and others in effective CPD.

WHAT IS CPD OR WHAT COULD IT BE?

There are three aspects to CPD, as the words imply. It:

1 connects with being a 'professional' teacher;
2 involves a teacher's 'development' within the profession; and
3 needs to be 'continuing'.

Professionalism and implications for CPD

Professionalism can be viewed as externally imposed, relying on society's perceptions and expectations of a profession's (e.g. teaching, nursing, social work) remit and responsibilities (Evans, 2011). This sees professions in a kind of service-level agreement with those who hold the profession to account. In the UK, as with many education systems globally, schools are judged on the attainment of their pupils in national and international tests, monitored by a government inspection body. Accountability extends to parents, further and higher education sectors and wider society for producing a highly educated workforce. The pressures of such external accountability help explain the performativity culture judged to have developed in UK schools (Jeffrey and Troman, 2012). This is demonstrated by schools' searching for quick-fix forms of PD aimed to help individual teachers address immediate issues, identified through analysis of pupil performance data.

An alternative definition defines professionalism as consisting 'of the attitudes and behaviour one possesses toward one's profession' (Boyt, Lusch and Naylor, 2001: 233). This grass-roots vision of professionalism connects with professional culture and collective identity development. It has been argued that the teaching profession needs to capture this sense of control-from-within to overcome the culture of compliance threatening its development (Whitty, 2008). Given the landscape of high-stakes testing and history of top-down policy-making driving such compliance, teachers need to develop a self-confidence and self-efficacy as their 'enthusiasm and innovation are reliant on these characteristics' (Bangs, MacBeath and Galton, 2011). This is important, not just for individual teachers, but for the profession as a whole. To move the profession forwards, a shared sense of what it is to be a teacher, based on agreed values, is needed. This assumes a teacher's identification with the profession, something not all training teachers feel they have developed as they take on their first post (Forde *et al.*, 2006). This is not surprising when a teacher's professional identity can be considered multifaceted – for example:

1 as a subject matter expert, based on self-perceptions of his/her subject matter knowledge and skills;
2 as a didactic expert, based on self-perceptions of his/her knowledge and skills related to planning, executing and evaluating teaching and learning;

3   as a pedagogic expert, based on self-perceptions of his/her knowledge and skills to support students' social, emotional and moral development (Beijaard, Verloop and Vermunt, 2000).

Although professional identity is considered to be more complex than this, involving an interplay between individuals and others (Beijaard, Meier and Verloop, 2004), these three facets are useful in thinking about becoming a teaching professional.

Task 9.2.1 Reflecting on your expertise

Reflect on how you see your developing expertise as a professional using Beijaard *et al.*'s (2000) three facets to professional identity development.

Rank yourself on a scale of 1–10:

- as subject expert (which, in primary settings, covers the full range of subjects you are expected to teach);
- as didactic expert (as defined above, rather than its more recent usage referring to a teacher-led teaching style);
- as pedagogic expert (again, as defined above, rather than its more recent usage referring to knowledge and skills about teaching approaches).

Mark your value on the sides of a triangle, with each side representing one facet, scaled from 1 to 10. Join your chosen values to help visualise your identity. Figure 9.2.1 illustrates what a 7, 3, 4 evaluation would look like. Add words to each facet describing how you feel about each expertise. Use one colour for words associated with how you feel now and another colour for your aspirations for the future.

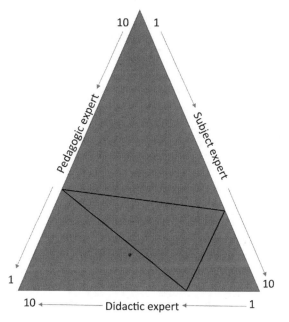

FIGURE 9.2.1 Visualising your professional identity

So, what does *development* within the teaching profession encompass, and how are teachers supported to develop?

Development as part of CPD

If we consider Teacher Professional Standards, interestingly, the Scottish Standards refer to 'Professional Learning' as compared with 'Professional Development' (PD) in the English, Welsh and Northern Irish Standards. What is the difference, if any? Owing to the poor reputation of teachers' PD provision noted earlier in this unit, there has been a shift towards referring to Professional 'Learning', rather than 'Development' (Timperley *et al.*, 2007; Opfer and Pedder, 2011; Cordingley and Bell, 2012). PD, however, is not necessarily limited to fragmented activities designed to transfer knowledge. It can be effective in supporting sustained learning. Practically, the term 'development' remains within policy documentation and, hence, the vocabulary of many English, Welsh and Northern Irish Schools and so is referred to as such in this unit, even though what we are discussing is better described as professional learning. Such learning relates to both individual teachers (for example, enhancing all three facets of teacher professional identity) and the school: one relies on the other.

In Northern Ireland . . .

The General Teaching Council for Northern Ireland (GTCNI) has consistently rejected any attempt to adopt a reductionist approach to professional development and the adoption of a competence based analysis underpins the Council's belief that professional knowledge is by its very nature organic, and to an extent evolutionary, reflecting a synthesis of research, experiences gained and expertise shared in communities of practice.

(GTCNI, 2007: 5)

Source: General Teaching Council for Northern Ireland (GTCNI). (2007) *Teaching: The Reflective Profession*, Belfast: GTCNI. Retrieved from www.gtcni.org.uk/userfiles/file/The_Reflective_Profession_3rd-edition.pdf (accessed 7 November 2017).

TABLE 9.2.1 Schools as professional learning environments

An expansive learning environment has:	A restrictive learning environment has:
Close collaborative working between colleagues, demonstrating mutual support	Individuals working in isolation
Opportunities to work beyond current role in other departments, working groups and school activities	No chance to boundary cross into other areas of school life, without a major job change
Support for personal development, beyond school or government priorities	Targets for development limited to external accountability agendas
A supportive atmosphere accepting diverse ways of working and learning	An expectation of standardised ways of working and learning
Opportunities to work beyond the school to experience different perspectives	Limited chance to work out of school, other than short training sessions

Source: Adapted from Figure 3.1, Fuller and Unwin (2006: 53)

One way to evaluate a school's CPD provision is to rate it as a professional learning environment on a continuum from restrictive to expansive; see Table 9.2.1.

When this framework was applied to beginning teachers' reported experiences (Fox, Wilson and Deaney, 2011), it was realised that different teachers can perceive the same school differently and engage differently with its CPD opportunities. This revealed the role teachers can play in their own development by proactively making connections with others, rather than passively relying on their workplace to provide opportunities. Effective PD is fundamentally social and requires a commitment to working alongside, listening to, watching and, most significantly, talking with other professionals and members of a school community.

The previous unit covered the statutory requirements for newly qualified teacher (NQT) induction to include the appointment of an induction tutor, regular observations and feedback on practice, progress reviews and formal assessments. However, although this implies that early career PD follows a standardised process, in practice, teachers report a range of experiences, as illustrated in Vignette 1, from research into primary school teacher development in mathematics.

Vignette 1: NQTs' development of their mathematics teaching

(With thanks to Alison Godfrey, PGCE Lecturer, University of Leicester)

Paula's first year of teaching was in a primary school with a strong focus on whole-school development in mathematics, following a 'mastery approach'. The subject leader led whole-staff input on teaching for mastery; a scheme resource was purchased; and teachers' planning was monitored, with staff given feedback on planning. Although not a confident mathematician herself, Paula proactively sought to implement new ideas in her practice and sought advice from the subject leader, her year group colleague and increasingly from other colleagues. She had intensive individual support, with several formal lesson observations providing targets to work towards, and was given opportunities to observe good practice in other classrooms. The advice she gained helped develop her confidence and subject knowledge.

Carrie taught a setted Year 1 group for mathematics in her NQT year. Coming into teaching with a very strong maths background, she proactively developed interesting, practical and well-resourced lessons, supplementing scheme resources with her own. A school focus on mastery gave her ideas for deepening children's understanding through different questioning techniques, enhanced by ideas and resources from courses. She considered a wide range of experiences as PD opportunities, including parents' evenings, pupil progress meetings and whole-school training. She also drew on more formal PD opportunities, such as lesson study cycles,[1] courses relating to KS1 SATs and formal observations. Her expertise in mathematics became recognised by colleagues, and she became increasingly consulted and asked to run pupil intervention sessions.

Task 9.2.2 Reflecting on your learning opportunities

Although both teachers' newly qualified CPD experiences were positive, use Evans *et al.*'s (2006) expansive–restrictive framework (Table 9.2.1) to conclude which teacher appeared to work in the most expansive learning environment. Were 'close collaborative learning' and 'mutually supportive' colleagues evidenced? Consider what these vignettes reveal about the roles of (a) personal motivation and (b) others in supporting the teachers' development, noting who was useful to them.

Turning to your own situation, who do you refer to and rely on to develop your thinking and practice as a teacher? You might create a learning opportunities map of those from whom you gain support, placing yourself at the centre and drawing links to all those who you identify, such as shown in Figure 9.2.2.

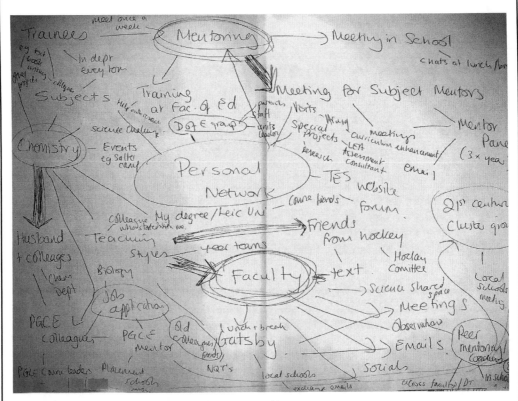

FIGURE 9.2.2 A beginning teacher's learning opportunities map

Source: Fox *et al.* (2011)

How is CPD continuing?

To counter the fragmented picture of CPD provision painted by the 'State of the Nation' review team (Pedder *et al.*, 2010), Bubb and Earley (2007) advocate that PD should be considered cyclically. Schools should be:

* identifying training and development needs among their staff;
* analysing these needs;
* planning and designing appropriate training and development activity;
* implementing activities;
* monitoring;
* evaluating impact as a way of identifying further needs.

However, just having a cyclical model in place, if it is imposed on teachers in a school, will not ensure it is effective. Teachers need personalisation and opportunities to be creative, and these are not guaranteed by a one-size-fits-all approach. Your development as a teacher needs to be an ongoing, continuing endeavour. It also needs to be a collective one.

Effective workplaces are those that can be considered learning organisations (Senge, 2006), in which the whole organisation learns as individual members of staff within it learn. You can hope that you will be welcomed into schools that operate as 'professional learning communities' (Lieberman and Miller, 2008), with 'ongoing groups of teachers who meet regularly for the purpose of increasing their own learning and that of their students' (Lieberman and Miller, 2008: 2), not only within a school, but also across them. In such communities, 'new ideas and strategies emerge, take root and develop' (Lieberman and Miller, 2008: 2). The Office for Standards in Education, Children's Services and Skills (Ofsted) has commented positively on such learning communities in action:

> Perry Beeches the Academy ... sees itself as a learning community and all members are expected to be acquiring further professional qualifications. All teachers are on MA courses and all teaching assistants are studying for foundation degrees ... The academy finds that the traditional model of training days and staff attending one-day INSET courses is simply not fit for purpose. These innovative approaches have led to rapid improvement in the quality of teaching and in turn to the achievement of students, which is outstanding.
>
> (Ofsted, 2014a: 1)

THE SCOPE OF CPD ACTIVITIES

Traditionally, PD takes the form of courses, and course attendance is still very much part of teachers' lives. These may be part-day, full-day or run on consecutive days. Less often, they are more sustained, requiring some activity between linked days. Courses can be offered by external providers off-site or, if there are sufficient participants, by visitors to a school (or school cluster, alliance, trust or chain). Increasingly, courses are organised by school groupings and may draw on expertise from within, rather than buying in external input.

There is nothing intrinsically wrong with courses. They can be beneficial and fulfil specific needs. Longer courses run by external providers might offer accreditation, either professionally – for example, as part of the NCTL's modular leadership curriculum – or academically, at Masters or Doctoral level, by universities. These can support career development. However, this unit highlights the potential value of less formal in-house, in-work opportunities for PD, including:

* reflective practice (or self-study);
* observing other practitioners;

- extending professional experience by engaging with new roles and activities;
- working with pupils as a resource for reflective practice;
- engaging in enquiry, ideally collaboratively (Bubb and Earley, 2007).

Importantly, activities should be relevant and meaningful and lead to changes in your thinking and practice. The question 'What makes great PD that leads to consistently great pedagogy?' was examined by thirty-one TS alliances as part of a national NCTL project (2012-14; Stoll, Harris and Handscombe, 2012) and evidenced nine claims:

Effective PD . . .

1   . . . starts with the end in mind;
2   . . . challenges thinking as part of changing practice;
3   . . . is based on assessment of individual and school needs;
4   . . . connects work-based learning with external expertise;
5   . . . opportunities are varied, rich and sustainable;
6   . . . uses enquiry as a key tool;
7   . . . is enhanced through collaborative learning and joint practice development;
8   . . . is enhanced by creating professional learning communities within and between schools;
9   . . . requires leadership to create the necessary conditions.

(Nelson, Spence-Thomas and Taylor, 2015)

Nelson *et al.*'s (2015) final project report offers a much rosier picture of the state of CPD in English schools than earlier studies (e.g. Pedder *et al.*, 2008).

SCHOOLS' RESPONSIBILITIES FOR PROFESSIONAL DEVELOPMENT: THE POLICY CONTEXT

A school's responsibilities for PD are explicit within the new Common Inspection Framework for schools in England and Wales, introduced by Ofsted in 2015. Schools need to show that they provide teachers with access to high-quality PD. A school's leadership is evaluated, as to:

the quality of CPD for teachers at the start and middle of their careers and later, including to develop leadership capacity.

(Ofsted, 2015)

Owing to concerns about teachers' early career attrition (Schaefer, 2013) and warnings of poor provision of CPD for such teachers (Pedder *et al.*, 2010), Ofsted now specifically focuses on:

the effectiveness of the support and PD put in place for NQTs and other teachers who are in the early stages of their careers, particularly in dealing with pupil behaviour. This must include the quality of mentoring and what the school has done to support their development in areas for improvement identified by initial teacher training providers.

(Ofsted, 2015: Item 73)

PD, leadership development and initial teacher development are three of the six responsibilities of every TS alliance in England and Wales, established in response to the White Paper *The Importance of Teaching* (DfE, 2010) 'to identify, develop and co-ordinate expertise for the benefit of pupils across a network of schools' (NCTL, 2016). All schools are encouraged to work towards these aims, either within or attached to an alliance.

However, formal PD responsibilities do not only lie with schools. Teachers' responsibilities for their own PD are built into all four nations' Teachers' Standards. The English and Welsh Teachers'

Standards refer to teachers' self-evaluating their own practice, using feedback from others and extending 'the depth and breadth of [their] knowledge, skill and understanding' through their careers.

(DfE, 2011: Item 14, p. 7)

The Northern Ireland Teacher Competences (GTCNI, 2011) are underpinned by teachers' responsibilities to become reflective practitioners, who engage in enquiry, and the Scottish Teacher Professional Standards' (GTCS, 2013) Standard 8 is entitled 'Standard for Career-Long Professional Learning'. PD is therefore a joint responsibility between teachers and schools.

In Northern Ireland . . .

Our strategic vision for teacher professional learning is, every teacher is a learning leader, accomplished in working collaboratively with all partners in the interests of children and young people. Our aim is to empower the teaching profession to strengthen its professionalism and expertise to meet the challenging educational needs of young people in the twenty-first century. Our objectives are to provide a structured framework for teacher professional learning; develop the leadership capacity of teachers; and provide practice-led support within communities of effective practice.

(DENI, 2016: 10)

Source: DENI. (2016) *Learning Leaders: A Strategy for Teacher Professional Learning*, Bangor, DENI. Retrieved from http://dera.ioe.ac.uk/25762/1/strategy-document-english.pdf (accessed 8 November 2017).

SETTING AGENDAS FOR PROFESSIONAL DEVELOPMENT: LINKS WITH APPRAISAL

There is an explicit link between Teachers' Standards and Teachers' Appraisal (previously called Performance Management, or Professional Review and Development in Scotland) in the UK:

All teachers are expected to use the Teachers' Standards instead of the previous core standards for appraisal, identifying PD, and other related purposes.

(DfE, 2011: Item 17, p. 8)

As the Standards were implemented, teacher unions, such as the National Union of Teachers, made clear that appraisers should start appraisal discussions from the premise that, once in post, all teachers already meet the Teachers' Standards (NUT, 2016). Appraisal should therefore focus on onward support to identify a teacher's training and development needs and link this to the school's CPD offer. Such strategic support is therefore your right as a teacher.

HOW DOES REFLECTIVE PRACTICE RELATE TO MY PROFESSIONAL DEVELOPMENT?

Notions of reflective thinking and reflective practice, covered in earlier units, underpin effective PD. Reflective thinking, traced to Dewey in the 1930s, challenges teachers to go beyond routinized ways of thinking to develop as a teacher. This is easier said than practised. Beginning teachers are socialised into their workplaces and 'the way we do things around here' in ways that are easily internalised with little conscious thought. This is where Schön's (1983) notion of reflective practice becomes important.

This involves reflecting on problems teachers have experienced in their practice – for example, children not able to settle to a task or fully understand a new concept or skill – to identify the underpinning issue(s) and consider the options for future actions. This goes beyond one-off problem-solving (sometimes termed single-loop learning), to identify how such problems can be prevented or solved in the future (double-loop learning; Argyris and Schön, 1974). Teachers need to reveal and challenge their assumptions, developing theories they can use to guide future practice. Hence, reflective thinking extends into reflective practice. This has become a central tenet of teacher professionalism, embedded within initial teacher education (ITE) in the UK, to support teachers in becoming reflective practitioners.

Vignette 2 reports how a group of teachers were supported in developing reflective thinking to guide future practice.

Vignette 2: The value of reflective diaries

(With thanks to Elizabeth Hewitt, PGCE Lecturer, University of Leicester)

Three Year 4 teachers were trying to develop more interactive teaching in their science lessons. After selected lessons, they audio-recorded short reflections to form a year's oral diary. These diaries revealed teachers' shifting beliefs and helped to capture their developing understanding of the value children gain from becoming involved in peer-group discussion. The diaries supported reflective thinking: a space to query situations, explore possibilities, create meaning and develop as a teaching professional. These spaces are not easy to incorporate into the general busyness of school life, and teachers benefitted from being prompted to recount illustrative excerpts and analyse significant moments. As this was part of a research project, transcripts of pupils in class discussions and group interviews provided further stimulus for reflection, allowing teachers to hear the reality of group talk and gain insights into the pupils' perspectives.

The oral diary revealed teachers openly questioning their views and their practice to develop plans for their future practice, as illustrated by extracts from Emma's diary as the year progressed:

> They [the children] didn't really question what they had produced necessarily and again looking ahead . . . that could be . . . peers being able to look at their work together.

> But I want them to be ready to do it themselves next time and I think if I keep giving it to them they are not going to make that step.

> I am more aware of not talking too much . . . The hardest thing was not to get involved but at the same time not to let them go off at the totally wrong tangent.

> I said to them I've not taught like this before and thought I'd just see what questions they could come up with and I was a bit unsure but I was just, go on, go with it . . . It gave them the courage and the opportunity to almost fly with it, to just have a go and learn from each other.

The diaries revealed the basis for practice changes and how teachers became aware of dilemmas and brought into consciousness their beliefs.

Studies have evidenced that teachers' practice is not easily aligned with what they value and believe about teaching. A values-practice-gap survey of more than 1,000 teachers from 338 primary and secondary schools, as part of the 'Learning How to Learn' project (Pedder and Opfer, 2013), found teachers often reported higher levels of values for statements covering a range of classroom and PD activities than they reported (on the same scale) for their practice of these activities. If what teachers value is not revealed and discussed, practices will remain unevaluated, and value-practice gaps will remain unidentified in schools. Under these circumstances, schools are in danger of staff developing routinised ways of thinking (and practising), as Dewey feared. We hope you find spaces and support in the schools you work in, for you and colleagues to challenge assumptions and develop reflective practice.

THE ROLES OF ENQUIRY AND OTHERS IN DEVELOPING AS A REFLECTIVE PRACTITIONER

The value of enquiry

The power of teachers individually and collaboratively being involved in enquiry has been well evidenced as the most effective approach to CPD, as it allows evidence-informed practice development (Timperley *et al.*, 2007; Whitehouse, 2011; Cordingley and Bell, 2012; Stoll *et al.*, 2012).

The use of evidence to inform school development comes back to Hargreaves's notion of schools becoming self-improving and is why research and development are built into the remit of TSs. Although the opportunities and benefits of teachers engaging in research are expanded upon in the next unit, we illustrate the significance and nature of such enquiry in a beginning teacher's development in Vignette 3.

Vignette 3: Reflections on the value of enquiry as CPD

(With thanks to Caroline Zwierzchowska-Dod, now headteacher at Clements Primary School, Cambridgeshire)

> In my early to mid-career, I became involved in a series of action research projects in partnership with the University of Cambridge. These were advertised by the local authority and my senior leaders and I were keen for our school to be involved. I felt that it was really important for my class to see me as a learner alongside them, as well as the obvious benefits to my CV. One of the most important outcomes for me though, was the chance to re-engage with the ideas I had covered during my training; to both remind myself of some of the theories of learning and to extend my understanding of them through enquiry.
>
> As there are so many demands on our time as teachers, I found it valuable to have a reason, almost an excuse, to go and read about education. It also gave me a licence to take risks in the classroom, testing a hypothesis or trialling a new approach. Failing and learning from this were just as important as the successes that arose.
>
> Becoming involved with enquiry allowed me to expand my teaching repertoire and try approaches that my more senior colleagues weren't using. It enabled me to push the boundaries of my teaching ability and repertoire whilst senior leaders were reassured that, because it was part of an enquiry, I would be soundly evaluating my teaching choices. This freedom to experiment was for me the most valuable aspect of becoming involved in enquiry as an early career teacher.

The next unit explores further the value and opportunities for research as part of a teacher's development.

The importance of others

You will have reflected in Task 9.2.2 on the potential role of a wide range of others in your development as a teacher. Some of these might be the mentors/coaches all early career teachers should be offered. There is a distinction between a mentor and a coach. A *mentoring* approach is directive, suggesting a relationship between a more experienced and a more novice practitioner. The support given through mentoring relates to passing on essential knowledge and skills developed from years of experience. *Coaching* is at the other end of a continuum (see Figure 9.2.3), where the coach could be anyone trained in coaching skills. A teacher is 'coached' by being encouraged to talk about the issues they are facing in a non-directive way and, using a variety of strategies, supported to find solutions to their own problems. This approach is a powerful way to develop a teacher's reflective skills and increase teacher independence.

Vignette 4 (Part 1): An effective mentoring relationship

(With thanks to Val Poultney, Senior Lecturer, Derby University)

Lauren took up her first primary school post in the same school as her final BEd placement. The school was a challenging one, serving a largely deprived ward of a city in the English Midlands.

Lauren's mentor was a member of the senior leadership team and an experienced teacher. She had mentored Lauren during her placement the previous year. They continued their strong, supportive working relationship, although now Lauren's mentor encouraged her to become more independent as a teacher. As they both had a Year 6 class, they jointly planned for teaching, with her mentor scaffolding planning so that Lauren became proficient in independently planning a series of lessons. Lauren's mentor regularly observed her teaching and offered her chances to observe her own and other staff's lessons. Lauren was encouraged and allowed plenty of time to critically reflect. When appropriate, Lauren and her mentor team taught together. Their discussions benefitted the children's learning in both Year 6 classes.

Mentoring is most commonly employed and embedded within teacher training and induction. However, schools are encouraged to consider developing coaching provision, illustrated in an Ofsted best-practice example:

> Senior leaders are clear in their rationale for developmental coaching. PD feedback is instrumental to improving the quality of teaching at the school. A key element of this is the use of 'Parrot on the shoulder' coaching, where teachers receive direct in-class support that provides real-time feedback on their teaching. This has led to rapid improvements and up-to-date and innovative practice is shared, refined and developed.
>
> (Ofsted, 2014b: 1)

Lauren's experiences extended into enquiry with her mentor, the forms and benefits of which will be covered further in the next unit. However, effective enquiry cannot be assumed to take place simply

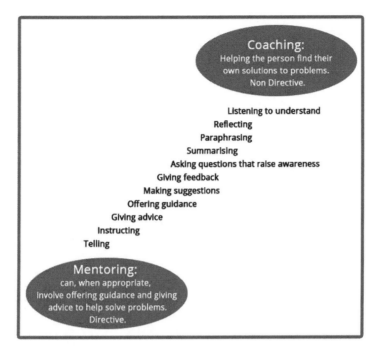

FIGURE 9.2.3 Coaching and mentoring as a continuum
Source: GTCS (2016)

by teachers being put together and expected to collaborate. For them to feel able to challenge themselves and one another as part of such enquiry, trust and a supportive environment are prerequisites (Little, 1990; Nelson *et al.*, 2015).

The biggest challenge is the mobilisation of learning from such enquiries to influence staff beyond those directly involved (Nelson *et al.*, 2015). Ideally, collaborative enquiry extends beyond single schools. 'Collaborative enquiry across school networks/alliances can be inspiring, empowering, engaging, and challenging for staff', but needs to be supported strategically if it is to develop a 'shared commitment to developing evidence-informed practice' (Nelson *et al.*, 2015: 62).

Vignette 4 (Part 2): Lauren's journey to practitioner researcher

As Lauren's confidence grew over her NQT year she began to share her pedagogical ideas with other teachers in her school, including the senior leadership team. Developing from Lauren's interests as a student around active learning, Lauren and her mentor were both keen to investigate the potential of adopting this in their classes. Together, they collected evidence of the impact of avoiding taking centre stage as a teacher and began to see improvements in the motivation of their children, particularly in terms of pupils' ownership of their learning.

Lauren was able to share with other staff their experiences of, first, researching practice and, second, the positive impact on the quality of pupils' learning. Although initially largely sceptical, many other teachers in the school went on to adopt similar approaches and found similarly good outcomes. It was Lauren's first-hand experience of enquiry that allowed her to allay other teachers' fears that more time and more resources would be needed to teach in this way. She could demonstrate ways of overcoming these issues, as well as showing her peers the benefits.

Task 9.2.3 Engaging with your professional development planning

Having read this unit, you will have seen how you can be active in your own PD.

To help you contribute to your appraisal/performance management meetings, prepare answers to the following questions:

- What do you need to achieve?
- What are you good at and want to build upon?
- What do you want to develop this year?
- What forms of CPD will help you in achieving your goals?

To get started, identify which Professional Teacher Standards relevant to your context you think you:

(a) are achieving well (colour *green*);
(b) feel you could develop further over the coming year (colour *amber*); or
(c) feel are high priority to tackle (colour *red*).

To help you, ask others, refer to feedback you have received and look at evidence you have collected. A professional portfolio is a great way to collate evidence of your achievements and progress. Don't forget these evaluations are based on the assumption that you are meeting all the standards, but are committing to a serious and honest self-evaluation of where you want to focus your efforts in the coming year.

SUMMARY: THE BENEFITS OF CPD

During ITE, teachers are assessed as competent to teach against the relevant Teachers' Standards. A standard pathway for PD during the newly qualified/induction year is then characterised by the setting of targets, regular meetings with a mentor and encouragement to take a full part in school life. There is also likely to be support for attendance at locally run meetings to share experiences with other beginning teachers. This chapter has shown how work with other, more experienced staff (including, but not limited to, mentors) can help a teacher grow in confidence and independence. Working within a school culture where staff are committed to professional learning offers the ideal conditions of support and challenge to develop practice and build professional relationships. Collaborative enquiry offers teachers the chance to understand the reasons why particular approaches do or don't work. This is relevant, in a profession as complex as teaching, throughout your career.

We have seen how it is important to avoid routinised thinking and welcome challenge to assumptions and beliefs. This requires individual teachers to commit to being proactive about their development, as encapsulated in the Teachers' Standards, and school leaders to commit to offering a conducive, 'expansive' learning environment.

NOTE

1 See http://lessonstudy.co.uk/

ANNOTATED FURTHER READING

Bubb, S. and Earley, P. (2007) *Leading and Managing Professional Development in Schools*, 2nd edn, London: Paul Chapman.

> This book offers a comprehensive and accessible overview of PD in schools. It is aimed at those responsible for school CPD provision and shows how individual CPD can contribute to whole-school goals and processes. It is a practical guide covering teachers at all stages of their careers, as well as support staff.

Guskey, T.R. and Yoon, K.S. (2007) 'What works in professional development?', Leading Edge Series, *Phi Delta Kappan*, 90(7): 495–500. Retrieved from www.keystoliteracy.com/wp-content/pdfs/orc-implement-science/What%20works%20in%20PD.pdf (accessed 7 November 2017).

> Thomas Guskey is a key name to whom people turn when they want to find out about evaluating PD. In this accessible paper, he reflects with a colleague on a review of more than 1,300 studies identifying connections between PD and student learning outcomes. Their conclusions re-evaluate the importance of workshops, external experts and time in offering effective teacher CPD and reinforce the value of enquiry.

Whitehouse, C. (2011) *Effective Continuing Professional Development for Teachers*, Centre for Education Research and Policy, London: AQA. Retrieved from https://cerp.aqa.org.uk/sites/default/files/pdf_upload/CERP-RP-CW-19052011.pdf (accessed 7 November 2017).

> This review of published research into teachers' PD highlights the importance of school structures and funding policies in supporting effective CPD. It outlines the features of effective CPD, illustrated with case studies, and presents a model for organising effective CPD in schools.

FURTHER READING TO SUPPORT M-LEVEL STUDY

Cordingley, P. and Bell, M. (2012) *Understanding what Enables High Quality Professional Learning: A Report on the Research Evidence*, CUREE and Pearson School Improvement. Retrieved from: www.dropbox.com/s/pzs2I07ksjjg6yz/Pearson%20CUREE-Report.pdf (accessed 7 November 2017).

> This comprehensive report brings together a wide range of evidence about the conditions needed for teacher development. It outlines effective models of professional learning, identifying those with enhanced student outcomes. The value of teachers' working with others in collaborative and enquiring ways is richly evidenced.

Sebba, J., Kent, P. and Tregenza, J. (2012) *Joint Practice Development (JPD): What Does the Evidence Suggest Are Effective Approaches?*, Nottingham, UK: NCSL.

> This report reviews models of professional development considered collaborative approaches to developing practice. Common characteristics of what make these practices effective are identified and link to the important role of enquiry in professional development, expanded upon in the next unit.

RELEVANT WEBSITES

Teacher Development Trust: http://tdtrust.org/
> The Teacher Development Trust is a charity set up to support and promote effective teacher professional development. It offers a free database of recommended CPD opportunities and live updates on advice about CPD.

Lesson Study UK: http://lessonstudy.co.uk/
> Lesson Study UK hosts everything a school would need to establish and run collaborative CPD using a lesson-study approach. There is a downloadable handbook, templates for data collection and case study videos to illustrate the various stages of lesson study.

International Professional Development Association: www.ipda.org.uk
> The International Professional Development Association is a membership organisation of an international community of academics and professionals committed to exploring effective approaches to CPD, offering a programme of seminars and a journal.

REFERENCES

Argyris, M. and Schön, D. (1974) *Theory in Practice. Increasing Professional Effectiveness*, San Francisco, CA: Jossey-Bass.

Bangs, J., MacBeath, J. and Galton, M. (2011) *Reinventing Schools: Reforming Teaching*, London: Routledge.

Beijaard, D., Meier, P. and Verloop, N. (2004) 'Reconsidering research on teachers' professional identity', *Teaching & Teacher Education*, 20(1): 107-28.

Beijaard, D., Verloop, N. and Vermunt, J.D. (2000) 'Teachers' perceptions of professional identity: An exploratory study from a personal knowledge perspective', *Teaching & Teacher Education*, 16(2): 749-64.

Boyt, T.E., Lusch, R.F. and Naylor, G. (2001) 'The role of professionalism in determining job satisfaction in professional services: A study of marketing researchers', *Journal of Service Research*, 3(4): 321-30.

Bubb, S. and Earley, P. (2007) *Leading and Managing Professional Development in Schools*, 2nd edn, London: Paul Chapman.

Cordingley, P. and Bell, M. (2012) *Understanding what Enables High Quality Professional Learning: A Report on the Research Evidence*, Coventry, UK: CUREE and Pearson School Improvement.

Department for Education (DfE). (2010) *The Importance of Education: The Schools White Paper*, London: HMSO. Retrieved from www.gov.uk/government/publications/the-importance-of-teaching-the-schools-white-paper-2010 (accessed 9 November 2017).

Department for Education (DfE). (2011) *Teachers' Standards*, London: HMSO. Retrieved from www.gov.uk/government/uploads/system/uploads/attachment_data/file/283566/Teachers_standard_information.pdf (accessed 7 November 2017).

Evans, K., Hodkinson, P., Rainbird, H. and Unwin, L. (eds) (2006) *Improving Workplace Learning*, London: Routledge.

Evans, L. (2011) 'The "shape" of teacher professionalism in England: Professional standards, performance management, professional development and the changes proposed in the 2010 White Paper', *British Educational Research Journal*, 37(5): 851-70.

Forde, C., McMahon, M., McPhee, A.D. and Patrick, F. (2006) *Professional Development, Reflection and Enquiry*, London: Sage.

Fox, A., Wilson, E. and Deaney, R. (2011) 'Beginning teachers' workplace experiences: Their perceptions and use of support', *Vocations & Learning*, 4(1): 1-24.

Fuller, A. and Unwin, L. (2006) 'Expansive and restrictive learning environments', in K. Evans, P. Hodkinson, H. Rainbird and L. Unwin (eds) *Improving Workplace Learning*, London: Routledge, pp. 27-48.

General Teaching Council for Northern Ireland (GTCNI). (2011) *Teaching: The Reflective Profession*, Belfast: GTCNI. Retrieved from www.gtcni.org.uk/userfiles/file/The_Reflective_Profession_3rd-edition.pdf (accessed 7 November 2017).

General Teaching Council for Scotland (GTCS). (2013) *Professional Standards*, Edinburgh: GTCS. Retrieved from www.gtcs.org.uk/professional-standards/professional-standards.aspx (accessed 7 November 2017).

General Teaching Council for Scotland (GTCS). (2016) *Coaching and Mentoring*, Edinburgh: GTCS. Retrieved from www.gtcs.org.uk/professional-update/professional-learning/coaching-and-mentoring.aspx (accessed 7 November 2017).

Hargreaves, D.H. (2012) *A Self-Improving School System: Towards Maturity*, Nottingham, UK: National College for School Leadership.

Jeffrey, B. and Troman, G. (2012) *Performativity in UK Education: Ethnographic Cases of its Effects, Agency and Reconstructions*, Stroud, UK: E&E Publishing.

Lieberman, A. and Miller, L. (2008) *Teachers in Professional Communities: Improving Teaching and Learning*, New York: Teachers College.

Little, J.W. (1990) 'The persistence of privacy: Autonomy and initiative in teachers' professional relations', *Teachers College Record*, 91(4): 509-36.

National College for Teaching and Leadership (NCTL). (2016) *Teaching Schools: A Guide for Potential Applicants*, London: NCTL. Retrieved from www.gov.uk/guidance/teaching-schools-a-guide-for-potential-applicants (accessed 7 November 2017).

National Union of Teachers (NUT). (2016) *NUT Appraisal Policy Checklist*, NUT Pay, Conditions and Bargaining Section. Retrieved from www.teachers.org.uk/sites/default/files2014/appraisal-checklist-final-feb-2016.pdf (accessed 7 November 2017).

Nelson, R., Spence-Thomas, K. and Taylor, C. (2015) *What Makes Great Pedagogy and Great Professional Development: Final Report*, London: NCTL.

Ofsted. (2014a) *Raising Standards through Professional Development: Perry Beeches the Academy*, Ofsted Examples of Good Practice in Schools, July, London: Ofsted.

Ofsted. (2014b) *Raising Standards through High-Quality Leadership of Teaching: St Mary's Church of England Voluntary Controlled Primary School*, Ofsted Examples of Good Practice in Schools, April, London: Ofsted.

Ofsted. (2015) *Ofsted School Inspection Handbook*, June, updated October 2015, London: HMSO. Retrieved from: www.gov.uk/government/publications/school-inspection-handbook-from-september-2015 (accessed 9 November 2017).

Opfer, D.V. and Pedder, D. (2011) 'The lost promise of teacher professional development in England', *European Journal of Teacher Education*, 34(1): 3-24.

Pedder, D. and Opfer, V.D. (2013) 'Professional learning orientations: Patterns of dissonance and alignment between teachers' values and practices', *Research Papers in Education*, 28(5): 539-70.

Pedder, D., Opfer, V.D., McCormick, R. and Storey, A. (2010) '"Schools and Continuing Professional Development in England – State of the Nation" research study: Policy context, aims and design', *Curriculum Journal*, 21(4): 365–94.

Pedder, D., Storey, A. and Opfer, V.D. (2008) *Schools and Continuing Professional Development (CPD) in England – State of the Nation Research Project Report*, London: TDA.

Schaefer, L. (2013) 'Beginning teacher attrition: A question of identity making and identity shifting', *Teachers & Teaching*, 19(3): 260-74.

Schleicher, A. (Ed.) (2012) *Preparing Teachers and Developing School Leaders for the 21st Century: Lessons from around the World*, Paris: OECD.

Schleicher, A. (2015) *Schools for 21st Century Learners: Strong Leaders, Confident Teachers, Innovative Approaches*, Paris: OECD.

Schön, D.A. (1983) *The Reflective Practitioner: How Professionals Think in Action*, London: Basic Books.

Senge, P.M. (2006) *The Fifth Discipline: The Art and Practice of the Learning Organization*, London: Random House Business.

Stoll, L., Harris, A. and Handscombe, G. (2012) *Great Professional Development which Leads to Great Pedagogy: Nine Claims from Research*, London: NCSL.

Timperley, H., Wilson, A., Barrar, H. and Fung, I. (2007) *Teacher Professional Learning and Development: Best Evidence Synthesis Iteration (BES)*, Wellington, NZ: Ministry of Education.

Weston, D. (2015) *Should We Stop Continuing Professional Development about Teaching Techniques*, 4 January. Retrieved from http://tdtrust.org/should-we-stop-cpd-about-teaching-techniques-2 (accessed 7 November 2017).

Whitehouse, C. (2011) *Effective Continuing Professional Development for Teachers*, Centre for Education Research and Policy, London: AQA.

Whitty, G. (2008) *Teacher Professionalism: What Next?* London: Institute of Education, University of London.

RESEARCH AND PROFESSIONAL DEVELOPMENT

Using research and enquiry to develop as a teacher

Cathy Burnett

INTRODUCTION

One of the most exciting – and perhaps challenging – dimensions of learning to teach is that the learning never stops. We cannot underestimate the complexity of teaching, of developing inclusive approaches to facilitate all our pupils' learning, while responding to their emotional and social needs, and organising classes of children, given limited space and resources. Moreover, we find that approaches that work well for one child or in one context do not work for others, that policy changes place new demands on us as professionals, or that there are broader shifts in society – such as developments in new technologies – that have implications for education. We never 'master' teaching, but rather engage in ongoing reappraisal as we review, interrogate and re-evaluate how we are supporting children's learning, and the values and beliefs that underpin what we do.

This unit explores how engaging with research, possibly through further qualification, can help you reflect on your practice more deeply and make informed decisions about your work. It is likely that you will engage with research and enquiry during initial teacher education, for example conducting small-scale investigations or child studies. This unit describes how research can support you throughout your career. Research will help you gain new insights, build your confidence to refine or innovate, and sometimes generate the evidence to justify why you should continue to do what you are already doing. After discussing different perspectives on teacher research, this unit explores how you can challenge your own assumptions about practice. It also provides guidance on critical engagement with existing research. Finally, it explores how you can become involved in research and considers the benefits of collaboration.

OBJECTIVES

By the end of this unit, you will be able to:

- identify how engagement with research will support ongoing critical reflection on your practice;
- engage critically with the work of other researchers;
- consider how your practice is underpinned by certain ways of thinking, values and beliefs;
- identify how you can use research to explore children's perspectives;
- recognise the value of engaging in collaborative, research-focused activities.

In Northern Ireland . . .

Teachers cannot be developed passively. They develop actively. It is vital, therefore, that they are centrally involved in decisions concerning the direction and processes of their own learning.

(Galanouli, 2009: 11)

Source: Galanouli, D. (2009) *School-Based Professional Development: A Report for the General Teaching Council for Northern Ireland (GTCNI)*, Belfast, GTCNI. Retrieved from www.gtcni.org.uk/publications/ uploads/document/School-Based%20comp_V3.pdf (accessed 7 November 2017).

In Scotland . . .

Teaching Scotland's Future recognises key strengths in Scotland as we continue to build a culture of career-long professional learning, owned by individual teaching professionals and supported by coherent and sustained systems. That includes the 35 hour per year commitment of every teacher in Scotland to continuing professional development (CPD), alongside other opportunities for professional learning across the working week and through in-service days.

(Scottish Government, 2011: 13)

Source: Scottish Government. (2011) *Continuing to Build Excellence in Teaching: Scottish Government's Response to Teaching Scotland's Future*. Retrieved from www.gov.scot/Resource/Doc/920/0114570.pdf (accessed 7 November 2017).

WHAT IS RESEARCH, AND WHY IS IT IMPORTANT TO PROFESSIONAL DEVELOPMENT?

Teachers constantly make choices and decisions. In doing so, they gather evidence through talking to children, observing what they do and analysing what they produce. As they make sense of all this, they draw conclusions about how children are learning. Teachers work in busy, complex environments, and consequently much of this sense-making is tacit, and decisions about how to respond are often rapid. However, these processes of gathering evidence and drawing conclusions are very similar to those we associate with research. Engaging in research is essentially about engaging in these processes more systematically. It means slowing down to look more deeply and perhaps differently at what is happening. This process involves being explicit about the questions you want to investigate and deciding which research approaches will generate the kinds of understanding you need to answer these questions. It means collecting and analysing data in an organised manner and considering different interpretations of what you find. Ultimately, it means communicating the results to others, so that they can learn from what you have found out. Much teacher research involves *action research*, through which teachers research and develop their own practice, collecting evidence and using what they learn from this to inform what they do. Julie Dutton, for example, conducted an action research project as part of her Masters degree:

> When the 2014 National Curriculum for Mathematics was published, it highlighted 'fluency' as one of three key aims. I was unfamiliar with this term and was concerned that if teachers did not have a shared definition, then it could lead to the curriculum being taught in very different

ways. My background reading led me to two main schools of thought: fluency as speed and accuracy of recall; and fluency as speed and accuracy of recall with an element of flexibility that comes from having a deep conceptual understanding of the maths. I held a discussion with teachers in my school and we concluded that fluency is more than quick recall and accuracy because concepts need to be embedded verbally, mentally and visually.

For my Masters project I therefore decided to focus on children's recall of times tables as this was one of the areas in which the National Curriculum expected children to be fluent. I wanted to find out how far their fluency in times tables was related to deep conceptual understanding. I began with a questionnaire to Year 3 and 4 pupils which asked them to rate how well they thought they knew the tables and what helped them to learn. Those who stated they were less confident mostly named counting and repetition as their approaches to learning, whereas those who stated they were more confident said they approached learning through searching for patterns and making connections. I also asked children to draw themselves learning times tables. The most common pictures showed a child working alone thinking or saying the tables, sitting at a desk writing them, or with a teacher at the front asking a question. The final question asked children to respond to a tables fact in three different ways: symbolic, pictorial and in context. When asked to draw what 4×3 looks like, the most common response was simply to draw the numbers in larger 'bubble' writing. I also gave small groups of children a range of mathematical equipment and asked them how they would use it to represent the times tables. I was surprised that although the children could recall times tables facts, they demonstrated little understanding of the concept of multiplication. This meant that they did not have the flexibility that I had come to realise was an intrinsic part of being 'fluent'.

The project was really valuable in helping us to understand pupils' and teachers' perspectives and to review our approach to teaching times tables. I found a diagram by Haylock and Cockburn (2013) that shows children need to make as many connections as possible between symbols, language, pictures and concrete experiences in order to gain a deep conceptual understanding of maths. This diagram has become central to all maths lessons that I plan. Visual representations have now become a part of every maths lesson in my school. I have rewritten the calculation policy to include visual images and manipulatives that can be used to help children to develop a deep understanding of the concepts rather than just the procedure or symbolic representation.

Over the years, there have been a series of government-funded initiatives designed to engage teachers in action-research projects focused on raising attainment. However, action research can also involve generating theory. Importantly, when we refer to theory, we do not mean something that is divorced from practice. We are talking about an ongoing, two-way, or reflexive, relationship between how we understand practice and our actions. As McNiff and Whitehead (2005: 4) argue, 'Practice (what you do) informs theory (what you think about what you do), and theory (what you think) informs practice (what you are doing). Theory and practice transform continuously into each other in a seamless flow'.

A focus on using teachers' research to generate understandings has led some to see practitioner research as a 'path to empowerment' (Kincheloe, 2003); engaging in research can enable teachers to take charge of what they do, going beyond implementing local or national policy or responding to research generated in other contexts. Indeed, following her project, Julie Dutton reflected that:

Engaging in a Masters allowed me to look more deeply at my practice and engage more with wider research. It gave me the opportunity to ask questions and look much more closely at classroom pedagogy than I feel I would have done in my usual daily practice. It has made me a better teacher and a better leader in school as I have become much more reflective and more confident. I can't imagine teaching without being involved in classroom research now.

From this perspective, teacher research should be driven by teachers' questions, rather than those imposed by their head teachers or the government, and a *critical* stance is important. Teacher research is not just about finding 'what works' to raise attainment in relation to existing frameworks, but about interrogating the assumptions, values and beliefs that underpin policy and practice (Carr and Kemmis, 1986). A critical stance emphasises the relationship between the specific contexts in which teachers work and broader social, cultural and political contexts. As Hardy and Ronnerman argue (2011: 462):

> Changed practice can only come about as a result of sustained and concerted inquiry on the part of teachers into the nature of their work, in specific locations, and in the knowledge that this work is being undertaken under broader, influential social conditions.

In Scotland . . .

The Scottish Government will ask the National Partnership Group to consider how Masters level work can be built into ITE courses, induction year activities and ongoing CPD activity. Alongside this the Government encourages universities to set up Masters accounts for students studying on ITE courses.

(Scottish Government, 2011: 29)

Source: Scottish Government. (2011) *Continuing to Build Excellence in Teaching: Scottish Government's Response to Teaching Scotland's Future*. Retrieved from www.gov.scot/Resource/Doc/920/0114570.pdf (accessed 7 November 2017).

Task 9.3.1 Considering relationships between research and teaching

Lankshear and Knobel suggest that a teacher who is involved in research is also a 'thinker, troubleshooter, creator, designer and practitioner' (Lankshear and Knobel, 2004: 11).

Discuss what you feel is meant by each of these terms in relation to your teaching role, using examples from your own experience or of practice you have observed or read about.

Next, order the terms from 'most' to 'least' to represent the extent to which you feel you have had opportunities to fulfil each of these roles in your teaching experience to date. Consider what has enabled you to do so, and any barriers you have faced.

Discuss how you think research might support you in carrying out these different roles as you embark on your career.

HOW CAN RESEARCH HELP YOU THINK DIFFERENTLY ABOUT PRACTICE?

Importantly, when individual teachers and researchers look at evidence, they often notice very different things and have different ways of interpreting what they do notice. In her book *Listening to Stephen Read*, Kathy Hall (2003) illustrates this powerfully by presenting interviews with four experts on the teaching of reading, all of whom have different beliefs about what reading involves and, consequently, how children can best be supported to become readers. The interviews focus on their analysis of evidence of 8-year-old Stephen's reading. They each draw different conclusions about him as a reader and the kinds of experience that might be appropriate for him. The book not only helps us understand different perspectives on reading, but also illustrates how different theoretical understandings mean that we arrive at different conclusions when we analyse evidence.

Task 9.3.2 Reflecting on your own assumptions when analysing practice

With a group of colleagues, watch a video of children interacting around a shared task. This could be a video of children you have taught or one of the many videos of classroom practice found on websites such as the Teachers TV video archive, available via the *TES* website (www.tes.co.uk). Individually, jot down what you notice about how the children interact and how this is supporting their learning.

Afterwards, draw two conclusions about these children's interactions based on what you have noted. Take turns with your colleagues to share and justify your observations.

Discuss reasons for any differences – both in what you noticed and in your explanations. Which theories – implicit or explicit – did you draw on as you made sense of what you observed? For example, did these relate to assumptions about each individual child, or to features such as the task or the setting?

As discussed above, all teachers draw on theories as they interpret what learners are doing and what they need. These theories may be explicit (based on values and beliefs that they clearly express) or implicit (evident in what they do and the assumptions they make as they do so).

Research can help us re-examine some of the implicit theories that underpin everyday practice. In their book *Turnaround Pedagogies*, Comber and Kamler (2005) describe how they worked with a group of teachers to develop a series of research projects through which newly qualified teachers collaborated with more experienced colleagues. The projects aimed to achieve a 'turnaround' in how teachers saw what was going on in classrooms and the resources children brought with them to school. Following work by Moll *et al.* (1992), Comber and Kamler supported teachers to recognise and investigate what children *could* do and *did* know, rather than what they could not do. They then used their collective experience to decide how to respond to what they found. In another project, led by Teresa Cremin and colleagues (Cremin *et al.*, 2015), teachers researched children's 'literacy lives' outside school in order to better understand 'the cultural, linguistic and social assets' they brought to school. The project shifted teachers' perceptions about schools and parents, strengthened relationships between teachers and families, and generated new approaches to working in partnership.

Another way of gaining a different perspective – or perhaps a turnaround – is to research children's experiences of school. Children will learn what counts in classrooms from what happens when they enter them, the resources they can access, the way their spaces are bounded and regulated, and the kinds of response given to what they do and say. In developing practice, Bath argues that teachers, therefore, 'need to constantly reflect upon and question what they do and the messages that practice transmits to the children in their care' (Bath, 2009: 3). Clark and Moss (2011) recommend using participatory methods to enable parents, children and practitioners to build a 'mosaic' of a child's experiences. This might involve, for example, inviting children to take photographs, give tours, create maps or role-play. The range of evidence is then used to stimulate reflection and dialogue about children's experiences and feelings and how to respond to these.

The following studies also used participatory methods to investigate children's perspectives:

- Veronica Hanke (2014) invited 4-7-year-olds to draw guided reading sessions. The drawings provided insights into the children's perceptions of guided reading, linked for example to the role of friends, ability grouping and their teachers' organisational approaches.
- Anne Kellock (2011) invited her pupils to take photographs and devise captions to present views on their school environment. As well as learning a great deal about what mattered to children in her class, she felt that her pupils gained from the opportunity to explore their experiences and gain insights into each other's perspectives.

Task 9.3.3 Thinking differently about a focus area

Identify an aspect of your teaching experience to date that has caused you concern or raised questions for you. This could, for example, be linked to an area of the curriculum, the experiences of a particular group of children, or the broader school environment. Summarise the evidence you currently have that has led you to identify this issue. Identify what you think you already know about this and your possible explanations for how things are. Try to represent these in diagrammatical form. Now consider what you could investigate to help you gain a deeper understanding of this area. Whose perspectives might you investigate? How might you involve children or parents and carers in this process? What kind of evidence might you collect? How might the wider context – such as school, local or national policy – be relevant here? Annotate your initial diagram with these areas for further investigation. It will help to talk through your ideas with a friend – can they provide other possible explanations? Or suggest other areas for enquiry?

USING EXISTING RESEARCH AND PUBLICATIONS

The previous sections have suggested that carrying out your own research is important for your professional development. You also need to continue to be aware of published educational research and other writing done by researchers in universities and/or commissioned by organisations. This is important because such work may provide new insights or introduce new approaches. For example, Adam Daly describes a collaborative project with academics from Sheffield Hallam University that explored contextualised approaches to teaching grammar:

> I worked with a colleague from within my school to plan two lessons to teach an aspect of 'grammar' from the National Curriculum. With the support of staff from Sheffield Hallam University, we looked at an article by Debra Myhill (Myhill, 2003) which described the reasons behind an author's use of passive voice and the importance of teaching this concept to children. Previously to this, our experience of teaching active and passive voice had been through worksheets that had required the children to convert from active to passive or vice versa. Using this article, we were able to create a lesson that taught the concept of passive voice whilst also

allowing the children opportunity to write creatively. Sharing ideas supported the process of creating an interesting and engaging context for learning.

Masters programmes will, of course, introduce you to research relevant to your particular interests. You can also find various digests written for teachers that provide summaries of research linked to particular topics (e.g. Hattie, 2009; MESH Guides: www.meshguides.org/). Such digests can be very useful in informing future developments, although many would argue that research can never simply provide us with evidence of 'what works' (Biesta, 2007). Learning is always highly contextualised, and what 'works' in one context may not in others. Moreover, summaries are inevitably selective. They are usually based on studies that have set out to look at the measurable impact of certain interventions on aspects of children's learning. You will find that qualitative studies are also valuable. They can provide rich insights into teaching and learning that allow you to better understand complex issues and the experiences of learners.

Critical engagement with published research

Just as it is important to adopt a critical orientation when enquiring into your own practice, so it is important to engage critically with published research, particularly when that research is being used to justify local or national policy developments. You need to consider how researchers' assumptions, values and beliefs shaped what they tried to find out, how they went about this, and what they concluded.

One aspect of being critical involves evaluating how the study was conducted and judging whether or not the ideas presented seem justified. This involves considering whether methods used were well chosen to generate the insights the researchers claim to have gained. You might review, for example, the research tools used, the range of participants or the scale of the study. It is important, though, not to dismiss a study simply because it is small-scale or because it used qualitative approaches. Critical evaluation of qualitative studies includes deciding whether the researchers' approach to the study enabled them to gain rich and detailed insights into the experiences or practices of the individuals, groups, classes or schools studied.

Another aspect of being critical involves considering how useful a study is in terms of thinking about or developing practice, and how it adds to what is already known about an area. There are various ways in which a study may be valuable. It may provide evidence that suggests that a particular approach is worth trialling with your class. Alternatively, it may generate a new way of looking at what you do, or lead to further questions relevant to your situation. In any case, as explored above, you need to try to identify the values, beliefs and assumptions (implicit and explicit) that informed the study and decide whether you feel these are appropriate.

Some questions to support critical reading of research articles and reports

- Which research questions did the researchers set out to answer? How far did their research approaches and methods enable them to answer these questions?
- Which claims do they make, based on their findings? How far are these justified by the evidence presented?
- How do the findings connect to your current understanding and beliefs relating to this area, or to existing research?
- What implications do any recommendations have for your and others' practice?
- Do any issues or questions remain unresolved?
- Which values, beliefs and assumptions have informed the choice of research question, research approaches, methods, data analysis and conclusions?

Task 9.3.4 Critical review of research

Identify a report or journal article based on a recent study that has been linked to a policy development at local, regional or national level. For example, you could investigate one of the approaches described in this book, such as mastery learning or systematic synthetic phonics.

Use the questions above to support your critical reading of the report or article.

Next, search for media reports that refer to the policy developments based on this research. How far do the media reports reflect the conclusions you have drawn through your own critical reading?

GETTING INVOLVED IN RESEARCH

In practical terms, teachers often become involved in research through a postgraduate programme of professional development, such as a Masters in Education. Indeed, you may gather credits towards a Masters degree during initial teacher education and have opportunities to gain further credits through modules aimed at those in their first year of teaching. Universities run a variety of Masters courses, including generic programmes with a broad range of options and those with a specific focus, such as literacy, inclusion or leadership. During a Masters programme, you are likely to engage in a series of practitioner-led enquiries designed to research aspects of your work. Programmes will support you in reflecting critically on your practice, exploring it from different perspectives and developing your skills as a teacher-researcher.

You may, however, find other ways of collaborating with others to investigate your practice. One increasingly popular approach is *lesson study*, which originated in Japan (Dudley, 2014). Although lesson study has been adapted in various ways in the UK, essentially it involves a group of staff working collaboratively to plan a lesson, drawing on appropriate research and shared expertise. The group then observes one member of the group teaching the lesson. Observers collect data about students' responses from different perspectives. These data are discussed in a post-lesson discussion during which colleagues reflect on what they have learned through the observation and how this will inform lessons (Takahashi and McDougal, 2016).

Other opportunities for research arise when schools become involved in major projects or lead research themselves. Teaching school alliances often coordinate research activity and enquiry-based activities designed to benefit schools across the alliance. Sometimes, schools take a national role in initiating and coordinating such developments.

Megan Dixon works at Ash Grove Academy, Macclesfield, and is Director of Research and Development for Aspirer Teaching Schools Alliance. She believes passionately that all teachers should be involved in research and that all development should be based on theoretical principles. Otherwise, she says, 'you don't get critical reflection unless we have a framework of principles on which to base our assumptions'. The school draws on available research whenever possible to inform what they do, and collects data to inform ongoing review and reflection on new initiatives. This information helps them to decide whether or not to continue with certain approaches. As Megan says, 'the information is always interesting and empowers our decision making. It helps us to engage in discussion and debate, constantly question what we do and challenge assumptions'. Ash Grove is one of five Research Schools that will work with the Institute for Effective Education based at York University, and the Education Endowment Foundation (which funds educational research). The school will be involved in helping to capture and describe elements of exemplar practice, raising the profile of research evidence, and supporting other schools to develop evidence-informed practice.

Collaboration beyond schools

Working with colleagues to investigate and develop practice can be very rewarding. For many years, local education authorities facilitated professional networks. Recent changes in the funding, organisation and administration of schools, however, have meant that groups of teachers may be more likely to meet together in other contexts – for example, as part of collaborative research projects like the ones Megan and Adam describe. Many teachers also increasingly exchange ideas and engage in professional discussion through events such as TeachMeets or through online communities, for example contributing to forums managed by the *Times Educational Supplement* (www.tes.co.uk), following teachers' blogs or using social media (Carpenter and Krutka, 2014). Ian Guest, who is researching use of Twitter for teachers' professional development, reflects:

> Social media increasingly permeate our everyday and professional lives. This is as true in teaching as it is in other professions, with many teachers 'flocking' to Twitter as their tool of choice. Many claim Twitter constitutes a powerful tool for professional development. In 140 characters or fewer, teachers converse with one another, ask for and respond to requests for help, reflect on practice, seek and provide emotional support, share and seek ideas and resources, and forge and maintain professional connections. As a consequence, they feel they have to access to experts on particular issues; can join communities for support; experience a sense of belonging and thereby reduce their sense of isolation; and keep up to date on educational issues. They might hear about guided reading strategies, maths challenges for pupils with SEN or a range of approaches to book scrutiny. Or they might SEE and be inspired by examples of classroom displays, quiet reading areas or pupil art. Crucially, learning opportunities on Twitter come in easily digestible, bite-sized chunks, to be consumed at a time and place of their choosing.
>
> (Guest, 2016)

As well as opportunities that arise to engage with research and professional development within a school or alliance, there are also organisations that work with teachers across the country. These include associations committed to the promotion and development of a particular subject. Joining a subject association or attending a subject association conference can provide you with rich opportunities to learn about recent research and/or present your own research, meet colleagues from elsewhere, and even work with others to play an active part in influencing policy. Subject associations also sometimes offer small grants for research projects. Julie Rayner and Daisy Rothwell reflect on their involvement with the United Kingdom Literacy Association (UKLA):

> As an experienced teacher, developing pedagogical subject knowledge and keeping up to date with theoretical viewpoints can be difficult. School-based professional development is usually directed by school development issues, linked to patterns of pupil attainment across the school. Working with those outside my school has given me an opportunity to reflect more broadly on how children learn and meant that I am more up-to-date with new developments. I have attended two UKLA conferences and this has allowed me to access innovative and thought-provoking practice from across the world. This in turn has helped me to question my own practice and curriculum.
>
> (Julie)

As a teacher, being part the UKLA is a great opportunity to step out of the classroom and participate in a much wider education community. It offers the chance to understand and discuss the development of English learning with a diverse range of professionals and bring back to school, and my own practice, new inspiration, initiatives and ideas. It is also the chance to contribute a current classroom perspective to UKLA discussion which is greatly rewarding.

(Daisy)

Task 9.3.5 Investigating subject associations

In a group, each select a subject association from the list below. Visit its website and investigate the support and opportunities the association provides. Report back to the rest of the group.

- Association for Physical Education: www.afpe.org.uk
- Geographical Association: www.geography.org.uk
- NAACE – the IT association: www.naace.co.uk
- National Association for Language Development in the Curriculum: www.naldic.org.uk
- National Association for Primary Education: www.nape.org.uk
- National Association for Special Educational Needs: www.nasen.org.uk
- National Association for the Teaching of English: www.nate.org.uk
- National Drama: www.nationaldrama.org.uk/nd
- The Association for Science Education: www.ase.org.uk
- The Association of Teachers of Mathematics: www.atm.org.uk
- The Design and Technology Association: www.data.org.uk
- The Historical Association: www.history.org.uk
- The National Society for Education in Art & Design: www.nsead.org/home/index.aspx
- United Kingdom Literacy Association: www.ukla.org

You can also identify subject associations through the Council for Subject Associations website: www.subjectassociation.org.uk

In Northern Ireland . . .

The Chief Inspector of the Education and Training Inspectorate, Stanley Goudie, stated:

There is proportionately insufficient investment in the development of the teachers and the educational workforce compared with that invested in changing structures and systems. The need to ensure a range of continuing professional development for those who lead, manage and teach has never been greater.

(ETI, 2009: 59)

Source: ETI. (2009) *Chief Inspector's Report 2006-2008*, Bangor, NI: Education and Training Inspectorate. Retrieved from https://www.etini.gov.uk/content/chief-inspectors-report-0 (accessed 7 November 2017).

SUMMARY

This unit has explored the role of research in supporting ongoing critical reflection on practice. It has emphasised that this involves, not only a process of asking questions and collecting and analysing evidence, but also being prepared to examine the values and beliefs that underpin what you do and how you think about your work. It has suggested that collaborating with others is an important part of this process and also highlighted the need to keep up to date with research conducted by others and review this critically. Research has an important role in professional development, and it is hoped that the examples provided here will inspire you to keep investigating and interrogating practice throughout your career.

 ## ANNOTATED FURTHER READING

Cohen, L., Manion, L. and Morrison, K. (2011) *Research Methods in Education*, 7th edn, London: Routledge.
> This gives practical guidance on designing and conducting research, including a very useful overview of research methods.

Cremin, T., Mottram, M., Collins, F.M., Powell, S. and Drury, R. (2015) *Researching Literacy Lives: Building Communities between Home and School*, Abingdon, UK: Routledge.
> This describes how teachers researched children's literacy lives outside school and, in doing so, strengthened relationships with children and their families, and developed new ways of working together to support children's learning.

McNiff, J. (2013) *Action Research: Principles and Practice*, 3rd edn, Abingdon, UK: Routledge.
> This provides an overview of approaches to action research.

 ## FURTHER READING TO SUPPORT M-LEVEL STUDY

Hanke, V. (2014) 'Guided reading: Young pupils' perspectives on classroom practice', *Literacy*, 48(3): 136-43.
> In this article, Veronica Hanke explores how children's drawings of common classroom practices can provide illuminating insights into what matters to them in classrooms.

Ellis, S. and Moss, G. (2014) 'Ethics, education policy and research: The phonics question reconsidered', *British Educational Research Journal*, 40(2): 241-60.
> This provides a critique of the way in which research evidence was used to support government policy regarding systematic synthetic phonics.

 ## RELEVANT WEBSITES

Collaborative Action Research Network (CARN): www.esri.mmu.ac.uk/carnnew
> CARN is an international network that aims to raise the profile of action research and support its development.

Education Endowment Foundation (EEF): https://educationendowmentfoundation.org.uk/
> EEF's website include summaries of education research projects it has funded, usually by conducting randomised control trials, as well as a Teaching and Learning Toolkit that aims to provide 'an accessible summary of education research on teaching 5-16 year olds'.

MESH: www.meshguides.org/
> This website provides summaries of research evidence that relate to a variety of topics and are written for teachers.

 # REFERENCES

Bath, C. (2009) *Learning to Belong: Young Children's Participation at School*, London: Routledge.

Biesta, G. (2007) 'Why what works won't work: Evidence-based practice and the democratic deficit in educational research', *Educational Theory*, 57(1): 1-22.

Carpenter, J.P. and Krutka, D.G. (2014) 'How and why educators use Twitter: A survey of the field', *Journal of Research on Technology in Education*, 46(4): 414-34.

Carr, W. and Kemmis, S. (1986) *Becoming Critical: Education, Knowledge and Action Research*, Lewes, UK: Falmer.

Clark, A. and Moss, P. (2011) *The Mosaic Approach*, 2nd edn, London: National Children's Bureau.

Comber, B. and Kamler, B. (2005) *Turnaround Pedagogies: Literacy Interventions for At-Risk Students*, Newtown, Australia: Primary English Teaching Association.

Cremin, T., Mottram, M., Collins, F.M., Powell, S. and Drury, R. (2015) *Researching Literacy Lives: Building Communities Between Home and School*, Abingdon, UK: Routledge.

Dudley, P. (ed.) (2014) *Lesson Study: Professional Learning for Our Time*, Abingdon, UK: Routledge.

Guest, I. (2016) Email correspondence.

Hall, K. (2003) *Listening to Stephen Read: Multiple Perspectives on Literacy*, Buckingham, UK: Open University Press.

Hanke, V. (2014) 'Guided reading: Young pupils' perspectives on classroom practice', *Literacy*, 48(3): 136-43.

Hardy, I. and Ronnerman, K. (2011) 'The value and valuing of continuing professional development: Current dilemmas, future directions and the case for action research', *Cambridge Journal of Education*, 41(4): 461-72.

Hattie, J. (2009) *Visible Learning: A Synthesis of Over 800 Meta-analyses Relating to Achievement*, Abingdon, UK: Routledge.

Haylock, D. and Cockburn, A. (2013) *Understanding Mathematics for Young Children*, 4th edn, London: Sage.

Kellock, A. (2011) 'Through the lens: Accessing children's voices in New Zealand on well-being', *International Journal of Inclusive Education*, 15(1): 41-55.

Kincheloe, J. (2003) *Teachers as Researchers: Qualitative Inquiry as a Path to Empowerment*, 2nd edn, London: RoutledgeFalmer.

Lankshear, C. and Knobel, M. (2004) *A Handbook for Teacher Research: From Design to Implementation*, Maidenhead, UK: Open University Press.

McNiff, J. and Whitehead, J. (2005) *Action Research for Teachers: A Practical Guide*, London: David Fulton.

Moll, L., Amanti, C., Neff, D. and Gonzalez, N. (1992) 'Funds of knowledge for teaching: Using a qualitative approach to connect homes and classroom', *Theory into Practice*, 31(2): 132-41.

Myhill, D. (2003) 'Principled understanding: Teaching the active and passive voice', *Language & Education*, 17(5): 355-70.

Takahashi, A. and McDougal, T. (2016) 'Designing and adapting tasks in lesson planning: A critical process of lesson study', *Mathematics Education*, 48: 513.

INDEX